Guanxi or Li shang wanglai?

—Reciprocity, Social Support Networks, & Social Creativity in a Chinese Village

關係抑或禮尚往來

—江村互惠、社會支持網和社會創造的研究

◆◆◆

Xiangqun Chang

常向群

airiti
press.

To whom I acknowledged in my postscript......

送給那些我在「後記」中答謝過的人們......

Xiangqun Chang

Dr Xiangqun Chang was born in Nanchang City, Jiangxi Province, China; and now lives in London as a UK citizen. She received a BA in Political Science and an MA in Sociology in China, and a PhD in Sociology and Social Anthropology in the UK. Before she left China in 1991 she was a lecturer at Chinese People's Public Security University. Subsequently, she had been worked and studied at City University, London. Since 2004 she became Visiting Research Fellow at London School of Economics and Political Science (LSE). She is now coordinator of the China in Comparative Perspective Network (CCPN) and managing editor of the China in Comparative Perspective Network (JCCP), LSE. Her publication in Chinese amounts to one million Chinese characters, e.g. On Marxist Sociology (1992), Henan People's Publishing House. Her English publications include: co-author with Stephan Feuchtwang, Social support in Rural China (1979-1991): A Statistical Report on Ten villages, London: City University, 1996; co-editor with West, Zhao and Cheng, Socio-economic Transformation in China and Chinese Women, Basingstoke and London, Macmillan Press Ltd., 1999; "Fat pigs and women's gifts" -- Agnatic and non-agnatic social support relationships in Kaixiangong village (1979-1996), in the above book. Her book Guanxi or Li shang wanglai?: Reciprocity, Social Support Networks and Social Creativity in a Chinese village is published in both Chinese and English in 2009.

Contents

List of maps, photos, figures and tables

Photos
This book includes a total of 133 photos, taken by the author in 1996 except where otherwise noted. 125 of them are in Part One, the remaining eight are in Part Two chapters V to VII. Photos are referred to where appropriate by number and chapter, e.g. "Summer-begins picnic" (*yehuofan* 野火飯), see photos III-38 and III-39.

Figure

Table

Recommendations from scholars (Alphabetical order)

Western scholars

►This book brings all of this work of the particularistic alongside the universal, the socially loaded gift alongside impersonal exchange together as never before, more comprehensively and grounded in the most thorough ethnography. Taking up the classical schema of reciprocal and impersonal relations produced by Marshall Sahlins, Chang Xiangqun extends it and gives it life by showing how such a schema can work dynamically. This enjoyment and the dynamics of the making of interpersonal relationships are the two main contributions Chang Xiangqun has made to the ethnography of reciprocity

---- *selected from the Preface by Professor Stephan Feuchtwang, Department of Anthropology, London School of Economics and Political sciences (LSE), UK.*

►Chang Xiangqun has provided a wonderful in-depth analysis of rural, central, Chinese social relationships. Building upon the pioneering work of Fei Xiaotong, her study of Kaixiangong retains a strong historical feel as it probes matters of the human heart. Her investigation of Chinese emotional and ethical considerations provides a rich informed and vibrant chronicle of ordinary village life. An excellent ethnographic account. This is how anthropology should be.

---- *Professor William Jankowiak, Department of Anthropology, University of Nevada, Las Vegas (UNLV), USA.*

►Based on extensive empirical research, Chang Xiangqun's book, *Guanxi or Li shang wanglai? – Reciprocity, Social Support Networks and Social Creativity in a Chinese village,* provides an invaluable overview of social relationships in the Chinese countryside, and puts forward an ambitious theoretical framework for thinking about them. Both scholars and students will benefit greatly from it

---- *Professor Charles Stafford, Department of Anthropology, London School of Economics and Political Science (LSE), UK.*

▶This book is a major contribution to one of the most dynamic research literatures in Chinese sociology and anthropology. Building on the many-sided significance of a phrase (*li shang wanglai*) used both in scholarly and everyday discourse, Chang Xiangqun develops a sophisticated framework for the analysis of interpersonal relationships in village China, bringing together phenomena often discussed separately as face, reciprocity or *guanxi*. She uses this framework to interpret her thorough and sensitive ethnographic accounts of social life in the area studied from the 1930s by Fei Xiaotong, emphasising both continuities and changes over time. This book will be vital reading for all sociologists who aim to understand the complexities of social relationships in this rapidly changing society.

> ---- *Dr Norman Stockman, Senior Lecturer, Department of Sociology, University of Aberdeen; Honorary Secretary of the British Association for Chinese Studies (BACS), UK.*

Chinese scholars

▶The great achievements in socio-economic development over the past three decades have attracted worldwide attention to China. Questions about China's development model are becoming a very popular topic with different social scientific disciplines in the age of globalization. Chang Xiangqun's book *Guanxi* or *Li shang wanglai*? can be seen as a "virtual icon" in which the so-called "China model" is embedded. This book is an excellent outcome based on the author's transdisciplinary training in both China and the West and long-term, in-depth empirical studies on contemporary China. It is the first Chinese scholar's book, in nearly 100 years, to systematically challenge important Western social anthropological theories of social exchange and reciprocity.

> ---- *Professor Deng Zhenglai, Dean of National Institute of Advanced Studies in Social Sciences, Fudan University; Editor of the <u>Chinese Social Science Quarterly</u> (Chinese); Editor of the <u>Fudan Journal of the Humanities and Social Sciences</u> (English),China.*

▶Dr. Chang Xiangqun, in this in-depth monograph, revisits the village that the late Professor Fei Xiaotong studied 60 years ago in the Yangzi River Delta. Elaborating on Dr. Fei's pioneering work on graded interpersonal relationship, Dr. Chang further articulates the concept of *lishang wanglai* as the analytical instrument to understand agrarian stability in traditional Han Chinese society. This work enriches contemporary understand of rural China.

---- *Huang, Shu-min, Distinguished Research Fellow & Director, Institute of Ethnology, Academia Sinica, Taiwan.*

▶ Though this is not the first book dealing with the establishment, reinforcement, and conditions of mutual benefit of interpersonal relations and its "*guanxi* networks" in ethnic Chinese societies, it is certainly the most ethnographic report on such social phenomenon in today's PRC society after reforms. It uses the everyday life phrase of "*li shang wang lai*" (reciprocity) to depict and to develop the prevalence and importance of personalized social relations in China. It both makes contributions on localisation of anthropological theory and brings local knowledge alive.

In particular the significance of its political and social perspective are to note the revival of the important caring role of "family" for its members, and the strategic role of "personalized relations" in maintaining ordinary people's quality of social life under the post-communist state, the socialist society without the "collective responsibilities". *Li shang wang lai* (reciprocity) is in fact a true portraiture of the "key relationships".

Although it is a serious anthropological study, this book reads with truth and liveliness, as though it were a work of reporting literature.

---- *Hsin-Huang Michael Hsiao, Professor and Director, Institute of Sociology, Academia Sinica, Taiwan.*

▶ I first came to know Dr Chang Xiangqun back in 1987. She was a lecturer of sociology in the Chinese People's Public Security University, one of the few sociologists with a master's degree in sociology since it was re-established in China in early 1980s. I was lecturing in sociology in the People's University of China, and enjoyed insightful communication with China Xiangqun at conferences in Beijing and national-wide, as well as through reading her papers from *Sociological Studies* and *Sociology* of the "Replicated Journals", by the Information Centre for Social Sciences of People's University of China. Chang Xiangqun participated diligently in the National Social Science Funded project "Marxist Sociology Studies", conducted under the auspices of the Institute of Sociology Chinese Academy of Social Science (CASS). I was deeply impressed that she had thoroughly immersed herself in such so-called "boring" theoretical studies in Beijing, against the background of the excitement of the time when tremendous changes were happening in China brought about by the Opening-up policy since 1979.

In 1992, a year after she went to the UK to advance her studies in sociology, her monograph *On Marxist sociology* (460,000 words) was published. I received a copy of the book from the publisher, and gained a comprehensive understanding of her research. I therefore selected the work as a reference book for my course of theoretical sociology when I worked in People's University and Tsinghua University successively. As regards the book, I cannot agree more with some opinions, summarised below, stated in a book review:

> The book is not only the remarkable fruit of the author's efforts, but also represents the generational scholars' collective intelligence on Marxist sociology... accomplished the construction of the theoretical system of Marxist sociology; the author offers historical insights on the main issues of Marxist sociology against the background of the development of Western sociology or scholarship; the author also provides explanations with a sense of reality on major events of the international society discussing their relevant factors and backgrounds. The book places Marxist sociology in an open system while it introduces and analyzes nearly 100 scholars of Marxist sociology. It is proposed, for the first time, that studies of Marxist sociology in China play an indispensible role in establishing the forthcoming sociology of China with its theoretical paradigm. (Wang Tie, *Social Science in China*, 1995(2):195-6)

Although Xiangqun was not actively involved in Chinese sociology circles after she left China, her influences are still profound: her articles boasting domestic awards, her book has been selected in the *China Year Book of Sociology* (1989) which is the first of such covering 10 year's important work after sociology was re-established in China. During the past two decades, I kept in touch with Xiangqun and met with her on visits to the UK in 1995 and particularly 2007. When I visited LSE to negotiate about the cooperative establishment of the Confucius Institute, I met Chang Xiangqun before leaving London. She was just back from her fieldwork village and talked to me for hours with great enthusiasms about her work on *Li shang wanglai* (reciprocity).

I realised that she had found what she had been seeking so unwaveringly. The "*lishang-wanglai* model" sets an example as an important theoretical paradigm for the sociology of China. It can be used as a key to understand and interpret Chinese society and the Chinese people. This book demonstrates Chang Xiangqun's indomitable will in searching for truth and her solid theoretical background. Based on in-depth empirical studies and nearly two decades of experiences living overseas Chang Xiangqun presents us with another high quality book which can go down in history like her *Marxist Sociology* (in Chinese, 1992). The publication of *Guanxi or Li shang wanglai?* in both Chinese and English versions, during the period of deepening reform of the Chinese cultural system, marks the transition of "Made in China" from material to cultural, specifically as regards forthcoming developments in social science.

> ---- *Professor Li Qiang, Dean of the School of Humanities and Social Science, Tsinghua University; Vice President of Chinese Sociological Association (CSA), China.*

▶ I have known Chang Xiangqun, a scholar of the greatest determination, since the early 1990s when I was in London. Xiangqun, whose masterpiece of *Marxist sociology* had exerted a far-reaching influence, initially was a visiting fellow, then a research assistant and researcher doing her PhD and carrying out various research projects in City University and later at the LSE.

Xiangqun's research interests focus on contemporary China studies, especially relationship systems, to which she devoted more than a decade. During the past years, she worked on social support systems in rural China, under Professor Stephan Feuchtwang's supervision, and co-authored the statistical report of the project.

She possesses not only splendid research experience, but also astonishing patience that enables her to be immersed in researches. She visited Kaixiangong village (the classical fieldwork site of Professor Fei Xiaotong) many times and conducted similar work outside China (e.g. UK) to form a comparative study.

Previously, Professors Mayfair Yang, Yunxiang Yan and others had made intensive studies of Chinese systems of relationship. Compared with these the book *Li shang wanglai* stands out with undeniable advantages and novelty. This book holding anthropological reciprocal theory as its breakthrough point, restudies the social life of a classical fieldwork site. The subtitle of the book includes the key words of reciprocity, social support and social creativity. I believe there are very few works linking anthropological classic theories of reciprocity with new theories of social support and social creativity. Xiangqun's work pioneered in this area. In particular, the concept of social creativity is very refreshing.

Among many noteworthy qualities of this book there are three that stand out especially.

(1) I would like to stress that based on in-depth empirical re-studying of previous studies and rethinking of reciprocity this excellent work has the characteristic of "critically inheriting" previous studies.

(2) The author demonstrates the approach to her subject of significant social scientific research by constant questioning both fieldwork methods and theories. This book is an inspiration to Chinese scholars and exercises a valuable influence on the international social science domain.

(3) Chinese social science "going abroad" needs both ideological resources and global views. Using traditional native Chinese concepts combined with theoretical resources from general knowledge, the author's approach on "*guanxi*" goes beyond studies of relationships in two dimensions, and provides a significant attempt at exploring this topic in a historical perspective with a dynamic approach.

> ---- *Professor Wang Mingming, Institute of Sociology and Anthropology, Peking University; Distinguished Professor of the Central University for Nationalities; Editor of the Chinese Review of Anthropology, China.*

Preface

Interpersonal relationships have been the hallmark of Chinese sociology and anthropology ever since 1940, when Fei Xiaotong proposed a distinction between the Western individual, defined by equal membership whether of a group or many groups, like a straw in a bundle, and the Chinese individual, defined as the centre of a widening circle of reciprocal and hierarchical relationships, like the ripples made by a stone thrown into a pond. A large number of scholars, Chinese and non-Chinese, philosophers and historians, as well as sociologists and anthropologists, have since that time examined and elaborated a number of key Chinese terms, central to the moral philosophy and character of Chinese social relationships.

At the same time, grand theorists of social evolution, in particular Talcott Parsons with his theory of evolution from particularistic to universalistic social structures, and Marcel Mauss with his theory of total social prestation giving way to socially embedded but impersonal money-mediated exchange, have been questioned and modified. Their evolutionary dichotomies have been turned into simultaneous dichotomies, the particularistic alongside the universal, the socially loaded gift alongside impersonal exchange.

This book brings all of this work together as never before, more comprehensively and grounded in the most thorough ethnography. I want to say something about each of these achievements, the bringing together of previous discussions and theories and the grounding of them in ethnography.

Li shang wanglai is a phrase that combines practice and principle. It is what others have discussed as Confucianism. But it is the summation of what is practised in daily life and without the leadership of an elite intelligentsia. With this phrase Chang Xiangqun has brought together what had been separately discussed: the social philosophy of *bao* (asymmetrical reciprocity), the central importance of *mianzi* and *lian* (face), the moral economy of *renqing* (human relationships of fellow-feeling), the art of making *guanxiwang* (social networks), and much else. She shows how they work together in what might be called a discursive constellation. Using sociological and anthropological theorisations of reciprocal relations in China and Japan, she creates a framework of four dimensions, namely, principled rational calculation, human-feeling, moral, and religious, and four kinds of relationships, namely, instrumental, expressive, negative and generous. This looks at first like a typology. But it is much more, because she shows how one kind of relationship can turn into another and how more than one type of principle can be in use at the same time in the same relationship. Indeed, taking up the classical schema of reciprocal and impersonal relations produced by Marshall Sahlins, Chang Xiangqun extends it and gives it life by showing how such a schema can work dynamically, as process rather than as map, as the way social distance and familiarity are created rather than acting as a fixed and determining structure.

This brings me to the ethnographic grounding of the schema. What brings it to life, and what shows how it is a dynamic process, are the ways people conduct their relationships. Chang Xiangqun has produced the most detailed ethnography of the same village and area where Fei Xiaotong did his fieldwork for his doctorate in 1936. From her initial fieldwork in 1996 until the present day, she has made and maintained contact with the village residents. From this intense and continuous relationship with them, she can show how they are their own intelligentsia, how they think about and enjoy the making, changing and unmaking of interpersonal relationships. At the same time, she shows not just what are the customary, learned rules of what to bring as a gift to whom on different occasions, but also how villagers adapt and change customary rules to deal with new situations and a changing economy. They enjoy the making of distinctions, which accord with those of the framework she has used to present them. They enjoy the creativity demanded of them in changing situations. This enjoyment and the dynamics of the making of interpersonal relationships are the two main contributions Chang Xiangqun has made to the ethnography of reciprocity.

I want to make one further recommendation of this book to its reader. The ethnography is about village life in contemporary China, a very dynamic and changing social setting. Chang Xiangqun embraces the facts of change, in particular the changing local political economy. During the years of her fieldwork, the village and township government has been changed a number of times and she describes how these changes can be understood in terms of the personalisation and moralisation of the relationships between villagers and their government. This is a micro-history of a village in what has become a very prosperous part of China and one which has its own peculiar culture, with, for instance, a greater stress on little sisterhoods and brotherhoods than in other parts of China. Nevertheless, this study illuminates, as a case study, what must be happening, although with quite different customary practices and in different economic conditions, in other regions of China. The rapid development of Chinese market economics has not diminished the importance in China of interpersonal relationships; while the extension of the moral economy of interpersonal relationships to relationships with government is not only worked out locally, but everywhere.

Stephan Feuchtwang

Department of Anthropology

London School of Economics and Political sciences

26 February 2008

Introduction

This study examines reciprocity and personalised relationships including personalised institutional relationships (see Chapter IX.I.2) by looking at social support arrangements in rural Chinese people's everyday life since the 1980s. It illustrates that *li shang wanglai*[1], a term rooted in Chinese culture, can be developed as an analytical concept, *lishang-wanglai*[2], and even perhaps make a contribution to general anthropology and sociology. To some extent the concept of "*lishang-wanglai*" can answer the question "What holds Chinese society together?" (James L. Watson 1988: 3), which has puzzled scholars for decades.

In this introduction I will first provide some background information about social support and the ESRC project, which formed the starting-point for my own research. I will then introduce *lishang-wanglai* (the term was used, during my fieldwork, by a Chinese villager). After explaining the general methods I have applied in my fieldwork I will make clear the scope of the research in time and space, and discuss the researcher's multifaceted rather than monotonic subject-position. The introduction is concluded with a section containing a brief introduction of how materials (fieldwork data and photos) were arranged and a summary of the organisation of the book. Part One will cover the fieldwork site – a portrait of Kaixiangong Village, in which its economic, administrative and informal systems will be introduced. Part Two will show villagers' practice of *lishang-wanglai*. Part Three will show the theoretical approaches in both Western and Chinese contexts, construction of the *lishang-wanglai* model, and highlight its great significance in studying Chinese society and China in comparative perspective with other countries and regions.

---

[1] Words in italics are phonetic translations (*pinyin*) of Chinese characters, phrases etc. in current usage in the People's Republic of China. This will apply throughout. This current usage of *pinyin* follows both the practice and principles which are set out in *A Chinese–English Dictionary* (Revised edition), 1995. In cases where phrases are not in the dictionary I follow my understanding of these principles. The form used is therefore consistent for any given phrase.

[2] The *pinyin* form of *li shang wanglai* came from *A Chinese–English Dictionary* (Revised edition), 1995: 598. It means "courtesy demands reciprocity", "deal with a man as he deals with you", "pay a man back in his own coin" and "give as good as one gets", in differentiation to the slightly different form *li shang wang lai* used by Charles Stafford (Stafford, 1995, 2000a and c), and also of course the form I use, *lishang-wanglai*, in describing and analysing my fieldwork data (see the section of "The villagers' usage of *li shang wanglai*" in the Introduction and IX.II, and XI.I).

I. The ESRC project on social support

The idea of studying personalised relationships first came to me from my participation in an ESRC project (1991–94) entitled *Rural social support arrangements and the transformation of local tradition in China* (1979–91).[3] Social support has for all countries been the basic way for most people to seek help, before state welfare or social security systems (see Chapter VI.II). About 80 per cent of China's population are rural people who have never been covered by a state benefit system. In order to show clearly how rural Chinese people support each other and arrange their everyday life and major events, I will start with the concept of social security[4]. To a Westerner, social security means government payments to people who are unemployed, ill, disabled and so on. In China it is common knowledge that there are different social security systems for urban and rural areas. Before the 1990s there were policies of high employment, high welfare and low income in urban areas. This meant that almost every employed person received an income that covered only food and basic materials. Their medical care, pension, housing, even their furniture, all kinds of subsidy and allowance were controlled by their workplaces. Urban people's lives were thus highly reliant on their workplaces. This employment-based welfare system has changed very much since the 1990s, along with a deeper level of social reform, but this topic is beyond the scope of this research.

In rural areas a different kind of social security policy obtained in socialist China, the relief system, which combined state relief with people's support of themselves, namely, people with problems could rely on the collective and the collective could rely on the state (Cao, 1991). In

---

[3] The Economic and Social Research Council of the UK from 1991–94, grant number R-000-23-2585. Seven researchers (for names see Acknowledgements) spent substantial periods of time during 1991 and 1992 interviewing 304 households in ten villages that were located in five provinces (for details see the section Introduction). A large number of documents, observational records and questionnaire returns were acquired as a result. This research is a pioneer in its field as well as in its definition (Chang and Feuchtwang, 1996: 5–6).

[4] I received many comments on why I didn't involve "social capital" in my work. In a recent discuss with Bian Yanjie, an expert on social capital, I realised the way how he used social support is similar to my usage of social support. It means people use different kinds of capital (Bian) / resources (Chang) through different links or ties (Bian) / sources (Chang) in different occasions (Bian) / events (Chang) to get maximum gain in return (Bian) / meet different needs (Chang). In this way both Western theories of social support and social capital are all useful to study Chinese people and society. However, I prefer to use social support for three reasons: (1) The term social capital is often misunderstood by interviewees, as happened with *guanxi* (X.VI), unlike the term social support; (2) There is no identical term in Chinese for social capital, whereas there is for social support; (3) Use of social capital applies a Western theory to Chinese society, whereas social support crosses the disciplines of psychology, sociology and anthropology, and not yet being a "mature theory", allows space for development in the context of Chinese people and society.

other words, the collective applied and distributed limited social security and welfare from the state to rural people. However, Table 0-1 shows that the coverage of the social security system by the state for rural people is very small. Up until 1990 only 0.83 per cent of rural people were covered by the social security system (SSB, 1991). This figure comprises temporary relief during major natural calamities, various schemes for chronically poor areas, relief funds for five-guarantee households (*wubaohu*)[5] and extremely poor households. So, only the people mentioned above with special difficulties were covered by the state welfare system. The majority of rural people arranged everything for themselves through social support based on local groupings: collective production brigades or households themselves within or after the Mao era.

Table O-1. Social security coverage in 1990 (million)

	Population*	Social security coverage **	%
Urban	301.91	150	49.68
Rural	841.42	7	0.83
Total	1143.33	157	13.73

*   SSB: *China statistics yearbook*, 1991.
**   Cao Guigen "Report IX: Development report on social security" (*Shehui baozhang shiye fazhan baogao*), in Lu, Xueyi and Li, Peilin, (Editors), *The development reports of Chinese society* (*Zhongguo shehui fazhan baogao)*. Liaoning People's Publishing House, 1991: 343.

By the mid-1980s the collective organisations of production were being dismantled, after which the collective was no longer significant in the distribution of limited social security and welfare. People with problems could not rely on the collective any more, although the system continued in name. But from then on households were responsible for their own security. So where does the rural population look for protection, whether for its basic needs or for extraordinary events and expenses?

The ESRC project explored these questions from the viewpoint of social support. It examined social support arrangements and the transformation of local traditions in ten villages from 1979 to 1991.

The significance of studying social support was acknowledged by the Communist Party two years after that study. Social support (*shehui huzhu*), together with personal savings (*geren*

---

[5] They are food, clothing, medical care, housing and burial expenses for the aged and infirm without family support.

chuxu), were added in the decisional document of the Third Plenum of the Fourteenth National Party's Congress in 1993. Thus the Chinese social security system includes: social insurance, social relief, social welfare, work of *youfu anzhi* (providing preferential treatment to families of soldiers, martyrs, and proper arrangements for the placement of demobilised soldiers)[6], social support and personal savings (Bianweihui, 1995). Personal savings is officially defined as any means of financial savings or investment (Duojicairang, 1998). One type of personal savings which relates to social support is a pension fund to provide for old age instead of depending on the traditional "rearing sons against old age" (*yang er fang lao*). Although there have been many studies about saving for old age in rural China, this financial saving has very little to do with rural people's everyday life. We found, in the ESRC project, that only about ten per cent of sampled households saved and even these had only small quantities of personal savings. The people preferred to store building materials and other goods rather than make financial savings.

The Communist Party recognised that social security and welfare actually covers only a very small proportion of the population in rural areas. People with special difficulties, for example five-guarantee households, are a very small group in the society, and also major natural calamities do not often occur in the same place. The nature of rural social support shows that the Party and the state encouraged the majority of people to look after themselves through sources such as household, neighbours and friends. Social support was listed as part of the social security system in 1993, but since then little research work has been done by officials or academics in China, apart from a few policy studies about elderly care in both rural and urban areas, or working mothers in urban areas[7].

The assumption of the ESRC project was that informal and household-based social support networks were performing much of the function of social security. These social support networks have become much more active since the Mao era, involving relationships of kinship, marriage, neighbours and friendship, and senses of reciprocity. In order to arrange sensibly the data from our survey we redefined the concept of **social support** in our Statistical Report (Chang and Feuchtwang):

Social support is a relationship in which basic living security and further social needs are

---

[6] These four items were clarified in the Seventh Five-year Plan of the state in 1986.
[7] Sociology tendency: Ruan et al., 1990, 1997; Yuen-Tsang, 1997; Olson, P., 1986; Kallgren, 1992; Schweizer, 1991, 1996; Bian and Ang, 1997. Sino-anthropological tendency: Fei, 1947; Walder, 1986; Oi, 1989, 1999; Davis and Harrell, 1993; Selden, 1993; Unger, 1993; Yang, 1994; Yan, 1997.

gained in one of four ways: (i) personally, as part of a reciprocal process in which individuals or groups provide material, financial, labour, information, technological, emotional and other resources; ii) impersonally as loans, grants and benefits from government; (iii) from savings (premiums) with an insurance company; (iv) through other market transactions, such as the hiring of labour and paid consultation with professionals (1996: 4).

This is the broadest definition of social support; applicable to any social context. In our survey, a narrower range of social support transactions was defined and used to arrange data in the statistical report. We classified transactions according to: (i) sources: household support, private support and public support; (ii) types of social support: finance, labour and information; (iii) events: family events, emergency events and investment events; and (iv) range: within village and township, and beyond township. Some of these items have been further subdivided. For example, private support includes kin, neighbours and friends. The friendship category includes seven different kinds of friend and so on. These categories will be used in this book.

One interesting figure from the ESRC project is that 74 per cent of the total number of contacts for social support in Kaixiangong came from non-agnatic kin[8] (see chapter I.III). I focused on this village because the higher proportion of non-agnatic kin played an extraordinary role in social support. After my fieldwork, when I became increasingly interested in the notion of *lishang-wanglai*, my Chinese version of social support and reciprocity (see Introduction-II), I found that it explained why non-agnatic kin were so significant in Kaixiangong as well as providing a framework to understand the full range of social support. *Lishang-wanglai* in this book will be based on the study of social support from my fieldwork, although I will introduce it in a more general way.

II. The villagers' usage of *li shang wanglai*

The motivation for using *lishang-wanglai* (see Part Three) as a key concept for my study is derived from my fieldwork. The phrase itself, *li shang wanglai*, came from a male villager in Kaixiangong Village, while a woman used the metaphor of fattening pigs (*yangzhu*) to mean the

---

[8] Agnatic kin are those related to the household through the direct male line, either as ancestors or descendants, plus the women who marry into the household and minus the women who marry out. Non-agnatic kin are related through a female link. Normally, in a three-generation household these include the male household-head's married-out paternal aunt(s)' relatives, his mother's relatives, his married-out sister(s)' relatives, his wife's relatives, his married-out daughter(s)' relatives and so on.

same thing (Chang, 1999: 156–174). In order to distinguish my terminology from the standard folk expression *li shang wanglai* I will use the form *lishang-wanglai* to describe my understanding of social support and reciprocity. The term *lishang-wanglai* is a literal rendering of the villagers' usage of the folk expression *li shang wanglai*, and the model of *lishang-wanglai* is my interpretation of patterns of social relationships based on implicit cultural models in Kaixiangong village.

1. Raising or fattening pigs

Here I will firstly relate the practice of fattening pigs to *lishang-wanglai,* to clarify the villagers' usage of *li shang wanglai*. The analogy of "fattening pigs" was provided by an old woman in the village. She explained that almost every household in the village has one or more pigs. Pig feed in 1996 cost about 500 *yuan* a year for a normal sized pig. The pig itself sells for about 600-650 *yuan*. The profit from raising household pigs is less than the overall cost including both pig feed and labour. Therefore one cannot expect to earn much money from fattening household pigs. But why are people still raising pigs? The villagers told me that the benefits from fattening pigs are many:

- Plenty of farmyard manure from a small daily amount of pig fodder; meat for a wedding or funeral feast; and immediate cash from selling the pig when money is needed urgently. These benefits can be described by *li* and *yi* which are villagers' versions of rational calculation.

- Fattening or raising pigs in Chinese is known as *yangzhu* which relates to a study of '*yang*' (Stafford, 1995, 2000a, 2000c). The villagers say "fattening a big fat pig" (*yang zhi da pang zhu*) in the same way as they say "fattening a big fat son" (*yang ge da pang erzi*). Raising pigs involves human feeling (*qing*). This explains why, as the villagers told me, some women would cry when their pig was killed.

- For the villagers the pig also has symbolic meaning, for example to have a big fat pig means to have good fortune (*youfu*).

- To offer sacrifices to the ancestors with a whole pig is better than half, and half better than an upper part of leg (*tipang*). There is a village saying that without the upper part of one leg of pork there can be no feast (*meiyou tipang bu cheng yan*), due to the *tipang*'s symbolic meaning.

Both a religious sense and enjoyment are involved. The above points show that although the process of raising or fattening pigs is an action or practice of feasting and gift-giving (*wanglai*), there are always a multiplicity of principles (*lishang*) behind the action.

2. *Li, shang li* and *li shang*

I always heard stories about how women brought different kinds of "*lipin*" (presents or gifts) to "*zou renqing*" or "*zou renjia*" (visit other households). They are all different kinds of *wanglai*[9], for example for a wedding, a visit to a sick person, or even to gain a job opportunity in a village enterprise. In maintaining relationships and arranging resources for their welfare the phrase "fattening pigs" is used to imply a set of criteria, *liyi* (benefit), *ganqing* (human feeling), *fuqi* (religious sense) and so on. The way in which the villagers use *lishang-wanglai* is concrete. They always count how often they visit or contact each other, whether or not they attend someone's wedding, how long they stay there, how many gifts and what kind of gift they should bring to the occasion and so on, to judge the quality of relationships.

The villagers have clear and readily comprehensible explanations for *lishang*. For instance, suppose a guest brings a gift which is inferior in quality or quantity, or his or her behaviour is bad (attending too late, wearing improper clothes, or not being polite to other guests). This guest, normally, would receive an even worse reply from the host, unless there is a special reason involved. According to the villagers, the host treating the guest in such a way is proper because:

- It is morally right – it would help the guest to realise he or she has behaved badly to the host without involving any words.
- It would remind the host to review whether or not this relationship should be maintained. If this is a sign of the end of *yuan* (fate, predestined relationship), he or she should happily see a natural ending to the relationship.
- The process of arranging gifts involves rational calculation. Wives of the agnatic kin normally sort out all the gifts received by a host. The same women also prepare the return gifts (*huili*).[10] This is a kind of important labour support because both the sorting out of gifts and the preparation of return gifts involves understanding local customs and the quality of the relationships with the guests.

---

[9] Stafford's *laiwang* is interchangeable with *wanglai* in a horizontal direction, and his *yang* can be understood as *awanglai* in a vertical direction, but his explanation about *yang,* such as filial piety, caring, can be seen as a part of "*lishang*".

[10] According to local custom nobody should bring an empty gift container back home. There are many detailed customs covering what and how many gifts should be presented in each event and what and how many things should be returned after the event. See Part One.

- There is always social creativity in the event. Apart from organising the event the host also needs to work out who wants to be close to him or her and who wants to keep a distance from him or her, according to information from gift giving and behaviour at the event. This is hard work because his or her policy in relationships with others should be applied in a proper way when he or she attends any of these guests' events in the future. Almost all my informants actually enjoyed the process of reviewing relationships because it is creative work.

Here, the element "*shang*" (uphold) of "*shangli*" (civility, propriety) and "*shangwen*" (advocate culture), or "*shangwu*" (warlike) is written with the same character, and is also grammatically correct. But, unlike the freestanding phrase "*laiwang*", the independent use of "*lishang*" from "*lishang-wanglai*" is grammatically incorrect. Moreover, both the "*shangli*" or "*lishang*" in oral and written form in everyday life are relatively unfamiliar. However, I found 100,000 and 500,000 entries respectively for "*shangli*" or "*lishang*" from the Google search engine, and their usage more or less agrees with that of my villagers'. "*Shangli*" or "*lishang*" are becoming phrases like "*wanglai*" and "*laiwang*" established by usage, and can be used independently and interchangeably. In this book, I will use "*shangli*" or "*lishang*" freely depending on situation and convenience.

3. *Wanglai* and *laiwang*

For Kaixiangong villagers, *wanglai* is also called *zouwang* (meaning to visit each other, to come and go, and to contact or to connect with somebody) and describes the condition of relationships with other households.[11] The villagers say that *wanglai* is the most important way to make and maintain personal relationships: *qinqi yue zou yue qin* and *pengyou yue zou yue jin* (the more *wanglai* with relatives the deeper the relationship; the more *wanglai* with friends the closer the relationship). For them, different kinds of relationships (kin, neighbour, friend, etc.) in the village and other places have varying qualities (close or loose, good or bad) of relatedness. For example, most people indicated in their responses to the ESRC survey that they would wish to treat their neighbours as relatives. As the old saying says: "a relative far off is less help than a

---

[11] In the ESRC project the concept of contact has been understood as *wanglai*. "Every transaction of social support for every event from every source to every household, and sub-categories of these. Note that contact is not the same as person, since the same person may have been contacted for different kinds of support and for different events many times" (Chang and Feuchtwang, 1996: 17).

neighbour close by; neighbours are dearer than distant relatives" (*yuanqin buru jinlin*). However, it is not easy to do so because of the large amount of obligations that would be involved in neighbourhood relationships. There are even a few extreme examples in Kaixiangong village of close relatives who live as neighbours but do not maintain a close relationship. For example, a mother and a son's family live as neighbours but never talk to each other (see the Zhou family example in chapter VIII.II). Some educated villagers quoted Lao Tzu's famous passage to describe such a situation. It says, "*ji-quan zhi sheng xiang wen, lao si bu xiang wanglai*", literally, people grow old and die without even going where others live close by. It is clear that the original meaning of the passage referred to two villages next to each other. However, the passage has had many interpretations over more than 2,000 years. The villagers' interpretation was that it is very inappropriate for brothers never to *wanglai* to each other even though they lived within the same village and their houses shared the same courtyard.

Wanglai*'s rich contents can be described in different ways. I found that rural people usually use *zoudong*, *zouwang* or *zoufang*, for long-term interactive relationships with other people or families, whereas urban people or well-educated people often use *wanglai* or *jiaowang* for the same thing. Here the *zou* of *zoudong*, *zouwang* or *zoufang* means walk. Perhaps this is because originally in rural society people lived closely together, with walking as the only means of contact, so walking was essential to *wanglai*. *Jiao* of *jiaowang* is also used in *jiaotong* (transport) and *jiaodao* (contact with others). These words appeared before socialist China in urban areas and have been used continuously until now. In urban areas relatives and friends normally live in different places between which transport is easy.[12] There are some other related terms used by people: *da jiaodao* (contact, or make contact with), *jiaowang* (contact), *jiaoqing* (friendly relations, friendship), but the term of *jiaoji* (social intercourse) was used less often. Yang and Peng (1999) found that from the 1990s more and more Chinese business people used *jiaoji* to describe the first stage of making relationships.

4. "*Li shang wanglai*" and "*lishang-wanglai*"

The way in which Kaixiangong villagers use the terms "fattening pigs" and

---

[12] In socialist China people who work in the same work unit (*danwei*) live in the same big court (*dayuan*) or big building (*dalou*), which belongs to the *danwei*. Although they sometimes visit each other (so-called *chuanmen*, not *zouwang*) within walking distance, their relationships are mostly those of colleagues rather than friendship because there is competition among them in sharing the same resources from the *danwei*. This is another topic.

"*lishang-wanglai*" is to describe the complicated creative process of making and maintaining relationships. As Kipnis noticed "no unchanging, single form of *guanxi* exists…each of these relationships (*guanxi*) carries its own connotations and its own social/historical specificity. The meanings of words like *guanxi* and *ganqing* cannot be fixed" (1997: 184).

However, the complicated relationships or unfixed meanings of different types of relationship, such as. *guanxi* or *renqing*, can be explained by noting the different principles of *li* of *lishang-wanglai*. There is a Chinese saying "*yi bubian ying wan bian*", that is to say, "meeting all changes by remaining unchanged – coping with a constantly changing situation by sticking to a fixed principle or policy". Any relationship can be changed, but the principles behind the change remain the same. The changes are based on different types of *lishang* and people's understandings of *lishang* change interdependently. Thus, relationships can be fixed by *lishang*, whether in loose, temporary, permanent, completed or continuous forms. In practice, people can choose different ways to have *wanglai* within different relationships. In chapters IV to VIII, I will show how, in rural China, villagers use local customs (*lishang*) in constant discussion and deliberate action (*wanglai*), which can change according to changing circumstances.

Lishang-wanglai, based on the understanding and perceptions of the villagers, both male and female, is the key concept of my study. It relates to a creative process of personal or personalised reciprocal relationships in which different types of reciprocities (*wanglai*) are judged by different criteria (*lishang*). I will show how the common usage of "*li shang wanglai*" and my interpretation of the Kaixiangong villagers' usage of *li shang wanglai* becomes *lishang-wanglai* in Chapter XI.

III. Research methods and research scope

Although the ESRC social support project provided a guide for studying social support, it is too general for an in-depth study, especially when one involves the notion of *li shang wanglai,* which is both complicated and central to Chinese culture. It is therefore necessary to set some boundaries for the usage in my study. After I describe how I conducted my own fieldwork I will then clarify three things about my work: its precise time, space and discipline. Since the topic of subject position of the researcher is very complicated I will discuss it in a separate section.

1. Research methods

(1) General methods

I conducted my fieldwork in Neiguan Village, Gansu Province (see Map 1-1), from late August to the middle of November 1995, and in Kaixiangong Village, Jiangsu Province (see Map 1-2), from the middle of February to the middle of May 1996. In my fieldwork I used a mixture of questionnaire surveys, interviews, direct observation, documentary research and case study methods. This is similar to the ESRC project methodology. I interviewed the households in the original study, which were selected by random probability sampling from the administrative village's household registrations.[13] I interviewed 30 households in Neiguan, the identical households as those used in the original study. However, the 32 households I interviewed in Kaixiangong are two less than in the original survey. One of the two missing households was that of an old couple who moved to a city and lived with their daughter's family. Another was a single father's family. The son left the village when he was aged 16, and the father died two years later (see Chapter VII.III).

There is little agreement about fieldwork methods and methodology on the topic of social support and *lishang-wanglai* in China. I had to develop my own methods while I was doing the fieldwork itself (see XII.I and II). In this section I will describe a few of these methods. I will also sometimes refer back to the ESRC project guide because it provides the baseline for a longitudinal study. When I do so will be to add more information to it, including the results of more intensive fieldwork on each household.

(2) Language

It is important to learn local languages to carry out fieldwork. I found that I had to learn the local languages at the beginning of my fieldwork because I only understood about 60 per cent of words spoken in the two villages when I arrived there. Apart from the many minority languages there are a few major Chinese language families in Han dominated Chinese society, such as *ganyu* in Jiangxi Province, *minyu* in Fujian; *wuyu* in Shanghai, Jiangsu, and Zhejiang; *yueyu* in Guangdong; and Mandarin which covers most of the rest of China. It is feasible for a Mandarin speaker to do fieldwork in most of China, although there are local accents and intonations in

---

[13] In two villages with dense populations, namely Jinxing and Kaixiangong of Jiangsu province, 36 and 34 households were chosen. In Xianfeng of Gansu Province, with a scattered population, only 24 households were chosen. In the other seven villages 30 households were chosen.

different areas. It would be difficult for a Mandarin speaker to do fieldwork in the non-Mandarin speaking provinces, which require special language skills. I learnt the local languages by checking the copies of "local language rules" from the general records of the two counties (*xianzhi*), while I was doing interviews with informants. These rules are mainly related to pronunciation. Rules of grammar are quite similar everywhere in China. It took me a few days' study to understand 90 per cent of both local languages. The local accent in Neiguan Village was not too difficult, because their language can be counted as part of Mandarin, whereas the Kaixiangong people spoke another family of languages (*wuyu yuxi*). Luckily I understood some *wu* language because when I was a teenager I spent a year living with some Shanghainese in a professional Ping-Pong training team. I can also speak one of the above most difficult local languages (*ganyu*), because I was born and grew up in Jiangxi Province. I thus have a foundation for understanding different dialects in China.

It is particularly important for external fieldwork researchers to catch the cultural flavours from local languages. Kaixiangong villagers use the character *yisi* in different contexts: for example *bugou yisi* (not properly express somebody's appreciation or gratitude), *buhao yisi* (embarrassed), *hen you yisi* (very interesting, fun), *meide yisi* (meaningless, tasteless, dull)*, shenme yisi* (meaning, opinion), *xiao yisi* (a token of appreciation or gratitude), *yisi yisi* (to express somebody's appreciation or gratitude in a reasonable way). After I worked out all these different meanings of *yisi* I understood more of the way in which social support worked in the village. Examples of this occur, in Kaixiangong, when villagers ask for payback from those people they have helped, or refuse those people who are asking for help even though they would really like to help, or delay the return of a favour to someone who has helped them before. The villagers describe the feelings involved in such situations with the term *buhao yisi* (feel shy, shame, embarrassed or humiliation). This relates to *mianzi* (face, see section IX.II.), although the villagers care more about their *lianmian* (*lian* + *mianzi*, cheek and face, moral reputation) than face (*mianzi,* prestige). I will use the *lishang-wanglai* model to demonstrate how I gained access to the fieldwork sites and got to know the informants in chapters XII.I and XII.II.

(3) Local guide, interviewee and informants

How to use a local guide is another issue. Fieldwork researchers would normally be introduced or accompanied by a local guide. It was not clear to me who my local guide should be and how I should use the local guide, because different researchers have had different relationships with them. The local guide can be an assistant who could come from any level:

province, county, township or village. The broadest understanding of a local guide's role would be to expect the local guide to take part in the interviews, to translate where necessary and sometimes to interpret meanings. This happened in the original study. According to the original fieldwork guide, researchers should be helped by a locally born village guide. It was clear, if I followed this, the local guide should come from the village, but it was still unclear how to use the local guide. After my fieldwork I have concluded that it is wrong to have such high expectations from a village guide. I found that the village guide could comprise one person (in Neiguan Village) or several people (in Kaixiangong Village). They normally would be village cadres, such as the treasurer in Neiguan, and the agrotechnician and the director of the Village Women's Federation in Kaixiangong. It was part of their "job" to introduce a researcher briefly to every sample household and to answer general questions about the village and their own fields. The cadres or guides were instructed to do so by the head of the village in the case of almost all researchers and visitors. So these kinds of local guides cannot be informants or key actors (Bailey, 1996) because they play a limited role. However, if their households are used as part of the sample, as happened in Kaixiangong Village, they could be much more helpful, because they would have been interviewed with a big questionnaire, would understand more of the research, be able to introduce more related detailed information, and so on. They then become real key actors, but the chance of this is not great because households interviewed are selected randomly. If they were experts in local customs or knowledge themselves they could also be key actors. Personally I found that village guides' roles, if they were village cadres, are limited and the key actors of a particular project cannot also be village guides or cadres. The identities of key actors in the village depend on the subject of the research, and they can only be found through interviewing all the sample households and by talking to many local people.

How to define a respondent, informant, interviewee, or key actor was another problem for me. I used the same questionnaire and fieldwork guide as for the ESRC project. The questionnaire mixed both sociological and anthropological elements and was made up of 111 questions, which included both closed and open questions. I would normally call people who filled or answered standard sociological questionnaires the respondents, and standard anthropological questionnaires the interviewees or informants. Informants can also be key actors who provide much more useful information, but not necessarily through answering a questionnaire, as I mentioned in the previous paragraph. I tended to avoid the term of key actors because there were so many people involved in my fieldwork who were "key" in different ways. I will use the term informant to refer to those people who either answered the questionnaire, or extra questions, or both, but I will make clear what each person's role was when I describe my fieldwork.

Interviewee is the broadest term for anybody of whom I asked any question, whether or not they answered the questionnaire, and whether they provided more or less information. One household can therefore have different interviewees. In the original ESRC study, the researchers often broke the long questionnaire into more than one session in order to complete it, and I followed this practice. However, I found that the same informant from the same household sometimes provided different answers to the same question on different visits! Therefore, I then checked with the informant for detailed reasons and found how he or she weighted different reasons in different situations. Instead of interviewing one person (aged above 18) in each household, as the previous study required, I also interviewed a representative cross-section of each household: male and female, old and young. When I asked a male informant about labour support he would advise me to ask his wife for details. What I define as "annual events" were not on my questionnaire originally, and could be omitted if the male informant did not notice this, or I did not pay attention to his referral. One important reason to involve female informants is that almost all the annual life events (see VII.I) involved labour support between women. However, when I put the same question to the female informants from my sampled households, they listed the above events naturally. This gave me the idea that interviewing different genders with the same questionnaire could get different results, and this could be considered as an addition to the general fieldwork method.

(4) Questionnaire

I will now move onto another issue relating to the contents of the fieldwork questionnaire used in the ESRC project. This mixed sociology and anthropology questionnaire was too long, and had too many open questions, to be considered a sociological questionnaire, and it was also too long, and too simple, for an anthropological questionnaire. I also found it inadequate for investigating the social support arrangements of rural Chinese. So I added more questions and instead of asking for information on only two major support events, I obtained the whole list of different types of social support (financial, labour and information) from all different sources (household, private – kin, neighbour and friend and public) for all kind of events (family, emergency and investment) from each household. This list includes each household's events from 1996 all the way back to 1979. I also obtained the whole structure of the kinship network of every sample household, and a large number of supporting documents and materials from the different types of organisations, the village committee and the different departments of the local government.

My observations were broader than the those of the original ESRC fieldwork in two ways. Firstly, I attended many different types of funeral, weddings and other important events to observe how social support works. I spent time with the local people on the official National Day and the Moon Day (the 15th of the 8th lunar month) in Neiguan, the Chinese New Year, Lantern Festival (the 15th of the 1st lunar month), Qingming Day (the day marking the beginning of the 5th solar term, the 4th, 5th or 6th April,)[14] in Kaixiangong. I also attended many feasts for the ceremony of house-building completion in Kaixiangong. Secondly, I visited all the temples around the villages and townships[15] and also those in neighbouring villages and townships, to get a feel for the social changes peculiar to the local culture and how they affected villagers' lives. I also visited many kinds of factory, works and institutes run by individual people, the village committee, and also the local government, to help me understand social change in and around the village.

(5) Post-fieldwork method

My original fieldwork had been focused on the key words social support, so I was now eager for as much new empirical data as possible, as I evolved my understanding of *lishang-wanglai.* I innovated a post-fieldwork follow-up with my informants, through telephone and e-mail interview from 1997 to 2004. There were very few households in the village with their own telephone when I was there in 1996, whereas in September 2002 more than 80 per cent of families had telephones. Although there are few people using e-mail, it's a very useful way to get documentary attachments. The cost of telephone calls from the UK to an informant in the village also went down significantly[16], from 19p (1998) to 2p (2004) per minute. Personal

---

[14] Traditionally observed as a festival for worshipping at ancestral graves, technically known as "sweeping the graves".

[15] Except one temple in Neiguan Village, where women were not allowed to enter.

[16] However, the rates to China were affected by changes of Chinese policy. For example, after the Chinese government suddenly increased the termination charge from 1st November 2002, Communication 2000 increased its rate from 5p to 15p per minute, Planet Talk from 10p to 19p and VoizFone from 7 US cents to 22 cents. From early 2003 all the related telephone rates adjusted downwards after complaints by overseas Chinese and foreign business people. Currently, the cheapest rate to China is 2p per minute through Telediscount and Call 18866. Note: in 2009 when I proofread the Chinese version I added WebCallDirect as the most up-to-date way to carry out telephone interviews. It costs 0.5 Euro cent to ring landlines and mobile phones in China via online access.

computer to phone calling provided an even lower cost, but at reduced quality. Both telephone and computer recordings helped to store the related information. If technology eventually allows high recognition voice to text transfer then this would make the process of sorting out such interview materials even easier and quicker. Initially I was using telephone interviews as an addition to my fieldwork. They were mainly used for the longitudinal study of some incomplete cases. If my description mentions something which happened after my fieldwork period, readers should assume that the information came from my telephone interviews.

As time went by, telephone and e-mail interviews became more and more important to my study. E-mail allows the transfer of tables and digital photographs as well as texts. The rapid advancement of technology allows researchers to apply it both during fieldwork and post-fieldwork. In 1996 digital cameras were not available. My study required recordings of events. The photographs only reflect a part of villagers' events because I was trying to take part in them and use my camcorder at the same time. Nowadays, the quality problem of my fieldwork photographs can be solved by using a better quality digital camera. In the future, it will be helpful if the quality of still photography in combination digital camera/camcorders can be improved. Beside, with technological advances, Kaixiangong has set up its own webpage which will benefit people who are interested in the village.

I have noticed a tendency in fieldwork duration and method of contact17; that is, the time lived in a field site has become shorter and shorter (from one year, to six months, to three months minimum) but more and more frequent. The information revolution has made it possible to do post-fieldwork interviews by telephone, e-mail and other means. This book has benefited from the usage of post-fieldwork methods.

2. Research Scope: time and space

(1) Time

In the broadest sense this study covers the historical period from 1946 to 2004, when my PhD dissertation was completed, continuing to 2009, when I proofread the Chinese version and updated some of its content.

More intensively, my work will focus on the post-Mao period from 1978 to 2004, which

---

[17] Some researchers also noticed this in a workshop on fieldwork research methods in contemporary Chinese society (Oxford, 18 – 21 September 2000).

covers the Deng and Jiang regimes and extends into Hu's. This period starts with the Deng regime and his economic reforms. After the June 4th Event in 1989 Jiang Zemin came into power and partly shared it with Hu in 2003. There is a huge difference in socialist China between the times of Mao and this post-Mao period. The former is characterised by the collective and the latter by the individual. In the latter the establishment of the household responsibility system in rural China coincided with the disintegration of the People's Commune System. Under the Commune System rural people lived in shared poverty. The Household Responsibility System broke away from the old mode of production, which was based on the production brigade or team, and provided the opportunity for rural people to arrange their lives for themselves. So many aspects of social relations can be seen more clearly in the freer post-Mao era than previously, when rural people's lives were highly controlled by their production brigades and their living standard was very low.

Chinese society and rural people's lives have changed almost beyond recognition over the twenty-plus years of economic reform after Mao. There were three major changes in this historical period. The first, dating from 1985, was the abovementioned establishment of the household responsibility system and replacement of the People's Commune System by a system of administrative townships and villages, leading to economic reform of the whole society.

The second change was the policy of "fast economic development" that was brought into the party's declared guiding principles in 1993. This new encouragement of privatisation and marketisation was initiated in talks by Deng Xiaoping in 1992 in Guangzhou, endorsing that city's fast capitalist development. There were to be no more pronouncements condemning bourgeoisification. Formalised repetitions of the Four Political Principles of adherence to Marxism-Leninism-Mao-Zedong-thought disappeared. 1992 was also the year that the number of workers in so called 'township and village enterprises' (TVEs) rose above the number employed in state-owned enterprises (Guo, 1993), an economic turning point in the development of rural industrial enterprise. The third change, in 1996, was the privatisation of the TVEs themselves. Their establishment had on the one hand given many villages additional welfare resources, for example Fanggan Village in Shandong Province and Jinxing Village in Jiangsu Province, which I visited in 1993 and 1996. On the other hand, many TVEs overstocked bad quality products and became stuck in heavy debt, as happened in Kaixiangong. The changes of ownership from TVEs to private persons (*gaizhi* – privatisation) provided opportunities of economic development to Kaixiangong Village.

These changes have very much enriched the fabric of social support during the period after

Mao. Social support as a way in which rural people arrange their life in rural China is a reciprocal process. One can only see the dynamics of this complicated process clearly by examining it over an extended period. Twenty-five years is an appropriate length of time for this study. The ESRC project and my own fieldwork's records of social support arrangements cover 1978 to 1996, with additional information gathered by telephone until 2004. Where it is relevant I will also use some materials from previous studies in Kaixiangong Village, which began in the 1930s. For example, I use information from Fei, 1939; Geddes, 1963; Hui, 1996a, 1996b, 1999; Li, 1996; Liu, 1996; Lu, 1993; Shen, 1993, 1996; Wang, 2002 and my own interviews with Hui when he visited London in 1999. My post-fieldwork material, obtained by keeping up contacts made during fieldwork by telephone and e-mail, is described in the previous section.

By supplementing direct fieldwork with this additional material it is possible to examine more clearly the ways in which *lishang-wanglai* adapts and changes.

(2) Space

My research is based primarily on the detailed study of one Chinese village – Kaixiangong. However, my views of social support and *lishang-wanglai* will also radiate to wider areas, for example, Neiguan, Gansu Province, my other fieldwork village[18] and other parts of rural China (e.g. materials from ESRC project villages[19]; He, 1992; Yan, 1996a, 1996b, 2003; Kipnis, 1997; Stafford, 1995, 2000a, 2000c). Given the many similarities between all these villages, side by side of course with differences, I feel justified in talking about rural China as a whole. Where appropriate, I will also use material from urban areas in China, and even my experiences of living in the UK.

Thus, previous researchers' work and my own fieldwork experience told me that it is possible to generalise studies of social support to a national level. I regret that I didn't visit Xianfeng Village, a neighbouring village to Neiguan, Gansu Province. I resisted my urge to go there whenever I passed by because I thought then that I should keep a very pure experience within one particular village. However, local officers of the county made it possible for me to visit many other villages after I finished my fieldwork, and this was very helpful. After I finished my fieldwork in Kaixiangong Village I visited Jingxin Village in the same province. Each

---

[18] Given the wealth of fieldwork I have accumulated, a full comparison of the two villages would be too large in scope for one thesis.
[19] The regional coverage of the 10 villages of the ESRC project is wide. They are administrative villages, which contain a number of natural settlements – hamlets or natural villages.

village is different, some markedly so, but there are common themes in their social support arrangements. My fieldwork was carried out as part of a re-study of the ESRC social support project, and my central framework of *lishang-wanglai* was refined during my writing up, after all the fieldwork had been completed. This fieldwork had not been designed to explicate underlying rationales. So this book omits much of my original fieldwork material, and supplements it with materials from other researchers and my own post-fieldwork.

I have been living in England since 1991 and married an Englishman in 1996. We lived in a small village, in a Conservation Area, in North-West London for six years. We were involved in the village residents association when we lived there. After we moved to the Moat Mount Nature Reservation area I became involved again in both the residents association and my son's school PTA (Parents and Teachers Association). My personal experiences of living in England and participating in local activities provide me with opportunities to observe how ordinary English people arrange their everyday life and relate to each other. Although this book will not make a scholarly comparison between Chinese rural villages and English urban villages, I will sometimes give examples from England, to form a contrast. It would appear that *lishang-wanglai* can be used in different cultural contexts, therefore ways in which it is common or different amongst different cultures and people make a fascinating object for further study.

IV. Researcher's multifaceted position

1. The subject-position of the researcher

I mentioned at the end of the section "The villagers' usage of *li shang wanglai*" that the vitality of *lishang-wanglai* comes from an enjoyment of creativity under uncertain conditions that can bring benefit and good fortune, and at other times trouble and disaster, into the same people's lives. It is not easy to maintain a lukewarm relationship with this powerful social force.

I never imagined I would find myself interested, even fascinated, by the subject of *lishang-wanglai,* because when living in China I had been a rebel against intricate social or human relationships, in particular *guanxi, renqing* and *lishang-wanglai*. My family, my friends and everybody I knew had had their own various experiences of escape[20] from the intricacies

---

[20] Some sinologists (Jin or King 1989a; Hwang 1982, etc.) use the term of "escape" to describe someone leaving a difficult situation when he or she recognises that the negative side of *renqing* or *wanglai* could destroy one's

of these aspects of social life.

When I was working out the methodological implications of *lishang-wanglai* from my own fieldwork experiences, I needed to treat myself as another interviewee (see XII.I and II). I found that however hard in the past I had tried to escape from the complexities of *lishang-wanglai*, my life required me to be involved with them one way or another. I found that the villagers had been using the basic principles of *lishang* for themselves to improve their lives, as well as obtaining enjoyment from the process of *lishang-wanglai*. I also found that they sometimes escaped from over-personalising relationships in order to keep distance and their own space. So, I am writing about *lishang-wanglai* as a practitioner, as well as somebody who wishes to escape it, and therefore, like the villagers, to keep my distance from it.

In order to integrate different partial understandings of the process of *lishang-wanglai* I intend to find a position or space where I am looking at it both from the outside and inside. What I am in that position is neither Chinese nor British. In this position my goal is more task-oriented, and not personalised. My judgement is based on merit but not on personalised relationships. This means I am, in my writing, moving away from the personal substance and enjoyment of *lishang-wanglai*. This is a social anthropologist's position. Although I cannot be a purely abstract person, I can use this space to move from one position to the other within a sociological and an anthropological discipline. This will be my subject-position.

2. From a masculinised feminist perspective

Ever since I was a child I admired masculinity. My imitation of male masculinity had earned me such epithets as tomboy or Lady Robin Hood. I see myself as a female who has been academically masculinised. Up to now, my Chinese publications that have amounted to nearly a million words have been invariably in a "masculine" style.

However, the awakening and development of my feminism has been taking its place in my life for more than two decades. For instance, as a postgraduate, I edited a volume of the *Journal of Postgraduate* with a column on women. In the UK, I coordinated an international conference on Chinese women and the conference collection was later published with me as one of the editors. I attended the UN 4th World Conference on Women (1995) in Beijing. One of my main reasons for choosing to go back to Kaixiangong Village was the statistical finding of the

---

work or life.

ESRC-funded social support projects, that the proportion of non-agnate kin support in Kaixiangong had been far higher than in the other nine villages.

During my field trips, I didn't specifically consider the issue of gender. However, upon the completion of this book, I began to see myself in a feminist context. Among the studies on Chinese relationships, Mayfair Yang (1994) is a female, whereas Yunxiang Yan (1996b) and Andrew Kipnis (1997) are male. Yang focused her attention on urban China whereas Yan, Kipnis and I are more interested in rural areas. In the Author's Preface of the Chinese translation of *Flow of Gifts*, Yan acknowledged that his studies lacked a feminist perspective. Mine do not.

This book can be seen as a result of a dialogue between male and female. Although it was written by an academically trained masculinised female, it is no longer a work of masculinisation, nor of feminism, but rather a combination of the two.

3. A mutual communication between an urban dweller and her village interviewees

Despite my insistence on independence in sociological and anthropological position, I'm nevertheless not an abstract non-entity. During fieldwork, I was often faced by interviewees with very personal questions on subjects such as my age and boyfriends. Then unmarried and already into my thirties, I felt very uneasy and unaccustomed to these sensitive questions. City born and city bred in China, I had lived in London for a few years. I had an English boyfriend (now my husband), but I neither wanted to lie to the villagers nor involve a "foreigner" to complicate their perception of me. However, my interviews covered a large amount of sensitive personal issues with my interviewees. I believed it must have been uncomfortable for them to be prodded with these questions. Therefore, I decided to open my heart to them. A researcher should not treat his or her interviewees as research subjects, but as friends, which I believe to be the only way through which is it possible to obtain truthful, in-depth information. One of my most significant discoveries was that fieldwork is a process of bi-directional communication, which can be regarded as a "*wanglai*" (my term) between the interviewer and the interviewee.

The bi-directional communication with interviewees is not only an important means to obtain information, but also an effective measure to ensure data accuracy. As I interviewed almost every adult of the sample families, in an amiable and friendly atmosphere, I found different responses from interviewees towards the same questions, or different responses by the same interviewee under different circumstances. At times I needed to check different responses. After explanation, they would sometimes add, 'I have already been so explicit. How can you not understand it at all?'[21]. In the initial stage of my fieldwork, interviewees from more than one case complained to me that I failed to understand them without requiring them to be very exact about what they were saying. In their eyes, since I was the one interested in them, it was my "work" to figure out what they meant. Therefore, I used to ask questions such as: "is this what you mean", or "is that what you mean", to check their responses. For them, a specific answer is incapable of capturing the complicated picture of manoeuvring resources. For one thing, all relevant answers to the same question can only be revealed by a variety of ways of looking at it. During fieldwork, different reasons and principles in enlisting social support have resulted in the diversity of rules governing "*lishang*".

4. A Dialogue between a not-yet-fully-Westernised Chinese scholar and Western sociology and anthropology

Two years ago, when I first started studying entrepreneurial relationships, I realised the biggest issue facing the delivery of this book is its lack of economic viability. In the simplest terms, it is too long. The draft was 300,000 words, which could have made three entire books on the themes of reciprocity, social support networks, and social creativity. In these circumstances most Western and non-Western scholars alike would make a rational choice to avoid trying to include too much material in one book. However, the subject-position of my book includes a dialogue between a not-yet-fully-westernised Chinese scholar and Western sociology and anthropology. On the one hand, as a relatively mature scholar who was trained in China, it is impossible to avoid the influence of the Chinese way of thinking during research. On the other hand, I admired and wanted to carry out Westernised sociological and anthropological methodology.

In this process, I discovered the essentially epistemological difference between Chinese social science and its Western counterpart. This can be captured by a metaphor. The service of Western cuisine includes three or up to seven courses, centring on a certain theme (meat, vegetable or seafood). By comparison, a Chinese dinner may include eight to twenty dishes with a representation of diverse themes in each dish. Similarly, Sahlins argued that the cosmogony of Western scholarship was based on monotheism, whereas Feuchtwang, among others, submitted that in China gods or sages exist everywhere, and many gods coexist in the same place (Stephan

---

[21] In his interview in Xiajia Village (Yunxiang Yan, 2003: 255), the villagers had similar expectations of being understood without their further explanations.

Feuchtwang, 2005). In the same year, there was an exhibition of "China: Three Emperors (1662–1795)". David Hockney, the Academician of The Royal Academy of Arts, commented that the Chinese paintings deployed multiple perspective points in a single painting, which is different from the single perspective point in Western painting. For him, the Western history of arts has long neglected the beauty and sophistication of the Chinese painting scroll[22], which bears close resemblance to cinema pictures by offering a sense of pleasure at being part of the painting. As the Chinese painting has no vanishing point, its viewer has to assume a participatory approach, rather than a static posture, through which to engage him or herself, including eyes, body and psyche into the story-telling and moving with the scroll part by part.[23]

So, generally speaking, Western social science is more focused on a detailed analysis of specific issues, while the Chinese way is to offer a combined approach to several issues together. This book is an attempt to present to its readers a huge painting scroll of the complicated relationships in the everyday life of a Chinese village. It is nonetheless not totally Chinese, just as sometimes in the West a few miniatures can be presented on one big wall. In this case they are embedded in the Chinese scroll. Hockney's prescription of how to appreciate Chinese painting might be helpful for readers in their approach to this book.

Now let's return to the metaphor of cuisines. In 2008 I interviewed Chinese restaurant managers or owners in Chinatown in London. They told me that Western customers always eat Chinese food in the Western manner: from starter, main course to dessert. But when eating the main course, Westerners also order different dishes to share with each other, which is a Chinese way of eating. In contrast, in China it is fashionable to eat Western or international food at a buffet in a five-star hotel or shopping centre, at a cost of 200 *yuan* per head. Over a dozen cuisines from different countries and regions may be presented. Western chefs are appointed at certain places for authentic offers of Western food. Chinese patrons can choose to eat from eight to any number of different kinds of Western food at the same time. This is eating Western food in the Chinese way.

The purpose of my metaphor is to illustrate that in spite of the typically incisive methods of presentation used by Western social sciences, such as detailed description, logical analysis,

---

[22] A typical example is the Qingming Riverside Painting, which was selected as the homepage background for CCPN, cf. www.lse.ac.uk/ccpn.
[23] David Hockney, "A Difference of Perspective", in "Three Emperors, 1662–1795", *RA Magazine*, Winter, 2005.

insightful arguments, critical reviews, independent thinking, a rational and equal approach to debates (these methods do of course partially overlap with Chinese social scientific training), they hardly exhaust the totality of social scientific researches taken the world over, especially in our current age of globalisation. A book such as this would have never been published in the West without cutting it into two or three pieces, at the cost of losing its Chineseness. It awaits challenges from and responses to complexity, synthesis and inclusiveness, as in the Chinese way of thinking.

Therefore, this book can be seen as an encounter of East and West, as it contains very detailed descriptions and in-depth analyses, but from a complex and inclusive frame of mind. It is an attempt at a dialogue with Western sociology and anthropology, however crude, by a not-yet-fully-Westernised Chinese scholar.

V. Arrangement of fieldwork materials and structure of the book

1. Methodology in writing

(1) Verification of facts and confidentiality

This book involves numerous people and incidents. During writing-up I have kept in close contact with interviewees to verify and constantly update my information and understanding of their situations. To ensure veracity, objectivity and accuracy, all the chapters from I to VIII were checked and confirmed by Fukun Yao, the key interviewee in my study. Parts of the book were also presented to other interviewees for comment. Local verification is I believe a very important part of the work's value.

In dealing with these materials, there is an issue facing me all the time: how to protect the privacy of interviewees as well as ensure the veracity of interviews. When a proofreader asked me whether or not I had obtained permission to publish someone's birthday, I checked with the person concerned and she wasn't at all disturbed because privacy of birth details are not an issue in the village; almost everybody knows each other's birthday within a group. An oft-used protection mechanism is anonymity, but due to descriptive details, interviewees can often be easily identified. To opt for a *nom de guerre* might make them feel uncomfortable. For this reason I have opted for pragmatism, sometimes using real names and sometimes disguising them.

If informants or actors are within the same family, the initials of names are used to differentiate family members. In the case of public figures or protagonists in well-known stories within the village, real names are used. Connection with an official post inevitably reveals the identity of the signified.

(2) Use of photos

Due to cost, technology and the nature of academic work, use of photographs is normally restricted. I faced a challenge when I was writing up my PhD dissertation: how many photos should I use from more than 1,000 of them? How do I use these photos? If cost and technology were no longer a problem would the nature of academic work prevent the use of many photos? My experience told me that photos shouldn't be just for providing evidence. They can literally flesh out information the reader has been given, providing a sense of these ordinary villages in their context as a "micro sociology" in a complicated society with a long history.

So, in the PhD dissertaion, I decided to use 124 photos, presented in thumbnail size on a few pages, and divided them into four groups, basic information, annual life cycle and production events, and life-cycle events, which are further sub-divided into birth and growing up, establishing a marriage relationship, house construction and family division, elderly care, the funeral ceremony and post-funeral rituals. Readers of my PhD dissertation have told me that these photos transcend the limitations of verbal description, providing a sense of place that enriches understanding. However, the scheme I then chose is not user friendly, since readers want to check photos as and when they are useful to the text. Inspired by Chinese academic books which creatively used a couple of dozen photos, I too follow in this fashion. There are 133 photos in this book, about 100 photos in Part One, the rest are distributed in different chapters.

(3) Abstract framework and application of the framework

However, how was I to describe and analyse the villagers' activities for mobilising different kinds of resources via social support and its inner operative mechanism? As shown in Table IX-1 in the ESRC Social Support, there are three sources of these resources: household support (from family members), private support (from relatives, neighbours and friends) and public support (from government or non-government organisations, such as the village collective, local government and bank). Guo Yuhua, an anthropologist from Tsinghua University, visited London in 1999 and scanned the draft of my dissertation which consisted of an introduction, social support theories, research methodology, household support, private support (3 chapters), public support and conclusion. She asked why I didn't submit it. I answered that it was merely a descriptive account that was incapable of explaining how everyday life is organised, how to deal with the reciprocal relationships with others or institutions during major events, and the inner operative mechanism of these relationships.

Frankly, it was a good enough dissertation for a PhD, but at that time, my fieldwork data was forcing me to look for a concealed pattern, a local practical social support model. It took me several more years to evolve *lishang-wanglai* (see Part Three) as a model which not only helped me to describe the complicated social intercourse involved in resources-seeking, but also to explain the reasons behind the process. I further found out that the villagers' management of these relationships is usually far from mono-causal, with many different considerations weighted against each other, often contingent or unpredictable. This fluidity is the reason behind the villagers' incessant and joyful weaving of relationship networks. Speaking personally, the spectator's pleasure in analysis and prediction cannot equal the surprise and excitement of discovering the outcome of the real game.

Therefore, this framework of *lishang-wanglai* was made, used and tested in a single continuous process.

2. The structure of this book

Compared to the Kaixiangong Village of 70 years ago when Fei conducted his fieldwork, Kaixiangong might now seem like an open book. When I first decided to carry out fieldwork on villages in Gansu and Jiangsu, a political scientist from Harvard suggested that I concentrate on Gansu, as Jiangsu was already over-explored. When I finished my doctoral dissertation on *lishang-wanglai*, a historian from Sun Yat-sen University gave me his own impression of Kaixiangong Village after making a field trip to it- it seemed to him that the Village had become entirely socialist, with hardly any vestiges of tradition. When I was in the village in 2007, a villager told me that a journalist visiting in the Chinese New Year had praised the village for being a "socialist civilised new village" with no trace of so-called feudalism and old customs. We both smiled. To me the better I had got to know Kaixiangong the more I found that its present life builds on the past rather than replaces it. But I cannot satisfy anyone's love of the exotic. I merely try to present a very ordinary village in as true a form as possible. The many photos in Part One ("Village Portraiture") depict very ordinary people engaged in ordinary lives, but for me this makes the hidden patterns of those lives all the more special.

Faced with an overwhelming quantity of fieldwork material and theoretical resources, the first question during writing up was how to transcend the disjunction that occurs when Western theories are used to study Chinese society. This book draws on the research model a la mode from recent studies (Yang, 1994; Kipnis, 1997), by placing the description and analysis of field materials in the first part, and the theorisation effort in the second part, as I had done with my PhD dissertation. Afterwards, in attempts to convert my 240,000 word thesis into two separate books, one confined to social support and the other to social creativity, I was constantly vexed by the problem of how to separate my Siamese twins. I was stuck in the operating theatre unable to wield the knife that would take the heart out of my work, no matter how much publication in the West required it.

It was proofreading the Chinese translation of this book that somehow allowed me to free myself from the impossible dilemma of how to combine or separate two intertwined themes, and instead follow the natural logic of the work. I found myself with a new "trilogy", representing the three steps taken in my research, namely introduction of the village and the study, description plus analysis, and finally theorisation (including methodology), incorporated in an Introduction, Parts One, Two and Three, and a Conclusion.

In the Introduction, I outline the ESRC social support project, villagers' use of *li shang wanglai* and methodological issues such as the multilateral position and structure of this book. Part One including Chapter I to III, provides an overview of Kaixiangong Village. A short history of the economy and governance of the village is followed by a discussion of such informal mechanisms as kinship, religion and relationships between villagers and the collective.

Part Two includes five chapters, focused on the social relationships amongst villagers, and how they manage them and how *lishang-wanglai* operates. Chapter IV deals with generous *wanglai*, with a relatively significant proportion of content due to its novelty. Chapters V to VII deal mainly with expressive *wanglai*, the core part of this book. My fieldwork had shown how expressive *wanglai* plays a central role in village life, with an ubiquitous presence at all events ranging from those related to life-cycle (Chapter V and VI), to annual cycle and to emergencies (Chapter VII). Chapter VIII deals with both instrumental and negative *wanglai* together, because the former has been well-researched, and my main concern is to facilitate comparison between them.

Part Three, the last four chapters (IX to XII), deal with reciprocity, social support networks and social creativity – the three major anthropological concepts related to *lishang-wanglai*. The discussion of these concepts is informed by terminologies and researches in Chinese studies, which is the theorisation in this book. Chapter XII then examines methodology and the application of *lishang-wanglai* to practical case studies. The conclusion returns to the research on *lishang-wanglai* by summarising the characteristics of previous researches on reciprocity and *lishang-wanglai*.

PART ONE

VILLAGE PORTRAITURE[24]

As explained in the methodology section of the Introduction, I went to Neiguan Village, Gansu Province and Kaixiangong Village, Jiangsu Province in 1995 and 1996 respectively. While I was in Gansu I felt deeply that there must be an inclusive and comprehensible model of social support and relationships to be found behind villagers' everyday life and cultural patterns. So when I had finished my fieldwork there, instead of going straight on to Kaixiangong I returned to the UK and discussed the relevant issues with Professor Stephan Feuchtwang, my supervisor. This led to my revising and expanding my research guidance and contents. I still used the ERSC project questionnaires in Kaixiangong Village, but obtained plentiful first-hand data based on the revised guide. During the long process of forging the lishang-wanglai model after returning from the field, I was able to use the telephone and e-mail from time to time to check and update my data with my informants. The material which I collected from my fieldwork plus the additional material gathered over the subsequent eight years via "post-fieldwork" gave me a solid foundation on which to build the lishang-wanglai model.

Part One consists of chapters I to III. The first chapter describes the village's economic development, changes of administrative system, kinship system, religious system and practices, and relationships between villagers, collective and the state. The second chapter describes the earlier part of the village's life cycle events from, growth, and marriage to the closely related local customs of house construction. The third chapter describes customs of the second half of life cycle events, from family division and elderly care to funeral and post-funeral; followed by annual cycle events and customs and emergency events. This material will I hope help readers to understand Part Two, which consists of five chapters describing villagers' interactions in everyday life firstly in terms of four categories of reciprocal relationship (*wanglai*), and secondly according to the four related principles or criteria (*lishang*) that govern these relationships. In this, I will show readers a model of social relationships in rural China based on local implicit cultural patterns, rather than the written records of the folk model basis. They provide the

---

[24] I will omit repetition in the overview of the village because details will be provided in four chapters in the book *Changes of Kaixiangong Village*, by Yunyun Zhu and Fukun Yao, will be published by Shanghai People's Publishing House, 2010.

foundation of this book, leading on to the theoretical approach and its applications in Part Three.

Chapter I

Economic, administrative and informal systems

Chapter I will briefly outline my fieldwork site – Kaixiangong Village's geographic location, transportation, village administrative system, land, income, population, education and other basic information. There are then five sections introducing the village's economic development, changes of administrative system, kinship system, religious practices, and relationships between villagers and the collective (including the state). My data can be traced back as early as Fei Xiaotong's study of 1936, and will be extended to cover the history of the past seven decades as well as possible. This material ranges from economics, politics and religion to social aspects and cultural practices. I hope it will help readers gain a picture of Kaixiangong village and the social setting of the book in its entirety.

Kaixiangong Village comes under the control of Qidu Township, Wujiang City, Jiangsu Province (see Map I-1). It is situated on the south-east bank of Lake Tai in the lower course of the Yangtze River. As Fei pointed out "The commanding position of this region in the Chinese economy is due partly to its superior natural environment[26] and partly to its favourable position in the system

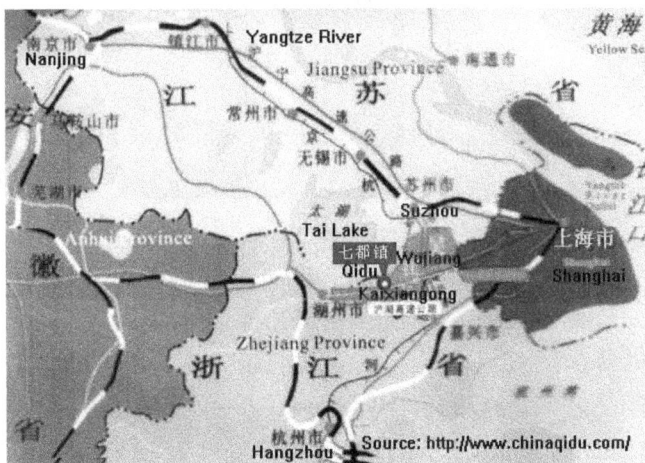

Map I-1. Kaixiangong Village and surrounding area[25]

of communications" (1939:11). Access to land and water transport remains an advantage today. Seen on a map the railway system looks the same as in the 1930s, but the old single track system was destroyed in the Japanese War and afterwards rebuilt as double track (Shen, 1993: 15–16).

---

[25] Source: http:///www.chinaqidu.com/
[26] The geography of the region containing Kaixiangong can be seen from Fei's citation from G.B. Cressey (Fei, 1939: 10–12).

The most significant change, compared to the earlier reliance on extensive use of canals and canalized streams, is the development of the road system starting from the 1980s.

The first bus station (Photo I-1) was set up in Kaixiangong in 1982 (see Map I-2). It now took ten minutes to travel by bus to Zhenze Township (which had been in charge of Kaixiangong in the 1930s) rather than two and half hours by boat; one and half hours to reach Suzhou City 40 miles north of the village, and three hours by bus to Shanghai rather than eight hours by boat in the 1930s (Shen, 1993:16; Fei, 1939:12). Map I-1 also shows there are highways around the village. The Lake Tai Circular Road connects with the 318 State Highway and 227 Provincial Highway.

Photo I-1. The bungalow is the bus station (photographed in 1996[27])

From 1996 onwards the village built more than six kilometres of a metalled Round Village Circular Road (*huan cun gonglu*) for vehicles, as a very important addition to the existing use of boats on village streams, as well as bridges and roads for walking and carts. Some families can now drive their own private cars to and from home. In 2001 another neighbouring village Xicaotian joined Kaixiangong (see Map I-2) and the related roads to and from it were built. In 2004 Kaixiangong Village raised money to build a better road on the existing narrow lane linking Xicaotian to Hengshan Township (see Map I-2). In 2007 a motorway was built near the villages linking Shanghai, Jiangsu, Shejiang and Anhui Provinces. This reduced the driving time to Shanghai from three hours to one hour. In 2009 another highway from Shuzhou City to Wujiang Township of Zhejiang Province is being built and it will cut through the East part of the

---

[27] This book includes a total of 133 photos, taken by the author in 1996, except those otherwise named or dated in their notes.

village. It is hoped the construction of extra roads will provide Kaixiangong and the surrounding villages with a more convenient road system and speed up the development of the area.

As a fieldwork village, Kaixiangong first appeared in Fei Xiaotong's (Hsiao-Tung Fei) book *Peasant life in China* (1939)[29] in which it is spelled "Kaihsienkung" using the old type of phonetics (*pinyin*). Kaixiangong's other famous name is *Jiangcun* (river village). This first appeared in Chinese characters on the cover of the Chinese version of *Peasant life in China* as *River village's economy – peasant life in China* (《江村經濟—中國農民的生活 (*Jiangcun jingji--Zhanguo nongmin de shenhua*)》 1986). According to Fei, this village is located around two streams which look like an arc and arrow forming the shape of an unstrung bow. In Chinese *kaixiangong*

Map I-2. Kaixiangong Village[28]

literally means "open-string-bow" (see Map I-2). This is how the village gets its name (Fei, 1939: 19).

Over the past 70 years the original Kaixiangong Village has changed in many ways: in 1956 it was divided into South and North Kaixiangong Villages during the Co-operative, which were renamed Hongwei and Lixin Great Brigades respectively during the Cultural Revolution. In 1982 both South and North villages were amalgamated into the original one. Kaixiangong Village has now expanded by taking in four small neighbouring villages: Kehuawan, Xicaotian, Tianzixu and Sifangyu. According to the village's statistics in 2008 the village occupied 4.5

[28] Source： http://jiangcun.net/E_ReadNews.asp?NewsID=119
[29] In recognition of this book Fei was awarded the Huxley Memorial Medal from the Royal Anthropological Institute in 1981.

square kilometres, with a total cultivated land area of 2,965 *mu* and lake area 1,400 *mu*. The village contained 25 groups, 773 households, 3,022 residents including 317 migrants. The average household consisted of 3.9 family members. The average income per capita was 12,054 *yuan*.

Let us return to 1996 when I was doing fieldwork there. According to the village's statistics the total cultivated land is 2,540 *mu*, total population is 2,416 in 613 households, organized in 19 groups. The average income per capita was 4,078 *yuan*. I will show details of the changes in cultivated land, population and income in the next section.

The most obvious change was that 510 new houses had been built since 1981, compared with 1980 when none were built at all (Figure V-1). As a result, in 1996 the social support and practice of *lishang-wanglai* in the arrangements of house construction could be seen much more clearly (see Chapter V.III). Every family had tap water and three out of four families had gas cylinder cooking, a significant change in villagers' lifestyle. Photo I-2 shows villagers changing their gas cylinders aboard boat on the village river. On the right is a photograph of villagers fishing on the river (see Photo I-3).

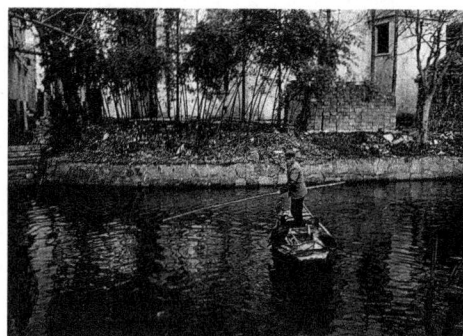

Photo I-2. Changing gas cylinders on board;   Photo I-3. Fishing in the village river

There was one school in the village consisting of 12 classes, 23 teachers and 471 pupils, and a nursery consisting of 3 classes, 3 teachers and 80 children. The pupils and children came from Kaixiangong and neighbouring villages. The school was in a three-storey block building built in 1991 (see Photo I-4) and the nursery was in a bungalow within the same courtyard. According to the Village Memorabilia (Wang, 2002), the school building was a replacement of a previous school which was a bungalow with 21 classrooms built in 1974. This was already much larger than in 1936 when Fei Xiaotong conducted his fieldwork. However, since 2004, more and more pupils from year 5 onwards have moved to a school in Miaogang Township to gain a better education, fetched by the school's minibuses. In 2007, when I visited this village, schooling was a very hot topic because the township government intended to close down the local school. The previous head of the Village, YG Zhou, represented the majority of villagers in calling for it to be kept open, but without success. Qidu Township (Miaogang Township was merged with it in 2006) disbanded the school, but the nursery remained open.

Photo I-4. The village school;   Photo I-5. The village clinic in 1996

After Kaixiangong School was closed in 2009 the school building was used by the Village Office, the library, Fei Xiatong's exhibition hall, the elderly activity centre, and the clinic[30] (Photo I-5 was the old clinic). In the 1930s informal evening gatherings were held around the bridges and there was no special place for public life (Fei, 1939:19–20). In 1996 these gatherings were still around the bridges, but the village's warehouses were used for Spring Entertainment (see Chapter IV.III). Apart from the two common rooms for the elderly mentioned earlier, there were plans to establish a folk museum, and to use the school yard and surrounding area as a central square for social and cultural events.

A village cadre has told me that in 2010 the village will establish a new school in the old village office building, for migrants' children in and around the village. Previously I have described the village as having 317 migrants, but these are village registered residents. In reality there have been 600 to 700 new migrants in the village since 2006.[31] Some migrants married villagers and established families in the village, others brought their parents and children and settled in the village. This kind of "rural to rural" migration has affected local customs. The way in which these migrants build their networks and integrate into village society, and how the village and villagers treat them, is another story, one that can't be told in this book.

---

[30] There are two clinics in the village: the one in the photo, and another which was brought in when Xiacaotian Village was merged with the village in 2000.
[31] Since 2008 it dropped down to about 400 which effected by the financial crises happened globally.

I.I. Economic development and villagers' standard of living

1. Cultivated land and population

It is not easy to make detailed comparisons of the population and land area of the village from the 1930s to today. As I have described earlier, over time official figures have varied with administrative changes affecting the size of the village (see details in Chapter I.II). I do however have the following figures relating to farmed land. In 1935 the village's total of farmland was 3,065 *mu* or 461 acres, total population was 1,458 (771 male and 684 female), with 360 households divided into 4 groups or *bao* (Fei, 1939:17–22; 106–114). In 1995 the village's total land under cultivation had decreased to 2,540 *mu* and the total population was 2,416, comprising 613 households and 19 groups. In 2003 the village had a total population of 2,942, comprising 787 households and 25 groups, and a land area of 3,049 *mu* as the result of the earlier merger between Xicaotian Village and Kaixiangong. The area per person appears to have halved. A different set of figures referring to the areas of Households' Contract Land with the state, 1,784 *mu* before 1956 and 2,356 *mu* before 2001, show land increasing with the increasing size of the village. This does not include the 1962 distribution of land by the state for permanent private use, which converts to a total, for the village, of about 380 *mu*. However none of these figures can be used to compare like with like. Land is increasingly used for factories, shops, school and nursery, roads and residential areas, as would be expected with increasing prosperity and reduced dependence on the soil. The matter is complicated, and I won't go into it further (see more details in Shen, 1993:17 and 1996, 321–391).

2. Income

It is even more difficult to make an accurate comparison of village income and expenditure from the 1930s up to the present. I accept W. R. Geddes's estimate based on his restudy of Fei's work in the village in 1956. According to Geddes one Chinese dollar in 1936 was more or less equivalent to 1 *yuan* in 1956 (see Appendix in Chinese in Fei, 1986:306). Hereafter I will use *yuan* whenever I mention the unit of money in 1936, with this implied conversion[32]. I have not been able to establish the figure of income per capita in Kaixiangong in 1936. Fei (1939) provided annual expenditure figures between a minimum of 263 to 350 *yuan* for an average

---

[32] In the Chinese version of Fei's book the money unit of dollar is simply translated into *yuan*.

4-person household (132–37). We also learnt from Fei that Kaixiangong Village was located in one of the richest areas of China. On Fei's second visit to Kaixiangong in 1956 he found that Kaixiangong's income per capita was 90 *yuan* compared to an average for China as a whole of 50 *yuan* (Fei, 1986:237). Fei said that the villagers' income increased but they still complained about a living standard decrease because a new policy restricted the development of "sideline" production (*fuye*)[33], such as raising silkworms, sheep, fishing and marketing. The proportion of sideline production reduced from 40 per cent to less than 20 per cent of their income (Fei, 1986:232). More details about the economic development of the village during the period of 1949 to 1956 can be seen in Hui Haiming's paper (1996a:192–415).

According to Fei's report on his third visit to Kaixiangong in 1981, the income per capita was around 114 *yuan* from 1966 to 1978, a small rise, due to the Cultural Revolution, but by 1980 income per capita had reached 300 *yuan*. This was a direct result of the new policy of rural social reform in the later 1970s. The proportion of sideline production, in particular raising rabbits, suddenly increased from 10 per cent to 20 per cent. Moreover, the village enterprises provided 40 per cent of overall income (Fei, 1986:253–61). In the 1930s there was only one silk mill in the village, which claimed to be the first rural joint-stock enterprise in China.[34] In 1980 there were four enterprises run by the village collective. They comprised: one silk-reeling factory, one silk weaving mill and two tofu mills. Compared with the proportion of 67 per cent rural industry or enterprises run by the collective, 20 per cent agriculture and 13 per cent of sideline production in the surrounding Suzhou Prefecture, it can be seen that the village's economic development had fallen behind that of its local area (Fei, 1986:261).

According to Shen Guanbao (1993:155), Fei's first PhD student whose study covered the period up to 1987, in Kaixiangong Village the proportion of collective run enterprises increased from 51 per cent to 62 per cent, agriculture decreased from 30 to 12 per cent and sideline production increased from 19 to 27 per cent from 1981 to 1987. Village income from enterprises was 30 per cent in 1981 and increased to 42 per cent in 1985, agriculture amounted to 36 per

---

[33] For the development of Kaixiangong's sideline productions over the past 60 years see Liu Haoxing's paper (1996:416–494).

[34] The source for this saying see: 「中國首家農村股份制合作企業」, 《江蘇絲綢》1999 年第 3 期 http://jfsilk.com/D-MJBD2.htm. In fact the experimental reeling mill was established in 1929 in Kaixiangong Village. It is still located in Kaixiangong but belonged to the Miaogang Township until 1997. Its current name is Wujiang City Miaogang Reeling Co. Ltd. I touch on its tense relationship with Kaixiangong Village in (5) of "Clarifications of *wanglai*" of XI.IV.

cent in 1981 and 28 per cent in 1985, sideline production more or less the same, just above 30 per cent during this period (Shen, 1993:170). The income per capita was 550 *yuan* in 1984 and increased to 873 *yuan* in 1987, according to the village's "Rural Economical Income and Distribution Form (*nongcun jingji shouru fenpei biao*)".

From 1989 to 2003 a 70 year old senior research fellow of Jiangsu Academic and Social Sciences, Wang Huaibing, carried out a "retirement leisure social survey" in Kaixiangong. During this period Wang visited the village eleven times and wrote eleven reports (Wang 2002:263–376). According to Wang, the village's income from enterprises increased to 58 per cent in 1989 from 42 per cent in 1985, agriculture decreased to 11 per cent in 1989 from 28 per cent in 1985, and sideline production was 31 per cent which was similar to that in 1985. The villagers' income per capita in 1989 was 1175 *yuan*. The income from enterprises and sideline productions was 40 per cent each and 20 per cent came from agriculture.

In 1991 Lu Feiyun, a team member of the ESRC social support project team, carried out fieldwork for the project. Village statistics have income per capita at 1,346 *yuan* in 1991, lower than Lu's finding of 1,834 *yuan* from the sample households. This figure is also lower than the SSB's figure of 1,664.65 *yuan* in the Shanghai region, which is the richest region in rural China (SSB, 1991: 296). According to Lu's fieldwork report, Kaixiangong Village had three enterprises run by the collective, two silk mills and one factory for rice wine. Of the total labourers in the village 48 per cent were engaged in industry, 22 per cent in handicraft industries (*shougongye*), and 30 per cent in agriculture and sideline production. For the sample households 11.25 per cent of their income came from land, 45.40 per cent came from sideline production and 43.35 per cent from enterprise and industry. Of their expenditure 28 per cent was on their own produce. An average family in the village consisted of five people: three and four generation families being 67.64 per cent of the total (Chang and Feuchtwang, 1996).

In 1996 I carried out a restudy of the ESRC social support project in the village. According to the village's "Rural Economic Income and Distribution Form", in 1995 Kaixiangong had a population of 2,416, comprising 613 households and 19 groups, and the average income per capita was 4,078 *yuan*. This figure more or less agrees with the figures for rural household net income per capita from the Chinese statistical yearbook. In 1995 it was 4,245.61 *yuan* in the wealthy Shanghai region (SSB, 1996:302). However, I found that my sample households' income per capita was 1,890, much lower than the official village and the regional figures. The village treasurer told me that the "Rural Economic Income and Distribution Form" was a very complicated matter. I won't go into details of how village statistics were worked out, and how I collected my own figures. However, village cadres and villagers both confirmed that my figures were closer to their real lives than the official figures (I will touch upon the "Income and distribution form" again in Chapter I.V).

3. Industry and enterprises

In 1929 Fei Dasheng, Fei Xiaotong's sister, established a silk factory in Kaixiangong Village. It was the first joint-stock limited company in rural China[35] (see photo I-6). The factory was destroyed during the Japanese War, and rebuilt later in the 1950s, but managed by the Miaogang Township from 1980 to 1997, and known as the Wujiang City Miaogang Jinfeng Filature Factory (see Photo I-7). Later I will show the complicated relationship between this factory and Kaixiangong Village (see Chapter XI.V). By 1980 there were four enterprises run by the village: one filature factory (photo I-8), one silk factory (photo I-9), one bean card (*tofu*) factory, and one rice wine factory. In 1996 the village established a chemical factory (photo I-10).

In 1996 the village had a few privately owned home weaving enterprises (photos I-11 and I-12). These were called "family" businesses (*jiating jingji*)[36]. One of them hired a few employees and so was large enough to be called a *geti jingji*, meaning a "self-employed" business or "individual business". Nowadays the preferred term is "people's enterprises" (*min ying qiye*), rather than "private enterprises" (*si ying qiye*). The villagers avoided using the term "private business" (*siying jingji*) because "private" was in opposition to "collective".

The large self-employed business was Miaogang Electronic Equipment Ltd. It was established in 1983and its current name is Wanda Electronic Equipment Ltd. The owner, YG Zhou, showed me photographs of workpeople demolishing the first floor of the workshop (Photo I-13). Zhou had got permission for the building, but just before completion of the first floor the township sent a gang of workers to demolish it, on the grounds that development of a private enterprise should be restricted to the ground floor. Photo I-14 shows the overall view of the bungalow workshop from a distance.

---

[35] Zhou Dehua, "The first joint stock limited company in rural China", Jiangsu Silk, No.3 1999. http://www.jiangcun.com/D-MJBD2.htm . [周德華：「中國首家農村股份制合作企業」,《江蘇絲綢》1999 3）]。

[36] See Li Youmei's paper on family businesses of the village (1996:195–530)

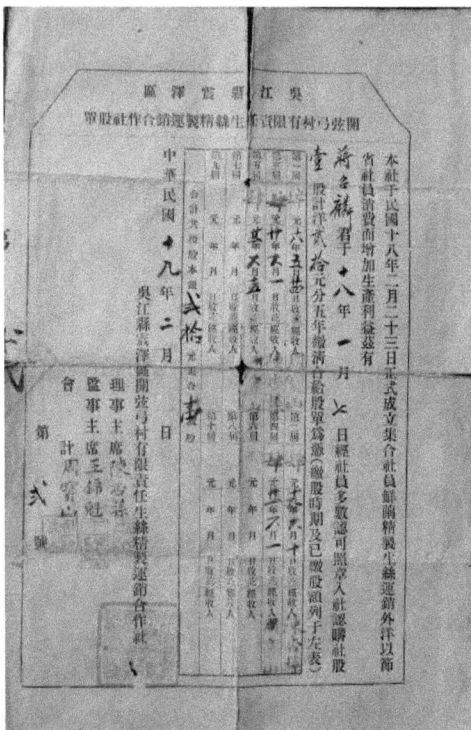

Photo I-6. The share certificate of the 1930s factory, provided by Yao Fukun

Photo I-7. Miaogang Jinfeng filature factory

Photo I-9. Kaixiangong silk factory

Photo I-8. The building on the left was part of Miaogong Jinfeng factory, the one on the right was Kaixiangong's filature factory

Photo I-10. Village run enterprises including a newly established chemical factory

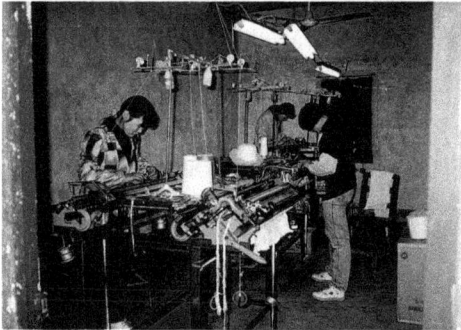

Photos I-11 and 12. Two households with a family business

Photo I-13. The process of demolishing the first floor, photographed by YG Zhou in 1995

Photo I-14. An overall view of the bungalow workshop in 1996

My attention was drawn to the question of family vis-à-vis collective business enterprise. By the mid 1990s, the so-called "Southern Jiangsu model" (*sunan moshi*) based on the development of business within the collective, was well-established in Southern Jiangsu Province. It propelled industrialization of the local area forward and increased the income of the villagers, the collective and the state. However, with the development of the market economy from the 1990s the limitations of collective run enterprises became clear. Mixed administrative and business managements and unclear responsibilities, power, rights and benefits were a severe hindrance to workers' productive enthusiasm. Kaixiangong's village enterprises were in a depressed situation. Villagers told me that the "Southern Jiangsu model" no longer suited this village and its neighbourhood.

The theory behind the "Southern Jiangsu model" had been put forward by none other than Fei Xiaotong himself[37]. It was interpreted by the state to mean that the collective economy always has, and always should, play a leading role in village industries. However, during the post-Mao era China had dual policies. One was to follow the logic of the Southern Jiangsu model because it represented the socialist direction. The other, based on Deng Xiaoping's slogan *"rang yi bufen ren xian fu qilai"*, was to "let some get rich first by any means including walking on the capitalist road." The situation in Kaixiangong Village was complicated by its role as a focal village for the Southern Jiangsu model[38], which the villagers now regarded as a misfortune. They believed that Kaixiangong had been overtaken by its neighbours because they did not have to be "show" villages of the model. A villager told me that they hoped Fei would use his political influence with local officials to get restrictions relaxed.

---

[37] The theory was established by Fei Xiaotong in 1983 (Zhu and Wu, 1994:15).
[38] It was "Civilized Village of Jiangsu province" in 1982 and "A Pearl of Lake Tai" of the Wujiang City in 1987 (see Kaixiangong Village Memorabilia, by Wang Huaibing, 2004).

On the 14 April 1996 Fei Xiaotong made his 19th trip to Kaixiangong Village. First he received a report from Wujian City and Miaogang Township officials about the development of Lake Tai. He then paid a special visit to Mr Baolin Xu's family to learn about its family business (Photo I-15). A few months later Fei Xiaotong publicly concluded that the historical mission of the collective economy based on the Southern Jiangsu model was over. All the areas that followed the model, including Kaixiangong, have since completed a smooth transition to privatisation.

Photo I -15. Fei Xiaotong accompanied by local officials visiting a household with a family business

4. Changing a system (*gaizhi*) and privatisation

To return to Kaixiangong in 1996: a few months after I left the village Fei's change of heart led to the introduction of a new policy, or system, for the privatisation of collective enterprises (*gaizhi*). The owner of the private enterprise whose upper floor had been demolished, YG Zhou, was suddenly appointed by the township government as the number one head of the village (fuze quanmian gongzuo), although he was not even a member of the CCP (Chinese Communist Party). Villagers called him "General Secretary Zhou" (Zhou *shuji*) of the Kaixiangong branch of the CCP. His task was to sort out the chaos caused by the bankruptcy of all the village collective enterprises, a task which this successful self-employed businessman completed effectively piece by piece.

The bankruptcies led to the unusual situation of "xiagang nongmin" (farmer-workers became the unemployed). Unlike xiagang gongren (urban workers became the unemployed) they received no unemployment benefit. For example, there were about 200 workers in the silk weaving enterprise. Although it was started up again as a private enterprise a year later, while they were unemployed they lost their income of between 5,000 and 6,000 *yuan*, with no unemployment relief. During this hard time many could not even find the 1,000 *yuan* required to buy one of the looms for work at home. However, two villagers who had their own business in Shengze Township, the so-called "oriental pearl of textile", and had access to capital, together with two of their business friends, managed to raise 140,000 *yuan*. This enough to take over what was one of the biggest village enterprises. In the contract negotiated by "General Secretary

Zhou" they became shareholders and managers, and about half of the unemployed went back to their old jobs. Their new average annual income reached about 10,000 *yuan*, considerably more than they had earned before. But about 40 per cent of them had been prosperous enough to buy themselves one or more looms from one of the former silk mills at about 1,000 *yuan* each, ten times less than the original cost. At the end of the year the income of this group had improved even more, being now slightly more than 10,000 *yuan* on average. I

They called this "profit by misfortune" (*yin huo de fu*) but it was not a gift from the gods (*xi cong tian jiang*) because it was the result they themselves had been attempting to reach for several years. The rest of the unemployed either worked on small parcels of contracted land, or turned to service businesses, such as a new cooking service (*chuishi fuwu*) preparing lunch for the self-employed who were too busy working to cook for themselves.

In 2002 there were twelve privately run enterprises. Most families, other than the 5 five-guarantee households (*wubaohu*)[39], were engaged in family industries. YG Zhou's private business also developed rapidly. Photo I-16 shows an overview of his premises, which finally realised the original design of 1995. On the left of the photo is the two-storey house which was the completion of the workshop partially demolished on the official order of the Township. The bungalows were built on land that had been planted with mulberry trees (Photo I-14).

The completion of privatization solved problems of ownership, management and village workers' employment, but the heavy burden of debt left over from the days of the collective now became a pressing matter. The collective had received loans of 4 million *yuan*

Photo I-16. Overall view of YG Zhou's premises after completion of the first floor (on left) showing further expansion. Photographed in 2004

only a few months before being bankrupted to the tune of 10 million *yuan*, amounting to an average for each household of nearly 18,000 *yuan*. In 1997, under their new management, the old collective enterprises began to pay off some of these debts, but the biggest, worth 4 million *yuan,* was not fully paid until 2004 (see Tables VIII-1 and 2). With the bankruptcy of the

---

[39] A household is given five guarantees by the social security system. They are guaranteed food, clothing, medical care, housing and burial expenses.

collective enterprises in 1997 the villagers thought they had got rid of the bondage of the Southern Jiangsu model but still found themselves disadvantaged. Sighing with emotion, a villager said that in the Spring of the market (1993–96) they were left stranded in the Winter of policy; but when they were ushered into the Spring of the policy they found themselves in the Winter of the market (1997–2000).[40]

Although the villagers complained about having missed chances of economic development, in the subsequent five years the improvements in their living standards after privatisation led to their being much more contented. According to the "Brief Introduction of Kaixiangong" from the Village Committee in 2003 the village had a population of 2,942, comprising 787 households and 25 groups, and the average income per capita was 5,632 *yuan*. This is quite close to the NBS's figure of 6,223.55 *yuan* in the Shanghai region, the richest region in rural China in 2002 (NBS[41], 2002:368). These figures can be summarized by saying that the villagers' income per capita had not increased significantly between 1995 and 2002, but their quality of life, and use of modern technology, had changed significantly. I was told by different village cadres that the village statistics were not always reliable because they could be influenced by policy. The 1995 official per capita income for the village was higher than the villagers' actual average living standard, but in 2002 it more or less reflected the real situation.

I.II. Changes of administrative system

From 2003 onwards, Kaixiangong Village has been administered by Qidu Township, Wujiang City (county equivalent), Suzhou City (prefecture equivalent) and Jiangsu Province. It was administered by Zhenze Township in the 1930s and from 1958 to 2003 by Miaogang Township. The territory and size of the village itself has changed several times over the last 70 years. Map I-2 shows what it was like in the 1930s. According to Fei, the basic administrative system in the village was a kind of *baojia* (*Pao Chea*); 360 households were divided into 4

---

[40] It is commonly known in China that the four seasons correspond to different characteristics. This idea can be traced back to Dong Zhongshu (Tung Chung-shu) in the Han Dynasty. According to Dong, "the sage in his conduct of government, duplicates the movements of Heaven. Thus with his beneficence he duplicates warmth and accords with spring, with his conferring of rewards he duplicates heat and an accord with summer, with his punishments he duplicates coolness and accords with autumn, and with his executions he duplicates coldness and accords with winter." *Ch'un-ch'iu Fan-lu*, chap. 13, p.1a-b; translated by Bodde in Fung, p. 48 .1948.

[41] The SSB (State Statistical Bureau) changed its English translation into NBS (National Bureau of Statistics), but the Chinese name is still the same: 中國國家統計局.

groups of *bao* and there were two heads of the village (*cunzhang*) (1939, 106–114).

From 1949 to 1955 during Land Reform the village retained the system of having two heads (*cunzhang*). It was divided into two big groups (*dazu*): the northern group and the southern group, separated by the stream in the middle of the village, with one head for each. From 1956 to 1961, under the Co-operation Movement, two neighbouring villages (Hehuawan and Huanxiqiao) joined Kaixiangong. The new name for the three villages was "Wujiang Third United Agricultural Cooperative" (in short, the United Third Cooperative, *liansan she*). In 1958 the United Third Cooperative was turned into the "United Third Great Brigade" (*liansan dadui*) which came under the Miaogang Commune. There were five cadres: the general secretary (*shuji*) of the local branch of the CCP, the head of the Great Brigade (*daduizhang*), the vice general secretary, the treasurer and the vice Great Brigade in charge of sideline production (*fuye daduizhang*).

During the "adjustment period" (1961–62), Huanxiqiao village separated from the "United Third Great Brigade." Nine productive brigades in the northern village of the United Third Great Brigade were organized into one Grand Brigade called Kaixiangong Great Brigade, while six productive brigades in the southern village united with four productive brigades of Hehuawan into the Hehuawan Great Brigade. The separation of the southern part from the rest of the village destroyed the bow shaped village structure. This configuration lasted for 20 years, from 1962 to 1982, under the People's Commune System. During the Cultural Revolution, Kaixiangong Great Brigade was renamed Lixin Great Brigade (Lixin is the second half of the term *pojiu lixin* – destroy the old and establish the new); whereas Hehuawan Great Brigade was called Hongwei Great Brigade (Hongwei being the characters *hongwei* of *hongweibing* – red guards). But as far as Kaixiangong villagers were concerned the two areas were Kaixiangong North Village (*beicun*) and Kaixiangong South Village (*nancun*). There were 10 cadres in each. Besides the five titles in the previous great brigade: general secretary, head of the Great Brigade, vice general secretary, treasurer and vice Great Brigade, in charge of sideline production, the newly added titles were militiaman, battalion commander (*minbing yingzhang*), general secretary of the CYL (Communist Youth League), head of security (*zhibao zhuren*), head of the Women's Federation (*funü zhuren*) and agricultural technician (*nongjiyuan*).

In 1983, under the Household Contract Responsibility System, the neighbouring village Hehuawan together with the southern part of six groups of the original Kaixiangong Village reunited with Kaixiangong. There was a population of 2,376, comprising 572 households divided into 19 groups. This organization lasted from 1983 to 2000. During this period the village cadres increased to twelve. The general secretary (*shuji*) of the local branch of the CCP was still at the number one (*yibashou*) position in the village and mainly had charge of village industrial enterprises. The number two was the head of the Village Committee (*cunweihui zhuren*) who played the head of village role as it was pre-1949. The number three was the vice general secretary (*fu shuji*) of the local branch of the CCP who held the post of the head of the Rural Economic Co-operation (*nongcun jingji hezuoshe*) and played the role of head of Grand Brigade. There were two vice heads of the Cooperation (*shezhang* and *fu shezhang*), who acted as Great Brigade vices in charge of agricultural and sideline productions, and all other positions remained as before.

This administrative structure covered the periods of the ESRC social support project carried out in 1991 and my restudy of it in 1996. In subsequent chapters whenever I mention "village collective" (*cun jiti*) it refers to these cadres as a group, and I will refer to individual cadres by name as the case arises.

In 1998 the village office (see Photo I-17) was sold and the village office premises were moved to a building where a chemical plant was located (see Photo I-18). In June 2009 I was informed that the village offices moved into the closed school's courtyard and building (Photo I-19).

Photo I-17. Village official court years before 1998

Photo I-18. Village official courtyard from 1998 to 2009

It is worth noting that during my post-fieldwork period (from late 1997 to early 2003) the post of the "general secretary" (*shuji*) of the local branch of the CCP was held by YG Zhou, who we have already met earlier in this chapter, both as the owner of a private business partially demolished, and as the "general secretary" who came to the rescue in 1997, and remarkably, a non-CCP member. This is an important transitional period for the village, which saw various reforms:

(i) The village completed the transition from the collective enterprise system to privatisation, as I have described in "Economic development".

Photo I-19. Kaixiaogong Party and Administrative name boards hanged on the previous school's gate. Photographed by Fukun Yao in 2009

(ii) Another reform was brought about in accordance with the new policy "Bring fees into tax system" (*feigaishui*).[42] For local villages this simplification had the direct major effect of cutting down on unnecessary administrative expenditure, such as the number of village cadres. The organization of Rural Economical Co-operation was revoked and village cadre positions reduced to nine for each brigade. These were "general secretary", (YG Zhou, but since he is not a member of the CCP I will now call him "head of the village" with his name to specify), actual head of village (JM Wang), two vice general secretaries of CCP (one for each of Kaixiangong and Xicaotian), vice head of the village in charge of agriculture (FK Yao who was Agricultural Technician of the village), treasurer, general secretary of the CYL, head of the Women's Federation and militiaman battalion commander.

(iii) Under another new policy of "Adjustment of Administrative Regions" (*xingzheng quyu tiaozheng*), the administrative system of the village changed yet again. In 2001 the neighbouring village of Xicaotian joined Kaixiangong. The status of Kaixiangong was changing from that of "administrative village" (*xingzheng cun*) to that of "central village" (*zhongxin cun*) because it covered a number of natural villages (*zirancun*), e.g. Tianzixu and Sifangxu which were part of Xicaotian (see Map I-2). Although the households increased from about 600 to 780 and the groups increased from 19 to 25, the numbers of village cadres gradually reduced. From 2003 the nine posts have in fact been held by five cadres. They are: the "General Secretary" of the CCP (YG Zhou); the head of the village, who holds three posts (the others are the vice general

---

[42] The policy of "Bring fees into tax system" was put into force in Kaixiangong Village from 2000. Its purpose was to remove unnecessary fees from peasants and at the same time strengthen the tax system. However, the policy miscarried a few months after it was put in force, when a local official wrote a report to the previous Premier, Zhu Rongji, that the policy was impossible to apply because although the principle itself was positive the target figures were all wrong,. However, Li Changping's saying "three *nong* (農民真苦，農村真窮，農業真危險 *nongmin zhenku, gongcun zhenqiong, nongye zheweixian*, literally, a peasant's life is so hard, rural area is poor and agriculture is so dangerous)" drew real attention from the government and society (see Li Changping, 2002 in Chinese).

secretary of CCP and militiaman battalion commander); the other vice general secretary of the CCP who holds two posts (the other is treasurer); the vice head of the village in charge of agriculture, and finally the general secretary of the CYL who holds two posts (the other is head of Women's Federation). Of the five cadres, three came from Kaixiangong and two from Xicaotian.

After completing all the above reforms in 2003 YG Zhou was dismissed from his post when there was a new head of Miaogang Township. (I won't go into the complicated details of the dramatic changes that resulted in a non-CCP member being chosen to be general secretary of the CCP of the village during a difficult period, and then of how he was removed when the villagers' lives had been restored to good order.) Currently, the village still has five cadres who hold nine posts. YL Zhou, the new general secretary (*shuji*) of the village branch of the CCP, is also a successful businessman. It appears he is also liked by the villagers to whom I talked by telephone.

I.III. Kinship system

The kinship system in Kaixiangong village is rather interesting. It includes agnatic kin (*zijiaren*), non-agnatic kin (*qinqi*), close relatives (*jinqin*) which means major non-agnatic kin and quasi kin, far relatives (*yuanqin*) which are relatives excluded from the close relatives list, new relatives (*xinqin*) which are relatives of a newly married wife or husband, and old relatives (*laoqin*) which means relatives of a focal family's grandparents or above. All the above relatives play different roles in social support events or *lishang-wanglai* activities, but agnatic kin, non-agnatic kin and quasi kin play the most positive role.

The explanation I now give of agnatic kin and non-agnatic kin is based on the relevant section in my previous paper, including Figure I-1 (Chang, 1999). Figure I-1 shows a household tree, where all the kin of a given household enclosed in dotted lines can be split into two classes: agnate (in bold) and non-agnate. Because of the institutions of patrilineal descent and patrilocal marriage, on marriage the agnatic relationships of a woman are changed: A becomes agnate to her husband's household; B becomes non-agnate to her natal household.

Figure I-1 Kinship diagram

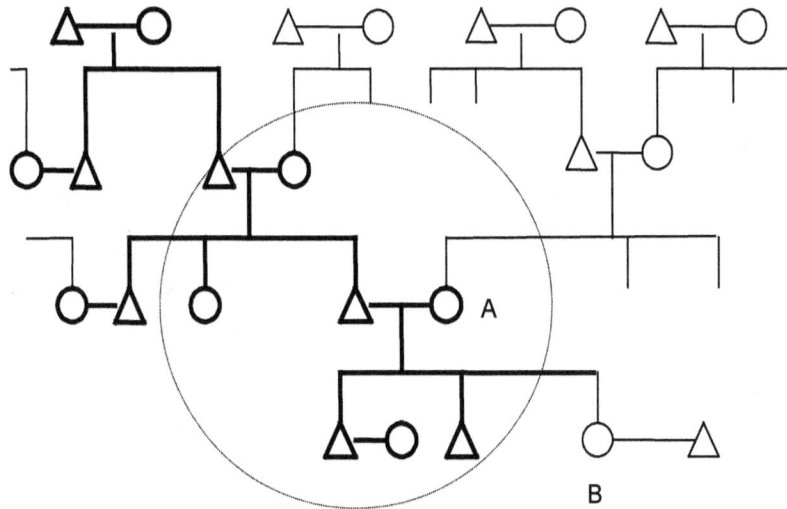

Figure I-1. shows the differences of agnatic and non-agnatic kin through a household tree:

- All the kin of a given family can be split into two classes: agnate and non-agnate.
- Agnatic kin are those related to the family in a direct male line, either as ancestors or descendants.
- Non-agnatic kin are related through a female link.
- Direct male ancestry is only one of the possible lines of ancestry in a family tree, so agnatic relatives are in a minority.

On marriage the agnatic relationships of a woman are changed:

- A means a woman becomes agnate to her husband's family
- B means a woman becomes non-agnate to her parent's family.

The relatives agnate to a family are thus:

> *direct male ancestors or descendants*
> *+ women who marry in to the family*
> *- women who marry out of a family.*

We can see from this that:

- Conversely agnatic relatives have a direct male linkage to the household.
- All non-agnatic kin are linked through a woman to the household.

Non-agnate support for a household will always be through a (genealogical) female link. This does not mean that the woman is necessarily directly in control of the support; it might come from either men (*Jiujui*) or women.

- A woman's status in a household is related to her understanding of local customs and ability to bring resources into the household via support from her own relatives (non-agnate).

1. Agnatic kin

Agnatic kin are those related to the household in a direct male line, either as ancestors or descendants, plus women who marry into the household, minus women who marry out. Agnatic kin support in Kaixiangong mainly comes from those households that share the same grandfather or the same great grandfather in the male line. The villagers call these households *zijia* or *zijia menzu*.

In Kaixiangong there is a custom for extending agnatic kinship. Some households lack *zijia* households in the village, because, for example, several generations in one line had only one son, or because the household moved from another place, or because there is hostility between brothers due for instance to an unjust division of household property. These households will enter another neighbouring agnatic kin group by means of *ren zijia,* namely, as adopted agnatic kin. Twenty-five per cent of households in the village sample have the relationship of *ren zijia*.

For those households which have no son at all, the village also has a custom called *zhaonüxu,* which takes two forms. Firstly, a son is adopted, raised and then marries the daughter of the household to continue the lineage with the same surname as the father's. This is the counterpart of *xiaoxifu* meaning small daughter-in-law, or *tongyangxi* more precisely meaning foster daughter-in-law (Fei, 1939:53). Secondly, the daughter of the household with no son will marry someone who agrees to marry into this household and allow their children to keep their mother's surname. This woman's natal relatives will remain agnatic kin and the *zhaonüxu*'s relatives will become non-agnatic kin even though they are linked through a man.

The phrase 'agnatic kin' used here includes all the above relationships, namely, *zijia* relatives, *ren zijia* relatives, and the relatives of the household which have *zhaonüxu*.

2. Non-agnatic kin

Non-agnatic kin are related through a female link. Normally, in a three generation household these include the male household-head's father's married-out sister's relatives, mother's relatives, married-out sister(s)' relatives, wife's relatives, married-out daughter(s)' relatives and so on. However, in Kaixiangong there are ways of extending the non-agnatic kin network, just as *renzijia* extends agnatic kin. The custom of *ren guofangqin* (quasi kin) allows a member of a household to have one or more adopted father(s), mother(s), son(s) or daughter(s), a relationship which Fei (1939:87) called a pseudo-adoption. Of the households in the village 68.8 per cent have a relationship of *ren guofangqin.*

Villagers need to limit the number of *guofangqin.* Too few, and they have insufficient support, too many, and they have to pay back too much in return. Some households want *ren guofangqin* for *chuxing*, that is to add a father's surname (the child still keeps its own) to guarantee the child will not die and will grow up healthy, but they do not want to increase the number of non-agnatic kin. Another way to protect a child is to ask the father's sister and her husband to be the child's *guofang* parents. This phenomenon, *qin shang jia qin*, "adding kinship to kinship", means adding extra responsibilities to those who are already non-agnates.

In Kaixiangong, the term *qinqi* includes all the kinds of non-agnatic kin listed above. In addition, villagers take the *zhaonüxu*'s natal household and its relatives, the *guofangqin's* relatives, the master or apprentice's relatives of a member of a household into account as non-agnatic kin. The phrase "non-agnatic kin" I use here includes all the above relationships.

No one in Kaixiangong can tell when these customs, the *ren zijia, zhaonüxu* and *ren guofangqin,* came into being, but they believe that they are necessary for meeting a household's different needs. Almost every household can immediately list the number of both its agnatic and non-agnatic households. Villagers always maintain a reasonable number of each for practical purposes, although because marriage and birth results in an increase in kin, they sometimes need to remove some agnatic and non-agnatic kin from their list.

The reasons non-agnatic kin are seen as especially important providers of social support for a household are as follows (I am once again quoting from a previous paper): "firstly, non-agnatic kin are always a large network offering security for different types of resource. For each household in my sample, the average number of agnatically related households is 5.72, and non-agnatically related households is 9.31. There is a common saying, *zhongren shi chai huoyan gao,* meaning 'the more people, the greater strength'. Secondly, non-agnatic kin have an obligation to provide financial support, while the limited number of agnatic kin share a local economic condition and are under fewer obligations. Thirdly, non-agnatic kin relationships can always be made by marriage or adoption. The villagers also told me they value *renqing* (human feelings) more then *renli* (labour), and value money and gifts more than materials. More evidence about this will be given later" (Chang, 1999:164).

Of my sampled households 69 per cent involved a relationship with one or more quasi kin.

Some were already non-agnatic kin, in which case the extra link was described as "to add a quasi relative on top of relative (*qin shang jia qin*)" to make the relationship closer.

3. Quasi kin

In 1930s the quasi kin (*guofangqin*) relationship was called pseudo-adoption (Fei's term). This is "to create a new social relation similar to kinship by metaphorical use of relationship terms and by ritual acts" (Fei, 1939:89). It's main purpose is support rather than enjoyment, which can be seen from the quasi relations' role in major family events. As will be made clear later, "support" will involve a moral obligation to help at some time in the future, unlike an instrumental purpose which involves a direct immediate quid pro quo.

There is a ritual for claiming quasi kin as non-agnatic kin. Villagers are very likely to claim one or more women as quasi mothers after a child's birth. The ritual is called carrying a small Chinese New Year's Eve feast (*dan nianyefan*). The quasi mother should *dan nianyefan* to the child for three years. Here the *nianye* of the *nianyefan* means the Winter Solstice (*dongzhi* – the day marking the beginning of the 22nd solar term on 21, 22 or 23 December), which is also called the small Chinese New Year. This can occur any time after the harvest season and before the Winter Solstice. For the first *nianyefan* the quasi mother should bring a big basket with a big bowl of rice and red or black beans, an upper part of pig leg (*tizi*), a carp, two pieces of half cooked pork, egg balls, meats balls, red eggs, oranges, a hat, and a red bag with 20 *yuan*. This gift was worth 100 *yuan* in 1990. The child's family entertained the quasi mother with a nice meal and returned a little bit of raw rice in the bowl. The second year the ritual was more or less the same except that the gifts were slightly different, a pair of shoes was brought instead of a hat. The third year was the finishing year (*mannian*). As well as similar gifts as before, the quasi mother should bring clothes and knitting wool for the child. The child's family should make different rice cakes: white and green colour rice balls with red bean fillings, savoury rice balls mixed with thin slices of radish and so on. The child's family should cook a nice meal with *tizi* for the quasi mother and some rice cakes as a returning gift.

Once a child claims a quasi mother her husband automatically becomes the child's quasi father. The child should address them as quasi parents and the two families become non-agnate relations (*guofangqin*). They put each other on their families' lists for Chinese New Year's feasts.

In practice, apart from claiming quasi non-agnatic kin, Kaixiangong villagers also claim quasi agnatic kin and even quasi neighbours (omitted here).

I.IV. Religious and spiritual belief system and villagers' practices

The statistics of the ESRC social support project show that among my sample households 95 per cent described themselves as having "general spiritual beliefs", 5 per cent as believing "Christians". This covers the Kaixiangong religious system in its entirety. Villagers' family life and religious life are closely mixed together in almost every event from life cycle to annual cycle events. Villagers regard ancestors and local gods as indispensable sources for meeting their spiritual needs in the same informal fashion as their kinship system. However, the village's religious system and religious practice are not in harmony with the state's formal religious system and ideology. Villagers have had to adapt their practices in order to keep a harmonious relationship with the state.

1. Christianity

I will now very briefly outline the position of Christianity in and around the village. According to Geddes, in 1956 there were 10 families of believing Christians in the village (see Appendix in Fei's book in Chinese, 1986). In 1996 I found there were 14 Christian believers, 4 male and 10 female, all of whom I interviewed. I was able to confirm that the 10 families recorded by Geddes as Christian are still believers after 40 years. The earliest Christian believer known in the village can be traced back to 1931.

Fei mentioned that in the 1930s the main religious activities were carried out at the township (1939:103). He was speaking of Zhenze Township, which used to administer Kaixiangong Village. In 1996 it was still a centre for Christian religious activity, as I discussed in I.IV (and see Photos I-20 and 21). Local people called Christianity a "State religion" (*guojia*

Photos I-20 and 21. The exterior of a Church in Zhenze Township and a service

jiaohui) because it had a real church and was registered with the local government. The church was built in 1915 and turned into a school in 1958. In the 1980s Christians held services at private homes, known as "underground church services" (*dixia jiaohui*) because there was no church building and these "gatherings" were not registered. In 1989 local government returned the Church to local Christians. Up until 1996 about 2,000 people attended church services, 400 of whom were baptised.

When I asked about Christianity in Miaogang Township I was given another term "local church (*defang jiaohui*)". This meant a fixed meeting place without a church building and no registration with the local government, which sounds similar to the "underground church service" (*dixia jiaohui*) before 1989 in Zhenze Township. I went to see the site – in fact the only "local church" in Miaogang Township – with a Kaixiangong Christian (see Photo I-22).   There were about 80 believers and a service was held every Sunday, set up in a believer's home. Two "brothers" (lay preachers) came from Zhejiang Province and worked (*chuan fuyin*) in this area. They led people in singing hymns, gave testimonies (*zuo jianzheng*), read the bible, preached the gospel, and prayed. One quarter of the 50 believers were male. People who wore a black hat had been baptised and called each other brothers and sisters, and were joined in friendship. After the rituals the baptised believers left to share red wine and small pancakes.

Photo I-22. A Christian in Kaixiangong; Photo I-23 A "local Christian service" in Miaogang Township

More details about "vertical *wanglai* with spiritual beings" can be seen in Chapter VII.III, where I will describe a Christian religious phenomenon with a Chinese characteristic, known as "praying for others (*daidao*)" (see Photo VII-1), which must be seen as a part of local social support arrangements. I will also mention a conflict caused by the differences between popular religious practice and Christianity

2. Popular religions

As I've already said, 95% of ESRC social support project interviewees described themselves as having "general spiritual beliefs". Amongst choices of Buddhism, Taoism, Christianity, general spiritual beliefs, and others, an outright majority of the interviewees chose "general spiritual beliefs". In their own words they "pray for Buddha (*baifo*)", "worship local gods (*bai dalaoye*)", "worship kitchen god (*baizao*)", "regularly worship local gods twice per month (*zuo chuyi yueban*)", "worship ancestors (*bai shangzu* or *guo sijie*)" (see Chapter IV.III). They confirmed that they believed there were local gods and goddesses, ancestors and ghosts having existence in a spiritual realm. If they worshipped them or engaged in religious activities with them on a regular basis they would be blessed by them and avoid bad luck. In Feuchtwang's term, these religious activities of "general spiritual beliefs" are a part of popular religion (2002). In the official view they are feudal superstitions (*fengjian mixin*).

Religion in Kaixiangong consists on the one hand of a whole panoply of popular religious beliefs, and on the other Christianity. Villagers' family life and religious beliefs are closely related. In almost every major family event (whether annual or life cycle events) we see villagers routinely using ancestors and local gods as sources of spiritual support for their family networks. Their "religious system" is an integral part of the village's own informal system. However, villagers' ideas and activities sometimes differ from the state's ideologies and policies. They needed to create ways to adjust their own spiritual needs and coordinate them with the relationship between themselves and the state. Below I will describe some religious settings in the village, township and at home.

(1)Temples in the village

Fei found there were two temples in the 1930s: "one at the west end and the other at the north end" of the village (1939:21). After the liberation in 1949 the two temples were no longer used as residences of local gods and priests as they were in the 1930s (Fei, 1939:20). However, according to Geddes, both temples still existed and were even repaired by villagers when he visited in 1956 (Appendix in Fei, 1986:306). But there was no escape for the temples during the Cultural Revolution.

At the time of my visit in 1996 one of the temples was located in the east end of the village, the so-called East Temple (*dongmiao*). During the Cultural Revolution all religious artefacts and symbols had been thrown out and destroyed.

As the main temple of the village, it was rebuilt in 1993 (see Photos I-24 and 25). It was a simple structure attached to one of the village's warehouses, divided into two merely by using two separate altar tables. That on the east side was for *Guandi* (*guandi laoye*) and that on the west was for Bodhisattva *Guanyin* (*guanshiyin niangniang*). On each altar table there were also various other small statues of Buddha or Taoist gods who in past lives had been Taoist masters.

Photo I-24 and 25. Outside and inside east temple which was rebuilt in 1993

I asked a villager why some of them called this temple the East temple, others the North. Even Fei himself once referred to the one as the other (1939:20–21) and (1939:104–5). I was told that the temple was actually located at the north-east end of the village. Fei lived south of the river where villagers called it the north temple, whereas I lived on the north side of the river where villagers called it the East temple. In this book I will do what I learnt first, and call it the East temple.

One day in April 1996 this temple was once more destroyed, at the hands of a gang sent by the Township government. This was part of a nation-wide tightening of the policy to restrict mass gatherings before the Qingming Festival (also called sweeping the graves). A few years later this policy was slightly relaxed, especially when large numbers of Taiwanese businessmen began coming to Southern Jiangsu Province and wished to take part in spiritual rituals. This had its influence on local cultural life, and rebuilding temples became popular again. Against this background, the East temple was rebuilt yet again in 2003 (see Photo I-26 to 29). Near it the villagers also built a little temple for the land god, based on old peoples' memories.

The other temple was located in the west of the village, the so-called West Temple (*ximiao*). During the Cultural Revolution this was replaced by a warehouse for the ninth group of the village. In 1993, since there was no space to build another temple, villagers simply set up an altar table and placed small statues of Buddha or Taoist gods on it in one end of the warehouse. Then in 1996 the West Temple, like the North, was abolished, and the altar table, statues and incense burner and so on were thrown out (see Photos I-30 and 31).

Photos I-26 and 27. Outside and inside the East Temple (photographed by Fukun Yao 2003)

Photos I-28 and 29. Villagers worshipping local gods in 2003 (by Fukun Yao) and 2005

Photos I-30 and 31. The so-called "West temple" inside a warehouse (photo taken on Chinese New Year Day), and the destroyed "temple" remains outside it (photo taken before Qingming Festival)

In 2002, one year before the new East Temple, a new West Temple was built, enclosed within an independent courtyard. Needless to say, as the temples once more increased in popularity, restrictions were re-imposed. Photo I-32 shows the gate of the West temple yard closed when Dr Haiming Hui visited Kaixiangong in 2003.

In 2004 I visited the West temple on my trip to Kaixiangong. In the courtyard there were a well, candle stands, and an iron basket for burning paper. The temple was divided into two rooms. On the east side there were two statues, one of Buddha Jiu Huang (Liu Huang *pusa*), the other of Master Cao (Cao *daren*), both local gods reputed to protect the neighbourhood from generation to generation. In the top centre of the screen curtain there were four characters "*you qiu bi ying*" meaning "give response to every prayer and grant whatever is requested". This was echoed by another four characters in front of the offertory table: "*fo guang pu zhao* (The local gods are spreading the glory of the Buddha" (see Photos I-33 and 34).

Photo I-32. West Temple was closed in 2003 (photographed by Haiming Hui)

Photos I-33 and 34. The courtyard and interior of the West temple in 2004

Meanwhile there were two small temples in the original Hehuawan village and two others in the original Xicaotian village. So Kaixiangong now has a grand total of six temples. Chapter III.III will show how the villagers *wanglai* with their ancestors and local gods.

(2)The temple in the township

For Kaixiangong villagers the popular religious centre was in Miaogang, where there was a temple called Grandpa Temple (*laotaimiao*) where grandpa Qiu lived, a half an hour's walking distance from Kaixiangong. The villagers told me that the temple had two other buildings around it, one with a skylight (*tianjing*) in the middle. It was located in a big courtyard within quite a large area of land belonging to the temple. Inside the courtyard was a stage for plays, and donors (rich local people) arranged for theatricals (*xiban*) to play local dramas. There were 14 resident monks. The buildings were partly destroyed at the time of the Great Leap Forward and completely destroyed during the Cultural Revolution. Rebuilding started in 1993 but was still was not completed when I was there in 1996. This can be easily seen from the shape of the temple and building materials around it. Photo I-35 shows the event at the Chinese New Year Eve.

Chinese New Year's Eve is the most important time for worship of local gods. This event is called "grabbing the first incense (*qiang tou Xiang*)", literarily, to worship local gods with full body and heart. I participated in this event and stayed there next morning (see Chapter III.III). However, like so many others, the unfinished temple was once more completely destroyed the day before the 1996 Qingming festival[43] (see Photo I-36).

Photo I 35 and 36. The Laotai Temple on Chinese New Year's Eve and its remains before Qingming festival 1996

As mentioned earlier, in order to attract Taiwanese businessmen to invest in Jiangsu Province the policy regarding popular religions was slightly softened. In 2001 the Laitai Temple was rebuilt. It attracts a large number of pilgrims and is very prosperous. However, in 2003, with renewed application of the anti feudal superstition policy, the temple was closed. But instead of being burned down, it was saved by local people arguing for it as a tourist attraction, as well as a venue for cultural entertainment. Photos I-37 and 38 were taken in 2003 by Haiming Hui and 2008 by myself. In both photographs the temple is closed, but for quite different reasons. In the first photo the closure was forced, but the latter was merely taken out of opening hours. The big tree, in front of the temple, (an important part of ritual, see Chapter III.III) was still there, but my photo excludes it in favour of showing the complete structure of the building.

---

[43] The day marking the beginning of the 5th solar term, April 4, 5 or 6.

Photos I-37 and 38. The Laitai Temple were rebuilt in 2001 (left photo were taken by Huiming Hui in 2003; right photo were taken in 2008)

(3)Religious activities at home

After all the temples were destroyed, what happened for people who normally attended them? I checked the reference materials I had brought with me to the field. According to Shen Guanbao, during his fieldwork period from 1985 onward there was always fresh ash from burned paper money and incense by an old ginkgo tree beside the temple[44] (Shen, 1993:19). Fei Xiaotong said that villagers' spiritual life was very much mixed in with their family life and "largely carried on in their own houses" (Fei, 1939:21).

When I walked around the village I found burning incense on burned honeycomb briquettes outside houses. I was told that this was a way they created to worship local gods after the temple was destroyed (see Chapter III.III and conclusion I; Photo I-39). Photo I-40 shows a religious ritual being carried out in XQ Wang's kitchen.

Photo I-39. Burning incense on a burned honeycomb briquette outside a house.

Photo I-40. A religious activity in XQ Wang's kitchen

It is clear to me that the removal of the temples did not stop the villagers' religious activities. Kaixiangong villagers treated ancestors and local gods as spiritual sources and resources, as a part of their family networks. Later chapters will describe villagers' religious

---

[44] There is no tree by the north or east temple in Kaixiangong Village, the old ginkgo tree where Shen saw incense ash must actually have been by the *Laotai* temple in Miaogang Township.

activities as an intrinsic part of their lives through every event, whether annual or life cycle.

In 2009, when he was proofreading some chapters of the Chinese version of this book, Yunyun Zhu[45] expressed the following ideas about local people's spiritual beliefs and activities. First, he thought, the purpose of worshipping local gods was pragmatic. Second, it was a way to express ideas of right and wrong. Third, it was an important part of local cultural life. His ideas came from observation over a long period, and accord with my own descriptions and analysis from my empirical data (see Chapter IV.II and IV.III, and Chapter VII.III).

I.V. Relationships between villagers and the state

Although the administrative structure changed, there was an unbroken informal system of beliefs and practices in Kaixiangong which actually held rural society together at the village level. As we can see from Fei's work, in the 1930s a far from successful new administrative system of *baojia* (*pao chea*) was imposed on the village (1939:109–116). The village had two heads in the 1930s, but during the Cultural Revolution the actual number of cadres increased to 20. In spite of the village being separated into two halves the villagers always considered the two Great Brigades to be one Kaixiangong Village. After a cycle of 60 years (*huajia*), the number of cadres reduced to five, an acceptable figure to villagers because the original Kaixiangong Village had increased its size by taking in Hehuawan and Xicaotian. The villagers did not actually need all these changes of administrative system over the course of half a century. They have their own ways to organize their lives and they knew how to update their systems from time to time according to changing situations. Subsequent chapters will show how the villagers' system of social support works through *lishang-wanglai*.

Kaixiangong villagers had their own family networks which consisted of members of family, relatives, neighbours, friends, fellow villagers, the collective, institutions, and even the ancestors, and the local gods and goddesses. Relatives were divided by the villagers into agnatic kin (*zijiaren*) and non-agnatic kin (*qinqi*). For how they claim quasi kin and include in this claim both quasi agnatic kin (*ren zijiaren*) and quasi non-agnatic kin (*guofang qin*), and even quasi neighbours (*ren linju*) see earlier in this chapter and Chapter V.I. For a focal family a son's friends are called "little friends" until he marries, whereas a married man's friends are called "old friends". A daughter's friends are called "little sisters" until she marries and the friendships

---

[45] one of the authors of *Changes of Kaixiangong Village* (to be published in 2010 by Shanghai Publishing House)

then end (see Chapter 2). Fellow villagers (*tongxiaodui renjia*) include households sharing the same surname but not agnatically related and the households which live in the same group or the same natural village (*zirancun*). The group is an important social support unit. Almost all the villagers have detailed knowledge of other households within their own group.

The collective and local institutions are another part of villagers' sources of resources. Villagers always say "*cunli*" (village collective) or "*changli*" (enterprises run by village collective) referring to the village collective, but they get limited support from it. In Socialist China about 80 per cent of rural people are commonly called "second class citizens" (*erdeng gongmin*) because they have never been covered by the state social security system. As I mentioned in the Introduction Part I "The ESRC project on social support", before the 1990s socialist China's official social security hardly covered rural areas at all, except for a system of relief limited to natural disasters and people with special difficulties, for example the five-guarantee households or extremely poor households. During that period it was the village collective that played the role of applying and distributing this limited state social security and welfare. From the late 1980s to the mid-1990s some village collectives became very rich due to highly developed village enterprise and industry and provided genuine welfare for villagers, for example Jinxing Village of Zhenze Township, one of the ESRC social support project fieldwork villages. From 1997 onwards privatisation reduced the village collective's power and property, but the villagers and the collective are still connected.

The major inter-reaction between the village and the collective lies in the collection of taxes. Basically, villagers are subject to more than 30 different taxes and fees, including Agricultural Tax, irrigation works, electric, medical co-operation, education, welfare fee for the poor, public welfare, administrative fees and so on (see Table I-1)[46]. The previous head of the village, YG Zhou, told me that the figures for tax and fees do not look big but are nevertheless burdensome. In 1996 the villagers owed a total of 120,000 *yuan* in unpaid taxes and fees, even though the collective and similar organisations paid out large amounts on their behalf. After a few years' hard work, the village cadres reduced this figure to 69,000 *yuan*, but it still involved 118 households. Among the reasons given for non-payment, 5 households refused because the level of taxation was "unfair", 8 of them lived outside the village, 16 extremely poor households were unable to pay, 24 of them were still in debt from the expense of recent family events, and 65 of them kept on delaying payment for no particular reason. The general consensus was that most

---

[46] Table I-1 shows details of more than 30 different fees that the villagers had to pay in 1998 (in Chinese)

villagers would agree to pay reasonable taxes and fees, but thought many fees were unnecessary. Their practice of delaying payment was a complaint about the State's unfair treatment of them as second-class citizens ever since the Liberation in 1949.

Both villagers and village cadres agreed that the eventual change of policy on tax and fees was the result of *wanglai* between village cadres and villagers, and village cadres and local officers, in the process of collection. This phenomenon of personalised institutional *wanglai* between villagers and village cadres and village cadres and local officials has been demonstrated again in an official form "2002 Rural Agricultural Tax and others" where I found an item for "fees for *wanglai* with households" (*nonghu wanglai e*). The village treasurer told me that the form covered all village.

Table I-1 Kaixiangong Village's financial budget (1988)

項目					預算			負擔	
					鎮糸口	村統籌	合計	村	衣'戶
支出部分	提留統籌	福利費		衣發基金	1.47		1.47		1.47
			優供補	烈軍屬優待金	3.11	0.5	3.61		3.61
				慰問軍屬		0.5	0.3		0.5
				徵兵費用		0.6	0.6		0.6
				五保戶供給	0.7		0.7		0.7
				困難戶補助		0.3	0.3		0.3
				小計	3.81	1.9	5.71		5.71
			文教衛生	教育附加	2.38		5.71		2.38
				電影廣播		0.2	2.38		0.2
				業餘教育		0.1	0.2		0.1
				醫療衛生		0.8	0.1		0.8
				計畫生育		0.5	0.5		0.5
				小計	2.38	1.6	3.98		3.98
			公益事業	橋梁道路					
				合醫保險	3.81		3.81	0.95	2.86
				獨生子女父母養老	0.71		0.71		0.71
				用電達標					
				民兵訓練		0.1	0.1		0.1
				小計	4.52	0.1	4.62	0.95	3.67
			社會福利	幹部養老金	0.4	1	1.4		1.4
				慰問老人		1	1		1
				賣葬補助		0.1	0.1		0.1
				家財保險		1.2	1.2	0.5	0.7
				聯防經費	2		2		2
				扶貧基金	0.24		0.24		0.24
				小計	2.64	3.3	5.94	0.5	5.44

（continued）

項目				預算			負擔	
				鎮紮口	村統籌	合計	村	農戶
支出部分	提留統籌	幹部報酬	幹部報酬	定工幹部		5	5	5	
				誤工幹部		5	5	5	
		管理費	電話電信		1.2	1.2	1.2	
			差旅費		0.5	0.5		0.5
			書報費		0.6	0.6		0.6
			辦公費		0.2	0.2		0.2
			茶水費		0.3	0.3	0.3	
			黨群活動費		1	1	1	
			小計		13.8	13.8	12.5	1.3
	稅金	二金一費支出合計		14.82	20.7	35.52	13.95	21.57
		農業稅		14.81		14.81		14.81
		農林物產稅		0.78		0.78		0.78
		漁業稅						
		小計		15.59		15.59		15.59
	農副業服務	關於水費		4.53		4.53		4.53
		水利工程費		1.55		1.55		1.55
		防洪保安基金		1.19		1.19		1.19
		水電費			7.6	7.6		
		機耕費			1.6	1.6		
		農機修添費			1.5	1.5		1.5
		服務誤工				0		
		組幹部等報酬			5.3	5.3		5.3
		小計		5.27	16	23.27		23.27
	其他費用	招待費用			4	4	4	
		利息支出			10	10	10	
		彌補上年赤字				0		
		其他開支			2	2	2	
					16	0	16	
		小計		37.68	52.7	90.38	29.95	60.43
	支出部分總計				30.6			

（continued）

項目			預算			負擔	
			鎮糺口	村統籌	合計	村	農戶
收入部分	上繳收入	企業利潤上繳		5.55			
		副業發包上繳					
		其他承包上繳		61.38	61.38		
		農戶承包上繳		97.53	97.53		
		小計			0		
	常規收入	生產經營收入			0		
		服務收入			0		
		其他收入			0		
		小計			0		
	收入部分總計				97.53		
收支相抵結餘					7.15		
農戶按承包耕地 2604 畝計，畝均負擔			232.07				
農戶按總人口 2382 人計，人均			253.69				

taxes and fees except for one item for irrigation, which was collected by the irrigation works institution independently from 2002 onwards. Village cadres no longer needed to collect this fee from the villagers but still needed to *wanglai* with them for the rest of the tax and fees. Village cadres hoped that the electricity fee might in future be paid directly to the institution by the villagers, to reduce the number of fees they themselves had to collect, but this would take time because systems of accounting for the use of electricity were very complicated.

If we zoom out from this period of "cutting down tax and fees" in 2002 to view the issue for the whole period of the Household Responsibility System (1984–2003) we can see how policies vary. Table I-2 covers just this period and shows Kaixiangong households' shares of tax and fees to the state, township and the village collective. Households sometimes pay more and sometimes less, as determined by changes of policy. Table I-2 shows that from 2001 to 2003 households' shares of tax and fees reduced by nearly one quarter. Moreover, the last row of Table I-2 shows that 191,537 *yuan* of state tax was waived by Suzhou government. In effect 40 per cent of the villagers' burden of tax and fees had been rescinded (*jianfu* short for *jianqing nongmin fudan*).

Table I-2 Population, income and households' shares of tax and fees to the state, town and village (*yuan*) *

Year 年度	Population 人口	Household 戶數	Income* 人均 收入	Tax & fees per household 戶交稅費	Fees to the institutions/ town/village 上交有關部門 /鄉鎮/村統籌	Tax to the state 交國家稅	Total tax & fee 共交稅費
1984	2,376	572	551.39	107.09	28, 583	32,671	61,254
1985	2,381	609	806.54	101.65	19, 955	41,952	61,907
1986	2,377	609	803.35	124.63	25,942	49,955	75,897
1987	2,394	612	872.79	107.79	20,910	45,059	65,969
1988	2,384	612	1,115	215.27	86,684	45,059	131,743
1989	2,411	613	1,181	292.01	121,537	57,464	179,001
1990	2,436	620	1,120	373.34	168,829	62,643	231,472
1991	2,441	620	1,346	496.41	245,219	62,556	307,775
1992	2,429	619	1,873	535.15	255,956	75,299	331,255
1993	2,428	619	2,222	539.42	258,601	75,299	333,900
1994	2,427	617	2,931	684.76	299,300	123,200	422,500
1995	2,416	613	4,078	798.63	376,658	112,900	489,558
1996	2,396	610	4,879	867.05	369,675	159,227	528,902
1997	2,382	604	4,945	971.52	425,400	161,400	586,800
1998	2,369	597	5,106	1,023.95	451,300	160,000	611,300
1999	2,356	589	5,117	1,054.50	466,583	154,520	621,103
2000	2,263	585	5,246	1,001.61	424,916	161,024	585,940
2001	2,953	789	5,466	697.73	354,956	195,555	550,511
2002	2,941	790	5,632	699.78	357,336	195,488	552,824
2003	2,942	787	6,073	638.24	310,758	191,537	502,295

* This table starts from 1984 which is the first year that the Household Responsibility System was applied to the village. In 2003 Suzhou City waived the Agricultural Tax of 191,537 (see Chapter I.II "Changes of administrative system"). Sources: Rural Economic Income and Distribution Form (《農村經濟收入分配表》 1984 – 2003); Agricultural Responsible Contracts Form (《農業承包合同匯總表 2000》); Agricultural Tax and other Fees (《農村農業稅及其它(2001－02)》); Households Turn in Statement (《農戶上繳款結算匯總表 2003》). The above data was checked by the Village Treasurer.

The village treasurer told me that the initial goal of the policy was to "bring fees into the tax system". As far as paperwork went this goal was realised with the village Rural Economic Income and Distributing Form. When I queried this the treasurer provided me with another set of forms: the Agricultural Responsibility Contracts Form (2000), Agricultural Tax and other Fees (2001–02) and Households Turn in Statement (2003). The figures for tax and fees in Table I-2, showing a reduction by one quarter from 2001, is based on these forms (for how the different forms work see an example on repaying a large amount of debt in Chapter VIII.I). However, the treasurer told me that a new local policy is having a real effect as regards cutting rural people's tax and fees by 40 per cent. This new policy is an application of Premier Wen Jiabao's "Report on the Work of the Government" delivered at the Second Session of the Tenth National People's Congress on 5 March 2004. According to Wen "Solving problems facing agriculture, rural areas and farmers is a top priority in all our work. … [We] will press ahead with the reform of rural taxes and administrative charges. …agricultural taxes will be rescinded in five years."[47] I was told by many village cadres that Suzhou Prefecture is the first area in the whole of China to decide to rescind agricultural taxes, because the urban area of this region is rich enough to support its surrounding rural area. Suzhou is once again realizing the famous saying "up above there is Paradise, down here there are Suzhou and Hangzhou (*shang you tiantang xia you Su-Hang*)". The villagers felt much happier for being treated more fairly. They see the reduction of tax as the result of reciprocal *wanglai* with local officials (see VIII.II).

This completes my short description of the village, its historical changes of economy, administration, kinship system, religious and spiritual system and practices, and finally the relationship between villagers and the state via the village collective.

---

[47] http://news.xinhuanet.com/english/2004-03/16/content_1368830.htm

Chapter II   **Local customs (I)**

Table V-1 shows 38 events normally experienced on the journey from birth to death. It consists of three main stages: the birth and growing up period, the establishment of marriage relationships, and funeral ceremony and post-funeral rituals. Chapter II has three sections which cover the first two stages, together with house construction. This includes 28 of the total of 38 events listed in Table V-1. They represent the raw materials of Kaixiangong villagers' everyday life and customs, and will hopefully lead to a better detailed understanding of the *lishang-wanglai* model. "House construction" is a special phenomenon produced by the socialist system. According to local tradition house construction is "an important task lasting for one century". Villagers build their houses based on their individual need. However, for 30 years after the People's Republic of China was founded villagers lived in the collectivization system. There was hardly any house construction until the early 1980s. However, since then villagers have built their own houses one group after another, and even one "generation" after another, with houses being ascribed to one of the three generations depending on the number of storeys, architectural style and quality. Third generation houses are often multi-storey, in the Western style ("*xiao yanglou*") and use high quality building materials intended to last over a century. The peak of house construction has now past, but the customs adhering to its different phases have revived, new ones have been created, and additional elements have accrued. They illustrate the mechanism of *lishang-wanglai,* and the social support arrangements for this major family event.

II.I. Birth and growing up

There are a number of important events in the growing up period in the village. They are the events before and after the birth; celebrations of the one-month old birthday and one-year old birthday; events of "being a guest" and "being visited"; events for a child pre-school and starting school; and celebration of the sixteenth birthday and seeing-off ceremonies. A major difference between village children and those in urban China or the West is that the latter have a birthday celebration every year, whereas special events for the former are attached to ideas of being a guest and being visited and getting ready for school and starting school. Village children do also have a birthday every year, but the celebrations for it are relatively simple.

1. Events before the birth (*Dan shengtang*)

An important event before a baby's birth is called *dan shengtang* (to carry soup for a woman when she has been pregnant for eight months). (*Dan shoutang* will mean to carry soup for a woman after she gives birth). *Dantang* is short for these two events of providing "soup" before and after childbirth. Fei found that "soup" (*tang*) in the 1930s referred to a herbal soup to help labour at a time when maternal death rate and infant mortality were both high (1939:35). However "soup" could change from time to time. In the 1960s and 1970s it meant sugar or sugar tickets. A sugar ticket was 150g sugar per person per month according to the then current state policy. The villagers believe that sugar is the best nourishment when food is scarce. But in the 1990s soup" signified a variety of goodwill gifts – for the pregnant woman's health, for the new baby's birth and growing up lucky, and for entertaining guests after the delivery.

I attended a dan shengtang event at HK Zhou's family's home on 21 March 1996. There were two feasts for two sets of Zhou's relatives.

According to the local custom the lunchtime feast was designed for Mrs Zhou's natal family and their relatives, as a part of the networking process of Mr Zhou's family. The guests came in the morning with *shazhao* (big bamboo steamers each of 50cm diameter) containing gifts of knitting wool, red/Chinese dates (jujube), the upper part of pig's leg with foot (*datizi*), eggs (hen and duck's), egg cake, noodles, lotus root starch, brown and white sugar, daidi (a thin glutinous rice crust) and so on. In addition, Mrs Zhou's natal family gave clothes for the new baby suitable for four seasons and for different uses, all made by Mrs Zhou's mother (See Photo II-2). The total cost of Mrs Zhou's natal family's gifts was about 400 *yuan*. Every non-agnatically related household, in respect of being newly established non-agnatic kin (*xinqin*) of the Zhou family, spent on average 100 yuan for gifts. Altogether 48 people attended the feast, seated around six tables: 37 women, six men and five children. During this feast Mr Zhou's relatives accompanied Mrs Zhou's natal family's relatives. I noticed that Mr Zhou's mother sat Mrs Zhou's natal family's relatives apart from each other at the best seats at different tables, accompanied by Mr Zhou's mother, his father's brother's wife and his father's patrilateral cousin's wife.

The suppertime feast was designed for Mr Zhou's relatives, both agnatic and non-agnatic. 72 people attended the feast. In contrast to the wedding banquet, for the *dan shengtang* event only those close agnatic kin who had invited the new couple for welcoming feasts after they themselves got married were invited, but all the non-agnatic kin within three generations were included They brought gifts with them for the feast which were similar to those of Mrs Zhou's natal family's relatives. Since Mrs Zhou's natal family's relatives became *xinqin* (new generation relatives) her husband's family's non-agnatic kin became *laoxin* (old generation relatives) and only needed to bring gifts worth 50 *yuan* each, according to local custom.

In the two feasts the Zhou family received gifts and red envelopes amounting to 2,500 *yuan* and spent about 3,000 *yuan* on tea and snacks, and return gifts including jujube, eggs, and instant noodle. So these events cannot be explained as financial support. Emotional support and caring, in this case, were more important than financial or labour support, because the people came to share the emotion caused by expectation of and fear for the birth, as Fei noticed in the 1930s (1939:34–35).

The event can be understood as the foundation stone ceremony of the Zhou family's *xinqin*, a new generation of non-agnatic kin, being joined in the

Photo II-1. Mrs Zhou's mother and relative visited her with gifts

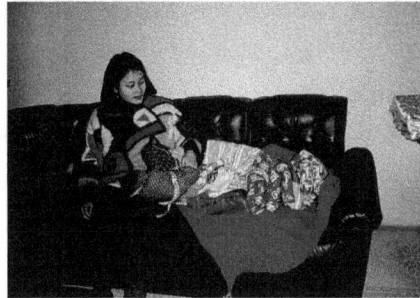

Photo II-2. Mrs Zhou was admiring the gifts: baby's clothing

Zhou family's *lishang-wanglai* networks. Mrs Zhou's mother reported that she felt that she was an important guest, noting that Mr Zhou's household treated her, her brother's wife and her husband's sister well as honorary guests. This is a great change in style of welcome from the 1930s, when Fei tells us that a pregnant woman's mother is bound by duty to look after her for several days (1939:35). Although participants in a new wife's natal family can vary in position from that of servant to honorary guest over the course of the event, the overall relationship between the new wife's natal family and her married-in family will consistently be that of an important new resource for the married-in family. After the *dantang* event Mrs Zhou's natal family and their relatives became important guests and sources of resource in Mrs Zhou's new family's list of close non-agnatic kin.

2. Events after the birth (*dan shutang* and *wangxinke*)

Ten days later, on the 31 March, I attended DQ Rao family's *dan shutang* event. Mrs Rao told me that since the family had already held a *dan shengtang* event when she was 8-months pregnant, quite similar to the Zhou family's above, the *dan shutang* would be much simpler. In the morning I saw Mrs Rao's natal family plus six other families of non-agnate kin, as well as Mr Rao's four close non-agnatic kin, bring gifts to see her and the baby. The contents of the gifts were more or less the same as the *dan shengtang* plus a bag of *yunpiangao* (a kind of rice cake in thin strips), except that there were no clothes or upper part of pig leg from Rao's mother, and no knitting wool from all the relatives. As in many events in the village there was also a standard value of gift for different categories of people. Both Mrs Rao's natal family and Mr Rao's *jiujiu* (mother's brother) should get 80 *yuan* each, the rest of the non-agnate kin 50 *yuan* each, and Mrs Rao's friends (little sisters) 30 *yuan* each. The Rao family held a lunchtime feast for all the guests. The feast was without *tizi* (upper part of pig leg), which is the way in which villagers describe the standard of a feast as being lower in rank than the *dan shengtang* feast, although the numbers of dishes looked similar.

As well as the *dan shutang* visits from the baby's mother's and father's close non-agnate kin and the father's agnate kin, other people would also come to see the baby. On this occasion there were about 40 visitors: the baby's parents' friends, neighbours and fellow villagers. They brought small gifts such as *yunpiangao*, and milk powder, and put a red envelope with 10 *yuan* on top of them. The baby's family entertained with tea and snacks for all the guests (see Photo II-3).

Photo II-3. Neighbours and friends participated in the "after birth event"

Rao's family spent about 1,200 *yuan* for the entertainment (feast and tea). But they received gifts plus gift money amounting to 1,680 *yuan*. Superficially it looked as though the Rao family received more in *dan shutang* gifts than they spent, but these figures include a mixed event of both *dan shutang* and *wangxinke* (visiting a newborn baby).

Dan shutang was only meant for those relations who attended the earlier *dan shengtang* event. They are the baby's father's family's both agnatic and non-agnatic kin, and the baby's mother's natal family's close relatives. Here *sheng* and *shu* in *dan shengtang* and *dan shutang* can be translated as raw and ripe, uncooked and cooked, unfamiliar and familiar, as an informant explained it to me, with the words "*yihui sheng erhui shu* (unfamiliar at the first meeting, familiar at the second)". The baby's mother's natal family's relatives were now classed as familiar visitors in this event, since on this occasion there were other unfamiliar people gradually being introduced into the baby's life. They were the baby's parents' friends, neighbours and fellow villagers. For them, to visit a new-born baby is called *wangxinke*. The *xinke* is formed by two Chinese characters meaning new guest. The *wangxinke* event lays the foundation of a newborn baby's status as a new guest in a society formed by *lishang-wanglai*. The term of *xinke* indicates that as soon as the baby is born it starts a lifelong journey of *lishang-wanglai*. The following sections will show how the baby started to visit others and be visited.

3. Celebrations of the one-month old birthday

The celebrations for the one-month old birthday are known by the name of a local goddess, *manyue baitai*, because the event involved a ritual of worshipping her. I attended a *manyue baitai* from 17 to 20 March in JP Ren's family's home. Two days before the baby's one month birthday the baby's grandfather carried a basket (*shazhao*) of dried rice cakes (about 100 *gaobing*) to visit the baby's *jiujiu*'s family to ask for a rabbit hat (*taomaozi*). This was a way of issuing an invitation to the *manyue baitai*. In place of the *jiujiu* himself, who was working in a township with his wife, the *jiujiu*'s father gave him a purple-coloured rabbit hat[48].

The baby's *jiujiu*'s family immediately distributed the rice cakes they had been given to their relatives, neighbours and fellow villagers. On the 18 March they went shopping for gifts in the township while rice balls were made for the *manyue baitai* at their home.

On the 19 March the *jiujiu*'s father[49] carried a shoulder-pole load of gifts and his mother carried a basket to visit the baby's family. They presented their gifts. They were a cot (150 *yuan*), a red cloth wrapping a silver padlock (150 *yuan*) and a silver dollar (80 *yuan*), a red paper bag with 100 yuan, a *tizi*, a bag of cake, and two big food steamers (*longti*) of wet rice cakes (80 of *shuigao*). A bunch of evergreen was placed on the red cloth covering the steamers. In the steamers there were 12 big white rice balls with fillings of red bean mashes (*atai tuanzi*) and 30 small green[50] and 30 small white rice balls without fillings (*atai yuanzi*). The former were for agnatic kin and the latter for neighbours, fellow villagers, and all the attendants. These gifts were

---

[48] If the child was a girl the rabbit hat should be a pink colour.
[49] Although the *jiujiu*'s parents are the baby's grandparents, in this case they represent his mother's natal family and play roles for the baby's mother's brother. So I would like to address them as the *jiujiu*'s father and mother.
[50] The green colour is made from the juice of pumpkin leaves.

Photo II-4. The baby's *Jiujiu*'s parents representing the *jiujiu* participate in the baby's one-month old birthday event with gifts

worth 600 *yuan* (See Photo II-4).

The baby's mother dressed him in a cloth (*ataiyi*) specially made for worshipping an *ataimo* (a goddess) and put the rabbit hat on his head and hung the silver padlock on his chest. *Jiujiu*'s father drew a line between the baby's eyebrows and painted both his cheeks red. This is called *tiaoshou* and symbolised wishing the baby a long life for. The baby's *jiujiu*'s father told me that the ritual has been simplified recently, in that it is no longer the custom for him to cut the baby's hair.

Meanwhile, the baby's grandmother was presenting offerings for the *ataimo* (goddess). She put a table[51] in the middle of the living/dining room, with a paper inscription representing the *ataimo*, in the centre at the back of the table. Two candles were on either side. There were five big plates of offerings in the middle of the table: a small live mandarin fish, a raw *tizi*, a whole raw chicken, some big green rice balls and small rice balls. The baby's grandmother and the mother carried the baby in turn making bows to the *ataimo* (see Photo II-5). The baby's grandmother then "sent the *ataimo* away" by burning the paper representation and "setting the fish free". This was originally a Buddhist custom.

Photo II-5. The baby's mother's mother carried him to make bows to the *ataimo*

The baby's father lit firecrackers and fireworks for 20 minutes. Children in the same group shared the firecrackers and ran around the family. The father gave the attendants small white and green rice balls, one of each. He then distributed the rice cakes and balls to their agnate kin, neighbours and fellow villagers. The baby's father left rice cakes and balls in a bowl on top of the stove in the kitchen or dining table in the living/dining room for those in the case of households with nobody at home (it is normal for villagers to leave their kitchen doors unlocked).

On the same day, the baby's grandmother carried him to visit his *jiugong* (father's *jiujiu*)'s

---

[51] When the table is for presenting offerings its grain should run from south to north, whereas for dining the grain runs from west to east.

family, namely, the grandmother's natal family. This was the first visit in his life. His *jiugong* put a tiny bit of sugar in his mouth, which symbolised wishing him a sweet life. He also gave him a red envelope. The baby's grandmother then carried the baby to his *jiutaigong* (father's grandmother's brother)'s family, who repeated the same actions.

At lunchtime there was a family celebration at which the baby's family held a feast with the *jiujiu*'s parents. After the feast there were many people who received rice cakes and balls and visited the baby with little gifts, such as a few sweets, a bag of instant noodles, and small red bags for congratulations on his one month birthday. In the evening, the baby's father's family started preparations for paying return visits to his *jiujiu*'s family.

On the morning of the 20th, the baby's mother carried the baby, his father carried gifts, and his grandmother carried their personal belongings, to pay a return visit to the baby's *jiujiu*'s family. When they were 100 metres away several fireworks were let off, which served the function of sending a welcome salute. In front of the *jiujiu*'s house there were three piles of firewood. The *jiujiu*'s mother held a big bamboo pan (*canda*)[52], a metre in diameter. The baby's mother put the baby on the pan and the *jiujiu*'s mother carried him into the house. This ritual symbolised the baby's safe arrival (*ping'an dida*) and that all should be well in his life (*yisheng ping'an*; see photo II-6).

The baby's father presented gifts on a table: 100 dried rice cakes, a bag of cakes, and 11 sets of gifts which each contained 2 *jin* of sugar and one bag of crisp pancake rolls (*danjuan*). The *jiujiu*'s mother presented offerings for the *ataimo*, roughly similar to those the baby's grandmother had offered in his home. This time the baby's *jiujiu*'s mother and his mother carried him in turn making bows to the *ataimo* (see Photos II-7 and 8).

Photo II-6. The *jiujiu*'s mother welcomes the baby with a big bamboo pan

---

[52] It was used for raising silkworms.

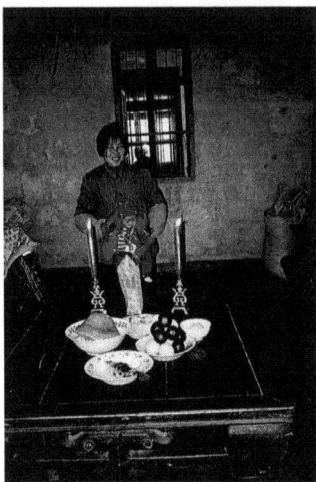

Photo II-7. The *Jiujiu's* mother carried the baby to make bows to Ataimo.

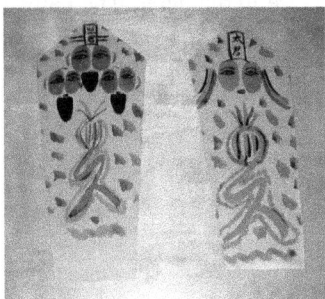

Photo II-8. Two paper inscriptions of Ataimo

After the ritual I asked the *Jiujiu's* mother for the *Ataimo* paper inscriptions. To my surprise she gave them to me, although the baby's father's mother had burned them "to send them off to the Heavens". The *Jiujiu's* mother explained her action to me with a little joke, "the *Ataimo* is supposed to go the West (*xitian*, namely the Heavens), and you will take them to the west when you go back there". So it seems to me that this practice has become more a question of ritual than of actual belief. The two *Ataimo* paper tablets were rolled together when they were presented on the table. One was inscribed Taijun (太君), the other Zhaojun (照君). I asked her who these figures originally were, but she said she did not know – in other words, no one really cared.

The baby's *jiujiu's* father lit firecrackers and fireworks again. Children who lived in the same group heard the fireworks and came running in to see the new guest and were given little rice balls. The baby's *jiujiu's* mother then distributed the dried rice cakes to relatives, neighbours and fellow villagers. After lunch the baby's father and his grandmother went back home. The baby and his mother stayed on in the *jiujiu's* family for a month. During their stay close relatives, neighbours and fellow villagers visited the baby with gifts. The baby and his mother also took 11 sets of gifts as described above and attended meals with the 11 close relatives of the *jiujiu's* family in turn. After the trip the baby and his mother returned home with gifts of knitting wool, rice cakes and so on. They distributed the rice cakes again to relatives, neighbours and fellow villagers.

After over a month of *wanglai* with different relatives the cycle of the one-month old birthday celebration is completed. This is the first event arranged for the baby himself, since the celebration of his birth was shared with his mother. Its importance can be seen as follows: (i) It is the first time religion has come into the baby's life. Two rituals have been held, separately, in both the baby's family and his *jiujiu's* family, which is also his mother's natal family, which why the event is known as *manyue baitai* (worship of a local goddess on the first month old birthday). The cloth the baby wore was called *ataiyi* (cloths of the goddess) the rice balls were called *atai tuanzi* (the goddess's big rice ball) and *atai yuanzi* (the goddess's small rice ball). (ii) It is the first time the baby has worshipped his ancestors and asked blessings from them. For the baby's family this was also a way of reporting to their ancestors that the family has a new member. (iii) At his one-month old birthday the especially important relations of "*jiujiu*" were introduced into the baby's life. The *jiujiu*'s family spends a considerable amount on the event. There were gifts for everyday usage, such as the cot; for spiritual purposes, for example a silver padlock which symbolised happiness and a silver dollar for getting rich; the upper part of pig leg for a grand family feast; the rice balls and cakes for establishing relationships with small friends, relatives, neighbours and fellow villagers. (iv) The one-month old birthday involves several episodes of *wanglai* between the baby's family and their relatives, neighbours, and fellow villagers. The cakes flowed reciprocally. Every family received cakes twice: the first time was for *manyue baitai* and the second time was for returning home as a little guest from *jiujiu*'s family. The baby was also involved in reciprocal relations with his father's *jiujiu* and his father's mother's *jiujiu*. These people are now officially familiar to the baby because this is the second time since birth that he has seen them. (v) It is the first time the baby is involved in a broader circle of kin related to the *jiujiu*'s family and relations. The *jiujiu*'s relatives, neighbours and fellow villagers receive cakes from the baby's family twice. The first time is when "asking for a rabbit hat" (at the start of the whole celebratory process) and the second is when mother and new baby pay their return visit to the *jiujiu*'s family. The baby's family also receives gifts and letters from the relations of the *jiujiu*'s family. (vi) The one-month old birthday is also the first time that "small friends" from both his own family and his *jiujiu*'s family's groups are introduced into the baby's life. The children within the group came to the family celebration as soon as they heard the firecrackers and fireworks, quite of their own accord, without needing adult direction. These children are potentially the baby's future friends, neighbours or fellow villagers. Thus, this little person has been knitted into his family's *lishang-wanglai* networks. At the same time, his family has been knitting his own *lishang-wanglai* networks for him.

4. One-year old birthday celebration

The one-year old birthday celebration is called *zhousui baitai,* since this event also involves worshipping the local goddess. But it is a much lesser event than the one-month old birthday.

On 3 May I attended a one-year old birthday event in JL Song's family's home. It was arranged by the birthday girl's grandmother, because the girl's mother was working in a village enterprise. The presentation of the offerings looked slightly different from the one-month birthday already described. As before a paper inscription representing *ataimo* was placed in the centre back of the table. Two candles were placed at the front of the table instead of on each side of the *ataimo*. On the table there were a small live mandarin fish, an upper part of pork leg (*tizi*), a whole chicken, some smoked bean curd, white and green small rice balls without fillings (*atai yuanzi*). The grandmother also set a small bench facing the table. The girl hung a silver padlock on her chest which had been given to her by her *jiujiu* on her one-month birthday. The grandmother carried the girl and made a bow with bended knees to the *ataimo* (see Photo II-9)

Photo II-9. The grandmother carried the girl and made a bow with bended knees to the *ataimo*

She also helped the girl to do it herself. Then the grandmother burned the paper inscription, and lit firecrackers and fireworks. After that she distributed small rice balls to the visiting children. At the end of the ritual the grandmother and the birthday girl "set the mandarin fish free". The grandmother then took the girl with her to distribute rice balls, which she had made herself the day before the event, to her relatives both agnate and non-agnate. After receiving the rice balls these relatives gave them sweets or biscuits in return for the celebration. The girl's grandmother also prepared a nice evening meal for the family celebration of the girl's one-year old birthday.

This event has two significant features: (i) The girl's members of close family and their relatives all shared the happiness of her one-year old birthday. As an extension of the members of the family only the agnatic and non-agnatic kin who lived in the village were involved in the celebration. The girl's grandmother told me that this is the way in which they limited the size and standard of the celebration. (ii) Although there were no new relatives introduced into the girl's life on the one-year old birthday, friends and the local goddess were involved in this event for her for the second time since she was born. It is important for her that by her one-year-old birthday all her relations are familiar to her. The girl's grandmother explained that after this birthday the girl would start another circle of *lishang-wanglai*, "to be a guest" (*zuoxinke*) and "to be visited" (*wangdouke*), from the next lunar Chinese New Year onwards.

5. To be a guest and to be visited

To be a guest is called *zuoxinke,* which means a child is a new guest of his or her family's close non-agnate kin, whereas to be visited (*wangdouke*)[53] means that the close non-agnate kin of the child's family visit him or her. Compared with the first-year's intensive knitting of her circle: making familiar relations with relatives, neighbours, fellow villagers, friends, ancestors and local goddess, the next *lishang-wanglai* circle of a child is knitted slowly, over more than fifteen years, from one to sixteen years old and onwards.

I saw a mother carrying a baby, with her mother who carried small gifts (Photo II-10). They told me that they were "visiting relatives as guests" (*zuoke*). I had heard about the custom in Song's family when I was observing the one-year old birthday. The grandmother told me that during the coming lunar New Year period the girl would visit all the Song family's close non-agnate kin in turn (including *jiujiu*'s family as well as quasi kin's), with her mother. The style of her and her family's visits to all the non-agnate kin is much simpler than

Photo II-10. A grandmother, her daughter and granddaughter on their way to visit relatives as guests

that of her first visit to her *jiujiu*'s family when she was one month old. There is no need to fire welcome fireworks or stay for a month when a guest of the close relatives. The usual practice was for them to have a nice meal with each non-agnate relative on different day trips. Each time when the girl and her mother came to be a guest of one or another non-agnatic kin's family they would bring a basket of dried rice cakes (*gaobing*) with them to distribute among the visited family's close kin, neighbours and fellow villagers. People who received cakes would pay a visit with a small gift to the family who had the new guest.

From three to five years old the girl would be visited because of her status as a new guest (*wangdouke*) by the close non-agnatic kin which visited during the lunar New Year periods. It is the female adults' job to pay a visit to the new guest of their non-agnate kin. They would bring a basket of dried rice cake (80 –100 *gaobing*) in turn in the same year or different years. Each visitor would be entertained with a nice meal. After the meal the girl's family would then

---

[53] I was asked by the proofreader why the baby was called a guest at its own home when visited by other visitors. The villagers explained that it is because the newborn was a guest to other members of the family.

distribute the cakes to its agnatic kin, neighbours and fellow villagers.

To sum up, in the events of "being a guest" and "to be visited", a child becomes involved in wider *lishang-wanglai* networks of his or her family's non-agnatic kin. If the child's family has ten close non-agnatic kin, he or she should "be a guest" by paying a visit to each of them with the appropriate dried rice cakes. These are then distributed by each non-agnatic kin to their own agnatic kin, neighbours, and fellow villagers. Equally, each of the non-agnatic kin families should pay a return visit to the child's family with gifts, which would also be distributed to the child's family's agnatic kin and their neighbours and fellow villagers. This time the child, not the child's family, takes the role of "being visited" by each. This is how the child and his or her close non-agnatic kin and their networks come to recognise each other. As the child grows up, its *lishang-wanglai* networks are gradually strengthened.

6. Events for a child pre-school and starting school

Starting school is a very important stage for a child in his or her life and involves two events. I did not get a chance to observe these because they would normally happen in early Autumn at a time when I had completed my fieldwork. The following description is based on information provided by many informants in my sampled households.

Qiu started to organise the event of "asking *jiujiu* for a book bag" (*tao shubao*) when her daughter was 5 years old. She made 120 dried rice cakes (*gaobing*), with help from one of each of her neighbours and fellow villagers. She took her daughter and the cakes with her to visit the girl's *jiujiu*. They had a nice meal with the *jiujiu*'s family. The *jiujiu*'s wife then distributed the cakes to her relatives, neighbours and fellow villagers. Qiu and her daughter went back home with some *zongzi* (a pyramid-shaped dumpling made of glutinous rice wrapped in bamboo leaves) given by *jiujiu*'s family.

A few days before school started, the girl's *jiujiu*'s wife (*jiuma*), representing the girl's *jiujiu*, visited the Qiu family. She brought the girl many presents: a book bag, a stationery box with a pen, pencils, a ruler, a pencil sharpener, erasers, notebooks, an ink-slab, a paintbrush, a calculator, a cloth, a pair of trousers, an umbrella and rain boots. Qiu told me that the symbolic meaning of the umbrella and rain boots is *feng-yu wu zu* (literally, to go to school regardless of wind or rain). *Jiuma* also gave the girl sweets. These were to be used for an introduction to children in the school. Qiu explained to me that, on the first day of the school, children dressed in new clothes and carried a new book bag which contained stationery, notebooks and sweets, which should all have been provided by the *jiujiu*'s family. They hand the sweets to their teacher.

The teacher then introduces each student while distributing his or her sweets to other classmates. Meanwhile, the child would be given sweets from other children which were also mostly from their *jiujiu*s.

Another event is known as "asking *jiujiu* for nephew or niece balls" (*tao waishengtuan*). Bao, another informant, told me that when her son was aged seven they visited his *jiujiu*'s family. They bought gifts of a bag of tea, smoked green soya beans, sesame seed, and a basket of dried rice cake. These gifts were mainly used for a tea party for her son's *jiujiu*'s relatives or friends who were involved in making rice balls for the nephew and niece (*waishengtuan*). They had a nice meal in the *jiujiu*'s family's home. Then the *jiuma* distributed the cakes to relatives, neighbours and fellow villagers. The *jiujiu* gave him a red envelope which contained 100 *yuan* before Bao's son left the *jiujiu*'s family.

A few days later the boy's *jiujiu* carried two loads of rice balls on a shoulder pole for the nephew and niece to visit the boy's family. The rice balls were made of 100 *jin* of rice powder. They were both white and green in colour, with sweet and savoury fillings. The white rice ball had fillings of mashed red bean and the green rice ball had fillings of pork meat mixed with sliced radish. The Bao family held a feast with *tizi* to entertain the *jiujiu*'s family. They distributed the rice balls to their relatives, neighbours and fellow villagers. The boy then brought lots of rice balls to school, sharing them one at a time. He would also receive rice balls from others in his network, some time during this period.

The main purpose of the two celebrations to do with starting school is to help children make friendly relationships there. Bao told me that villagers believed sharing sweets and rice balls is generally seen as a good way for children to get together, just as sharing meals is a good way for adults. Her son's class had 46 children. The flow of sweets and rice balls among children also provided a basic foundation for them to give and share things. This can be seen as an extension of the flow of rice cakes among the *jiujiu*'s relations. I asked many people why the *jiujiu* is so important for special occasions. Qiu's answer related to knitting *lishang-wanglai* networks. The *jiujiu*'s family normally lived in a different village nearby, and the relationship between a child's family and its *jiujiu*'s family increased opportunities for a child to make school friends who might come from the *jiujiu*'s village. This could explain why on these two occasions the child's *jiujiu*'s family distributed rice cakes to its relatives, neighbours and fellow villagers.

7. Celebration of the sixteenth birthday and seeing-off ceremonies

The sixteenth birthday celebration (*shiliusui baitai*) starts when a child passes its 15th birthday. Peng's mother told me that her family's close non-agnate kin visited her son and gave him gifts, such as a watch, a bicycle, clothes, shoes and so on during this period. The style of giving was similar to that of their visits to the child when he was between two and four years old (*wangdouke*). The family entertained these visitors with a feast of 12 dishes without *tizi*.

On the 20 April, the day before the birthday, I saw five women making different rice balls (*atai tuanzi* and *atai yuanzi*), Peng's grandmother and her friends and neighbours. In contrast to the one-month old and one-year old birthdays, on the sixteenth birthday, although there were the white and the green rice balls, the green rice balls must be in the shape of a peach (*shoutao*) to symbolise a long life for the boy (Photo II-11).

Photo II-11. Two different colours of rice balls with different shapes

On the morning of the 21st Peng's mother set the altar tables. Two tables were joined together. At the north end were two paper inscriptions side by side. One was *ataimo* and the other was *nannü xingan* (the pronunciation of *xingan* is similar to the heart and liver goddess, but here a mixture of a god and a goddess were referred to). There were six small bowls and three handleless wine cups in front of them. They were for double cups of tea (sweet and savoury) and cups of wine. Two candles were in front of the cups. There were 12 big plates of offerings laid on the table. One was a big live mandarin fish, one was a bar of pork and one was a whole raw chicken. There were three plates of different kinds of rice balls, three plates of peach-shaped birthday cake with fillings, and three plates of fruit (bananas, apples and orange). A table extended from north to south.

Soon someone said "the *Jiujiu* are coming!" I saw them walking towards the house carrying gifts (Photo II-12). On the extended table the *jiujiu*'s families' gifts were presented. Each set of gifts was held in two big bamboo steamers wrapped with red cloth. They were 90 square-shaped dried rice cakes with toppings (*fanggao*), fruit, firecrackers, fireworks and a red envelope with 100 *yuan* (Photo II-13). Peng told me that the day before the birthday his family had already received one upper part of pork (*tizi*) and 400 *yuan* for clothes from each *jiujiu*.

Peng's grandmother put a small wooden bench facing the altar tables. Peng made a bow with bended knees with closed palms in front of his chest to the paper inscriptions of *ataimo* and *nannü xingan*. Peng then served a cup of wine to each in turn. After all his cousins had finished making bows Peng made another bow to the paper inscriptions (Photo II-14). Then Peng's grandmother "sent the inscriptions off" by burning them. While Peng's mother rearranged the tables Peng's father lit two strings of firecrackers and eight fireworks. Peng's mother then set the mandarin fish free by sliding it into the river (Photo II-15).

The standard of the feast of the 16th birthday was one level higher than that earlier in the year, because an upper part of pork (*tizi*) was involved when individual non-agnate kin came to see Peng with their gifts after he reached the age of 15. Apart from the *tizi* there were whole chicken, rice-field eels, red eggs, bean cut and vegetables. The firecrackers were also lit during the feast. Five close non-agnate kin (including three *jiujiu*'s families, one aunt's family, and one quasi mother's family), and three agnate kin attended the feast, including Peng's grand aunt's family (father's father's sister). After the feast all the guests took home their share of returning gifts. Peng's grandfather then distributed rice balls (*atai yuanzi*) to neighbours and fellow villagers. During the 16th birthday celebration Peng received a total amount of 300 *yuan* of gifts and 1,500 yuan of gift money from three *jiujiu*, 200 *yuan* gifts from each of his aunt's (mother's sister)'s family and his quasi mother's family, and 50 *yuan* from Peng's great aunt, which was her share as an old generation relative. The host family spent 1,000 *yuan* on the feast and the rest of the expenditure amounted to 200 *yuan*. This was the first time Peng received considerable financial support from his relatives.

Photos II-12 and 13. *Jiujiu*s carrying gifts, and the gifts themselves

Photo II-14. Peng making bows to the ataimo paper inscriptions

Photo II-15. Peng's mother setting the fish free

A few days later I was told that Peng's family held another little birthday party for him and invited all his little friends and classmates, a total of nine children[54]. They came to the party with gifts. In this case, an informant told me that the term "little friends" had a narrow meaning, indicating only those little friends who had grown up together. When children were school age, villagers distinguished classmates from little friends. But when the children get married the term of "little friends" would be used to cover all kinds of their friends. Children normally started to make other kinds of friends from 16 years old onwards.

After the 16th birthday, children are expected to have completed their middle school education. They would go on to high schools or specialised secondary schools or start work in enterprises or business. This would be a first separation from existing little friends or little sisters, but there would be opportunities of making new friends. Three years later they would either go to universities, find other jobs, or perhaps join the army. This would be the second such life experience. Thus their little friends' networks could be increased from little friends from the same village, to classmates, to work colleagues, army comrades and so on. Based on our sampled households in a wedding banquet there are 22 per cent little friends and 13 per cent old friends out of total guests on average per household[55].

However, there is a special kind of seeing-off ceremony (*huansonghui*) for children who go to specialised secondary schools, universities, or serve the army, all of which involve leaving the township. All close agnatic kin and non-agnatic kin, little friends and classmates would be invited for the seeing-off ceremony. They should bring gift money (*lijin*) varying in amount from 50 to 100 *yuan* each. There was a difference between a person joining the army and the other cases, because the latter are voluntary but the former is an obligation, and the village collective is involved. An informant told me that her son received about 2,400 *yuan* gift money from a "seeing-off" ceremony when he left for the army. He also received 1,000 *yuan* in a red envelope and 400 *yuan* gifts, such as a suitcase and watch from the village collective. This was the first time he had received significant financial support on his own account, with the village, his friends and the collective being among the gift money donors.

These two events from sixteen years old onwards mark the transition of a person from a

---

[54] Some families invited the birthday child's little friends and classmates for the birthday meal if their close relatives were few.

[55] This figure came from wedding gifts and gift money, which excludes little sisters and old sisters, because according to local custom they kept gifts and gift money for themselves.

child to an adult. The 16th birthday party is a review of relationships for a young person. Peng's case is an example. All the relatives including old generation relatives, friends including little friends in the village and close classmates, even the goddess (*ataimo*) and her companion (*nannü xingan*) had to be invited. Meanwhile, the neighbours, fellow villagers of both Peng's family and his *jiujiu*'s families' are included by the giving of rice balls. Moreover, a new kind of relationship is involved in a person's life when he has to serve the army. This new relationship was with the village collective, even the Township Civil Affair Bureau.

In these ways the basic *lishang-wanglai* network of a person is knitted.

II.II. Establishing the marriage relationship

1. Pre-wedding *wanglai* between the fiancée's and the fiancé's families

In 1996 pre-wedding *wanglai* between the fiancée's and the fiancé's families contained two important betrothal rites. The first is the small betrothal rite (*xiaoding*). Here the Chinese character *xiao* means small and *ding* is an abbreviation of *ding hun* (betrothal rite or engagement). The second the large betrothal rite (*dading*) which means a formal engagement. There are different ways of addressing and arranging betrothal rites for a boy-fiancé's family and a girl-fiancée's family.

(1) Small betrothal rite (*xiaoding*)

For a boy's family the small betrothal rite includes *taotiezi* and *dan xiaopan*. The purpose of the event *taotiezi* is to ask a girl's family for a red paper on which eight characters defining the year, month, date and hours of her birth are written. A red paper (*tiezi*) from the girl's family or red envelopes (*hongfengtong*) with bridewealth and gift money from a boy's family are normally placed on a container such as a plate or tray, the so-called *dan xiaopan* (*pan* short for *panzi*, namely, plate or tray). For a girl's family the small betrothal rite includes *chutiezi* and *shou xiaopan,* which means to provide a red paper and to receive the bridewealth.

On 16 April 1996 I attended a small betrothal rite in the Yao family. I saw two women, walking matchmakers (*xingmei*), who carried gifts, arrive at 13:30 pm. They presented a boy's family's gifts and gift money on a table (Photos II-16 and 17).

Photos II-16 and 17. Two matchmakers carried gifts for a small betrothal rite

There were three classes of gifts: *li, wu* and *liwu. Li* is *li* of *liwu* (gift) which relates to gift money/bridewealth for the fiancée's family and its close relatives' families. The gift money was itemised in different red envelopes. They were 3,066 *yuan* for the fiancée's family as bridewealth; 488 *yuan* to be spent on small gifts for more than twenty of the relatives; 40 *yuan* for each of the three matchmakers. Besides two walking matchmakers (*xingmei*) there was a sitting matchmaker (*zuomei*). The sitting matchmaker should be the girl's mother's brother, or his wife or father's sister's wife. According to local custom the sitting matchmaker does not need to appear at the occasion of asking for a red paper or small betrothal rite.

The second kind of gift is *wu,* which is the *wu* of *liwu* (gift) and/or *wuzhi* (materials), or *lidan* (gift list) in Xiajia's case (Yan, 1996b:55). It listed what the fiancé's family pledged for the dowry: wedding rings, watches, bicycles and woollen sweaters for the future bride and groom. Some families would put real gifts (*liwu*), for example a pair of gold rings and watches, or red envelopes with money for rings, watches and bicycles, in a little box (*wushihe*) which means surety for their safety in case the arrangements should go wrong. The *liwu* (gifts) are called additional gifts (*fuli*). They were 120 small soft crunchy rice cakes (*songgao*) with Chinese characters on top representing gold, jade, flowers, grass and so on; two boxes of knitting wool, one red and one yellow, two balls of bright red knitting wool, a big box of sweets (5kg), a bag of crunchy candies (*sutang*), a bag of biscuits, two washing towels with red and green strips, and a red and a green string. The crunchy candies were for the elderly and the biscuits were for the children of the Yao family.

According to the local custom all the gifts need to be checked by one of the Yao family's agnatic kin who was expert in local customs (Photo II-18). After everything had been checked Mr and Mrs Yao gave the red paper with the eight "characters of their daughter" to the two walking matchmakers. The girl's eight characters are "*kuichou eryue chuqi wushi*" which means the girl was born at 09:00 am the 7th day of the second lunar month, 1973.

The Yao family then held a tea party for the matchmakers, accompanied by a few of its agnatic kin. Meanwhile the Yao family asked the two matchmakers to bring their return gifts to the boy's family together with the red paper. The return gifts were prepared by Mrs Yao. She put 20 small soft crunchy rice cakes (*songgao*) brought from the boy's family in the bottom of the basket, and filled it with slightly different-looking rice cakes. This is called *gao jia gao,* which means the

Photo II-18. Yao family's agnatic kin checking the gifts

two families joined together would raise their living standard. She also left one third of the sweets for the returning gifts. She then added 20 *yuan* each to three red envelopes, making a total of 60 *yuan* each, for the matchmakers. She gave each of the two walking matchmakers a red envelope with 60 yuan and saw them off.

Mr and Mrs Yao then held an evening feast with the upper part of a pig's leg for celebration. They invited close relatives: three families of agnatic kin and seven families of non-agnatic kin, including the sitting matchmaker. The non-agnatic kin brought gifts such as sweets and cakes (about 16 *yuan* of each) for the feast. Gifts were not requested from the agnatic kin because they had helped at the feast. After the feast the guests brought their share of gifts back home.

Afterwards Mr and Mrs Yao distributed the rice cakes and sweets to a broader list of the family's agnatic and non-agnatic kin, Mr Yao's friends, and the neighbours, but not yet to fellow villagers. A broader list of agnatic kin included families sharing the same surname and living in the same group with the family (*tongxing*), and non-agnatic kin included families in the older generation (*laoqin*): Mr and Mrs Yao's parents' parents' sisters or brothers and so on. The fiancée distributed cakes and sweets to her own friends, or "little sisters".

Let's go back to the fiancé's family. As a welcome rite the family set off a string of small firecrackers as soon as the matchmakers appeared. After the matchmakers had handed the red paper (with the girl's 8 characters on it) to the fiancé's parents they placed it on the stove by the kitchen god[56]. On top of it they put two rice cakes to keep the red paper safe. It should stay there

---

[56] This is the same in the 1930s (Fei, 1939:41).

for one year before being moved to a suitcase where the family's treasures were stored. During this period nobody is allowed to mention the red paper at all (*xiukou*) in order to avoid anything going wrong with the arrangement. Some families also pray to the kitchen god, asking him to guard the red paper.

They then set up a feast for celebration of the small betrothal rite. The fiancé's family invited the matchmakers and close relatives for a lunchtime feast. Afterwards they also delivered rice cakes and sweets to the wider list of relatives, neighbours, and both the fiancé's father and her own friends. The details were more or less the same as for the Yao family.

(2) Large betrothal rite (*dading*)

The large betrothal rite (*dading*) is a formal betrothal rite or engagement. So this occasion normally should happen on a lucky date, for example during a lunar New Year period, May Day holiday, or the National Day. Again, there are different events for both fiancé and fiancée's families.

For the fiancé's family the large betrothal rite is also called *taorizi* and *dan dapan*. In order to fit the marriage relationship (*dingqin*) into the event a date for the wedding (*dingrizi*) should be booked, the "deposit" (*dingjin*), the large amount of bridewealth, should be delivered to the fiancée's family, the so-called *duan dapan*. For the fiancée's family the large betrothal rite is also called *churizi* and *shou dapan* which means to give the date of the wedding and receive the bridewealth.

There were no large betrothal rites while I was there, but I collected data about the event from several families. The Xu family had held a large betrothal rite on the 2 May 1995. For the Xu family this event was called *shou panzi* (accept a plate or tray with formal bridewealth). After the two matchmakers arrived Mr and Mrs Xu's brother checked details of the bridewealth.

Again, the bridewealth divides into three parts: *li, wu*, and *liwu*. *Li* included many itemised red envelopes: 6,660 *yuan* for the fiancée's family, 1,880 *yuan* was for more than twenty of the relatives, for example, *jiujiu* (mother's brothers), *guma* (father's sisters), *yima* (mother's sisters), *guoniang* (quasi-mothers), *jiuli* (brothers), *bogong* (father's older brothers), *shugong* (father's younger brothers), *waitai* (mother's mother), *zengtai* (father's father) and so on, wrapped separately. Each of them contained gift money varying from 80 to 120 *yuan*, and 60 *yuan* each for the three matchmakers. These items should be provided by the fiancée's family. *Wu* consisted of gifts and a gift list. The gifts were especially for the engagement: a pair of golden rings and watches, or an equivalent amount of money in red envelopes in the safe box (*wushihe*) if a fiancé's family had not already sent it to the fiancée's family on the small betrothal rite. The gift list listed what the fiancé's family proposed for the future bride's dowry: jewels including a golden necklace, a golden bracelet, golden earrings; electrical home appliances including a sewing machine, a colour TV, a video player, a refrigerator, a washing machine, a standard fan, a bicycle; bedding and clothes. *Liwu* (gifts), the additional gifts, consisted of a basket of rice cakes, two cartons of cigarettes, and two boxes of sweets (5kg of each), four *jin* (500gm) of silk, four *jin* of knitting wool, and a woollen sweater.

After they accepted the gifts, the matchmakers, the Xu family and its relatives had a lunchtime feast to celebrate the engagement. To this feast a broader list of the Xu family's agnatic and non-agnatic kin were invited. These people would all be invited again for the seeing-off ceremony. The non-agnatic kin brought gifts worth about 30 *yuan* to attend the ceremony, whereas agnatic kin brought only 10 *yuan* of gifts because they helped at the ceremony. After the feast the guests brought back their return share of the gift money and return gifts of rice cakes and sweets.

At the same time Mr Xu added 30 *yuan* to each red bag, making a total of 90 *yuan* each, for the matchmakers, in respect of their "taking away the wedding date" and returning gifts to the fiancé's family. In this case the Xu family only returned half of the sweets because the proportion of the returning gift was based on the amount received from a fiancé's family. Again, Mrs Xu sorted out the returning rice cakes with the principle of *gao jia gao,* meaning that to join two families together would raise their living standard.

The fiancé's family invited two matchmakers for a small tea party in the morning and then sent them off to the fiancée's family. When the matchmakers arrived back from the fiancée's family, the fiancé's family set off a string of small firecrackers to welcome them, followed by a ceremonial feast. Instead of the lunchtime feast for the small betrothal rite this was a supper feast, because the matchmakers had had a lunchtime feast with the fiancée's family. This high standard feast involved an upper part of pig leg, as well as 18 different dishes for each table. The family invited a wider list of their agnatic kin and non-agnatic kin for the feast. As in the small betrothal rite, the agnatic kin brought a small portion of gifts for the feast and took their share of the preparatory work, as kitchen assistants, setting up tables, entertaining guests and so on. The non-agnatic kin came with gifts, such as apples, pears, and peaches, and a sum of 30 *yuan* each. After the feast all the guests brought their share of returning gifts back home.

After the large betrothal rite both the fiancée and fiancé's families distributed the rice cakes and sweets to the fiancée or fiancé's fathers' friends, and fiancée or fiancé's friends. The fiancée herself or fiancé himself distributed a bag of crunchy candy (*gaotang*) to each of her "little sisters" or his "little friends" and invited them to the wedding. If their friends worked outside the township they sent them invitations. They should also remind them of the invitations closer to the date of the seeing-off or wedding ceremonies. The cakes and sweets were also distributed to neighbours and fellow villagers who would be involved in post-wedding tea parties.

The significance of the engagement ceremonies for the relationship between the fiancé and fiancée is as follows: (i) To involve all the possible relations of their families as a moral restraint. If either the fiancé or fiancée broke off the engagement (*tuiqin*) they and their families would lose great face (*diuren*) in front of their relations. Here the villagers used the character *ren* (human being) rather than *lian* or *mianzi* (face) because the matter is so serious as to upset the whole family. (ii) To lessen potential embarrassment as regards the bridewealth. According to local custom, if the fiancée breaks off the engagement her family and relatives should return all of the red envelopes with the bridewealth, plus 10 per cent extra. If the fiancé breaks off the engagement his family would lose all the deposit they have paid on the two occasions, the gifts and money in small and large betrothals. On top of this his family should bring apology gifts to the fiancée's family. (iii) If all goes well the relatives involved in the two ceremonies establish a marriage relationship between the bride's and the groom's families, as Freedman (1970) noticed, rather than only for the "new family" (Fei, 1939) or the "conjugal couple" (Yan, 1997).

The remaining sections will show details of how this wider relationship is established.

2. Pre-wedding *wanglai* between the fiancée's family and its relations

After the large betrothal rite the wedding date is fixed. All the people related to the fiancée and her family should make arrangements for "seeing-off" the fiancée. Different kinds of relations express themselves in different ways, such as giving her gifts (dowry gifts), gift money, or by inviting her to seeing-off tea parties and feasts.

(1) Dowry gifts and gift money

I found that dowry gifts are part of the bride's dowry which comes from her family's agnatic kin, non-agnatic kin and her own friends. I checked with some villagers. It appeared to be no problem that relatives and little friends always gave marriage gifts. Tan's mother, a 76-year-old woman, told me that when she was young her "little sisters" gave each other gifts when they got married, though in those days the overall amount was smaller. Women in the village always have their own private savings (*sifangqian*) as Fei had noticed:

> Theoretically, according to the ideal system, other members, whenever they get money from other sources, must hand it to the head; and when they need things must ask the head to buy them. It is a very centralised economy. But in practice the earner usually reserves the whole or a part of his or her earnings. For instance, a girl who works in the factory usually gives her wage, not to her grandfather, but to her mother to save for her own future use (1939: 62)

According to the local custom, Xu told me, nowadays gifts of this kind normally account for nearly half of the dowry. For example, the reference rate in 1996 is that if a fiancé's family gives 10,000 *yuan* of bridewealth to the fiancée's family, on the wedding day the groom's "welcome bride" team should take 20,000 *yuan* of dowry back with her to the groom's family. In other words, of the 20,000 *yuan* dowry, about 10,000 *yuan* of dowry gifts should have come from the bride's family's agnatic kin, non-agnatic kin, and her own friends. MrsYao told me that her family received dowry gifts of about 10,800 *yuan* which came from 5 families of agnatic kin, 16 families of non-agnatic kin, and her daughter's 32 friends. I worked out that on average each family or person spent an amount of 212 *yuan* on the gifts.

However, this was not what the villagers would have calculated. Tan told me that by local custom there were three points to take into account: (i) The total of 10,800 *yuan* included 2,000 *yuan* of itemised small red envelopes given by the fiancé's family at the large betrothal rite. People who had received these gifts were supposed to add 50 per cent to their value and give this increased sum as a new gift to the bride one month before the wedding, meaning that if they received 100 *yuan* at the large betrothal rite they should spend 150 *yuan* on dowry gifts. Therefore 3,000 *yuan* of the total sum should be counted as a kind of return of gifts to the groom's family. (ii) On top of the increased sum they gave back, receivers should also give their personal share of gifts to the bride, which varies from 50 up to 500 *yuan*. The value depends on the closeness between the givers and the fiancée's family. However, there is a further division between agnatic and non-agnatic kin. The fiancée's family's agnatic kin are normally required to send gifts of between only 50 and 80 *yuan*, in acknowledgement of the fact that they are also responsible for holding a seeing-off feast for the fiancée (see the next subsection "(2) Seeing-off tea parties and seeing-off feasts"). In this case the dowry gifts from 5 families of agnatic kin were about 350 *yuan*. In contrast, the 16 families of non-agnatic kin sent 4,450 *yuan* of dowry gifts. Non-agnatic kin provided a larger amount partly because they were three times more numerous and partly since they were not required to hold a seeing-off feast. (iii) The fiancée's 30 friends gave her about 3,000 *yuan* gifts, on average 100 *yuan* each. As well as the dowry gifts, the fiancée's friends should also give money wrapped in red paper (*hongbao*) at her seeing-off ceremony. For example, Yao had 32 "little sisters" who were the bride's childhood friends, school classmates, and work colleagues of a village enterprise. About half of them had already married and lived in different villages. The bride's list shows she received 4,600 *yuan* from them. As her friends, as well as giving gifts and gift money, they were also companions of the bride to the groom's family on the wedding day.

The significance of the gifts is as follows. (i) It is a way for the bride to remember these earlier relationships. The gifts were called "objects to be accompanied alive" with the fiancée (*peijia*), the term *peijia* being used in much the same way as *peizang* (objects to be buried alive with the dead). As Martin (1998) noticed, many researchers (Baker, 1979; Liu, 1986; Watson, 1981) have shown that in south China, from a woman's point of view, marriage was associated with death, dirt, darkness, confusion, cold, poverty, meanness and sterility, rather than life, purity, light, order, heat, prosperity, plentitude and fertility (169–171). I have no intention to make a farfetched comparison. Mr Zhou did tell me that marriage for his daughter meant losing an old life and gaining a new one. By local custom, after a fiancée married out from her natal family she had no more dealings with most of her relations except a few very close family members, such as her *jiujiu* and her parents' sisters. She made a list of which gift was given by each family or friend and whenever she used the gifts they would remind her of the givers. This is how she remembered her former relationships.

(ii) The gifts function as a kind of financial support. As I have shown in II.I, during the growing-up period a person is involved in his or her family's *lishang-wanglai* networks from the time he or she was born. The child's families knitted the *lishang-wanglai* networks for him or her when they were very young, and they carried on knitting the networks themselves as they got older. This process of knitting networks is just like fattening pigs. A girl is expected to receive a big pig from her natal family's relations and her own friends when she marries out from her natal family. The process of fattening the first pig is now complete. After she gets married she will be involved in fattening another pig with her husband and his family. For a boy, if he left the village for the army he would receive a small pig as I show in Chapter V.I. When he takes a wife into his family he also receives a pig via his wife. After he gets married he will fatten another pig with his wife.

(2) Seeing-off tea parties and seeing-off feasts

Just as actors and actresses come out in reverse order of importance when responding to curtain calls at the end of a show, the same applies when seeing-off a fiancée in the village where she has grown up. I did not attend any of these events because my informants told me that they did not bother to invite me to them because they happened too often and were too small to be noticed.

According to my fieldwork notes, the seeing-off tea parties were held by neighbours and fellow villagers' families in a fiancée family's group. Mr Rao told me that there were 30 households in his group. Reckoned geographically, 7 families were his family's neighbours including 3 families of agnatic kin, and 22 families can be called fellow villagers (*tong xiaoze de renjia*) including 2 of agnatic kin. The 5 close families of agnatic kin were not necessarily close in location. Among the 29 households 10 families' surnames were the same as his own family's. So there is another category of "*tongxing de renjia*", which means sharing the same surname and living in the same group. Among the 10 families there were 5 of agnatic kin, 2 neighbours, and the rest of them were sometimes categorized as agnatic kin, sometimes as fellow villagers. For example, in the ceremonies of weddings, funerals, or house construction they were invited as agnatic kin; in other events, from births to betrothals, they were counted as fellow villagers. On the occasion of seeing-off or a wedding ceremony, the same-surname families were required to give gift money – the first required of them in connection with the wedding- but also were to provide a tea party before or after the wedding, as were other neighbours and fellow villagers.

Mrs Zhou told me that two months before the wedding day she and her mother were invited to tea parties in turn by her family's neighbours, those with the same surnames, and fellow villagers. They did not need to bring any gifts because they had already given rice cakes and sweets after her betrothal rites. Each family provided different snacks for the tea party, such as sunflower seeds, pumpkin seeds, sweets and candied fruits. It is the custom for some families to have double teas of sweets and savouries if the time is close to a lunar New Year. If the time is close to the fourth lunar month then some families would make the savoury tea with newly produced tea.

The seeing-off feasts held by a fiancée's family's close agnatic kin are called *chaiguroujiu* (similar to *liniangrou* in a Northwest Chinese village, Stafford, 2000a) in which *chai* is for separate, *gurou* for flesh and bone, and *jiu* means feast. Some people said it was called *cuiguroujiu* in which *cui* means to hurry (literally to accelerate the ripening of the marriage). This event, from the agnatic families' point of view, is a formal way of ending their relationship with the fiancée. So this kind of feast must have an upper part of pig leg. The feasts normally started two months before the wedding. All the agnatic families should take turns to invite the fiancée and her mother to the seeing-off feast. The feast itself costs about 150 to 200 *yuan*. Each family would also give the fiancée 20 *yuan* wrapped in a small piece of red paper (*hongbao*, red bag).

There is also a kind of seeing-off feast held by non-agnatic kin. Mrs Rao said her natal family had 16 families of non-agnatic kin. Among them 6 families were distant non-agnatic kin who only attended her seeing-off ceremony with gift money, and 10 families on the list for the lunar New Year's feast attended her betrothal rites, gave her dowry gifts, and gift money on the seeing-off ceremony. Within the 10 families 4 of them were closest of all. They were her mother's brother and sister, her father's sister, and her quasi mother's families. These four very close non-agnatic kin also held feasts for her before she got married not in respect of ending the relationship, as with the agnatic kin, but because they would be keeping up their relationship with her (*daizou de qinqi*) after she married out. For example, they were part of the team of the before and after birth events and would also be part of the distant non-agnatic kin of Mrs Rao's son's future wedding feast. Among the four close non-agnatic kin Mrs Rao's *jiujiu* (mother's brother) was the closest. We will see the differences in the next section.

(3) Seeing-off ceremony (*chujia*)

In the village the seeing-off ceremony is called *chujia*. Here the Chinese character *chu* of *chujia*, *chutiezi*, *churizi*, or *chufenzi* is the same word which means to give, that is to give a red paper with a girl's eight characters, give the date of the wedding, give a share of gift money and give the daughter to her new family. This ceremony is mixed with part of the wedding ceremony because it includes a party sent by the groom's family to meet the bride at the bride's home. It is called *yingqin* before the bride is escorted to the groom's home for the wedding. In 1996 I attended two such ceremonies on 23 February in the Yao family and on 1 May in the Zhou family. My descriptions in this section are mainly based on these ceremonies.

On the day before the seeing-off ceremony the bride's mother worshipped ancestors (*qingshangzu*), which is different from *baishangzu* during festivals. Here *shangzu* are ancestors, *qing* means invite or welcome, because this was the way in which the family invited its ancestors to join the family ceremony. The background of the central living room was decorated as a ceremony hall (*zhongtang*). In the middle of the wall there was a big painting of the god of longevity (*shouxing*) with a boy and a girl, and a pair of antithetical couplets on each side of the picture (this is a well-known Chinese literary form). A big red paper-cut of double happiness (*shuangxi*) was on each side of the back wall. Under the picture stood a big sideboard against the back wall. On top of the sideboard there were two big, red wooden bathtubs full of special long rice cakes (*dagao*), each wrapped with red paper. In between them there were a set of big candlesticks.

Mrs Yao, the bride's mother, set up the altar table in front of the sideboard with 12 big dishes with different foods in the middle of the table and lots of handleless wine cups with Shaoxing wine, rice bowls and chopsticks around them. She moved the set of big candlesticks to the front of the table and lit candles. She knelt on a big mat and bowed to the ancestors with both hands in front of her chest. Then she burned some papers. For the mother this was the way in which the family reported to its ancestors that a member of the family was going to leave. For the bride, this was a seeing-off ritual in honour of her ancestors and at the same time she believed that she would get blessings from them.

After a ritual/feast with the ancestors, on the seeing-off ceremony of the wedding day, there were three feasts with the family's relations. The breakfast feast is the main feast (*zhengjiu*), which must involve the upper part of pig's leg. In the Yao family the bride's family invited a full list of the family relations and the bride's "little sisters"/friends for the feast. They came with small red bags (*hongbao*) of gift money. There were 164 guests: 16 agnatic kin, 76 non-agnatic kin, 40 friends of the bride's father and 32 of the bride's friends. This was a way for the bride's parents to express their feelings by holding as grand as possible a feast and organizing as many as possible of their relations to share the special moment. It was also a special occasion for those attending to express themselves to the bride by bringing small red bags.

After the breakfast the bride's parents and helpers set up tables and chairs for the next part of the ceremony. They put two joined dining tables from north to south in front of the sideboard. On the table there were eight big plates covered with different snacks such as sweets, pistachios, peanuts, sunflower seeds, watermelon seeds and candied fruits. Ten tea bowls were along the edge of the table. Two main chairs faced south and four chairs were on each side of the big table.

Around 10:30 the groom's team arrived in two decorated boats. People set off big firecrackers from both the bride's family and the groom's boats. The groom's oldest agnatic kin (*laozhangbei*), guided by the male matchmakers and the groom's friends, carried silver plates with itemised gift money wrapped in red envelopes (*hongfengtong*) to the bride's home. These plates are called *zhuangyuan pan*. *Zhuangyuan* meaning "Number One Scholar", the title conferred on the one who came first in the highest imperial examination. The *Zhuangyuan pan* are the highest-rated plates that the groom's family carried to the bride's family, not in size or value but for their symbolism.

The bride's mother lit two candles and opened the scene by checking the bridewealth on the *zhuangyuanpan*. She then served the guests green tea with smoked soya beans. The bride's father, *jiujiu*, two male matchmakers and some close male relatives sat around the big table. They started to check the *li* (gift money) by counting each red envelope (Photo II-19).

Photo II-19. *Jiujius*, matchmakers and agnatic kin are counting gift money

The *li* consisted of: 5,880 *yuan* for the bride's family; 550 *yuan* for a chef who cooked for the seeing-off ceremony for the bride; 350 *yuan* for a tailor; 150 *yuan* for a lacquerer; 300 *yuan* for the matchmakers (100 *yuan* each)[57]; 100 *yuan* each for the chief witnesses at the wedding ceremony, who were the bride's mother's brother (*jiujiu*) and the bride's father's sister's husband (*gufu*); 60 *yuan* for her *jiujiu* to put the flower on the bride's hair (it is a custom similar to "*jiujiu* cut baby's hair" on its first month birthday); 20 *yuan* for a person who brought news of the arrival of the groom's team (*baomen*); and a small red envelope of 10 *yuan* for each of the groom's friends who helped load and unload the dowry. The *wu* (gifts) were the silver plate itself, two big flower candles, small fire crackers, two cartons of cigarettes and two boxes of sweets (5kg each) for the fiancée's family. The total gift money and gifts amounted to 8,000 *yuan*.

At the same time the groom's friends distributed sweets and cigarettes to the rest of the guests. The bride's relatives set up six imaginary fences one after the other to stop the groom's team from getting into the house (*baishan*). The team would get through them by giving the relatives sweets and cigarettes.

After a discussion between the bride's father, *jiujiu*s and other close male relatives they agreed the value of the gift money and gifts and then decided the amount required for returning gifts. The climax of the ceremony now approached.

---

[57] Two of them were empty bags because the "groom"'s father would pay a thanks visit to the matchmakers on the second day after the wedding.

However, the second seeing-off ceremony, for the Zhou family, did not go so smoothly. The bride's *jiujiu* did not arrive in time, so the counting of the bridewealth had to be postponed. Meanwhile the bride's grandmother (father's mother) started swearing loudly because the sweet boxes had been emptied and there were still many guests waiting for their share. The groom's friends immediately went away to buy some more sweets.

When the bride's *jiujiu* finally arrived everything took more or less the same course as in the Yao family. Let us stick with the Zhou family from now onwards. After the bride's father, *jiujiu* and others had approved the bridewealth the groom's friends were allowed to load the dowry onto the boats. While this was happening big and small firecrackers were set off again. At the same time there was a deafening sound of gongs, drums and trumpets while the dowry was being loaded.

Before and during the loading I made a full list of the dowry. This was much more complicated than in the 1930s when it only consisted of furniture, ornaments, clothes and sometimes a sum of money (Fei, 1939:68). In this case, the dowry included a colour TV, a video player, a standard fan, an electric heater, a pair of chairs, a pair of sofas, a tea table, a pair of flower vases, a desk, a bookcase, a pair of wooden chest boxes, a pair of leather suitcases, 18 duvets with covers, 8 sheets, 8 pillows, a pair of towelling coverlets, an iron, an ironing board, two dozen clothes hangers, a pair of bronze foot warmers, a big doll, a big soft toy dog, a set of 5 wooden boxes, 2 pairs of wooden tubs full of peanuts, broad beans, sweets, a pair of basin bowls, a pair of spittoons, a chamber pot, a hair drier, half a dozen bottles of shampoo, half a dozen bottles of hair mousse, a refrigerator, washing machine, a pair of gas cookers, four dining chairs, a pair of wooden buckets (*tangtong*) full of peanuts and broad beans, an electric kettle, a bucket of dried fruit, a pair of woollen blankets, a pair of plastic containers, a pair of measuring cups (*shuiyao*), a pair of baskets (*shazhao*), 8 thermos bottles, a big saucepan, 20 bowls, 8 cups, an electric rice cooker, a set of teaspoons, a 5-piece stainless steel cookware set, a 5-piece non-stick cookware set and a bicycle (Photos II−20 and 21).

Apart from the above dowry the bride's *jiujiu* also brought two big, red wooden bathtubs full of special long rice cakes (*dagao*), each wrapped with red paper, which were displayed on top of the sideboard, two big red boxes full of rice, 100 small square-shaped rice cakes, ten big fire crackers, two big flower candles[58] and one double mosquito net. As I mentioned at the end of the

---

[58] The candles with dragon, phoenix patterns and flowers were usually used in the bridal chamber on the wedding night.

last section, as the closest non-agnatic kin, during the establishing of a marriage relationship the bride's *jiujiu*'s family give her gifts and gift money five times. The last time they gave these gifts to the bride was on the day before the wedding day and the gifts would also be taken away with the bride together with the rest of the dowry.

Photos II-20 and 21. Dowry in the hall and on the leaving boat

While the dowry was being loaded, some of the groom's friends were busy getting ready for the next big event. They laid straw mats on the ground in front of the big table and in the middle of the hall. Then they put a chair by the north end of the mat facing south and put a duvet (*zhuangyanbei*) on top of it. In front of the chair they placed a bronze foot warmer with warm stove-ashes.

The bride's mother placed two new candles in holders and lit them. Then the bride, accompanied by her "little sisters", walked down the stairs. Her father carried her from the end of the stairs onto the chair (Photos II-22 and 23).

Then the bride's mother put a small piece of glutinous rice cake (*songgao*) into her mouth. This cake together with a large plate of such cakes was brought by the bride's *jiujiu* and would be taken away with the dowry to the groom's family. Her *jiujiu* then put a flower on her hair. If the groom had formed part of the team, he would put the wedding ring on her finger and the bride's mother would put a wedding ring on his. He would be given a red bag with gift money from each of the bride's parents. However, on this occasion the groom followed a traditional practice, giving her the wedding ring in advance and so did not come to the bride's home. Then firecrackers, drums, gong and trumpet went off again. The bride walked to the boat accompanied by her 32 "little sisters". The bride's mother was weeping after she left.

After the bride and groom's teams left, the bride's family held lunchtime and supper feasts without the upper part of a pig's leg. Most guests stayed for the lunchtime feast. About half of the guests who lived in the village stayed for the supper. They believed it was important to stay as long as possible to keep the bride's parents company, because they had just lost their beloved daughter.

Between the feasts the bride's *jiujiu* and *gufu* (father's sister's husband) started counting the gift money and writing down a list (*yinqingbu*) for the bride's family. Here the character of *yin* is silver meaning money, *qing* is human feelings, and *bu* is a booklet. It is more precise than "*renqingbu*" which I heard in Shandong and Gansu provinces, and "*lidan*" in Yan's Xiajia village (1996b). The total sum of the *yinqingbu* was 3,145 *yuan* from all the relatives of the family and the bride's father's friends. The difference between this list and the groom's family's list is that the "little sisters'" gift money would not be included in this list because the bride would make her own list of it for herself. The bride's list shows she received 3,150 *yuan* from her friends.

After the seeing-off feasts all the guests took back home their share of returning gifts, like "party bags" in England. Unlike the betrothal ceremony, after the seeing-off ceremony the bride's parents did not distribute any cakes or sweets to their neighbours and fellow villagers. Mrs Zhou explained to me that there is no need to do so because she had lost her daughter., and according to local custom such a distribution is to share gain rather than loss.

Photos II-22 and 23. The bride's father carried the bride all the way to the special chair

(4) Wedding ceremony (*quqin*)

The wedding ceremony is called *quqin* in the village. Here the Chinese character *qu* is pronounced the same as *qu*, which means to collect something. The *qu* of *quqing* was designed specially for collecting a woman and is formed by the *qu* of collecting a thing plus a Chinese character *nü* for woman. *Qin* means blood or marriage relations and in this case *quqin* means to take a woman as a wife and get married. *Qu* is different from *tao* of *taotiezi* and *taorizi* which means to ask or beg for something. The former is for collecting somebody after special permission and the latter is for asking permission for somebody.

I attended two wedding ceremonies on 21 and 23 February 1996, one in the Tan family and one in the Qiu family. The Tan family took a man into their family as a son-in-law (*zhaonüxu*)

and the Qiu family took a girl who came from outside of the province, and worked in a village enterprise (*dagongmei*), into the family as a wife. Neither of these events represents a typical wedding. However, the style of the former more or less follows a standard form of wedding according to local custom, whereas the Qiu wedding represents an adaptation of the wedding ceremony. To help the reader understand the normal style of a wedding ceremony I have chosen the Tan family's case and use "groom" for the woman and "bride" for the man.

Although worshipping the ancestors is a part of the local wedding ceremony just as much as is the ritual of "seeing-off", in this instance the Tan family did not perform this worship because the "groom"'s mother was born in Wujiang County and had little knowledge of local customs. She was introduced into the village by one of her family's relatives because her natal family was poor, with four sons and four daughters including her. The "groom"'s father did not see the point of the ceremony because he had problems in the relationship with his own two brothers after his father passed away in 1991. With the Qiu wedding, Qiu's mother's description of worshipping ancestors was similar to the Yao family's practice in the seeing-off ceremony. However, the event was staged at dinnertime on the day before the wedding day, in the middle of the decorated central hall, and although the ritual is more or less the same as that of the seeing-off ceremony, the meaning was different. This time, worshipping the ancestors was a way of reporting to them that a woman was being brought into the family to continue the family line (*xianghuo*, literally, incense and fire).

Let's return to the Tan family now for the wedding ceremony. The Tan family's central hall was also decorated with a big picture in the middle of the wall in which the main figure was the god of longevity (*shouxing*) with a boy and a girl. Different families choose different prints in different styles, with different pairs of antithetical couplets on each side of the picture. The Tan family's antithetical couplet read "*qianzai fugui fuguang man fuzhai, baifeng hehe fuwang ju shoutang*" (the light of happiness shines on the happy family for a thousand years, the hope of happiness gathers to the family central hall with hundreds of peaceful people and plenty of everything). The heart-shaped bright red double happiness paper cuts were on each side of the back wall. A big sideboard was against the back wall under the picture. A set of big candlesticks were in the middle of the sideboard. On both sides was a large red wooden bathtub full of special long rice cakes (*dagao*) each wrapped with red paper.

There were three feasts on the wedding day. The breakfast feast was designed for the matchmakers and the "groom"'s 22 "little friends". The "groom"'s father sent two people to the matchmakers' homes and accompanied them back to the "groom"'s home. They sat in the big living room next to the central hall in the seats facing the east (*zuoxi chaodong*), which were the best. After the feast the "groom"'s friends went upstairs accompanied by the "groom". The "groom" distributed sweets and snacks to them. They also helped her put the wedding dress on. At 10:00 the welcome "bride"'s team (*yingqindui*) got ready. They were the "groom"'s father, two male matchmakers, 8 male helpers, a band of 8 children, the "groom" and his 22 friends. The 8 male helpers would not normally be required, but they were needed in this case because the "groom" was female and her female friends would not be able to do jobs such as unloading and loading the dowry. The "groom"'s father carried a big tray (*zhuangyuanpan*) containing a great many red envelopes and various gifts. The male helpers carried a chair, a rolled up straw mat, a folded up duvet (*zhuangyuanbei*), two big bamboo trees with roots and leaves decorated with lots of small red bows[59], and a bronze foot warmer with warm stove-ashes, boxes of sweets and so on. The band was formed by 8 children, boys and girls between 11 and 12 years old, who were pupils in Kaixiangong Primary School. They played a trumpet, a gong, a pair of small cymbals and drums for the Young Pioneers at the school. They were paid 20 *yuan* each for the wedding ceremony.

Unlike at the seeing-off ceremony the welcome-bride team came with the boats because both the groom and bride's families lived in the same village, but in different groups.

The Tan family's "bride" lived in a different village so they hired two cars and two coaches as transportation for people who took part in the ceremony (Photo II-24). They also hired a boat for carrying the dowry.

As soon as the vehicles and the boat arrived at the "bride"'s house the big firecrackers were set off from both sides. The children played the music and drums and so on. The "groom"'s father and matchmakers went into the "bride"'s house and presented the gift money and gifts to the "bride"'s parents. They sat around a large table drinking tea and eating snacks (Photo II-25), while the "bride"'s father, *jiujiu*, and father's sister's husband counted the gifts money. Meanwhile, the "groom" and her friends sat in another living room around a large table eating, drinking, and chatting, as did the "bride" and his friends in yet a different living room upstairs.

The remaining steps of the ceremony were more or less the same as I have shown for the Zhou family at their seeing-off ceremony. The "bride's" family distributed sweets and cigarettes to the guests, loaded the dowry, and put in place a straw mat, a chair, a duvet, and a bronze foot

---

[59] See religious sense of *lishang* in Chapter V.II.

warmer with warm stove-ashes. After the dowry was loaded the boat left ahead of the "bride" and "groom". At the same time a string of small firecrackers was set off and the band played music.

Photo II-24. The "groom"'s welcome "bride" cars and coach

Photo II-25. The "groom" was accompanied by her "little friends"

When everything was ready the "groom" held a bunch of flowers accompanied by her friends and went upstairs. She gave the flowers to the "bride" and then they held arms and walked downstairs. The "bride"'s brother carried him all the way to the chair. (The reason his father did not do it was because in this case the "bride" was too heavy for him.) The "groom" stood beside him (Photo II-26). The "bride"'s mother put a ring on the "groom"'s finger and gave her a little red bag of 200 *yuan*. Then the "bride"'s female, close non-agnatic kin also gave "the groom" red bags in turn. The red bags contained money varying from 100 to 180 *yuan*.

Photo II-26. The "groom" stood beside the "bride"

In this case the close non-agnatic families gave money to the "groom" in response to the "bride"'s goodbye, because he chose to not take them away with him after he married out from his natal family. This was not a special custom for this kind of marriage (*zhaonüxu*) but quite normal. Custom allowed villagers to choose whether or not to keep their natal family's close non-agnatic kin after she or he married out from her or his natal family. Mrs Rao in chose to take them with her, and Mrs Zhou and the "bride" here chose not to do so (see Chapter II.I). In this case, the red bags represented the close non-agnatic kin's response to the end of the relationship between them.

The band played again, and the firecrackers went off when the "groom"'s team set off. The "groom" and "bride" walked in front of the team followed by the "groom"'s father, matchmakers, the band and friends from both sides. Apart from carrying the straw mat, a chair, a duvet, and a bronze foot-warmer they also carried one of the bamboo trees with them back home.

By the time they got home the dowry had been completely unloaded (Photo II-27) and each item placed perfectly in its designated position. Even electrical home appliances were unpacked and connected. All the wrappings had been cleared away. The bridal chamber looked like a one bedroom flat within the house[60]. It contained a bedroom with en suite bathroom and a separate sitting room, but no kitchen. The "groom"'s family supplied a double bed with basic bedding, bedside chests stood by two decorated sugarcanes with roots, and built-in cupboards occupied one side of a wall. The rest of the things came from the dowry from the "bride"'s family. The helpers were watching the new TV in the sitting room and eating snacks from the new containers which they had just brought back from the "bride"'s family.

The central hall had also changed a bit. There were two big plates of food with decorations placed on the sideboard. One contained white and green rice cakes with fillings and another contained fresh-made noodles. In front of the big table there were two big "flower candles" (*huanzhu*) which were specially designed for a wedding. All these were given by the "bride"'s *jiujiu* and brought back by the helpers, together with the dowry.

Photo II-27. Unloading dowry from boats

Outside in the courtyard two old men were getting ready to welcome the "bride"'s team. One was preparing a string of firecrackers, and another was arranging three bunches of straw for them like a tripod, which they set off as soon as the team appeared. The "bride" and "groom" and the team walked through them. When they reached the central hall, the "bride" and "groom" sat on the main chairs facing south. The representatives of the "groom" and the "bride"'s friends sat around the table. The "groom"'s mother lit the special flower candles. They drank tea, ate snacks, and teased the new couple. For example, they asked the "groom" to light a cigarette for the "bride" and they blew it out again and again; they asked them to drink tea without spillage with their arms tangled together; they asked them to bite one sweet without letting their lips touch and so on.

---

[60] This design related to a typical stem household composition in the village (see Chapter VI.I)

After they had had enough fun the "groom"'s parents moved the flower candles to the upstairs corridor by the bridal chamber. The "groom" changed her wedding dress for a bright red woollen suit and then the main wedding feast started. There were about 184 people at 23 tables. During the feast the new couple proposed a toast to each table. After the feast people started to play cards, chat and watch TV.

At the same time the "groom"'s father and his brothers, the "groom"'s *jiujiu,* were counting the gift money and writing the list (*yinqingbu*), in order from top to bottom according to the amount of money. For example, the amounts from the 4 *jiujiu*s varied from 420 to 400 *yuan*. After they wrote them down they did a calculation with the gifts sorted into 4 groups: 12 families of non-agnatic kin gave 2,300 *yuan*, 5 families of agnatic kin 400 *yuan*, 4 father's friends 290 *yuan*, and 22 "groom"'s friends 2,210 *yuan*. The total sum was 5,180 *yuan*.

The "groom"'s mother prepared the "party bags", which contained a bar of special long rice cake (*dagao*), a pack of cigarettes, sweets and so on. She also distributed two pieces of small square shaped rice cakes and sweets to the family's neighbours and fellow villagers.

The day after the wedding day the "groom"'s father paid thank you visits to the two sitting matchmakers' families with a red envelope of 100 *yuan* and an upper part of pig leg for each. As I mentioned in a note of Chapter V.II, the two red envelopes of 100 *yuan* for the two walking matchmakers were empty because, according to the local custom, a groom's father should pay a thank you visit to each of them (*xiemei*). This is how they ended the relationship that had lasted a few years between a groom's family and the matchmakers'. In some cases, one of each of the matchmakers was invited by a groom and bride's families, and then both their fathers should pay thank you visits to the matchmakers separately, immediately after the wedding.

3. Post-wedding *wanglai* between the bride's natal family and the groom's family

After the wedding the show of establishing a marriage relationship is far from ended. Qiu's new wife told me her story. Although her mother and younger sister were working in Shenze Township within a one-hour bus journey to the village, rather than a ten-hour train journey from her home town, custom forbade the bride's natal family's members appearing at the wedding ceremony. However, her older sister's family was invited to the wedding because she had married a villager two years previously. This was a compromise, because according to local custom fellow villagers were not on the invitation list for the wedding. This section and the next section will show how relationships between a groom's family and a bride's family are established, and how the groom and the bride establish a relationship between their new family and the surrounding villagers.

(1) Briefly visit a bride's natal family (*huimen*)

The first scene of the act is called *huimen* (briefly visit a bride's natal family), which is the opposite of the *guomen* (the bride goes out of her natal family's door on the wedding day), rather than *huijia*. Here the characters of *hui* is for returning, *guo* for over or passing, *men* for gate or door, and *jia* for family or home. *Guomen* is a special term designed for a woman who has got married. In theory, it means that after she passed through her husband's family's gate or door she would no longer be a member of her natal family. When she came back to her natal family for a visit she passed through their gate or door, but this did *not* mean she was a member of the family again. In other words, the married-out daughter became a close relative of her natal family, and vice versa. In practice, before the bride got married when she returned to her natal family she said "*huijia*" (go home) and after she got married she would say "*hui niangjia*" (go to mother's home). This is the same everywhere for a nuclear family when either wife or husband visits their parents' families. However, the difference is that the wives in Kaixiangong village normally lived in their husbands' families, therefore they lost their right of inheritance from their natal families by the local custom, although not by law. The way in which they gain their natal family's property back is by following local customs throughout life-cycle events. At the same time they enjoyed themselves in attending and arranging those events.

I did not attend a *huimen* myself. However, Mr Rao told me that on the second or third day after the wedding the bride and groom should visit the bride's natal family (*huimen*). She and her husband brought two bottles of liquor, cigarettes, fruits, and a basket of small circle shaped rice cakes as gifts to her parents. The gifts cost about 200 *yuan*. Her parents held a feast of two tables, with an upper part of pig's leg on each, to entertain them. The bride's family members and male agnatic kin were invited for the feast. The feast cost 600 *yuan,* including drink and cigarettes. At the feast the new couple received 180 *yuan* gift money in little red bags: 80 *yuan* from the bride's parents and 10 *yuan* from each of the agnatic kin. At the same time they asked the male agnatic kin to bring red bags of 4 *yuan* gift money to each of the agnatically related children. The meaning of the visit is to reassure the bride and her parents that their daughter will be all right after leaving her natal family. The new couple also invited the bride's parents, brother(s), and male agnatic kin to visit the bride's new family. Afterwards her mother distributed the small rice cakes and sweets to her neighbours and fellow villagers.

(2) Uniting two families by male kin (*zuo manyue*)

The next scene is called *zuo manyue* (uniting two families). The *manyue* has the same characters as *manyue* for a baby's first month birthday but with a different meaning. Here it takes another meaning of *manyue* (full moon) which means that one family is a half moon and two families make a full moon. As I have mentioned at the beginning of the section, according to the local custom, the members of a bride's natal family are not allowed to come to the groom's family on the wedding day. This event and the following one is the way in which the two families gather together. If the representatives of the bride's natal family pay a visit to the bride's new family and are entertained properly by the groom's family members, the two families will be united as one big family (*manyue*).

Normally on the third or the fourth day after the wedding day the bride's father and close male agnatic kin visit the bride's new family with gifts. I attended such an event with the Tan family (Photo II-28). I saw the bride's father and five other male agnatic kin carrying gifts in big steamers on a shoulder pole come to Tan's house. The gifts were small square-shaped rice cakes (*songgao*), sugar canes and so on which cost 150 *yuan*. The Tan family held a feast, that included the upper part of a pig leg, with its male agnatic kin who were placed at two tables. After the feast the groom's mother distributed the rice cakes to the family's agnatic kin, neighbours and fellow villagers.

Photo II-28. The "bride"'s father and five agnatic kin visited the Tan family for the after one-month married event

(3) Uniting two families by female kin (*shier zhao*)

Although a bride's brother came with his mother for this event, the event is mainly designed to unite the female members of the two families. *Shier zhao* originally means that on the twelfth day after the wedding the bride's mother and brother visit the groom's family with gifts. Nowadays this event would happen on the sixth day after the wedding. Some villagers also called this event "to be new guests" (*zuoxinke*) of the groom's family.

On that day Mrs Rao's mother and brother brought a big cloth bag of gifts to visit her new home. It contained a bag of tea, a bag of smoked soya beans, a bag of *daidi* (crust of cooked glutinous rice powder), sugar and jujube. Mrs Rao's mother-in-law held a feast with an upper part of pig leg because this was the bride's mother and brother's first visit. This time it was her mother-in-law and female agnatic kin's turn to be companions at the feast. The groom's family's agnatic kin's children were also invited. Mr Rao's mother and brother also brought five bags of gifts, including egg cakes for old people and biscuits for children, to the Rao family's five agnatic kin families. At this occasion Mrs Rao's mother gave each of the children little red bags with 10 *yuan*. One child was absent and his mother took the red bag for him. The gifts and gifts money cost 200 *yuan*. After the feast the bride's mother-in-law put 10 per cent of everything back in the bride's mother's cloth bag as return gifts.

Mrs Rao told me that perhaps the meaning of this visit is that her natal family wanted to support her to make a friendly environment around her new home, because the gifts which her mother and brother brought would be used in a tea party for the neighbours and fellow villagers later (see next section). On this occasion her brother was also introduced to the female agnatic kin as *xiaojiuzi*, another way to address the *jiujiu* who would be Mr Rao's future child's *jiujiu*. The *xiaojiuzi*'s appearance and the above gifts can be seen as a kind of *renqing* investment from Mr Rao's natal family.

4. Post-wedding *wanglai* between the new couple's family and its relations

After the relationship between a bride's natal family and the new couple's family has been established it is the turn for the new couple to start knitting their own family's *lishang-wanglai* networks.

On a new couple's list the most important relationship is with the wife's natal family, which has been categorized as new non-agnatic kin (*xinqin*) as soon as the above events (see Chapter V.II were completed. At the same time the list of the husband's family's agnatic and non-agnatic kin would be slightly modified. Very old generation relatives (*laoqin*) would be removed from the family list, for example the husband's father's mother's mother's brother's family. For some families the wife's natal family's close non-agnatic kin would become less important non-agnatic kin of the new couple's family (*niangjia de qinqi*) if she brought any of them with her, for example Mr Rao in Chapter V.I. In the case of the "bride" in the Tan family of Chapter V.II, he only kept his natal family as new non-agnatic kin. In this section I will show how a new family is involved in different relationships at the later stage of the period of establishing a marriage relationship.

(1) To be new guests of a bride's natal family and its relations

Here the characters of "to be new guests" (*zuo xinke*) are the same as the "to be guests" when a child passes his or her first birthday and becomes a new guest of his or her family's non-agnatic kin's families (see Chapter V.I). "To be new guests" means both: (i) to be a new guest of a bride's natal family and its relations, and (ii) to be a new guest of a groom's family's relations.

For the new wife's family, in theory, after a bride marries out from her natal family she is no longer a member of it. In practice, for the villagers, only after the bride's mother's visit to the groom's family was the bride no longer a part of her natal family and instead its new guest (*xinke*). The event of *zuo xinke* normally happens around one month after a bride gets married. Some people also called this the "return to the bride's natal family after she was married for one month" (*manyue hui niangjia*). This visit makes a starting point for the new couple to be the new wife's natal family's new non-agnatic kin.

Mrs Zhou told me that she and her husband carried a set of steamers on a shoulder pole with gifts: crunchy candy, liquor, fruits, egg cakes, biscuits, oatmeal and so on, for the new wife's parents. Other gifts, such as crunchy candy, egg cakes and biscuits wrapped up individually, were for attending feasts held by each agnatic kin. The event of "to be new guests" cost about 400 *yuan* for the new couple, who brought gifts to all the families and gift money to the children. The cost was less than it might have been because she did not bring any families of non-agnatic kin from her natal family with her to her married family, so there was no need to spend anything on the non-agnatic kin. They stayed at Mr Zhou's natal family for about a week to attend the feasts held by the above 10 families of agnatic kin and 2 feasts by her natal family.

The first scene of being new guests was to attend a feast that included an upper part of pig's leg at Mr Zhou's parents' home. Her natal family's agnatic kin were invited. The new couple then took turns to visit each family of agnatic kin for a feast with the same gifts as for the new wife's parents. This was the first and also the last time the new couple were invited to their families for feasts, because these feasts are the agnatic kin's way to end the relationship with them.

During the feasts each family's older-generation adult gave the new couple a little red bag with 10 *yuan* and the new couple gave a little red bag of the same amount to the children who were of a younger generation than them. If an agnatic kin family was without an older generation or younger generation, such as a newly married couple living apart from their parents, then according to local custom they did not need to exchange little red bags. In this case the 10 families all had an older generation and only 4 of them had a younger generation so they spent less than they received. In some cases the gift money they gave and received is balanced. The giving of little red bags in this way, an exercise in generational identity, is so that the new wife can learn related rules of preparing little red bags for different occasions. It is also a way to end the relationship between the new couple and the wife's natal family's agnatic kin with a balance of obligation.

During their stay Mr Zhou visited her "little sisters" and friends who lived in the village, she even visited friends who had married and lived in different villages. This is the way in which she expressed her thanks for their support during her wedding ceremony. It is also the way to end each relationship with them.

As I have mentioned in the section on the seeing-off ceremony, brides were supposed to keep a list of gift money given by their friends. Mrs Zhou remembered *wanglai* details between herself and each of her friends. If she had already given gifts and gift money to them in the past, then the rice cakes and sweets was her way of ending the relationship between them. Otherwise she would return them the same amount of gifts and gift money when they got married. By then, in theory, she would have ended the relationship between herself and her friends from her childhood.

However, there is a difference in relationships with friends between a bride and a "bride" who was taken into his wife's family as a son-in-law. Mr Tan told me that although his son-in-law chose not to bring close non-agnatic kin into his married family, he would bring other resources. For example, according to the local custom, the relationship between the "bride" and his friends from his childhood should last until after the house completion ceremony of his married family (see Chapter V.II)

The "to be new guests" event in Mrs Zhou's natal family ended with another feast held by Mrs Zhou's natal family. Again, all the agnatic kin were invited, but this time did not need to bring any gifts. This feast for the members of Mrs Zhou's family represented starting a new relationship and for the agnatic kin meant saying goodbye. After the feast Mr Zhou's father accompanied the couple back to their home with a shoulder pole of rice balls with sweetened red-bean paste fillings. The rice balls are called son-in-law rice balls (*nüxu tuanzi*) because this is the first time the new couple return home from the new wife's natal family after visiting it as new guests. The rice balls were for distribution to the couple's agnatic kin, neighbours and fellow villagers, and the husband's friends. This is an announcement that *wanglai* has started in the new non-agnatic kin relationship between the new wife's natal family and the new couple.

However, the final ending of a relationship between married-out daughters and their natal families during the period of establishing a marriage relationship is the event of *xiexia*. This denotes the holiday (or time of rest) in their natal families that new wives should take in the first summer after they marry out. Mrs Rao told me that she prepared gifts and returned to her natal family for a few days. The gifts were fruits, steamed buns, and small pancakes with fillings (*jiuniang bing*). The buns and pancakes were for her mother to distribute to her agnatic kin, neighbours and fellow villagers. Afterwards her mother sent her back to her husband's family with gifts: two feather fans, an electric fan, a double-size summer sleeping mat of woven split bamboo, summer clothes for both the new wife and her husband, an umbrella, mosquito net and so on. These gifts cost about 400 *yuan* in 1996. Mrs Zhou said she received more or less the same kind of gifts from her mother as Mrs Rao but without the mosquito net because her *jiujiu* had already given her one as an additional dowry. The new wife's mother-in-law's family would entertain the bride's mother for a nice meal, costing about 100 *yuan*. This meal was without an upper part of pig leg, there were no other guests, and no return gifts for taking away. Some families would have a different arrangement. Instead of the new wife visiting her natal family there might be reasons for her to stay at the husband's home. Her mother would visit her in her married family with the gifts mentioned above.

After the summer holiday event the dealings between the newly married-out daughters and their natal families would gradually change into dealings with their brothers instead, namely, the relationship between their children and the children's *jiujiu*.

(2) To be a new member and new guests of a groom's family's relations

After completing the events to be new guests in a wife's natal family it would be the turn of the new couple to become involved with the husband's family's relations. The relations included agnatic kin, non-agnatic kin, neighbours and fellow villagers. For events between a husband's family's relations and the new wife she would be a new member of the family, and for her husband's family's close non-agnatic kin the new couple would be new guests.

Local custom provides for the arrangements for the event of becoming a new member of the husband's family or new guests of the husband family's close non-agnatic kin to be held at different times. If the wedding was held during the lunar New Year the whole thing can happen very quickly. If the wedding was held on the National Day, 1 October, the feasts would be delayed to the following lunar New Year period. If the wedding was held in the middle of the year then the feasts could take a few months to complete. If the numbers of the new couple's agnatic and non-agnatic kin were small it could also happen quickly. One informant said she had three families of agnatic kin and seven of non-agnatic and she was married during the lunar New Year period, which made her life much simpler, but less fun.

In contrast to the seeing-off feasts held by the agnatic kin of the fiancée's family before the wedding, there are welcome feasts held by the agnatic kin of the groom's family after the wedding. After a new couple complete *wanglai* with the wife's natal family and its relations they are invited by the husband's family's agnatic kin for welcome feasts in turn. Mrs Zhou told me that she and her husband brought the same gifts to her husband's agnatic kin as they brought to her natal family's agnatic kin. Although there were upper parts of pig legs involved in the feasts and the little red bags flowed more or less in the same way as with her natal family's families of agnatic kin, the feasts had a different meaning, the former being for ending a relationship and the latter for renewing one. The purpose of the feasts is to welcome the wife as a new member of the clan. This is also a way to introduce the new wife to the closeness of the families of the husband's family's agnatic kin. During the feasts there were also little red bags of gift money, as there were in the wife's natal family's agnatic kin's feast. But there is a difference in that this new amount of gift money can help the new wife revise the list of agnatic families in an order based on feelings of closeness rather than closeness of blood tie or geography, depending on the size of the gift.

After the couple complete the cycle of feasts with the husband's family's agnatic kin it is the new wife's turn to be the hostess. According to local custom the new wife should only invite her mother-in-law's generation's females of her married family's agnatic kin for a feast. For example, the Qiu family invited 10 female representatives of the 10 families of agnatic kin to attend the feast. This is practice for the new wife to be a hostess. During the feast time the women would offer her all kinds of help. If she had any problem in arranging household events she was encouraged to consult them. It is also a way for the new wife to get to know more about the relationships between her new family and its agnatic kin. According to local custom the females of the older generation should bring little red bags for the feast. On this occasion they are free to put more or less gift money into the red bags. As I mentioned in the above paragraph the new wife can determine who likes her or not from the amount of gift money, rather than by their words.

As a new member of the family the new wife also invited female neighbours and fellow villagers for a post-wedding tea party (*kai chaguan*) to liven things up. Mrs Zhou said she entertained them with double teas, both savoury and sweet teas. The savoury teas were made of smoked soya beans and green tea. The sweet tea was made of crust of cooked glutinous rice powder (*daidi*) and sugar. The ingredients were brought by her mother and brother on their visit a few days after her wedding. There were also snacks of sunflower seeds, sweets and so on. During the tea party Mrs Zhou and her mother-in-law also showed them the new couple's newly decorated bridal chamber (*xinfang*).

At the same time the female neighbours and fellow villagers also invited the new wife and her mother-in-law for tea. She accepted the invitations. When Mrs Zhou had settled down a little in her husband's family, she started to visit neighbours and fellow villagers' families for tea, accompanied and introduced by her mother-in-law. This was how she started *wanglai* with them.

Finally I will move onto a relationship between a new couple and the husband's family's close non-agnatic kin. Before a man married he was a member of a family related to his family's non-agnatic kin. After he married and took a wife into his parents' family he and his wife would gradually become representative of his parents' family. The interfamily relationship between the new couple and the rest of the family resembled the relationship between the bridal-chamber and the whole family house (see Chapters V.I and VI.I). Therefore, for the family's non-agnatic kin, the new couple, who lived within one house with their parents or siblings (in stem or extended families), were treated as a newborn nuclear family on some occasions.

For example, the new couple was invited as new guests of the husband's family's close non-agnatic kin families in turn. These feasts were for the new couple's first visit and upper parts of pig legs must be involved. Some people explain feasts of this kind as feasts in return for the wedding feast. During the feasts the little red bags flow. The rule for giving little red bags is the same as when the new couple were guests in the new wife's natal family's agnatic families, but different from feasts between the wife's married-in family and its agnatic families. If the host family has older generation member(s) they should give the new wife a little red bag which varies from 10, 40 to 100 *yuan*. If the host family had a younger generation member(s) the new wife should give him/her/them little red bags of the same amount. If the generations in the host family are the same as the new couple's then there is no need to give red bags. Generally, the amount of little red bags flowing between the new couple and their close non-agnatic families is greater than with agnatic families of the wife's natal family's.

When the new couple attend such feasts they should bring gifts costing 40 *yuan* to each family, which include crunchy candy, fruits, egg cakes, biscuit, and a basket of small square-shaped rice cakes. The reason they bring doubled gift amounts to close non-agnatic kin's families is because the small square-shaped cakes were for the non-agnatic kin to distribute to their agnatic kin, neighbours and fellow villagers. This distribution of rice cakes is similar to the practice when a child is to be a new guest in each family of close non-agnatic kin. The rice cakes create an association between the child with his or her parents, and the non-agnatic kin's agnatic kin, neighbours and fellow villagers.

This is how the new couple started to "feed pigs", or, in other words, knit their own *lishang-wanglai* networks.

II.III. House construction events

In order to see the different kinds of house construction event clearly I need to describe styles and functions of houses before and after the new wave of house construction began. The old-house style was the same as in the 1930s, see the old-house style in "a typical front view of a house" (Fei, 1939) (Photo II-29).

According to my fieldwork notes, part of the structure was made of bricks, with wooden panels

Photo II-29. One of the old houses in 1996

with a door and windows in them covering the front, and a roof covered with thin layers of tile. Such a house is a south-facing detached bungalow which covered an area of 56 to 80m^2 (or 180 to 260ft^2), namely, 7 (D) x 8m (W) or x 11m (W), plus a rear extension *longshao* (dragon tails) as a kitchen[61]. The house would normally be divided into two or three parts (*jian*) from west to east. For example, a 56m^2 house would be known as two *jian*. If the kitchen is on the west part of the house the dining and living area would be on the west, and the east part would be a bedroom area which could be divided into two bedrooms.[62] However, as Fei (1939:60) reported:

> The house is used for the silk industry, for threshing rice, for cooking, and for other productive work. It is also used for shelter, for sleeping and comfort... In the case of silk raising, much space is needed especially during the last two weeks of the raising period. In that period, all the rooms, except the kitchen, may be used for sheltering silkworms.

---

[61] Some houses have kitchens on the west side of the front of the house, which are called *daotou longshao* (turned around dragon tail).
[62] The dimensions are approximate and together with the description came from my fieldwork notes based on a few existing old style houses.

> All the members of the household will crowd in one bedroom. The individual allotment of bedrooms disappeared temporarily. (Fei, 1939:60)

The new house style kept the same functions of eating, sleeping, living and productive work as the old houses, but living standards were raised by changing from bungalows (*pingfang*) to two-storey buildings (*loufang*) and building with brick throughout. Recently some villagers have even called their rebuilt houses *xiao bieshu* (little villas). The new-style houses have increased their quality of life[63] without altering housing functions. For example, for the same covered area of 56m² in a detached two-storey building the ground floor is the same size as with a bungalow, but the east part is an empty area for living or productive work instead of being divided off into bedrooms. The first floor becomes an entire en-suite flat including a bedroom, a living room, and a bathroom in one half, with two further bedrooms and a family bathroom in the other. Villagers considered this kind of house as four *jian* whereas they considered a bungalow as two *jian*,[64] and a two-storey building with a covered area of 80m² was considered as six *jian*. In order to use land efficiently there were also some semi-detached two-storey buildings, whose style and structure were the same as those of detached two-storey buildings.

In the different stages of house construction villagers arranged finance, materials and labourers using resources from their families' *lishang-wanglai* networks. In 1996 the process of house construction (Photos II-30 and 31) is as follows: one week for pulling down an old house and sorting out reusable materials, two weeks for laying a foundation and putting up the first floor, two weeks for fitting roof-beams and laying tiles, and six weeks for plastering, decoration, wiring, plumbing and painting. But after 2001 house construction took five to eight months (Photos II-32 and 33) because the new "little villa" style of houses are taller, with two floors for more living space and storage places in the loft, and the decorations are rendered with more care.

In the introduction to this chapter I mentioned "three generations" of new houses. The first-generation new house (Photo II-30) is much simpler. Villagers singled themselves out from their neighbours by differing the materials used in the windows and door, and in the types of roof material. Two different types of house, one described as current in 1996 and the other since 2001, are regarded as the second-and third-generation new houses. I touch on the topic of the three generations of house building here because I will be analyzing cases of social support

---

[63] For example, the little villa style has a loft area for storage, which gave more rooms for living.

[64] This is a standard structure of a family house in the village, as I have shown in the Tan family (see Chapter V.II).

arrangements for building houses of different "generations" in Chapter V.III.

Photos II-30 and 31. Typical style of second generational houses in 1996

Photos II-32 and 33. Third generational houses (little villas) in 2005 and 2008

The stages of house-construction involve the following events, which include laying a foundation stone (*baidipan*), putting up the first floor (*jialouban*), putting up the roof-beams (*shangliang*) and moving into the new house (*shengqian*). According to my informants these events all belong to local tradition, except the putting up of the first floor (*jialouban*) – because the first two-storey building did not appear in the village until 1982.

1. Ceremony for setting a foundation stone (*baidipan*)

I was only allowed to attend part of the event of laying a foundation stone for the Huang family on 9 April 1996. In order to avert misfortune some of the event was not allowed to be witnessed by anybody, including me. Mr and Mrs Huang told me that the event started at 03:00 by setting off big firecrackers. Mr Huang drove four stakes into each corner of the foundation boundaries. Each stake was wrapped in red cloth, which would stay in place all the way through the house construction, to avert evil. At the same time Mrs Huang placed two benches in the south middle of the ground as an "altar table", covered with a big red cloth. She then placed a few plates on top of the benches with a whole fish, a big bar of pork, some eggs cut into half, and a basket of diamond-shaped rice cakes (*tuyuan*), especially used for a land god (Photo II-34). Mrs Huang also burned candles, incenses and paper money. She also made a bow facing the "altar table". This ritual signifies worshipping a land god (*tudi gonggong*). It is important particularly for houses that were not built on exactly the same foundations as the original.

If a house was located beside a road, according to *fengshui*, a screen should be built in front of it with a millstone built into the screen (Photo II-35), or a millstone pattern should be carved on the screen or an outer wall. It is believed this can keep evil spirits away from the house.

Photo II-34. An event of laying a foundation stone

Photo II-35. The screen with a built-in millstone.

At 08:00 helpers gathered in a village warehouse which was borrowed by the Huang family for general use throughout the period of house construction. These helpers consisted of the Huang family's agnatic kin, neighbours, fellow villagers, as well as a few bricklayers. They drank tea and ate the diamond-shaped rice cakes (*tuyuan*). A few big firecrackers were set off for breaking the soil (*potu*), and then they started digging the foundations. While people were digging the foundations, at around 09:00, Mrs Huang's brother (her son's *jiujiu*) brought along a shoulder pole of congratulatory gifts, two upper parts of pig legs, one basket of steamed buns, two *jin* of sweets and six big firecrackers. Mrs Huang displayed them at the "altar table" for a few minutes while the firecrackers were set off. She then moved them away. She also distributed sweets to all the people around the site. The steamed buns were tea for the helpers later in the day. The celebration feast was held at suppertime. It contained ten dishes, but without an upper part of pig leg. As well as the above helpers, Huang's agnatic kin's families and some close non-agnatic families attended the feast: Mr Huang's brother's family, Huang's married out daughter's family and his mother's quasi-daughter's family. They brought *zongzi*, steamed buns, firecrackers and sweets for attending the feast and took away one quarter of *zongzi* and steamed buns of whatever they brought as return gifts after the feast.

2. Putting up the first floor (*jia louban*)

On the 1 May 1996 I attended the event of putting up the first floor (*jialouban*) in YM Zhou's family. YM Zhou told me that it took nearly 20 days to get to the stage of putting up the first floor of the house. Everybody close to his family wanted a ceremony for the success of the halfway stage of the building work. The ritual of putting up the first floor was simple, requiring only the setting off of big firecrackers at the start and finish. Most of the people attending the feast were the same as for the feast of laying the foundation stone, except for the different sets of non-agnatic kin with different types of gifts: YM's married out brother's[65] two sons' families. Each of them brought 20 *jin* of egg cakes, one upper part of pig leg, 2 *jin* of sweets, 10 big fire crackers and 200 *yuan* cash. The gifts and gift money amounted to 320 *yuan* from each family. YM's mother's quasi-son's family brought 100 steamed stuffed buns (*baozi*), one upper part of pig leg, 2 *jin* of sweets, 6 big firecrackers and 160 *yuan* cash. YM's mother's quasi-daughter's family brought 1,000 *yuan* gift and gift money. The gifts are more or less the same as the YM's mother's quasi-son's family, plus 100 small square-shaped rice cakes halfway through the feast for when YM set off the firecrackers. After the feast the non-agnatic families took their share of returning gifts away with them.

3. Putting up the roof-beams (*shangliang*)

On 20 April 1996 I attended an event of putting up the roof-beams (*shangliang*) in FL Wang's family's house. The event started at 07:30 when four decorated boats with gifts arrived near to FL Wang's house. They were a magnificent sight. They carried the family's four close non-agnatic families: Mrs FL Wang's natal family, the married out daughter's family, their son's quasi-mother's family and Mr FL Wang's *jiujiu*'s family. The gifts included live pigs, a set of bathroom facilities, a ceiling fan, a washing machine, many duvets, a mosquito net, different kinds of food and fruits, sweets and lots of big firecrackers. Helpers unloaded the gifts and presented them in the middle of the house, and they also put the duvets and mosquito net on top of the decorated roof-beam for a while. The triangular shaped roof-beam was decorated by

---

[65] Who counts as *gugu*, namely, father's sister.

wrapping a piece of red cloth (*baoliangbu*) around its top end which had a set of copper coins fixed to it, and then a red string with a small wooden block wrapped in a red cloth was hung from it. Then they fixed the roof-beam into position while big firecrackers were set off. People gathered on the first floor to catch *zongzi*, steamed buns, sweets, oranges and cigarettes thrown up by a carpenter and a bricklayer. They each received one red bag containing 20 *yuan* for performing this ritual of *paoliang* ("through up to roof-beams") (see Photo II-36).

At 09:00 people had a break for tea, *zongzi*, fruits, cigarettes and sweets. The rest of the morning was for tiling the roof. At the end of the event there was another ritual "*zuojie*", which consists of putting a solid flowerpot with an evergreen plant in it on the top middle of the roof (Photo II-37).

Photos II-36 and 37. Rituals of "through up to roof-beams" and "a solid flowerpot"

The big firecrackers were set off again and followed by a lunchtime feast. Tidying up work was in the afternoon. At 15:00 there was a tea. A formal feast with an upper part of pig leg was held in the evening, involving nearly 200 guests: 80 non-agnatic kin, 40 agnatic kin, 8 bricklayers, 4 carpenters, 50 fellow villagers, 10 friends and members of the family. Mr FL Wang set off firecrackers for the ceremony of putting up the roof-beams. The non-agnatic kin and friends brought gifts and gift money for the feast and took away returning gifts after the feast.

4. Moving into the new house (*shengqian*)

Moving into a new house is the last main event during the period of house construction. Again I was only allowed to attend part of the event on 28 April with XK Zhou's family. This was for the same reason as in the laying foundation stone event; moving into a new house also involved religious activities. XK told me that the first ritual is called *anchuang* (moving beds and placing them in designated places) and performed at 06:00, before sunrise, to prevent people from seeing it. His family members moved beds, a table and benches from a village storehouse into the new house. Then he set off big firecrackers.

The second ritual at 10.00 was called *zhuangmen,* meaning to fix an entrance door for the new house. Big firecrackers were set off again followed by a tea. Apart from *zongzi,* white and green rice balls (*tuanzi*), deep fried glutinous rice cakes with sweet fillings (*jiuniangbing*) were needed for the symbolic meaning of the project of house construction being rounded off satisfactorily (*yuanman*). Before lunchtime Mrs XK Zhou set up an altar table for worshipping the family's ancestors (Photo II-38) and after lunch people did the winding up work.

The moving into a new house feast was held at suppertime and 52 people attended, including 24 non-agnatic kin, 8 agnatic kin, 16 fellow villagers and members of the family. The non-agnatic kin brought gifts for the feast, large intestines of pig, fresh noodles, fruits, sugar, sweets and firecrackers. A custom of lifting pig's intestines as high as possible above a wok was performed, symbolizing the length of time the new house will stand (Photo II-39). Firecrackers were set off again during the feast. Once again the non-agnatic kin took away their share of returning gifts after the feast.

Photo II-38. A ritual of ancestor worship before lunchtime

Photo II-39. An elder woman taking intestines of pig out of a wok

5. Completed house tea party

The last event of the house construction should be a completed house tea party. It normally happens within one week after a family moves into a new house. I did not attend such a party. Mrs Yao told me that all the wives who lived in the same group should be invited and 28 of them attended her family's tea party including agnatic kin who lived in the same group, neighbours and fellow villagers' families. She served smoked soya bean tea, snacks and sweets for the guests. Although some of them had come to the house for feasts during its construction, Yao said it was nice for her to have the opportunity of showing them around the new house. He told me that she went to many such tea parties and learnt a great deal from them.

Chapter III   Local customs (II)

Chapter III consists of three relatively independent parts. The first two sections are a continuation of Chapter II, life-cycle events from later life, from family division and elderly care to funeral and post-funeral rituals – 11 different events in all. Section three will turn to annual cycle events. It includes annual production cycle events, annual everyday cycle events, festivals and customary events, ancestor worship and worship of local gods. Finally, section four will introduce non-routine issues, which I call emergency events. It includes natural and man-made disasters, illness and injury. Over generations, Kaixiangong Village developed all kinds of customs providing guidance for villagers' routine and non-routine life. Over time these customs have been updated and re-created by the villagers according to changing situations.

III.I. Family division and elderly care

1. Family division

The old ideal Confucian family (seldom realized perhaps) would consist of up to 5 generations living and eating together under the same roof and of course working on the shared family holding, under the authority of the senior male. Breaking up such an organization involves not just separation of hearth and of property but of responsibilities including social responsibilities. I won't go into the details of how family organization changed during the period of collectivisation, or the modern pressures continuing to exert influence. However, family division is now rare in Kaixiangong Village. The event could last for two years, unlike Cohen's "serial division" (1992) and Yan's finding in Xiajia that the timing of family division has been shortened (1997:194–95, 1998:75). I attended a final part of the family division in HL Wang's family in May 1996, and will describe the related customs based on this case which I partly witnessed.

Mr HL Wang gave me an account of this event. According to him the main event had started in March 1994. The reason the family had decided on that date was because the whole family believed it would be much simpler to have the main event before the second son's wedding. It lasted two days.

On the first day HL Wang's family invited four *jiujiu*s (Mrs HL Wang's wife's brothers including one quasi-*jiujiu*), one *gufu* (Mr HL Wang's sister's husband), and three male agnatic kin to be helpers (witnesses or mediators) and guests. The oldest *jiujiu* was in charge of the event. A major part of family division is that the family property should be divided fairly. After people discussed details of the family property one of the *jiujiu*s wrote two copies of the family division contracts for the two sons, with the same contents. After the two sons agreed the contents they signed as holders of the contracts. All the relatives present signed as witnesses. At the end, the oldest *jiujiu* joined the two contracts together, affixed his seal to the join, and handed a copy to each son (Photo III-1).

Photo III-1. HL Wang family division contract

Then there was a simple worship for ancestors. Offerings were laid on the dining table, everybody bowed and burnt candles. This was followed by a family feast (*qieqiekai*) which translates as "cutting off each nuclear family from the joint family." In this feast an upper part of pig leg must be involved, as a good-luck symbol for each small family to grow well after the family division. All the relatives who had been helpers and witnesses and their families were invited.

On the second day villagers moved furniture and large items to the sons' share of family property as prescribed in the family division contracts. In the case of HL Wang's family the only big item was a motor vehicle, which was mainly purchased by the younger son, used by him, stored in his house, and agreed to belong to him by everybody. So the main activity on the second day was a family feast in the older son's home with the older son's parents-in-law's family. The guests carried a shoulder pole of gifts to HL Wang's family for the meal. The gifts included rice cakes, upper part of pig leg and some kitchenware. These gifts were for the ceremony of the older son's family eating separately from the joint family.

Before the feast a ritual of worshipping the kitchen god had to be performed when the new kitchen was used for the first time. The feast marked the joint family passing of one of its non-agnatic families to the older son's nuclear family, with all the responsibilities and expectations of support that this involved. HL Wang told me that before the family division his family networks included 19 families of non-agnatic kin. Apart from the above relatives which already, on the first day, took part in the family division feast, the rest of them came for a feast individually within a few days after the event of family division. The last step of family division wasn't completed until two years later after the second son got married and a new kitchen was built.

Two years later, in May 1996, after the younger son got married and the new kitchen was built, the son's parents-in-law's family carried gifts to HL Wang's family for the ceremony of the younger son's family eating separately from the joint family, and I witnessed the ritual for worshipping the kitchen god. In the morning the younger son's mother-in-law and sister-in-law[66] carried a shoulder pole of big gift baskets to HL Wang's house (Photo III-2).

These gifts were some kitchenware: a crate full of rice, two bamboo wire strainers, two dustpans, two brooms, eight rice bowls, eight medium bowls, eight large bowls, ten plates, some cooking utensils and chopsticks. The gifts also included some food: a big upper part of pig leg, a large intestine in a silver pot with a silver coin on top of it, a bag of egg cakes, a bag of sweets, two bags of egg products, eighty wet rice cakes in a big bamboo steamer covered with red cloth and with an evergreen on top. After Mrs HL Wang had served the in-laws tea and snacks she performed a simple worship of the kitchen god by placing some of the gifts and additional fruits on a new stove, burning incense sticks and bowing.(Photo III-3). That was all.

Photo III-2. The carrying of gifts to the younger son's home for the kitchen god worship

The worship of the kitchen god was called *baixinzao,* and required a new stove and new wok, symbolising good luck for the new family's fresh start because a good start is half of success. The

Photo III-3. Offerings on the new stove

presentation of gifts also involved a religious sense, such as the even numbers of 2, 8, 10, 80 for

---

[66] Since the *jiujiu* (the younger son's wife's younger brother) worked outside of their village, his older sister, accompanied by her mother, brought the gifts, in the same way as Mrs Ren's father represented her brother for her son's one-month old birthday event in Chapter II.I.

luckiness; colours of red (keep away evil) and green (long life); production of an upper part of pig leg (*tipang tishang*) and large intestine (*dachang chang*) for raising living standards and a long-lasting marriage; a silver coin for a wealthy and satisfactory life (*yuanman*) and unison (*tuanyuan*). The eighty rice cakes were for distributing to agnatic-kin, neighbours and fellow villagers as an announcement that the worshipping of the kitchen god had been performed and the family division been completed.

Finally, the younger son's mother started use of the new stove to cook a meal for the younger son's family, his parents and in-law's family. This was an "eating separately meal" (*chichikai*), which was the younger son's family's first meal after the family division. At the same time the joint family passed another set of the non-agnatic relatives to the younger son's family. This ended the family division. There are further details of how the 19 households of non-agnatic relatives were divided, and further analysis of family division, in Chapter VI.I).

2. Elderly care

There is a famous Chinese saying that "raising sons can provide for old age"; it seems that elderly care is the sons' responsibility. In Kaixiangong village there are some divisions between children. If one family has two sons, the elder son is responsible for the father's elderly care and the younger son for the mother's. This is because younger sons always get married later and their children will be younger and more likely to need their grandmother's care. In return, when their mothers get older it is the younger sons' responsibility to take care of their mother. For married out daughters, the local custom also had detailed stipulations of their responsibilities and obligations for elderly care, such as doing housework whenever they visit their natal families, preparations for parents' birthdays, and they play important roles in parents' funerals (see Chapters VI.II and III.II).

Let us have a look at the family division contract. Among the five items two of them relate to elderly care: one is where parents are to live after family division, and the other is daily elderly care after they pass their 60th birthday. The contract has two copies for each of the two sons to keep. The contents were:

> (1) House. This is a two-storey, four-bedroom building to be divided into two semi-detached, self-contained houses. The east part belongs to WQ (the older son) who should build a separate staircase himself; the west part belongs to ZQ (the younger son) who should complete the bedrooms himself on the first floor. He can also keep the motor vehicle for the balance of the building cost. The semi-detached

bungalow behind the main house divides into two parts: the east part belongs to WQ and the west part belongs to ZQ for their kitchen and dining rooms.

(2) Additional buildings. The detached bungalow with one living room, two bedrooms, and one kitchen and dining room belongs to HR (HL Wang's unmarried brother). The semi-detached piggery divides into two parts: the east part belongs to HL (HL Wang), and the west part belongs to HR.

(3) Parents' accommodation. Parents live in one of WQ's bedrooms temporarily. After ZQ completes the bedrooms the father remains in the bedroom and the mother moves into one of ZQ's bedrooms. If the parents feel uncomfortable at some point they may swap these bedrooms for the semi-detached bungalow behind the main house.

(4) Foundation base. The east part of the yard in front of the house and east side of foundation base (5 x 4m²) belongs to WQ, but ZQ is allowed to access it for rubbish and manure. The west part of the yard in front of the house and the back yard belongs to ZQ.

(5) Elderly care. After parents pass their sixtieth birthdays both WQ and ZQ provide 150 *jin* of grain, 500 *jin* of firewood, and 200 *yuan* of cash to each of them per year.

The figures of elderly care look low, but they were based on the standard of the state policy for "five guaranteed households"[67], and the elderly care home in Miaogang Township, in 1994. Chapter VI will show details of how the elderly couple lived and all the changes that happened afterwards.

According to local custom, married-out daughters visiting their natal families should always do whatever housework they can for the elderly. Photo III-4 shows a married-out daughter carrying her mother's nightstool to wash in a river near the house. Some adopted daughters who married outside the village would treat their foster parents the same way. "Adopted daughters" are supposed to marry these families' sons when the families adopted the girls, but during the Great Leap Forward campaign and its consequent famine many of these girls had to leave their foster families to survive. When things improved they came to visit their foster families and helped their adopted parents, although this was not demanded by custom. This kind of behaviour merited special approval.

In theory in the village the elderly are entitled to receive help from their daughters, even "married out adopted daughters". In reality, I noticed that the elderly were actually very

---

[67] Households receiving the five guarantees, i.e. childless and infirm old persons are guaranteed food, clothing, medical care, housing and burial expenses by the local government.

independent, and took care of their everyday lives themselves either on land or field or at home. Photos 5 and 6 respectively show an old man who works on a farm and an old lady picking up firewood from around the village.

The elderly in the village were not only independent, they were also very supportive to their children's families. Photo III-7 shows the charming courtyard picture I spotted through an open gate − nobody has noticed me except the little boy. The three elderly people in the photo were the boy's grandmother and his great-grandparents. They looked after him while doing a great deal of the housework. In the photo the great-grandpa is cuddling the little boy, while behind him are a pair of big baskets full of grass cut by the two old ladies to feed the rabbits. When cutting the grass they also picked wild vegetables used especially for making "Beginning of Summer" (7th solar term) rice cakes (called "*lixia tabing*", which is made of glutinous rice mixed with wild vegetables), as well as cooking supper and feeding the rabbits.

Looking after children has its time limit; it ends when they go to nursery or to school. However, throughout this book we show how the elderly play important roles in both life-cycle and annual cycle family events. Their positive participation in these events can be seen as their way of preventing themselves from getting old and as self-provision for their old age.

Just as the ESRC social support project divided social support into "household support", "private support" and "public support", elderly care in Kaixiangong Village can be seen as "self support", "family and private support" and "public support" (see Chapter VI.II).

Photo III-4. A daughter carry a nightstool to wash.

Photo III-5. An old man carrying a pair of buckets full of farm manure to his land.

Photo III-6. A 90-year old woman picking up firewood

Photo III-7. Three elderly people doing housework and looking after a child at the same time

III.II. Funeral ceremony and post-funeral rituals

I attended four funerals, including some post-funerary rituals, in Kaixiangong village in 1996. Three were traditional funerals and one was Christian (omitted here). Although they had completely different styles, they all involved social support and *lishang-wanglai* networks in different ways. I will describe them based on XQ Wang's mother's case and add variations when necessary.

1. Funeral ceremony

XQ Wang's mother passed away on the morning of 5 March 1996. Before she died her son and son-in-law carried her onto the temporary bed, as is done in North China (Naquin, 1988). After death she was washed and completely dressed in brand new clothes by her daughter and daughter-in-law. The deceased had two sons and lived with the elder son. The younger son had married out of the family as a son-in-law in the village and had died in an accident a few years previously. The younger son's wife came round just before the death, bringing her share of gifts for setting up the altar table as soon as her mother-in-law had breathed her last.

The family sent a member of its agnatic kin, wearing a strip of white cloth in a trouser pocket, as a messenger to announce the sad news (*baosang*). Based on the Wang family's list he visited houses inside and outside the village where XQ Wang's agnatic kin, non-agnatic kin and friends lived. At the same time the family prepared the mourning hall (*lingtang*), which was in the family living room. The corpse lay on the temporary bed with her head to the east and her feet to the west, and the body covered by a duvet with a red silk cover. The bed stood by the end of the hall against the northern wall, with a stool beside it for seating mourners. In front of the bed two tables were joined together to make an altar table. On the table were offerings: a pig's head, fruit, oval-shaped rice cakes with filling (*tabing*), wonton, glutinous rice dumplings (*zongzi*), incense, candles and yellow paper. In front of the altar table was another stool (Photo III-8). Later on, they drew a large white curtain between the bed and the tables, which performed the function of separating the nether world from the world of the living.

Photo III-8. The body on a bed behind the tables on which offerings were presented

(1) Paying condolences to the deceased (*puxiang*)

As soon as people received the sad news they came to pay condolences to the deceased (*puxiang*), in the same way that mourners pay their last respects (*xiang yiti gaobie*) in urban China. Instead of using red coloured containers for gifts as for weddings, the colour green and natural baskets are used in funerals (Photos III-9 and 10).

Photos III-9 and 10. The containers must be green or a natural colour for funerals

Women coming to pay condolences to the deceased brought bags in which the contents were wrapped in a green shawl and did as follows. The woman opened the bag which contained a sheet of white cloth, some yellow paper and incense. She put the white cloth on the body of the corpse and the yellow paper under the feet, then she sat on the stool by the bed and wailed. Other female family members joined in the wailing with her. She then removed the white cloth and yellow paper from the corpse and gave them to the daughter-in-law. She then walked away from the corpse and bowed with knees bended on the stool facing the altar table. Other mourners repeated the same practice throughout the day.

Taoist priests are required during the event of paying condolences to the deceased. A group of five of them arrived before lunchtime. They hung a wide painting on the white curtain, showing the jade emperor and the god of longevity (*shouxing*). They then placed religious equipment on the altar

table and played music with different instruments: gong, tambour and two stringed bowed instruments (*huqin*). They also sang songs and chanted the salvation litany from time to time throughout the day. After all the closest female kin had performed the ritual of paying condolences to the deceased, the Taoist priests set up their table and put on Taoist robes and hats, and played music, sang songs and chanted the salvation litany again (Photo III-11).

After lunch two women came with their husbands, one after the other. They carried, on a shoulder pole, a pair of baskets full of gifts. They placed the gifts, more or less the same as the existing gifts, on the altar table. They then paid condolences to the deceased, in more or less the same way as earlier mourners. The only difference was that they presented their gifts on the altar table with big trays pointing east and west. A third couple, who I was told were the closest kin

Photo III-11. Taoist priests performing their ritual

of the deceased, brought an almost equal quantity and style of gift and repeated the same ritual. The first women and their husbands were the deceased's daughter and son-in-law and quasi daughter and quasi son-in-law, and the man with his wife was the deceased's late husband's carpentry apprentice. According to custom the quasi daughter and the apprentice played the roles of daughter and son throughout the funeral and post-funerary ritual.

For the rest of the afternoon mourners came to pay their condolences to the deceased (*puxiang}* with gifts similar to those brought by the relatives in the morning,. Around supper time up to 100 mourners gathered in the house. They were the deceased's and the family's agnatic kin and non-agnatic kin, including close and distant kin, newly established and old generation's kin. They all came with baskets full of gifts. The contents were more or less the same, except that there were no pig heads, and they were of a much smaller quantity. They also brought red bags (envelopes) with gift money. The supper contained twelve dishes. Before and after the supper the Taoist priests played music, sang songs and chanted the salvation litany. Agnatic kin's families' women stayed in the house for the whole night, as well as the Taoist priests, keeping vigil (*shouye*). During the vigil they made paper money with different types of paper (Photo III-12) that would be used the following day. This can be seen as a kind of labour social support because this custom applies to every family.

Photo III-12. Female agnatic kin making paper money during vigil

(2) Funeral feast (*sushijiu*)

The second day in theory was a funeral day. On the day more mourners came to pay their condolences. Some had come from far away, and others had not had time to come the day before. On this second day, all the fellow villagers in the same group sent their senior female to the house. The deceased's daughter-in-law gave a bag of tofu, so called "elderly tofu", to each senior female of the group. The supper was called the formal funeral feast (*shushijiu* or *zhengcan*). An upper part of pig leg (*tizi*) and 18 dishes were served. The 120 guests included the agnatic kin, the non-agnatic kin families which shared the same surname (*tongxing*) and the deceased's son's friends. They brought red bags (envelopes) with gift money. The Taoist priests came again and played music, sang songs, chanted the salvation litany before and after supper and stayed overnight as well.

(3) Cremation (*huohua*) and ash box burial

Before the 1970s the dead were buried, but since then the practice of cremation has spread in this area. The event has become complicated because it now consists of two parts: seeing off the deceased to the crematorium, and the burial of the ash box. Taoist priests played music, sang songs and chanted the salvation litany before and after breakfast. After the big breakfast everybody put on their mourning dress. People moved one of the altar tables together with sacrificial offerings to the northwest end of the living room and set a spirit tablet (*lingpai* or *lingwei*) at the middle end. Others bowed on bended knees in front of another altar table, one by one. Behind the altar table and inside the white sheet used to the corpse, the corpse was tied with the red duvet and transferred onto a stretcher or hearse. Meanwhile women were wailing mournfully (Photo III-13).

The deceased's daughter wailed in a heart-stricken manner and collapsed onto the floor. One of the priests burnt a bunch of straw outside the house. The "temporary bed", made of one side of double doors, was stood in front of the main entrance. The younger son's wife smashed a tile on the door (*qiaomen tuanzi*), which is similar to smashing a bowl in other parts of China. Firecrackers were set off. A large white sheet was held high to form an arch or bridge. The deceased's son, son-in-law, her late husband's apprentice and one of the close cousins carried the stretcher with the corpse on it and left the house. Other people carried something (which I could not see) after the stretcher. The women quickly swept the floor to drive evil spirits from the house. Taoist priests played music and followed them, and then the rest of the mourners followed. They walked all the way through the village to the hearse, which had stopped by the main road (Photo III-14).

All the mourners got onto a big truck behind the hearse to go to the Wujiang City Crematorium. Once they got to the Crematorium the women wailed again. They planned to have a ceremony in the Crematorium and had brought mock money, candles and firecrackers with them. However, they did not use them because there were signs in the Crematorium saying "Burning mock money is forbidden" and "Superstitious

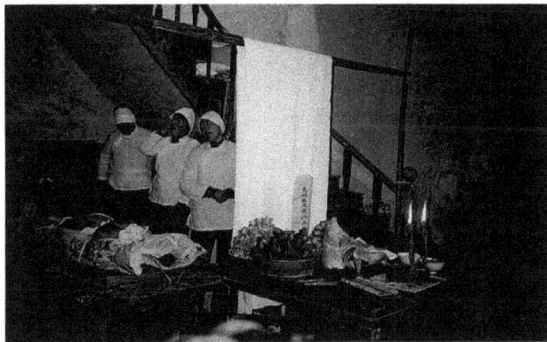

Photo III-13. Women wailing mournfully

Photo III–14. The body was carried through the village to the hearse

activities are forbidden" and so on. So there was no ceremony at the Crematorium, just the burning of the corpse in the furnace. While they were waiting to collect the ash they bought a bone ash box for it together with mini plastic wreaths (*huaquan*) and flowers.

The mourners returned to the village in their truck and the priests played more music, after which they and most of the mourners went home. This local custom is different from that in Guansu province, my other fieldwork village, where the priests stayed to perform a ritual in the graveyard. In Kaixiangong, only the close members of Wang's family walked to the graveyard: Mang and his wife, daughter, second's son's wife and the quasi-daughter. Wang set off firecrackers to start the burial ritual. They wailed again, drank sugar water, poured water around the grave place, bowed with bended knee one by one, and then left. Four men remained to bury the bone ash box. They placed the deceased's ash box next to her late husband's so that it looked like a mini detached house. They then turned the grave into a semi-detached house with bricks and cement, so they could keep their mother's ash box next to their father's. They also fixed the plastic flowers on top of the new part of this joint grave and the plastic wreaths (*huaquan*) in front of it.

JH Zhou's family's ash box burial ritual was slightly different from XQ Wang's. As soon as the truck with the mourners came back to the village everybody including the Taoist priests got down. Two grandsons carried a lantern each and walked in front of the group of mourners, followed by the deceased's son who carried the ash box that was covered with a piece of red silk, then the Taoist priests and the rest of the mourners followed them (Photo III-15). Firecrackers were set off and music played and people walked all the way through the village and into Zhou's house. The close members of the Zhou family then walked to the grave site to bury the bone ash box. The rituals of firecrackers, wailing, sugar water and bowing were more or less the same as those of the Wang family with the difference that they played Chinese official funeral music bought from Wujiang Crematorium while they built the grave.

Photo III-15. JH Zhou's family return to the village from the crematorium

The Taoist priests did not come to the gravesite, the universal practice for every household in Kaixiangong but different from that in Neiguan, Gansu province, my other fieldwork village. The mourners also threw a handful of coins on top of the ash box before they covered it. It is clear that at the stage of welcoming (*ying*) the ash box back home (*lai*) and burying it, the dead person's social relations were no longer involved in the ritual of burial and only intimate family members were present, indicating that the dead person's social relationships had already ended, but close family relationships remain.

Back to XQ Wang's case. After the close family members finished burying the ash box they came back to the dead woman's home (also the family home) wailed and bowed to the altar table that was located in the northwest corner of the house. A picture of the dead person hung on the west wall and the spirit tablet stood on the altar table against the west wall. Instead of candles, as for ancestors, (ie she's not yet an ancestor) there was an oil lamp by a spirit tablet on the altar table, together with sacrificial offerings of rice balls, tofu, wonton, vegetables and fruit.

After they had all had lunch the deceased's son and close family members carried various items used by the deceased, such as a big straw mat, clothes-stool (*matong*) and clothes, outside the village and burned them by the east temple. Thus the funeral was completed.

2. Post-funeral rituals

I have described how after a wedding ceremony there were a series of "post-marital activities" between husband and wife and their families, with the purpose of helping the newly established family to settle. This includes ending old relationships, for example between the wife and her little sisters and old generational relatives beyond four generations, and updating existing family relationships and networks. Kaixiangong Village extended these practices symbolically from this life to the afterlife, as can be seen from their post-funerary rituals (*zuo houshi*). The following post-funerary rituals will show what the villagers do to help a dead person end the relationships they had when he or she was alive, and start establishing new sets of relationships in the nether world.

(1) Doing the sevens (*zuoqi*) and the first seventh

The first post-funerary ritual is called "do the sevens" (*zuoqi*). The villagers normally do three "sevens": the first, third and fifth seventh-day after the person dies. The first seventh-day ritual (*touqi*) is to send the dead person to join his or her dead relatives, that is the late wife or husband and ancestors and settle them into their status of ancestor. The third seventh-day ritual (*sanqi*) is for when the deceased as a new arrival meets all the heavenly gods and spiritual beings, and the fifth seventh-day ritual (*wuqi*) is to help, and mark, their finally being settled in the nether world.

However, XQ Wang's mother's case differs slightly from the typical ritual described above. According to local custom, the deceased's fifth seventh-day ritual should be finished before the Qingming Festival. Wang's mother died on the 5 March 1996. Her fifth seventh-day ritual should have been on 8 April, which would be after the Qingming Festival (4^t April 1996). Under this circumstance the local custom was for the family to perform the third seventh-day ritual instead of the fifth one, and then it could carry out the sweeping of the deceased's grave for the first year at the Qingming Festival on 4 April. So the Wang family performed the first seventh-day ritual as usual and combined the third and the fifth into one.

On the first seventh-day the Wang family's members and close relatives gathered in the morning, his older son, his wife, the older daughter, the younger son's wife and the quasi daughter. They placed fresh food on the altar table and bowed in front of the mother's tablet. They then put on their mourning clothes and walked out of the house with a basket and bag filled with incense sticks and paper money. Having walked around the village they stopped at one end of a bridge, put sticks of incense sticks on the ground, burned paper money and bowed (Photo III-16). This was where the ritual started because it was the place where a little temple for deceased souls (*lingwumiao*) had once been located. Although the little temple had been gone for several decades it remained in village memory and was remembered by one generation after another. They repeated the same actions at the other end of the bridge.

Then they walked around the river, passing another two bridges, at each of which they performed these same actions. In this way they accompanied the deceased on her journey to meet her late husband and ancestors, finishing at the imaginary meeting-place, the East Temple. Here they put the rest of the incense sticks on the stick holder and the rest of the paper money in a burner, and bowed with bended knees.

After they finished the ritual everybody stroked the wooden column inside the temple (photo III-17), which appeared to be similar to the actions of local people at the big gingkgo tree outside Laotai temple near the Miaogang Township on Chinese New Year's Eve.

When they returned home they wailed, burned more paper money, bowed and changed into their normal clothes. They had tea that included various kinds of sweet rice balls (*yuanzi*) and savoury rice cakes (*tabing*), which symbolised the deceased's reunion with her late husband and ancestors. At lunchtime the rest of the family members joined them and bowed to the altar table. The ritual ended.

Photos III-16 and 17. First seventh-day rituals on the road and at the temple

(2) The third or the fifth seventh

The third seventh-day ritual should have been held on 25 March 1996 but the Wang family changed it to the 24th. When "double sevens" happened, custom allowed the villagers to hold the event a day before or after to avoid unlucky numbers. The third seventh-day was on the 25th March which is the seventh day of the second lunar month. It doubled the sevens of the third seventh day and the day of the lunar month and so the family decided to hold the third seventh-day ritual on the 24 March. This change was determined by religious feeling, rather than the practical concerns which had led to combining the third and fifth seven-days events.

The ritual of the third seventh-day (bear in mind that normally it should be the fifth seventh-day ritual) started at 08:00. A Taoist priest chanted scriptures (*nianjing*) by a table against the west wall but a metre away from the altar table. On the table the Taoist priest set a number of inscription tablets which represented the death god (*dizangwang*), land god, Jade Emperor and so on (Photo III-18). There were also incense sticks, scriptures and a wooden fish – a percussion instrument made from a hollow wooden block, originally used by Buddhist priests to beat a rhythm when chanting scriptures (*muyu*). On the altar table there were nine small dishes containing offerings: two big apples, two big pears, pickled tofu, cooked green vegetables, pickled vegetables, steamed rice, rice balls, steamed egg custard and dried fish. Around the table there were many sets of clothes made out of coloured paper for the four seasons, a shawl, apron, bedding (silk padded quilt, bed and foot warmer (*jiaolu*), paper houses, and two big parcels containing all the deceased's clothes and shoes. There was also lots of mock paper money and mock *yuanbao* (a shoe-shaped gold and silver ingot used as money in feudal China) and incense sticks. The mock *yuanbao* were sorted into piles of 16 (making 1 *jin*) and the mock paper money was also sorted into piles of 100 *yuan* each. These items had been given by the family members and close relatives who had attended the first seventh-day ritual. They sorted out who gave what based on a list, just as when preparing a daughter's dowry.

Five families of agnatic kin and 12 families of non-agnatic kin were invited for the event. As in other major family events the agnatic kin were helpers and came with 10 *yuan* gift money and much lesser gifts than each non-agnatic kin family. Each non-agnatic kin family came with 25 *yuan* gift money and a basketful of gifts such as fish, pork, tofu, eggs, rice cakes, steamed stuffed buns and paper money. They were given some returning gifts in their basket: two rice cases and two eggs, and 10 per cent respectively from the 10 and 25 *yuan* for their efforts in dressing up in mourning clothes and performing in the ritual .

At 11:00 the Taoist priest put the deceased's tablet (*paiwei*) into a small box. He also wrote a few envelopes with letters of introduction to the god of the dead, the land god and so on. The Taoist priest guided all the people through the rest of the rituals (Photo III-19). They put on mourning clothes and wailed around the altar table. They burned some paper money and mock *yuanbao* together with the envelopes, which the priest had written earlier inside the house. They then blew out the oil lamp and removed offerings from the altar table and brought the paper items into the courtyard (Photo III-20). There they burned more mock objects: money, paper clothes, foot warmer, bedding, beds and houses, together with some real clothes in front of the house. While the things were burning XQ and his wife, sister, sister-in-law and quasi sister walked around and around the fire after the priest. They also chanted with him. Finally they took off the mourning clothes they had worn while they were walking and shook the dust from them into the fire (Photo III-21).

Then they set off firecrackers. This is how they sent off their mother's soul and possessions into heaven and separated themselves completely from her. At the same time they prayed to the heavenly gods and other spiritual beings to bless them.

In order to celebrate XQ Wang's dead mother's reunion with her dead husband and other dead relatives the family invited 5 families of agnatic kin and 12 families of non-negative kin for a family feast. As with other family events, their male and female agnatic kin helped with the feast before and afterwards, and brought 10 *yuan* gift money from each family, and small gifts. Each non-agnatic family brought 25 *yuan* gift money and a basket full of gifts: fish, pork, tofu, egg, rice cake, steamed bun and mock paper money (the plain baskets in photo III-10 were used for this event). After the event the guests took their baskets home with them with small returning gifts from the hostess, such as two pieces of rice case and two eggs. In addition, everybody would return with 10 per cent of 10 *yuan* or 25 *yuan* as a tip to thank them for wearing mourning clothes during the events.

Photos III-18 and 19. The Taoist priest releases souls from purgatory for the dead person and guides family members in their performance of the ritual, respectively

Photos III-20 and 21. The paper house and bedding were burned and they took off their mourning clothes

After lunch the priest moved his paraphernalia from the living room to the kitchen. He set up 6 small wine cups, 6 pairs of chopsticks, 6 rice cakes, 3 apples, 3 smoked tofu (*xundougan*), 2 candles and a bunch of incense sticks on the stove. He then chanted scriptures and burned two sets of mock *yuanbao* (eight per set) and kitchen inscription tablets. The son and grandson bowed with their knees bended three times. This ritual was to report to the kitchen god.

It was then time to worship the ancestors. They all went back to the living room. In the middle of the room was a table with four small wine cups, and four pairs of chopsticks, on each side of both its east and west ends. On the north side there were three wine cups and three pairs of chopsticks and on the south there were two bowls. There were three steamed stuffed buns and two cakes on each plate at the four corners of the table. On the middle was a bowl of soup and four dishes of food. There was also a candle. Everybody bowed, facing to the north of the table. They then hung their deceased father's picture on the west wall beside pictures of the newly deceased mother and bowed to them. This meant that from then onwards the father and mother would live together again in the underworld.

This ritual was mainly attended by family members, close agnatic kin and close females among non-agnatic kin. The evening feast was the main meal. All the non-agnatic kin's male members and children now joined in as well. The feast is to celebrate that the deceased has settled in the nether world.

3. Wearing the mourning material (*daixiao*)

Different mourning clothes and materials were worn during the funeral and post-funerary rituals. Some traditions had been kept from fthe time of Fei's *Peasant Life in China*, 1939, such as the son, daughter-in-law, daughter and son-in-law's heads being wound with a long white belt reaching down to the ground (Photo III-22), and short belts being worn by grandchildren (Fei, 1939:75). But instead of the son's generation wearing coarse hempen cloth and the grandchildren wearing white clothes I saw that they all wore white clothes and long and short white clothes to distinguish between male and female. This adaptation is for a practical reason. Long white clothes are a doctor's and chef's uniform, which are much easier to buy or borrow than to get coarse hempen cloth. During the funeral period all the agnatic kin and non-agnatic kin are asked to wear mourning clothes, but friends only need to put a piece of black cloth on their arms.

Photo III-22. A traditional mourning cloth

On the ritual of the fifth seventh day (in Wang's case, the third), family members and close agnatic kin and non-agnatic kin were also requested to wear mourning clothes. After the ritual only members of the family and close relatives continued to wear them. In the Wang family's case I saw the son wear mourning shoes (shoes specially made with white cloth on the front of the upper) after the third or the fifth seventh-day ritual. I was told he would continue to do so for six months or a year depending on how well the shoes were made. The son must wear them all the time until they wear out. Each daughter or daughters-in-law wore a small bow of knitting wool on their hair for one to three years. The grandchildren's generation wore a little black cloth on an arm, and the great grandchildren's generation wore a little red cloth on an arm. Wearing the mourning materials served the functions of remembering the deceased, accompanying the deceased in his/her separate world and averting evil from evil spirits for both the living and the dead.

4. Sweeping a grave at the Qingming Festival for the first three years (*shangfen*)

On the 4 April it was the first time for the Wang family to sweep the grave for the newly passed away mother who had joined her ancestors. According to the local custom "do the sevens" and sweep the grave, the participants must be an odd number. One reason XQ Wang's deceased father's apprentice did not take part in the "do the sevens" ritual was because there were five people already. He would have had to come if XQ Wang's younger brother had not died, which would make seven of them in total. In theory all the people who attended the ritual of the first seventh day should all come again for each of the three sweepings of the grave. However, XQ Wang's younger brother's wife, his sister-in-law, couldn't make it and the quasi daughter gave up sweeping the grave as well in order to make an odd number. So three adults, that is XQ, and his wife and sister, went to sweep the grave. Children were also allowed to join them if they kept to an odd number, but they didn't come because they were in school.

On the morning of the Qingming Festival I saw that XQ, carrying a gravestone on his shoulder, walked ahead, followed by his wife who carried a basketful of fruit, incense sticks, candles, paper money, sugar and bowls in one hand, and a thermos flask of boiled water in the other. His sister carried a plastic bag with apples, bananas, incense sticks and mock *yuanbao* (shoe-shaped money) in one hand, and a stool in the other. They went to the graveyard. XQ fixed the gravestone in front of the grave, side by side with his father's. They put offerings on the stool, burned incense sticks, candles, mock money and bowed. Lastly, they drank sugar water and poured the sugar water around the grave. Thus the grave sweep finished. They needed to carry this out for a further two years before the sweep grave ritual would be completed. The post-funerary rituals are then completed (Photo II-23).

Photo III-23. Sweeping a grave at Qingming festival

According to custom they do not need to do anything any more for the grave, but should let their parents rest in peace and never disturb them again.

III.III. Annual cycle events

I lived in Kaixiangong Village for only three months, too short a time to observe everything throughout a year. Therefore, the list of annual cycle events comes partly from my observation and partly from my informants records that were made either when I was there or after I came back to the UK via post-fieldwork. There are many different kinds of yearly based rituals or events which I have placed into five categories: annual production cycle events, annual everyday cycle events, festivals and customary events, ancestor worship, and worship of local gods.

1. Annual production cycle events

Among the many yearly based production events there are three kinds which normally involve social support: agricultural production, raising silkworms and raising rabbits.

(1) Agricultural production

When I was there from February to May the main agricultural products were rapeseed and wheat (Photos III-24 and 25).

Photos III-24 and 25.Rapeseed and wheat

Fei Xiaotong (1939:152–53) listed two busy seasons in farming. There still are, but at different times of year and for different products. In 1996 the first busy season was from 20 May to 30 June for harvesting wheat, barley and rapeseed, sowing seeds, planting young shoots in nursery farms, transplanting rice, and raising spring silkworms. Labour support was important at this time. The second busy season in farming was from 20 October to 15 November, and involved harvesting rice, reaping, husking, storing rice and sowing seeds of wheat, barley, and rapeseed, all however almost without labour support.

The wheat, barley and some of the rapeseed were needed by villagers to pay their obligation to the State in respect of their contracted State-owned land. Threshing needed labour help because there were only 1 or 2 big threshers for wheat per group, and 4 or 5 families share one small thresher within a group of about 30 households. Normally this kind of support would involve 4 or 5 households and they would help each other in turn. They called this kind of labour support labourers' exchange (*huangong*). However, it has recently changed (see "Social creativity" in section IX.III).

Sowing seeds, planting young shoots in nursery farms, and transplanting rice seedlings are important because this is only a once a year plant grain for eating. This work involved less labour support from others. Traditionally, after harvest and before the rice seedling transplant, villagers would hold a feast for the people involved in the labour support. They can be relatives, both agnate and non-agnate kin, neighbours and fellow villagers. This feast cannot be considered grand because an upper part of pig leg (*tizi*) is not required.

(2) Raising silkworms

The history of raising silkworms in the area goes back 4,700 years (Liu, 1996:429). It is an important sideline production. Silkworms were normally raised four times a year, spring silkworms, summer silkworms, early autumn silkworms and late autumn silkworms. However, villagers had not raised summer silkworms for many years because silkworms produce far fewer cocoons in hot weather. The most important period is the raising of spring silkworms from 20 May to 30 June.

In mid-May before I left the village I saw many red ribbons shaped like small bow ties hung on trees around villagers' houses, a bit like Christmas decorations. The villagers told me they were called "silkworm flowers" (Photo III-26). This custom is for keeping evil spirits away from the silkworms and to ensure easy production from the period of incubation all the way to harvest. They also told me that there is a temple for the Silkworm Goddess Leizu in Shengze Township. People who lived there would pray to the goddess, but Kaixiangong villagers would only go to the temple if it fitted in with other business in Shengze. On the 1st or 15th of a lunar month a minority of villagers will go to local temples to pray, but most families simple follow the custom of hanging silkworm flowers.

Photo III-27 shows women worked in a hatchery sorting silkworms' eggs. They were redistrabuted by their head of group in the dawn. I was told that at the stage of hatching eggs social support is involved. In the village every 3 to 4 or 7 to 8 households on average share each hatchery, which is a small room in a private house. The facilities in a hatchery were well sterilised and disinfected, and temperature and humidity were well controlled.

Photo III-26. "Silkworm flowers" on trees

Photo III-27, Women sorting out silkworm eggs

BY Zhou told me that 11 households shared her hatchery. Two of them were agnate kin, two non-agnate kin, two fellow villagers, and five households from a neighbouring group. They sent their share of eggs from a group head's house to her hatchery as soon as they had collected them. The newly-hatched silkworms needed to be fed four times a day around 09:00, 15:00, 21:00 and 03:00. During the first few days BY got up at 03:00 to feed the silkworms. Other families made appointments for the other three feeding times. Normally they collected their silkworms and brought them back to their own houses to raise after two weeks. If a family had any kind of family event the silkworms had to stay in BY's house for one more week. This kind of support happened twice a year, in the spring and late autumn. It was not needed in the early autumn because the weather was warm enough for households to hatch eggs without hatcheries. BY and the 11 households supported each other using an exchange involving labour, materials and even premises.

(3) Raising rabbits

Raising rabbits had become an important sideline production in the village. On his second visit to Kaixiangong in 1956 Fei found a shift from raising sheep to raising rabbits. Instead of 1,000 sheep in 1936 there were 1,000 rabbits in 1956. Rabbits provided a reasonable income with much less risk and costs (1986:230). On his third visit to Kaixiangong in 1981 Fei noticed that 50 per cent of total villagers' income was derived from sideline production including the raising of rabbits (1986:259). In 1981 Wujiang County's export of rabbits' hair was equal to that of silk. According to Liu, from the 1980s to middle of the 1990s the State purchasing price of rabbits' hair remained steady at between 60 to 80 *yuan* per kg. In 1995 there were a total of 5,500 rabbits in the village which produced 2,200 kg of hair (1996:464-65). In my sampled households, 91 per cent of families raised rabbits, varying from 6 to more than 23.

I observed the cutting of rabbits' hair in Ni's family. Four women including Ni were working together. Ni told me that her family raised 14 rabbits, which brought 1,750 yuan income in 1995. They needed to shear each rabbit's hair every 55 days, which means 7 times per year on average. It needed three or four people to cut the hair and it was normally women's job to do this. After the shearing, Ni held a tea party for her helpers (Photos III-28 and 29). During the teatime they told me the tea was a reward for their hard work. They helped each other in turns. The three helpers were one agnate kin and two neighbours of Ni's family.

Photo III-28 and 29. Four women in Ni's family cutting rabbits' hair and having a tea party afterwards

2. Annual life cycle events

The annual life cycle events I will describe are those which relate to the lifestyle of the villagers and which are repeated on a yearly basis and which engage an element of social support. They are: peeling soya beans, making rice cakes and conditioning silk-quilted roll-neck jerseys.

(1) Peeling soya beans

Peeling fresh soya beans (*bo qingdou*) was normally done from 20 September to 15 October every year. It is not a large event but did involve labour support. As a speciality of the village, smoked soya bean (*xun qingdou*) is an important ingredient served with tea throughout the year. Since peeling fresh soya beans is a very boring task women would normally gather together to chat while they worked. Jin told me that to get 5 *jin* of smoked soya bean 30 *jin* of fresh soya beans must be peeled, taking half a day's work for 5 women. After they had finished peeling the beans she held a tea party (*xinkucha*) in recognition of the helpers' hard work. Note that this kind of tea party is similar to the one after cutting rabbits' hair, but unlike that after the Harvest of Green Beans (*xinkucha*) which was purely for enjoyment (Chapter IV.I).

As a reciprocal task she peeled soya beans with five other families. Jin's partners were more or less the same every year. The team can be formed by agnate kin, non-agnate kin, neighbours, friends or fellow villagers. In my sampled households 87.5 per cent of them had such yearly based labour support.

The way in which the villagers arranged such an event makes me think of a notice in a school's newsletter in London, which reads "We need volunteers to cut out the 'free books for schools vouchers' from the crisp packets we have collected so that we can send off for more books. Come with a friend to chat as you work. Coffee will be provided!" The difference is that in Kaixiangong this arrangement is regarded as a kind of labour exchange and the helpers worked in turns with each other's families, whereas cutting out the free books vouchers was a one-off occasion.

(2) Making rice cakes

"Rice cakes flow" (*gaolai gaoqu*) is another analogy for *zou renqing* or expressive *wanglai* in Kaixiangong. I spent one afternoon watching four women making rice cakes, and learnt the names of the different types of rice cakes and their different usages (photos III-30 and 31). There were different types of rice cake for different events, both annual cycle and life-cycle events. These rice cakes can be classified into three types: dried rice cakes, rice balls and *zongzi* (a pyramid-shaped dumpling made of glutinous rice wrapped in bamboo leaves).

Photos III-30 and 31. Four women making two differently coloured rice balls together

Dried rice cakes include *yunpiangao*, *shuigao* and *gaobing*. *Yunpiangao* is a kind of rice cake in thin strips which is used as a gift for visiting newborn babies or as a return gift after a wedding banquet. *Shuigao* is a flatt-ish rectangular (4x4x2cm) rice cake with or without fillings inside or with different patterns on top. *Shuigao* can be used in the one-month old birth celebration; on this occasion it has a red square pattern made of thin dried fruit slices on top. It has one small red spot in the middle for a completed house celebration, fillings of red bean mash and mixed dried fruit thin slices for a family division, 16 Chinese characters on each cake with 4 of them joined as one group for betrothal rites. These characters are *changming fugui* (long life, riches and honour), *chenxin ruyi* (very gratifying and satisfactory) and *zaosheng guizi* (have a child sooner). *Gaobing* is a kind of circular rice cake similar in size to the *shuigao* but with different kinds of small flowers patterned on top of each. However, among these different kind of rice cake only one involved labour support, because it could not be bought on the market. I watched three women spend a whole afternoon making *gaobing*. They were made using a wooden model about 3 inches wide and one foot long including the handle. Each model had three different patterns which made a full set of these rice cakes.[68] According to local custom, a household should distribute a set of such *gaobing* to neighbours or fellow villagers whenever it holds an event. Thus labour support is involved whenever a family needs to make a large quantity of *gaobing*.

Rice balls include *tuanzi* (a 6 cm diameter big rice ball with red bean mash filling) and *yuanzi* (a small 3 cm diameter rice ball without fillings) which has two different colours: white and green dyed with pumpkin leaves. They were given different names for different events, such as *atai tuanzi* or *atai yuanzi* for the one-month birthday celebration, *waisheng tuanzi* for asking for a school bag from *jiujiu* (mother's brother), *nuxu tuanzi* for parents-in-law to give to a son-in-law after the newly married couple's first visit. A child's sixteenth birthday, completing a house and so on also involved rice balls. Making them would normally involve labour support from three or four people.

Zongzi is a pyramid-shaped dumpling made of glutinous rice wrapped in bamboo leaves and is eaten every year during the Dragon Boat Festival. As well as this, in Kaixiangong *zongzi* are made on many other occasions, for example the Pure Brightness Festival (the 5th of the 24 solar terms on the 4, 5 and 6 April, see Chapter III.III, three events of house construction,

---

[68] The model is not available from a market. Qiu told me that her grandfather, a handyman, made it for her family and also made it for others.

funerals and so on. All the above events need a large quantity of *zongzi,* which naturally involves labour support. Liu told me that unlike making rice balls which almost everyone can do, *zongzi* requires special skill. and labour support is especially important. So in her family the team for making rice balls or rice cakes was different from the team for making *zongzi.*, and more difficult to arrange. Photos III-32 and 33 were taken randomly when I passed two houses: in one house *zongzi* are being made for an event in house construction, and in the other for the Pure Brightness Festival.

Photos III-32 and 33. Two occasions when villagers help each other making *zongzi*

(3) Conditioning silk-quilted roll-neck jerseys

Wearing silk-quilted roll-neck jerseys was a new fashion in the village from the early 1990s. The villagers wore them underneath a normal jacket or suit. Dressing in this way, for everyday winter use, replaced traditional cotton-quilted overcoats, being warmer, lighter in weight, more comfortable, convenient and slimmer looking. In contrast, I looked cumbersome and even more of an outsider because I always needed to wear a down jacket, both outdoors and indoors indoors because the villagers never close their main entrance door. Villagers don't condition new quilted roll-neck jerseys for each member of the family every year, but in a 4-person family each member would get a new silk-quilted jersey on average once every four years, making it a regular annual task involving labour support.

The jersey was made of two cotton roll-neck jerseys with a silk quilt in the middle as a sandwich. Zhou told me that she conditioned silk-quilted roll-neck jerseys (*fanyi*) in October and removed the quilt to wash the jerseys (*chaiyi*) in April every year. *Chaiyi* could be done all by herself, but *fanyi* needed another person to help because two people were needed to stretch and smooth the silk quilt. Each jacket needs 3 to 5 *liang* (150 to 250g) of silk, depending on the size. Her family has 5 people and she needs to condition 5 such tops, and a pair of trousers for her

70-year old father. Silk-quilted roll-neck jerseys had become part of the village lifestyle so it is natural that women would help each other as a labour exchange. After the work they had a cup of tea – not a "tea party" because only two people were involved.

3. Festivals and customary events

I now come to annual cycle festivals and customary events, in seasonal sequence.

The Chinese New Year period is from the lunar New Year's Day to the 15th day of the 1st lunar month. Traditionally on the 1st day of the 1st lunar month people let off a string of small firecrackers as soon as they get up. This is for keeping evil away and for having a good harvest and happy life. Traditionally the villagers eat rice balls with fillings (*tangtuan*), small rice balls without fillings (*xiao yuanzi*), or rice cake with sugar (*tangniangao*) and noodles for breakfast, a meal that symbolises the reunion of family members and a sweet and long life. I was told this was a customary day for people to worship local gods and the kitchen god. Some families would have a reception for the kitchen god. The day should be a quiet and relaxed time during which no tools should be touched and no people should be met.

From the 2nd day onwards people start to have feasts and tea with relatives, neighbours, friends and fellow villagers. Weddings also take place during this period. In 1996 villagers told me that their family events, such as weddings or Chinese New Year's feasts between relatives, started from the 1st day of the lunar month and all the way through to the 15th day of the lunar month. It was also customary for all the neighbours to invite each other to chat and eat snacks at tea parties. Photo III-34 shows a tea party at the Shen's family. Unlike most tea parties which are normally held in the afternoon, this one was in the evening because Mrs Shen worked at a village-run enterprise and had to work there in the afternoon. The photo shows that there were two men at the party. They told me they were representing their families because their wives were doing housework at home.

Photo III-34. A tea party was held in the Shen's family home during 1996 Lunar New Year period

An old man told me that in the old society (before 1949) there were two religious events during this period. One was called *jielutou* (birthday of five road gods: east, west, south, north and middle) and was held on the 5th day. Villagers met in the streets to burn incense, light fireworks, and beat drums and gongs boisterously. They hoped that the road gods would bless them so that business would go smoothly. The next was called *mengjianghui* (*mengjiang* is another way to address *liuwan* or *liuhuang*), on the 13th day. *Luiwan* spells *liuhuang* in modern *pinying*. "*Lui* being the personal name of the god and *wan* meaning king…The god, *luiwan*, is the supernatural protector against the local menace" (Fei, 1939:103). There is another slightly different version, which has it that originally Liu came from Liu Rui, a General of the Song Dynasty, famous for driving off plagues of locusts (Xu, 1996:195). People met at temples to burn incense, candles, paper money and to pray for the harvest.

On the 15th day is the *yuanxiao* festival or lantern festival. I was surprised that the villagers were very quiet at this festival, marking it only by making rice balls with different fillings (*yuanxiao yuanzi*). Some families worship local gods and the kitchen god twice a lunar month, on the 1st and 15th days. A villager told me that they never play with lanterns because it would be dangerous. This is borne out by the county general records. In 1915 the lantern festival was forbidden by the local government because it caused a serious fire (Wujiang Xianzhi, 1994:792).

On the 2nd day of the 2nd lunar month the villagers cut dried rectangle-shaped rice cake into slices and fry them in shallow oil. The rice cake should be eaten with brown sugar and walnuts. This is called *eryue er cheng yaogao*. This practice improves adults' waists and backs, according to local custom. The 29th day of the 2nd lunar month is the Buddhist Guanyin (*guanyi niannian*)'s birthday. Some women go to the temple to burn candles, paper money, and to bow to the goddess.

On the 3rd day of the 3rd lunar month the villagers place mustard flowers (*jiecai ua*) at various vantage points (*sanyue san cha jiecaihua)*: in women's hair (of any age) to cure headache, on the top of the stove to keep ants away from it, on bedsides to keep evil under control (*yaxie*), and so on.

Qingming festival (the 5th of the 24 solar terms) for worshipping ancestors is later on in the 3rd lunar month. A new practice has sprung up to use this season to pay respects to parents-in-law, and prospective parents-in-law. New tea comes onto the market immediately after the *qingming* festival. A male fiancé should bring new tea and fresh fruit when he visits his future parents-in-law. Married couples should visit the wife's parents-in-law (*niangjia*) together, with new tea and fresh fruit. The symbolic meaning of these acts is to wish that their lives be full of youthful vigour. A villager told me of another new custom dating from 1995, that the mother-in-law also gives the son-in-law gifts, such as the upper part of a leg of pork, or a handkerchief.

When the new tea becomes available every female villager would arrange tea parties for neighbours, friends and fellow villagers (see section of "Neighbours and fellow villagers" later). Photo III-35 shows one of the tea parties held to enjoy the new tea. All the families in the same group took a turn to be hosts. Some people said the best tea would be the tea-leaves that were just picked off from the tea tree before the Qingming Festival or Sweeping Grave Day (between 4 and 6 April) (*mingqiancha*). Others said the broader meaning for *mingqiancha* can be three days before and after the Qingming Festival. They commented on how the same variety of tea could have a different taste according to when the leaves are picked. They also talked about different varieties of tea and ways of serving tea. This kind of tea party had the nature of being for pure enjoyment, in contradistinction to the tea parties held after peeling green beans or cutting rabbits' hair.

Photo III-35. A tea party held after new tea became available on the market

During the period of the 3rd and 4th lunar month there used to be a local play (*chuntaixi*, see the section about the Spring Performance). Some performances were still held as village public entertainment during this time of the year, but the time could also vary. In 1996 I watched two kinds of performance. One was on the ground by a bridge, just as Fei Xiaotong describes: the village had no specific place for public life and informal gatherings were held on open ground by a bridge (1939: 19–20). Another took place in a warehouse. Photos III-36 and 37 show such performances (for details see Chapter IV.III "Cultural life" in the section of vertical *wanglai*).

Photos III-36 and 37. Performances on the ground and stage in March 1996.

The Beginning of Summer (*lixia*) is the day marking the beginning of the 7th of the solar term (5, 6 or 7 May) on the 4th lunar month. It is the second festival "for human beings" according to local custom (the first is the Spring festival)[69]. It is also the wine god's birthday and men may drink as much rice wine as they like at the family feast. Villagers also call this feast the fresh food tasting (*lixia changxin*). The food includes *tabing* (a steamed, small, round thin green-coloured cake made with malt, *ziniantou* – a fresh herb, mashed soya bean and glutinous rice powder), *doufan* (boiled rice with fresh broad beans), salted duck eggs, yellow crackers or rice-field eel, deep fried bean curd, fried fresh vegetables such as three-coloured amaranth, and garlic cloves. A newly married-out daughter should visit her natal family with summer clothes and a summer sleeping mat of woven split bamboo. Some children go by themselves to visit their mother's brother (*jiujiu*)'s family for the feast of the Beginning of Summer. On that day children under the age of 16 are weighed. They also gather together for a picnic which is called *yehuofan* (Photos III-38 and 39).

Photos III-38 and 39. Children picking up broad beans and cooking *yehuofan*

The 5th day of the 5th lunar month is the traditional Chinese Dragon Boat Festival. It has never been a big event in this village. The villagers present ball-shaped rice cakes (*tuanzi*) and deep fried peach-shaped rice cakes with red bean paste fillings (*shoutao*) to the kitchen god. They also burn incense and candles on their stoves. There is normally a family feast. They eat *zongzi* (a pyramid-shaped dumpling made of glutinous rice wrapped in bamboo leaves) and *zhizhudan* (boiled egg with a spider in egg white which is put in while the egg is raw). The spider is not for eating but for good luck. There is a saying *wuyue wu mai tiao huangyu guo duanwu* which means that this is the day for yellow crackers at the family feast. At the feast

---

[69] There are four days or festivals designed for dead people, they are called ancestor worships (*bai shangzu*) or festivals for the dead (*siren jie*).

there are also dishes such as fried bean curd with garlic leaves. Some older children would wear a necklace made of garlic cloves. Children under one year old should wear a tiger hat, clothes and shoes. A villager N told me that the materials for making the tiger suit should be provided by the child's maternal uncle (*jiujiu*). Its construction can involve labour support because some people do not have this skill and have to ask others to do it. Recently, people can now buy these suits from the town market. The reason for wearing the tiger suit is to keep mosquitoes away from the child (Photos III-40 and 41).

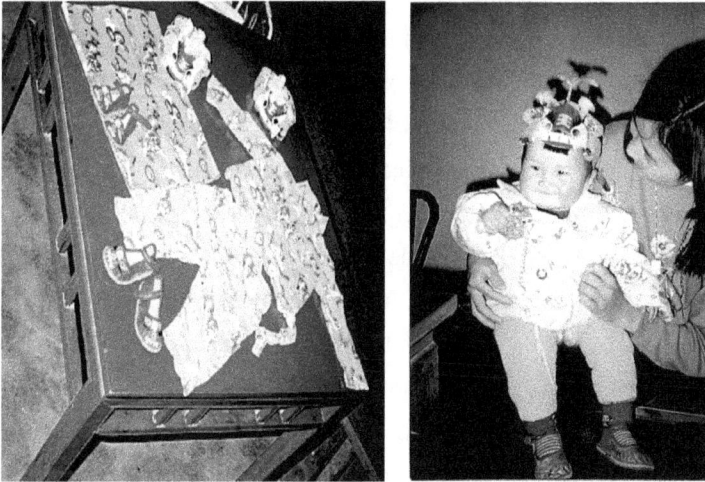

Photos III-40 and 41. A tiger suit and a baby wearing a tiger hat

On the 6th day of the 6th lunar month there is a saying *liuyue liu mai lai huntun liu yi liu*. *Liu yi liu* is similar to *liuyue liu* (6th of the 6th lunar month) in pronunciation and means to visit informally. *Huntun* is a speciality of Southern China. In comparison with dumpling (*jiaozi*), a similar speciality of Northern China, it has much thinner wrappings and is eaten with flavoured soup. *Huntun* and noodles are normally eaten on this day. It is the birthday of pets, cats and dogs. On this day villagers have a shower for cats, dogs and themselves. The y also lay items such as beds, clothes and books out to freshen in the sun.[70] During this month there is another custom called *jiujiu mai qizi*. *Qizi* means seven kinds of fruit or nuts with *zi* (seed or core): oranges (*juzi*), pears (*lizi*), peaches (*taozi*), plums (*lizi*), Chinese dates (*zaozi*), red bayberries (*meizi*) and

---

[70] However, for some reason in 1996 I saw very few pets, hardly ever dogs, although when I was there in 2004 dogs were everywhere. I was told this is because so many outsiders / strangers (migrants) worked in the village since 1998. Dogs could keep strangers away if they were thieves.

watermelon seeds (*guazi*). From 2000 onwards the villagers have also included items without "*zi*", such as bananas and candied fruits, that have become fashionable. Normally a mother's brother should buy seven kinds of fruit for his sister's child or children. The mother's brother (*jiujiu*) should also bring firecrackers together with the fruits. If a child's father has been taken as a son-in-law, the father's sister (*gugu*) should buy *qizi* for the child.

On the 7th day of the 7th lunar month people should cut a watermelon according to the saying *qiyue qi nage xigua qie yi qie*. This is the way in which the villagers celebrate the harvest of watermelons and keep cool on hot days. Also girls and women should gather balsam from their own courtyard and use it overnight to paint their fingernails red. An old woman remembered that when she was young her mother showed her how to put an embroidery needle into a big bowl and beg from the Weaving-girl star (Vega) for wisdom. The 15th and 30th day of the 7th lunar month are important days for ancestors and land gods.

The 8th day of the 8th lunar month is in the harvest season of *ling* or water caltrop (*bayue ba nage ling lai bo yi bo*). The day is set aside for people to pick and enjoy it.   On the 15th day of the 8th lunar month there is a traditional Chinese Moon Day festival or middle moon festival, *tuanyuanjie*, at which local gods and the kitchen god are worshipped. People normally present apples, pairs, and peaches, and of course some moon cakes on their stoves. They also burn incense, candles, and bow to the local gods including the kitchen god. A villager told me that the Moon Day Festival has been an official traditional festival for a long time so they just simply fit it in their everyday life without creating any special food for their dinner on this day. According to local custom, on this day the youngest generation (*xiaobei*) should give moon cakes and fruits as presents to older generations (*zhangbei*), and married-out daughters should visit their natal families with similar presents for their parents.

On the 9th day of the 9th lunar month the villagers make rice cakes with newly harvested glutinous rice which is called *jiuyue jiu chongyang gao*. A villager told me this day is designed in autumn for celebrating the harvest. Villagers call autumn "gold autumn" for two reasons: the colour of mature grain is similar to a that of gold and autumn also illustrates that a person is becoming older. So the custom is in accord with a traditional Chinese Double Ninth Festival (*chongyang jie*), which in particular marks respect to the elderly.

In the 10th lunar month people make rice wine known as *shiyue zhong niangjiu*, which they drink with their family feast, again to celebrate harvest.

Dongzhi (the winter solstice – 22nd of the 24 solar terms; 21, 22 or 23 December) is normally in the 11th lunar month. As well as performing ancestor worship (see next section) villagers hold a family feast and invite any married-out daughters' families to join it. Villagers believe it is the longest night in the year so they finish the feast early and sleep early. There is also a custom called *dan dongzhi fan* which means people giving presents of a basket of food to each other. This normally happens on the *Dongzhi*'s Eve among relatives, neighbours, friends and fellow villagers.

On the 8th day of the 12th lunar month people eat *laba zhou* (rice porridge with beans, nuts, and dried fruit; eaten on the day). This food originally came from the temple. Buddhist monks and nuns cooked such porridge mixed with vegetables, peanuts, ginkgo, red date and rice to ward off calamities and remove illness from worshippers. On the 23rd day is the ceremony for the kitchen god (see related section). There are several ceremonies around the end of the 12th lunar month. I will omit the ceremonies for local gods, ancestors, and family reunion feasts here and show instead a ritual related to a local goddess. On 28th, 29th or 30th day of the 12th lunar month a few families worship a goddess (*lizimo*). *Lizi* is a popular name for *jili* (good luck). *Mo* is the local way to address a lady, in this case the local goddess. A woman told me that she presents offerings on a table in the front living room. At the end of the table she lays twelve handleless small wine cups in a line with Shaoxing wine in each cup. In the middle of the table a whole pig head is presented. Around it are fruits and cakes. At the front of the table there is an incense burner on the left and two candles on the right. A little wooden bench is set one metre away from the front of the table and faces the middle of the table for people to kneel down (*guibai*) to worship the goddess. On the right-hand side some paper money is burned in an enamel basin or simply on the cement ground surface. The woman also told me that not many families worship the *lizi* goddess in the village. So, according to local custom, there is a flexibility that allows different arrangements to each family during the period from the end of the lunar year and beginning of the lunar New Year, as I mention in the section on kitchen god worship.

All these annual events and rituals show that the villagers' everyday life is varied and colourful. There are supplements to the main rituals for local gods, ancestors, and people. For example, both the worship for *lizimo* at the lunar New Year Eve and birthday of Buddhism Guanyin at the 2nd lunar month are for goddesses. On the day of the Dragon Festival the villagers also worship their ancestors. The events regarded as being for human beings are of many types from the baby's tiger hat, girls painting their fingernails, the children's picnic, women's flowers, men's *yaogao* (a kind of rice cake), to parents-in-law's new tea, elderly day, swapping around gifts to neighbours, friends and fellow villagers, to family reunion and harvest ceremonies.

4. Ancestor worship

In the village, ancestor worship was called "*jizu*", "*baishangzu*", "*sirenjie*" (festivals for the dead), and "*guo sijie*" (four festivals for ancestors). The four festivals are on four special dates: Chinese New Year Eve, the Qingming Festival (between 4 and 6 April), the 15th day of the seventh lunar month and the Dongzhi Festival (between 21 and 23 December), dates based sometimes on the lunar calendar and sometimes on the twenty-four solar terms.

The first ritual of ancestor worship is on the lunar New Year's Eve. I spent my first day with the family of the head of the Women's Federation of the Village, BY Zhou. BY's stepfather[71] was preparing the lunar New Year's Eve feast (*nianyefan*). Before the meal started I noticed that he was setting up a table for a ritual, which he told me that it was for the worship of ancestors (*baishangzu*). The table was a standard size of a square metre (*baxianzhuo*), which allows a maximum of eight people to eat together. It stood in the middle of the hall (a living / dining room). Three long thin wooden benches were placed on the back, left and right sides of the table. Four small handleless wine cups and four pairs of chopsticks were at the back edge of the table, three cups and three pairs of chopsticks were on both left and right sides. At the front side of the table there were candle sets on each side. There was a small stool facing the middle of the table. On the right-hand side next to the stool was an old enamel washbowl for burning papers. The offering sacrifices were presented in the middle of the table on five large dishes: an upper part of pork leg (*tizi*), fish, pork meat balls, bean sprouts and Chinese leaves (Photo III-42)[72] 。

---

[71] Her mother passed away.

[72] This is a not the original photo because it was damaged and the replacement came from another occasion.

The worship of ancestors[73] was very simple. BY's stepfather poured liquor and rice wine into the wine cups, lighted candles and burnt paper. He then bowed three times with palms put together held in front of his chest (*baibai*), facing the dining table where the sacrifices and candles were presented. He also knelt at the wooden bench to bow three more times (*guibai*). The rest of the family members took turns to worship their ancestors in the same way. After the worship

Photo III-42. A standard table setting for worshipping ancestors

BY reset the table for the family's New Year's Eve feast. There were seven more dishes carried on the table and the lunar New Year's Eve feast started. They told me that all the members of the extended family, namely, a brother or his family, were requested to share the feast, and in this way maintain relationships between each other through reference to the ancestors.

The second ritual of ancestor worship is the Qingming festival. It is traditionally observed as a festival for worshipping at ancestral graves, technically known as "sweeping the graves or Tomb-sweeping Day". The festival itself is very simple but lasts for a few days. It was said in the village that the 5th of the solar term can be any day of three days, the 4th, 5th or 6th April, but the festival itself always lasts for four days (*santian qingming sitian jie*). For example, in 1996 the 5th solar term was on the 4th April and the villagers started the preparation for the festival on the 1st April. The sacrifices offered to their own ancestors must be *zongzi* (a pyramid-shaped dumpling made of glutinous rice wrapped in bamboo leaves) and fruit. It would take at least one or two days to wrap a large quantity of them. The ritual on the Qingming is very like that on the lunar New Year's Eve. Members of the family light candles, burn paper and bow to the ancestors with bent knees, followed by a family feast. According to local custom if a family member has died within three years then all the members of the family should gather together to sweep the graves (*shangfen*), but not otherwise. There are many other customs related to sweeping the graves.

The third ritual of ancestor worship is *qiyue ban* (the 15th day of the 7th lunar month),

---

[73] The ancestors included BY's mother.

which is traditionally a ghost festival. According to the villagers, in the nether world gods are always represented as good beings and ghosts as bad beings. Villagers also believe that people's ancestors cannot turn into gods, but could be turned into ghosts if they are treated badly, and the ghost would bring bad luck and evil into their descendents lives. So the ghost festival is a day especially designed for the villagers to express their feelings to their ancestors. They first go to the local temple to burn incense sticks and bow. Then they set up a table for offerings, light candles, burn paper and bow with bent knees. The sacrifices offered to their own ancestors must be *húntún* (a kind of dumpling in Southern China)[74] and square-shaped rice cakes with a red spot on top of each. The ritual ends with a family feast.

In August 2005 when I was in the village I observed such a ghost festival. Photo III-43 shows a feast set up for worshipping ancestors. Photo III-44 shows both mock paper money and *yuanbao*-shaped paper money in the box and basin. After every member of the family had bowed, the offerings were burnt and thus sent to their ancestors. In the Yao family they repeated the same process to worship their former neighbour's ancestors, because after the previous neighbour left they had taken over their courtyards and regarded it as their responsibility. This happened to many families when new houses were built, shared foundation land was no longer shared after family division, or villagers' migrated.

Photos III-43 and 44. A feast and *yuanbao*-shaped paper money for worshipping ancestors at a ghost festival in 2005

The last ritual of ancestor worship is *dongzhi* (the Winter Solstice, the 22nd solar term – 21, 22 or 23 December), which is the day marking the beginning of the 22nd solar term. This time

---

[74] wen ten in Cantonese.

the offered sacrifices are big rice balls with sweet and savoury fillings. As well as offering sacrifices, lighting candles, burning paper and bowing with bent knees, villagers invite married-out daughters' families to join the family feast. They also give small gifts to neighbours, fellow villagers and friends. Fei's comments:

> The general view is that the spirits live in a world very similar to ours, but that economically they are partially dependent on the contributions of their descendents which are made by periodically burning paper money, paper cloths, and paper articles. Therefore it is essential to have someone to look after one's well being in the after-world. (1939:30)

This ritual is very like one that I witnessed in Neiguan village, where it was prescribed that villagers should send clothes and money to their ancestors (*shiyue yi song hanyi*) on the 1st of the 10th lunar month, with the difference that this is one and half months earlier than in Kaixiangong. This difference in custom might due to climatic variations; Neiguan is located in Northwest China, which is much colder than Kaixiangong.

5. Local gods' worship

Local gods' worship includes one "big" (lunar New Year Eve), one "medium" (30th of the seventh lunar month for land god) and 24 regular worships, two a month. For the kitchen god there are two large and two medium worships, plus regular worships twice a month. Figure III-1 shows a comparison of sizes and types of local gods' worships.

Figure III-1 Worship of local gods by size and type

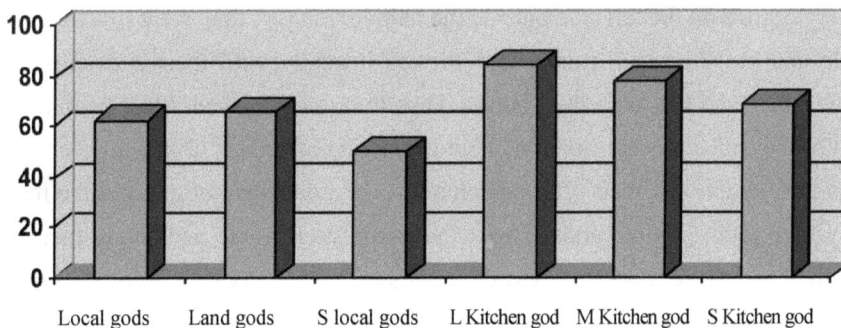

1. Local gods
2. Land gods

3 .S local gods

4. L Kitchen god

5. M Kitchen god

6. S Kitchen god

The biggest ceremony or ritual (*dabai*) for local gods and goddesses is known as *niansanshi qiang touxiang*, which translates as "grab and burn the first incense at the lunar New Year's Eve". After the lunar New Year Eve's feast in BY Zhou's family's house I went to the Grandpa temple (*laotaimiao*) in Miaogang Township with her son, QF Zhou. We got to the temple at around 20:00 and left at 05:00. Inside the temple there were many statues placed on a long, wide altar table. Apart from *Qiu laotaiye*, the local lake god, there were a son and a grandson of his, Bodhisattva Guanyin (*guanshiyin niangniang*), and Maitreya. Local villagers presented many offerings, such as fruits, cakes, and wine. I found that they were almost all brought by women. The women visited the temple and took part in the ritual individually.

I followed many of them through the ritual from beginning to end. It was very simple and informal. They firstly presented the offerings on the altar table. Then they burnt a bunch of incense sticks and held them in front of their chests with both hands and made a deep bow facing the statues of the local gods and goddesses. Some of them performed *kowtow*. They left the rest of the incense sticks in a big incense burner outside the temple. Then they burnt candles and put them on a big candlestick frame and made another bow facing the temple. The candlestick could hold several dozens of candles at a time. Underneath the candlestick there was a big basin half full of water for storing the candle ends safely. Afterwards the women burnt paper money in a big open-style stove on the left side outside the temple. Finally, they went to a big ginkgo tree by the temple and put their hands on it and stroked it gently with their eyes closed. Then they stroked their face and hair with their hands. Thus the ritual finished. Most people went through part or all of the above process, some without presenting offerings, or in a different order. People who came later simply left their offerings on a few extended altar tables after the main table was full. They then took off old candles from the candlestick frame and threw them into the big water basin. There were thousands and thousands of people from different villages continually going to the temple for the ceremony from 19:00 until the early morning of the next day. At that time there some "early birds" who had already arrived with their handcarts to sell spiritual goods （PhotoIII-45）.

A medium-sized ceremony is for the land god on the 30th day of the 7th lunar month, the land god's birthday. Two thirds of the sampled families said that they burned incense sticks and offered sacrifices to the land god (*shang diwangye xiang*). A woman, JY Yao, told me that the reason for worshipping the land god (*bai tudi gonggong*) was because they needed to ask him to forgive them for urinating and defecating everywhere when they were young. So this ritual always involves children who are one year old and above. Normally a grandmother, or a mother if one has no grandmother, leads the ritual.

Photo III-45. A man was selling spiritual goods in the dawn of the lunar New Year

JY told me that she took her grandson to the East Temple. They presented offerings such as apples, pears and lotus root on an altar table and burned candles and paper money there. She also explained to the child that "it was *tudigongong* (grandpa land)'s birthday". They then bowed to the land god, one after the other.

There are twice monthly small worships (*xiaobai*) for local gods and goddesses on the 1st and the 15th days of each lunar month (*chuyi yueban*). The most important small worship that on the lunar New Year's Day, the 1st day of the 1st lunar month. I went to the East Temple at 10 in the morning. It was divided in two. The main statue *guanyin*, a goddess, stood on an altar table in the west side of the temple, and *guandi* was presented in a commanding position on the east side of the temple. Many women worshipped the local gods. One was selling incense sticks, candles, and paper money. I watched another woman who bowed to the statue of *guanyin* on bent knees in front of the altar table. She then burned candles and put them on the candlestick outside the temple. There were two uncovered oil drums full of water underneath the candlestick. Afterwards she went inside the temple again, burned a bunch of incense sticks and held them in front of her chest and bowed to the curtains behind *guandi* and the other statues on the altar table. Then she left the ends of the incense sticks in an incense burner outside the temple. Finally she burnt paper money (*huangtongzhi*) in an open stove by a warehouse wall outside the temples. Other women performed similar actions. For the rest of the small worships throughout a year the villagers repeat the same things in more or less the same way.

The kitchen god is particularly important. Villagers distinguish kitchen god worship (*baizao*) from other kinds of worship (*baishen*, *bailaoye* or *baitai*). In his book *Peasant life in China* Fei has anecdotes about worship of the kitchen god (Fei, 1939:99–102), so I wanted to examine the current relationship between villagers and their kitchen god. There were two big and two medium yearly worships for the kitchen god, and two regular small monthly worships.

The two big worships for the kitchen god are the 3rd day of the 8th lunar month and the 23rd of the 12th lunar month[75]. The first is for his birthday. People present sacrificial offerings such as peach-shaped birthday cakes (*shoutao*), apples, oranges, noodle, lotus root and water caltrop. They also present three small handle-less cups of wine to the kitchen god because they believe he has three heads with three mouths. Then they burn incense sticks, candles, paper, and bow to him.[76] The second big worship is the day on which villagers send the kitchen god on his annual trip to heaven (*songzao*). Instead of a peach-shaped birthday cake, noodles and lotus roots in the sacrificial offerings, people offer rice balls mixed with pumpkin (*huang nanguagao*) and fermented bean curd (*hei doufugan*). This particular day is also called small lunar New Year's Eve (*xiaonianye*) and there is usually a family feast. After the feast people burn incense sticks, candles, paper money, and bow to the kitchen god. With the paper money they also burn the paper inscription of the kitchen god. In this way the kitchen god returns to heaven.

There are two medium kitchen god worships. The first is on the 29th or 30th day of the 12th lunar month, or on the 1st day of the 1st lunar month, when the kitchen god is welcomed back from heaven: the paper inscription of him kept by the stove is replaced with a new one (*jiezao*). Offerings such as small rice balls without fillings (*yuanzi*), fermented bean curd (*hei doufugan*), noodles, and fruits are presented on the stove. They also burn candles, incense sticks, and bow to the new inscription. The second medium worship is actually made up of three ceremonies on separate days, the 3rd, 15th and 24th days of the 6th lunar month. Although this ranks as a "medium" worship villagers treat it much less seriously. Only two-fifths of the sampled families bothered with it. Those that do simply burn candles, incense sticks, no offerings are needed. On these dates it is considered healthy for both males and females to wear shorts in the morning and in the afternoon old men strip to the waist.

Two small kitchen god worships are on the 1st and the 15th days of every lunar month (*chuyi yueban xiaobai*). On these two days the villagers only burn incense sticks and candles on their stoves. This kind of ritual can be held in temples in the Township or in the village, or even at home. Fei also observed this in his fieldwork in the 1930s. He said that each family sends its representative to visit the temples and make sacrifices individually (Fei, 1939:104). Nowadays,

---

[75] Fei said it was on 24th day of the 8th lunar month (1939:100) and it was also the birthday of the kitchen goddess (1939:153).
[76] The ban against paper being burnt in houses or courtyards no longer obtained (Fei, 1939:100–101).

more and more people combine regular worships of the kitchen god with those of other local gods.

III.IV. Emergency events

The ESRC social support project looked at three types of event: family events, emergencies and investment. I omit investment because in 1996 private business was strictly controlled (see section "Kaixiangong Village" of Introduction) and, unsurprisingly, there was very little to observe. Family events have been discussed in Chapter II and the earlier part of Chapter III, so we now come to emergency events, and show what they were, and how they were handled by Kaixiangong villagers.

1. Natural and man-made disasters

Expected natural disasters in Kaixiangong Village are floods, plagues of insects or infectious diseases of animals. Drought is seldom a problem due to the village's location on Lake Tai.

(1) Flood

From the end of June to the middle of July 1991 Wujiang County suffered from the biggest flood of the century. During this 3-week period rainfall was more than 500mm and the water in Lake Tai a full one metre beyond the warning level. Along the embankment beside the village flood-relief channels were needed in some places and higher dams in others.   The Kaixiangong Village Collective enlisted the villagers to fight the flood. Wang, a head of the fifth group, acquired material, thick bamboo tubes for pilings and straw sacks for filling with stone or brick pieces or soil which he brought in by boat. The collective also required each household to contribute five large bags (*shepidai*) filled with soil or broken bricks for reinforcing dykes and dams. Dong, a former head of one of the groups, told me that he led the villagers of his group who worked on the dam day and night for about 20 days to minimise loss of property.

Compared with other villages where many houses collapsed losses at Kaixiangong could have been much worse. But hundreds of *mu* of farmland were inundated. Dong told me that in his own group only 30 *mu* were flooded, ruining 1 *mu* of rice fields and spoiling 1 *mu* of his household mulberry fields. An extra batch of fertiliser for the rice fields cost 150 *yuan*, but the loss from the mulberry field was very much greater. The direct cost of the flood was about 500 *yuan*, from 6 pairs of loads (*dan*) of fallen mulberry leaves, and much reduced production of silk worm cocoons that year. The indirect loss was significantly greater. It took him 3 years to fully recover the mulberry field, and involved costs of fertiliser, farmyard manure, replacing dead mulberry trees, labour and his own time.

Kaixiangong had suffered far less damage than other areas in Wujiang County was because it had a protective embankment. The village agricultural technician, Yao, told me that flood control work was carried out on an annual basis, arranged by an informal committee formed by six neighbouring villages, organised by the Township. The agreement between the villagers and the village collective goes back to the time when household responsibility first came into effect in the village in the mid-1980s. Each household was required to contribute one labourer for reinforcing dykes and dams, and contribute to a flood control fund, financed according to how much farmland each household contracted with the village collective. This system stood the test of floods in 1995 and 1999. In 1991 most households had suffered at least some damage, but in 1999 only five per cent of the village's farmland was flooded.

Yao was a firm believer in flood protection. On his own contracted farmland he dug a linked system of deeper ditches and drainage and had no losses, and he was able to convince other villagers to do the same. However, in 2000 the township brought in new measures. The head of fifth group, Wang, recently told me that the local government had appropriated special funding to buy five dredgers with five or six people employed on each. Their job was to dredge up silt and mud and use it to reinforce the dykes and dams on a regular basis. If this is successful the villagers will be freed from the burden of protective work during the flooding season.

(2) Plague of insects

Protection from plagues of insects is also regular work. Yao, the agricultural technician, told me that locusts, mentioned as a common disaster by Fei (1939:167), had been fully controlled since the 1950s. As part of his job, Yao often walks around farmland to monitor the pest and disease situation. He also attends about 20 different meetings in the Township for reporting, exchanging information and training. Whenever necessary Yao makes announcements through the village wired broadcast. He also writes notes and instructions on a blackboard outside the pesticide and chemical fertiliser station of the village. Normally villagers need to apply for pesticide to control pests and disease nearly 20 times a year:

- 6 times for mulberry trees from June to September against snout moth's larva (*mingchong*), wild silkworms, caterpillar and so on;

- 5 times for rice from late July to September against rice borer, bacterial blight of rice, rice blast, sheath and culm blight of rice, and rice leaf roller and so on;
- 4 times for wheat from late November to April against wheat midge, wheat aphid, gelechiid, armyworm and so on; and
- 3 times for rapeseed in the same season.

The average overall cost of pesticide is 120 *yuan* per household, and the wide variety of agricultural pests and diseases are kept more or less under control. Even for some families who take less care of thir land and field their losses are not significant.

(3) Disease of farm animals

For diseases of farm animals there is an epidemic prevention station in the Township and a veterinarian in the village. The veterinarians from both the Township station and the village provide a service for prophylactic inoculations of pigs and sheep twice a year in spring and autumn. Meeting a stiff target of healthy pigs available for sale to the state is the responsibility of the Township epidemic prevention station. Treating the animals is done for free, but the cost of chemicals is 3 *yuan* per head, including young, which villagers pay for themselves.

However, villagers arrange epidemic prevention for rabbits themselves, because raising rabbits, as purely a sideline production, has nothing to do with the state, and preventive injections cost only 0.30 yuan per rabbit. Zhou told me only half the villagers asked the village veterinarian for injections for their rabbits. The rest made their own arrangements, which involved labour support. For example, she bought two bottles of epidemic prevention chemical herself from the Township station and asked a former colleague of her husband in the village enterprise to do the injections for her rabbits (Photo III-46). In exchange she helped his family in cutting the rabbits' hair. She then gave the remaining one and half bottles of the chemical to one agnate

Photo III-46. Villagers found their own way to give injection to rabbits

kin and one fellow villager's family. They asked somebody else to give injections to their rabbits.

(4) Man-made disasters

To my surprise, many informants lost their patience when I asked them for details of natural disasters, preferring to raise the subject of those made by man, such as war, unsuitable policies, political campaign. BS Yao, a former head of the village, told me that in 1995 the village had 813 *mu* mulberry land but only 459 *mu* in 1985, because nearly half of it was used for planting rice during the Cultural Revolution. Yet in 1958 the villagers even grew vegetables, corn, pumpkin, sweet potato, wheat, barley and highland barley to provide for themselves on limited mulberry land, further restricting the growing of mulberry trees, because most of their land was being used to grow rice taken by the State. Man-made disasters during the Great Leap Forward made the natural ones that followed even worse than they should have been. In 1961 villagers were so poor they were reduced to begging. Yao's wife was forced to let one of their daughters be adopted into another family. I asked him what was the biggest man-made disaster during the post-Mao era? He said that the policy of restraining private business in the village would cause a great disaster within a year. His words were borne out only a few months after I left the village.

When I was there the village had four collective enterprises, two for silk products, one for rice wine, and a chemical plant. They were built with funds pooled by all the households in the village. However, villagers complained about the losses incurred by enterprises drawn into larger and larger debt because of management problems and political corruption. After I came back to the UK, YG Zhou, the outgoing head of the village, told me that in November 1996 all the village enterprises had gone bankrupt with debts of up to 10 million *yuan*. If this debt was passed to the villagers every household would carry a debt of 18,000 *yuan*. This had been a cause of anxiety since 1991, as recorded by Lu, a previous fieldwork researcher.

The bankruptcies became a catalyst for the systematic privatization (*gaizhi* or *qiye zhuanzi*) of the TVEs (town and village collectives) in accord with relevant local policy. There were now villagers and workers prepared to snatch property from the bankrupt collective enterprises. The offices in the township had to close for a few days to avoid conflict − not to speak of saving the running cost of a few thousand *yuan* per day. Action that restored social order was taken just in time: replacement of the head of the village, contracts for the enterprises with private owners, sale of equipment to individuals (see Introduction-II.)

2. Illness and injury

(1) Village Clinic (*weishengshi*)

The Village Clinic (*weishengshi*) was a basic health unit in rural China. Dr Ni explained how the rural co-operation medical system changed over the past 25 years. Before 1984 the clinic charged 5 *fen* per visit for registration, plus the costs of medicines. In 1984, when the rural reform policy of the responsibility system was applied to the village, the collective charged 3 *yuan* per person per year for a medical fund, effectively a kind of insurance, the fund being used in case of serious illness when claims could be made for up to 30 *yuan* for medicine from the collective. However, Rao's family spent 40,000 *yuan* for Rao's son's medical treatment for leukaemia in 1993. Apart from private support the family also borrowed 6,500 *yuan* from the village collective. I asked Rao how much a villager was allowed to borrow from the collective. He said there was no clear regulation, and his case was unusual. It was well known that the expenditure for his son's medical treatment was very large. Any household incurring heavy expenses for hospital treatment was allowed to apply to the Township Civil Affair Office for aid for the poor. After seeking private support and village collective support, Rao applied for reimbursement from the township (*gongjia baoxiao*) for 9,000 *yuan* through the Civil Affair Office, which granted 22.5 per cent of their total medical expenses, making a significant difference for which he was grateful.

From 1984, when rural reform was put into effect, Ni, as a village doctor, was paid about 2,000 *yuan* a year by the village collective. In 1991 Ni received 3,600 *yuan* a year from the village because there were now only two doctors in the village (there was less local need for midwifery because pregnant women were being encouraged to give birth at the Township hospital). When I was there in 1996 Ni told me he was paid only 3,000 *yuan* the previous year because a new reform of medical insurance was introduced (see next section) and he now lived on fees from dual sources, partly from the collective and partly from his own charges for treatment.

With this new introduction of the medical insurance system, the registration fee to the clinic increased to 50 *fen*. If a doctor paid a visit to a patient he or she could charge 3 *yuan* per visit by day and 5 *yuan* in the evening, as laid down by the Township Medical Management Association (*yiguanhui*). On top of that villagers needed to pay the cost of medicines themselves, and the doctor was allowed to pocket the difference of 15 per cent between market and wholesale prices. In return the doctor must give part of his profits to the Medical Management Association. Later, in a telephone interview, Ni said that over the previous four years his average direct pay from the village was only about 2,000 *yuan*.

However, from 2001 the village did not pay him directly at all. A deeper level of rural reform was now being applied in the village, known as "*feigaishui*" (change from collecting fees from peasants to a system of taxation). Its purpose is to reduce the peasants' burden and improve relationships between peasants, collective and the state. In 2000 the village collected fees amounting to 490,000 *yuan*. The introduction of *feigaishui* reduced by 40 per cent, the main reduction coming from cuts in salaries for village cadres. Instead of paying him a salary the village collective contracted for Ni to keep the business license, and waived his rent for using the clinic to continue disease prevention work. Ni attended a meeting of the Township Medical Management Association in May 2001 at which the issue of fees charged to patients was discussed, in view of the change from a rural medical co-operation system towards a free market system. Since his salary from the village collective had ceased he had increased his charges for visiting patients, and did not think it would be difficult for him to make a further increase under the new circumstances, because the good relationship he had with villagers would help them understand his situation.

(2) Medical insurance (*yiliao baoxian*)

Medical insurance (*yiliao baoxian*) means making claims to the Medical Foundation of the Township. It was a new phenomenon in rural China, although a well-developed commercial system in many developed countries. Xie, the head of Wujiang Civil Affairs Bureau, told me that the Bureau conducted an experiment in one township described as "foundation of a large amount of medical expenses based on different shares" (*gaoe yiliao tongchou jijinhui*). From 1991 onwards the institution of a Medical Foundation spread to all the townships of Wujiang County, in varying forms. That in Miaogang Township was known as the Township Medical Management Association (*yiguanhui* for *yiyao guanli jijinhui*). Villagers in Kaixiangong paid 6 *yuan* per person per year for it in 1995, increased to 12 *yuan* in 1999 and 16 *yuan* in 2003. They were allowed to make a partial claim in case of serious illness or injury. The village treasurer told me that claims could be made of 30 per cent of 1,000 *yuan*, 40 per cent of 2,000 *yuan*, up to a maximum of 4,850 *yuan* of 10,000 *yuan*, to the Township Civil Affair Office for hospital treatment of a serious illness.

Han was the first villager to benefit from medical insurance. He told me that he fell off a roof when he was helping a fellow villager build a house in 1995. A vertebra was injured and he was sent to Wujiang hospital for treatment, at a cost of 3,000 *yuan*. Since his family had a furniture business, it did not need to seek financial support from outside the household. So he was surprised to receive 800 *yuan* from the Township Medical Management Association, to which each of his family members had that year paid only 6 *yuan*. Han told me that in the past he hadn't been clear as to the difference between the medical insurance and a relief fund or aid from local government agents. In particular he did not like being obliged to pay medical insurance because he was healthy. Han thought that many villagers, as he did before the accident, would resent the local government for forcing them to join the system. But after the accident, he had learnt that medical insurance was a fair way to gain something back from what they have paid. "Accidents are inevitable", Han told me, "although I did not see any point of paying for the medical insurance when the policy was introduced to the village, because I was reasonably healthy just like many others".

(3) Public financial support

The disabled living allowance was another source of public financial support. It appeared in the village around 1995, with the reform of the rural co-operation medical system. The relationship between the allowance provider and receivers is supposed to be an institutional relationship, by which I mean that it should not depend on or be influenced by personal networks and the mechanisms of *lishang-wanglai*. Recently, more and more villagers have gained such disabled living allowances. An unusual case was of a villager who cut off his own finger to meet the criteria. However, at a very early stage of implementation, Liu's family gained a disabled living allowance in circumstances that can be seen to display all the characteristics of *lishang-wanglai*. Liu, a 52-year-old housewife, told me that she was not qualified to claim for the disabled living allowance from the township because her particular problem wasn't listed.

However, when she made her case to village cadres she used special pleading clearly based on *lishang* criteria. (i) Morally Liu was proud of herself for raising two sons for the Country (*wo yang erzi wei guojia*). The older son worked in Shengze Township and was financially independent from the family after he graduated from a university. The second son went to serve in the army and could be promoted there. So the State (*guojia wei wo yanglao*) owed it to her to provide living expenses when she lost the ability to work. (ii) Human feeling had gained her wide sympathy inside and outside the village. She only started to seek public financial support when she lost her job in a village enterprise because of serious, worsening arthritis in her knees. Her second son was serving in the army and could not help with the household responsibility for the farmland. Her sister-in-law, who lived next door, helped her with much of her housework. (iii) Rational calculation also helped. Liu told me that she had had two operations, in 1983 and 1988. For the first operation her family did not seek any support from outside of the household, although her older brother gave her 500 *yuan*. Her husband was a farmer and fisherman and she was working in a village enterprise. She had two brothers, one a carpenter and group head in the village, and another a lacquerer. They both lived in the village and were well-off. But for the second operation, which cost 3,000 *yuan,* she had to seek financial support from private sources. Her elder son started work at that time and was able to give her 1,000 *yuan*. Her older brother loaned her 1,000 *yuan*. But with both her sons away from home, and she herself unable to work whether inside or outside of the house, she still needed to go on spending money on her knees.

Hence the decision to seek long-term medical support from the village collective. (iv) Finally, as she told me, the heavenly gods saw her difficulty (*laotian youyan*) and gave her a chance. The village head introduced a new fund providing living allowances of 30 *yuan* per month for disabled people, raised by township welfare factories for the Township Civil Affair Bureau. The allowance increased every so often with the development of the welfare factories.

(4) Support for the extremely poor

A funeral for the poor was an extreme case which involved a vertical expressive *wanglai* from the Director of the Village Committee, Wang, to a villager Gao, of household no. 14. In 1991 this family comprised two persons: a father and a son. At that time it was one of the sampled households, but in 1988 the son left the village and the father, Gao, passed away in 1992. According to fieldwork notes by Lu Feiyun in 1991, his wife had died many years ago and his son had left three years previously because his family was too poor to arrange a marriage for him. Gao contracted lung cancer in 1991 and died in 1992.

During Gao's last days Wang made himself responsible for everything, arranging for a doctor when the time came and engaging a funeral specialist from Miaogang Township. The funeral was a simple version of what was local custom required. Wang told Gao's relatives, neighbours and friends the sad news, and they paid condolence calls with gifts, which amounted in value, including gift money, to 400 *yuan*. There was a feast after the cremation costing 1,200 *yuan,* part of which was paid for by gifts from Gao's relatives, the rest from Gao's own limited savings. About 30 people attended. The funeral was thus financially supported by Gao himself together relatives, with some private support including labour support, and public support because the funeral was arranged by the JM Wang in his capacity as Head of the village.

When I heard that Gao was a distant of relative of Wang's, I asked him what would have happened if Gao had not been related to him. Wang told me it made no difference at all. This was his explanation: (i) Wang regarded such arrangements as part of his job. It was morally right that he should take care of his villagers nicely and he would take responsibility for all poor and unfortunate people if it was necessary. When Gao suffered from lung cancer in 1991, he had hospital treatment which cost 8,000 *yuan*. Wang arranged had social and financial support for him from both public and private sources. He applied grant-in-aid from the village collective and the Township to pay his hospitalisation expenses. The village collective then paid 4,000 *yuan* from the relief fund and 2,000 *yuan* were claimed from the Township Civil Affair Bureau. After Gao left the hospital Wang organised about 30 relatives, neighbours and fellow villagers of his group to visit him with gifts. As well as material, emotional and spiritual support, the neighbours and fellow villagers also offered labour support with his housework and even his land work, because he could not work on the land for both his own grain and contract tasks.

(ii) According to Wang he had a natural human feeling of sympathy (*tongqing*) with Gao independent of kinship (*qinqing*). The relationship between the two families was very distant. Gao's grandmother had some link to Wang's family but this had not been acknowledged on his family's non-agnatic kin list since his grandparents' generation. Gao was grateful, according to Lu's fieldwork notes, that villagers not only worked for him but also spent money on his expensive medicine. Gao understood that people who did not find poverty a reason for helping would nevertheless do so in the case of ill fortune, and this accorded with local custom (one of meanings of *renqing*). But in this case, the human feeling of sympathy (*ganqing*) was the weightiest factor.

(iii) The simplified arrangements for Gao's funeral were based on local custom which accorded with rational calculation. It wouldn't be proper for the villagers if Gao didn't have a funeral at all, but it was proper for the funeral to be kept simple.

(iv) Wang told me that although he never expected anything directly in return from Gao, he could gain villagers' trust by treating a poor and sick person kindly. Although he did not worship any particular god, he had a general belief, with religious undertones, that people's behaviour would get its just deserts.

PART TWO

THE PRACTICE OF"*LISHANG-WANGLAI*"

PART TWO will present Kaixiangong villagers' practice and experience of dealing with social relationships in a contemporary Chinese village, in accordance with *lishang-wanglai*. Based on Kaixiangong villagers' own accounts, using terms such as "*bao en*" (gratitude), "*zou houmen*" (go through back doors), "*la guanxi*" (pull relationships), "*bu xiao*" (unfilial) and "*wanglai*" (come and go), I will categorise their complex reciprocal social relationships into variations and combinations of four basic types: generous *wanglai*, expressive *wanglai*, instrumental *wanglai* and negative *wanglai*. In section I of Chapter IX, I will explain how my understanding of the typology of such relationships was influenced by previous researchers (see Table XI-1), and how in building the *lishang-wanglai* model I have borrowed the concepts of expressive, instrumental and negative relationships from Befu (1966–67) and Sahlins (Sahlins, 1965a and 1965b, 1972)

According to my fieldwork records and statistics of the sample households, generous and negative *wanglai* (denoted by interviewees' usage of terms such as "gratitude" or "unfilial"), comprised only a small proportion of total resource-seeking related activity, 11 per cent and 9 per cent respectively; whereas instrumental *wanglai* (what is broadly understood as *guanxi*) accounts for about 20 per cent, and the remaining 60 per cent of activity is expressive *wanglai* (often described as *renqing*). In this chapter I will show the operation of generous *wanglai* in the village. But since expressive *wanglai* has received little attention from sociological research, and in anthropological studies it was categorized in the broadest sense of *guanxi*, I will use not one chapter but three, Chapters V to VII, to make an in-depth exploration of this important topic. There are already many studies on instrumental *wanglai*, which per se needs no further exploration, but in practice instrumental and negative *wanglai* are always mixed. To help readers understand their similarities and differences Chapter VIII reviews them together in one chapter. Village practice of *lishang-wanglai* can be analysed not only into the different types of *wanglai* mentioned above, but also according to the underlying principles that govern their choice, evident from villagers' explanations and local customs (*lishang*). I will introduce these basic principles in Section III of Chapter IX: moral judgment, human feelings, rational calculation and spiritual belief, and show how they determine the maintenance and change of type of *wanglai*. It will be seen that these changes are not haphazard or random, but governed by principle. Each chapter in Part Two will follow the same pattern: to describe the various relationships (*wanglai*) and how they changed, and then to analyse them with a set of criteria or principles (*lishang*), in order to demonstrate how these complex different types of relationships change or co-exist.

Chapter IV   **Generous *wanglai***

Chapter IV will introduce the first type of *wanglai* (reciprocity) of the four that I postulate: generous *wanglai*. It relates closely to the idea of "gratitude" in Chinese culture, as well as the practice of "giving" in everyday life. It is also close to the second type of *wanglai* (expressive *wanglai*) which will be demonstrated in Chapters V to VII. These two types of *wanglai* can co-exist in any one particular relationship, whether between individual and individual, or between individual(s) and organizations or systems. They can also change from one *wanglai* to another or vice versa dependent on changes of situation.

Generous wanglai relates to people giving without expecting any kind of exchange in return (see Chapter IV). In other words, it is to do something for nothing, or for no obvious reason or for the pure enjoyment of giving. Instances of this are most clearly visible in the villagers' festivals or rituals where everyday and religious life is mixed. The villagers categorise these occasions as being between people (huoren jie), between villagers and ancestors (bai shangzu or siren jie, see Chapters III.III and IV.III.2), or between villagers and the local gods (bai shen and bai zao).

I found that in the village generous wanglai works both horizontally and vertically. When such wanglai happens between family members of the same generation, or a family with its relatives1, neighbours, friends and fellow villagers it can be regarded as horizontal wanglai, whereas the wanglai that happens between different generations of members of a family, or in the relationship between the village collective and villagers, or ancestors and family members, can be seen as vertical wanglai. In this section I will show related cases within one family, and between two or more extended families, which illustrate how such wanglai works in everyday life. I will then extend this concept of generous wanglai in villagers' everyday life to see how it works between villagers horizontally, and vertically between villagers and ancestors/gods in their religious life.

IV.I. A case study of horizontal and vertical *wanglai*

An old lady called FY Tan told me her life story in which she had experienced many

---

[1] See section III of Introduction for kinship system.

different and changing kinds of relationships, some forming a vertical cycle in her life, others horizontal. She had been born in 1926. She told me that she came to the Tan family when she was 16 years old as a daughter-in-law-to-be (*tongyangxi*). After she got married she gave birth to three children. The oldest was a girl who died two weeks after she was born. In 1945 she had a boy, XR Tan. FY adopted a two-year-old girl as a daughter-in-law-to-be in 1950. In 1957 FY gave birth to her youngest boy, JR Tan. However, the Tan family became very poor during a series of natural disasters that were exacerbated by the social policies of the Great Leap Forward. They were forced to give two-year-old JR to the Gu family for adoption and agreed never to claim him back. Thirty years later, during the lunar New Year's holiday of 1990, XR Tan at last discovered his long-lost brother JR, now a director of the county hospital. XR told JR how much their mother and the Tan family had missed him over the 30 year period and how much he wanted to satisfy his dead father's unfulfilled wish (*yiyuan*) for reunion and his mother's continuing, long-cherished wish (*suyuan*) to be reunited with her youngest son before her death. Surprisingly, JR's response was cold: "It is better that you do not claim me at all since we have not *laiwang* (come and go) for so many years according to the adoption agreement". XR felt utterly disappointed in JR.

However, seven years later, in 1997, these two brothers and their families began to *wanglai* with each other expressively. In August of that year JR brought his wife and son to pay the first visit to his own mother and brother's family for a family reunion. He came again for XR's younger son's wedding in 1999, at which he assumed the role of a close relative. In 2000, after a conference in Suzhou City, JR made a detour and visited his mother and brother's family again. XR brought his family to pay a visit to JR Tan's family in 2001 during the period of the Mid-autumn Festival (*zhongqiujie*, 15th day of the 8th lunar month), which is also called Moon Day or Family Reunion Festival (*tuanyuanjie*). XR told me that six members of his family attended this important family reunion, his mother, two sons, the oldest son's wife and daughter and himself. XR's wife and the younger son's wife could not come because they needed to look after the younger son's baby girl who was ill. In 2002 JR's son spent his Moon Day holiday with his birth grandmother and uncle's family in Kaixiangong Village. During 2003's summer holiday JR's son visited XR's family in Kaixiangong. XR took him to Wujiang City to see XR's wife who was helping to look after their younger son's child. Then they went to Suzhou City for sightseeing together. In recent years XR and JR's families talk to each other by telephone two or three times per month.

This case exhibits a horizontal generous wanglai between the Tan family and the natal family of the two-year-old girl taken into the Tan family as a daughter-in-law-to-be, and the Gu family with the Tan family when the Gu family adopted the Tan family's two-year-old son. In both cases there is a strong element of generosity, because the adopting families were more influenced by the thought of saving the children's lives than of any return. The case of FY's own adoption had been different. She had been taken into the Tan family as a 16-year-old daughter-in-law-to-be as part of a marriage arrangement, and the relationship between her natal family and the Tan family who adopted her can be described as expressive wanglai (see Chapter IX.I). However there was another difference, in that FY's two-year-old daughter-in-law-to-be was allowed to stay in contact her natal family, but FY's son was not. Because of this, the initial generous wanglai between the girl's natal family and the Tan family could be developed into different types of wanglai. After the girl was married to XR, FY's older son, FY's relationship with her moved down from generous wanglai to expressive wanglai as was usual.

The relationship between the FY Tan's family and the Gu family which had adopted her son JR is less simple than it looks. After the little boy was handed over to the Gu family any type of laiwang between the two families was stopped, whereas for FY, inside her heart the relationship between her and JR and the Gu family was eternal. This can be seen as a quiescent relationship which could be mixed with different types of wanglai and could be reactivated into any type of wanglai.

A few years after JR was adopted it became the turn of the Gu family to suffer misfortune. During the Cultural Revolution their status sank to the lowest level of society (I will explain this later) and FY thought it could be a good time to reclaim her son. But she refrained, and the relationship (or rather lack of it) between the two families remained the same. By 1990 when her son XR met his brother, she felt that now was truly a good time to claim her relationship with him, but JR refused. According to Lu Yinghao's fieldwork notes for the ESRC social support project, in 1991 the relationship between the Tan family and Gu family (JR's new name is Gu YM) was one of negative wanglai. If the Tan family had given up the attempt to claim JR the relationship could have been ended. However, FY decided to create a new type of wanglai between the two families. After many efforts made by both sides, when I was there in 1996 the relationship had begun to be positive, with each side understanding the other much better. From 1997 onwards the relationship between the two families has grown into an expressive wanglai. Following the local custom, the Tan family categorised JR's family as non-agnatic kin or close kin (jinqin) rather than agnatic kin (zijiaren) because JR was treated as a married-out daughter. This means that whenever the Tan family had family events the JR family would be invited and treated as relatives.

The mobility of the above different types of wanglai between Tan and Gu families horizontally can be explained in terms of lishang criteria as follows:

(i) FY firmly believed in the Chinese moral code which declares "good is rewarded with good, and evil with evil" (*shan you shan bao, e you e bao*), so that if her family accumulated merit by hard work and good intentions towards other people it would be rewarded with good. When and how to reclaim JR involved a moral judgment. FY told me that it would have been morally wrong if she had claimed him when the Gu family was in trouble. During the Cultural Revolution, Gu was denounced as a capitalist and he and his family were repatriated to his home town. Although this would have given her a good chance to reclaim JR, she did not do so. She said she would not requite kindness with enmity (*en jiang chou bao*) because Gu was the Tan family's benefactor. For her, to abide by this moral code added to her accumulated merit (*jide*) and would lead to a good future.

(ii) FY said she was heartbroken when her younger son was adopted by the Gu family. She would feel much happier in her remaining life if she could make some compensation (*baochang*) to JR, whether for the material loss of the care that his natal family should have given him or for his feelings when he was forced to leave his natal home. FY made it clear that she never expected JR to provide for her in her old age in the traditional manner. On the contrary, she and her family worked very hard to be wealthy enough to reclaim JR and compensate him for his original loss of his real parents by providing love for him and his family. This was what JR should be repaid and compensated (*zheshi JR yingde de baochang*).

(iii) FY's decision to let her younger son be adopted can be explained as a rational choice because it was the only way he could survive, but of course she always dreamt of claiming him back. However, she kept the adoption agreement for 30 years without laying any claim to JR, also by rational choice. FY told me when she eventually claimed JR it was in the situation that a new agreement had been reached between the Gu and Tan families. Without this she would only have broken the agreement if Gu had died prematurely, or if the Gu family had been unable to survive during the Cultural Revolution.

(iv) FY had quite a strong religious sense. She believed in accumulated merit (*jide*). She also believed that if she broke the original agreement without a proper reason she could receive evil (*zao baoying*). Here retribution (*baoying*) functions as a warning for people to avoid a negative result by accumulating merit. FY thought that fortune and misfortune could be changed in a circle either within one's lifetime or in another life in the other world, as a process of retribution or karma (*yinguo baoying*). In her case, it happened in different periods within her life in which the ups and downs of fate were cyclical. She told me that when she was 16 years old her family was very poor and she had had to be contracted as a daughter-in-law-to-be of the Tan family, which was a kind of poor families' marriage arrangement. When she knew a family in a neighbouring village was so poor that they had to let a two-year-old girl be a daughter-in-law-to-be, her heart went out to the girl, and she adopted her as a daughter-in-law-to-be for her five-year-old son. Nine years after that it was the Tan family's turn to feel too poor to survive. They had to let their own two-year-old son be adopted by the Gu family. However, the hope of reclaiming JR never died. She also planted this seed into her older son's heart and encouraged him to be successful because this would make him more fit to claim his younger brother. Thirty years later XR tried to reclaim JR for a family reunion and failed. But this was not a sad ending for FY. It didn't stop her son from seeing her forever. She told me that her heart told her that JR would forgive his birth parents gradually and eventually acknowledge his birth family, since she had been praying devoutly to the local god and the god would help her. After many years' efforts FY has her son JR reunited with the Tan family. XR told me recently that his mother is 78 years old now and lives in happiness and health. The villagers said she has good fortune (*youfu*) now, although she suffered from cruel fate (*kuming*) when she was young. FY said the gods had turned her bitter life into a happy one (*tuo laotian de fu*), she had suffered enough hardship and it was her turn to enjoy her old age. FY thought this was deriving gain from misfortune (*yin huo de fu*).

This case also exxhibits a vertical generous *wanglai* between the elder son XR and FY, and FY's younger son with his adopted parents the Gus. This can also be described in terms of *lishang* criteria. I didn't interview JR but am inferring his motives from his mother and elder brother's explanations.

(i) To pay a debt of gratitude to parents is a question of moral judgement. XR told me that he worked very hard, as his parents expected, because this was the best way to pay a debt of gratitude to beloved parents for their sacrifice in bringing him up (*bao'en*).[2] And the reason he wanted to claim his younger brother was mainly for *bao'en* to his parents. He remembered his father's words before he passed away in 1985; that he would "take with him to the other world his lifelong regret at giving up JR, and pray there for the reunion of JR with the Tan family." XR said that to fulfil his parent's unsatisfied longing, as he had told JR when he first met him, was his responsibility as a filial son (*xiaozi*). As for JR, after his refusal to meet her *wanglai* with both JR and his adoptive parents, by letters and telephone calls, led her to understand him. She said JR is a filial son (*xiaozi*). Just like his elder brother, JR's actions came from the root of "pay a debt of gratitude" (*bao'en*) to his adopted parents. He refused his natal family's initial attempt to reclaim him because of his obligation (*yiwu*) of filial duty to his adopted parents (*jinxiao*).

(ii) When XR was first refused by JR he told his mother that JR still hated his own parents for leaving him with other people. This human feeling of hatred was interpreted by FY as "a kind of revenge" (*baofu*) because JR was hurt deeply. FY understood that it was human nature for JR to have negative feelings of hatred for his own parents, who gave him away and appeared to not want to see him again. That negative feeling could have determined a negative *wanglai* between the two families, but she made strong efforts to create a positive *wanglai* with the Gu family and with JR, and was vindicated. Over a seven year period from 1990 when XR had first met him to 1997, during which he remained unresponsive, JR was involved in a struggle between his great gratitude to his adopted parents for his upbringing (*yangyu zhi en*) and his feelings (*gurou zhi qing*) towards his blood relatives who gave him life. The way in which JR refused XR when he tried to claim him back for the Tan family can be described as "embodied *ganqing*" (Kipnis's term 1997). Later he told his brother his feelings had been very complicated when they first met. He didn't mean to hurt XR but he couldn't help but express his feelings in that way. JR told FY and XR that now that he was older the reunion with his birth family helped him get over his feelings about having been given away, and eased the loss of his now-deceased adopted father.

---

[2] When Tan XR was 17 years old he became a treasurer in one production team and nine years after that he became a treasurer of the production brigade (Kaixiangong Village). X. Tan became one of the heads of the brigade from 1974 to 1986. From 1986 onward X. Tan was promoted to head a township enterprise, then a managing director of the Industry Company of the township, and finally a vice-director of the township (*fu xiangzhang*) until his retirement.

(iii) In this case rational choice can be seen in different ways. XR had the rational idea that the best time to claim JR was when he had achieved high enough social status and accumulated enough wealth to be on an equality with the Gu family. So in 1990, when he became a vice-director of the Miaogang Township (*fu xiangzhang*), XR judged that the time had come to go to Sheyang County of Jiangsu Province to see his younger brother. When he was refused by his younger brother, one of the reasons XR gave his mother was that JR did not want to be involved in any financial trouble by having a relationship with a poor relative from a rural area, because JR and his family were urban people. However, this was a misunderstanding. JR's point of view was that he should honour the agreement of adoption that he should not *wanglai* with the Tan family, an agreement that had been kept by everybody for a long time. JR told FY that he was moved when his adopted father Gu told him that the agreement was less important now since JR was grown up, and it was JR's choice whether or not to claim his own flesh and blood – his mother and brother. The agreement adapted to a changing situations, also by rational choice. Thus, with his adopted father's permission, JR decided to keep to the original agreement only until his adopted father passed away (in April 1997).

(iv) Both XR and JR had a religious sense that it was fate that brought them together.

So far I have shown how horizontal and vertical generous *wanglai* between families and generations can be treated separately. But this case has an extra dimension. The relationship between FY and her younger son JR should be vertical *wanglai*, but for her the whole business of letting JR be adopted and claiming him back is to do with the Gu family, which determined the nature of such a relationship to be horizontal. Although in both cases all four criteria of *lishang* had been involved, I should point out their relative importance varied. For example, FY's religious sense is much stronger than her sons', whereas for JR the reconciliation with the Tan family was mainly determined by moral judgment and rational choice.

IV.II. Horizontal *wanglai* in annual life-cycle events

I am now moving on to villagers' practices of generous *wanglai*, as shown in various customs. There are three major customary festivals for human beings (*huoren jie*), as well as the four festivals for ancestors (*xiren jie*, see Chapters III.III and V). The major human festivals are the Spring Festival (also called Chinese New Year or lunar New Year), the Beginning of Summer (*lixia*) and the Moon Day Festival (*tuanyuanjie*). There is also at least one ritual or event per lunar month throughout a year (see Chapter III.III). These were embedded in the four seasons, different intervals in the solar year, different times of the lunar year; for people of different ages and sexes, and for different kinds of local gods. But many rituals were less religious than recreational (Fei, 1939: 104), and can be treated as a supplement to village cultural and social life (Xu, 1996: 194–197), (Wujiang general records: 1994: 791–793). There was much entertainment only slightly coloured by religion. These festivals and events exhibit a wide variety of practices involving ancestors and local gods or goddesses. The relationships people have with each other has the character of generous *wanglai* because people enjoy providing nice feasts to members of a family, extended families, guests and non-agnatic kin without expecting anything in return. I would now like to show horizontal generous *wanglai* at work in villagers' everyday life.

1. Agnatic kin (*zijiaren*)

Local customs pay little attention to agnatic kin in terms of generous *wanglai*. However the lunar New Year's Eve feast (*chi nianyefan*) involves the reunion of close agnatic kin. Traditionally the family reunion feast at the lunar New Year's Eve is the most important time for members of a family to enjoy themselves together. As the Chinese saying goes "a second of a fine moment is worth a thousand grams of gold" (*liangxiao yike zhi qianjin*). I found that 87.5 per cent of sample families celebrated the lunar New Year's Eve feast. Among them 47 per cent were stem families[3] who enjoyed New Year's Eve feasts themselves, 6 per cent were nuclear families without brothers who invited their parent(s) for the feast, and 34.5 per cent were nuclear families divided from joint families who invited brothers' families and their parent(s) for the feast. Only 12.5 per cent of sample households with close agnatic kin did not hold the New Year's Eve feast. This group consisted of four households: one family had two sons who lived in the village but had stopped having this kind of *wanglai* (Case 3), and three families had sons living outside of the village who could not come back for the New Year's Eve feast (this included BY Zhou's family).

My fieldwork started on the lunar New Year's Eve with BY Zhou's family. BY's parents had no sons of their own but had two adopted sons. One became BY's husband. Another, BX, had not yet married and had been working in another township for many years and came back

---

[3] A stem family refers to a married couple or surviving spouse in each of at least two generations and unmarried children.

once or twice a year. Although this family was not a typical case for agnatic kin, it was categorised as agnatic kin and should have shared a lunar New Year's Eve feast. But, contrary to the custom, BX was not present at the family reunion feast. Of the four families which did not hold family reunion feasts three cases were due to geographical distance. The case of BX's failure to reunite with BY's family is more complicated. When I asked for reasons they all felt embarrassed. As BY's husband pointed out, it was BX's obligation to make an effort to join the feast. This involved a moral judgement. BY's father said that given the complicated family background BX's behaviour was not a surprise because he would feel little interest or fun (*mei shade yisi*) in a reunion with the family. This is another criterion of *lishang-wanglai* relating to human feeling. BY's adopted daughter said BX must prefer to earn holiday double pay in the tortoise farm where he worked rather than come back to the village for the family reunion. This kind of explanation is a typical rational calculation. BY was clear herself that BX "had no luck" with his family (*yu zhege jia wuyuan*). So there was no point in making him return to the family if he did not want to *wanglai* with them.

However, these reasons for BX's absence for the New Year's Eve feast changed in 2003. From 1996 to 2003 there were many big events in BY's family: BY's father passed away; and her son became engaged, bought a flat in a Zhenze township where he worked, got married and had a son of his own. During the last few years BX attended every lunar New Year's Eve feast regularly. He also took his share of fulfilling obligations according to local customs in each event on his own initiative. He even gave his nephew, BY's son, 40,000 *yuan* for his wedding. This behaviour won high praise. But none of this had happened when I was there in 1996. According to BY's daughter, QZ, all her family members had felt embarrassed by her uncle's absence for the New Year's Eve feast. Now the family dynamics had improved. AM, BY's husband, said the way in which BX gave 40,000 *yuan* to his son was just like the return of a "big pig" for his daily "pig feed". AM farmed BX's share of the grain ration field (*chengbao de kouliang tian*) and allowed BX to take his share of grain from the household once or twice a year, free, for many years. This was just like giving a small amount of feed to a pig everyday, then when BY's family needed money BX returned it with a big amount all at once (4,000 *yuan*), like giving a whole pig. Although there was not any kind of agreement between them, the principle behind their behaviour was analogous to saving small coins in a piggy bank for later use and therefore based on rational calculation. However, according to BY, the big pig from BX was much more valuable than his wife's pig feed. She herself always believed that the good relationships between members of the family was in fact thanks to her mother (*tuo niang de fu*), in effect regarding the family's happiness as her mother's reward from heaven. This typical religious statement refers to her mother's accumulated merit (*jide*) gained through adopting BX and working hard to raise four children; merit which benefited her descendants.

For the villagers, whether or not to attend the Chinese New Year's Eve family reunion feast is a way of expressing (or failing to express) generous *wanglai* between family members. In 1996 my view was that the relationship between BX and the family had dropped down to a kind of instrumental *wanglai* because he only visited once or twice a year when it was convenient to collect his share of grain. However, since then the relationship between BX and BY's family has improved to one of expressive *wanglai,* as can be seen from his taking part in major family events (funerals, weddings and so on) as well as attending the annual family reunion feast. The turning point of the relationship between BX and the Zhou family had been his stepfather's death.

2. Non-agnatic kin (*qinqi*)

As I have shown in Chapter I.III, non-agnatic kin are much more numerous than affinity relatives because they include relatives by marriage, un-married sisters, married-out daughters, the natal family of a married son-in-law's, quasi relatives and so on. According to local custom, the New Year's Eve feast is for family reunion between brothers' families or members of the extended family based on agnatic kin. The feast on New Year's day is used for a married-out son or daughter, as close non-agnatic kin, to reunite with their natal family as equals. FK Yao told me that during the period of the lunar New Year his family would prepare a few more such feasts for the rest of the families on the non-agnatic kin list, and his family would attend several such feasts too. All these feasts between close non-agnatic kin are categorised as generous *wanglai* by the villagers. Here I will illustrate a case of generous *wanglai* with non-agnatic kin in a lunar New Year feast.

I attended a feast on the lunar New Year's day (*xinnian fan*) in FK's family. This is a stem family with five members, FK himself, his parents, and his wife and daughter. So FK's father's married-out sister and FK's three married-out sisters' families should all have been invited. At around 11:00 one of FK's sister's family arrived with gifts. Soon afterwards FK's other sisters' families and his father's sister's family arrived with their gifts. The gifts of cake, general medicinal tonic (*zibupin*), sugar, and fruit were for FK's parents. The rest of the gifts included sweets, biscuits, fireworks and so on and were for his daughter. The gifts embodied a moral code of respect for the elderly and love for the children (*zunlao aiyou*), although they can be shared with all the members of the family.

As hostess, FK's wife provided the highest standard of service to their guests. It started with a double cup of teas. One was sweet tea made with fine glutinous rice crust (*daidi*) and sugar. The other was savoury tea made with green tea, smoked dry green beans (*xun qingdou*)[4], dried carrot chips and so on. The feast was held as a late lunch rather than an evening meal. There were 12 different dishes, made of an upper part of pork leg (*tizi*), fish, prawn, chicken, duck, goose, eggs, bean curd and different vegetables. The event ended after the main meal with a pure green tea.

Everybody seemed very happy with their feasts. Villagers dressed up in their best clothes, saw many relatives, and enjoyed many feasts and gifts. They enjoyed playing the roles of both host and guest. I saw many people walking around the village carrying baskets covered with red cloth who told me proudly and happily that they were going to be guests (*zuo keren*). Their enjoyment of the flow of gifts and banquets reveals the villagers' true attitudes: the chief purpose of this behaviour is pleasure. Kipnis (1997) regards *ganqing* as an activity mainly concerned with propriety, which might however also involve genuine pleasure. My own observations are similar to his, but there is a significant difference in my interpretation. For Kipnis, the obligatory element of *ganqing* is primary; and from my observations the natural expression of real pleasure is more important.

On many occasions there are local customs that conflict with each other. Interpreting them so as to make a right decision involves rational choice. FK told me that according to one local custom his elder sister's family should come for the New Year Day's feast. They had not come this year because she could not bring her whole family with her. According to another local custom, after FK's older sister's son got married he and his wife also needed to attend the lunar New Year Day feast arranged by their in-law's family. So the arrangement for the feast had to be changed. From now on FK's older sister's family would make their visit on a different day, because establishing a new generation of non-agnatic kin is more important than maintaining an existing relationship (see Figures VIII-2 and 3).[5] Rational calculation can also be seen in a family labour division. As I mentioned earlier, FK's wife was in charge of entertainment at the

---

[4] Fresh soya bean after treatment remained a green colour: the villagers call it *qingdou* – green bean.
[5] Compared with Figure VIII-2, a patrilineal family tree, I obtained Figure VIII-3 from MY (No. 28 of Figure VIII-2 and No 3. of Figure VIII-3). Figure VIII-2 includes 9 families of the close kin who are the most positive relatives of the family's *lishang-wanglai* networks, but one can't find them from Figure VIII-2.

feast. FK's mother's job was sorting out all the gifts from the guests. At the same time she put small items back as returning gifts, such as different kinds of sweet and biscuit, because nobody is allowed to take an empty basket back home. FK's wife and mother did their work on a basis of proper treatment for each guest according to local custom, so that the guests could interpret the way they had been treated correctly. If FK's wife served only one kind of tea before the feast, or FK's mother did not put little things into a gift basket, these actions or omissions would have a consequent effect on the relationships concerned, both for guest and host. And if FK's older sister's family could not attend the feast she must give a proper reason.

The modification of non-agnatic kin also involved rational calculation. FK's father listed 10 families of non-agnatic kin for the New Year feast. Besides the four families discussed above these were FK's mother's brother's family, FK's wife's sister's family, and both her older and younger brothers' families, and two quasi kin's families. One of them was FK's mother's quasi daughter and another was FK's wife's quasi mother. The reason for claiming a quasi relative is not only to increase the numbers of non-agnatic kin, it can also be for a health reason, or to make the relationships of the families concerned even closer, as in this family's case. A village saying refers to adding closeness on top of the kinship relations (*qin shang jia qin*). Both FK and his wife had enough sisters and brothers so they claimed two of FK's sisters and FK's wife's sister to be their daughter's quasi mothers. This means FK's daughter has three quasi mothers who were also her aunts. At the same time this kind of arrangement limited the numbers of their close non-agnatic kin.

The religious sense can be seen from the meanings of gifts. For example, the fruit from guests must be apples and oranges. The pronunciation of apple is similar to *ping'an* which symbolised peaceful life, whereas the pronunciation of orange is similar in the local accent to *jili* which symbolises luck and good fortune. The whole period of the lunar New Year is coloured with religious sense. It starts from the 23rd day of the twelfth month to the 15th day of the first month of the lunar year, which is called the New Year ceremony (*guonian*). Here *guo* means passing a moment with ceremony and *nian* is a general designation for different kinds of spiritual beings. For example, on the 23rd day of the twelfth month villagers hold a ceremony for the kitchen god, which is also called "passing a moment with ceremony for a less powerful spiritual being" (*guo xiaonian*). The events on the New Year's Eve such as the family reunion feast, ancestor worship and villagers going to local temples to worship local gods and so on (see Chapters VI.II and III) are called "passing a special moment with ceremony for a powerful spiritual being" (*guo danian*).

3. Friends

In Kaixiangong Village everybody has a list of friends. For a male, his friends are called little friends (*xiao pengyou*) before his son or daughter marries, or old friends (*lao pengyou*) after his son or daughter marries. For a female her friends are called little sisters (*xiao jiemei*) until she gets married. After a female marries, in theory she should stop *wanglai* with her little sisters. In practice if the female and her little sister(s) live in the same village or group they can keep their relationship, although this is unlikely to happen. The difference is expressed as "they *were* little sisters" instead of "they *are* old sisters" (see Chapter XII.II for more details). Friends are made through playing, studying or working together. The Beginning of Summer (*lixia*) is the second festival for human beings. It is the day marking the beginning of the 7th of the solar term (5, 6 or 7 May). Apart from the family event on that day there is a kind of picnic (*yehuo fan*) which in children under 15 years old involves generous *wanglai* among friends (see Photo III-38 and39). It will illustrate how friendship networks form and join to family *lishang-wanglai* networks, and why part of friendship relationships can be counted as generous *wanglai*.

On 5 May 1996 I arrived at XL's house around 09:00. XL's five-year-old daughter JY had reached the age to have fun with other children without an adult's supervision. The girl asked her mother to make the arrangement for her. XL invited five children from her group to her house on the day before the Beginning of Summer. I saw that the child guests brought a little bit of rice mixed with oil and salt in different containers to XL's house. They comprised three girls and two boys. XL gave her daughter JY a basket which contained a few bowls, spoons and a box of matches. Another girl carried a saucepan and a bottle of water. A boy, DM, carried a bunch of rice straw. Six children were there at the start of the picnic trip. The oldest girl was 10 years old and was in charge of the gang. On the way to a field two boys joined them. Some of the children picked broad beans, peeled them and threw them into the saucepan. Others collected sticks and small branches. DM dug a pit and placed rice straw inside it. Then they lit a fire with the rice straw, but it did not burn properly. Two bigger girls came from 100 metres away where they were having their own picnic, and helped them with the fire. Soon it burned well and the broad bean rice was cooked. They enjoyed themselves very much. They let me try a bit of the rice and it was really delicious.

I then went to the older girls' picnic site. There were four girls. They had just finished their broad bean rice. They were drinking coca cola, eating snacks and playing cards. They told me that they all lived in the 16th group of the village and had grown up together. They had started having such picnics when they were about five years old, following some older children. This was the last picnic for them because they were now aged 15. According to the local custom once children pass their 16th birthday they are not allowed to play in this way. NI, one of the girls, told me that they were little sisters. They had formed their gang after they passed their tenth birthdays. According to local custom, at this age children were allowed to decide who would be their little friends or little sisters. This means they were no longer just playmates, they were also committed to help each other whenever it was needed. There was even a ritual for the establishment of such a sister relationship. With their parents' help, they took turns to be hosts and guests at each other's houses for feasts, at which they made their promises. From then onwards they invited each other for their birthday feasts.

I will now consider *lishang* criteria to show how the friendship relationship is formed and why some *wanglai* between friends can be seen as generous *wanglai*. According to local custom, children under 11 years old cannot form a relationship of real friendship, because that involves responsibility. Before they are eleven they are not considered to have any obligation to each other, and parents always help children to make friends. At this stage their *wanglai* is mainly generous *wanglai*.

(i) The moral sense behind it is that villagers generally believe it is right to encourage children to play and make their friends freely. I saw that the children gathered beans as soon as we got to a broad bean field. I asked them whose land it belonged to? They told me that it doesn't matter whose land because children were free to pick anybody's broad beans on that particular day. I checked with the older children afterwards and they confirmed that this was a local custom. The older girls came to light the younger children's fire on their own initiative. To help others is a moral code which is put on children from a very young age (see Chapter V.I). By 11 years children show they have learnt about committing themselves. Friends go to school together and come back home together. They collect lunch boxes for each other and eat lunch together in school. They do homework together after going home. At school they help each other with the general cleaning of a classroom (*dasaochu*) and on Sunday often have a day out together. Of course they share each other's birthday parties. They also talk lots among themselves on all sorts of different topics. Moreover, on the busy seasons' holiday they help each others' families with housework and farming, such as cutting grass to feed rabbits, feeding chickens and ducks, picking up leaves of the mulberry tree for silk worms and so on.

(ii) Human feelings affected friendship a great deal. On the one hand, children enjoy each other's company. I noticed the two children who joined the younger children's group on their way to a field for the picnic. They worked hard to pick broad beans and enjoyed themselves very much, even sharing spoons and bowls with the other children. The older girls told me that when they were playing together or entertaining others, everybody took turns. This part of the whole relationship among friends can be counted as generous *wanglai* because they enjoyed giving to others rather than asking from others. The dominant feeling is enjoyment. On the other hand, emotional attachment also strengthened their relationship. They enjoyed each other's company very much and felt attached to each other just like real sisters. The girls told me that they really missed each other if they could not meet, especially after a row. They would sometimes use emotional blackmail against each other. The girls also helped each other solve problems, although sometimes a problem could not easily be solved. For example, originally there were six girls in their gang. One of them had a boyfriend when she was aged 12. She was showing off about this in front of them. The other girls thought it was not a good idea to have a boyfriend so early. One year later the girl who had the boyfriend dropped them. They said it was difficult to know whether or not she would be friends with them again. But although she was no longer one of their gang they still kept the secret about her, because if the school found out she might be expelled.

(iii) Although it was not easy to lose a little friend from one's friends' list, little friends or little sisters necessarily changed along a life journey. This kind of modification was mainly based on rational choice. QN, a 42-year-old man, had 8 little friends when he was a boy; he dropped three of them and added two others. He started his gang from primary school in the village, and went on to middle school in the township. After he passed his 16th birthday the above friends became part of his family's guests and came every year for a feast during the period of lunar New Year. During the Cultural Revolution when he was working to reclaim the Lake Tai with some villagers from another village he made another little friend. When he was serving in the army he made one more little friend who came from a neighbouring township. All the above friends formed his current friend networks.

(iv) There was much less religious colour in gangs of little sisters or little brothers in socialist society than there was before the Liberation in 1949. An old lady told me that when she was young she was a member of a gang of little sisters. Apart from playing together they also joined a bigger group called the Buddha Guanyin group (*guanyinhui*). Almost all the girls would attend this group. They went to worship Buddha Guanyin twice a year: on the

19th of the 2ndlunar month and on the 19th of the 9th lunar month. Boys and men would join another group called the group of sons and grandsons (*zisunhui*). They met twice a year: on the 20th of the 1st lunar month and the 20th of the 8th lunar month. They first went to a temple, then walked around fields carrying statues and afterwards settled in a host's house where they would have a feast. They carried the statues back to the temple when the event was over.

Emotional attachment and enjoyment of human feelings were the overriding factors in their friendly relationships when they were younger. But when they got older practical considerations, such as sharing housework or farming in the busy seasons, weighed more heavily. This part of the relationship can be counted as expressive *wanglai* (see "Events for a child starting school and under sixteen years old" of Chapter V.I).

4. Neighbours and fellow villagers

As part of family *lishang-wanglai* networks Kaixiangong villagers also had lists of neighbours and fellow villagers. My sampled families can easily provide lists of their neighbours and fellow villagers, just as they provide lists of agnatic kin, non-agnatic kin, little friends or sisters. Unlike Fei's geographical finding that "Conventionally people take the five households on each side of their residence as being their neighbours" (1939: 98), a village neighbourhood network can be formed with vertical and horizontal lines. One of the former heads of the village, Yao, told me that there was a custom called *zoudai* which means an older generation can pass its family's neighbours to a younger generation. In other words, a newly established family can inherit neighbours from its parents' family and pass them to its younger generation forever in a vertical way. This cycle is broader than the *yang* circle (Stafford, 2000a) because the *yang* circle limits its object within a family system. The local custom requires villagers to keep inherited neighbours wherever they move within the village, but also encourages a household to make new neighbours in a place it settles in. As a Chinese saying goes, "neighbours are dearer than distant relatives"; a relative far off is less help than a neighbour close by (*yuanqin buru jinlin*). The two translated versions of the saying show two sides, of generous and expressive *wanglai*. Thus any family can have vertical inherited neighbours as well as newly made neighbours in a horizontal line. The list of fellow villagers in a family *lishang-wanglai* network was the easiest one. AL told me that on average there were about 30 families in one group. Apart from her family's agnatic kin, non-agnatic kin, if there are any living in the same group, and neighbours, the rest of the families who lived in the same group were fellow villagers (*tong xiaozui de ren*).

This can be any number between 10 and 20 families.

After the villagers finished lunar New Year's feasts among close families of non-agnatic kin, they would hold tea parties (*kaichaguan*) for their neighbours and fellow villagers. I attended one such tea party held by JF Shen. It was in the evening because JF was working in a village enterprise during the daytime. There were eight people including two children, two men, and four women. The adults came from different families who were neighbours and fellow villagers. JF served double cups of tea for her guests, as FK's wife had done before and after the feast on the lunar New Year Day. One was sweet tea and the other savoury tea. There were also many sweets, watermelon seeds and so on. Throughout the tea party they enjoyed themselves with drinking, snacking, talking and laughing.

I was told there were 10 to 20 different kinds of tea party throughout a year. But only three of them can be counted as generous *wanglai*, with no additional element of instrumental purpose.[6] They are after the lunar New Year, after the Qingming festival (later than the 3rd lunar month) when the fresh tea went on market, and after the harvest of green beans. The tea party after the green bean harvest is purely for pleasure, unlike a tea party held after villagers finish helping each other peel green beans, which may be very enjoyable but is also an acknowledgement of labour support as part of an expressive *wanglai* (see Chapter V.I) In the above three tea parties women treated each other nicely and enjoyed themselves just like they did with the feasts among close non-agnatic kin during lunar New Year and after harvest.

Different *lishang* criteria can be seen from this kind of generous *wanglai* amongst neighbours and fellow villagers. For the villagers the moral judgment is that a tea party is an important form of socialising with each other. Fei had mentioned a kind of teashop (*chaguan*) in the township for men to enjoy themselves (1939: 129),[7] but in the village the tea party is supposed to be a social event for women.[8] Women are always busy with their everyday housework so a tea party is a way especially designed for them to relax and enjoy themselves. Apart from tea parties women sometimes pop into somebody's house in the afternoon and they serve each other a cup of tea. This kind of socialising is so important to the villagers that even in

---

[6] I will show the rest of the types of tea parties in chapters on Expressive *wanglai*.

[7] There is another kind of teashop which provides a service to set up tea parties for different family events as happened in Kaixiangong Village in the old society, and still existed in other villages up to 2002.

[8] For men there is another way of socialising. A woman Gu pointed at her door and explained to me that her house's main door never closed from the time she got up until she went to bed. This meant anybody is free to pop in (*cuanmen*) for a chat or a rest, without warning. In fact, usually it was men who normally popped in after dinner and she always offered them a cup of tea.

the most difficult period tea parties of this sort did not cease. In the hard times of the early 1960s they infused salted vegetables rather than tea and smoked soya beans to entertain their guests. Several old women continued this custom when they left the village. FY Tan, the old lady introduced in Chapter IV.I, currently lived in Miaogang Township with her older son and older grandson's family. She and four other old female villagers who lived in the same township took turns to hold tea parties every day. This was an important part of their life.

Human feelings in the custom of the tea party show in the villagers' enjoyment of tasting tea and being company for each other. I attended another tea party during the Qingming festival, held by AL. There were eight other people attending the party, including one little boy and one baby. The adults were all female. The purpose of the tea party was to taste a fresh tea they had just bought from the market, buying a   tasteful tea and sharing it with others is part of their tea culture. As well as a cup of fresh tea for everybody on the table there were peanuts, watermelon seeds, sunflower seeds and sweets. The party lasted for two hours from 14:00 to 16:00. During the tea party some of them chatted while drinking their fresh tea and eating snacks, while others fed a baby, sorted out yarn, or knitted a sweater. They said it was more fun to do the boring work with others than to do it at home.

Rational choice can also be seen clearly in such a tea party. Although the villagers told me that a tea party is supposed to include neighbours and fellow villagers within the same group, one can hardly gather more than 10 people at one party. Whether or not to attend a tea party involves rational choice. In a tea party after the lunar New Year, I asked the two men why they came to the tea party when it was supposed to be a women's activity? They explained that they represented their families for the tea party because their wives were either busy with children or housework in the evening. The choice of holding a tea party in the evening instead of afternoon also is the result of rational choice, since the host would have to take a day off from work in order to meet the custom of holding it in the afternoon. In the Qingming tea party, AL explained to me the reason the attendance was so low was because she chose a bad date, which was a day before the Qingming festival, and most of her guests decided not to come because they needed to stay at home to wrap *zongzi* (a pyramid-shaped dumpling).

I didn't find any evidence for drinking tea that related to religion in the village, even when I checked out a custom of Anhui Province, where in rural areas villagers were said to believe tea can purify one's heart or mind. They put a tea bag on a hand of a dead body rather than pour a magic potion (*mihuntang* or *yao*) into a dead person's mouth in order to prevent them from being bullied by ghosts in the other world. This custom serves as a contrast to Kaixiangong, where drinking tea is mainly for enjoyment of villagers' everyday life and a way of socialising.

IV.III. Vertical *wanglai* in villagers' festivals and religious life

Vertical generous *wanglai* relates to relationships between the village collective and villagers, or ancestors and members' families. They flow downwards and upwards reciprocally. Among them, the vertical generous *wanglai* between the village collective and villagers during periods of the village's festivals is to between human beings, but vertical generous *wanglai* in villagers' religious life is more complicated. Although there are already a multitude of studies about rituals, ceremonies and worship for ancestors and gods (see Chapter IX.I), I touch upon this field because Kaixiangong villagers extend their ideas about their everyday lives into the nether world. In other words, religious life is a special part of villagers' everyday life. It forms endlessly circulating *lishang-wanglai* networks. I will show during such occasions how vertical generous *wanglai* works with *lishang* criteria between the villagers and their ancestors (*bai shangzu* or *siren jie*) and the local gods or goddesses (*bai shen* and *bai zao*), and leave the vertical expressive *wanglai* between villagers and their ancestors, local gods and goddesses for the next chapters.

1. Cultural life – village festival

In Kaixiangong Village there wasn't an annual festival on a fixed day, like the Village Day in Roe Green Village in London where I lived. I've already mentioned the Spring Performance (*chuntaixi* – a stage play or drama in the Spring). It normally happens during the period of the 3rd and 4th lunar month. I am not sure when this custom started. Fei (1939) mentioned there was a *degi* (*taiji* – the foundation of the stage), ten years before his fieldwork there, which served both religious and recreational functions annually in autumn (103–104). An informant told me that in the old society (before 1949) there were sometimes two such events, in spring and autumn. It involved vertical generous *wanglai* between organisers and the villagers because rich persons paid for it as presents to fellow villagers. A villager told me that nowadays in the neighbouring townships successful business executives did the same. In Kaixiangong now the situation is a little more complicated. The village collective's involvement seems like a vertical generous *wanglai* with villagers, but the villagers are not very grateful.

I witnessed two completely different kinds of performance (see Photo III-36 and 37). On 8 March, Chunlei Shaoxing Opera Troupe (*yuejutuan*) came to the village from Shanghai and stayed for about 20 days. The Troupe was formed of 20 people, 14 female and 6 male. They lived in different villagers' houses but cooked and ate in XQ Yao's house. The village collective provided a warehouse that can hold 200 people free of charge The Troupe built a stage in the warehouse themselves. They performed twice a day and the places were always all taken. On 10 March a circus came from Fuyang Prefecture, Anhui Province. The 13 people in the circus were all related. The village collective provided one of the village's warehouses for their accommodation and a village ground for their performance free of charge. The circus ate and slept together in the warehouse. After each show a clown closed his fists in front of his chest and asked the audience to show their appreciation either by money or by their cheers if they had little money (*you qian peng qian chang, mei qian peng ren chang*). The villagers left tips. On top of that the village collective donated 80 *yuan* to them as expenses for the villagers' cultural life from the village account. The play and the show both presented what could be described as a combination of "Spring Snow" and the "Song of the Rustic Poor",[9] and very much enriched villagers' everyday life. As a yearly event the Spring Performance in Kaixiangong was similar to the Roe Green Village Day where I lived in London, though the former is more focused on a particular theme and the latter is much more mixed, with individual performers, games and sale of different goods. On the Roe Green Village Day the relationship between residents, resident association and performers or helpers in selling different goods can be counted as generous *wanglai* with each other because the profits would be spent on the village's Children's Christmas Party. Similarly, in Kaixiangong Village some villagers told me that in the matter of the Spring Performance the relationship between the village collective and the villagers can also be counted as generous *wanglai* because the collective helped the villagers' enjoyment of the cultural life.

Strictly speaking the relationship between the Troupe or Circus and village collective mixed an institutional relationship with generous *wanglai*. It is clear that both the Troupe and the Circus made a living as actresses[10] and performers, which involves market exchange. However, the relationships between the Troupe or Circus and village collective are not a strict market exchange because the village collective provided warehouses to them free of charge. There are slight differences between the village collective's treatment of the Troupe and of the Circus. The relationship between the Troupe and the village collective consists of an institutional exchange.

---

[9] *Yangchun baixue xiali baren* (Spring Snow melodies of the elite in the State Chu – highbrow art and literature, the Song of the Rustic Poor – popular literature or art).

[10] There are no male actors in the Shanghai Opera, which always uses a woman to play a man's role.

The relationship between the village collective and the Circus contains an element of generous *wanglai* because it treated the Troupe as a family business and gave them a tip of 80 *yuan* on top of providing a warehouse for them to live in for free.

I was surprised that there was no gratitude (*bao'en*) from villagers to the village collective over the matter of providing the villagers with Spring Entertainment, because this was not at all what I had been taught to expect during the course of my education. I sought to confirm this idea with the villagers. They told me that the idea of gratitude (*bao'en*) to an institution is not suitable for their everyday life. Their replies, below, demonstrate *lishang* criteria:

(i) The villagers believed that individuals or groups in higher positions are more likely to bestow favours on others, for instance rich people sometimes make donations for the public good. From the villagers' point of view, the moral judgement applicable to this situation is the idea of good being rewarded with good, and evil with evil (*shan you shan bao e you e bao*). They never entirely go along with the popular Chinese saying *di shui zhi en dang yong quan xiang bao* (to one who gave you a drop of water when you were in difficulties you should give back a whole spring of water in return when you get better).

(ii) When asked about the human feeling of paying a debt of gratitude to a higher placed individual or organisation, the villagers' examples always related to rich people who hold grand funerals for their parents. It can be a way of paying a debt of gratitude (*bao'en*) to their parents and at the same time showing off. I asked them how they felt about *enqing* (loving-kindness or gratitude) to the party and the government. OM told me that the party and the government always use the language of human feelings when they call people to do something voluntarily, although he never believed there is any human feeling between the party and villages. He speculated that this might be the way in which the government mobilised resources from people.

(iii) OM's reply involved rational calculation. He admitted that the village collective, as part of *lishang-wanglai* networks for a family, played a relatively important role because it controlled resources, as many researchers (i.e. Djilas, 1957; Szelenyi, 1978; Walder, 1983, 1986; Yan, 1996b) pointed out. But OM said he couldn't see how they owed anything much to the party and the state. All he saw was that the village collective took money and goods from the villagers and controlled resources from the higher level (*shangji*). In this case the villagers paid fees to the local government through the collective and it was the collective's duty to provide cultural life for the villagers.

(iv) There could be no religious sense involved in a relationship between the village collective and the villagers. During the period of Spring Entertainment, the village collective as an executive organ always prevented religious activities, which before 1949 had been a routine part of the old social order.

2. Worship of ancestors[11]

The reason ancestors are counted as part of a family's *lishang-wanglai* networks is because a son inherits the family name, property, and everything from his ancestor. He does not have absolute title, but rather holds these things in trust from the ancestor and must pass them on to the next generation, one after another in a reciprocating circle. Therefore, ancestor worship (*bai shangzu*) is a kind of vertical *wanglai* within a family. The internal relationship between family members and their ancestors is a personal relationship. In the villagers' words "our own ancestors are members of one's family after all" (*zijia xianren zonggui shi zijiaren*). It is very similar to Rubie Watson's statement that "Ancestors are, after all, members of the descent group; they are not 'outsiders', like gods and ghosts" (1988: 226). Since the ancestors are no longer corporeal both *wang* and *lai* between villagers and their ancestors actually involve the actions of villagers themselves and the imaginary reactions of their dead ancestors. I shall refer to the ancestors as imaginary because their responses are imagined by their descendants. Without the reactions of their imaginary ancestors the vertical *wanglai* between villagers and their ancestors would stop.

The villagers used two different terms of *bai shangzu* and *qing shangzu* to distinguish generous *wanglai* and expressive or instrumental *wanglai* with their ancestors. The purpose of *bai shangzu* means to pay their respects to ancestors through worship without asking anything in return, whereas *qing shangzu* means to ask or invite ancestors to take part in different family events for instrumental purposes (see Chapters IV to VII, and VIII.II). Amongst many rituals for ancestor worships there were only four such events related to generous *wanglai*, corresponding with festivals for human beings; villagers called them celebrating four festivals (*guosijie*, details see Chapter III.III). They are *qingming* festival (grave-sweeping day), *qiyueban* (ghost festival), *dongzhi* (the Winter Solstice) and *nianye* (lunar New Year's Eve). Here I will use *lishang* criteria to show why the villagers' imaginary ancestors react to ancestor worship with vertical generous

---

[11] I use the plural because the villagers worshipped many of their ancestors by using many wine cups and several pairs of chopsticks whenever they presented sacrifices to them.

wanglai:

(i) About 90 per cent of my sampled households replied that they celebrated all four of the annual festivals for ancestors[12]. This embodied a strong moral sense that it was their duty to continue the family bloodline, property and especially family tradition (*jia feng*). Frankly I didn't see much property inherited from their ancestors, but I heard villagers quoting lots of sayings from their "ancestors" – in a very broad and loose way. It might be that family traditions were more important and more respected than any others. The local *zongzi* (a pyramid-shaped dumpling made of glutinous rice wrapped in bamboo leaves) can be expressive of this. Traditionally, *zongzi* is popular in many areas of China for the Dragon Boat Festival (*duanwujie*, the 5th day of the 5th lunar month).[13] However, the villagers adopted it for the *qingming* festival by specifying two kinds of fillings in two types of *zongzi*. They are candied date (*mizao*) and cured meat (*larou*), which symbolised the sweet and bitter in their life. JF Tan told me that eating these fillings of *zongzi* was the way in which they shared weal and woe, comforts and hardship, or joy and sorrow with their ancestors (*tonggan-gongku*). This seems to me just like the morality of *yiku-sitian* when I was in primary school during the Cultural Revolution. *Yigu-sitian* was when a school invited a poor person to tell of his sufferings in the old society (before 1949) and his happiness in the new (after 1949), or recall the sorrows of the past and savour the joys of the present. The purpose of it is to keep people in their current position and encourage them to work hard for a better life.

(ii) The four festivals for ancestors were imbued with villagers' human feelings. An English translation for *wenhan-wennuan* is "to inquire with concern about somebody's well-being or welfare."[14] The Chinese characters of *wen* mean inquire with concern and *han* and *nuan* mean cold and warm. The term represents concern with someone's basic well-being. The villagers' four festivals for their ancestors vividly evoke the origin of the term. On the brightest day of spring villagers pull weeds and sweep the graves for their ancestors. In the hottest summer the villagers gave their ancestors *wonton* soup with rice cakes. In the coldest winter they sent their ancestors food, clothes and money. In the longest night

---

[12] Except one woman who stopped it after she became a Christian in 1987.
[13] It always refers to Qu Yuan, a famous patriot and poet of the state of Chu.
[14] Cidianzu, *A Chinese-English Dictionary* (Revised version), Beijing: Foreign Language Teaching and Research Press, p. 1059, 1995.

they gathered together to celebrate the New Years' Eve with their ancestors. Human feelings can also be seen from feelings of veneration, reverence, awe and fear towards their ancestors. This can be confirmed by my sample households' most common reason for the continuance of their ancestor worship, fear of stirring up their ancestors and getting themselves into trouble .

(iii) The villagers respected and loved their ancestors, but also made many adaptations based on rational choice in order to carry out the above festivals, which sometimes conflicted with their everyday life. For example, BY Zhou's stepfather set up a table for ancestor worship and BY set up a New Years Eve' family feast at the same table (see Chapter III.III). This was a new way of setting a table for worship. In the village traditionally every family has a fixed *zhongtang* in the main room of its house. *Zhongtang* consists of a long thin side table against the central northern wall of a main living room and a central scroll of painting hung above the table. The ancestral shrine was kept on the side table, as well as all the offering sacrifices and candle holders. They also had a separate dining table for everyday eating. But with changing lifestyles, a side table can now hardly be seen in the village.[15] Villagers put their dining table in the middle of the dining/living room, surrounded by four benches on each side. BY said this was convenient for their family life and social life.

Villagers also created new local customs in order to keep their traditions of ancestor worship. In regard to sweeping the graves, if a family finished the ritual of *sanqi* (three weeks after the person's death) one month before the festival then it should perform the ritual of *wuqi* (seven days after the person's death) on the day of the festival. If a family has just finished the ritual of *wuqi* before the festival then the family does not have to sweep the grave again during the festival. Villagers also had arrangements to balance the different rituals of local gods and villagers' everyday life events. If the festival period, within four days, covered a *yueban* (the 15th of any lunar month), for example the 2nd April 1996 was the 15th day of the 2nd lunar month, the villagers should go to a temple to burn incense and offer sacrifices to the local god as well as offering sacrifices to ancestors at home. If the festival period covered a ritual of *shengqian* (ceremony for completion of building a house)

---

[15] In Neiguan Village they kept the form of *zhongtang* with a replacement of the dining table to the side table. Villagers normally eat at a small short-legged table (*kangzhuo*) on *kang* (a kind of bed).

the family has to hold two separate feasts for different people and to offer sacrifices to ancestors separately with different kinds of offerings.

(iv) The four festivals for ancestors themselves are an expression of villagers' religious sense, even though one can still see the sense in other ways. During the *Qingming* Festival period and on the *Dongzi* Day only the older generation (*laobei*) is allowed to visit the younger generation's (*xiaobei*) families because it shows they are full of activity and health. The younger generation is only allowed to visit families whose older generation has died. They are not allowed to visit older generation's families because at these times it would bring bad luck (*bu jili*) to the older generation, symbolising that the younger generation wish them to die quickly (*cuiming*). Religious sense can also be seen from the symbolic meaning of food. The upper part of pig leg (*tizi*) means increasing life standard. Fish is for year after year with surplus (*niannian youyu*), which is almost everywhere the same in China because the pronunciation of *yu* (fish) is the same as *yu* (surplus). Meatballs symbolise family reunion, due to their shape and the pronunciation (*tuantuan yuanyuan*). The shape of a single bean sprout[16] looks like *ruyi* (an S-shaped ornamental object, usually made of jade, formerly a symbol of good luck) and they symbolise good luck (*jixiang ruyi*). The Chinese leaves symbolise the relationship between the villagers and their ancestors as evergreen. The sacrificial offerings for the four festivals are always odd numbers, for example 5 or 7 dishes, whereas those for human beings are even numbers, for example 8, 10 and 12. For the villagers the even numbers are lucky numbers in this world and in the nether world the lucky numbers are odd numbers. The distinction between human beings, ancestors or gods in some details of the rituals also involves religious sense. For instance, they treated ancestors as part of the family, which can be seen from the details of how they set the offerings table. They also applied this to local gods by treating them as home gods and visiting gods by calling the land god grandpa *tudi* (*tudi gonggong*), the kitchen god grandpa *zaoju* (*zaojun gonggong*), but the goddess lady *atai* (*ataimo*) or lady *xingan* (*xinganmo*).

Villagers distinguish between home gods, such as a land god (*tudi gonggong*) or a kitchen god (*zaojun gonggong*), and visiting gods such as a life goddess (*ataimo*) or a medicine goddess (*xinganmo*). The home gods were established when the house and kitchen were built, whereas

---

[16] In China there are two different types of bean sprouts: soya bean sprouts (*huangdouya*) were made of soya bean, and green bean sprouts (*laoye*) were made of green beans which are commonly seen in UK.

the visiting gods are only invited for special occasions. They worship the established gods by facing inwards into their house and face outwards for the visiting gods or goddesses. The villagers also varied the directions of worship for ancestors and gods. Sometimes they faced north to worship ancestors and faced south to worship visiting gods, and sometimes they faced west to worship ancestors and faced north for established gods. The importance of the directions of north, south, east and west is a typical idea relating to *feng shui*, although the houses are not always laid out strictly north-south facing.

3. Worship of local gods

Compared with ancestor worship, worship of the local gods is an external relationship for a family with the nether world. The different rituals form another vertical *wanglai* in the villagers' *lishang-wanglai* networks. The villagers classified the many rituals into different types. To me they can be best described with generous, expressive and instrumental *wanglai*. It seems nobody wanted to have negative *wanglai* with the local gods and goddesses on purpose, because they are too powerful and sacred. In the course of a year there was almost one ritual for a particular local god in each lunar month (see Chapter III.III). They were common customs with religious colour as part of villagers' everyday life. The generous *wanglai* related rituals or worships between the villagers and the local gods or goddesses (*baishen, bailaoye* or *baitai*) are as follows. In every year there was one biggest worship for the local gods as a general group (*qiang touxiang*), one medium worship for the land god (*baitudigong)* and twice each lunar month small regular worships for particular local gods and goddesses (*xiaobai*). Also, the villagers set their system of worship for the kitchen god (*baizao*) a little apart from others. Amongst kitchen god worship there were two big, two medium, and twice monthly regular worships (see Chapter III.III and Figure III.I).

Here I will use *lishang* to explain how generous *wanglai* between villagers as individuals, a family or a group of people and the local gods or goddesses worked in the village. Mayfair Yang described Chinese people as acting according to popular opinion (*heli*) or agreed principles, human feelings (*heqing*) and rules and regulations (*hefa*) (1994: 326). In Kaixiangong, the term *hefa* included accordance with those customs known as "old laws (*lao fa*)". All of this is true. But in addition, Kaixiangong villagers' actions were in accordance with human nature or heart (*hehu renxing* or *renxin*), which can be seen in particular in *wanglai* with gods and spiritual beings. Such actions can be explained with the four criteria of *lishang,* which will be presented below.

(1) Moral judgement

One of the most important judgements for the villagers in maintaining a relationship with local gods or goddesses through the relevant rituals is that they believed it was morally right, based on local agreed principles or popular opinion (*heli*), to do so. The villagers believed that the gods should be thanked for either averting evil or blessing them throughout the past year. Some acted as caretakers doing voluntary work in the temples to accumulate merit (*jide*). The term of *jide* (accumulate merit) was first given to me by the old man whom I mentioned in the Chinese New Year's Eve event (see Chapter III.I). He was taking the ends of candles from the big basin with a big strainer in order to let more people burn candles. A woman who worked in the East temple on the Chinese New Year's day also mentioned *jide* (accumulate merit). She told me that she was one of the people who started to rebuild the temple in 1993. She sold incense sticks, candles, and paper money on special occasions. She also did voluntary work to look after the temple by presenting offerings and selling the above things at cost price.

Ordinary villagers also followed local popular opinion and carried out religious rituals even under extraordinary circumstances. On the 15th of the 4th lunar month 1996, a few days after the local temples were destroyed, I went to the temples but saw nothing happening. However, I did see bundles of incense burning on burned honeycomb briquettes outside different houses around the village (see Photo I-39). I went into one and asked the woman there, JF Tan, for an explanation. She told me that it was her way of worshipping local gods at the middle of the lunar month. She also told me that the people who destroyed the temples were committing a sin (*zuonie*), which is the opposite of accumulating merit (*jide*). She said that she wouldn't give in to governmental policy which changed all the time like a baby's face or weather in June (*zhengce duo bian xiang xiaohai de lian he liuyue de tian*), although one should be careful to survive different political campaigns.

I also interviewed a local official in the township about the destruction of the local temples. He told me that the Miaogang Township was praised by higher-ups as a "non-religious township" in the 1950s. He couldn't understand why those feudal superstitions (*fengjian mixin*) always revived (*sihui fu ran*). A village leader also complained that it was very difficult to collect fees from the villagers, but there was never any problem getting them to make donations to the temples. This happened in Neiguan Village too. The villagers complained heavily about fees from the local government, at the same time as they willingly donated money and materials to the temples.

Although the local official and village cadres wondered at the above phenomena,

Kaixiangong villagers understood the reason. Those days villagers always said to each other with a jocular tone that *Miaogang mei miao le* (the "temple port" township has got no temples now)[17]. They were all laughing because they sensed the others' meaning. This meaning was explained by an old man. According to him the temples can be destroyed temporarily by the Communist Party but people's religious sense cannot be killed. The villagers can worship the kitchen god by the stove at home instead. Because the temples were destroyed during the Great Leap Forward and the Cultural Revolution, villagers still carried out their local traditions with their heart for they believed they were morally right (*youli*).

(2) Human feelings

The case of burning incense on a burned honeycomb briquette outside houses involved two types of human feeling. JY Yao told me that on the one hand, they were afraid of getting into trouble if they sang a different tune from the government (*yu zhengfu chang fandiao*), so nobody went to the temple for the ritual of *yueban* (15th of a lunar month). Similarly, a villager Tan explained to me that some villagers didn't admit to going to the township temple for the Chinese New Year's Eve event because they were afraid of being accused of superstitious behaviour (*mixin huodong*). This is why Figure III-1 showed fewer families at such an occasion than those worshipping the kitchen god at home.

On the other hand, JY Yao also told me that she and a number of neighbours adopted the practice of burning incense on honey briquettes outside their homes after the temples were destroyed, so as to keep their routine of worshipping local gods in the middle of the month. And they really enjoyed (*you yisi*) creating a way to carry out their religious observances under special circumstances. The human feeling of enjoyment can also be seen on other occasions. JY Yao told me she always enjoyed different kinds of worship and even more the creation of ways to deal with the changing situation. She saw that some of the children enjoyed them in the same way, even asking for the ritual a few days in advance because they treated this as their game. More commonly, villagers dressed up and came happily to the temple in a spirit of what they called *haobaixiang* (to be cheerful and have fun). There is a local saying that also reflects this point. It is *chanzui de poniang qin baizao,* which means housewives who are gluttonous like to worship the kitchen god often. In Neiguan, my other fieldwork village, the villagers made

---

[17] The name of the township Miaogang means temple port because it was located by the Lake Tai and used to have hundreds of temples in the past.

different paper statues to represent local gods and ghosts. A villager told me that the most enjoyable thing (*zui haowan de shi*) was to hit the ghosts with a stick or shout at the ghosts because that is the way for people to get rid of the anger stored up from everyday life.

(3) Rational calculation

Apart from political interference, there were always conflicts between villagers' everyday life and their religious life, so the way in which they dealt with them embodied rational choice. According to local custom, villagers should have something with rice and noodles for breakfast on the lunar New Year's day. This food symbolises the reunion of family members, and sweet and long life. However, BY Zhou's family, where I had my breakfast, had simplified this custom and only ate small rice balls with sugar, and had only rice or noodles, one at a time, each day of the Chinese New Year. There were many other cases where practical concerns simplified local customs. For example, JY Yao explained to me how worship of the land god was simplified. In the past she took her grandchild to the East temple for the worship. After the 1980s the villagers stood a honeycomb briquette or an aubergine outside the main entrance of their houses in order to insert incense sticks. But now she presented offerings on a stove, burnt candles and incense sticks and bowed by the stove at home. Recently, honeycomb briquettes are no longer used in everyday life so villagers simply stick incense into the soil in their courtyard to worship the land god.

Local customs as well as styles of worship can be modified. Like many villagers, Mrs Tan told me that she was too busy to go to temples for so many worships. So she worshipped the kitchen god mainly at home and occasionally worshipped the local gods in temples. From the 1990s she followed a way of combining the worship of local gods and the kitchen god on *chuyi yueban* (the 1st and 15th of each lunar month) at home which specified that if the ritual of worshipping local gods was performed at home then one should burn candles and incense only, not incense and paper money as at the temple. Mrs Tan felt more comfortable with the new custom because it fitted well with her everyday life and as well as religious life.

Again, instead of having a quiet relaxed New Year's day, as dictated by local custom, I found a family holding a wedding on that day. Mr Tan told me the custom was only a guide and people can make slight changes depending on their circumstances. He told me that when he was young the New Year's day had to be a quiet and relaxed day because people always *shousui* (see the Old Year out and the New Year in) until midnight, hold a reception for a new kitchen god (*jie zao*) on New Year's day, and prepare food for feasts for the following days. So they wanted to have a peaceful day. When he got married the custom changed slightly because the reception for a new kitchen god (*jie zao*) on the New Year's day was less important, which meant one could either hold it at a different time or not do it at all. So a new custom appeared and the villagers agreed to move the date of *hui niangjia* (for a married-out daughter's family reunion with her natal family) from the second day to the New Year's day. Tan told me he only had one daughter and decided to take a man as son-in-law (*zhao nuxu*) from a neighbouring village. His daughter and her little sisters (*xiao jiemei*, namely friends) preferred the New Year's day, therefore, they chose that day. The reception of a new kitchen god is not on a fixed day because they have so many other festivals to arrange, worship of ancestors, weddings, family feast with closest agnatic kin, around the lunar Chinese New Year. So local custom allowed villagers to choose a quiet day for the reception of a new kitchen god on any day around the period of the lunar New Year.

The above examples came from my observations. I believe that some local customs had different versions, which I did not take part in, but which are changed by the villagers creatively and rationally in order to cope with changing circumstances. For example, the 6th day of the 6th lunar month used to be the birthday of pets, cats and dogs. However, a villager told me that this custom has changed, a good twenty years ago. The saying *liuyue liu mai lai huntun liu yi liu* (See Chapter III.III) is still there but the meaning has now changed completely. This is a day for both fiancé and fiancée and married couples to bring *huntun* wrappings, pork meat and fresh fruit to visit their future or present parents-in-law.

(4) Religious sense and spiritual beliefs

Religious sense can be seen in various ways. The old man who was a voluntary caretaker at the *Laotai* temple told me the following story. He said that the grandpa Qiu was a very powerful lake god. People normally called him Qiu *laotai ye* respectfully. The lake god is also called "scalp ringworm Qiu" (Qiu *lali*) because he suffers from the condition. Whenever great wind and waves appeared on the Lake Tai people shouted "Qiu *lali*" and the storms would stop immediately. I checked grandpa Qiu with many people of different ages and sexes who went to the temple. They did not know much about him except that he could bless them and keep them safe and sound on their life journey, year after year. So it was very important to worship grandpa Qiu, the local god, to keep all well and lucky and auspicious before the start of the next Lunar New Year. Another ritual that invoked good luck was to stroke particular trees and then stroke their own face and hair to get energy, luck, shelter, blessings and so on from the local gods through the spiritual tree.

When I use the term "religious sense" I am referring not to the explicit performance of religious activities, consciously performed acts of vertical *wanglai* from the villagers to their ancestors or gods, but the general beliefs behind such activities whether articulated or implicit. Religious sense is a *lishang* criterion related to beliefs in *fu* (luck, fortune), *yuan* (predestined relationship), *ming* (fate), and implicit in the symbolic meanings that villagers ascribe to food and decorations.

The four criteria of *lishang* have all impacted on the instances of generous *wanglai* in this chapter. They are not of course of equal importance. Villagers told me that they placed differing weight on one or another of these ideas depending on the situation. When I asked random interviewees "why do you come to worship?" at the temples on the lunar New Year's Eve and New Year's day I got different answers. (i) Some villagers said they came because it was the custom. They put their palms together in front of their chest and shook them, made different kinds of bow, or even kowtowed. They offered sacrifices, burnt incense, candles and papers. This kind of activity is rational, based on deliberate obedience to "old law" (laofa), a conscious, thought-out decision. Some of them said "*laile jiu yisi daole*", meaning that going to the temple in person shows one's sincerity to gods, part of a similar conformity to old law. (ii) Some people wished to make an obeisance to the gods to express gratitude for keeping away bad luck or evil spirits. This was linked to their moral judgement. (iii) At the same time most villagers prayed to the gods to go on blessing them with good fortune (*fuqi*). They said that "*laile jiu you fu*" (only one coming here to the temple can be blessed)."(iv) Some villagers said that they came to the temple simply for enjoyment (*hao baixiang, wanwan ma*): "one enjoys the lunar New Year by remembering to worship the local gods" (*zijia guonian wu wangle baibai shen*). This shows that the four *lishang* criteria co-exist in a particular *wanglai* but not necessarily in the same order of importance. Sometimes they are in opposition to each other, sometimes one or two criteria count for more than others. Going to the temple is governed more by religious sense (reverence or awe, even at a low level) than moral judgement (a sense of what is right or wrong regardless of divine reward or punishment). Villagers' usage of *lishang* criteria provides a space for creativity in changes of situation. The villagers call it *yi bubian ying wan bian* (coping with a constantly changing situation by sticking to a fixed principle or policy, namely, *lishang*) wherever they go, whatever they do, or however things change.

So far I have shown how "pigs were fed" at the stage of laying a foundation or investment for having a rewarding relationship whether with human beings or supernatural beings. I often use the word "enjoyment", and I'd like to clarify this usage. (i) The broad sense can be a deep level of motivation for *lishang-wanglai* as a whole, as an enjoyment of social creativity (see IX.III). (ii) The narrow sense can be one of the positive human feelings, for example happiness or enjoyment related to *lishang* criteria. (iii) It can also be a characteristic that distinguishes generous *wanglai* and expressive *wanglai*. If enjoyment for its own sake predominates, the *wanglai* is generous, whereas if expectation of material return or obligation is more important, then the *wanglai* is expressive. Note that both elements are almost always found together. According to the Kaixiangong villagers, festivals and annual cycle events are life-cycle events with generous *wanglai* and expressive *wanglai*. For them the gifts and feasts given during the festivals are generous *wanglai* because they enjoy giving to others without expecting any kind of material return at that time. This is different from expressive *wanglai* in life-cycle events and house construction (see Chapters V to VII) because that kind of *wanglai* requests certain returns of finance, labour, materials and information. It is a part of social support. In other words, the reciprocal visits with gifts and feasts during the festivals (generous *wanglai*) can be seen as investments for maintaining relationships. The reciprocal visits with gifts and feasts during the life-cycle events and house construction (expressive *wanglai*) can be seen as outcomes of the investment.

Chapter V

Expressive *wanglai* in life-cycle events (I)

Expressive *wanglai* is embedded in the whole process of life-cycle events from a person's birth to death. The social support arrangements for those life-cycle events reveal the course of how *lishang-wanglai* networks (see Chapter X.I and II) are established, maintained and changed. Since the effects of expressive *wanglai* in life-cycle events are so rich I will spend two chapters (Chapters V and VI) to introduce them. Chapter V consists of sections on birth and growing up, establishing a marriage relationship, and house construction. Chapter VI covers family division, elderly care, funerals and post-funeral rituals.

V.I. Birth and growing up

This period, in theory, starts as early as when a child is an 8-month-old foetus and extends to after the child's 16th birthday when there are celebrations for seeing-off a person who is starting work, entering further education, or joining the army and so on. As the child grows there are many events involving *lishang-wanglai*: before and after the birth (*dan shengtang* and *dan shutang*), celebrations for the one-month old birthday (*manyue baitai*), the one-year old birthday (*zhousui baitai*), to be a guest and to be visited (*zuoxinke* and *kantouke*), events for a child pre-school and starting school (*taoshubao* and *taotuanzi*), celebration of the sixteenth birthday and seeing-off ceremonies (*shiliusui baitai* and *huansonghui*). Chapter II.I shows details of all these events and how different relationships are gradually built up around the individual through these different events during childhood. All the contacts between a focal person and his or her different relations manifest expressive *wanglai*. On such occasions the various relatives express their care and attention by visiting each other with gifts or entertaining each other with feasts, The process of making such relationships can be described as "fattening pigs" or knitting *lishang-wanglai* networks (see Chapter IX.II).

1. Expressive *wanglai*

Table V-1 shows the workings of expressive *wanglai*. The first 10 rows of the table relate to the growing-up period. It shows that by the age of 18 the individual has more or less fully formed his or her *lishang-wanglai* networks. They consist of agnatic and non-agnatic kin, neighbours and fellow villagers of both a child's family and of his or her *jiujiu*'s family, possibly also including all the close non-agnatic kin's families, friends including little friends or sisters and classmates, the village collective, ancestors and a local goddess and gods.

Table V-1. Expressive *wanglai* in life-cycle events

Events	Agnatic kin	Neighbour	Fellow villagers	N-Ag. Kin**	Mother's brother/ wife's natal family	Father's sister/ married daughter	Old Friends/ Little friends	Coll./ Others ***	Ancestors	Gods / goddess
Before birth event (*dan shengtang*)	← →	-	-	◄··· ◄	◄··· ← →	◄··· ← →	-	-	-	-
After birth event (*dan shutang*)	← ⇒	← →	← ⇒	← ↓	← ⇒	← ⇒	← ◄··· ⇒	-	-	-
One month old Birthday at home (*manyue baitai*)	···⇒ ⇒ ←	→ ···⇒ ⇉	···⇒ ⇒ →	⇒ ← ◄	⇄ ← ⇒	-	← → →·	⇄	⇒ ←
One month old birthday at mother's brother's home)	⇒ ◄···	⇆ ◄···	⇆ ◄···		→ ⇄	-	←-- ···⇒	-	-	···⇒ ◄···
One year old birthday (*zhousui paitai*)	⇒ ←	-	-	⇒ ←		-	← ⇒	-	-	⇒ ←
To be a guest (*zuo xinke*)	···⇒ ⇒	→··⇒	→··⇒	→ →	→ →	⇒ ←			-	-
To be visited (*wang touke*)	⇒ ⇒	← →	⇒	← →	← ⇒	↔		-	-	-
Asking book bag (*tao shubao*)	···⇒ ⇒	···⇒ ⇒	→··⇒	→ -	← ⇒	-	→	-	-	-
Asking rice balls (*tao waisheng tuan*)	···⇒ ⇒	···⇒ ⇒	···⇒ ⇒	-	← ⇒	-	⇆ ⇄	-	-	-
The 16th birthday (*shiliusui baitai*)	◄ ⇒	→ ···⇒	→ ···⇒	⇆ ⇒	← ⇒	⇆ ⇒	← ⇒		-	⇄
Seeing-off ceremony (*songxing jiu*)	← ⇒	-	-	← ⇒	← ⇒	← ⇒	← ⇒	← ⇒	-	-
Small betrothal rite (*xiaopan*)	◄··· ···⇒ ← ⇒	···⇒ ⇒	-	◄··· ···⇒ ← ⇒	◄··· ···⇒ ← ⇒	◄··· ···⇒ ← ⇒	···⇒ --⇒ ← →	◄··· ···⇒ ⇆ ⇆	-	⇄
Large betrothal rite (*dapan*)	···⇒ ◄ ⇒	···⇒ ⇒	···⇒ ⇒	···⇒ ◄ ⇒	◄··· ···⇒ ← ⇒	◄··· ···⇒ ← ⇒	···⇒ --⇒ → →	◄··· ···⇒ ⇆ ⇆	-	-
Seeing-off feasts, teas, & gifts etc. (*chaigurou jiu,*)	···⇒ ◄···	···⇒ ◄···	···⇒ ◄···	◄···	◄···	◄···	←--	-	-	-
Seeing-off ceremony (*xinniangzi jiu*)	← ···⇒	-		← ···⇒	◄··· ···⇒	◄··· ···⇒	◄··· ···⇒ ⇆ ⇄	◄··· ···⇒	···⇒ ◄···	···⇒ ◄···
Wedding ceremony (*xijiu*)	← ⇉ ···⇒	→ ··⇒	→ ··⇒	◄ → ···⇒	← → ···⇒	← → ···⇒	← ⇄ ⇉ ⇆	⇄ ◄ ⇒ ◄··· ⇆	⇒ ←	⇒ ←

Events	Agnatic kin	Neighbour	Fellow villagers	N-Ag. Kin***	Mother's brother/ wife's natal family	Father's sister/ married daughter	Old Friends/ Little friends**	Coll./ Others*	Ancestors	Gods / goddess
First call for bride's natal familiy (*huimei*)	⇉→ ⇇···	⇉↘ ···↗	⇉↘ ···↗	-	-	-	-	-	-	-
Wife's father and his agnatic kin's visit (*manyue, etc.*)	···→ ← ⇇··	⇉→ →	⇉→ →	-	-	-	-	-	-	-
Wife's mother and brother's visit (*shier zhao*)	···⇉↘ ← ⇇··	-	-							
To be new guests in bride's natal family (*zuo xinke*)	⇉→ ◀··· ◀···	-	-	-	-	-	--→ ←--	-		
Welcome feasts & teas parties for a new wife (*zijiaren jiu, etc.*)	⇉→ ← ←	← ⇉→ ⇉↘	← ⇉→ ⇉↘	-	-	-				
To be new guests in groom's non-agnatic kin (*zuo xinke*)	⇉→ -	← -	← ←	⇉→ ←	⇉→ ←	⇉→ ←		-	-	-
Paying a foundation stone (*bai dipan*)	← →	← →	← →	-	← →	← →	-	→ ←	-	→ ←
Putting up the first floor (*jia louban*)	← →	← →	← →	← →	-	-		⇄		
Putting up the rooftrees (*shangliang jiu*)	⇐ →	← →	← →	⇐ →	← →	← →	← →	→ ←	-	-
Moving into the new house (*shengqian jiu*)	← →	← →	← →	← →	← →	← →	-	→ ←	⇄	⇄
House completion tea party	← →	← →	← →	-						
Family division (*fenjia*)	-	-	-	← →	← →	← →			⇄	⇄
Elderly care (*yang lao*)	-	-	← →	-	-	← →		← →		
Pay condolence to the deceased (*pu xiang*)	← →	-	-	← →	← →	← →	-	← →	-	⇄
Funeral feast (*sushi jiu*)	⇐ →	← →	← →	⇐ →	← →	← →	⇐ →	← →	-	→ ←
Cremation (*huohua*)	← →	-	-	-	← →	← →	-	← →	-	→ ←
Bury ash box	-	-	-	-	-	← →	-	← →	-	→ ←
The first seventh days (*zuo touqi*)	-	-	-	-	-	← →	-	-	→ ←	⇊←
The third seven days (*zuo sanqi*)	-	-	-	-	-	← →	-	-	⇄	⇊←
The fifth seven days (*zuo wuqi*)	← →	-	-	← →	← →	⇆	-	← →	⇄	→ ←
Wear the mourning material (*daixiao*)	-	-	-	-	-	⇆			⇄	-
Sweep a grove at Qingming Festival for first three years (*shang fen*)	-	-	-	-	-	← →	-	-	⇄	-

* This table is based on a person's life-cycle events from before birth to after death. It contains three parts: from before birth to 16 years old, the period of pre- and post-marriage together with house construction, and family division, elderly care and before and after death. For the first part the solid arrows could be for either a boy or girl, the bold solid arrows for his or her family and their relations, the dotted arrows for indirect relations through a child's mother's brother. For the second part the solid arrows are for a fiancé/groom/husband and dotted arrows for a fiancée/bride/wife, the bold solid arrows for the male's family's relations, and the bold dotted arrows for the female's family and its relations. For the third part see key below.

**The column of Non-agnatic kin refers to the broadest range of a given family, which include close non-agnatic kin (*jin qin*) and distant non-agnatic kin (*yuan qin*), older generational non-agnatic kin (*lao qin*) and younger generational non-agnatic kin *(xin qin)*, as well as quasi kin (*guofang qin*) and master or apprentice relations for artisans or craftspeople (*shitu guanxi*). The columns of mother's brother or wife's natal family and father's sister or married-out daughter are close non-agnatic kin. They are separated from other non-agnatic kin because they are more important and sometimes involved in an event separately.

*** "Collective and others" refers to the village collective and other sources which could be involved in events of a family, for example matchmakers for a wedding or priests for a funeral.

Directions and orders of arrows

→ The arrow pointing right indicates the action is outwards from the family.

← The arrow pointing left indicates the action is coming into the family (except matchmakers who are connected to two families and play one role)

⇄ The top arrow signifies the person who starts *wanglai* action, the second is for the person's response, either then or a little later.

⇆ The top arrow means other relations give gifts or attend feasts to/for the given person or family first, the bottom arrow is for the reaction of the given family or person

Key to arrows

⇐ A family's broadest list of agnate or non-agnatic kin which include close and distant relatives, older and younger generations involved in the given family's events

⇐⋯ Matchmakers are formed by both fiancé and fiancée's families

⇐ A person with his or her family when they were under 16 years old; or a fiancé/groom/husband with his family

⇐⋯ A person and his or her mother's brother's relations before 16 years old, or a wife's mother and her brother after she got married

⇐⋯ A fiancée/bride/wife with her natal family

⇐ A new wife with her mother-in-law

⇐ A new couple visit their relatives together

← Relations of parents' or married children who arrange events from birth to death

◀··· Relations of a fiancée, wife's natal families

← Relations of oneself from as baby/child/fiancé/groom/husband

◀- A fiancé/bride/wife's natal family's relations

(1) The bold arrows in Table V-1 indicate the importance of different events

The bold arrows in the non-agnatic kin column show that both "before the birth" and "one-month old birthday" are important events because they involve three or four generations of non-agnatic kin. The former is the ceremony at which a new generation of non-agnatic kin joins the focal family's network. The latter is mainly to establish a basic *lishang-wanglai* network for the focal child. This comprises the child's relatives, neighbours, fellow villagers, friends, ancestors and local goddess (see related events in Chapter II.I). On the row for the 16th birthday event there are two bold arrows, in the columns for both agnatic and non-agnatic kin. This event is the largest and grandest of the life-cycle events during childhood. It involves three or four generations of both agnatic and non-agnatic kin, because this is locally regarded as the most important event to mark the child becoming an adult.

(2) Whereas the solid arrows represent basic relations of a focal person or family's network, the dotted arrows are relatives of the person or family's close non-agnatic kin

Although relatives of the person or family's close non-agnatic kin might or might not become part of the person or family's network, it is important to acknowledge their existence. For example, Zhou, the husband of a before birth event (see Chapter II.I), told me his own experience of this network. Zhou said although his family could have arranged a marriage for him with or without love, they were content with his choice of a marriage based on true love. But he would never have met and got to know his future bride, who lived in a different village, without the networks made through the local systems of "to be a guest" or "to be visited".

Zhou's wife is a daughter of a neighbour to one of Zhou's little friends. On the one hand, those neighbours can be seen as one of the dotted arrows leading to Zhou's family's relations. On the other hand, Zhou's family and its close relatives can be seen as one of the dotted arrows of the little friend's family's relations because he is a nephew of one of the neighbours of Zhou's mother's natal family in Kaixiangong Village. When the little friend was five years old he visited his aunt's (father's sister) family and was introduced to Zhou, who was playing with his mother's natal family. When the little friend was seven he became Zhou's classmate in Kaixiangong Primary School, there being no school in his village. When Zhou was eight years old he paid his first return visit to the little friend. This was also the first time he met the girl who was his little friend's neighbour's daughter. Since then Zhou, his little friend, and the girl played together over many years. They all graduated from the Miaogang High School together when they were 16 years old. Zhou told me that eventually the girl became his wife, and the little friend is one of the closest friends among the 45 who were invited for his wedding banquet. Thus the relationships among Zhou, his little friend, and the girl changed from the dotted arrows of Zhou's family to solid arrows.

(3) The directions of arrows in Table V-1 show the direction of gift giving

Following the rows, it can be seen that the gift flow changes between balance and imbalance several times over the events during the growing-up period. The rows corresponding to the before and after birth events and the seeing-off ceremony show how all the relations visit the focal family with gifts on their own initiative. The case study of the "after birth event" (see Chapter II.I) shows how the Rao family received gifts and money totalling 1,680 *yuan* from relatives, friends, neighbours and fellow villagers and spent 1,200 *yuan* for entertainment at the event. How could the gift givers be sure they would receive return for the gifts they gave? Mrs Rao explained to me that the imbalanced figure always reminded her that the Rao family "owe some *renqing*" to their friends, neighbours and fellow villagers. When the next opportunity arises she will balance it. If we concentrate on the columns of "neighbours" and "fellow villagers" we can see that the rows of "one-month old birthday" and "to be visited" show that the focal family gave gifts to neighbours and fellow villagers which balanced each other. This balance is in both the quantity of gifts and order of action, namely, it completed a round of visiting and hosting each other. The rows of "asking for rice balls" and "the 16th birthday" show only a one-way gift flow from a focal family to its neighbours and fellow villagers – this time it is the focal family that gave gifts first and stored some *renqing* with their neighbours and fellow villagers. Thus the all-important imbalance of the expressive gift relationship is re-established.

(4) Table V-1 divides all relations into four groups by social and spiritual support resources

The four groups are agnatic kin, neighbours and fellow villagers; non-agnatic kin, friends; collective and others; ancestors, gods and goddesses. For agnatic kin, neighbours and fellow villagers, the support normally provided is labour, together with a token of money or gifts and materials. In the case of the "before birth event", Zhou's male and female agnatic kin offered different types of support throughout the day, in the form of shopping, kitchen assistance, dish washing, cleaning, sorting gifts, serving tea or meals and providing company for the guests (Photo V-1). The agnatic kin also brought tables and benches and other equipment for the event. They also provided a little financial support in the form of *fenzi*, which consist of about ten *yuan* wrapped in a red paper bag per household. At the event neighbours and fellow villagers provided support by giving gifts or lending tables or benches for feasts.

PhotoV-1. This set of photos show how both male and female agnatic kin provided labour support for different family events

Non-agnatic kin should include a child's mother's brother's (*jiujiu*) family and a daughter who has married out of the family. In Table V-1 the columns "mother's brother" and "daughter married out" show that these two relations sometimes play a more positive role than other non-agnatic kin. The events of the "one-month old birthday", "asking book bag", and "asking rice balls" would happen in particular between a child and *jiujiu*'s family and then be extended to other relations. The events of "house construction" and "elder's birthday" would involve *wanglai* between a daughter who married out of the family and her natal family. In the "before birth event" the significant gifts from non-agnatic kin can be understood as indirect financial support. At this event they also express their sense of caring by chatting with the pregnant woman and her mother-in-law, to share the complicated feelings before her birth and exchange experiences of labour and birth, and so on. This chatting serves a similar function to that at an antenatal class in Northwich Park Hospital, London which I attended in preparation for my own baby's birth.[18]

Friends served a similar function to non-agnatic kin. In the growing-up period little friends were mostly classmates, which originates as an institutional relationship. It is very likely to be personalised as expressive *wanglai* in the village. The two events of pre-school education and starting school allow relationships with classmates to be personalised because everybody expresses their feelings of wanting to get to know and be closer to others by giving others gifts on their own initiative. For Zhou, close classmates can be counted as little friends and distant classmates remain in an institutional relationship. Once a classmate becomes a little friend of a focal person, and the focal person is old enough, he or she is obligated to provide financial and emotional support when requested.

Although a relationship between the village collective and a household is supposed to be an institutional relationship, it can also include financial and emotional support. When occasion presents, the relationship between villagers and their collective (through a representative) can be personalised reciprocally, for instance a representative of the Village Collective might use charm to personalise villagers in order to gain trust from them for the Collective. In the growing-up period the only event which involves such a relationship is the seeing-off ceremony for someone joining the army. Before the rural reform of the 1980s, a youth looked forward to joining the army because this was one of best ways of improving his prospects. But after rural reform villagers believed that to serve in the army would waste time that could otherwise be used to get rich. Sending people to the army was one of the tasks of the village collective, and it had to work very hard to fulfil it, often needing to personalise the relationship with candidates and their families.

---

[18] The difference is that in the UK the husband is requested to participate in an antenatal class. Both wife and husband work together for exercising deep breathing and discussing pain relief methods. This means that the husband is also participating in the process of labour for both emotional support and sharing the experience of labour. But in the UK the wife doesn't need to have a "confinement in childbirth for one month" (*zuo yuezi*), which is a common practice in China in both rural and urban areas, where it is believed to be vital for the woman who has suffered great pain during labour to stay at home for one month to avoid wind getting into suture joints before they have settled.

Ancestors, gods and goddesses provide emotional and spiritual support. There is no objectively provable exchange relation between villagers and their ancestors and local deities, but villagers regard it as a given. Nearly all my sampled households said that they had general spiritual beliefs, and this is borne out by the way they involved themselves in many kinds of event involving spirits. The grandmother of the Song family told me that although it took some effort to prepare the worship for her granddaughter's first birthday's events, it was important for her to feel they could get the *ataimo*'s (a life goddess) blessing through its performance. Two weeks after the Song family's daughter's one-year old birthday event I went to visit another family with a nearly one-year-old daughter. The girl's mother told me that she had held a nice one-month old birthday for her daughter, which took care of all the relationships in her family including that with the goddess. To my surprise she then said "But I am not going to give a ceremony for my daughter's one-year-old birthday because I am less superstitious (*bu name mixin*) than other villagers." It is clear that she saw the one-year old birthday ceremony – *zhousui baitai* – in terms of an exchange with the goddess, of no interest to her because she was not superstitious.　There will be more about the religious sense of this in the next section.

2.　*Lishang* criteria

I will now use *lishang* criteria to explain how expressive *wanglai* operates during childhood. I will also show how the criteria of *lishang* vary in their relative importance during this part of the life cycle.

(1) Moral judgement

The moral sense of giving and sharing is embedded in the flow of gifts. Zhou's wife told me how she started making friends with her classmates by giving and sharing. When she was seven years old she went to Kaixiangong Primary School because the village where she was born and grew up did not have one. She felt it was difficult to fit in with the class to begin with because the majority of children came from Kaixiangong Village. However, what she learnt from the flow of rice balls and sweets is an idea that giving gifts could make friends, even though she could not remember which were whose because everybody gave sweets and rice balls to each other. After that whenever she had sweets and snacks she would bring them to school and share them with others. She also gave manual help to others on a cleaning day when the child on duty was absent. This kind of behaviour was encouraged by her teacher who always praised the children for being good pupils and doing good deeds (*haoren-haoshi*). Gradually she made a few friends through giving and sharing. When she went to Miaogang High School and even after she married into Kaixiangong Village from a neighbouring village she remembered how she had first learnt to make friends.

In 2000 Ren's wife, whom I met at her "after birth event" (*dan shoutang*), told me how parents or grandparents carry out and pass on to the younger generation local customs by encouraging them to give and share with others. She learnt this from her son who learnt this in fact from his grandmother. A child is expected to bring his or her younger cousin(s) of non-agnatic kin to visit a younger child or children who lived in the same group. Mrs Ren had a son Ming who lived in group 7. A little boy Ban was three years older than Ming. When Ban was young he attended the events celebrating Ren's babyhood and had received rice balls from Ming's family since he was born. So he knew a little about Ming and to some extent was obligated to Ming's family. He also knew all the cousins' details through "being a guest" and "being visited" and other kinds of *wanglai* with his non-agnatic kin. One day, when Ban was 7 years old, he realised that one of his cousins who lived in group 9 was the same age as Ming of his own group 7. They were both four years old. So he brought the cousin, a girl, to visit Ming's family. Mrs Ren's mother-in-law, Ming's grandmother, entertained them very well. All the children very much enjoyed each other's company and started to play together regularly. One year later, Mrs Ren continued, Ming and the girl who went to the same nursery in the village became close friends.

Mrs Ren also told me another story about how Ming made his little friends. Ming and Jia had been good friends since birth because Ming was 40 days older than Jia, who lived in group 6, a neighbouring group to that of Ming. In 2001, these two little boys, both aged five and a half, rode bicycles in the village and saw a girl in a village shop. She was one of their nursery's little friends who lived in group 4. They decided to take her back to Ming's home. Ming's mother, Mrs Ren, gave them a big tea and the children played happily together. Just before Mrs Ren took the girl back home her grandmother came to collect her. The grandmother had found a message from the village shop saying that her granddaughter had gone away with the two little boys Ming and Jia. Since then the girl became another close friend of Ming. This story illustrates that making friends can be spontaneous and does not necessarily follow the local customs. However both cases of Ming making little friends from other groups show how parents generally encourage children to make friends.

This caused me to reflect about how relationships are established between my son and his little friends in the UK, where there are similar but different systems for mothers and babies making friends. When my son was a few months old I made a few friends for my son: two through the antenatal class, two from the National Children Trust's (NCT) mothers' and babies' networks, one from the village where we live and one from a local clinic's waiting room. When he went to nursery school, and the reception of his first big school, he made four new friends. However, three of them moved to other countries and we ourselves moved to another part of London, where my son found himself in the same class in his new school as one of the children we had met in the NCT group. They became best friends until this child too moved. After losing the last friend of his early childhood my six-year-old son faced the problem of making friends for himself independently. One day I saw him sending a little present to our neighbour's son, XJ. I was interested in why he did so. He told me that it is good to give to others because that was one of the Ten Commandments that God gave Moses. I suppose he might have learnt the idea of "giving to neighbours" from a Western culture, as well as having been influenced by his Chinese mother and neighbour. Our neighbour gave us a present when the family moved in, and soon afterwards I gave her something in return, because we were both Chinese and had a common understanding of reciprocity. A few months later when the neighbour's son got a place in his class, my son gave him a small present, but was then badly teased by him a few days later. I found it is very difficult for a child to make new friends when they get older. Others have either formed their own friendship circles, have siblings which involve complicated arrangements for each of them, are busy with after school clubs, and one way or another are fully occupied. My point is that it is common for mothers to put effort into helping their children to make friends from a very young age, but their understanding of how to do it varies from place to place.

The case of the elder cousin bringing his younger cousins into his group in Kaixiangong Village fits perfectly into the local system of *lishang-wanglai*. Although Ming and Jia brought a girl back home, which is not part of any local custom, the way in which Mrs Ren encouraged them is based on the principle that giving or offers of help are a virtue in making friends. I can't simply apply the village's way of making friends to my own life on the other side of the world, the principle of giving to others can be shared everywhere in the world.

(2) Human feelings

The degree of emotional attachment often depends on frequency of *wanglai*. After the "before birth event" (*dan shengtang*) Mrs Zhou told me that it was very important for her that her natal family lived only one hour's walking distance away from Kaixiangong Village, because it would be much easier for her and her married in family to *zoudong* (another local term for come and go or *wanglai*) with them. This allowed the relationship between Mrs Zhou's married-in family and natal family to be maintained more easily, and for them to feel closer to each other. As the local saying goes, "*qinqi yue zou yue qin, linju yue zou yue jin*" (literally the more *wanglai* the closer between relatives, the more *wanglai* the nearer between neighbours).

Here the meaning of "neighbours" can be as broad as fellow villagers and little friends in the village. Mrs Zhou told me that although her son's best little friend lived in a neighbouring group, they in fact lived as close as neighbours since both families lived on the adjacent edges of their own groups. They have contacted each other frequently since their babies were born. Over the past five years both the parents and children became strongly attached to each other and the children were called little brothers. Especially, Mrs Zhou added, as her son's generation would not have any siblings so such little brothers or little friends are particularly important to them.

It is not difficult to imagine that the relationship between the above two little friends could become like the relationship between Mr Zhou and his special little friend who brought Mr and Mrs Zhou together. I would like to reflect on the village's custom to show how little friends or little sisters get closer through expressive *wanglai*. As I mentioned in the section on annual life-cycle events, at the Beginning of Summer (*lixia* is the day marking the beginning of the 7th of the solar term -- 5, 6, or 7 May) there was an event called *yehuo fan* (a kind of picnic), which involved generous *wanglai* among little friends. According to local custom, once children passed their 11th birthday they were expected to form gangs of little friends or little sisters with mutual obligations, making their relationship mainly expressive. They shared everyday school life, such as going to school together, eating lunch together and doing homework together, and also shared each other's birthdays, shopping or outings on weekends and holidays. In particular, they helped each other's families do housework and farming on the busy seasons' holiday (*nongmang jia*). For example, they cut grass for feeding rabbits, fed chickens and ducks, and picked leaves off mulberry trees for silk worms. These are the initial stages of labour support in their lifelong friendship. This part of the relationship between little friends and sisters can be counted as expressive *wanglai* compared with generous *wanglai* when they played together or entertained others.

On the summer picnic a girl told me that they enjoyed each other's company very much and felt attached to each other just like real sisters, although they sometimes had rows. The gangs of little friends or little sisters could be modified as they grew up. However, after they had grown up and the little friends or little sisters lived apart the concentrated attachment from their childhood would be loosened as necessary. But as Yang found in her fieldwork, such close friends do not need *guanxi* to gain help from each other when needed because the special childhood relationship stores up enough emotional resources to last for many years. (Y. Yang, 1995: Chinese article). This kind of input and output forms a vertical circle in one's life cycle. When their son or daughter gets married they address each other as "old friends" (*lao pengyou*) and "old sisters" (*lao jiemei*). More details about how this kind of relationship plays a positive role in villagers' *lishang-wanglai* networks can be seen in the rest of this chapter.

(3) Rational calculation

Rational calculation can be seen from the quantity of gifts, size of events, use of etiquette and style of arrangement. There are always clear quantities of gifts for each event from different relations. For example, in the "before birth event", Mrs Zhou's natal family had to bring gifts worth 400 *yuan* each, her agnatically related kin brought gifts worth 100 *yuan* each, Zhou's old generation non-agnatic kin only brought gifts worth 50 *yuan*, whereas Zhou's agnatic kin each gave 10 *yuan* plus labour support. The value of gifts indicates the different position of different relatives in Zhou's family's *lishang-wanglai* network. Mrs Zhou told me that the local custom provided guidelines which divided relations into different groups and specified a value of gift. People need to work out the correct amount for a given event, and usually get it right. When this calculation is made incorrectly it can cause conflict (see Chang 1999: 167–168).

Since there are so many events in villagers' lives, when annual cycle events of a family are added to the life-cycle events of each individual member, balancing the size of events involves rational calculation. Table V-1 shows that during childhood the one-month old birthday and sixteenth birthday are the largest events and involve three or four generations of relatives and all the other relations. The before birth event involves both agnatic and non-agnatic kin; the after birth event also involves neighbours, fellow villagers and friends; the one-year old birthday only involves close agnatic and non-agnatic kin and little friends within the village; the "to be a guest" event only considers the hosts' relations which include the hosts' agnatic kin, neighbours and fellow villagers; the "to be visited" event takes the focal family's agnatic kin, neighbours and fellow villagers into account; "asking for book bag and rice balls" are concentrated relationships with classmates. an understanding of who should attend which event can be seen even in young children. One day, I saw three children, just before suppertime, who went to attend a family feast of house completion and left one child behind. This child told me that he should not go with them to the feast because his family belonged to a neighbouring group. So children from a very young age understood which occasions they could or could not be included in according to local customs, and applied this understanding to their own lives without needing to be advised by grown ups.

The "size" of an event is chosen not only according to the nature of the relationships involved, but is also related to the standard of treatment, which involves prescribed etiquette. For the Zhou family in the before birth event, Mrs Zhou's natal family were on this occasion the most important guests because it was the first time they had been invited for a feast since Mrs Zhou got married. So the standard of the feast was very high. There is a saying involving a rational calculation in family management: parents' responsibilities extend up to three years after their children marry and it is then the children's turn to be responsible for the rest of their life for the elderly (*yeniang guandao hunhou sannian, zinü guan tamen hou bansheng*). As I mentioned at the end of "before birth event" (see Chapter II.I), this event laid a foundation for a new wife's status in her married family. After a child is born, the wife becomes the main manager of family events. The new wife/mother is supposed to have an updated list of agnatic kin, non-agnatic kin, friends, neighbours and fellow villagers. She is also expected to learn the arrangements and customs of all the family events. Although the process of learning about so many events can extend through a lifetime, the wife/mother is expected to be competent at this within three years of her marriage into the family.

The contents of gifts contain different meanings: some for the pregnant woman's health, others for the new baby's birth and luck in growing up, and for entertaining guests after the new baby is delivered, and so on. However the customary details of gifts can be adapted based on rational choice. When I was in an informant's family I saw a woman give the informant a bag of biscuits. The informant told me that the giver was one of her neighbours. The biscuits were brought by the neighbour's non-agnatic kin when she visited the neighbour's son. I then asked why she brought biscuits rather than dried rice cakes as the local custom demanded. My informant told me that the visitor was too busy to make the dried rice cake so she had brought a case of biscuits instead, which she learnt how to make from another village. She enjoyed this innovation because she liked the taste of the biscuits. This also happened in other events. In the asking *jiujiu* for a book bag event, the *jiujiu* should customarily give an abacus to his niece or nephew; instead of this a calculator is now given.

Nowadays, some *jiujiu*s even give a bicycle to their niece or nephew, instead of the customary rain boots. Arrangements for events can be changed based on rational choice. For example, "asking for a book bag" and "asking for rice balls" are normally two separate events.

BL told me that although his own family, like most families in the village, kept the two events apart, some families combined them together to make one big event. According to BL the overall cost for the two events varies from 100 to 300 *yuan* each. In the "asking for book bag" event a focal family could spend 7 to 13 *jin* on rice powder which can make 120 to 180 rice cakes, depending on the size of *jiujiu*'s family's networks. In the "asking for rice balls" event a focal family could spend 50 to 100 *jin* on rice powder, for 120 to 180 rice balls, again depending on the size of the child's family's networks, with further gifts perhaps required. This new custom of combining the two events started in the late-1990s. The focal families spend 300 or 400 *yuan* on making rice balls and additional gifts and make one visit to the *jiujiu*'s family and distribute rice balls to everybody. So the combined event is less effort than the two separate events. Having one big event had the advantage of saving energy and time spent on arrangements, but required a large amount of money to be paid all at once. BL also told me that if a child has two or more *jiujiu* they should work out a system of shares. If a child has no *jiujiu*, when the child is young his or her mother would create a quasi *jiujiu* for ḯ.

(4) Spiritual beliefs

Religious sense can be seen from the symbolic meanings of gifts, details of rituals, and the degrees and variety of the believers' belief. At every event the symbolism of different kinds of gift embodies a religious sense. Examples are as follows. Jujube in Chinese is pronounced as *zaozi* which is short for *zao sheng guizi* (this means to have a treasured son earlier). The gift of a jujube is particularly important before the birth event. In the after birth event everybody should visit the mother and baby with a bag of *yunpian gao* (a kind of rice cake in thin strips). I was given different explanations for the *yunpiangao*. The baby's mother told me that the pronunciation of *gao* is the same as in *gaogao xingxing* which means happiness. It is also the same as *gao* (tall) which symbolises that the child will grow up healthy. An informant told me that *yunpiangao*, among so many different cakes in so many other events, is confined to this one. It is made of about 100 thin strips and is completely different from any other cake, the number of strips symbolising a life of a hundred years, and is used to express good wishes for a newborn child. Another visitor said although he did not count how many strips were in the cake, so many strips means wishing the child to have lots of friends in his or her life. *Atai yuanzi or ataituanzi* (goddess rice balls) and *waisheng tuanzi* (nephew or niece rice balls) in the events of the one-month old birthday and asking *jiujiu* (mother's brother) for rice cakes also have their symbolic meanings. *Yuan* of *yuanzi* is the same pronunciation as circular, tuan of *tuanzi* means ball or rolling something into a ball. *Tuanyuan* is a term specially used for family reunion. So such rice balls symbolize having a happy family life. In the 16th birthday event *shoutao* (peach-shaped cakes) symbolise a long life, the traditional meaning of the peach.

Religious sense is also embodied in details of different rituals and events. For example, there is a taboo in the event of asking a mother's brother for a book bag. This taboo is that if a year is *mangnian* – one in which the Beginning of Spring (the first of the 24 solar terms, normally 3, 4 or 5 February) is earlier than the lunar New Year Day – then the event must be moved to the year before or after in order to avoid bad luck. An informant Yao told me that *mang* of *mangnian* is the same character in Chinese as blind, which has many negative meanings: worship blindly, obey blindly, act blindly or aimlessly, and so on. It is especially important to avoid this at events that mark a child's start at school. Colours in the wrapping and decoration of gifts also involve religious sense: gift money, silver dollars or necklace are put in red paper bags, and wrapping re cloth around big steamers as gift containers is for averting evil; decorating gift containers with green is for long life.

Religious sense is demonstrated in a great variety of beliefs and varies in degree. In Chapter II.I I mentioned in the section on the one-month old birthday ceremony that Mr Ren's family did not worship ancestors for reasons of practical family convenience. Mrs Ren admitted that her married family took ancestor worship less seriously than some other families in the village. Again, the Song family did not have a ceremony for the one-year old girl's birthday and did not worship the local goddess because her mother had "less superstition than others". However, Mrs Ren told me that she learnt about the one-month old ceremony from other families. In 2003, when I was checking details with Mrs Ren she told me that having a son for the family is a very important thing. She hoped my account would not neglect such important relations as ancestors, even though her own family did not perform customary worship to them (*qing zuxian* including *zuzong* – ancestor, and *xianren* – forefather) because of her mother-in-law's serious arthritis in her knees. She told me that there were many families that still continued the tradition of asking ancestors to bless the new baby.

Villagers combined ancestor worship with the worship of the local goddess by worshipping the ancestor(s) first, then the local goddess, at the same altar table. They set up an altar table for the ancestor and bow to him. They then remove all the offerings and set off firecrackers. Then they reset the altar table to worship the local goddess. Mrs Ren however had been taught to orient the table differently for the two purposes. The altar table for ancestors should have the grain oriented from east to west, because this would keep the ancestors at home, and for worshipping the goddess the table should face south and the grain should travel from south to north because the goddess is an honoured guest, and this will let her come into the house smoothly along the grain. Mrs Ren sounded as though she approved of this slightly simplified version. She told me that if she became a grandmother she would help arrange her grandchild's one-month old day in just such a proper way.

Here is another case, involving necessary creativity. Zhou told me that his family did not hold a ceremony at his baby's one-month old day at all because all the members of his family are Christian, which is in conflict with superstitious beliefs. He counts worship of ancestors, local gods or goddesses as *mixin* (superstition). Instead of this, unlike the majority of the villagers, his family had a ceremony for his son's one-year old birthday. Zhou and his wife invited all the members of the child's *jiujiu*'s (his mother's brother) family for the birthday party. *Jiujiu*'s family brought a big cake, sweets, and clothes for the party boy. They sang a happy birthday song to the party boy and helped him blow out the candle. They also prayed to god before they ate the cake and had the lunchtime ceremony feast, which was set up by the boy's parents and grandparents. Afterwards they distributed sweets to the children of neighbours and fellow villagers. This case indicates that although in Zhou's family the nature of the religious belief changed, the *lishang-wanglai* did not.

Mrs Ren told me that details of rituals varied over time. For example, in the past people burned *huangtong zhi* (a kind of rough straw paper) in their rituals. The ash looked like fine dust coloured black and white. From 2000 onwards villagers burned *lianfang* (a kind of special paper) and the ash looked like a yellow *yuanbao* (a shoe-shaped gold or silver ingot used as money in feudal China). Burning paper money signifies sending money to the ancestors. Mrs Ren told me that as villagers' standard of living improved they would like to spend more on buying such special papers for the ancestors, in the belief that the more they offered to them the better the care the ancestors would give back to them.

V.II. Establishing a marriage relationship

Having attended many wedding-related events, I made the calculation that on average it took about five years and 50,000 *yuan* to complete the whole process of establishing a marriage for a boy/fiancé/groom/husband's family in 1996, and 40,000 *yuan* for a girl/fiancée/bride/wife's family. This process involved complicated financial and family relational transactions. Among many scholars' writing on Chinese marriage[19], Fei (1939), Freedman (1966), and Yan (1996a and b) have findings similar to mine in two ways. (i) Both Fei and Yan stressed the issue of the new family or conjugal relationship. Based on his fieldwork in Kaixiangong Village, Fei (1939) suggested:

> The marriage gifts and dowry are, in fact, the contribution of the parents on both sides to provide the material basis for the new family, and a periodic renewing of material basis of the household for each generation. (43)

60 years later Yan (1996b) made it clearer that in Xiajia village:

> The marriage transaction is no longer a cycle of gift exchange between two families, but has become a means of claiming one's share of family property employed by individual brides and grooms in their pursuit of conjugal independence (198–199).

(ii) Freedman raised the issue of kinship relationship between the two families of the boy/husband and girl/wife, describing one of the objects of marriage as "the successful absorption of a 'foreign' woman into the family and the smooth regulation of ties created between two sets of kin" (1970: 11).

My observations in Kaixiangong will show these two issues from vertical and horizontal viewpoints:

(i) Although bridewealth and dowry provide the material basis for the new family in a vertical circle of generational relationship, as Fei and Yan observed, they overlooked the fact that the bridewealth and dowry can also be seen as a kind of investment made by parents on both sides for their care in old age and burial after their death. Also, the tendency that Yan (1996b, 2003) found in Xiajia, that the brides and grooms who claim bridewealth were seeking conjugal independence, is not the case in Kaixiangong (see Chapter VI.II).

(ii) Although the bridewealth and dowry provide the material basis for the newly established marriage relationship between two families and their kinships in a horizontal circle, Freedman did not show how the relationships are established or reviewed, and overlooked other kinds of relationships. Chapter V.I has already shown how both a new couple's

---

[19] Chen, C., 1985; Cohen, 1976; Croll, 1983; Freedman, 1966, 1970, 1979; Harrell 1992; Johnson 1983; Parish and Whyte 1978; Wolf 1985; Yan, 1996b, 1997, 1998, 2003.

families strengthen their relationship and build up new relationships for the younger generation. Chapter II.II shows how a marriage relationship is established between two families and how this new relationship modifies the existing family networks through major events. I have shown in Chapter V.I that the children in Kaixiangong Village are involved in large family-based *lishang-wanglai* networks from the time they are born. By the time they are sixteen years old, Mrs Zhou told me, most children expect to find their own partners in marriage (*duixiang*). The establishment of a marriage relationship requires a succession of stages: from asking for the red paper envelope, the two betrothal rites, the seeing-off ceremony, wedding, and other pre-wedding/post-wedding activities. All the events relating to the marriage relationship serve the function of ending or renewing different parts of the family's *lishang-wanglai* networks. Once all the relationships have been reviewed the process of establishing a potential marriage relationship has been completed.

Here I will show how all the different parties to these events participate with *lishang-wanglai* and, in some cases, social creativity.

1. *Lishang-wanglai* in the period of establishing a marriage relationship

Table V-1 is formed of three parts divided by triple lines. In Chapter V.I I have discussed the first part, how *lishang-wanglai* networks were knitted for/by a person from his or her birth to sixteen years old. I will discuss the third part in Chapter VI.II. In this section I will show how the creation and management of networks resemble "fattening a pig" through different events among different relations during the period of establishing the marriage relationship. I will first demonstrate the operation of expressive *wanglai*, and then analyse the underlying *lishang* criteria that motivate it.

(1) Expressive *wanglai*

Here I will firstly explain different events and relations according to Table V-1 and then point out how the various *wanglai* are mobilised.

The bold arrows in Table V-1 show that the most important events during this period for both fiancée/bride and fiancé/groom's families are the betrothal rite and wedding ceremony. These events involve the broadest lists of the given families' relatives, people with the same surname who live in the same group (*tongxing de renjia*) but are not so close as to take the part of neighbours, nor so close by blood tie as to be a part of the agnatic-kin; or people who have moved back one rank on a family's non-agnatic list (*laoqin*) due to a marriage relationship being established. The fiancée/bride's and fiancé/groom's fathers, the fiancée/bride and fiancé/groom themselves and their friends are not invited to the betrothal rite feasts. They are the most important guests and kept for the most special occasion (see related paragraph in next section).

The solid and dotted arrows represent fiancé/groom/husband and fiancée/bride/ wife and their families and relations separately. The events of seeing-off feasts, tea parties, and gifts show different *wanglai* between the fiancée and her relations because the fiancée, but not the fiancé, has to end large numbers of relationships. Thus the fiancée receives gifts from them, which can be seen as a payback from those with whom the relationship (with her but not her family) will be broken. This payback is analogous to the final payback, on the slaughter of a pig, after many years fattening, and can be seen in two ways. From a vertical point of view the process started when the fiancée was born. The food for fattening the pig is *renqing* and *ganqing* rather than finance or materials because the *wanglai* among the relations over a certain period are already balanced. From a horizontal point of view the pig can be seen as a gain from families who received feasts, tea parties, or gifts from the fiancée's parents in the past, or investment from other families who would be involved in the same events in the future. Either way the period of preparing gifts varies from a few months to more than one year and relations could take their time to arrange their gifts based on the fiancée's family's dowry list.

The thin solid and dotted arrows represent fiancé/groom/husband and fiancée/bride/wife themselves separately. From the post-wedding events of Table V-1 we can see that sometimes these two arrows are joined together and at other times the thin dotted arrows and solid arrows are joined together. This signifies that the new wife has started a process of "fattening" another "pig" in her life with her husband or mother-in-law and their relations, from now on to be hers. This is the process of knitting her married-in family's *lishang-wanglai* networks.

A. Different relations

Leaving aside the broadest list of a given family's relations shown above, I will now concentrate on the occurrence of *wanglai* among the two families themselves and their most important relatives during the period of establishing a marriage relationship.

(a) Agnatic kin are the most positive relations for both fiancée/bride/wife and fiancé/groom/husband and their families

There is no visible ancestral hall or temple (*zongci*) and no lineage system in Kaixiangong Village. The activities of agnatic kin or people sharing the same surname embody the idea of a patriarchal clan's existence. In the period of establishing a marriage relationship the agnatic kin's involvements are especially very high and on many occasions unique. Apart from the involvement of finance, materials and labour, their position of being of the same clan (*jiazu, zongzu*) and close agnatic kin of both a new wife's natal family or a new couple's family plays a unique role. For a fiancée/bride there is a separate flesh and bone feast for seeing off the bride before she gets married, and the agnatic kin also accompany the bride's father as a clan to take part in a feast held by the groom's family for uniting the two families after the wedding into one big family. The agnatic kin are included again in the bride's house when the bride and the groom visit the bride's natal family, and they in return are invited back for a feast in each of the agnatic kin's families. For the fiancé/groom/husband agnatic kin play an equally important role, mainly in the post-wedding events. They accompany the bride's father to the groom's family as guests. In return each agnatic family invite the bride and the groom for feasts to welcome them into the clan.

(b) Non-agnatic kin obviously play an important role in this period

In the Yao family's dowry (See Chapter II.II), non-agnatic families made up 76.2 per cent of the total number of gift givers from among the kinship source, whereas 23.8 per cent were agnatic kin. This is similar to the finding from the ESRC project in Kaixiangong Village. It shows 77.14 per cent of contacts in financial support came from non-agnatic kin, and 22.86 from agnatic kin (Chang and Feuchtwang, 1996: 17). Apart from the absolute number of non-agnatic kin always being larger than agnatic kin I found another reason for this. The lesser quantity of agnatic kin's financial support compared to non-agnatic kin's is also caused by a local custom which deducts the costs of labour in helping at feasts, hosting feasts, gift money, as well as the post-wedding welcome feasts that agnatic kin are supposed to provide.

Among non-agnatic kin, *jiujiu* (the mother's brother) and his family play a very important role. As one of the wife's non-agnatic kin, the *jiujiu* represents her natal family because he inherits his family property, including his sister's who has lost the right to inherit due to being married out of the family. The way in which his parents transfer some of the family's property to their married-out daughter is to let him give a greater number of more expensive gifts to her. At the same time he gains honour as the most important person among all the relations who attend the wedding (*jiujiu wei da*). However, the *jiujiu* can't be the richest guest among them so the local custom laid down guidance for different relations in order to avoid the situation of a "river being higher than a bridge" (*heshui moguo qiao*).

As we have seen in earlier related paragraphs the reason villagers care about numbers of non-agnatic kin is because they are important resources for emotional and financial support. The following case will show how crucial is such a resource for a poorer family. HL Wang told me that his family had two sons. The older son got married in 1989. It took his family another six years to get ready for the younger son to be married. The total cost was 35,000 *yuan*, from asking for a red paper envelope, right up to the wedding. The family had to borrow more than one third of the money they needed. The sources were 4,000 *yuan* from his sister's daughter (for whom Wang was *jiujiu*) who lived in the village; 2,000 yuan each from his father's brother's two sons who lived in Zhenze Township; 1,900 *yuan* from his *jiujiu*'s sons and daughters who lived in Xicaotian village; 1,500 *yuan* from his wife's brother who lived in the village; 1,000 *yuan* from his agnatic kin who lived in the same group; and 600 *yuan* from his sister's son who lived in the same village. The total sum was 13,000 *yuan*. Of this sum 93 per cent of the lenders were the Wang family's non-agnatic kin who were on the Wang family's list for lunar New Year's feasts.

Wang told me that the above order for the list of borrowed money is based on the quantity borrowed rather than the closeness of relations. This is the same order as the donation list which was published in the rebuilt East Temple. It was customary to list in order of amount, but to repay distant relatives first and then closer relatives. By May of 1996 the Wang family had repaid 7,100 *yuan* and left 5,900 *yuan* for 1997. The only items unpaid were two items from Xicaotian village and Zhenze Township. Wang said that if his second son had been taken by a family as son-in-law the marriage would have cost 10,000 *yuan* less.

(c) Friends played multiple roles on the wedding day

The fiancée's friends gave her gifts and gift money, and accompanied the bride to her married family, whereas the fiancé's friends provided labour for the performance on welcoming a bride's party, loading and unloading dowry, and so on, and also paid a significant amount of gift money at the wedding feast. Apart from the bride and groom's friends, both the bride and groom's fathers' friends are also involved in the event. On the wedding day the friends make up more than half of the guests. For the bride and groom and their families it is the highest honour to have lots of people for the wedding: this means that they have rich human resources. My informants always gave numbers of guests proudly for the feasts. If some families had less than 15 tables of guests (120 people) for the wedding they would explain the reason, so as to save face before being asked.

(d) For neighbours and fellow villagers the most obvious point is that the seeing-off ceremony had nothing to do with them, according to Table V-1

The reason for not involving neighbours and fellow villagers in the Zhou family's daughter's seeing-off ceremony was because a daughter's marriage away from the village meant the family loses a daughter and should therefore keep the event low key. However, immediately after the wedding day, the Zhou family distributed rice cakes to its neighbours and fellow villagers when the bride and her husband paid a brief visit to it. It is very important to distribute the rice cakes and sweets because they were left out of the big family event of the seeing-off ceremony. The cakes and sweets from the daughter and her husband meant she was reborn as a closer new non-agnatic kin of her natal family. This is the only transaction between Zhou's family and its neighbours and fellow villagers during the period of the post-wedding, and can be seen to compensate them for not being a part of the ceremony. In contrast the *wanglai* between the new wife and her marriage family's neighbours and fellow villagers was strong. First the new wife and her mother-in-law invited their neighbours and fellow villagers for a tea party and then they paid each family a visit in turn. Thus the foundation of a relationship between the new wife and her new neighbours is laid.

(e) The column "others" of Table V-1 refers to matchmakers

For villagers it is very important for a matchmaker to take part in the marriage process. There is a traditional Chinese saying that a proper way of contracting a marriage should be based on "the command of parents and the good offices of a matchmaker" (*fumu zhi ming, mei shuo zhi yan*). Fei tells us that in the 1930s matchmakers were approached by girls' parents and randomly distributed red paper bags containing their daughters' "eight characters" to boys' families. A boy's family could receive several red paper bags and make a choice with the help of a fortune-teller. The matchmaker then played a role as negotiator of bargains between the boy's and the girl's families until an agreement was reached (1939: 40-43). This custom changed greatly in the 1990s. I was told that there are usually three matchmakers involved in establishing a marriage relationship: two walking matchmakers (*xingmei*) and one sitting matchmaker (*zuomei*). The walking matchmakers' job was to go between the two families with requests for red paper envelopes, making arrangements for small and big bridewealth, and guiding the groom's team to welcome the bride from her home to the groom's family on the wedding day. The sitting matchmaker ensures everything runs smoothly. There were still fortune-tellers outside of the village but villagers hardly ever used them. For them the importance of matchmakers in establishing a marriage relationship is as follows:

(i)   Morally it is right and honourable for parents to arrange a boy's and a girl's marriage properly through matchmakers (*mingmei-zhengqu*) according to *lifa* (rules of etiquette) or local customs. The three matchmakers were addressed as *huahong* (blooming flower), *jianxiu* (change bad luck into good luck), and *yuelao* (the god of marriage) on the red envelopes of gift money at the occasions of betrothal rites and wedding. They also used the terms of *qingmei* (inviting matchmakers), *xiemei* (thanks to matchmakers), *meiren zuo da* (the best seats for matchmakers). For example, on the wedding day the groom's father should invite the walking matchmakers for a big breakfast with a whole duck or whole chicken. On the day after the wedding day the groom's father should pay a thank you visit with an upper part of a pig's leg to each matchmaker's family.

(ii) For the matchmakers, as Qiu said, he felt he didn't have the heart to turn down his nephew's parents' request to be a matchmaker because normally the matchmakers are the closest relatives or friends of their "clients". According to the local custom the two walking matchmakers should each be invited by one of the boy's and girl's families. The sitting matchmaker should be a girl's *jiujiu* (mother's brother), guru (father's sister), or a person who is very close to the girl's family. Walking matchmakers can be male or female. Normally it is the wife of a family who is a walking matchmaker for the small betrothal rite and a husband for the big betrothal rite and wedding. So the three matchmakers can come from three different families.

(iii) As an intermediate or go between, to be a matchmaker is a kind of sideline occupation that would bring some income. According to the standard rate in 1996, payments to matchmakers were 40, 60, 80, 100 each for asking for the red paper envelope, the two betrothals, and the wedding from a groom's family, and 20, 30, 40 and 50 from a bride's family, plus some thank you gifts from both groom and bride's families separately. Thus each of the matchmakers' families can receive about 600 *yuan* for being a "go between": 400 *yuan* from a boy/fiancé/groom's family and 200 *yuan* from a girl/fiancée/bride's family. Since matchmakers are necessary in establishing a marriage relationship, Tan said,

"I would rather pay for my close relatives than others", as in the saying *feishui buliu wairen tian* (do not let fertilized water flow to outsiders' paddy fields).

(iv) For villagers, it does not very much matter who plays the role of matchmaker and how things are arranged, the important thing is to have a third party to represent the will of a marriage god (*yuelao*) to bless the new couple to live to a ripe old age. This example of religious sense is still rooted in villagers' unconscious. Yao told me that the root is so deep in the village that even during the Cultural Revelation period (1966–1976) village cadres were asked to act as matchmakers and Chairman Mao's portrait was used as the god of longevity's (*shouxing*) picture and revolutionary slogans as a pair of antithetical couplets[20].

(f) The reason some villagers involved the village collective in this biggest of family events is that they needed financial support

Such families normally were either relatively poorer than average or had better knowledge of using collective resources in the village. For example, JG Wang, a head of one group of the village, told me that he had two daughters and incurred debt in arranging his older daughter's wedding. JG Wang has two sisters who had married out of the family and he was the only son of his family. However, he has two daughters but no son. In this situation it was essential for his elder daughter to take a man into the family as a son-in-law, but this made the marriage more expensive. JG Wang's list of family expenditure differs substantially from HL Wang's. The Wang family spent about 50,000 *yuan,* from the small betrothal in 1994 to the wedding in 1996, 40 per cent of this was spent on the two betrothal rites and 60 per cent on decorations and the wedding. They incurred a debt of 50 per cent of the total, that is to say 25,000 *yuan*. JG put lenders in 5 groups: 6,000 *yuan* came from 5 families of non-agnatic kin, 3,000 *yuan* from 3 families of agnatic kin, 6,000 *yuan* from 6 friends who had grown up together in the village, 2000 *yuan* from a bank, and 8,000 *yuan* from his work colleagues and friends (*yaohaode*) made through links at work. Among all the lenders only 60 per cent came from private sources because JG's wife came from north Jiangsu (*subei*), which is the poorest area in the province, and 40 per cent came from public sources including bank and work colleagues. Although the money was not directly borrowed from the village collective, the way in which JG arranged the money was through his knowledge and ability to use village collective resources. For example,

---

[20] Antithetical couplets are a millennia-old verse form unique to China.

applying for money from a local bank requires an application form, and two guarantors at the village cadre level, approved and stamped by the Village Committee. One applicant is allowed to apply for 2,000 *yuan* at a time for six months. This complication and the limitations of borrowing money from the local bank puts off many villagers. However, as the head of one of the groups in the village, JG did not feel it was too much for him because he had many dealings with the village cadres in person because of his job, and found them helpful. The money lent by his work colleagues or village cadres was also given because JG had a friendly relationship with them; they helped him with administrative formalities and even with their own money. JG's case is close to being an example of villagers' understanding of *guanxi,* as I will show later.

However, one of the lenders said this was a "*renqing guanxi*" between him and JG because they were more like friends rather than colleagues, even though it was work that had linked them, he being head of another village group. Such a mixture between human feelings and work position is not unusual. In HL Wang's case above, HL borrowed 1,000 *yuan* from JM Wang, who was connected to HL Wang in three ways: he was close to being agnatic kin, had the same surname and he was also a vice Director of the Village Committee. The reason HL Wang categorized him as agnatic kin is the understanding way in which he had loaned the money, saying "please accept this small amount of money as a token of agnatic kinship without feeling embarrassed" (*yidian xiaoyisi, buyao buhao yisi, doushi zijiaren ma*). For HL Wang the amount of money itself was not large but the way in which JM Wang handled the matter deeply moved him. He thought that he gained great face from him because to be poor and to borrow money from others, especially from those whose position is higher than one's own, is not a comfortable business. As I will show in Chapter VII.III, JM Wang also helped when a very poor old man, whose son went away from the village, died from lung cancer. Many people told me different stories about how kindly JM Wang had treated them. I asked him what he would have done if he had had no money available when HL Wang came to him. He said he would still have agreed to lend to him and borrowed a small amount of money from his relations to do so, because he had more resources than HL Wang. His kindness towards his kinsmen and fellow villagers won their trust and gratitude, so that, to use a Cultural Revolution term, as head of group he had a "solid mass foundation". This kind of giving and receiving is the top-down component of the vertical circle of reciprocity, in marked contrast to the bottom-up type that Yan found in Xiajia village (1996b).

(g) Ancestors and local gods account numerically for a relatively small proportion of the *wanglai*

Ancestors and local gods account numerically for a relatively small proportion of the *wanglai* between a fiancée/bride/wife and a fiancé/groom/husband and their families and relations. But the key point is how much importance is ascribed to them during this period of the life cycle. I was surprised that at two weddings I attended I did not see the brides and grooms *baitiandi* (make a ceremonial obeisance to gods in heaven and Earth), which is a popular performance during the wedding. I asked why not. The replies were all the same, that "it is no longer fashionable (*bu shixing*)". After I discussed the matter with them we all agreed that the form of paying respect to the local gods had changed, but the same sense of respect was still felt and expressed in the decorative central hall: a big painting of the god of longevity (*shouxing*) with a boy and a girl (*tongnan tongnu*), and a pair of antithetical couplets on each side of the picture. The young couples believed from the bottom of their hearts that they hoped the heavenly gods would bless them (*laotian baoyou*) to have a long life, a child, and a happy family. In spite of the picture none of them wanted to have two children, explaining that nowadays to rear more than one child meant to reduce the quality of their own life.

B. Mobilising of different *wanglai*

This whole chapter is concerned with expressive *wanglai* − one aspect of which is that like any form of *wanglai* it can change or develop into another. As I have shown in the previous sections marriage involves many relationships: between a fiancée and fiancé, a daughter and her parents, a son and his parents, a wife and a husband, in-laws' families and their relations before and after the wedding, and so on. Villagers asked the kitchen god to keep the red paper envelope safe, or involved matchmakers, because things could sometimes go wrong, in consequence changing one type of relationship to another and affecting many. I will show three very extreme examples.

Xie contracted a marriage in the 1950s. The relationship between Xie and his parents could be categorised as expressive *wanglai*, like most parent and son relationships in the village. As required by morality, he married a girl who had been adopted into the family as a daughter-in-law-to-be (*tongyangxi*), as a part of a family arrangement. The relationship between him and his wife just managed to keep going (*couhe*). I would call this instrumental *wanglai* because they stayed together just for the sake of keeping the family together, without love. However, Xie met a girl with whom he fell in love, and she with him. Xie tried and failed to persuade his parents to let him give up his marriage, and the girl was forced to marry another man as arranged by her family. The relationship between Xie and his parents deteriorated into instrumental *wanglai*, with no real positive feeling. A year later Xie's lover ended her unhappy life. Since then Xie's relationship with his parents and wife deteriorated even further to negative *wanglai*. He decided to end the family line (*duan xianghuo*) by separating from his wife. His wife then had an affair with another man and became pregnant. Xie's family refused to accept the baby so she committed suicide by hanging from a beam. Xie's wife's death improved his relationship with his parents from negative to instrumental *wanglai*. A few years later he agreed to marry another woman and had a daughter. However, Xie never walked away from the shadows of the two dead women. Eventually his new wife divorced him and left their daughter with Xie's family. The relationship between Xie, his daughter, and his parents remained at a level of instrumental *wanglai* until Xie's daughter grew up and Xie's parents passed away.

The second example is from the 1970s. Fang had an expressive *wanglai* with her parents until she became engaged. However, she fell in love with a different man. Her family had held a large betrothal rite for her, and so had her lover's parents for their son with a different girl. They both failed to persuade their parents to break off the engagements. Fang's relationship with her parents became more and more tense, one of merely instrumental *wanglai*, finally negative. Fang tried to persuade the matchmakers to help but they had committed themselves to her parents' side. She even went to her fiancé's family to find a solution. The fiancé's family's response was to organise its male agnatic kin to trap her in a storehouse and beat her badly. Finally Fang gave up hope and told her boyfriend that she wanted to die, and her boyfriend decided to die with her for love. They both committed suicide by hanging themselves on a tree. Thus the relationship between Fang and her parents entered into negative *wanglai*. Notice that the relationship has not ended. As Yao told me in a recent telephone conversation, he saw a relationship of this kind as negative *wanglai* because the effect of Fang's death on her parents would last to the last moment of their lives as a continuing act of revenge.

The third example is from the 1990s. An informant Xu told me that her ex-daughter-in-law eventually divorced their son because the Xu family's financial situation was never satisfactory to her. In her words "this marriage was very much grudging (*mianqiang*) from the very beginning". She agreed with me that during the period of establishing the marriage relationship, the relationship between her ex-daughter-in-law and her family could be seen as instrumental *wanglai*. Xu's family's situation had been quite good before her son's marriage. Her husband had been a hero in the "War to Resist U.S. Aggression and Aid Korea" (1950–53) and he worked in Miaogang Township (employment in the township being a big step up from a farmer in the village.). The two families held betrothal rites before her son followed in his father's footsteps and joined the army. However, after they got married the family's situation worsened. Xu's husband lost his final chance to be promoted due to his lack of educational qualifications and he returned back to the village with only a small pension. Her son demobilised from the army and worked in a depressed village enterprise. The young couple lived together and rowed constantly. Eventually the ex-daughter-in-law divorced Xu's son, leaving their child in the Xu family. The relationship between the ex-daughter-in-law and the family moved down to negative *wanglai*. Although the ex-daughter-in-law never came back even once to see her own child, the villagers counted the relationship as continuing negative *wanglai* because the negative effect on the family still remained.

These three cases are instances of different types of *wanglai* moving up and down within the same relationship, for instance that of son or daughter with their parents, or husband with wife. My reason for recounting them is to point out that Sahlins's (1972) model, according to which the closer the relationship the more generous the attitude, is incomplete (see more in Chapters VI.II and IIIV.II), and omits realities of life as experienced in Kaixiangong.

2. *Lishang* criteria

One or more criteria of lishang have been touched upon again and again in this chapter. Here I will show the lishang that operated during the period of establishing a marriage relationship − the same principles at work in knitting relationships as in the process of fattening pigs.

(1) Moral judgment

Moral judgment can be seen at work in Kaixiangong in villagers' respect for local customs (*laofa*) or understanding of *lifa* (rules of etiquette; the proprieties). *How* gifts flow is practice, but *why* they flow in particular ways involves principle. For example, why did villagers sometimes put gift money in red envelopes, and sometimes gift wrap it with a small piece of red paper? This telling detail seems not to have been noticed by anthropologists before, but the distinction between *hongfengtong* (red envelopes, size 110 × 220) and *hongbao* (little red bags) carries real significance. Qiu told me that if a fiancé's family wrapped the bridewealth and gift money in small bags made out of many pieces of red paper, (*hongbao*) to give to the fiancée's family and her relatives, the fiancée's family should refuse to accept them, however large the amount of money. By contrast, if a person attending a wedding feast brought their gift money in a red envelope (*hongfengtong*), he or she would be laughed at. These ill-chosen presentations of gift money are not in line with *lifa* (rules of etiquette; the proprieties). According to *lifa* the gift-giver using a red envelope for his or her gift money is merely muddle-headed (*linguini*) because they fail to remember local customs that are so often repeated. It would be more complicated if the giver of bridewealth (quite different from a "gift" of money) used little red bags for the gift money. This could be interpreted as (i) the fiancé's family did not show respect for the fiancée's family, by being too informal; (ii) the fiancé's family did not take the relationship seriously which is why they did not bother to make envelopes- money is folded to be put in a bag, but can be put flat in a red envelope; (iii) the fiancé's family did not understood *li*, which dictates that different gifts of money have their own appellations which should be inscribed on each red envelope with paint brush writing. The appellations were *wei li* (small gift) for the fiancée's family, *qinggeng* (invitation) for the fiancée's father's friends, *yuelao* (marriage god) for payment to a matchmaker and so on.

For Kaixiangong's villagers the red envelopes are normally only used for betrothal rites and in a wedding for delivery of bridewealth between a fiancé/groom and a fiancée's families and their matchmakers, a fiancée's relatives, and different kinds of helpers. The red envelopes are called *hongfengtong* because the money is too much to be folded on this formal occasion. The red bags relate to gift money from individual givers to receivers because the money is limited and can be folded and wrapped in a small piece of red paper. This is called *hongbao*, which can be translated as "little red bag". This division might relate to rational calculation in a quantity of money or the size of paper. However, the significance of the division between red envelopes and little red bags is for existing rules of etiquette and the proprieties, the observation of which is a matter of moral judgement. This does not mean that every villager should know all about every event, but it does mean that they should seek advice from a specialised person qualified to advise them.

Moral judgment is very much involved in creating new ways to interpret local customs (*laofa*) or rules of etiquette and the proprieties (*lifa*) because in practice there are so many things not covered by the *laofa*. For example, the girl, Fang, was beaten up by her fiancé's male agnatic kin. She and her family did not make a complaint because according to *laofa* the fiancé's kin had a right to hit her when she broke the engagement. The tragedy of the lovers' suicide woke the villagers to the potential cruelty of the existing custom, which has since evolved to provide better solutions. In 1996 if a fiancée wanted to break off an engagement, the practice was for her family to return all of the red envelopes with the bridewealth plus some extra by way of recompense, whereas the fiancé's family should lose the small and big betrothal gifts and give additional apology gifts.

Adaptation of local customs can be seen on many occasions. For instance, all the wedding photos which I saw were taken in a photo studio in Wujiang City. However, instead of being dressed in accordance with the studio's standard sample picture of a groom wearing a formal suit or a swallow-tailed coat and a bride wearing a white wedding dress in Western style, wedding photos in the village show the brides wearing pink. For the villagers the white wedding dress is in conflict with the *laofa* which demands a bright red colour cloth or dress. More seriously, according to the *laofa* the colour white is not a lucky one, being only worn during funeral periods. So the compromise arrived at is a Western style of dress, such as the dress in the sample of the photo studio in township or Wujiang City, but in pink, which is in-between bright red and white. This new custom has been widely accepted.

(2) Human feelings

Many different human feelings come into play during the marriage period. The most hopeful is that of true love between the conjugal couple, most evident when expressed in physical terms. An old Chinese saying has it that spouses should "get married first then have a courtship" (*xian jiehun hou lianai*). However, nobody can tell whether or not the married couples have a courtship or are in love after they get married, since after marriage overt displays of feeling between the couple would be indecorous. The tragic stories of Xie and Fang show the power that feelings of love can exercise in forcing changes of types of family relationships.

The second feeling is of pain at separation mixed with *renqing*. It is very difficult to express such a feeling directly in public. Some villagers expressed their pain at separation by embodying it (Kipnis's term) in local customs. For example, in the Zhou family's seeing-off ceremony the bride's father's mother swore loudly about a shortage of sweets, the bride's relatives set up six rows of human fences one after the other to stop the groom's team from getting into the house (*baishan*), the bride's mother wept after the bride left. Sometimes a bride's close male relatives would complain that the red envelopes were not enough and tell the groom's team to return to the groom's home, which is called "*dahuigui*". The groom's team would have to go back to the groom's family to collect more money. "The symbolic expression of antagonism on the part of the girl's relatives often causes unpleasant feelings between the newly established affinal relatives, especially if they have not a sense of humour" (Fei ,1939: 45).

It is very difficult to express such feelings appropriately. Villagers preferred to express themselves with a bit too much exaggeration on those occasions. If the girl's natal family members or relatives did not show such feeling, especially in front of the groom's welcome team, it would be interpreted that the family did not care for the girl enough. Fei claimed that the feeling "we cannot let them have our girls without making a fuss" is a psychological expression of conflict between mother-love and patrilineal descent (1939: 43). In order to show such feeling in public everybody who is involved in different roles has to play with exaggeration. In the division of the wedding ceremony work, some people helped with the labour, even though this was not required by a particular local custom, because according to the general local custom it is always good to do too much rather than too little. The grandmother said the way that she expressed herself was through her share of gift money in a red envelope being larger than that of the other relatives. She was expressing her feeling of pain at separation from her granddaughter, and at the same time doing her job properly.

The third kind of feeling of closeness can be expressed by giving different amounts of gift money in post-wedding feasts with families among close agnatic kin. The amount of gift money given by each family of agnatic kin to a groom's family on the wedding day is called *fenzi qian* (share of gift money), and is based on the standard obligation of agnatic kin. The local custom provided reference figures for each type of agnatic kin, for example in 1996 a groom's father's brother paid 160 *yuan*, a groom's father's father 120 *yuan*, a groom's father's father's brother's sons 100 *yuan*, and so on. It would be improper to give more or less than the guideline on this occasion. However, in post-wedding feasts these agnatic families were free to give any amount of gift money to the new wife. This is a way to tell the new wife the real closeness and distance among these families. If one of them decided she did not like the new wife she could reduce the amount of gift money. If another liked her and wanted to make a closer relationship with her new family they could put some more money into the little red bag. The rule is that the amount of the gift money should be an even number for double happiness and for the couple to remain happily married to the end of their lives. There is no need to say anything. Based on the amounts of gift money and rules the new wife should be able to update the list of agnatic families. This is not simply to increase or reduce the number on the list; it is a matter of ordering the list according to closeness and distance. So the updated agnatic kin list is based on a feeling of closeness rather than the closeness of blood tie or geography.

(3) Rational calculation

Rational calculation can be seen everywhere during the establishment of a marriage relationship between two families. Here I will start with Table V-2 to show three major points.

A. Table V-2 shows the expenditure of Mr Rao's family and Mrs Rao's natal family during the period of establishing a marriage relationship from 1992 to 1995. The figures are approximate. From the table we can see two points.

(i) The column for Mr Rao's family shows that the Rao family provided 20,000 *yuan* for decoration of the bridal chamber and basic materials. Mrs Rao's natal family provided 22,000 *yuan* dowry for the new couple. The total sum was 42,000 *yuan*, which was 43 per cent of the total expenditure from the two families. This expenditure bears out Fei's (1939) observation that it is for the "material basis of the new family". In Kaixiangong the majority of new couples lived with their parent(s). Yan found that in Xiajia village, where this is not the case, the raising of bridewealth and dowry is for the "conjugal family" (1996b, 1997).

Table V-2 Two families' expenditure during the establishment of a marriage relationship (*yuan*)

Mr Rao's family		Mrs Rao's natal family	
10,000 bridewealth, 6,000 feasts, and 1,000 gifts for betrothal rites	16,000	Feasts and gifts for betrothal rites	8,000
Decoration of bridal chamber	20,000	Dowry including contents for the bridal chamber and jewels	22,000
6,000 welcome bride party including 4,800 bridewealth, and 10,000 wedding feast	16,000	Seeing-off feast and return gifts	10,000
Post-wedding activities	2,000	Post-wedding activities	4,000
Total	54,000	Total	44,000

(ii) Table V-2 shows that the rest of the expenditure was 56,000 *yuan*, namely, 57 per cent of total expenditure used on expressive *wanglai* among their relations for feasts including food, drink, cigarettes, sweets, gifts and return gifts to different relations, and ceremony-related expenses including decoration of the central hall, tips for labourers, firecrackers, different kinds of gift money during post-wedding feasts, tea and snacks for tea parties and so on. Of the two families Mr Rao's family spent 36 per cent and Mrs Rao's natal family spent 50 per cent on expressive *wanglai*. The main reason Mrs Rao's natal family spent more on this item than Mr

Rao's family is because it occurred in pre- and post-wedding activities. So Yan Yunxiang did not see a large expense on the updating of *lishang-wanglai* networks of the wife's natal family and he husband's family.

B. Financial support is necessary for almost all families during the period of establishing a marriage relationship. The ESRC social support project shows that in Kaixiangong Village, 72.2 per cent of financial support for family events, emergency, and investment is provided by a household, 18.4 per cent is from private sources, and 9.3 per cent from public sources (Chang and Feuchtwang 1996: 8). These figures are very similar to those of households which take wives or son-in-laws into the family to establish a marriage relationship. Table V-3 shows that Mr Rao's family's household's financial support amounted to 62.6 per cent of the total, those from other private sources 33.7 per cent, and those from public sources 3.7 per cent.

Table V-3 Sources of financial support during the establishment of a marriage relationship (*yuan*)

Mr Rao's family			Mrs Rao's natal family		
Sources	Sum 54,000	100%	Sources	Sum 44,000	100%
Household	33,800	62.6	Household	17,400	39.55
Private	-	33.7	Private	14,800	60.45
	13,000			8,000	
	5,200			3,800	
Public	2,000	3.7	Public	-	-

(i) For the Rao family the sum of 35,800 *yuan* was accumulated over many years from 1988 to 1995 by the working members of the family. In the row of private sources there is a figure of 5,200 *yuan* for gift money from guests at the wedding feast. This can be seen as a pig received from the family's networks. It would take another a few years for them to repay the debt of 13,000 *yuan*. The main reason for seeking financial support was for decorating an en-suite flat style of bridal chamber within the family house. Unlike the old style of bridal chamber, which is one double bedroom within a family house, the new flat style appeared in the late-1980s. The new bridal chamber is like a one-bedroom flat without a kitchen. It contains a bedroom with en-suite bathroom and basic furniture including bed and built-in cupboards, and a separate sitting room. The cost of decoration varies from 10,000 to 30,000 *yuan*. The rest of the domestic contents were the dowry worth 22,000 *yuan*, which was received from the bride's family.

(ii) Mrs Rao's natal family spent only 17,400 *yuan* of family savings, about two-thirds of the total expenditure, during the period of establishing a marriage relationship. There was no need to seek financial support from public sources because her natal family already had rich private resources of their own. More than half the money came from Mr Rao's family, although it would return back to his family eventually in a different form as bridewealth. Gifts came from the family's relatives and the girls' friends worth 8,000 (See Chapter II.II for details of how gifts were made up). 3,800 *yuan* came from the family's relations, excluding the daughter's friends, at the seeing-off ceremony feast. The bride brought 3,400 *yuan* of cash from her friends' gift money with her to her husband's family.

Although both Mr Rao's family and Mrs Rao's natal family received a large amount of gift money during the wedding/seeing-off ceremony feasts, the families are part of the networks of other families. Kaixiangong had a long tradition of high ceremonial expenses. Fei (1939) mentioned that these varied from 5 *yuan* to 20 *fen* according to the closeness of kinship and friendship, and on average the amount per family per year was at least 10 *yuan*. At that time the basic expenditure per year per family was 263 *yuan*, marriage expenses were 500 *yuan* including bridewealth and wedding ceremony (133–137). In the ESRC social support survey ceremonial expenses (overall expenditure on maintaining or creating relationships) averaged per year per family 4,873 *yuan* (Chang and Feuchtwang 1996: 6) in 1992, whereas marriage expenses were 20,000 *yuan* including bridewealth and wedding ceremony. It seems that marriage expenses were twice a family's annual total out-going expenditure in the 1930s and four times in the early 1990s. However, my findings show that the main reason for the increase in marriage expenses is the cost of decoration and outfitting a modern-style en-suite flat for the new couple – still called a bridal chamber – which reflects changes of family composition and lifestyle.

C. The majority of two-children families in the village normally reach a balance between a married-out daughter and a married-in wife. There is a village saying that if a woman, for example, A, gave birth to a daughter B, her family would pay for three generations (*sheng yige nu'er pei sandai*). The first generation is A's parents, the girl's grandparents. From just before B was born A's parents would start to prepare events for before and after a child's birth, and throughout the growing-up period events are carried out by A's brother (who is B's *jiujiu*), up until B marries out from her natal family. The second generation affected is A and her husband, who pay for B's upbringing until she is married out from the family. After B has a child her natal family, through B's brother, would become the third generation to support B's son's growing up. Their role in this would be similar to that of the first generation. So A's parents, A's brother's family, and A's son's family form three generations working in relays one after the other in complete circles of giving birth, giving support, to giving up the daughter. Such circles flow in both vertical and horizontal directions.

As a reciprocal circle, the family that takes a wife into it and establishes a marriage relationship between two families, gains three generations through the daughter-in-law and her natal family and her son's family in both vertical and horizontal ways. This is how over three generations a family with one daughter and one son through marriage reaches a balance. If families have two sons or two daughters this model can still be applied by either taking a man into the family as son-in-law for a daughter (*zhao nuxu*) or letting a son be taken into another girl's family. In the past women had no right of inheritance, since both the land and house are paternally inherited. When a daughter marries she receives dowry from her parents, but at the same time loses considerable rights over property in her natal household. Although women have equal rights including the right of inheritance with men under the post 1949 Constitution, this is not implemented in the village, which still prefers local custom (Chang, 1999: 168). So the mobilisation of materials is based on a complete set of local customs. On the one hand, a woman gives up the legal right of inheritance of the natal family's property after she marries out from it. On the other hand, the local customs provide protection for married-out daughters to be recompensed for losing their share of the natal family's property throughout life-cycle events.

Since the Chinese state's one-child family policy only applies to urban areas the above model is fully developed in Kaixiangong Village and works quite well. However, nowadays more and more young generation families want to have one child only, on their own initiative. This model therefore met a challenge. I will show how villagers created new customs to deal with such changes in the section "Social creativities and enjoyment in marriage relations" later.

(4) Religious sense

Religious sense can be seen everywhere throughout the period of establishing a marriage relationship. Villagers used symbolic meanings of even or odd numbers, colour, date, food, pronunciation of words for different things, and so on. For example, in every event returning gifts are required. The rules for returning gifts are "*feng dan huan yi*" (return one item if the number of gift is odd) and "*feng shuang bu huan*" (return nothing if the number of gift is even) for cigarettes, and to return half of the sweets from the fiancé's family's gifts. One should always keep an even number because the meaning is two, double, a pair, the lucky numbers. In 2000 I found one reason why a gift receiver always returned a little piece of a token gift in a gift sender's container. It was explained with the well-known symbol of Taoism by Yao. The logo combines two parts yin (black) and yang (white) in one logo in which a white spot is in the middle of the black part and a black spot is in the middle of the white part. The spots are turning points for changes from white to black or vice versa. So the gift giver's container shouldn't be filled with gifts in full. The gap can be seen as the white point in the black part. The gift receiver puts a little bit of return gift in the empty gift container to represent the little black spot in the white part. In this way both parties can see that the other wishes to continue their relationship. Not to return the little token gift in the empty container would signify that one is stopping *wanglai* with the other.

On the plate or tray for the small betrothal rite there were two threads of knitting wool. The red colour is for a girl from a boy and the green one is for a boy from the girl (*nan hong nu lu*). The meaning of the threads is to link two people together, as Fei said:

> This is facilitated by religious beliefs. Human marriage is believed to be held together by the old man in the moon (*yuelao*), with invisible red and green threads. This knitting together is symbolically performed in the wedding ceremony. The paper inscription of the god is in evidence in every marriage ceremony. Human helplessness breeds such religious beliefs and help to relieve the situation. (1939: 46)

The colour red used to be very popular. In order to avert evil almost everything was wrapped with pieces of red cloth. A piece of red decorative cloth was put on top of gifts, the anchors of the groom's boats were wrapped with red cloth, the envelopes and the little red bags for gift money were made from red paper. Red bows were used for decoration, on two sugar canes standing by the bed of the bridal chamber and on the roots of two bamboo trees.

The sugar canes are for a deepening relationship and the happier life of the couple because the taste of sugar cane is sweeter towards the root. The bamboo trees are called *shangrenzhu*, which means to climb the bamboo tree bit by bit up to the top, to raise the living standard bit by bit.

In the "welcoming the bride party" there is a custom of *bao xinniang* which means a bride's father carries her on a chair covered by a red duvet (*zhuangyuanbei*). This is actually adapted from an old custom of *bao xinniang* in which a bride's father or her closest male agnatic relative carries the bride in a sedan chair (Fei, 1939: 45). Since the sedan chair (*jiaozi*) has not been in use since 1949 the villagers replaced it with an ordinary chair. In Tan's case they used a decorated car (*jiaoche*) to collect the "bride". The *jiao* of *jiaoche* and *jiaozi* is the same character as, and means, sedan chair, the *zi* of *yizi* and *jiaozi* is also the same character and meaning. So to collect a bride with a car and have the ritual of *bao xianxiang* is an integrated ritual.

An old man told me that the reason for the ritual of "throwing the bride into the air" is because the bride should not take away her natal family's soil with her when she left home. If she did, she would be "*bai niangjia, liang fujia*", or making her husband's family prosperous at the expense of her natal family. This custom can be seen in other parts of China. As Freedman described, a bride should take her dowry with her and leave food and riches behind her as she leaves her parents' house. She should be "borne out of the house into the sedan chair, or if she walks to it, then her feet must not touch the uncovered ground" (1966:16).

3. Social creativities and enjoyment in marriage relations

There have been ever changing situations over the past decades since Fei conducted his fieldwork in the 1930s. I will show not only how villagers have been coping with the changes by adapting and creating new customs, but also how they have enjoyed what they have been doing.

(1) A stack of plates

Changing situations have brought change to the process of establishing a marriage relationship in Kaixiangong Village. According to Fei, the first step of establishing a marriage relationship is to ascertain the time of birth of the girl through matchmakers. Initially the girls' families arranged matchmakers to send red paper envelopes (*tiezi*) with eight characters defining the year, month, date, and hour of the birth to different boys' families and let them choose. The second step was for a boy's mother to bring the red paper envelope to a fortune-teller. This was both a means of reaching a decision and of shifting responsibility for human error to the supernatural will. Once the girl was selected, the third step was for the matchmaker to persuade the girl's parents to accept the match. After the agreement, the bridewealth would be sent spread over three ceremonial occasions before the wedding (1939: 40–43).

However, this changed in the 1990s. Normally there were three events to establish a marriage relationship between a fiancée and fiancé's family, to ask for a red paper envelope (*dan tiezi*), the small betrothal (*dan xiaopan*) and the large betrothal (*dan dapan*). At these events the red paper bags and the envelopes of gift money are all placed on plates (*pan*). Instead of three events the villagers simplified this to two events or even one. For example, the Tan family held an event of equivalent size to a small betrothal's rite for the "asking for a red paper envelope" (*dan tiezi*) event in 1992. The family then combined the small and large betrothal into one in 1994. This was called "carrying a stack of plates" (*dan yiluopan*) which means to join the small and large betrothal rites in one ceremony. Tan's family displayed social creativity in these two events. They changed the custom in this way because Tan's wife's natal family lived in Wujiang City. It would be very difficult for the family to arrange two betrothal rites based on the village custom without considering their situation. What they did for the "carrying a pile of plates" (*yiluopan*) was simply to put *li* (gift money or bridewealth) into three big red envelopes: 800 *yuan* for *jikou*, 4,800 *yuan* for the small betrothal and 6,800 *yuan* for the large betrothal. There were also lots of red envelopes on the big plate for the fiancée's relatives and matchmakers. The rest of the gifts, return gifts, feast and distribution invitations and the news were more or less the same as in the usual large betrothal rite.

By 1996 the Tan family was still the only family to have arranged its engagement in such a way. However, in recent telephone interviews I discovered that the creation of "a pile of plates" had been widely accepted as a new adaptation of local custom. An informant told me that the villagers simply combine the events of asking for a red paper envelope and small and large betrothal rites together because two plates cannot be called a pile of plates. He said that some older villagers referred to the old custom of "three plates", namely, small, medium and larger plates in pre-1949 to prove that "a pile of plates" is, in fact, a proper adaptation based on the local tradition.

(2) A wife's natal family lived outside the province

I attended a wedding on the 5th of the first lunar month 1996. The groom Qiu was getting married to his bride Jiang who came from Henan Province in 1993. Qiu met Jiang in the village enterprise when she first came to the village. Jiang had lived with Qiu's family since they became boyfriend and girlfriend. However, they could not get married for two years because Jiang was somebody else's fiancée in her hometown. Thus the way in which the marriage relationship was established is different from the standard arrangements in many ways (See Chapter II.II).

The wedding ceremony was also different, and adapted to the family's situation. On the wedding day there were three formal feasts. The first feast was at breakfast time which normally is a seeing-off ceremony held by the bride's family. In this case it was held by Qiu's family because Qiu's mother, Mrs Qiu, claimed she was Jiang's adopted mother. In order to make a distinction between the seeing-off feast and wedding feast Mrs Qiu decided the main meat was whole duck instead of upper part pig's leg. She chose duck rather than chicken because it was bigger and nicer. Mrs Qiu organised her agnatic kin to kill 26 ducks and clean their feathers the day before the wedding day to get ready for the feast. All the agnatic and non-agnatic kin and some of Qiu's little friends who lived in the village attended the feast with little red bags of gift money. The main wedding feast was at lunchtime with the upper part of a pig's leg, in line with the local custom. In this feast Mrs Qiu played a mother-in-law's role with the bride. Apart from the above attendants the groom's other friends who lived outside the village and the bride's friends attended the wedding feast with their little red bags. In the evening feast all the above guests attended again except those who lived outside of the village.

After the lunchtime feast I noticed they ate cream cake for dessert. Qiu told me that this way was influenced by Wujiang City. The reason for the combined cakes for the feast is because Qiu had four *jiujiu*s. They decided two of them would provide the long rice cakes and the other two, the cream cakes. Qiu's mother then placed them on a longer sideboard in the middle of the back wall of the central hall. Apart from a set of big candlesticks and two big red, wooden bath basins full of special long rice cakes (*dagao*) there were also four boxes on top of each other at both ends of the sideboard containing a generous supply of cream cakes. Qiu told me this was a good combination of traditional and modern, East and West.

Mrs Qiu told me that the total cost for establishing the marriage relationship between Qiu and Jiang was 30,000 *yuan* which included decorating the couple's room, making furniture, buying a TV, hi-fi, refrigerator, bicycle, clothes, watches, golden necklace, rings, earrings, and wedding feasts. The Qiu family managed this without borrowing money because all the expenditure came from the family's savings over the years, including Jiang's, who gave most of her wages to Mrs Qiu. Obviously the reason why the Qiu family spent 20,000 *yuan* less than the average expenses in establishing a marriage relationship was because it had no need to pay for bridewealth and a welcome bride party in the bride's family.

Mrs Qiu told me that although the wedding feast cost 7,500 *yuan* including feasts, drinks, cigarettes, and sweets, she expected the expenses on the wedding day to be balanced more or less by gift money from the guests, as happened in other weddings in the village. After the lunchtime feast the groom's *jiujiu*s (mother's brothers) counted the gift money and wrote down the list on a red paper envelope. The total sum from the list was 6,936 *yuan*. Of this .746 *yuan* was given by 10 agnatic kin, 2,360 *yuan* was given by 15 non-agnatic-kin, and 3,830 *yuan* was given by 35 friends. However, the gift money list was different from that of a standard marriage in the village in many ways:

(i) The above figures show friends were the largest financial providers. Among 35 friends, 33 were Qiu's friends, including 9 of his little friends in the village, 13 classmates in primary school and high school, and 11 colleagues in the enterprise. From Qiu's point of view about two-thirds of the ones who gave little red bags in Qiu's wedding can be seen as an outcome of his input since he was born (see Chapter II.II). One third of them gave little red bags to Qiu based on a friendship between work colleagues. Qiu told me that there is a kind of informal mutual aid group between work colleagues. They provided such resources naturally because everybody would get married sooner or later and they enjoyed each other's presence during the biggest event in their life. For Qiu some of the friendly colleagues that appeared at his wedding with little red bags were an outcome of his input, because he had attended weddings with little red bags for about half of the 11 colleagues in the past. He was sure he would go to the others' weddings whenever they got married. Out of Qiu's 33 friends there was only one female friend, who was Qiu's childhood little friend. Qiu told me that if his father had not died earlier and his family situation had been better then this female friend could have become his wife. This is another instance in Kaixiangong of children making little friends of mixed sexes from a very young age like Mrs Rao's son and his special female friend, and of these early relationships leading to a marriage relationship as with Mr and Mrs Zhou.

(ii) Normally a gift-money list only lists gifts from the groom's family's relations. However, in Qiu's case, gift money from the bride's sources was added, comprising 200 *yuan* from the bride's sister's family who lived in the village, 70 *yuan* from her master, and 100 *yuan* from a colleague at the enterprise where she worked.

(iii) Normally a groom's sister's friends are not invited to the wedding. However, Qiu's older sister's best friend was invited. She gave 200 *yuan* in gift money. At the beginning she was categorised in the friends' group. One *jiujiu* questioned the relationship. After discussion the *jiujiu*s decided to move her into the non-agnatic category as quasi-sister (Photo V-2). Thus the family's non-agnatic kin increased from 14 to 15.

(iv) I asked them why the bride's femal master (*shifu*) at her workplace only gave her 70 *yuan*. They explained to me that the relationship between a master and apprentice would be very special if they had individual tuition, such as a carpenter, lacquerer, bricklayer, or chef with their apprentices. If the bride' relationship with her master had been of the above kind, she should have been given 200 *yuan*, the same amount as the groom's father's sisters' families or quasi-parents if he has them. For the *jiujiu*s it was reasonable that the master only gave her 70, because more would be burdensome: her work group had many unmarried apprentices and she would have to give each an equal share when they got married. But she could not expect any return because she was already married.

(v) The 100 *yuan* from all the bride's colleagues was a standard rate, which is the same amount as just one of Qiu's work colleagues. The bride told me that she received less colleagues' gift money for two reasons. On the one hand, half of them came from outside of the area and did not intend to establish a marriage relationship in the village and so they would not create the same kind of mutual aid group as male colleagues. On the other hand, the other half of the colleagues had already married and had no need to involve themselves in such a relationship. They expressed their congratulations on Jiang's marriage by collecting a small token amount of money from everybody and bought her a present. Jiang distributed her happiness sweets (*xitang*) to them afterwards. This practice was created by the female workers in the village enterprise. It is normal in the majority of urban areas, and in my own former work units at Shenyang and Beijing.

From the above paragraphs we can see that adding the bride's gift money on the list and putting the groom's sister's best friend's gift money into non-agnatic kin category were creative activities, an adaptation to different circumstances. As I have shown earlier, Mrs Qiu organised the wedding event and combined the ceremonies of seeing-off and the wedding, which were both creative activities, but their success is due to their basis in local traditions. Qiu's *jiujius* modified the wedding gift money list because the relationships involved were more like quasi-sisters than work colleagues, although they did not claim each other to be so. As Mrs Qiu explained, there were customs of *tongyangxi* (a girl taken into the family as a daughter-in-law-to-be) or *tongyangxu* (a boy taken into the family as a son-in-law-to-be) in the village before 1949. Although Jiang's case was different from *tongyangxi*, there are references in dealing with different kinds of relationships before, during, and after wedding among them, which could be adapted to apply to Jiang's case. Therefore, such innovations can be seen more or less as adaptations of local customs or other practices. They happened everywhere and all the time and provided opportunities for people to create and enjoy their own innovations in human relationships.

In this case everybody in this family played two or more roles, shifting from one to another. For example, in the seeing-off ceremony feast Mrs Qiu played the adopted mother's role and from the lunchtime feast onwards her role changed to that of mother-in-law. For Qiu and Jiang the situations were much more complicated. They started with a relationship of boyfriend and girlfriend. After Jiang moved into the house they had to change their roles to be a brother and a sister, so that they were not allowed to make love. On the wedding day they were groom and bride and afterwards they became husband and wife.

I was interested in the special relationships among the members of the family and conducted another interview after the wedding. Qiu told me that he fell in love with Jiang and established a relationship of boyfriend and girlfriend soon afterwards. One day Qiu brought her back home and asked his mother's permission to let her live with his family. Mrs Qiu agreed with this, with one condition that they should never make love before they got married. They kept their promise. Qiu was proud of his girlfriend, using the phrase "*jie shen zi hao*" (preserve one's purity; refuse to be contaminated by evil influence).

I found that their unusual and difficult situation could be explained with the four criteria of *lishang*: moral judgement, human feelings, rational calculation and religious sense.

(i) Qiu told me that it would be wrong morally if he made love with Jiang without marrying her, but she was already somebody else's fiancée. Jiang told me she escaped from her family before the wedding because that marriage had been arranged by her parents. For Qiu, it also would be wrong morally to make love with her because his family provided free accommodation for her. Jiang had to control her feelings to avoid an embarrassing situation.

(ii) Although Jiang had already had a fiancé, she had never loved him. Qiu and Jiang did love each other very much. They expressed their love by treating each other nicely in everyday life but living in the same house as brother and sister. Qiu also tried his best to control himself. Mrs Qiu told me that she liked Jiang very much and treated her as her own daughter. Her husband had passed away when Qiu was 4 years old. Since then she and her children, two daughters and one son, had been dependent on each other for survival. One of Qiu's sisters married out from the family a few years previously. Another sister lived in Wujiang, although she had not yet married. Jiang came to the house to brighten the family. All of them were emotionally attached to each other more and more as time went on. However, Qiu could not marry her without a certificate from Jiang's hometown to prove that she was either unmarried or divorced in order for them to be registered as a legal couple. Jiang's fiancé's father was an official in the township where she came from and stopped Jiang from getting the certificate by using his work connections. If Jiang had cared about material gains or social status more than love she could have accepted her family's marriage arrangement. However, she escaped, and eventually realised her ideal family relationship based on love.

(iii) Qiu said he could ignore the fact that Jiang was somebody else's fiancée, and there were even many old women who fled from famine in the village and married again with male villagers in the 1960s. However, Qiu also thought of his case rationally. The worst thing for his family would be if they were unable to register their child's birth due to its parents' marriage being illegal. Jiang and her natal family tried again and again over a two-year period and finally persuaded the fiancé's family to accept the returned bridewealth and apology gifts. Eventually she obtained the certificate. Qiu was proud of his wife, "our marriage is now in accordance with reason and popular opinion (*heli*), in accordance with human feelings (*heqing*), and in accordance with rules and regulations (*hefa*)."

(iv) To conclude this discussion of the marriage relationship Qiu said he was lucky that *laotian* (heavenly god) sent him such a wonderful bride. Jiang said that they had a predestined relationship (*yuanfen*) to be married. Mrs Qiu said that she believed that the circle of the bitterness had ended and the sweetness had begun in her life. These sayings are all grounded in a religious sense.

(3) A marriage "hanging on two sides"

Since the application of the State's one-child family policy, more and more young generation families want to have one child only of their own accord. The local marriage custom system has met a challenge. Here I would like to introduce a case that reflects many changes in establishing a marriage relationship between two families and their relations. Although this case was not itself of a single child family, it could also be a new model for such, as a villager told me.

The case started with a conflict in the Shen family about taking a man into the family as a son-in-law (*zhao nuxu*). Shen and his wife had two daughters and had been thinking of this process for the older daughter for a long time. According to local custom (*laofa*), if a family has two daughters the older daughter should take a man into the family as son-in-law, if a family has two sons the younger son should be taken into somebody else's family as son-in-law. However, the older daughter's boyfriend's family had two children, one older daughter and one younger son. According to another *laofa* the son should take a wife into the family because his older sister should be married out of the family (and in fact she was already married out of the family). However, Shen's daughter persuaded her parents to allow her to *liangtougua,* according to another local custom. Here *gua* is short for *guafan* (hang a streamer), *liangtou* means they live independently but would visit both her and her boyfriend's families in turn occasionally.

All three of these patterns of marriage were in line with different local customs (*heli*). They reached agreement on the idea of *liangtougua* but made a slight change and called it *gualiangtou*. Shen's daughter and her boyfriend were free to "hang" (*gua*) themselves, namely, to live with either family for any amount of time. All the betrothal rites and wedding ceremony were adapted accordingly, which they called "*laofa xinban*" (literally, to do a new thing based on old ways).

Instead of small betrothal and large betrothal rites the two young people and their parents agreed that they would have a single combined rite (*dinghun*). In the middle of April 1996 the engagement ceremony was held in Shen's family's home. Two *jieshouren* (intermediaries, which is a new name for matchmakers) came to the village by car, carrying two big baskets of gifts wrapped in red cloth: two bottles of liquor, four cartons of cigarettes, six big rice cakes with lucky words on top, a bag of tea, a bag of candied dates; a pair of rings with a diamond on both the golden ring (*huangjin* - yellow coloured gold) and the platinum ring (which they called white gold, *baijin,* because it was as valuable as gold), a gold bracelet, a gold necklace, a pair of silver bracelets, 10,000 *yuan* cash, and four empty red envelopes（PhotoV-3 and 4）.

Photos V-3 and 4. Two male "matchmakers" bringing "betrothal" gift money and gifts to the Shen family.

Normally, Shen told me, for either small or large betrothal rites the bridewealth would be wrapped in different itemised red envelopes. His understanding was that the empty red envelopes were the fiancé's family's goodwill gesture of adaptation of the old way of *liangtougua*. Shen was not surprised by the above gifts which were all discussed in advance, except for the 10,000 *yuan* cash. He and his wife discussed this with their older generation relatives and decided to refuse the money, because acceptance of the fiancé's family's bridewealth would change the relationship. However, the intermediaries refused to take the money back. They insisted that the money was not for the fiancée's family, but for the girl herself to buy clothes as had been agreed in advance, all they had done was double the amount. Shen and his wife agreed to accept the money on condition that the fiancé's family also accepted 10,000 *yuan* for the fiancé's clothing. However, acceptance of the 10,000 *yuan* meant their daughter would be considered to have married out according to the local custom. So, on one of the occasions when the fiancé visited the Shen family they made him take the 10,000 *yuan* back to his home.

After the ceremony feast the fiancée's mother handed return gifts to the intermediaries. They were two big steamers of small rice cakes for the fiancé's family to distribute to its agnatic kin, neighbours and fellow villagers; a bag of soft crunchy rice cakes (*songgao*), two bottles of liquor, two boxes of candied dates, two towels, a platinum ring, 3,000 *yuan*, and four empty red envelopes.

One year later the couple got married. Shen and his wife told me through telephone conversations that the wedding was also a "new thing based on old ways". They explained that the old way is for both the bride's and groom's families to hold wedding ceremony feasts. The new way is for two families to hold a joint wedding banquet in a restaurant or hotel, as people did in urban areas. For their daughter, the adapted way was that both the bride's and the groom's families should hold one feast each on the wedding day. The lunchtime feast was held by the bride's family. The groom accompanied by seven friends attended this feast. In the supper feast it was the groom's family's turn to hold the wedding feast. The groom and his friends, the bride and her seven friends went to the groom's family. Both the groom's seven friends and the bride's seven friends were their high school classmates who had known each other very well for many years.

Both families agreed that the numbers of guests, types of gifts, and standard of the two wedding feasts on the wedding day should be similar. They chose seven friends each for both bride and groom for the following reasons. (i) Morally, it is right one should choose those friends who would be most likely to live and work in the same city, Wujiang, and therefore become lifelong friends. This idea is based on a Chinese saying that *zaijia gao fumu, zaiwai gao pengyou* (at home one can rely on parents, away from home one can rely on friends). (ii) Those chosen were very close friends from the bride and groom's boarding-school. The bride and the groom came from different townships and went to yet another where the school was located, as did their other friends. Over a six year period they had become very close emotionally. (iii) Practical considerations were also taken into account. The groom plus his seven friends could just fit in two cars. When the bride went to the groom's family for the second wedding feast they hired two cars. Also the wedding party could be fitted on one dining table at both feasts. (iv) In addition, the bride's mother said the number 8 was a lucky number. Apart from this table there were two other tables, eight on each, of the bride's "little sisters" who either lived in the village or were primary school classmates.

Since Shen's older daughter and her husband lived in Wujiang City all the pre-wedding and post-wedding *wanglai* between the in-laws' family became very simple:

(i) The bride did not have a large dowry. She brought engagement gifts worth 20,000 *yuan*, her parents' gift money of 16,000 *yuan*, and her friends' gift money of about 2,800 *yuan* given at her wedding feast. The Shen family gave the son-in-law engagement gifts worth 20,000 *yuan*, and his family and friends also gave him more or less the same amount of gift money as the bride had received from her family and friends. The young couple explained that they wanted to make their new family with the above money based on their own preferences. However, her natal family still made a bridal chamber for her and her husband. All the gifts from relatives and her friends were kept there.

(ii) This marriage did not involve a relationship with ancestors because Shen's wife said her daughter insisted the marriage was a new arrangement and she did not want to involve them. The same happened in the groom's family. However, the Shens decorated the central hall for the wedding ceremony for good luck and a family happiness.

(iii) The in-laws' families invited each other for lunar New Year feasts once a year. They addressed each other as non-agnatic kin and added each other as non-agnatic kin to their family lists. If Shen's daughter had been taken into her husband's family as a wife then the Shen family would have been non-agnatic kin of her husband's family, and the new couple should not bring the husband's parents for the annual lunar New Year's feast held by the Shen family. However, in this case, her husband's parents could attend the feast with the young couple because they were non-agnatic kin of the Shen family as well.

(iv) Shen's daughter and her husband attended feasts held by Shen's agnatic and non-agnatic kin's families. Equally the young couple also attended the husband's family's agnatic and non-agnatic kin's families' feasts together, as well as tea parties with neighbours and fellow villagers in both the Shen family's group and the husband's family's group. The difference from the norm was that they were both of them new guests to every family, because neither of them had become a member of the other family.

(v) The young couple then had a baby who was sent to a full-time nursery from six months old, so there was no need for both sides' parents to look after him. Shen's wife needed to look after her little shop at home so she hardly ever visited her daughter's family in Wujiang. Shen's daughter and her husband brought the boy to visit them about once every two weeks and did the same with their son-in-law's family.

Shen and his wife told me that their younger daughter and her boyfriend were also working in Wujiang. They would make similar arrangements for the engagement and wedding of this younger daughter. Shen's wife admitted that however equal the relationships in this kind of "hanging over two sides" (*gua liangtou*) marriage there were still some things that could not be shared equally. For example, in a marriage of taking a man into family (*zhaonuxiu*) the wife's agnatic kin would remain as agnatic kin. If the new couple had a child he or she would carry on the wife's surname. The child would call his or her mother's sister *guma* (father's sister) rather than *yima* (mother's sister), and call his or her mother's brother *shushu* (father's brother) rather than *jiujiu* (mother's brother). The child's father's natal family and its relatives would be non-agnatic kin of the new family. His brother would be his child's *jiujiu*, and his sister would be his child's *yima*.

In the Shen family's case, these forms of address to relatives made Mrs Shen feel her daughter had married out from the family. Her daughter's son carried his father's surname because, as her daughter said, "I have to follow the local custom wherever I am" (*ruxiang suisu*). She lived in an urban area where nuclear families' children almost all used their father's name as surname. Thus, when a conflict of local customs occurs between a rural area and an urban area the resolution can be reached based on where the new couple resides.

The whole process of establishing a marriage relationship is like a drama which contains prologue, acts, scenes and epilogue. In this process mainly horizontal expressive *wanglai* is involved, compared with the vertical expressive *wanglai* from birth to sixteen years old. Although the process of knitting *lishang-wanglai* networks sometimes involved the villagers' lives in tragicomedy, the variations of *wanglai* are always determined by the varying criteria of *lishang*.

V.III. House construction

House construction became a main event for Kaixiangong villagers during the period from 1981 to 2000 (see Figure V-1). Following rural reform in the early 1980s villagers at last had state permission to build new houses and could afford to do so. I include house construction as a life-cycle event because Kaixiangong villagers treated it as a family event rather than a family investment as the ESRC social support project assumed. I found the complex project of house construction made a showcase for villagers' talent for arranging resources through expressive *wanglai* in family networks. House construction also relates to family division and elderly care, which affects family structure and composition in the village.

Figure V-1 Number of houses built from 1981 to 2000

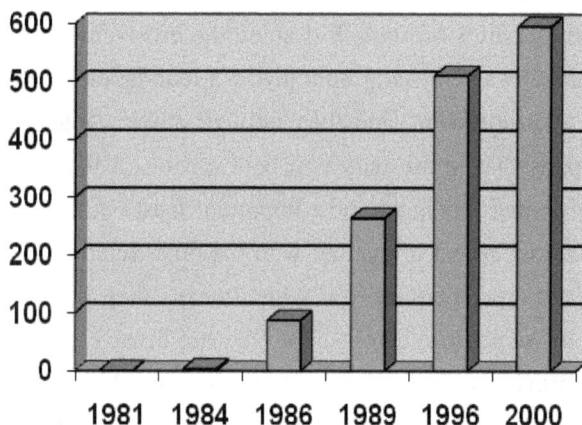

* See Fei, 1986:,258, Shen, 1993:,262; Hu, 1996:,15 and Wang, 2002 for the first three numbers, the fourth number came from my fieldwork notes, the last number was given by Wang, the Director of the Village Committee, in a telephone conversation in 2003. I won't provide the latest date because a neighbouring village joined into the village.

1. Expressive *wanglai*

In 1996 it took two to three months, using from 20 to 30 labourers per day, to build a house as far as raising the roof-beams, with a total cost of about 100,000 *yuan*[21] for building materials, food for labourers, payment to bricklayers, carpenters, and a chef, as well as many associated events. Chapter II.III shows the major events of house construction. "Ceremony for setting a foundation stone" (*baidipan*) offers respect to the land god. "Putting up the second storey"

---

[21] My informants told me that, on average, the cost of construction of a house was 20,000–30,000 *yuan* in 1982, 40,000–50,000 *yuan* in 1990, 100,000 *yuan* in 1995, and 15,000–20,000 *yuan* in 2000. The most expensive house nowadays costs 50,000 *yuan*.

(*jialouban*) is a new way to demonstrate that one's standard of living has increased. "Putting up the roof-beams" (*shangliang*) shows that a new house is nearly complete. "Moving into the new house" (*shengqian*) tells the ancestors and everybody else that the new house is ready for occupation. "Completed a new house tea party" (*kaichaguan*) is the way in which women show each other their new houses and exchange ideas. The arrangements of the events in house construction involve almost all the relations in a family's *lishang-wanglai* networks. *Lishang-wanglai* and social support, therefore, can be studied at work within a short timescale by examining the process of house construction.

The first five rows of part 3 of Table V-1 show the involvement of expressive *wanglai* in both horizontal and vertical ways. It starts from laying a foundation stone through putting up the first floor, putting on the roof-beam, and then through moving into a new house down to a completed house tea party. There are only two bold arrows in the row of the putting up the roof-beam feast. It shows that this is the most important feast because the old generation, both agnatic and non-agnatic kin, attend it together with the other relations. The columns of agnatic kin, neighbours and fellow villagers are full which means they have been invited for all the events throughout the house construction because they are involved in the process as helpers or household equipment providers. The columns of non-agnatic kin, mother's brother or wife's natal family and father's sister or married-out daughter show they take part in the major events and provide important financial and material support (see Chapter II.III).

Friends only appeared on one occasion, that of putting up roof-beams during the house construction period. The obligation of a friend on this occasion is either to give the upper part of a pig leg, a big piece of pork, or equivalent gift money, say 50 *yuan*. In terms of whose friends should be invited to this occasion, according to the local custom the family should invite only one set of friends: either the father's friends if the family's son has not got married, or a newly married son's friends. However, the villagers have created a new custom to take a son-in-law into the family. Tan told me that the reason friends of son-in-laws were invited on this occasion might be because they are male and can accompany the male helpers, neighbours and fellow villagers during the meal time. This new custom was confirmed by two other informants when they told me the difference between married-out daughters and sons. As I mentioned in Chapter II.II, a new wife and her friends normally ended their relationship at the visit to her natal family one month after she got married, whereas for a family taking a son-in-law into it the son-in-law is supposed to end the relationship with his friends after the feast for putting on the roof-beam of his house.

The row of the completed house tea party shows that only wives of agnatic kin, neighbours and fellow villagers are invited for this. It is a new event which first appeared in the village in the middle of the 1980s. In my sampled households 96 per cent said they had had such tea parties, the exception being one family which still lived in an old house. Although I did not discover which family started it, this small event adds the finishing touch to the different kinds of events in which women have special importance in the arrangement of the rituals. The women were in charge of the rituals and showed a new generation how to deal with all kinds of relationships, with the land god, the ancestors, and with people (kin, neighbours, friends etc.). It was the women who invited different people to attend the various rituals on behalf of their families. Women knew how to perform the rituals. They asked men to help them to put all the gifts from the non-agnatic kin in the middle of the foundations or in the hall of a new building, and to take the gifts away after the rituals. They burned incense and paper money, lit candles and put offerings on tables for the land god or the ancestors, and at the same time they asked an appropriate man to let off firecrackers. Women also knew how to offer different food for labourers at the break. The wet rice ball (*tuyuan*) was for the "ceremony for setting a foundation stone" (*baidipan*); the egg cake (*dangao*) was for "putting up the second storey" (*jialouban*); the pyramid-shaped dumpling made of glutinous rice wrapped in bamboo leaves (*zongzi*) was for the "putting up the roof-beams" (*shangliang*); the dumpling ball made of glutinous rice flour (*tuanzi*) was for the "moving into the new house" (*shengqian*). Although the above food as gifts is carried by men with a *longti*, a handcart or a small boat, women always determine and arrange the gifts for them. The organisation of gifts, both practically and socially, is a complicated matter, in which women need to take great care to avoid giving offence. I have described a case of changing a relationship from expressive *wanglai* to negative *wanglai* between a given family and in-law's family due to lack of consideration of the correct gifts (see Chang, 1999:167–168).

For a given family in house construction vertical expressive *wanglai* is also involved. This is *wanglai* between different generations of family members (see section of "elderly care" later), between villagers and village cadres, collective and local officials of the township, between villagers and ancestors and gods. The column for the collective in Table V-1 shows it has been involved in house construction from laying the foundation stone to moving to a new house. The way in which the village collective affected house construction materially was by letting its warehouses to villagers, free of charge. Every house-building family had to borrow a group's warehouse for the family to live in from the beginning to the end of house construction. In terms of financial support, before the 1980s the village collective used to be a source of welfare for houses seriously damaged by natural disasters. This still holds, according to the head of the Village Committee, but no such event has occurred in the past two decades. The village collective's involvement in house construction can also be seen in mediating neighbourhood disputes at house sites and going through administrative formalities for the villagers (see Chapter VI.I: "Top down vertical instrumental *wanglai*").

The column for ancestors in Table V-1 also shows them to be invited once for the moving to new house feast, whereas the column of local gods or spirits shows they are involved in house construction twice. The rituals of worshipping ancestors and gods are performed in more or less the same way as for other family events but have a different significance. Villagers invited their ancestors (*qing shangzu*) for a celebration when the family moved into a new house. At the same time this settles them into the new house, where it is hoped they will protect the family's peace in their new dwelling. As I mentioned in Chapter II.II the villagers distinguish between residential gods and visiting gods. The two worships of gods during the house construction period were to establish residential gods in the new house. The first was for the land god (*tudi gonggong*) and to ask other spirits including ghosts their forgiveness for touching the land (*dong tu*). The second was for both land god and kitchen god, to settle them into the new house and ask a blessing and protection from them. Having a ritual for ancestors and gods during house construction indicates that the villagers regard them as an important part of their relationships and resources (see more from "religious sense" of *lishang*).

2. *Lishang* criteria

The reasons behind this complicated series of events in house construction and the prevailing system for mobilising the resources of family *lishang-wanglai* networks can be seen more clearly through the criteria of *lishang*.

(1) Moral judgement

Moral judgement played an important role in sorting out disputes. During the house construction period problems were bound to arise in arranging different relationships, such as quantities or varieties of gifts between a close non-agnatic kin to a given family, boundary disputes with neighbours of the new house, or from public spaces. As explained in "instrumental *wanglai*" in the Chapter V.III, in 1983 the village collective issued a regulation on villagers' house construction based on the township government's related regulations. Moral judgement is sometimes more powerful than a regulation. This one demanded that:

All new houses must be fitted into the "new countryside plan" (*xin nongcui guihua tu*): 7.1m (D) x 3.5m (W) per *jian* for a house site, 2, 3 or 4 *jian*, 3m (D) x 7m (W) for a pigsty or sheepfold site which should be kept 6m away from a house... one-child families are allowed to have 4 *jian* and two-child families 6 *jian*. If the second child is 17 years old the family is allowed to have 7 *jian*, but if the second child of any family with two children was born after 1st January 1973 then the family is only allowed to have 4 *jian*, due to the One-Child Family Policy... Any over-large foundation site would be fined 3 *yuan* per square meter per day, etc.[22]

This regulation caused many disputes between villagers and the village collective because the villagers felt "*lizhi qizhuang*" (literally, the villagers were bold and assured with *qi* of justice on their side). These disputes rested on three arguments from the villagers' points of view: (i) it was morally wrong to pay for a foundation site where their families had lived for generations; (ii) it was also wrong to make definite measurements for foundation sites of houses, courtyards, and pigsties or sheepfolds because the village is located around a winding river and by the meandering Lake of Tai; (iii) it was even more wrong to vary standards for foundation sites according to numbers of children and their dates of birth. So the villagers ignored the regulations because they thought they were in the right (*youli*). The village collective did not impose any fines because it was unable to advance any further argument. As one of my informants told me "the law is unable to punish the masses" (*fa bu ze zhong*). In other words, if a law or regulation is wrong it is weaker than the power of morality and will eventually be changed.

The villagers were proved right within two years. The village collective issued a new regulation in 1985 specifying:

Building site: a house covers a ground space of 20m^2 per person, an extra 20m^2 preferential treatment for a one-child family, 20m^2 for indoor production, 20m^2 for a pigsty or sheepfold site, a fine for exceeding space 130 *yuan* per square metre; courtyard site: 40m^2 per person, a fine for exceeding space 106 *yuan* per square metre.[23]

JM Wang, the head of the Village Committee, told me that it was easy to implement the new regulation because the villagers thought it was reasonable (*heli*), although some villagers still complained that they did not see the reason why a one-child family should live in a bigger

---

[22] A copy of a document in the Village Archives: *Kaixiangong dadui dang zhibu guanyu sheyuan jianfang de youguan guiding* (The related regulations of villagers' house construction by the Party Branch of Kaixiangong Great Brigade), 1983.

[23] A note came from Kaixiangong Village Archives.

house. This case shows villagers' judgement for the above regulation based on *li* (right or wrong, reasonable or not) rather than law or policy because they believed a rational argument covered by a moral cloth was a stronger case.

For villagers, the process of creating a new custom or discarding outdated customs in house construction is regarded as an honourable endeavour, and as a way to accumulate merit (*jide*). In 1982 when the first two-storey building, the Xu family's, appeared in the village the events in house construction were not fully developed. There was no event of putting up the first floor, nor the custom of one helper from each family for house building, nor the "completed house tea party" and so on. These customs appeared gradually. Tan, the father in the case of taking a son-in-law into the family (see Chapter II.II), told me proudly that he was the person who proposed a way to use labour support in 1984, namely, one of each family within the same group to help each other in turn. It was almost immediately accepted and spread quickly in the village, although the situation changed again a few years later. In 1996 when I was there I heard that a family hired a construction contract team (*jianzhu baogong dui*)[24] for house construction. I asked Tan what he thought about this departure from his proposed mutual help in house construction. Tan admitted that discarding an outdated custom – even if it had been proposed by himself – accumulates merit (*jide*). I then quoted an ancient moral statement that "*shi shiwu zhe wei junjie*" (a wise man submits to circumstances). We all laughed. Then Tan pointed out that the family who hired a construction team for house building was a rich family and rebuilding an already "new" house. Under this circumstance fellow villagers should not be involved in labour support according to the villagers' moral judgement "*bang qiong bu bang fu*" (help the poor rather than the rich). It is certainly true that a few other richer families started to rebuild their houses when I was there, as did the Zhou family, which caused a big problem in a relationship with its in-law's family (see Chang, 1999: 167–68). Handling a given changing situation is purely a skill in the art of personal relationships: but moral considerations play a considerable part in developing the adaptation in the first place.

(2) Human feelings

Human feelings played a large part in the events of house construction. An informant told me that he always helped people to set off firecrackers because this was one of the ways that

---

[24] It was a model in Neiguan Village, Gansu Province, my other fieldwork village, due to the implication of the State aid-the-poor programme.

villagers expressed happiness. The feasts were also villagers' way of enjoying their successes in the different stages of house construction. The purpose of the completed house tea party is, in particular, for women to share their happiness with others by showing the new house to their neighbours and fellow villagers. The newly adapted custom between in-laws' families of a whole pig, half pig, and a quarter of a pig respectively for the first, second and third time of building of a new house seems to partake of both rational calculation and moral judgement: the richer people are the less help they will gain. But villagers saw it as a question of human feelings, based on a sense of helping the weak and small, as expressed in the Chinese phrase "*tongqing ruozhe*" (sympathy with weak and small) which they often used.

Multiple house construction could give rise to embarrassment or anger. I found a few women who helped with a family's house building. Asking why, I was told that their husbands had already helped the family at its first time of building a house and when it was time to rebuild they felt uncomfortable providing such help again. But they also felt embarrassed (*buhao yisi*) to refuse the family which requested labour support. The compromise was to send a woman. In their turn, households which rebuilt their houses also felt uneasy about asking for repeated labour support. With the introduction of the free market system the problem of labour support in house building has solved itself. JM Wang, the head of the Village Committee, told me that some families who had already rebuilt a house simply hired a construction team for the next rebuild instead of asking for fellow villagers' help. This practice spread in the village from 1998 with the privatisation of the collective system. However, Wang said this did not mean that the previous custom of labour support in housing was out of date. It was commonly agreed that if any family was building a new house for the first time it could still get labour support from agnatic kin, neighbours and fellow villagers. The villagers have the saying "*renqing haishi yao jiang de*" (always have consideration for villagers' human feelings and customary practice however the situation changes). Note this saying is different from that "*renqing hashi yao huan de*" (one should always repay to others for whatever one owed) which is considered as *renqing* ethic.

(3) Rational calculation

Rational calculation is an inevitable part of arranging resources for house construction. On average, the cost of building a new house in the village in 1995 was 100,000 *yuan*. As in many other major family events, in house construction on average the villagers sourced more than 65 per cent of the financial resources from themselves and the rest through social support from their *lishang-wanglai* networks. There were two ways to arrange financial sources in house construction. One was vertical, using stored resources. Almost all the households interviewed by me purchased building materials over a period of years, and they also reused materials from the old house to avoid lump sum payments. The other was horizontal, through social support. There were divisions among different relations for different resources in their family based on *lishang-wanglai* networks. This was also true in house construction. The villagers normally arranged financial support from non-agnatic kin and friends, unless in an emergency when they would go to the collective or other sources. Labour and materials support mainly come from agnatic kin, neighbours and fellow villagers.

Just as there was a division among a given family's relations for financial support in weddings and other events, so there was also such a division in house construction. For example, Table V-4 shows that YM Zhou received 10,360 *yuan* financial support from the family's relations. This can be seen as a big pig, which came from 32 families. Among them, agnatic kin only gave 180 *yuan* for the putting up roof-beam feast since they were also labour providers. Gifts and gift money worth 720 *yuan* came from friends of a male head of the family. The gifts and gift money were partly used up, for example a big piece of pork was cooked for the feast. There were 14 families of non-agnatic kin. According to local custom Mrs Zhou's natal family should play an important role in events throughout the period of house construction. However, her natal family lived in Wanping Township which had different customs. The family had to find a proper arrangement based mainly on a rational calculation. They invited two families for the foundation-stone laying event. They were Mrs Zhou's quasi-daughter's family and Mr Zhou's mother's quasi-son's family. They brought gifts worth 120 *yuan* from each family of the same type. They were 100 small square-shaped rice cakes, one upper part of pig leg, 2 *jin* sweets and 6 big fire crackers. Three families were invited for the putting up 1st floor event. Mr Zhou's mother's other quasi-son and Mr Zhou's father's married-out brother's two sons' families. They brought gifts and gift money totalling 300 to 320 *yuan* each (see "laying 1st floor" for details). Some of the above families were invited again for the putting up roof-beam event at which considerable amounts of gifts and gift money would again be given. As an adaptation of the usual custom, Mr Zhou's natal family's resources were only mobilised once, because her brothers were busy with their work as officials, technicians, drivers and businessmen. They brought 600 to 800 *yuan* of gift money each for the putting up the roof-beam feast.

Table V-4 Y. Zhou family's financial support in house construction (*yuan*)

Relations	Laying foundation	Putting up 1st floor	Putting up rooftrees	Moving into new house	Total
Mr Z's mother's quasi-daughter	-	-	1,000	30	1,030
Mr Z's mother's quasi-son	120	-	500	30	650
Mr Z's mother's quasi-son	-	300	-	30	330
Mr Z' father's brother older son	-	320	500	30	850
Mr Z' father's brother younger son	-	320	500	30	850
Mrs Z' quasi-daughter	120	-	600	30	750
Mrs Z's older brother	-	-	800	-	800
Mrs Z's younger brother	-	-	600	-	600
Mrs Z's younger brother	-	-	600	-	600
Mrs Z's younger brother	-	-	600	-	600
Mrs Z's younger brother	-	-	600	-	600
Mrs Z's younger brother	-	-	600	-	600
Mrs Z's younger brother	-	-	600	-	600
Mrs Z's younger sister	-	-	600	-	600
Z family's agnatic kin x 6	-	-	180	-	180
Mr Z's friends x 12	-	-	720	-	720
Total	**240**	**940**	**9000**	**180**	**10,360**

Necessary material support is always provided by agnatic kin, neighbours and fellow villagers. There are ways of obtaining and outfitting housing through social support, which do not require money. For example, borrowing a hall for carpentry from agnatic kin or neighbours; borrowing a storehouse with a stove from their group head to use as temporary living space; borrowing tables, benches, dishes, bowls and chopsticks from their agnatic kin.

Labour support is mostly provided by agnatic kin, neighbours and fellow villagers. In 1996 building a new house needed 20 to 30 people per day on average for the building work.

Normally a household needs to hire the craftspeople, such as bricklayers, carpenters, a chef because the workers need to be fed, and also pays for consultation with professionals. However, it is not necessary to pay for most of the general labour needed. For example, unloading building materials such as sand, crushed stones, bricks, reinforcing bars, wood, cement from boats, digging foundations, putting up scaffolding, mixing crushed stones, sand, and cement mixture, delivering bricks to bricklayers and so on, can all be done casually through non-paid labour support. Otherwise the cost of hire of these helpers can be 5,000 to 8,000 *yuan*. A household can get two labourers from each agnatic family and one from every household in the same group, according to local custom. This kind of arrangement of labour support saves some cost.

This support given from one family to another is like growing and fattening a pig. What is given or obtained gradually over a period of time can be recovered or repaid all at once when required. However, the appearance of contract construction teams seems to have led to a real change. According to rational calculation the contract construction team was the most effective way of using labour to build a house towards the end of the 1990s. In 2000, Wang, the head of the Village Committee, gave me some calculations during a telephone conversation. The construction team normally includes 3 to 5 carpenters, 8 to 10 bricklayers and one chef for cooking lunch, who are called *da gong,* and 10 to 14 helpers for carrying materials who are called *xiao gong*. *Da gong* cost 35 *yuan* per day and *xiao gong* cost 20 *yuan* per day. The total cost per day is therefore about 600 *yuan*. The building work normally takes 20 to 30 days dependent on the size of the house and the decoration takes a further 3 to 5 months dependent on the house size and standard. In the decoration period only a few specialists, such as plasterers, painters, lacquerers, electricians, plumbers would be involved, which requires less organisation. There is no doubt that the house construction team replaces the function of labour mutual aid between agnatic kin, neighbours and fellow villagers. Together with the compatible customary practice of reducing support for the second and third time of a family building a house, this practice altered the contents and quantity of the gifts flowing among non-agnatic kin families. They mark the ending of the "house construction wave". Financial and labour support in major expenditures in house construction will be reduced significantly, because the hired builders are more professional and, from their point of view, the third generational houses will last forever.

(4) Spiritual beliefs

I now will show how a religious sense was embodied in the events of a house construction period. Although financial and labour support ended as more and more families hired construction teams, it didn't stop the villagers from having the five events (see Chapter II.III), even during the second or third waves of house construction. A helper building FN Wang family's house told me that building a house is a dangerous business. In order to reduce risks of accident all the heavenly gods and ghosts should be prayed to (*laotian xiaogui dou yao bai*) throughout the process, any part of which could be the cause of an accident. This kind of religious sense was very common for the villagers. In order to avoid evil (*bixie*) villagers worship the land god before laying the foundation stone, eat a rice ball (*tuyuan*) especially designed to keep them safe from ghosts (*yegui*) before starting work on the foundations, wrap red cloth on top of the four boundary stakes and hang up a red flag throughout the construction period, set off big firecrackers, and put a millstone in the lower middle of a screen wall in order to lay ghosts (*zhengui*) if a house is located by a road. The customs of worshipping the land god and moving the bed into the new house before sunrise also comes from the same concern to ward of misfortune.

A common religious sense that fortune, luckiness and happiness are supernaturally influenced can be seen in other ways. There was no ritual for pulling down the old house, but the date of it was important. The Huang family got a date for pulling down their old house from a fortune-teller, who chose the 16th of the second lunar month. Both date and month were an even number, symbolising everlasting peace for the family in the new house. During the ritual of throwing various consumables up to the roof-beam (*paoliang*, *zongzi*, steamed buns, sweets, oranges, cigarettes) a carpenter and a bricklayer repeatedly recited "*paoliang mantou pao de gao, daidai zisun jie de lao*" – meaning, the higher these objects were thrown the better for continuing the family line.

Almost all the houses were located south-facing based on the *Feng shui* principle, for they believed such a position would have an influence on the fortune of a family. Almost all the houses had a round solid flowerpot in the middle of the rooftop, which symbolises everlasting peace for the family, left over from the ritual of "*zuojie*" in which an evergreen is planted in the flowerpot when the roof is completed. In the "move into the new house" event there was a ritual of raising the large intestine of a pig high in the air (*tiaodachang*). It should be cooked whole and then lifted with chopsticks as high as possible. The length of the intestine symbolises the longevity of the house.

Chapter VI

Expressive *wanglai* in life cycle events (II)

Chapter V showed how a person's family builds a huge family-based *lishang-wanglai* network about them during the first half of their life. Each member's network from the same family would be slightly different. The obvious example is a boy or girl who would have a different set of friends. Marriage marks a new start for the married person and his or her family at the second half of the life journey. Chapter VI consists of the sections of family division (although not all families do this), elderly care, and funereal and post-funeral rituals. Looking at family social support arrangements for the above events I will demonstrate further how *lishang-wanglai* networks are maintained and updated, including the ending of distant relationships.

VI.I Family division (*fenjia*)

The meanings of "family division" in rural China can differ. A typical meaning relates to family property flowing from parents to married children (Cohen, 1976) or members of a family dividing into "two stoves" within a joint family (Hu, 1991). Some later research has shown that family division mainly relates to the transfer of power from parents to married children, since there was not enough family property to be divided in rural Chinese families during the Socialist society post-1949 (Yan, 1997, 1998 in Chinese). Other divided families continued working as one organization corporately in rural China (e.g. Ma, 1999). My findings will support Yan and Ma's ideas of power transfer from parents to married children, and continuity and cooperation of divided families as one organization. I will also show the difference between Kaixiangong and Xiajia, where Yan Yunxiang describes "the triumph of conjugality." (Yan, 1997, 2003).

Initially I found that the Kaixiangong Village collective's statistics for the average number of members in a family dropped from 4.15 in 1985 to 3.94 in 1996, which looked similar to Yan's finding in Xiajia, which dropped from 5.3 in 1980 to 4.2 in 1991 (1997:194–195; 1998:75). Yan also found that the percentage of nuclear families in Xiajia increased from 59 per cent in 1980 to 72 per cent in 1991 and claimed that family structure moved away from joint and stem families towards nuclear families (1997: 194–95, 1998: 75). Is there a move towards the nuclear family in Kaixiangong as well?

My sampled households' average number of family members was 5.31 in 1996, which was substantially higher than the village collective's statistics of the same year. I found three reasons for this:

(i)   There were two households that counted their future daughters-in-law as members of the family. QM Zhou's family members included him, his wife, son, and their future daughter-in-law. XH Yao's family counted himself, his mother, his son and his future daughter-in-law, but not his wife who had died a few years previously.

(ii)   Some families counted parents who lived separately but were financially still dependent on their families as members of the family. The RM Tan family counted his mother as part of the family because the family paid tax and fees and some living expenses for her, although physically she lived with her younger son after her husband passed away. JG Wang counted his mother as a member of his family because he was the only son of his parents and it was his responsibility to provide for her old age, although she lived separately from him because she did not get on with his wife.

(iii) Some families still included those members of an officially divided older son's family that would have been members before the division. For example, in March 1996 HL Wang told me that his family included 10 members: HL Wang himself, his mother, brother, wife, two sons and their wives and two grandchildren (Figureee VI-1). But one of his sons said this family had already divided into three families in 1994 (I will demonstrate and analyse this case in this section later). This agrees with the village collective's statistics, which counted the two sons' families as two families. The reason the two sons' families registered as two nuclear families as soon as they got married was because their wives could then receive their share of fields and land from the collective.[25] It is clear that just because the Kaixiangong Village collective's figures looked similar to Yan's finding in Xiajia, it doesn't mean there is necessarily a great increase in nuclear families in Kaixiangong.

---

[25] The village collective redistributed the land and fields from time to time by taking the dead people's land and fields and distributing it to new wives.

Figure VI-1 HL Wang's family structure in 1993

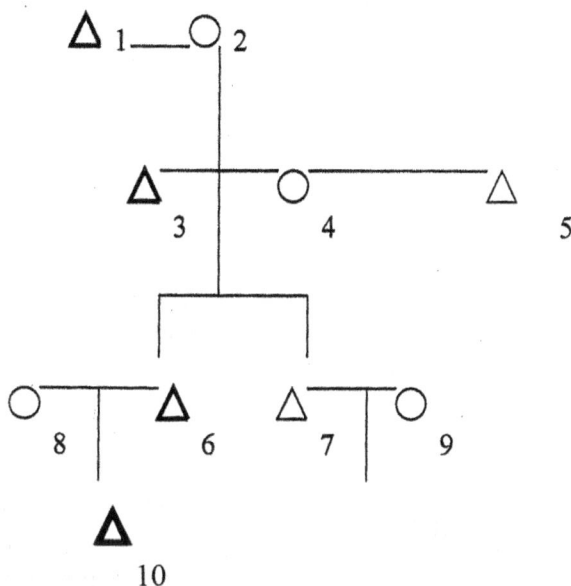

In Kaixiangong in 1996, my sampled households were 78 per cent stem families, 18 per cent nuclear families and 4 per cent joint families and incomplete families. Although the joint family divided into three families which included two nuclear families, more than half of the nuclear families had turned into stem families by the end of 2004. In 2006 village cadre Fukun Yao, previous agricultural technician, carried out a survey of 790 households of the village. He used a standard, whether parents, grandparents and married children lived in the same house and the same courtyard, to measure different types of family. This definition is the villagers' idea. He found that there were 63 per cent of household parents who lived with one of their children's families, 23 per cent in nuclear families and 14 per cent in other types of families in the village (Table VI-1). This means that the majority of married children still lived with their parents. The family structure seems not to have changed since the 1930s when according to Fei this was the result of a kind of obligation of the *yang* from the younger generation to the elderly (1939: 73–74). However, Yao's other data show there are huge differences between 1960 and 2006 due to the Great Leap Forward's campaign that caused a large increase in the number of incomplete families. Nowadays, villagers' life is much longer than it was in past decades which increased numbers of stem families accordingly.

Table VI-1 Differences in family structure between Kaixiangong and Xiajia Village (1991-2006)

	Xiajia Village Committee 1991	Kaixiangong Village Committee 1996	Kaixiangong sample households 1996	Kaixiangong Yao's survey 2006
Stem family	-	-	78	63
Nuclear family	72	62	18	23
Joint or incomplete family	-	-	4	14

In summary, nuclear families in Kaixiangong still play a relatively small part in villagers' everyday life. According to Yan there were two reasons that caused the difference between Xiajia and Kaixiangong. They are: (i) Xiajia is located in Heilongjiang Province where the farmland is plentiful, which allows the married couples to build their own houses and live separately from their parents (Yan, 2003: 253). (ii) Families in Xiajia have more children because the villagers' houses occupy much larger plots (Yan, 2003: 197, 253).

Due to the above differences from Xiajia village, Kaixiangong villagers arrange their family life differently. The main difference affects the ways of family division and elderly care (see Chapter VI.II). In "Establishing a marriage relationship (see Chapter V.II.)" I have shown that the marriage system in Kaixiangong Village makes vertical reciprocal relationships between parents and children amongst the majority of families with one or two children. However, for some families with two or more sons in which the sons either do not want or have no possibility of being taken by a girl as a son-in-law, they have simply kept the traditional family arrangement, namely, both sons taking daughters-in-law into the family which results in family division. According to a 37-year-old male villager interviewed by telephone in 2002, there were seven families with two sons involved in a family division between two brothers among about 700 families[26]. My fieldwork findings will show that family division is a rearrangement of family life between parents and the families of married sons or (if they have taken a son-in-law into the family) daughters. It involves input from both parents and married sons or daughters for dividing family property, contracted land, responsibility for care of the elderly, childcare, housework,

---

[26] The increasing numbers of families was caused by the amalgamation of a neighbouring village into Kaixiangong in

family networks, even debt. The process of family division will show vertical and horizontal reciprocal *lishang-wanglai* among parents and children and their relatives.

1. Vertical and horizontal *wanglai*

In Kaixiangong this process of family division involves an expressive *wanglai* between parents and children. Family division, as a rearrangement of family life, mixes passing on family property generously to married children from parents with exchanging elderly care from married children instrumentally. There were written and unwritten items in family division contracts (*fenjia qiyue*) for both parents and married children. Expressive *wanglai* with a given family's networks would be involved in both the family division event and the process of practice of the family division agreement, which can be seen through the written and unwritten items in family division contracts.

The "family division" row of Table V-1 shows how family division uses vertical expressive *wanglai* between parents and married children (see Chapter VI.II), the given families (from one joint family to three families) and their ancestors and kitchen gods (see Chapter III.III and the religious sense of *lishang* later). The same row also shows that no agnatic kin, neighbours, fellow villagers and friends are involved in family division. Table VI-2 shows how HL Wang's stem family divided into three families after their family division in 1996: 1 to 4 was the elderly family; 5, 7 and 9, and 6, 8 and 10 were two nuclear families. 2001.

Figure VI-2 HL Wang's family structure after family division in 1996

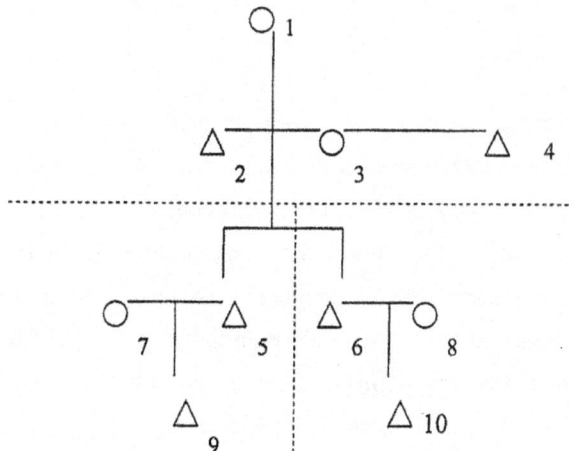

The non-agnatic kin are involved in family division horizontally. The joint family had 19 non-agnatic families (see Figure VI-3). They belong to Mr HL Wang's father's sister's son and daughter (who took a son-in-law into the family), his father's brother's two sons, his mother's three brothers' five sons, his sister's daughter (who took a son-in-law into the family) and two sons, Mrs HL Wang's four brothers (including one quasi-brother), the older son's son's quasi-mother, and both son-in-laws. The first nine families are the old generation of non-agnatic kin. For them the significance of the family division was that their close relationship with the joint family would be ended after the family division feasts. They would still be invited to weddings or funerals, the major family events, but would no longer be invited to the annual Chinese New Year feasts. After the family division, HL Wang would no longer host the joint family's annual Chinese New Year feasts for the close non-agnatic kin.

Figure VI-3 Structure of the Wang family's non-agnatic kin

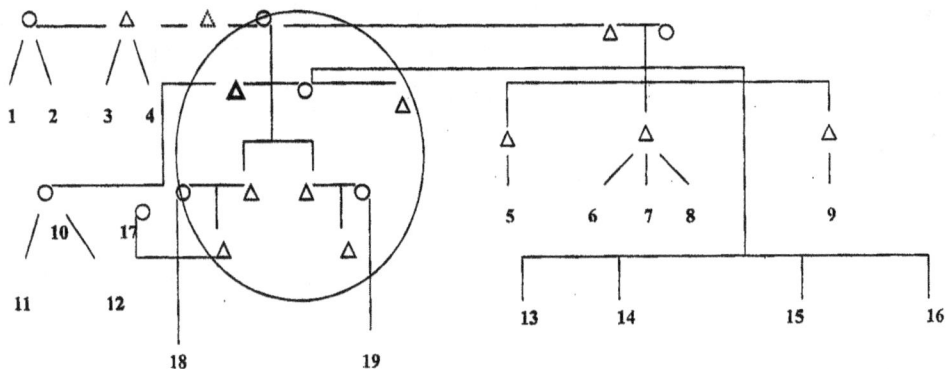

The rest of the 10 close non-agnatic kin were inherited by the two sons' families. The two son's families hosted Chinese New Year feasts from 1997 onwards. After the 2002 Chinese New Year feasts the older son told me that his family's non-agnatic kin included eight families. They are his parents-in-law, three *jiujiu*s, his son's quasi-mother, his wife's quasi-daughter, his quasi-son, and his father's sister's older daughter who took a husband into the family. The younger son's wife told me that her family had seven families on their Chinese New Year feasts' list. They are her natal family, three *jiujiu*s' families, her father's sister's older daughter who took a husband into the family, her father's sister's younger son's family who lived with her father's sister, and her son's quasi-mother's family.

The above lists for Chinese New Year's feast are slightly different to the two sons' inherited lists. From the inherited lists the older son's family lost three close non-agnatic families, which are the quasi-jiujiu's family and his father's sister's two sons' families. At the same time his list gained two more families: those of his wife's quasi-daughter and of his own quasi-son's. The younger son's family in turn lost two families, his quasi-jiujiu's, one of his father's sister's son's, and gained their son's quasi-mother's family. The close non-agnatic families ended the relationship by declining the invitations for the first Chinese New Year feasts hosted by the sons. They said "do not bother with it" (bu yao mafan le). This is a common way to stop a relationship between two families without saying "no". The two sons then recognised that the close non-agnatic families did not want to have a close relationship with them any more and they removed them from their families' lists. They did not feel hurt or sorry at the loss because "*laiwang* can not be forced", the older son said. The younger son's wife said "one can always make a new relationship if both sides are happy to be related" (*gaoxing laiwang*).

2. Implications of *lishang* criteria

Four basic *lishang* criteria of morality, human feelings, rational calculation, and religious sense can be seen in family division, as follows.

(1) Moral judgement

Everybody agreed that morally it is right for family property and elderly care to be clearly divided in a written contract in order to avoid any future disagreement between the two sons after the parents give up the family property and power. It is also morally right to divide the family property fairly between the two sons. This is why all the *jiujiu*s are formally involved in the event (see Chapter III.I). In contrast to the normally implicit speech of polite manners, at this event they make it clear or in the villagers' words "I must tell you bluntly" or "I must tell you bad or ugly words" first (*chouhuo shuo zai xian*), so should anything go wrong the responsibility is clear.

(2) Human feelings

Human feeling can also be seen from the family division. Normally family divisions relate to human feelings between parents and married children vertically. The following case shows that family division can provide an opportunity to resolve an old couple's negative feelings by letting them live separately with different sons rather than get divorced. An old woman told me that four years ago her joint family divided into two families instead of three families. According to local custom, a joint family with two sons dividing into two families where parents live separately, one with each son's family, is called *fen ren* (divided parents into two persons). In theory, the father lived with the older son and the mother lived with the younger son because the latter was more likely to need childcare from his mother. In practice, physically there were different ways to handle the real situation. If the parents love each other or get on well (*ganqing hao* or *hedelai*) they would live together physically but separate in name, this is similar to HL Wang's case. If the parents no longer love each other (*ganqing buhao* or *hebulai*) the family division would be a chance for them to live separately both in name and in practice, as in the old woman's case, because there was no such thing as divorce for her age group in the village. The old woman told me happily: "it was great that the family division finally separated me from that old man" (*fenjia zhenhao zhongyu ba wo he laotouzi fenkai le*). This case shows the villagers divided "people" as well as property. The reason the parents lived separately with different children was because they did not get along well with each other or were temperamentally incompatible (*xingge buhe*), rather than any particular custom. Villagers never used the word 'love' to each other. If they said *xingge buhe* it meant they did not love each other anymore. If there is a new wife the family relationship is even more complicated. The best solution was to let the no longer loving parents live separately. This example shows that even for the older generation, feelings of love, or its reverse, can have an important effect on family structures.

(3) Rational calculation

Rational calculation was a basic criterion in family division. Although a family division contract (see Chapter III.I) specifies ownership of the family property clearly based on rational calculation of a fair division, the uses of the family house, outbuilding, and curtilage change along with the change in situation, and this involves rational choice. Recently, HL Wang's older son told me that two years ago he and his brother turned the semi-detached bungalow behind their main house into another semi-detached two-storey, two-bedroom building. His family moved into the east part and his brother's family moved into the west part. Both families lived on the first floor and turned one part of the ground floor into a kitchen and living area, and the other part was used as a workshop for knitting woollen sweaters. Both his parents lived in the old house comfortably. Although the new arrangement of the divided families' living situation was very different from the family division contract, everybody was happy with it due to the fairness of redistribution of the divided joint family's property.

Villagers even tried to involve a rational principle to explain the way of drawing lots (*chouqian*) in family property division. HL Wang told me that some families could not divide their property fairly between two sons. Drawing lots seemed the only way to stop their complaints because if one of them said it was not fair everybody could tell him it was the will of the heavenly god (*laotian de yisi*). However, drawing lots can be subject to cheating. The common way was to make the two sets of lots with the same contents on each. This made sure that a particular son got the share of family property which the parents wished, whichever lot he drew. To prevent cheating one of the *jiujiu*s (mother's brothers) has the task of supervising the drawing of lots (*jian qian*) by making sure the two lots represent different shares of the family property fairly.

Although villagers applied the rational principle to family division in many ways, HL Wang's younger son told me that such division could not be done 100 per cent fairly because the east location, which belongs to his brother, symbolised that his brother's situation would always be better than his. However, he did not argue for the east location because the village custom made clear that the older son should occupy the east side and the younger son the west side. Although his family is much poorer than his brother's family, he attributed this to his fate, which touched upon another criterion of *lishang,* which is religious sense. This shows that the rational consideration of fairness is not the only factor that influences property division.

(4) Spiritual beliefs

Religious sense is also involved in family division in many ways. HL Wang's younger son gave me another reason to explain why his family did much less well than his older brother's family. He told me that there was a local custom that a family division should be on the 16th of the sixth lunar month of the year because it was in the middle of the year. The meanings of the date are that the even numbers symbolise luckiness in their family life after family division and the middle of the year means that it is even-handed between two brothers. If the date of family division were earlier than this date of the year it would be suspected of being partial to the older son, and vice versa. Wang's family division started on 23rd of the third lunar month of 1994. Both date and month were odd numbers and in the first part of the year. Although he did not care much when this happened, recently he reflected that the dates did mean something to him. The way in which the younger son believed in fate can be seen from another angle. He said he would not have had to be involved in a family division if he had been taken by a richer girl's family as son-in-law and his life could have been much easier. However, his wife came from a poorer family because her father died when she was young and she had a younger brother. According to local custom she had to be married-out from her family, although she worked hard and became a nursery teacher in the village school. The younger son told me that as one of his little friends he always admired her when they were younger and she could easily have married a man from a richer family in the village. However, he believed it was fate that linked them together and they loved each other so much that they got married eventually. The younger son's parents and his mother-in-law also hoped the heavenly god (*laotian*) would help this loving couple. They did not just say it but also they behaved devoutly in the last part of the family division ritual which I observed (see "worship of the kitchen god" in Chapter III.I). Their wish had been largely realised as evinced by a new house, when I visited the village again in 2004.

As I mentioned at the beginning of this section, HL Wang counted his older son's family as members of his joint family even two years after the family was divided from it. He insisted that the older son's family could not be calculated as a separate family before the family division was completed. The family division could only be finished after the end of the ritual of worshipping the kitchen god, even though officially the older son's family divided from the joint family in 1994. For him, based on village custom, the joint family should count as one until the end of all rituals of family division in May 1996. The phenomena can also be seen in a Hebei village as Ma claimed that it would not be counted as family division without a religious ritual of family division, even if members of the family ate from separate stoves and property was divided (1999: 114).

VI.II. Elderly care

In 1995 when I conducted my fieldwork in Neiguan Village, Gansu Province, I heard an extreme case of a daughter-in-law who eventually killed her father-in-law "accidentally" after torturing him for two years. A few years later Guo Yuhua gave a talk at Department of Anthropology, London School of Economics on an elderly father who was tormented by his sons in a Hebei village (also see Guo, 2001). Yan Yunxiang (2003) even reported several tragic cases of suicide – an elderly couple (2003: 86) and an old man (2003: 162), and other forms of abuse by sons and daughters-in-law, for example an old woman who was forced to climb out of a back window on a dark night, as a thief, to get remarried (2003: 169). He argues "[The] traditional mechanism of intergenerational reciprocity has broken down, mainly in response to the introduction of values associated with the market economy" (2003: 163). However,

Kaixiangong's case will show that the traditional mechanism of intergenerational reciprocity still exists. I will show this with their everyday life, including changes of house structure, living arrangements between elderly parents and adult children and elders' birthday ceremonies. I will then show how elderly care among Kaixiangong villagers is mainly expressive *wanglai*, although there are some phenomena that can be seen as instrumental expressive *wanglai*, for example family division. Finally I will show that although the villagers used social support as a supplement to rural elderly care, it remains the case that intergenerational reciprocity still works.

1. Expressive *wanglai* in elderly care

Among his rich observations and surveys, Yan's argument is that the change in domestic space (2003: 112–124) and living arrangements (163–167) mean that the traditional mechanism of intergenerational reciprocity has broken down. Although Kaixiangong's house structures changed very much in similar ways to Xiajia's, the Kaixiangong villagers still kept the same family structure (e.g. stem and joint families made up 65 per cent of households in 2003) and arrangements of intergenerational reciprocity.

The old house structure in Xiajia (Yan, 2003: 114–15) was very similar to Kaixiangong's (see Chapter II.III) before the 1980s. The only difference was that the east room had two beds (*kang*) in Xiajia, but two bedrooms were divided in Kaixiangong, where the parents and married son always slept in different rooms. Yan's three house plans from 1985 onwards show the bedrooms increased from two to four and separate living areas increased respectively (2003: 118–21). This is also very similar to Kaixiangong's (see Chapter II.III). The only difference is that the prevalent house style in Xiajia is the bungalow and in Kaixiangong it is the two-storey house. The downstairs in Kaixiangong is an eating, living and working space, whereas the bedrooms are upstairs where there is typically an en-suite flat for a middle aged or newly married couple, and the other two or three bedrooms are for the couple's parents and children separately. Both Xiajia's bungalow and Kaixiangong's two-storey house styles are similar to ordinary family houses in the UK. To live in such a house was a dream lifestyle for ordinary Chinese people before the 1980s. There was a popular saying that one's dream life is to eat Chinese food, to marry a Japanese wife, to earn an American salary and to live in an English house.[27] Although along with the introduction of the market economy the dream (at least with

---

[27] This saying changed a bit in the 1990s, such as to eat French food, to earn a Germany salary, but to live in an

respect to housing!) is more and more realised, the traditional mechanism of intergenerational reciprocity of respect for the elderly and love for the children (*zunlao aiyou*) also remains.

House construction events in Kaixiangong Village provide an opportunity to see the vertical expressive *wanglai* between parents or grandparents and married children (mainly sons). In Xiajia parents gave bridewealth to married children for them to build their own houses, therefore the family property transferred to the conjugal families and increased the proportion of nuclear families (Yan 1996b, 2003). Kaixiangong villagers either used a certain amount of dowry or bridewealth for decorating a bridal chamber (see Table V-4) within a family house after the family's new house was built, or a house was built sometime after the marriage and shared between the elderly parents and the adult children. In short, in Xiajia the gift of a house from the parents is a new separate house for conjugal families, whereas in Kaixiangong the gift of a house is a bridal chamber in enlarged houses for both parents and married children. But in either case a new house is the most important gift from a parent to the next generation.

This gift contains material property, spiritual values, responsibility and the obligations of a given family. The vertical reciprocal circle works by the older generation giving a house to the younger generation and the acceptance of the gift entailing in particular the promise that the new generation will take responsibility for the care of the old. Yan's bottom up *xiaojing* gifts (1996b) from children to parents only show half of the process of gift giving. From the parents' point of view the *xiaojing* gifts can be seen as a shareholders' dividend from their investment (dowry, bridewealth, a house, etc.) to their children.

The way in which Kaixiangong's family structure mirrors its house structure is similar to some families in urban areas where stem families commonly live in three- or four-bedroom flats. It is also similar to many overseas Chinese families where the elderly always live with their married children and their grandchildren. Although Xiajia's family structure (e.g. 81 per cent nuclear families, Yan, 2003: 89) does not match its house structure, the way in which the parents' and married children's houses are close to each other is similar to other families in urban areas where many nuclear families and empty-nest families live in different flats close by. This was called "joint families living as English house never changed. neighbours" (*jinlin shi zuhe jiating*) by Chinese sociologists in the late 1980s. It is also similar to many English families' arrangements where married children buy houses near to where their parents live or elderly couples sell their houses and move to be near to their married children.

My point is that the increase in material living standards or living in different houses or having different lifestyles would not necessarily worsen the elderly care or even break the

Chinese traditional mechanism of intergenerational reciprocity. The traditional mechanism of intergenerational reciprocity of respect for the elderly and love for the children (*zunlao aiyou*) can be seen as bottom-up elderly care and top-down child care. Nowadays more and more Kaixiangong villagers live in flats with their sons' or daughters' families to carry out this intergenerational reciprocity. This can be seen from many examples. In Chapter VII.I I mentioned an old woman withdrawn from a labour support team for peeling soya beans because she and her husband moved to Suzhou City to live with their daughter's family in a flat. I have shown the FY Tan family case in Chapter IV.I. I will use this family again here. FY had her own house in the village, which now is mainly used as a holiday house for major family events when the sons' or grandsons' families are reunited. FY's elder son XR has his own flat in Miaogang, but he and his mother FY live in a flat with XR's elder son's family in Miaogang, because they collect FY's great granddaughter from school and give her lunch; FY's elder son's wife lives in a flat with her younger grandson's family in Wujiang City to look after her younger grandson's daughter. The former head of the village Women's Federation BY Zhou resigned from her post after her grandson was born, when she moved to Shengze Township and lived with her son's family in a flat there. To live in a flat is a fashionable thing for anyone in the village. Many villagers, including both nuclear and stem families, happily agreed to give up their houses and foundation land and move into flats above the shops when the village's market place doubled in size in 2005.

So in Kaixiangong the family structure didn't change much along with the change in house structure, nor was it in 2004 much different from my findings in 1996 (see Chapter IV.I). When I put Yan's broken down figures together I found my finding was also close to Yan's own finding, that only 28 per cent of families headed by an adult aged above 45-year-old were involved in nuclear family types of living arrangement[28], whereas 72 per cent of them lived with either parents, married children, or unmarried children (2003: 164–66).[29] This means that in Xiajia the majority of families with elderly or middle-aged couples actually arranged their everyday life in a traditional intergenerational reciprocal way.

---

[28] The nuclear family type of living arrangement refers to nuclear households – a couple with one or two children, or single-parent families.

[29] Although Yan (2003) shows there is 81 per cent nuclear family, 16 per cent stem family and 3 per cent incomplete family of overall families in Xiajia in 1998 (89), I am not sure whether or not the above general figures of family structure came from the village collective's statistics. I trust his disaggregated figures more (164–66).

Intergenerational reciprocity in elderly care or expressive *wanglai* can also be seen horizontally between elderly parents and married-out daughter(s) and her or their families. In the row of "elderly care" in Table V-1. there is one event that involved daughter(s) in the life-cycle events. According to local custom the birthday ceremonies of old people are normally arranged by a married-out daughter(s). Traditionally, villagers only celebrate the 66-year-old birthday for their parents. Married-out daughters should come back to their natal families with their own families for the celebrations. They should bring two *tizi* (upper part of a pig leg) and from 4 to 5 *jin* of noodles for the birthday celebration feast. The symbolic meaning of the *tizi* is to raise their standard of life and the noodles are for their parents to have a long life. The daughters should also bring a new suit of clothes for their parents. After the birthday meal the elderly parents should give the daughter a red envelope with 20 *yuan* for best wishes for her life in her husband's family.

When asked why the elderly only have one birthday ceremony a villager told me that there is a special day that can be seen as an annual celebration for the elderly (see Chapter III.III). It is the Double Ninth festival (*chongyangjie* – on the 9th day of the 9th lunar month). According to local custom, on the Double Ninth Festival members of the family should express their respect in particular to their elderly. On both the above occasions a vertical expressive *wanglai* exists between the adult children and their parents or grandparents. They express their respect with emotional concern and by giving materials (good food and new clothes) to the old people. Yan's (1996b) *xiaojing* gift in Xiajia can also be seen as expressive *wanglai* between adult children and their parents. However, in recent years some villagers in Kaixiangong have also started to celebrate their parents' birthday every five years from the sixtieth birthday onwards. The gifts and feast of the ceremony are more or less the same as for the 66-year-old birthday, but without a new suit of clothes. This phenomenon shows that along with the introduction of values associated with the market economy the villagers' lifestyle has changed greatly, with the inclusion of a new way of celebrating old people's birthdays which has been influenced by urban people.

2. Analysis with *lishang* criteria

I shall now use *lishang* criteria to provide further analyses.

(1) Moral judgement

Whenever I asked villagers how they treated their elderly parents I always got replies quoting the popular slogan that respect for the elderly and love of children is a Chinese traditional virtue (*zunlao-aiyou shi Zhonghua minzu de chuantong meide*). This is a moral judgement by the villagers. Yao told me proudly, on my revisit to the village in 2004, that his daughter gave birth earlier in the year and his family became a four-generational family (*sishi tongtang*). To be able to hold four generations in one house and live peacefully in harmony is also a virtue and honours their family ancestors. However, in contrast to the Yao family, many families in 1996 reported that their sons were not reliable, and here it seems to me that moral restraint played a less important role. This can be seen from the way they fulfilled *bao'en* (paid the debt of gratitude). The cases of generous *wanglai* reported in Chapter IV.I show that only about 10 per cent of families were praised as models of *bao'en* to their parents by the villagers. Villagers also used the Chinese character of *xiao* (fulfil filial duty) in a negative way, that is to criticise a son who treated his parents badly (*ta dui fumu bu xiaoshun*), as FL Zhou's younger son did (see Chapter VIII.II). As Yan (2003) has observed, moral standards throughout China appear to be declining with the rise in the market economy. Although it may also be true in Kaixiangong, I have no evidence that care of the elderly is affected more than any other area in the moral sense.

(2) Human feelings

There are many local sayings that relate to human feelings. In contrast to the saying that a married daughter is spilled water (*jia chuqu de nu'er ru po chuqu de shui*), several women told me that a daughter is a mother's padded body vest (literally, a daughter is truly close to a mother compared with a son, *nuer shi mama de tiexin'ao*). I noticed that the villagers used the word "children" (*kao zinu*) rather than "son" to answer my question of who should be relied on for care of the elderly. This means that dependence is also on females. In contrast to showing filial respect to one's elders (*xiaojing*), filial duty or obligation (*xiaodao*) or filial obedience (*xiaoshun*), the villagers are more likely to invoke filial sentiments of heart (*xiaoxin*). For example, they sometimes quoted a Chinese saying "have a heart of parents' limitless benevolence and love of their children" (*kelian tianxia fumuxin*). Here *xin* (heart) of *xiaoxin* is the same character as *xin* of *tongqingxin* (sympathy) which has the same meaning as Liang's (1975/94) human heart (see Chapter IX.III). The movement from showing filial respect to one's elders (*xiaojing*) to using filial sentiments of heart (*xiaoxin*) internalises the younger generation's behaviour towards the elderly. The former means "I have to do it due to the moral code of filial piety", whereas the latter means "I want to do it and enjoy doing it". Yan (2003) also discussed the strategies of parental investment for old age. He found many cases indicating parents' efforts to improve the emotional bonds with both their sons and their married daughters (Yan, 2003, 163, 178–182). Therefore, Yan and I back up each other's view that the parents' emotional resources worked reciprocally with their children.

(3) Rational calculation

The principle of the older generation giving a shared house as a gift to the younger generation can be seen as a kind of rational calculation. For the older generation, accumulating many years of building materials and building up resources from the broadest family networks can be understood as fattening pigs. As soon as the new generation has received the gift of a new house, this big pig, it starts another cycle of fattening pigs and looks after the parents in their old age, including giving *xiaojing* gift on their birthdays or on Double Ninth Day every year, and giving them a proper burial after they die. The parents can't get any guarantee from their children as to whether they will be well cared for and buried well. It is therefore necessary to emphasise this commitment in associated events (see Chapter II.III). Although there had been only a few cases of house construction in the past hundred years before the liberation in 1949, JM Wang, the head of the Village Committee, explained that as part of family property the house gift between older and new generations played an important role of reciprocal support, just like other life cycle events. The older generation's gift of a house to the younger generation is like fattening a pig in reverse, in that what is given over a period of time can be recovered when required, the main difference being that the younger generation receives the biggest gift first and returns it to the older generation in daily care and so on in the future.

(4) Spiritual beliefs

Religious sense can also be seen in many events. In house construction the different rituals indicate a religious sense in many ways (see Chapter II.III). The rituals mark this transaction between generations, invoking the land god, the ancestors, and, of more practical importance, all of the assembled people. They demonstrate that house construction in Kaixiangong is not just connected to finance, materials or labour, but it is also a good way of transferring the local customs and family networks to the new generation.

I was given two reasons by the villagers for why the 66-year-old birthday is so important. One is its symbolic meaning. The number six itself is a lucky number, the double six as an even number means more lucky, which is also true in many other areas in China. I also heard another saying "when an old person gets to 66 years old he or she could lose weight heavily (meaning get a serious illness) if he or she doesn't die" (*liushiliu bushi yeyao diao shen rou*). This means that in one's life journey the 66-year-old birthday is regarded as a big bridge. If one didn't pass the bridge the new suit of clothes was used as grave clothes. If one passed it one would have double happiness in later life.

3. A case study of family division for elderly care

In Kaixiangong Village family division normally happens in families with two or more sons. Family division sometimes also happens in a family with only one son in which the stem family is divided into one empty-nest family and one nuclear family after the son gets married. In any case family division pokes "window paper" between parents and married children, which makes the hidden instrumental sense between parents and married children more visible. In other words, it pulls a veil of benevolence off the traditional Chinese saying that one rears children against old age (*yang er fang lao*), which in fact embodies the instrumental idea between parents and children. Here, I introduce an "instrumentalised expressive *wanglai*" to distinguish expressive *wanglai* and instrumental *wanglai* between parents and married children.

Although the instrumentalised expressive *wanglai* is more likely to happen in families with two or more sons, it doesn't mean that intergenerational reciprocity in elderly care or expressive *wanglai* between elderly parents and sons' families must get worse after family division. As I mentioned in Chapter VI.II, according to HL Wang's older son, only seven families with two married sons were involved in family division in 2002, which comprises one per cent of the families in the whole village. His family division case is typical. Let's examine again the relationship between parents and sons. As I mentioned in Chapter IV.I, HL Wang's family division contract form is both written and unwritten. The written contracts made clear the ownership and uses of house and additional places, courtyard, and elderly care, and so on. Among many details of the contracts the important written items are in two parts: the family property is transferred from parents to married sons and the responsibility for elderly care (in the form of providing a regular pension) is also transferred to the sons. This can be seen as a vertical instrumentalised expressive *wanglai* between parents and sons. The property transfer is a top-down gift from parents to married sons because this is the last investment in their children after the engagement, wedding, building and/or decoration of a house, provided for both sons, according to the parents' points of view. The old-age care is a bottom-up gift from married sons to their parents because elderly care is a kind of complicated giving.

The unwritten items include childcare, elderly care in everyday life as distinct from regular agreed pension payments, the parents' work for the responsibilities towards land which will be already divided between two sons' families, housework including arrangements for family events, family debt, family networks, arrangements of funerals. The unwritten items in the contract also involve a vertical reciprocal *wanglai* between parents and married sons' families. Childcare and elderly care in everyday life is never written into the family division contracts. In the joint family the parents looked after their grandsons before they went to nursery. When I was there the younger son's son was only one year old and was sometimes even looked after by his great grandmother, who died later in 1999 (see Photo VI-1).

Photo VI-1 HL Wang's mother was sorting out vegetables and looking after her great grandson

Childcare and elderly care was a typical vertical reciprocal *wanglai* between members of a stem or joint family. However, the time of childcare is limited because after both older son's and younger son's children go to nursery, earlier or later, such support from the grandparents becomes much smaller, whereas elderly care is a much longer process for the married sons, which is not included in written contracts. However, some of the elderly in Kaixiangong felt very strongly that their life was just like a silkworm with endless work until their death (*chuncan dao si si fang jin*), because they worked all the time. Normally they continue to help their children by looking after grandchildren, doing some housework, raising pigs or rabbits, and so on. This means that after family division they have little property left but if they are healthy enough they can exchange resources with their children or look after themselves. This is not purely instrumental *wanglai* because the elderly told me that they enjoyed this kind of family arrangement because it kept their life busy. They actually valued this and felt useful and satisfied with their burden.

The older son of HL Wang told me that it was not so important whether or not some items were written in family division contracts. All of the contractual items can be changed along with the changes of situation. On the one hand, the written contracts have been modified by the sons in the last few years. It would be much easier for the two sons simply to provide the elderly care specified in the contracts, that the older son should look after the father and the younger son should look after the mother after they pass their 60th birthday by giving each of them 200 *yuan* of cash, 150 *jin* of grain, and 500 *jin* of faggot per year. However, after the family division they created new ways of vertical *wanglai* between their parents and the sons' families. For example, when their parents were strong enough (up to 70 years old or more) to work on land and field, he and his brother lent their shares of responsibility for land and field to their parents for as long as they were able to, and instead they did not have to pay the above figures of cash or grain to their parents. The parents kept all the income from the land and field for themselves, and this was much greater than the figures in the family division contracts.

HL Wang's older son told me that this informal switch of responsibilities was actually done by many other people locally, before and during the period of family division. The reason the above new arrangement was not written into the family division contracts is because the land and field belong to the state. My fieldwork notes show the joint family contracted responsibility was a paddy field (*tian*) of 6.3 *mu* and land (*di*) of 2 *mu*. The paddy field is mainly for rice and the land for mulberry trees. The land and field is divided so that both the older son's and the younger son's families have 2.8 *mu* paddy field and 0.6 *mu* land each, with the remaining land and fields allocated for the other family members. In addition both of the sons can also get their wives' and children's shares of land and field from the village collective.

When the parents got too old or too ill to work on land and field the sons would provide elderly care, which would be much greater than the figures in the written family division contracts. Thus the written contracts cover a limited amount of the necessary elderly care. It seems this worked quite well between parents and married sons' families among the majority of villagers in both stem families and divided joint families in my sampled households. Many researchers noticed such a phenomenon. Ma (1999) claimed one important element of rural Chinese family division is cooperation (*he*) which can be seen in different ways, for example economic and cultural among parents' family and married children's nuclear families (115–117). From my point of view such cooperation (*he*), or "aggregate family" (Croll's term, 1987b), and "network family" (Zeng Yi, et al., 1993; Yan, 1998) can be understood as horizontal *wanglai* between them, although they can be different generations if measured by age.

I will now use *lishang* criteria for more explanations.

(1) Moral judgement

Morally some villagers still used *bao'en* (pay a debt of gratitude) towards their parents, although in practice married children didn't use the character of *bao'en* when they considered elderly care as a written item in family division contracts. This is because when everybody faced the facts that family division not only divided family property but also family debt there wasn't much space for *en* (great debt of gratitude to parents). When the HL Wang family division started in 1994 the younger son's wedding had not yet been held. The family discussed wedding expenditure and debt with relatives during family division feasts. Everybody agreed the debt should be divided into two parts and repaid by the two sons. There was 40,000 *yuan* debt in total. 10,000 *yuan* came from the older son's wedding, and 30,000 *yuan* was budgeted for the younger son's wedding. Although the older son's wedding debt was already paid off by the joint family, it was agreed that both sons should take their share of 20,000 *yuan* each to repay the debt. I asked HL Wang why the items of debt was not written in the family division contracts? He told me that it was not honourable to put such things into the contracts because they could be kept for generations. "How can you guarantee that the two sons would pay back the debt?" He explained to me that most of the debt came from the relatives in the family networks. During the family division feasts these relatives of the family networks were also passed onto the two nuclear families and it was agreed that from 1997 onwards both the older son's and the younger son's families would invite the non-agnatic kin for New Year feasts separately. This was how the parents passed their relationships to their younger generation and at the same time guaranteed the debt to be repaid by them. The reason the meals with relatives during family division are so important is because the family rearrangements were announced and approved within broader family networks which would play an important role in supervising fulfilment of the arrangements. This means that although generally moral restraint played a less important role, the horizontal *wanglai* between the given family and its family networks had the same effect as moral restraint.

(2) Human feelings

Human feelings in family division can be seen from HL Wang and his wife. Within 10 or 15 years after the family division, HL Wang and his wife expected to find it difficult to work on land and field and to pay for their yearly taxes and fees by themselves. HL Wang told me that his family (he meant joint family) had a good relationship between all the members. His family also had more complicated arrangements which could help his and his wife's later life. This family chose to divide one joint family into three families (*yi fen wei san*): two nuclear families and one stem family. He and his wife lived with his mother and his unmarried brother, who worked in a private industry, and formed a stem family. It was his and his brother's duty to pay for their mother's elderly care and funeral[30]. They could also work hard for their own pension. In 2003 I asked HL Wang's two sons how they were going to take care of their parents when they got too old to work on the land and field. They told me that although their parents belonged to a different family from them in name, they actually divided into two persons and belonged to the sons' families in practice. In other words, although their parents slept in different rooms in the next door houses which belonged to each son, they worked together during the daytime and ate at the same stove. The elder brother said that in the future they would take their share of paying for their parents' living expenses because the relationship between parents and sons is a very intimate relationship of bone and flesh (*gurou qinqing*). The younger brother agreed happily with this. HL Wang said that his parents treated him and his sisters very well when they were young, so he will treat them very well when they get old. He believed confidently that his sons would treat him and his wife very well in the future because they had treated them very well when they were young, and vice versa.[31] This saying accorded with Chen Jieming's (1988) survey of urban Chinese families. According to Chen there is an interrelationship between parents' investment in their children and elderly care from them later on. When parents transferred the knowledge of how to take care of the elderly (*shanyang laoren*) to their children over many years' training, embodied in different kinds of investment, voluntary elderly care would become an obligation within members of a family (134–135).

(3) Rational calculation

Rational calculation is also involved in family division between the parents and their married children and the children's children. If the middle-generation son's family is divided away from the joint family the rest of the family would be a stem family. The interfamily

---

[30] They did it until their mother died in 1999.

[31] HL Wang told me about such a case in the village, when a married son divided from his parents and lived separately, which, on the surface, was caused by bad feelings or the relationship (*ganqing buhao*) with their daughter-in-law. The underlying reason was the parents didn't treat the son well when he was young. The old couple's (husband is 75 years old and wife is 73 years old) son's family divided from the stem family 20 years ago because the daughter-in-law and mother-in-law could not get on well (*hebulai* or *mei ganqing*). It was not too bad for the old couple when their son's family first divided from the stem family because they were strong enough to work and support themselves. The problem started when they got older and were not able to work on the land or field any more and hadn't enough savings. They even found it difficult to pay for the yearly taxes and fees. A village cadre tried to ask their son to pay for them but their son refused to do so because they divided into two families such a long time ago. The relationship between the old couple and their son's family went beyond instrumental *wanglai*, and became negative *wanglai* by the village's standard.

relationship between the younger son's couple and the rest of the family can be represented physically by the relationship between the bridal-chamber and the whole family house. According to the local customs a new couple was expected to take over the family's power within three years, which includes arrangements with all the family relations. It says "parents take responsibility for their children up to three years after a new couple's marriage and they should in return look after them in their old age and give them a proper burial after they die" (*yeniang hunhou guan sannian, zinü guan tamen hou bansheng*). None of the villagers knew when this rational custom first appeared in the village. It obviously helped elderly parents adjust their position in the family with their married children, especially where they lived in the same house. A retired township cadre also told me that after his retirement his priorities would be changed to take care of his own health rather than gaining materials for the whole family. He believes if he is healthy he would bother his children much less. Although the local custom requests the new couple to take charge of running the whole family within three years, this was not what everybody wanted or was able to do. A young mother told me that she didn't think she would be able to take charge of the family within three years because as an only daughter of the family she took a husband into the family. She already had a baby and couldn't work away from home to earn a large amount of money. Besides she didn't think she wanted to move away from her parents' family, to which she was very much attached. For all the above concerns she would rather stay at home and take care of her parents when they got older. So the local custom is a guideline, which can be modified, and provides room for expressive *wanglai* between elderly parents and married children.

(4) Religious sense and spiritual beliefs

Religious sense can be seen from references to fortune or luck (*fu*). Villagers normally admired some families which took good care of their elderly parents in sickness with the characters of *fuqi* (fortunate, lucky lots). By contrast, in Neiguan, my other fieldwork village in Gansu Province, I heard an old man say that traditionally there is a saying that the more sons the more fortunate (*duozi duofu*), but nowadays this has become that the more sons the more unfortunate (*duozi duohuo*). In Yan's Xiajia there were many cases of negative *wanglai* between parents and their sons (2003: 168–71), which supports this idea. However, from 1993 onwards there was no third birth in Xiajia village (197), which might reduce the abuse of parents and intergenerational conflicts. In Kaixiangong, I found that one of the important reasons for fulfilment of the care of the elderly related to a religious sense. The two nuclear families can be influenced by agnatic kin since most of them live nearby and can have frequent horizontal *wanglai* with the given families in many kinds of family events, especially in events related to ancestor worship. This can be proved from Ma's (1999: 114–117) study. From his fieldwork in a village of Hebei Province Ma found families combined *ji* (continuity), in particular continuation of the family surname, and elderly care (*ji zhong you yang*) as well as ancestor worship. According to local custom the oldest son can have an extra share of family property for the expenses of ancestor worship (Ma, 1999: 115).

4. Social support as a supplement in elderly care

In Kaixiangong the broadest view of elderly care involves family support and social support. The family-based support for elderly care is the traditional elderly care idea that one rears children against old age (*yang er fang lao*). It involves relations between parents and adult children – married or not, son(s) or daughter(s), living together or separately. According to Lu's fieldwork notes in the ESRC social support project in 1991, about 90 per cent of respondents showed that they expected to rely on their children. One childless respondent expected to live in the old people's home (*yanglaoyuan*), and a few young couples said they were going to consider social insurance for the aged. Thus in 1991 the majority of Kaixiangong villagers still carried out the traditional family-based elderly care. However, in 1996 my re-study of the ESRC project showed 82 per cent of the elderly did not want to rely on their children to look after them in their old age (*yanglao*). Some of the elderly complained that their sons were not reliable (*erzi kao buzhu*) because they always forgot their mothers after they had got wives (*qu le laopo wang le ma*). This is similar to Yan's finding in Xiajia that the most common complaint from elderly parents was the lack of respect and concern or even lack of filial piety (*buxiaoshun*) from their adult children and daughters-in-law (2003: 170). It seems that with the introduction of values associated with the market economy the parents' and adult children's relationship or intergenerational relationship is getting worse. Yan and other researchers (e.g. Guo, 2001) even reported many cases of negative *wanglai* in elderly care in rural China since the 1990s. The question is whether or not "the traditional mechanism of intergenerational reciprocity has broken down" in rural China (Yan, 2003: 163).

As I argued earlier, more than half of the villagers still carry on expressive *wanglai* between elderly parents and their children and grandchildren. I have also touched upon instrumentalised expressive *wanglai* in house construction and family division cases. Yan's extreme cases (1997 and 2003, and 1998 in Chinese), as well as Guo's in Hebei (2001), might be atypical, and apply to just one generation in which there was insufficient family property to be divided in rural Chinese families during the socialist society (Yan, 1997, 1998 in Chinese). They seem to have some historical basis because, in Yan's own words, the unusual cases of abuse to parents existed in the families that had always had a history of disputes (2003: 170). This backs up my finding that negative *wanglai* in elderly care within family members and close relatives only comprises a small proportion of cases (see Chapter VIII.II). Here I will argue that an ego-based family takes care of its elderly through social support just as it does for weddings or funerals, and this doesn't alter the meaning of intergenerational reciprocity. In other words, social support can be a supplement to family elderly care.

In 1996 when I looked at social support for elderly care this mainly related to those elderly people who were without children and family (five guarantee households, *wubaohu*) [32] and involved sources from fellow villagers and the collective. However, I found a case of children who paid for Miaogang *jinglaoyuan* (home of respect for the aged) to care for their mother. Miaogang *jinglaoyuan* is located in the town, like most of the *jinglaoyuan* in rural areas. Cui, a head of the *jinglaoyuan*, told me it was built in 1986 to implement a policy. According to the policy it is a virtue that all the elderly should be looked after in our society (*lao you suo yang*). In order to establish the *jinglaoyuan* the town government appropriated fixed assets of 50,000 *yuan* including property and daily necessities, plus 20,000 *yuan* cash. It was the only such elderly home in the whole township and was designed for the five guarantee households living alone with difficulties. The local government mobilised (*dongyuan*) eight old people who came to register (*baodao*) to live in the *jinglaoyuan* from the whole town. By 1996 there were 22 old people, 13 male and 9 female. The oldest was 93, and the youngest was 62 years old. Four of them came from Kaixiangong. Living expenses increased to 200 *yuan* per month. The *jinglaoyuan* has a common room, one washing machine, and two chefs to cook for the old people. If they become ill the *jinglaoyuan* pays the fees for medical care.

In the *jinglaoyuan* I interviewed an 89-year-old woman who was BY Zhou's aunt. The old woman told me that she had three children who moved to Shanghai a few years ago. They rented a room for her because she did not want to live in Shanghai. In 1993 her children sent her to the *jinglaoyuan* because she had difficulties living alone. The arrangements were especially made by her children, who offered to pay for the *jinglaoyuan* and signed a contract with it. Apart from

---

[32] The five guarantees are guaranteed food, clothing, medical care, housing and burial expenses for the elderly without children.

paying living expenses of 210 *yuan* per month for her, they also took some share of the donation to the *jinglaoyuan*. This was the first such case of *jiyang* (financial self-support) in the *Jinglaoyuan*. This case can be seen as indirect elderly care via bottom-up expressive *wanglai* from the children. In 1996 there was a total of two such cases in the *jinglaoyuan*. In addition, BY told me that she offered emotional support to her aunt by visiting her from time to time, because she was obligated to her aunt who had looked after her for two years when she was young (*yangyu yiwu*). This kind of emotional support is also considered to be *yang* of *yanglao* (a kind of care of the elderly) according to the villagers.

Whether or not the elderly live in the *Jinglaoyuan* is not solely determined by the willingness of the old person's adult children to take care of them. From 1986 to 1996 there were six old women who transferred back to *wubaohu* and returned to their villages because they argued strongly that, according to the policy, they were able to live alone. The reasons some elderly did not want to come were because they had misgivings about losing their freedom and would receive less money than when they stayed outside. At that time they could only receive expenses of less than 100 *yuan* per month in the *jinglaoyuan*. The return of the six old women to their own homes shows clearly that they didn't want to live away, as is similarly the case for many of the elderly in the UK.

However, there was also a different case. A retired official made a case for getting into the *Jinglaoyuan* by following the example of the children who paid a fee to it for caring for their mother. He wanted to live in it but he was disqualified because he was not a *wubaohu*. He also argued that since the pre-1949 *yanglaoyuan* (elderly home) was open to all the elderly (this is similar to a kind of nursing home in UK), why should the *Jinglaoyuan* (home of respect for the aged) in post-1949 society discriminate against the elderly with money? So the retired cadre got into the *jinglaoyuan* by paying 210 *yuan* per month. He lived in a single room, which was of a much better standard than the shared rooms.

In 2000 the *jinglaoyuan* moved to a much bigger place, big enough for 40 old people. The necessary funds came from the civil administration of the Wujiang City, the local government, welfare factories, and self-employed donations. In recent years a new policy was issued which allowed the *jinglaoyuan* to take more elderly for *jiyang* from the society. The *jinglaoyuan* has become more popular also because it receives more regular funds from different sources including individuals' payment.

Children who pay for their parents to live in an old-age home consider this to be vertical expressive *wanglai*, whereas villagers paying fees for the elderly without children consider it to be horizontal expressive *wanglai*. The row indicating elderly care in Table V-1 also shows fellow villagers and the collective involved in those elderly without children, namely, the five guarantee households. I interviewed an old, single man called Aming in 1996. His main financial support came from the relief fee of 1,000 *yuan* per year from the Miaogang Township. He lived in one of the guestrooms of the village and looked after other rooms. He charged 4 *yuan* per night per bed because these rooms were shared. The fee was paid to the village. He charged 3 *yuan* per day, per head, half board at the cost price. Both the charges were paid for his upkeep of the rooms and therefore partly came back to him, which made additional income on top of the 1,000 yuan from Miaogang Township. He also raised a few pigs including a male pig for insemination. He charged 10 to 20 *yuan* per insemination. The success rates from this natural copulation were higher than from artificial insemination, and his business was successful. Aming's total income was about 2,000 *yuan* per year. However, his pig insemination business was disallowed by a policy from the township because it was "a base act"; Aming had to stop it while I was doing my fieldwork.

Aming's case involved fellow villagers' support indirectly. His relief fee of 1,000 *yuan* per year from the Miaogang Township was actually raised from fellow villagers and redistributed from the township to him. The villagers told me they had to pay for more than 30 different kinds of fees to the local government. They couldn't remember what they were but one item was called the welfare fee (*fuli fei*), for looking after people with special difficulties including those who are elderly and without children. They complained about all the above fees except the fee for those elderly, because they believed that it is a misfortune for a person to be without a family and a child. This is in line with a traditional idea that the greatest misfortune is to be without male offspring (*wuhou wei da*). The additional way that Aming made a living, looking after the guestrooms, was provided by the village collective. However, in 1998 the village collective sold the guestroom house so Aming moved back to his own old house. However, his living standard didn't drop because his skill at inseminating pigs was allowed due to a new policy of privatisation. Aming's skill at inseminating pigs not only supplemented his living standard but also provided more chances for him to have expressive *wanglai* with fellow villagers directly.

VI.III. Funeral ceremony and post-funeral rituals

No matter whether in the West or the East, in urban or rural China, a funeral or related mortuary event (*zangli* or *jili*) is required for any death, although the procedure and detailed arrangements can be very different. Based on his and other anthropologists' related work James

Watson was "convinced that there is an overarching ritual structure that is distinguished from non-Chinese rites" (1988: 133) and specifically considered that the related study would be helpful to understand the question of "What held Chinese society together?" (1988: 3). For me, Watson's structure of funeral rites that contains the ideological domain and the performative domain can be interpreted with *lishang-wanglai*. On the one hand, "the notion of continued exchange between living and dead is the foundation of late imperial China's ideological domain" (1988: 9) states there is a *wanglai* relationship between the living and dead in a vertical direction or the living with each other in a horizontal direction. On the other hand, there was "a prescribed set of ritual actions that had to be performed before a corpse could be expelled from the community and buried" (11–12), which can all be explained with *lishang* criteria.

In the UK I participated in two types of funeral services. One type is simply called a funeral which is held either in a chapel or a church. Families, relatives, friends and colleagues are invited but anyone (for instance neighbours, patients of a doctor, employees of a business may all wish to show their respect) is free to attend without special invitation. After the funeral service there is a tea party or reception, confined to invitees. Another type with the practice of cremation consists of a visiting period for a small numbers of visitors, mainly close family, to pay their respects to the deceased in their coffin, followed by a small funeral service for family and close relatives in a chapel or church, followed by a large memorial service in few weeks time in a large church for all the social relations of the deceased.

In Kaixiangong, the funeral rites are different from those I saw in urban China or in the UK. I will use the villagers' terms to describe the process from the person's death to completion of settlements for the dead. It consists of two steps. The first step is called funeral affairs (*sangshi*), the second one can be called post-funeral ritual activities (*houshi*). As I have described in "Establishing a marriage relationship"(see Chapter V.II) which involved many steps before and after the wedding, the same applied to dead people. In this section I will introduce how their social relationships were ended after their death and new relationships were established in the nether world through funereal and post-funeral activities. The vertical and horizontal expressive *wanglai* with different kinds of relationships will be demonstrated together with an analysis linked to *lishang* criteria.

However, the difference between James Watson's summary of funeral activities in rural China (1988: 12–15) and Kaixiangong is that the former excluded all the post-funeral ritual activities (Cohen's term, 1988: 181) apart from some descriptions from Feuchtwang (1974), Naquin (1988) and Kipnis (1997). I also noticed that the difference between urban China and

Kaixiangong is that the former's funeral and memorial ceremony is always combined as *zhuidaohui* (memorial meeting), and the difference between the cases I witnessed in the UK[33] and Kaixiangong is that the UK's post-funeral ritual is a memorial for the deceased amongst the living. So instead of entitling this section "funeral" I examined the funeral ceremony and post-funeral rituals side by side, just as I titled the section on weddings "Establishing a marriage relationship" in Chapter V.II, and considered the process as an entirety. In this section I will show how vertical and horizontal expressive *wanglai* is involved in the whole process of mortuary events and give explanations using *lishang*.

1. Expressive *wanglai*

In Kaixiangong the various activities during the mourning period are called *zuo sushi* (compared with colourful weddings which always use red colour materials or decoration, funerals are always in a plain colour) and *ban houshi* (for post-funeral affairs for settling the death in the nether world). Based on the case of XQ Wang's mother's death, Chapter III.II. shows that the whole mourning process includes the death announcement (*baosang*), paying condolences to the deceased (*puxiang*), funeral ceremony (*shushijiu*), cremation and burying the ash box (*huohua*), "do the sevens" (*zuo qi*)"(Feuchtwang, 1974: 327; Naquin, 1988 :59), wearing the mourning material (*daixiao*) and sweeping a grave at Qingming Festival (*shang fen*). It can last for a few weeks, a few months, or even up to a three-year period. The above death rituals are consistent with Stuart Thompson's three prevalent facets:

> First, the ritual aims to transform. In the case of the mortuary ritual the main problem is transforming the discontinuity of biological death into a social continuity, of transforming the corpse into an ancestor... Second, the ritual involves exchanges between the living and the dead, on more or less reciprocal bases... Third, the ritual is concerned with identity. To be Chinese is to perform Chinese rituals and vice versa... (1988: 73)

Here I will demonstrate how the dead person discontinues its mortal relations and establishes its *yin* being (Feuchtwang's term[34]) relations.

---

[33] The point of omitting a big literature review on funerals in the UK is that I want to make a simple comparison on the procedure of mortuary events between rural Chinese society and the UK, based on my observation of two cases in the UK, as I have summarized briefly at second paragraph in this section.

[34] "The Yin being is represented 1) as a body, to be well situated in the coffin and grave, 2) as efficacious soul (*ling*) to be pacified and housed, 3) as a fate and span of life, 4) as soul (*hun*) to be saved, and 5) to be converted

The first three rows of Table V-1 show that among the above rituals funerals mainly relate to the dead and his or her family's social relations. The rituals consist of paying condolences to the deceased, taking part in the funeral feast (*sushi jiu*) – a send-off party, and cremation of the corpse. On the one hand, it is "the last-stop for individuals in this world and also the final opportunity to be involved in the networks of social exchange" (Yan, 1996b: 59). The funeral feasts, like wedding feasts, provide the living with an opportunity to maintain social networks (Naquin, 1988; Thompson, 1998) or "manipulate *ganqing*, social hierarchies, and magnetic fields of human feelings" and building, producing or creating *guanxi* (Kipnis, 1997: 97, 98, and 102). On the other hand, for Kaixiangong villagers a funeral event is one way of *song* (seeing off) in the reciprocal *wanglai* circle of human beings. After the funeral the *wanglai* relationship between the deceased (XQ Wang's mother) and most of her social networks had stopped.[35] The discontinued horizontal relations are with all the fellow villagers who lived in the same group, villagers who shared the same surname, her son's friends, her late husband's apprentice, agnatic and non-agnatic kin of the family, except the intimate family members.

The last six rows of Table V-1 show the post-funeral rituals which started with the burial of XQ Wang's mother's ash box and ended with sweeping the grave at the Qingming Festival in the third year. The starting point of burying the ash box is different from what the villagers used to do in the past, when burying a corpse was the end of the funeral ritual. Nowadays from the villagers' point of view the cremation of the corpse ends the funeral because from then on the corpse has gone forever. This is why the villagers simply named *huohua* (cremation) as the last step of the funeral. The last step of *song* (seeing off) is actually mixed with *ying* (Stafford's term, welcome) due to the cremation system which has been introduced to this area. It can be described with a Chinese phrase of seeing off those who depart and welcoming those who arrive (*songwang-yinglai*). In this case *song* (seeing off), *wang* (go), *ying* (welcome) and *lai* (come) happened at the same occasion, but mean different things: as I mentioned in the previous paragraph the cremation event ended the dead person's social relationships, whereas the burial of the ash box started her spiritual relationships. Borrowing Feuchtwang's imagery the last step of the funeral constitutes a process of *songwang-yinglai* "simultaneously of cutting threads and of tying threads of continuity" (1974: 375). To me it means that as soon as the corpse was burned

---

into a male or female ancestor" (Feuchtwang, 1974: 330).

[35] This is similar to the relationship between her and her "little sisters'", which stopped after she married into XQ Wang's family (see Chapter V.II).

her social *wanglai* had been cut off from her and at the same time a spiritual *wanglai* has been tied up between the deceased and her intimate family members.

The participants involved are intimate family adult members: her son and his wife, the wife of the deceased married-out son, daughter (husband is not required) and quasi daughter, in a horizontal direction; and Taoist priests, ancestors and spirits in a vertical direction. The post-funeral rituals are mainly for establishing different types of relationship for the deceased, that is to join with other ancestors, to keep ghosts away from her, to ask the land gods to accept her, and to ask other gods, such as the Jade Emperor, to protect her in the underworld. The row relating to "the fifth seven-day" of Table V-1 shows that on the last day of the period agnatic and non-agnatic kin took part in the event. It is a celebration of the deceased turning successfully into one of the ancestors. This is how XQ Wang's family added his mother to his family's list of ancestors.

The way in which the villagers settle the deceased in the nether world is very similar to what they do to settle a new arrival, such as a baby or a wife, in a new family in this world. But this time XQ Wang's family didn't invite the family's old generational agnatic and non-agnatic kin, that is both XQ Wang's passed away parents' uncle and aunt's generation, for the event of "the fifth seven-days". This is how XQ Wang's family removed them as close relatives from the family *lishang-wanglai* networks (see Chapter IX.II) without a word. At the same time the others removed his family from their families' networks. Therefore, the completion of the whole process of the mortuary events upgrades the dead person's family's *lishang-wanglai* networks: not just living social networks in this world, but those with the nether world as well.

2. Analysis with *lishang* criteria

There are many rituals in mortuary rites, such as wailing or laments of women, kowtowing, bowing, mourning dress, gifts, music, chanting by monks or priests, banquets, sacrificial offerings, burning paper money and materials, candles, incense and oil lamps. Charles Stafford's (2000c) ritualised etiquette – separation and reunion, provides an important new angle of view. It is in particular helpful to understand the performative domain (J. Watson's term) related to the *wanglai* between living and dead of this world and the nether world. Stafford shows details from his two fieldwork villages of how people performed rituals of summoning (*qing*), receiving (*jie*), detaining (*liu*), and sending off (*song*) gods, the dead, ancestors and ghosts (2000c: 70–86). He states: if care is not taken for the dead they:

will become ghosts and suffer terribly, but they will also bring suffering to the living. By contrast, properly buried and worshipped ancestors – by definition those properly "sent off" and then routinely "welcomed back" – bring blessings to their descendants. (2000c: 82)

For me this statement involves all the criteria of *lishang*. I illustrate this by using *lishang* criteria as an outline to find out more information in order to understand why the rituals of separation and reunion are important in *wanglai* between the living and the dead. I will also show how each *lishang* criterion is mobilised and weighted and altered in different types of *wanglai* relationship between the living and the dead.

(1) Moral judgement

It is right morally that one should correctly bury and care for one's ancestors. This is why James Watson argues that "Chinese state had no effective means of controlling beliefs regarding the afterlife" (1988: 11). However, there are different understandings of burying well in different parts of China. Watson found in two Cantonese villages that it was the corpse handlers' job, which is the lowest job, to carry corpses because of the danger that death pollution would affect the male essence (*yang*) (1988: 112–115, 124–126). In other parts of China people didn't care about the "death pollution" because they believed morally that to carry the corpses of one's parents or close relatives was the last chance to express faithfulness and attachment to their beloved. As I have shown in Chapter III.II, XQ Wang and the closest male family member carried his mother's corpse, as was determined by a traditional moral code of filial piety (*jinxiaodao*). It was the same in Shenyang. When I was doing my fieldwork in Gansu village one of my mother's older sisters passed away. My brother and three of my cousins, as her closest nephews, carried her body on a stretcher. As the closest male relatives carried the corpse the closest female wailed very hard by or over the corpse without consideration of the "death pollution". This is also a proper way of expressing oneself physically while burying one's parents.

Financially the villagers considered that a reasonable expenditure on a proper burial for their parents is not an extravagance. For example, XQ Wang paid the Taoist priests 660 *yuan* for their two nights' and half a day's work. They didn't stint on the expenditure because the ritual of turning the dead person into one of the ancestors and settling it in the nether world is very important. The family also paid 260 *yuan* for hiring a hearse from Wujiang Crematorium and 650 *yuan* for the cremation. They could also have saved on the expenditure for hiring the hearse because the village collective provided a vehicle free of charge, and they could have got a refund on the cost for cremation from the local government. According to the local policy the cremation fee could be refunded in full in the 1970s and in half from the 1980s on to the late 1990s. This was one way that the government introduced cremation in this area. However, XQ Wang's family, as with most of the villagers, insisted on paying in full for the cost of cremation because they thought, again, it was the last chance to show filial piety. They even behaved very well in terms of obeying regulations in the crematorium when their local custom conflicted with the regulations. I noticed that they brought lots of mock money, candles and firecrackers with them, which the villagers used when they buried the corpse in the ground in the past, but they didn't use them at all in the crematorium because there were signs saying "Burning mock money is forbidden" and "Superstitious activities are forbidden". They even bought some plastic flowers and wreaths from the crematorium shop. This is how they learnt a new way of burying their beloved from the urban people. They placed them on the grave after they buried the ash box (see Chapter III.II).

All the mourners' quick responses to pay condolence to the deceased, take part in the funeral feast, and accompany the corpse to the crematorium were counted as moral support because the more people who came the more honour the deceased and the family gained. It is the same in Xiajia that "the more guests who attend and the longer they stay, the more the host gains social prestige and 'face'" (Yan, 1996b: 95–96). For them these occasions provided arenas to express their moral judgment: if you treat others badly you could receive your lesson of losing a big face, and vice versa. Instead of "spiritual support" used in Xiajia, Kaixiangong villagers used "moral support" for the idea of giving someone face at funeral or other crucial occasions.

However, unlike some onlookers around during the funeral event in other parts of China (Yan, 1996b; Stafford, 2000c) there were hardly ever any onlookers in Kaixiangong because nearly all the mourners were involved as participants because they were part of their family networks. This is an outcome of the family's input of yearly based generous *wanglai*. The number of mourners is dependent on the size of the family networks, and whether the deceased is male or female. I noticed there were many fewer mourners at the funeral for the father of Huang the village vet, because his family had fewer interests and was not good at making *lishang-wanglai* networks (see "Disease of farm animals" in Chapter III.IV).

(2) Human feelings

People can't bear their ancestors to suffer and are afraid themselves to suffer or they expect a blessing from ancestors. Stafford's second point mainly relates to the post-funeral activities which relate to human feelings. Weddings and funerals, the two biggest life events, in a Chinese popular saying are called red and white happy events (*hong-bai xishi*). The reason the human feeling of happiness is involved in funerals is because people generally felt it is a relief for both the living and dead when it is the time for them to depart. However, in Kaixiangong villagers used the term of *sushi* for the funeral. It means a funeral event involving a plain colour and vegetarian food. It reflects the involvement of complicated human feelings at a funeral. They are: grief of losing the beloved, dread from fear of the corpse, expression of one's own depressed feelings, as well as happy relief for both the living and the dead.

It is natural for mourners, both male and female, to cry when seeing off the deceased. The natural expression of human feeling forms a sharp characteristic of expressive *wanglai* in the funeral situation. In this the mourners express the feeling that they are reluctant to part with the deceased or as a Chinese saying puts it: see off somebody a part of the way and another and another (*song le yicheng you yicheng*). Apart from wailing at the funeral the periodical mourning is regarded as an expression of kinship tie's affection (Fei, 1939: 77), which can also be understood as the human feeling of *lishang*. However, some women also express their own depressed feelings by wailing in a funeral. This is similar to Elizabeth Johnson's (1988) finding that women's funeral laments use other people's funerals to release personal sorrow (*yong bieren de zangli xuanxie ziji de beishang*).

"The rituals associated with settling the soul reflect in some way the ambivalent feelings of mourners as well as the dread arising from fear of the corpse" (Watson, 1988: xii). This can also been seen in Kaixiangong's case. In the previous chapters I mentioned two cases involving suicides (e.g. Chapter VIII.II) who were buried with honours (*houzang*). The hidden reason for the lavish funerals is fear of the dead. An informant told me that the dead suicides are more likely to turn into ghosts. So it is necessary to settle their bodies and souls well to avoid trouble from them. This was also noticed by other anthropologists (e.g. Martin, 1988; Wolf, M., 1975).

(3) Rational calculation

The rituals of "sending off", routinely "welcoming back" and "visiting (sweep grave)" must be properly done as they are determined by rational choice. Whereas the most important guests at weddings are *jiujiu*s (mother's brothers), the most important guests at funerals are daughters (sons play other important ritual roles). When XQ Wang's father passed away the older daughter, XQ Wang's older sister, played an important role. She smashed the tile on the door (*qiaomen* *tuanzi*), she paid the related cost of cremation, she provided the largest quantity of gifts, and she cried and fell over. This time when XQ Wang's mother passed away it should have been the younger daughter's turn to do this. XQ Wang only had one older sister and one younger brother. The younger brother was married out of the family as a son-in-law to another villager's family. Local custom decreed that he should be treated as a daughter. Unfortunately, he died in an accident a few years ago so his wife played his role at his mother's funeral, for example smashed a tile on a door. However the costs relating to cremation were shared with the older sister and older brother, since her family was poorer. The reason daughters should be the most important people in the funeral was determined by rational calculation. For instance, XQ Wang was his older sister's son's *jiujiu* and he made contributions to his nephew before he was born until he got married (see Chapters V and VI on life cycle events). Therefore, XQ Wang's older sister should play the important role in looking after her parents in their old age and give them a proper burial after death (*yanglao songzhong*). The activities required are: the old-age birthday ceremonies, physically taking care of the disabled elderly or when he or she is near death, and contributions to the funeral and post-funeral rituals.

Rational calculation can also be seen from social support:

(i) Material support was the first thing I saw in 1996. All the mourners brought gifts for condolence (*puxiang*). The sheets of white cloth can be used for making mourning clothes and belts, the yellow and silver paper for making mock money, candles, incense and food.

(ii) Labour support was also involved. After the condolence the women made gold and silver shoe-shaped objects (*yuanbao*) with yellow and silver paper which looked like money in feudal China. They also prepared materials for the mourning dress, e.g. cut white cloth in various sizes, belts 6 inches wide by 5, 7, 9 or 11 feet long; or cut black cloth and wool in pieces. At the same time in the courtyard the men carried tables and benches into the living room. Male agnatic kin borrow them from the houses of neighbours who have not been invited for the funeral because they are not agnatic kin and do not share the same surname. Although a chef was hired for cooking six meals and feasts over the three days, the kitchen assistants were agnatic kin: males killed hens or fish, whereas females peeled quail eggs or sorted out vegetables. After lunch, the female agnatic kin did all the tidying up and washing up, whereas the males returned the tables and benches to the neighbours' houses. It was not a simple job to return 60 benches (4 for each table) and 15 tables and sort out which belonged to which family, e.g. I saw a person checking marks and names under benches in the weak light.

(iii) Financial support came from XQ Wang's family's broadest list which contained 34 families. Amongst them 562 *yuan* came from 12 agnatic kin, 1209 *yuan* from 15 non-agnatic kin and 147 *yuan* from 7 friends. So the Wang family received 1918 *yuan* gift money in total and repaid 412 *yuan* to the above relatives wearing mourning clothes or materials (see next point). According to the local custom the friends are not requested to wear mourning clothes or materials.

(iv) Spiritual support also occurred. I noticed everybody got his or her red bag back with 10 or 20 per cent of whatever was his or her gift money. It was paid with thanks for the participants who wore mourning clothes or materials. According to the local custom the more people who wore mourning clothes or materials the better for both the dead and the living of the family, hence to wear unpleasant mourning clothes or materials is considered as a kind of spiritual support for the family. In fact this kind of social support in the village has its tradition. Even Fei noticed two kinds of social support in the funeral period. According to Fei (1939) the ceremonies not only related to the dead person's social relations sentimentally, they performed an essential function in social life, such as financial support through kinship tie over a long period (131–132) and immediate labour support from neighbours because the family members are under heavy mourning and not able to work (75).

Although during the funeral period rational choice influences the arrangements according to local custom, the local customs change over the years. Kipnis (1997) reviewed how Fengjia's funeral activities changed due to political interferences after 1948 (141–143). For Kaixiangong villagers the adaptation of funeral rituals for whatever reasons is also a practice of rational choice. For them, although the local custom of details of funeral, mourning and sacrifice can be changed along with changing situations, villagers adapted their arrangements rationally from time to time.

- The villagers kept some traditions from Fei's (1939) time, such as that the son, daughter-in-law, daughter and son-in-law's heads should be tied with a long white belt down that reached down to the ground, and short belts are worn by grandchildren (75). But instead of the son's generation wearing coarse hempen cloth and grandchildren wearing white clothes I saw they both wore white clothes and distinguished between the males and females by long white and short white clothes. This adaptation is for a practical concern because the white long clothes are a doctor's and chef's uniform, which are much easier to buy or borrow than to get coarse hempen cloth.

- In Fei's time after a person died "a packet of clothes will be burnt with a paper chair before the front door" (75) before the funeral. In my fieldwork this happened after a funeral and the corpse was burnt in an incinerator. This adaptation occurred after the cremation system was accepted from the 1970s in this area. The villagers also burnt all the deceased's clothes, bedding, bed, the wooden board laid with the corpse, and paper house, paper chair and so on, because this was the way to send them together with him or her to heaven.

- The replacement of a system from inhumation to cremation also led to other adaptations. Instead of the eldest son holding the head of the deceased and the younger son the feet to put the corpse into a coffin (75), the corpse was laid on a wooden board and the son and a son-in-law carried the head end of the board and another son-in-law and a close cousin carried the tail end onto a vehicle to go to a crematorium. Instead of moving the coffin onto land among the mulberry trees and covering it with a shelter built with or without bricks and tiles (75), they buried a bone ash box of the deceased in land among the mulberry trees and built a little house-shaped grave with bricks and cement and put a concrete gravestone in front of it.

- During Fei's fieldwork in the 1930s villagers repaired the shelter of their ancestors' coffins for up to five generations and conducted complicated periodical mourning activities (76–79). The villagers told me that now the custom is very much simplified and the young generation should only offer sacrifices for three years. After the three years they do not need to look after the grave anymore, even at Qingming. In Fei's time the daughter and daughter-in-law wore yellow headwear for two years and 60 days (78), now they wore yellow or orange headwear for one year. They only mourned for the first seven days (*touqi*), the third seven days (*san qi*) and the fifth seven days (*wu qi*); and Grave-sweeping Day (*qingming* festival) for the first three years and their birth and death days.

(4) Spiritual beliefs

Funeral and post-funeral activities are rooted in the villagers' religious sense. This can be seen from many customs. For instance, in Kaixiangong a dying person had to be transferred to a special bed, a flat board, which was then moved to the living room or hall of the house because to die in bed was unlucky. This also happened in North China. According to Susan Naquin (1998) it was unlucky for anyone to die on the communal *kang* (a brick platform commonly used as a bed in North China)– instead they would be moved away from this to a flat board (39). In

Kaixiangong I found various reasons behind these judgements of lucky or unlucky. Villagers regarded someone who died in their own bed as unlucky because it shows the person was without relations to make proper provision, like one of the disappeared sampling households, where the father died in his bed a few years after his son had left home, and JM Wang, head of the village, had arranged a simple funeral for him (see Chapter III.IV). But to die in one's own home – as opposed to one's own bed – would be considered lucky, as in the case of such as FY Tan, whose second son was adopted by Gu's family, and eventually claimed back (see Chapter IV.I). I was told while I proofread the Chinese version of this book that FY Tan died in April 2009 at age 84. Two days before she passed away she said to her son that she wanted to go home because she needed to say goodbye to all her relations in Kaixiangong. Two days later she left the world in her home, but in a temporary bed, as with XQ Wang's mother, who was also laid on a temporary bed before she died (see Photo III-13). Some Kaixiangong villagers even seated the dead on special simple chairs made of wicker (called *kaolao*) for being dressed. In the past, some families even erected a separate room, next to the main dwelling, to house the dying. Villagers gave various reasons for these customs. Some believed that death pollution could affect the living, as Watson found in Guangdong (1988), so it was a rational choice to avoid it. Others, in an equally rational spirit, thought it would be wasteful to burn a real bed, or impractical to pull down a *gang* in Naquin's case (1988). However the custom of removing and immediately burning the clothes (*suishenbao*) of the deceased had a religious motive, of sending a message to the ancestors in the nether world. This extended to other rituals, for example after burying the bone ash box, the close family members would also burn the deceased's used possessions as if sending them to the dead to use in the nether world.

I would like to digress from Kaixiangong Village for a while. There are lucky and unlucky deaths also in the West. In a funeral speech in the UK I heard that my husband's grandmother was lucky to have died in her own home in her own bed, rather than in a nursing home or hospital. It is a kind of counterpoint to the Chinese idea. In 2003 on the Chinese internet news I saw another use of the word "luck" in the case of a Chinese lady – Mayling Soong, Madame Chiang Kai-shek, who died in her sleep at her New York home. So, it is clear that no matter whether Chinese or Western, if one dies at home and has been well looked after before death that is good fortune (*you fuqi*). The difference is whether or not it is good fortune if one died in one's own bed, which Kaixiangong villagers regard as highly unfortunate. This is something that will only happen when elderly people have no family and to be without children, according to a traditional saying, is one of the three most unfortunate things life can offer.

There were many instances involving religious sense in colour, shape, number, directions, symbolic meanings and so on. The messenger who announced the news of the death (*baosang*) to related families should put a piece of white cloth into a pocket. He should go into exactly the correct houses. It would be seen as a big misfortune if the person went into a house which was not related to the dead person. The villagers decorated the family mourning hall with a little bit of red paper or cloth on the window bolts and nails on the wall to avert evil spirits. The dead person's family gave "elderly tofu" to each senior female of the group to keep their life healthy in old age. This is similar to the practice of the people in Mountain Street in Taiwan, who gave spring onions and dried squid in abundance to their non-agnatic kin for the luck of living (Feuchtwang, 1974: 329).

Direction was also important. The corpse was laid by the northern wall of the family mourning hall. Its head pointed east and its feet to the west. After the corpse was taken from the house family members set up an altar table for the dead person by the northwest end of the living room. The picture of the dead person hung on the west wall and the spirit tablet stood on the altar table against the west way. The movement from east to the west means sending the dead person to the Western Heaven (*xitian*). Instead of candles to honour ancestors there was an oil lamp by a spirit tablet on the altar table, together with sacrificial offerings. The oil lamp is called *changmingdeng* and is kept burning day and night until the end of the ritual of the five seventh days. It is for lightening up the road in the underworld for the dead person to meet the family's ancestors.

In terms of numbers the obvious example is "seven". Not only Kaixiangong villagers use sevens in post-funeral activities, although it is reduced from seven "seven days" to five "seven days"; other parts of China also do it. In North China, where they still do seven "seventh days" for the first three years, the longest mourning was supposed to last for twenty seven months (Naquin, 1988). In Kipnis's (1997) Fengjia village the funeral itself lasted for seven days before 1948 (141). All these "sevens" mean the family protects its dead from being attacked by ghosts while crossing dangerous places or from being turned into a ghost in the underworld. Among suitable offerings were oval-shaped rice cakes with filling (*tabing*), wonton, glutinous rice dumplings (*zongzi*) which were built in a pyramid shape which symbolised a tomb. The upper part of the little tomb for a single dead person's ash box also looked like a pyramid. The structure of the little tomb for a dead couple looked like a standard suburban London semi-detached house, although there wasn't any real house of that shape in the village. The villagers put an evergreen plant on the tomb just as they put an evergreen on top of the roof when they completed a new house. It symbolised that the house and their life should last forever, in this case, the dead person lives in the nether world forever.

The most important thing in funerals and post-funeral rituals is the participation of priests of religion. The villagers called priests *heshang*. The Chinese characters for this term imply Buddhist monks, but from their clothes and rituals it is clear that they were actually Taoist priests. The villagers do not care whether they are Taoist or Buddhist. It is simply important to have professional religious people of one sort or another to perform funeral and post-funeral activities,[36] because the rites performed by religious specialists could raise the soul of the deceased to salvation, pay the soul's way through purgatory by burning spirit money, and give hope that the soul would be reborn in the western heaven (Feuchtwang 1974: 326; Cohen 1988: 180). Throughout the funeral and post-funeral period, food, paper money, and especially on the "fifth seven" days paper clothes, bedding, house goods and so on were burnt. These sacrifices were not only to help the dead person settle in the afterworld, but included hopes of being given progeny, wealth and luckiness for the living in return.

The villagers' religious sense was consolidated in their everyday life. I heard that a quarrel broke out on the evening before SM Yao's mother's corpse was sent to Wujiang Crematorium. One of the combatants (SM Yao) told the other that his ill health had been a punishment from the Heavenly gods (*zao laotian baoying*). SM Yao was angered because could not find his father's grave, which was sited on land used for building by the other man's family. According to local custom a grave should be located on high land at a distance from residential areas. SM Yao's father's bone ash box had been buried in 1980, when the plot was used by his own family (*ziliudi*). After the Household Contracted Land Responsibility System came into force in this area in 1985 land use changed. The residential area was greatly extended. SM Yao's family burial ground was granted to another person for building. The new householder promised SM Yao that he would move his father's bone ash box into a safe place and build a new grave and SM Yao believed him. But they never visited the new grave because they did not hold any rituals for the resettlement of SM YAO's father. Custom dictated that after three years of sweeping the grave his family should let his father rest in peace (*anxi*) and not disturb it any more. Also, his mother had just became a Christian and did not want to be involved in any non-Christian customs. Photos VI-2 and 3 were taken in 1996 when SM Yao's mother passed way, and the family held a local Christian style

---

[36] It is the same in my other fieldwork village, Neiguan Village, Gansu Province, where *feng shui* master (*yinyangshi*) is always involved.

funeral for her. SM Yao's failure to notice that his father's grave had not been resited according to the agreement takes a bit of excusing. But as a dutiful son, it was reasonable not to go against the wishes of his mother after her conversion to Christianity.

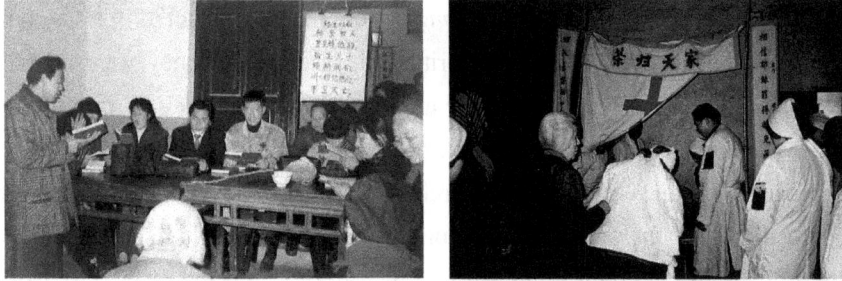

Photos VI-2 and 3. A Christian style funeral for SM Yao's mother in 1996

When his mother died SM wanted his parents' graves to be together and discovered that his father's bone ash box could no longer be found, due to negligence on the part of the new householder. He suddenly realised why this person had become paralytic (*zhongfeng*) as soon as he moved into his new house, and had been confined to his bed for a whole year. It had been the punishment of the Heavenly gods (*laotian baoying*) for his failure to keep his word and build a new grave for SM Yao's father's bone ash box. The new householder admitted he was guilty and told SM that his family worshipped the land god, stove god and general Heavenly gods for the whole year while he was suffering from the paralysis, until he fully recovered, contrary to nature. In the end he bought a new bone ash box, placed soil from the original burial spot inside it and sent it to the plot where SM Yao's mother's bone ash box would be buried.

In the village the unpleasant curses that can be made in the course of a quarrel are to wish the other person a "bad death" (*bu de hao si*) (cf. Thompson, 1988; Whyte, 1998; Kipnis, 1997), or a short life (*daduanming*), or punishment by Heavenly gods (*zao laotian baoying*), or "may you die without sons" (*duanzi-juesun*). "May you die without sons" is an accusation as well as a malediction, Mencius.[37] having said that failure to produce an heir is to be the worst kind of son. These maledictions relate to moral judgements, i.e. good or bad, and filial or unfilial, as well as religious sense. Some people told me they believed that such a curse might be fulfilled either this world or in the nether world. According to local custom a person who died after a long life would have a very

---

[37] There are three ways of being a bad son. The most serious is to have no heir (*buxiao you san, wuhou wei da*), 《孟子》.

good death. Death in illness without pain is also a good death, death in illness in pain is not a very bad death, but to die in an accident or at a very young age is a bad death. When I went to JH Zhou's mother's funeral everybody admired her blissful condition (*you fu*) because she died at age 92. I also heard people lament that XQ Wang's parents died in their sixties and not too long after their younger son's death. They were both involved in one of the three greatest misfortunes possible, according to the Chinese common saying "for a white-haired person to attend a black-haired person's funeral" (*baifaren song heifaren*). XQ Wang's younger brother's death in the village was called a "bad death". When I asked them why a good person would have a bad death, their explanation was he must have done something morally very wrong in his previous life in the other world.

In this second chapter on the life cycle I have shown how some customs were changed and others unchanged by social reform and the introduction of the market economy in the late 1970s. I would like to draw out two points to conclude this chapter. (1) Although moral standards declined in China in general, the Chinese traditional mechanism of intergenerational reciprocity – to take care of the elderly and love the children (*zunlao-aiyou*) continued – operating with instrumentalised expressive *wanglai*. The new head of the village YL Zhou quoted a Chinese saying that there are 30 years on the east side of the river and 30 years on the west (*sanshinian hedong sanshinian hexi*), meaning that at any one place situations don't last for longer than 30 years but rotate with that of other places. It reminds me of one of Yan's (1996b, 2003) description of the generation of old people in China who lived under socialism for thirty years, from 1949–1979, and so had little property to exchange for old-age care with their sons. Will the middle-aged parents who were able to store up property from 1979 onwards complain of the same thing when they are old? YL Zhou went on to tell me that situations always change and in a particular historical period elderly care might have historical peculiarities, but the nature of the relationship between parents and children would be always determined by positive human feelings in accordance with expressive *wanglai*. The current histoical trend is towards more instrumentalised expressive *wanglai* compared with the period before 1979, as is shown with Kaixiangong villagers' creation of new arrangements for family life, increasingly using money as a method of exchange, for example hiring a construction team for rebuilding new houses, paying for rebuilding temples, paying for parents' elderly care.

(2) The traditional Chinese intergenerational reciprocity – care of the elderly and love for children (*zunlao aiyou*) – continues to operate, but there has been a movement towards a greater valuation of daughters compared with sons. I noticed that the idea of rearing sons against old age (*yang er fang lao*) has changed from relying on sons to relying on children including daughters.

This is apparent in many ways:

(i) Traditionally in Kaixiangong Village a marriage that involved taking a son-in-law (*zhaonuxu*) into the family was seen as a misfortune. It meant that the family had no son, and the son-in-law's social status was low since he was poor. Nowadays more and more families accept this kind of marriage. Some people even admire such marriage arrangements, for example HL Wang's younger son said that if he was taken into a richer family he wouldn't feel poor. Uxorilocal marriage was always for the sons of the poor, so acceptance of such marriages by villagers is an obvious change. The transition to favouring daughters rather than sons, or to feeling easy without sons might, may have been brought about or encouraged by the one-child family policy, which applied from the early 1980s. The fact that about one half of all families had just one daughter changed the villagers' attitudes to uxorilocal marriage and also impacted on arrangements for elderly care.

(ii) Young women who have married out, into other families, are expected to take on responsibility for arranging family events and updating the families' *lishang-wanglai* networks. This implies a markedly higher status than that of new wives in the 1930s (Fei, 1939: 45–50). Their new status and responsibilities offer daughters-in-law a considerable challenge: if they get things wrong a mistake would cost their new family loss of face or even of a source of resources. But it is not unwelcome. Women told me they very much enjoyed being in charge of such arrangements.

(iii) Married-out daughters also created opportunities to stay close to their natal families. Traditionally the villagers only celebrate the one month, one year and 16-year-old birthday for children, and 66-year-old birthday for the elderly as family events. But nowadays some families celebrate children's birthdays every year and an elder's birthday every 5 years from 60 years old onwards. This change is as a result of the influence of towns. Although the birthday ceremonies are relatively small and low key, and have not yet been widely spread in the village, they give married-out daughters the opportunity to involve their natal families in their new lives.

(iv) Like girls in Beijing or Shanghai, who normally wouldn't want to move away to other parts of China, Kaixiangong Village's girls also preferred to get married and settled in their life locally. This facilitated *wanglai* with their natal families for both annual events and life-cycle events. For the natal families the daughters are no longer "spilled water that cannot be gathered up" as in Fei's time (1939: 46). Instead they are now mothers' padded body vests (literally, a daughter is truly close to a mother compared with a son, *nuer shi mama de tiexinao*). All in all, their status is significantly different from that in the thirties.

Chapter VII

Expressive *wanglai* in annual cycle and emergency events

Previous chapters have introduced and illustrated generous *wanglai*, and traced the use of expressive *wanglai* in many aspects of villagers' lives. We have also seen how close these two distinct types of *wanglai* can be. Generous *wanglai* can both enter into and result from expressive *wanglai*, which is embedded in villagers' activities in seeking resources for all the major events of their lives. Villagers do not regard these activities as instrumental (see Chapter VIII.I). In their eyes, expressive *wanglai* are interactions between members of families and different kinds of relations, over generations, for building individual and family-based networks which include friends and neighbours, a process guided and informed by human feelings. Previous researchers' studies on *ganqing* and *renqing* (see Chapter X.VII) have arrived at results very like my own. This chapter will discuss expressive *wanglai* to show how it operates in annual cycle events and emergency events. Of their nature, some annual cycle events generate a high input of generous *wanglai*, a predictable result of labour exchange.

VII.I. Annual cycle events

Kaixiangong villagers separated annual cycle events into annual life-cycle events and annual production-cycle events. As an input to social support most of the annual life-cycle events have been described in generous *wanglai* (see Chapter IV). Only those annual events involving social support (*shenghuo shang de xiangbang* and *shengchan shang de xiangbang*) can be seen as expressive *wanglai* and will be discussed in this section, peeling soya beans, making rice cakes, and conditioning silk-quilted roll-neck jerseys (*fanyi*)[38] (see Chapter III.III). Production in Kaixiangong Village fell into three main product groups, agricultural production, sideline production including raising silkworms, rabbits, pigs and sheep, and industrial production. Social support and expressive *wanglai* are involved in events of busy seasons in

---

[38] The last item does not happen on an exact yearly basis.

agricultural production (*nongmang jijie*), raising silkworms, and cutting rabbits' hair (see Chapter III.III). For a farming community such annual production events require labour support only, from sources that include relatives, friends, neighbours and fellow villagers. The relevant events can show how different types of *wanglai* are related to each other and the how different principles of *lishang* come into play.

1. Horizontal expressive *wanglai*

In Kaixiangong Village each family had relatively fixed teams for each activity in annual life and production events. Teams are formed mainly horizontally with agnatic kin, non-agnatic kin, neighbours, fellow villagers, or friends from their family networks. Liu told me that, "especially to wrap *zongzi*" (a pyramid-shaped dumpling made of glutinous rice) "it is not easy to pick up people to help randomly. Similarly the threshing has to be well organised with other families given limited time and available threshers". The establishment of the mutual labour support teams is based on a generous *wanglai*. As I have shown in Chapter IV, in most annual life-cycle events villagers concentrated on entertaining others and enjoying themselves, which can be seen as a generous input into an essentially expressive relationship. When they needed help in other annual life-cycle events the arrangement of labour support can be seen as the natural outcome of their input of generous *wanglai*. Yao said that she "would feel embarrassed (*buhao yisi*) if she had to arrange people to help with every annual event from scratch, needless to say more effort would be involved". She cared about the feeling of embarrassment more than the effort because she believed only those people who were invited for meals or tea parties during festivals could be asked to help with different events and become relatively fixed teams of her household.

For a household it is just as important to maintain mutual support teams as to form them in the first place. Besides annual life cycle events or festivals, every other event can be an occasion to express their appreciation of the help. Meals or tea parties before or after the events are forms of expressive *wanglai*. Jin told me that, although she likes to have fixed teams for the various events, her lists needed to be modified sometimes. For example, a woman was on her list for peeling soya beans. But in 1993 Jin was reluctant to ask her to peel soya beans because that year the woman did not grow her own beans, and so Jin would have been unable to pay her back. But the woman offered her help of her own accord. As soon as Jin had smoked the fresh soya beans she gave her a bag to thank her. This was also an allusive way for Jin to end the partnership in the peeling of soya beans, without involving any spoken words. I asked Jin how sure she was that the woman could understand her meaning? Jin said if she came again Jin would treat her in the same way– afterwards she would give her a bag of newly smoked soya beans. But she guessed that the woman might feel too embarrassed to come because this could be interpreted by villagers as her asking for the smoked soya beans with minimum effort – only peeling for another rather than growing it for herself. Jin was right. The woman did not come to offer help again in the following year, and one year later she and her husband moved to live with their daughter's family permanently, away from the village. This case shows both the woman and Jin wanted to give the other more, by either offering the other help or by giving a larger present, when ending the partner relationship. This way of ending a relationship was based on the local custom which said "do not owe each other any *renqing* (*shui ye bu qian shui*)" which can be measured by a scale fixed in their hearts . Jin enjoyed this elliptical way of dealing with different relationships. Whenever she recalled the experience to mind and pondered over it she tasted different flavours of *renqing*. For her it would be boring (in fact a reaction to something distastefully crude and heavy) if they spoke to each other directly, simply with words.

For the villagers, this mutual labour support within close relationships was considered as expressive *wanglai*, not instrumental *wanglai*. Qiu said, while she was making rice cakes, that "making different rice cakes or peeling soya beans is partly for the festival, partly for enjoyment, as well as to strengthen the families' relationships". Obviously, work like making rice cakes or peeling soya beans was related to generous *wanglai* because they did it mainly to entertain others and enjoy themselves. Other work, such as conditioning jerseys and helping in annual production events, "does not need to look for a special *guanxi* but does need proper arrangement because almost all the households can provide a labourer with reasonable skill and ability. So nobody is asking for a favour from anybody (*shui ye bu qiu shui*)", said Ni. The common understanding of how this mutual labour support worked is that households share tasks and resources equally. A request beyond this common ground, for example to ask someone's help in order to get into a hospital quickly or to buy cheaper building materials, would be considered as making instrumental *guanxi*.

2. *Lishang* criteria

Expressive *wanglai* in labour support was also found in Xiajia village. Yan (1996b) observed that, on the one hand, the cost of entertainment in mutual labour assistance increased and, on the other, villagers preferred to work for free in order to claim credit later (90). However, he did not explain why. For Kaixiangong villagers, the cost of entertainment and whatever kind of labour support can be offered or accepted are much clearer and more reliable for having been gradually cultivated over a long period. We shall see however that in annual events there are different *lishang* criteria behind the expressive *wanglai* between villagers.

The villagers are quite clear on what should or should not be done according to moral judgement. There were a few specialised households in the village which each raised more than 100 rabbits. These households did not engage in labour support with others because it was beyond the boundary of social support. As a villager said there is a strong sense embodied in a local saying that *bang qiong bu bang fu* (support for poor people but not for rich). It means villagers should only help others in a similar economic situation to themselves as a regular labour exchange. Some informants gave me an illustrative example. This anecdote comes from 1987 when the village began to experiment with economies of scale for agri-production, to try and narrow the huge gap between rural industry and household agri-production. One household contracted more than 20 *mu* of cultivated land with the village collective and had difficulty in the busy season due to problems with a sowing machine. However, nobody responded to the collective's call to help the household because they believed that it is morally wrong to help others for the sake of money.

Human feelings were also involved. Although the local custom makes clear boundaries for labour support, there is also an optional space for human feeling. An informant told me that even if a household contracted much land with the collective, if its main labourer became seriously ill some villagers including himself would offer to help out of sympathy. This feeling is mixed with *renqing*. Under this circumstance the sick person, whether he likes it or not, must show his appreciation in order to maintain an expressive *wanglai*. In such a case this means hiding his true feeling (*ganqing*) if he did not like others' help, otherwise they would be hurt and the relationship would be ended. And of course there is another kind of human feeling, namely enjoyment, which I have characterised as adding an element of generous *wanglai*, involved in some annual events. The significance of the tea party indicated such a human feeling. Although women helped each other to peel fresh soya beans and cut rabbits' hair as a labour exchange, the tea parties are treats for themselves as well. This is how they turned boring work into something enjoyable. Serving the same purpose, traditionally the villagers held feasts for helpers after they sold silkworm cocoons (*canba*).

These cases obviously involved rational calculation. In Jin's case the rational calculation can be seen from the way in which the other party helped her once but not twice, and she gave a larger present when they ended the teamwork relationship of peeling soya beans. In "raising silkworms" (see Chapter III.III) I discuss how mutual help is involved in BY's silkworm hatching room's case. She explained why villagers had to engage in personal mutual help in this way rather than by carrying out the advanced practice created in 1930s, when there were eight common rooms specially built for hatching eggs and shared by the villagers (Fei, 1939: 214–15). She said the collective hatcheries weren't a good idea because silkworms were such fragile creatures that they could easily become ill if the raising area was too big and they were not carefully looked after. This was a purely rational judgement of how to hatch silkworms, at the same time it showed how personalised expressive *wanglai* took place. The idea of rational choice not only appeared in agricultural arrangements, it was also used in household industrial work. It is normal to hire labourers if some household industrial work is needed. This is pure market exchange and is nothing to do with social support and expressive *wanglai*. However, the villagers carefully chose the Chinese character *pinyong* (engage somebody as – with a positive connotation) rather than *guyong* (employ – more negative, similar to exploitation) when hiring or employing labour, which saved them from any implication of being involved in private business, which was then not allowed.

Moreover, there is religious sense involved in such expressive *wanglai*. BY Zhou, the woman who owns a hatchery, told me about local customs related to raising silkworms. Before the work started, traditionally, people went to the temples to pray to the silk goddess (*canhua niangniang*), then addressed locally as *leizu* (wife of the legendary Yellow Emperor and reputed discoverer of sericulture). Nowadays her worship in temples has reduced, but is still conducted either in temples or at home. During the silkworms' month (May, or the 3rd or 4th lunar month) villagers should close their main entry door and fasten red paper on it (*bihu*). This means that nobody is allowed to drop in on others' houses with or without warning.[39] Couples are not even allowed to have intercourse because it is symbolically unclean. When people talk to each other they should avoid ginger and bean curd, which are regarded as taboo and unlucky. Ginger is pronounced as *shengjiang* and *jiang* sounds like a stiff corpse (*jiangshi*), and bean curd (*doufu*) is pronounced the same as decomposed flesh (*fulan*). Instead of *shengjiang* (ginger) and *doufu* (bean curd) they say *lakuai* (hot cube) and *baiyu* (white jade). Many informants confirmed that it is very important to respect the above local customs to avert disaster.

The principles of *lishang* can be mixed and interchangeable. This is when social creativity

---

[39] Only in periods of raising silkworms do the villagers close their doors. The rest of the time the main entrances of their houses are always open, as I mention in Chapter IV.II.

can come into play and one kind of relationship can be changed into another, or the proportions of each can change. The following example related to changes of agricultural production arrangements in the busy season. Villagers used labour support in the busy season because they needed to thresh wheat and barley with threshers within a limited time, in order to turn over the crop to the state as their dues for taking responsibility of the land. They used the term: selling public grain to the state (*jiao shou gongliang*). Others used a different term: selling surplus grain to the state (*mai yuliang*). Noticing the change I asked a former head of the village for the reason. He said the term of *jiao shou gongliang* (selling public grain to the state) came from the term of *jiao gongliang* (delivery of public grain to the state) before the rural reform in 1979. It was a very serious matter and the delivery was also called "loving the motherland grain" (*aiguoliang*), a political task which involved both morality and extension of human feelings from human beings to the motherland. To deliver loving the motherland grain was an effective way to arouse the enthusiasm of the peasants and at the same time strengthen political control. Although spiritual resources of morality and human feelings were mobilised, this would not last for a long period. The head of the village's experience shows that at that period the relationship between the state and the villagers was maintained by morality, human feelings including universal love, and fear and accusations of lack of patriotism, principles of *lishang*. Villagers' creativity was inhibited. The change in these terms illustrated a relationship between the state and the villagers in a vertical context over the past three decades. Although the relationship between the state and villagers is not *lishang-wanglai*, local officials and village cadres played a role and the relationship was personalised by both sides. By contrast, the market, the invisible hand, also played a positive role in the relationship between the state and the villagers, although this is beyond *lishang-wanglai*.

In the early stages of rural reform in the 1980s, selling grain including wheat, barley and rice was the villagers' duty in return for taking responsibility for the land from the state. However, a few years later, methods of repaying this agricultural tax were much more flexible, for example grain, silkworm cocoons, or even cash. The villagers found easier ways to meet the task of selling wheat, barley and the overwintering crop to the state (*jiao shou gongliang*). For example, there were two rice crops a year before 1990: the early one was in February and the later one was in June. They stopped growing the earlier rice in February because rice was no longer a "hard task to the state" (*ying renwu*) and they wanted to save more time for other work. When I was there, villagers started using the term "selling surplus grain to the state" (*mai yuliang*), because they had enough food to eat. The informant who used the term of *mai yuliang* explained to me that before the 1990s his family needed 1,500 kg rice for 5 people, whereas now with the same people they only needed 1,000 kg, because they had a much wider variety of other food. So they sold the remaining 500 kg to the state to pay part of the agricultural tax.

So the changing of villagers' *wanglai* with the state from meeting the political hard task of handing over "loving the motherland grain" (*jiao aiguoliang*) to selling surplus grain to the state (*mai yuliang*), indicates the movement of *lishang* criteria. The moral judgement of fulfilling the state's political task and human feelings of love of country gave way to rational calculation. With privatisation villagers wanted to arrange their lives more sensibly by themselves. Some villagers attributed this state of affairs to the heavenly gods and said "without heavenly gods's (*laotian*) blessing we could not keep our everyday life happy and auspicious". A woman told me proudly that they bought two big statues made of marble, each two meters high, to stand on the East Temple, which represented the heavenly god protecting them. This formed a sharp contrast with my memory of the shabby temple building in 1996. The changes that followed privatisation at the end of the twentieth century seem to show that expressive *wanglai* in annual life and production events has reduced. Rational calculation is the most positive criterion, although this co-exists with other *lishang* criteria, for example moral judgement, human feelings or religious sense.

VII.II Emergency (1): Natural and man-made disasters

Social support through expressive wanglai is especially important during critical periods as benefits that can be gained through interaction with others (Deaux and Wrightsman, 1988: 245). For rural Chinese people a critical period or emergency means a situation requiring immediate action, for example a famine, a natural disaster, illness and injury, market collapses, and man-made disasters. Kaixiangong villagers consider man-made disasters the worst of all, both more harmful and needing more urgent action. The phenomena of natural and man-made disasters form a contrast with the annual cycle events of the last section. Instead of private and labour support, in this section, public support accounts for a large proportion of the sources, and finance, information and especially policy are more important resources of lishang-wanglai networks. Although the nature of the relationship between the local officials and village cadres and the villagers is administrative, lishang-wanglai can be involved through the contacts between the authorities and villagers. In this section I will show how the villagers arrange their life during emergency situations, but will omit the topic of famine40 since Kaixiangong's case won't add more to the many existing studies. I will also leave illness and injury to the next section.

1. Expressive *wanglai* and its varieties

In emergencies brought about by natural or man-made disasters different types of wanglai can be involved in the relationships between the state via its representatives at the grass-roots level, and villagers.

The orthodox idea about the relationship between the state and the villagers in emergency situations is that it comprises generous wanglai, because the former provide different resources to give relief to the latter when they are in difficult situations. So the representative at the topmost level of the state and the party is claimed as the people's great liberator, emancipator, or saviour (da jiuxing). The famous song of "The East is Red" (dongfang hong) indicated Chairman Mao was such a da jiuxing. This orthodox idea remained from Mao Zedong, to Deng Xiaoping, Jiang Zemin and Hu Jintao. The yearly based performances of Chinese New Year by CCTV (Chinese Central TV station), started at the beginning of the social reform, and it takes as one of its main themes praises of heroes who fought against natural disasters. At the end of each performance the credit always went to the party and the state and their leader, either Deng Xiaoping or Jiang Zemin.41 I asked a few village primary school students from my sampled households for opinions on the this orthodoxy and confirmed that it was still taught in school textbooks. However, their parents had different opinions about it. Only 16 per cent of informants of sampled households agreed with the orthodox view. This 16 per cent could not give specific examples to back up their view, but they gave credit to the state and the party spontaneously. They believed newspaper propaganda reports of extreme situations in which institutional support was absolutely necessary for survival.

However, 75 per cent of villagers were sceptical. It was not that they were not appreciative of the local government's emergency support. For example, in the flood period of 1991, one

---

[40] Bernstein, 1984; Chang and Wen, 1997; Freedman, 1966; Lin, 1990; Lin and Yang 1988 and 2000; Mallory, 1926; Peng 1987; Potter and Potter, 1990; Skinner, 1971; Torry, 1984; Yan, 1996b. Yang 1996.
[41] However, in 2004 the CCTV's Chinese New Year's performances didn't glorify either Jiang Zemin or Hu Jintao, which seems a reflection of the uncompleted power transition from Jiang to Hu.

informant told me that his relatives lived in another township in which the loss caused by the flood was much more serious. The county and township officials visited them to give comfort. They also sent specialists to find report on problems and losses, distribute materials for victims, and help them in resettling and recovering from the flood. Another informant said that Miaogang Township officials came to the village and took part in the work of fighting the flood. The villagers also noticed that village cadres and heads of groups worked much harder than usual. As Chapter III.IV shows, Wang, who was head of one of the groups, rowed a boat and purchased materials for the whole village to fight the flood, which was not a part of his job as a head of the group. The agricultural technician also voluntarily worked overtime very hard for the dam. Villagers told me that one could only see such moving scenes in emergency situations, when almost all the village cadres and heads of groups worked very hard. Again, in other difficult situations villagers could get support from different institutions, for example the agriculture service station of the township and agricultural technician, epidemic prevention station in the township and a veterinarian in the village. So, villagers were grateful for these different kinds of institutional support, but explained that this kind of gratitude was quite different from the great kindness (enqing) experienced they from and to their parents. The relationship between the villagers and the state, through its representatives, in emergency situations can be counted as expressive wanglai, according to villagers' common sense.

In emergency situations, instrumental wanglai and negative wanglai can also be involved. I did not hear related examples in Kaixiangong. However, the head of the Wujiang Civil Affairs Bureau, Xie, told me that some township officials overestimated the flood situation and made guanxi with the Bureau in order to gain more relief funds. Facing this kind of phenomena the Bureau increased security and warned officials never to release relief funds for guanxi or renqing, at pain of disciplinary measures against the transgressor. Furthermore, Xie also told me that if the relief fund was not well controlled it could cause more serious problems. For example, a township official of a Northern Jiangsu County applied for a greater share of the relief fund than he needed for an emergency occasion. He diverted money to other purposes, including lending some to his in-law's family for house construction.

Xie's account show that administrative relations co-existed with lishang-wanglai. On the one hand, Wujiang Civil Affairs Bureau heightened their sense of discipline to prevent the relationship from being personalised by some township officials. This is not a lishang-wanglai relationship. On the other hand, the official from Northern Jiangsu personalised the administrative relation, which can be explained as both instrumental wanglai and negative wanglai. Xie's opinion was that if the extra fund was purely used for the township's public good even if not directly for the natural disaster, it can be seen as instrumental wanglai because he made use of guanxi for his own work in his own department for his own interests. However, this official had diverted funds for his relatives, in-laws, who lived in the disaster area but were no more needy than others. This should be counted as negative wanglai because the township official gave priority to his relatives (see Chapter VI.I), and why he was given a reprimand circulated to the whole of the county (tongbao piping).

I have no detailed information about this case because my interest when I was conducting my fieldwork lay elsewhere. I assume, however, that the township officials distributed a "circulated notice criticism" because they received complaints from neighbours of the offender's beneficiaries that they were much worse off than the favoured family and they did   not get any relief funds themselves. Normally this was the way in which feedback went to the township government or the county government. If a voice was loud enough or the township official's problem big enough it would draw the local government's attention. The circulated notice criticism was the reaction of local government to put right the wrong. The township official might become an honest and clean official after the criticism, or he might be removed from his position and replaced by another. Thus a balance was reached again between the villagers, the township official, and the local government.

Although in emergency situations the relationship between the state through its representatives and the villagers involved different types of wanglai, in Kaixiangong Village it mostly appeared as expressive wanglai. I will provide further explanations when different lishang criteria are considered below.

2. *Lishang* criteria

As I have shown in the previous section, people in an emergency or a difficult situation have an experience of renqing vis a vis public sources of aid. This kind of renqing can be categorised as expressive wanglai in which different principles of lishang are involved.

The moral obligation to help others in an emergency is the first criterion of lishang, which seems the same everywhere. For example, the Civil Affairs Bureau of the county collected a donation of about 2,700,000 yuan from people who were not affected by the flood, according to an annual report of the flood of 1991 by Xie, head of the county's Civil Affairs Bureau. Again, during the 1991 flood even overseas Chinese scholars and students in the UK donated about 120,000 yuan for the flooded areas and victims along the Yangtze River. Donors felt the same generosity towards victims is the same as the agricultural technician and many villagers who voluntarily provided labour support for other villagers, although their own farmlands were not threatened by the flood. Villagers' support for each other in an emergency is based on a local custom that jiu ji bu jiu pin (help for emergency but not for poverty). According to the local custom, everybody has an unshakable duty to help others when they are in an emergency situation, but nobody is obliged to help the poor because this is long-term work that can become an endless burden. Although support for emergencies and poverty are both part of the work of the County Civil Affairs Bureau,42 the cohesion of the different people voluntarily involving themselves in helping others in an emergency mainly comes from moral obligation. A former head of the village, BS Yao, said that when people suffered from natural disasters the government normally appeared tongqing-dali (reasonable, sensible, and understanding human feelings). The term of tongqing-dali includes qing (human feelings) and li which is the same as Neo-Confucianism's li (reasonable or sensible)43 but different from Confucius's li (propriety, rites, etc.). In this case villagers' understanding of the li is that the local government should be eager to support those in an emergency. In return, villagers always responded positively to the local government's calls, which accorded with local custom. Thus the relationship between the villagers and state via its representatives can be a virtuous circle.

The second criterion of lishang is sympathy and human feelings, although this can hardly be distinguished from moral judgement in the above situation. It was the dominant feeling in emergency situations, which can be mixed with other feelings among the Chinese. In 1991 when I had just arrived in the UK I saw the slogan "blood is thicker than water" (xue nong yu shui) everywhere among overseas Chinese who were collecting donations for the Yangtze River flood. I was moved by such patriotic feelings. Over more than 10 years' experience living in the UK I saw innumerable donations for different disasters all over the world but this was the only time I met that particular slogan. However my own reasons for donating owed more to human sympathy than patriotism. And of the sampled households, 75 per cent felt grateful for the local government's emergency support without feeling that they owed any great debt (enqing) to the state and the party or had any sense of patriotism. It was Yao, a former head of the village, who

---

42 Their basic works covered a larger range, i.e. social relief, relief for poverty or aid-the-poor programme (*fuping*), social welfare and security, and support for the army and giving preferential treatment to families of army men and martyrs.

43 A rationalistic Confucian philosophical school that developed during the Song and Ming Dynasties.

first used the term renqing to describe a relationship between the party or state and villagers. He said, "[Over] the half-century different kinds of policies have been implemented without understanding renqing and this has caused man-made disasters much bigger than natural ones". Here renqing relates to the will of the people more than human feeling but is still related to human feeling. Yao continued "villagers felt much happier (xinqing shuchang) when they were allowed to apply the policy of household responsibility in 1983, but they felt depressed in 1996 because private business was still not allowed in this village". Thus the relationship between the state and the villagers can be moved into a vicious circle. In the end he pointed out that "policies inconsistent with renqing would finish sooner or later" (bu tong renqing de zhengce zaowan yao wandan). I added his point as an additional question and checked with my sampled informants. All of them shared Yao's opinion.

Rational choice is the third criterion of lishang which can be seen in arrangements made for protection from natural and man-made disasters. According to the village income and distribution table of 1995, net income was only 17 per cent from agriculture, 31 per cent from sidelines, and 52 from industrial production. The industrial production included some villagers who worked for village collective enterprises, other households engaged in processing materials or supplying manufactured goods for enterprises outside the village, and others who worked in enterprises outside the village. Among the sideline productions, raising silkworms, rabbits, pigs and so on took 21 per cent of the total income. How villagers arranged a variety of kinds of production, which diverted risk from one particular product, is certainly a rational calculation, but not a criterion of lishang in expressive wanglai because there is no personal involvement. However, for the villagers, a diversified economy (duozhong jingying) is not only a model of all-round development, it is a way of protection from emergency as well. As Dong, one informant of my sampled households, said "however rational they are at balancing the proportion of different products the lack of security from uncertainty in policy always threatens the villagers". In other words, the villagers' rational calculation was limited by the degree of rationality exhibited by the government and its representatives.

As for the fourth criterion of lishang, there was almost no direct religious sense involved in emergency work in natural disasters during the post-Mao era. Fei's description of attitudes to threats of disaster shows the beginning of change:

> The occasions for magical performances are threats of flood, drought and locust plagues. Whenever the occasion arises, the people go to the district government and appeal for magical help. By ancient tradition the district magistrate was the magician

of the people. In the case of flood, he would go to the river or lake to demand the receding of water by throwing his official belongings into the water. In the case of drought he would issue an order to stop killing pigs and would organise a parade with all the paraphernalia suggesting rain, such as umbrellas and long boots. In the case of locust plagues he would parade with the idol of *luiwan*. (1939: 167).

However, the district magistrate was no longer the people's magician in the 1930s, when Fei was carrying out his fieldwork there. "The present magistrate... not only denies his traditional function to be the people's magician, but is supposed to enforce the law against magic. But the natural menaces of flood, drought, and locusts continue to threaten people" (168–69). Other researchers in other areas of China during the same historical period find that rural people did still employ religious activities to avert natural disasters (e.g. Luo, 1997: 693–694, 2000: 216–220; Mai, 1998: 231–247).

Although up to the late-1990s natural disasters appeared less serious than man-made ones in Kaixiangong, villager Qiu's claim that the destruction of the temples by local government was a kind of man-made disaster related to a religious sense indirectly. According to her, natural and man-made disasters, on a scale to disrupt villagers' everyday lives, can be a reason for each other. She explained to me in a telephone conversation after my fieldwork, that many villagers believed the two big events of 1996 were interlinked: the destruction of the temples was a reason for both the collective enterprises' bankruptcy and the changing of the economic system from collective to private (gaizhi). The villagers used two Chinese terms to describe this: yin huo de fu (profit by misfortune) and xi cong tian jiang (a gift from the Heavenly gods). The villagers said that it was they themselves who achieved the policy changes, with their persistent demands, but the fu and tian of the above two terms seem rather to indicate arrangement by supernatural beings. However brought about, the relationship between the state and villagers moved to a virtuous circle again after the crises.

3. *Lishang-wanglai* networks

The above cases of emergency and difficulty also show there were many vertical circles between the local government via its representatives and villagers in *lishang-wanglai* networks. In theory these are administrative relationships with no element of *lishang-wanglai*. However, in practice they can be partly personalised by *lishang-wanglai*, from both sides, which can be explained with *lishang* criteria as a reciprocal process between two parties.

(1) The starting point of one such big circle of the 1991 Yangtze River flood was when the victims needed support and ended with the victims who received support

The resources, donations in this case, came from different people including overseas Chinese through local government agents, up to the central government, downwards via local or overseas government agents, and ordinary people everywhere. As I mentioned earlier the relationship between the Chinese Embassy and overseas Chinese in the UK is a part of this big circle. The donations from overseas Chinese in the UK during the flood situation can be counted as expressive *wanglai,* due to complicated human feelings in which long-term benefits in return are expected in different ways. For instance, a newsletter from the CSSA-UK (Chinese Scholars and Students Association) published a list of donations. It also highlighted a UK-based Chinese scholar who donated £400 to the flood relief in 1991. He was then introduced to Chinese Embassy officials, as a model of repaying the motherland's kindness. This provided a chance for him to personalise his administrative relationship with the Embassy. I heard afterwards that he did indeed use the chance to make a closer relationship with Embassy personnel to create opportunities to work with his hometown in the Yangtze Delta. I noticed another donation list for the 1995 flood, which has been published on the internet. Almost all the "calls for a donation" would mention "a list will be published". Publishing such lists was a standard way for any Chinese institution to give credit to people who donated more (*biaoxian hao*) and encourage those who gave less. This might be one reason why Chinese people like to keep records of a variety of transactions between individuals and institutions when an element of *lishang-wanglai* is involved. Examples are *lidan* (gift lists) in Yan's Xiajia village or *renqing bu* (*renqing* notebook) in Kaixiangong, *heimingdan* (black list) by a government agent, *biantianzhang* (restoration records of usurious loans, former land holdings, etc., kept secretly by members of the overthrown classes dreaming of a comeback), and so on. Others can be published as a list of names posted on notice boards, for example *guangrong bang* (poster of honour), *gongdebang* (donation list for building a temple), *and mujuan mingdan* (donation lists for flood, etc.). For the Chinese the above lists can be stored over a long period as part of the relationship between an individual and an institution. In these relationships *lishang-wanglai* can be worked in both directions: top down or bottom up.

In the UK, the giving of a prestigious dinner in return for charitable support is a clear case of *lishang-wanglai*. But some of the charity appeals I met personally in the UK are very different. In spring 2001 my son's nursery school arranged a donation for an Indian earthquake. I had no idea whether or not the teacher would keep a list of the children's donations. After the donation there was no list posted, and it was completely finished as an individual action. For me, this kind of donation can be counted as generous *wanglai* due to its lack of expectation of any kind of return, but the donors gained better feelings by helping others. I asked some parents what they thought of it. One merely said that this kind of donation was based on people's generosity. Another said that it is commonly agreed that there would be unwanted side-effects if the list was kept or published. Some pupils donated more because their parents are richer but this did not mean they were better people. Others donated less because their parents were poorer, but they should not be embarrassed. This is how the sense of equality takes place.

(2) The relationship between Wujiang Civil Affairs Bureau of the county and welfare factories[44] is also a part of a big circle

Xie, the head of the Bureau, told me how a vertical expressive *wanglai* worked between the Bureau and welfare factories where disabled people worked in Wujiang County. The reason this case involved *lishang-wanglai* is because some workers in the welfare factories were flood victims or had relatives in the disaster area. When the Bureau collected donations from the welfare factories they also collected many complaints and comments on related policy through personal contacts. Xie told me that compared with their very limited financial support, policy support is a major resource from the state. For instance, in 1991 the Civil Affairs Bureau received about 200,000 *yuan* as a relief fund from the state, but the loss was 443,000,000 *yuan* in the 1991 flood. The state relief fund took on only 7.4 per cent of this. The rest was covered by donations raised from the welfare factories by the local Wujiang Civil Affairs Bureau of the county. The tactic used by the Bureau in raising so much money from the welfare factories was to promise lenient policies for their long-term development. Local officials can use policy making as an important and rich resource for gaining materials from individuals and organisations. In the case of providing lenient policies to the welfare factories the Civil Affairs Bureau had a double win. On the one hand, it raised a relief fund for the victims of the flood. On the other hand, it promoted the county's welfare factories' development which supported the Civil Affairs Bureau's work by raising more funds for poverty relief. The total number of welfare factories has grown from 67 in 1991 to 130 in 1995, and their total output value was 27.5 hundred million *yuan* in 1995.

---

[44] Welfare factories are factories established for people with different kinds of disabilities from 1980s. There were flexible policies of taxes and fees for welfare factories since this new phenomenon appeared in rural China.

(3) The relationship between Kaixiangong Village cadres and the villagers is also a part of the big circle

The relationship between Kaixiangong Village cadres, for example the village agricultural technician FK Yao, and the villagers, is also a part of the big circle. Yao told me that he gained support and trust from both local officials and villagers due to the credit he stored when they were in difficult situations such as the 1991 flood. An informant gave me another example about Yao to back this up. When I was there I heard some villagers complain that the pesticide and chemical fertiliser was not effective because the station purchased some supplies of bad quality. Yao reported this to the township immediately. Soon a new policy was made that the village station had to lay in new stocks of quality-controlled pesticide and chemical fertiliser from the township. Yao's good work in preventing a plague of insects also won credit from local officials. This is why he could affect the policy making of the township. He used his influence on public policy to help the villagers when necessary. He then used his influence on the villagers to gain influence with the local officials. This behaviour repeats itself in endless cycles. Yao said that in order to keep the circle running smoothly he should go on and on working hard and storing credits. But, he continued, the greatest impediment was interruption by man-made disasters such as the Cultural Revolution, which not only interrupted the continuity of the virtuous circle but also destroyed the order of villagers' everyday life.

(4) Not everyone wishes or is able to use vertical *lishang-wanglai* in an institutional relationship

The relationship between the village veterinarian and the villagers is in marked contrast to that with the agricultural technician who had worked so hard during the flood. Zhou told me that many villagers did not much like the village vet because he would only help them with preventative inoculations for big animals, pigs or sheep. She noticed he had not given a large enough dosage to the rabbits and they caught a disease in spite of the preventative inoculation. Another villager told me that the vet's wife always showed her cold face to them whenever they turned up to the vet's house asking for such help. The vet said that making inoculations for big animals was part of his job. He was paid 2,500 *yuan* by the village collective in 1995. Both the vet and his wife believed that inoculations for rabbits were largely a favour because the amount of work disproportionately high compared to the gain. He told me he was allowed to charge 3 *yuan* for the cost of the vaccine per inoculation for each pig or sheep but only 0.30 *yuan* for a rabbit, according to a reference guide from the township epidemic preventative station. It is clear that the vet wanted to keep his relationship with the villagers within a work boundary, so he did well with the big animals. But he has had difficulty with the relationship between the township epidemic preventative station, the villagers, and himself and his family. He felt the villagers did not understand the difference between his job and doing favours but tended to mix them together. So the vet's perfunctory manner and his wife's cold face were actually ways to avoid unwanted business without directly saying "No" to the villagers, which would have made them consider him an enemy. Until 1996 this method worked, because it stopped the demands of more than half the village households.

Thus the relationship between the vet and the villagers involved two circles. One is an administrative circle, outside of *lishang-wanglai*. Another is expressive *wanglai* with the households of the village for whom he did do small-animal inoculations. As I mentioned earlier in the previous paragraph, both the vet and his wife believed they were doing these households a favour by only charging for the cost of the chemicals but not his labour. This provided credit for his family's *lishang-wanglai* with the households who benefited. I have not got further material to prove this, but I believe it is shown indirectly.

Zhou told me that her family had 22 rabbits, which provided nearly a quarter of their income. It was very important for her to have the inoculations done properly. However, she felt it was very difficult to see the vet and his wife's cold faces when she asked him to vaccinate her rabbits. One day she bought two bottles of chemical (3 *yuan* each) from the township and asked one of her husband's workmates to help with the inoculations. In exchange she joined his wife's team for cutting rabbits' hair. Thus a private support link was established, forming a circle of expressive *wanglai*. I asked Zhou whether or not who had instigated such an arrangement. Zhou said she was one of the first people who felt they needed to do so – and that she had introduced a neighbour and a fellow villager to such a practice by giving them the unused chemicals. Recently, Zhou told me through telephone conversations that the person, who helped her with injections changed his job in 1998, now work outside the township. Since then, she asked her nephew who was the vet of a neighbouring village to do it. He only charged the chemical cost of the injections, and in return she cooked him a nice meal each time. Zhou also told me that although the cost of the vaccine for injections recently increased to 0.50 *yuan* per rabbit, still about half of the villagers continued to arrange this matter by themselves, mainly through relatives and friends in and outside the villages who knew how to do the injections. In exchange the villagers either entertained them with nice meals or helped their families to cut rabbits' hair. I believe that the Kaixiangong vet had a similar relationship, of expressive *wanglai,* with the half of the village households whose rabbits he injected.

These two kinds of arrangements for injections for rabbits described above can be seen as two circles which are interchangeable. After the implementation of the policy of changing fees to taxes (*feigaishui*) the vet's income was reduced from 2,500 *yuan* to only 300 *yuan* per year from 2001 onwards, which is the same amount as a village doctor. One of the previous heads of the village told me that the village collective stopped organising pig-raising in the village and the villagers now dealt directly with the township slaughterhouse, where they settled pig fees. Epidemic prevention for pigs was no longer part of the work of the village vet, because the villagers were provided with this service directly from by the township, which sent people out to the villages to do the inoculations. This of course affected the vet's position in the two circles between administrative institutions and villagers. The changed policies reduced his importance and relationship with administration, and his income from the administration was cut down. He continued the prophylactic inoculations of big animals in the village, but his relationship with villagers was now a market relationship, in which *lishang-wanglai* plays no part. But the expressive *wanglai* between the vet and the villagers in injections for rabbits, which mixed a little bit of administrative and a lot of *renqing* with some households, changed to a mixture of a little bit of market and a lot of *renqing*.

Let's find out the causes of the mobility of *wanglai* through *lishang*. Tan, the head of group 7 where the vet lived, told me that the vet does not like *lishang-wanglai* in general, although his family are partly involved in it. From Tan's point of view this was morally wrong, showing that the vet lacked a sense of social responsibility. Using the example of rabbit vaccinations, Tan said, if he were the vet, he would try to give feedback to the township epidemic preventative station about the unfairness of the policy relating to injections for rabbits, even by personalising it, in order to improve the policy. This would benefit many people. It would also improve the vet's situation in the village instead of losing so many villagers as his potential customers by providing inferior services. The vet's unpopularity in the village was also caused by his perfunctory manner towards villagers with whom he did not want to have close relations because he was not interested in *lishang-wanglai*.

Both the vet and his wife were put in a difficult situation when dealing with villagers' demands for injections for rabbits. They could not separate *ganqing* (human feelings) from *renqing* (human feeling and social rules) so when they defended themselves from using *renqing* networks in the village, they hurt the villagers' feelings, and lost them as friendly neighbours and fellow villagers. In Yao's words the vet lost his "*qunzhong jichu*" (mass basis).

The problem in the relationship between the village vet and the villagers was originally caused by the official guidelines from the township epidemic preventive station. The vet and his wife's decision to keep some households for expressive *wanglai* and drop others was largely based on the rational calculation that they should not work for too little gain with too much effort.

When the vet's wife complained of him as a "worthless wretch", as some villagers told me, I do not know whether or not he would say it was determined by fate (*mingzhong zhuding*) that he had no interest in *lishang-wanglai*. This happened to some village couples when they had a row. Fate is a religious term. It is difficult to tell how much the vet's relationships with the institutions and villagers were determined by this. It would be interesting to see how the vet improves his relationships with villagers and lives independently from the support of the village collective and the township epidemic preventive station under new circumstances.

VII.III. Emergency (2): Illness and injury

Table VII-1 shows there were 19 households and 22 persons in the sampled households involved in illness or injury from 1979 to 1996. The above cases involved resources of finance, labour, emotional caring and spiritual support, coming from members of households, family relations and fellow villagers, and different institutions including medical insurance. Apart from this, there was a system of worshipping gods or goddess for protection against illness or help in coping with long-term chronic disease. Although *lishang-wanglai* in illness and injury situations mainly involved expressive *wanglai*, other kinds of *wanglai* or relationships could also be involved. This section will show how different *wanglai* and relationships mobilised around a basis of expressive *wanglai* with explanations of *lishang* based on vertical and horizontal *wanglai* with different sources of *lishang-wanglai* networks.

1. Vertical and horizontal *wanglai* between members of the household

Normally a member of a family with chronic disease or permanent disability would rely on household support from other family members. This kind of arrangement would work as a vertical *wanglai* between older and younger generations. Table VII-1 contains information of illness and injury in sampled households from 1979 to 1996. For example, Han, head of household 7, told me that in 1995 he fell off a roof when he was helping a fellow villager build a house. His vertebra was injured and it took him one year to recover after hospital treatment.

Table VII-1 Illness and injury from 1979 to 1996 of sampled households

House hold No	Year	Who*	Illness or injury	Hospital	Yuan	Visits to patients	
						People	Yuan
4	1995	Wife	Lymphosarcoma	Suzhou	2,000	50	800
5	1985	Oneself	Pleurisy	Pingwang	600	100	500
	1993	Son**	Leukaemia	Suzhou	40,000	150	2,000
7	1995	Oneself	Injury of vertebra	Wujiang	3,000	100	1,000
8	1984	Father	Cerebral haemorrhage	Miaogang	500	100	600
	1982	Father	Tumour in chest	Suzhou	2,000	100	500
9	1994	Daughter	Tumour in abdomen	Zhenze	1,500	150	2,000
10	1995	Grandson	New born with too much hydramnios	Suzhou	2,200	200	4,000**
11	1988	Wife	Gastropathy	Suzhou	3,000	120	1,000
12	1986	Oneself	Pleurisy	Miaogang	800	150	1,000
13	1983	Wife (1)	Knee joint arthritis	Suzhou	1,200	90	300
	1988	Wife (2)	Knee joint arthritis	Suzhou	3,000	100	500
14	1991	Oneself	Lung cancer	Miaogang	8,000	30	500
15	1992	Father	Cancer of the oesophagus	Suzhou	7,000	40	1,000
16	1991	Mother	Kidney operation	Pinwang	1,300	120	1,500
21	1994	Mother	Gastropathy	Miaogang	1,300	50	1,200
27	1992	Mother	Myocardial infarction (died in hospital)	Zhenze	1,500	20	500
28	1995	Father	Cholecystitis	Miaogang	1,300	50	1,000
29	1990	Mother	Tracheitis	Miaogang	1,000	30	600
32	1995	Oneself	Fracture	Suzhou	2,000	50	1,500
33	1995	Daughter	Fracture to her arm	Wujiang	1,000	30	700

* Relation to the head of the household, who normally is male, but in household number 12's case the head was female.

** The gifts mixed with *wangxi* (visit a patient), *wang xinke* (visit a new arrival), and *dan shoutang* (visit the woman after she gives birth)

Moreover, he would never fully recover from the injury, which meant his family lost a full labourer. Han said, luckily his family had had a furniture business since 1980, which required less physical work than work on the farm. Han was also proud of having a filial and capable son who took responsibility for the family business and would take care of him for the rest of his life. Household 15's case demonstrated another responsible son in the village. The housewife of the household told me that her husband, Fang, spent 7,000 *yuan* on his father's cancer of the oesophagus in 1992, and 4,000 *yuan* for a lavish funeral in 1993.

If families had no sons they would make similar arrangements by taking a man as son-in-law (*zhaonuxu*) to serve the function of *yanglao-songzhong* (look after one's parents in old age and give them a proper burial after they die).

Household 11 illustrates a horizontal *wanglai* between couples. The family have spent more than 20,000 *yuan* since 1988 for Tan's wife. Tan told me that his wife suffered from gastropathy and went to hospital for an operation in 1988 which cost 3,000 *yuan*. Since then she has spent more than 2,000 *yuan* per year for medicine until 1996.

There is another case of *zhao nuxu* (taking a man as a son-in-law into family), also involving horizontal *wanglai,* which related to household support for chronic disease. When I was passing one of a few old houses in the village, a retarded girl drew my attention. After interviewing the family I learnt she was the only daughter of the family and had very limited ability to live without help.

A young man lived with them. He came to the village from a poor village in Zhejiang Province a few years ago and was very well looked after by the family. The young man also worked very hard with the other members of the family and they got on very well, as if he were a real member of the family. The retarded girl's mother told me that "I wish the young man

would live with us forever, but I do not think *laotian* (Heavenly gods) would bless my family with such *fuqi* (fortune, a happy lot)". Recently, I heard that they had built a very nice new house and the young man married the retarded girl as a *zhao nuxu* of the family. Yao, a neighbour of the family, told me that after I left the village the young man became a carpenter and earned a reasonable amount of money. One day he announced that he wanted to marry the retarded girl and became a *zhao nuxu* because he liked the family and wanted to live with the family and the village forever.

The above vertical circle is mainly mixed with generous and expressive *wanglai*. Parents should be generous to their children when they are young, and the idea of looking after one's parents in old age and giving them a proper burial involves generosity. When children get older and their parents are not yet too old the relationship between them is mainly expressive *wanglai* (see Chapter V). However, the idea of rearing children against old age including illness in the vertical *wanglai* is not a form of guarantee as is the insurance system in the West. The relationship between children and their sick elderly parents can move from generous, expressive, to negative *wanglai* and vice versa. For instance, there is a popular saying in the village that "*jiu bing chuangqian wu xiaozi*" (in cases of chronic sickness, there are no filial children at the bedside). After Rao's mother passed away he told me he understood more of the saying. According to Rao, if his mother was sick for a very long time and he took care of her less well he would be forgiven, and not called un-filial. This is why such a death in such a situation was called *baixi* (white happiness) in the village, as in the rest of China. This means the person's death extricated both the person and his or her closest family members from a predicament. If he did not take care of his mother, or even treated her badly, then he would be called an un-filial son. Luckily, he won the name of filial son because he took care of his mother very well for two years.

The mobilising of different *wanglai* can also be seen horizontally. The relationship between the young man and the retarded girl's family started with generous *wanglai* from the girl's family to the poor boy: at this time the girl's family never expected the boy would marry their retarded daughter in return for their taking care of him. During the period that they lived together the relationship moved to expressive *wanglai* because they liked each other and worked hard to keep together as a real family. When the boy decided to marry the retarded girl the relationship between him and the family became generous *wanglai* again because "the young man sacrificed his whole life for the family" as Yao said. However, if the young man had married another girl in the village after he got richer and kept a relationship of quasi son with the family the relationship between him and the family would have been seen as an instrumental *wanglai* because he used the family when he was in difficult situation. If he was a dutiful quasi son after he established his own family and kept an expressive *wanglai* with the retarded girl's family the relationship could then be improved. If the young man left the family and the village the villagers would describe him as *wang'en-fuyi* (devoid of gratitude) and the relationship between him and the family would then be negative *wanglai*.

I did not know the details of the young man's personal story. His choice to marry the retarded girl is consistent with traditional moral codes: *zhi en tu bao* (one is aware of a great debt of gratitude and understand to pay it back), or even *di shui zhi en dang yong quan xiang bao* (one should return a full spring of water for a drop of water received when one was in a difficult situation). However, the extent to which such moral codes are binding is unclear. Han of household 7 told everybody that his son would take responsibility for him after his back was injured and he was disabled permanently, for two reasons. On the one hand, it is normal for parents to internalise a popular idea of returning one's parents' great debt of gratitude and loving-kindness of upbringing (*baoda fumu de yangyu zhi en*) by praising their children. The idea of *en* is commonly agreed by the villagers to relate to generosity between parents and children. On the other hand, Han told everybody that his son would look after him to put additional external pressure on the son, because he was not so sure how long the above traditional idea would work in his case.

Human feeling is another *lishang* criterion. The above cases show loving-kindness involved in both vertical and horizontal ways, as Fang to his father, Han's son to him, Tan to his wife, and the young man to the retarded girl. I asked Tan why he spent more than 20,000 *yuan* for his wife's gastropathy. He told me that they were "an affectionate couple" (*en'ai fuqi*). For him, love meant putting in a lot of hard work into their life. He was proud of himself and paid the money all by himself, which he could do because he was a famous galvanised ironsmith in the township.

Rational calculation is another criterion. I also asked Tan why he did not seek financial support from public sources. He told me that he never expected he could claim anything from these and it was not worthwhile to spend much energy for limited money. Household 15's case also shows that it was too much hassle to claim financial support from public sources. Fang, the head of the household 15, told me that although he spent 7,000 *yuan* for his father's cancer of the oesophagus at one time, he did not bother the village collective or local government because there was not a clear regulation for him to follow. Fang was a manager of a construction company of the township and also one of the richest people in the village. Fang said that he hated to *la guanxi,* meaning to involve himself in an unclear relationship for instrumental purpose, because he was a businessman and wanted everything to be clear.

The sick and injured people in the village are considered to be unfortunate. All the members of the households I interviewed mentioned the term *fuqi* (good fortune). The main reason determining whether an unfortunate person could have a happy ending depends on whether or not there is a *fuqi* (good fortune) in their life. In particular the retarded girl's mother repeated again and again that her daughter "*youfu*" (has good fortune) and was blessed by the Heavenly gods (*laotian*). This idea of *fu* is imbued with religious sense.

2. Vertical and horizontal *wanglai* with personal relations

The highest expenditure on medical treatment in Table VII-1 is in the household No. 5, the RD Tan family. Tan's son suffered blood poisoning in 1993 when he was 27 years old and the father of a four-year-old boy. He was sent to Suzhou City hospital, which charged 40,000 *yuan* for the medical treatment. This was "snow and frost" for the family. The Tan family had 10,000 *yuan* of debt from building a house in 1992, bringing the total debt up to 50,000 *yuan*. The way in which Tan arranged financial support for the huge expense of his son's hospital treatment was as follows. He gave the bad news to his close links in the family's networks. He then received 22,000 *yuan* with no interest from their relatives. This comprised 5,000 *yuan* from his older daughter, 3,000 *yuan* from his younger daughter, 6,000 *yuan* from Tan's son's in-law, 1,000 each from Tan's sister and Tan's wife's brothers, which are old generation relatives, and 3,000 *yuan* each from Tan's quasi-sons. Rao also borrowed 500 *yuan* from each of three friends. The above private support made up 59 per cent of the total expenditure. Tan also borrowed a non-interest loan of 6,500 *yuan* from the village collective and submitted an expense account of 9,000 *yuan* to the township. Furthermore, the Tan family received about 100 people's visits (*wangxin*) and gifts equivalent to 2,000 *yuan,* after Tan's son came back from the hospital.

The above case shows the Tan family arranged and received financial support from criss-cross networks, which mainly involved horizontal private support. As I have shown in the section on "non-agnatic kin" of Chapter I.III, it is important for villagers to keep and maintain their lists of non-agnatic kin. I checked the relatives who loaned money to Tan's son for his hospital treatment. They are exactly the same families on the list of Tan's family's close non-agnatic kin. Since their relations were maintained well during festival periods, when the Tan family were in trouble he received financial support from them automatically. This process of maintaining relations which are used in an emergency can be understood as input and outcome. According to Tan, he did not ask their close kin for specific amounts of money when he told them the bad news. They worked it out themselves by following the local custom. So the sum of financial support was more or less expected by him, for example new kin which is of the in-law's family gave 6,000 *yuan*, 1,000 *yuan* each from two old generational kin, 3,000 *yuan* each from the sick person's younger sister and two quasi brothers and so on. I asked Tan how these families had spare money to loan to him? He said each of them had their own lists of close kin and they could borrow money from them. For example, his older daughter was the oldest child in the family. She got married in 1986 and established well-maintained family networks, whereas the younger daughter only got married in 1991. So the older daughter offered double the amount of the younger daughter. However, since the older daughter had already loaned 3,000 *yuan* for her natal family's house building, which she saved over a few years, she had to borrow money through her family networks for her brother's illness. Thus the money received from Tan's oldest daughter should be understood as one share (*yifen*) from her, who arranged it through her family networks.

The above case also shows the quasi kin's function in an emergency situation. One of them, Peng, was the son of the former head of the group when Tan was his assistant. Since these two families got on well, when Peng was two years old he claimed Tan and his wife as quasi parents. According to the local custom to "claim quasi kin", the quasi parents cooked three years' New Year's Eve meals (see Chapter I.III) for Peng and Peng should fulfil his duty as a son for Tan's family. Another quasi son, Jiang, lived in a neighbouring village. His mother was a little sister of Tan's wife when they were girls. The two girls lived in different villages but became good friends because they both enjoyed watching the Spring Performance. Sometimes Jiang's mother came to Kaixiangong Village to watch and vice versa. When Jiang was one year old he was made to claim Tan and his wife as quasi parents by his mother. Jiang became a bricklayer when he grew up. Tan's son claimed him as master, which meant a doubled closeness of a relative (*qin shang jia qin*). Since then Tan's two quasi sons and their families are part of the Tan family's close kin list. For Tan it was natural that the two quasi kin loaned Tan's son 3,000 *yuan* each, which was the same amount as Tan's own younger daughter. Thus the relationship between the Tan family and the two quasi sons was one of criss-cross networks because it involved different families horizontally and crossed older and younger generations vertically.

As another instance of private support, visits to patients are a popular custom in China. It is called *tanbing* in Yan's Xiajia (1996b: 63) and *wangxin* in Kaixiangong Village. After his accident Han, of household No. 7, enjoyed very much the *wangxin* from his relatives, neighbours and fellow villagers. Han told me that his relatives, neighbours, friends and fellow villagers visited him with lots of gifts during and after his stay in the hospital. For example, they brought him eggs, chicken, pork, pigeon, instant noodles, sugar, fruits, cakes and different types of general tonic. Han told me that the gifts which people chose were in particular good for patients. This can be regarded as material support.

In household No.12's case the *wangxin* involved a more complicated relationship. Zhou provided a full list of people who visited her when she suffered from pleurisy. To my surprise Zhou remembered all of the visitors, though this happened 10 years before my interview. She told me that she received about 150 people's visits. They were 15 close relatives, 100 fellow villagers from three groups, 10 village's cadres' wives, 19 assistants, one of each in 19 groups of the village (*xinxiyuan*), 5 people who came from the diversified economic service company of the township, 3 researchers from Shanghai University. Zhou told me proudly that "the gifts cost about 1,000 *yuan*, which can be calculated, but the *renqing* of caring was priceless".

It is easy to understand why the people from her work link visited her. This can be seen as a mixture of institutional relationship and expressive *wanglai* because in her work circle she always takes her share of care for others on similar occasions. It is normal for fellow villagers from her own group to visit her according to the local custom. But it was unusual to receive visitors from the other two groups, numbers 5 and 7. Among them the group 7's case is not too difficult to understand. Zhou told me that she started to create a relationship with villagers in her sister's group since her sister committed suicide (see Chapter VIII.II) in 1972, in case her nephews needed help. As time went on, she won all of them to be part of her family's network. It can be seen as an outcome of her input over a long term. Thus this kind of *wanglai* between Zhou's family and the fellow villagers in group 7 can be understood as a mixture of expressive and instrumental *wanglai*.

The reason Zhou helped many villagers beyond her own and neighbouring groups in the village boils down to a wish to be a good cadre (*haoganbu*). As a head of the Women's Federation, her job involved little formal work, so she often helped women who lived in other groups of the village. For example, some women were afraid or felt shy when seeing doctors in the township hospital for gynaecological examinations and asked her along as company. This was beyond her duty. She met their requests because she thought they could be her "mass basis" (*qunzhong jichu*). Some people thought this was her job and others understood these were favours she provided to them. Afterwards they gave her little gifts in return. Zhou told me that these women didn't visit her when she was ill because it was the wrong place (*changhe budui*) for them to do so. According to the villagers' common sense this kind of relationship between the women and her can be counted as instrumental *wanglai*. Zhou said it does not matter whether or not the women she helped gave her gifts. The important thing for Zhou is that she could win their trust and support for her work. This was the same argument the agricultural technician used, as well as the former head of the village YG Zhou: "we worked very hard in everyday life to win over villagers one by one (*yige yige di zhengqu*) and gain their support." The praise the village cadres gained as good cadres (*haoganbu*) showed how much credit they had won. Villagers called this relationship "state relationship with mass" (*qunzhong guanxi*), an example of vertical expressive *wanglai*, even though the power of village cadres was limited. It can be seen as downwards *wanglai* to the villagers, the opposite of the upward pattern that Yan found in Xiajia (Yan, 1996b: 171).

For both Han and Zhou the satisfaction of emotional care from their private links was very helpful for recovery. Han said he was very happy that visitors to came to see him because it proved that his family had a good reciprocal relationship with them. Zhou told me that she felt honoured that she received visits from so many people when she was ill. And she enjoyed all these visits because it proved that all her links felt grateful (*lingqing*) for her hard work in maintaining different kinds of relationships in the past.

Zhou's answer as to whether or not she would expand her mass basis is typically rational in its motivation. She said that there was no need for her to have the maximum number of villagers in her *lishang-wanglai* networks because her position was tiny compared with the head of the village and local officials. However, it was necessary for her to make a broader relationship with another neighbouring group, group 5, although she did not expect all the fellow villagers from the group to visit her, because the neighbouring group 5 villagers could be her potential supporters as her personal networks of mass basis for her work. Zhou told me about the ways she helped group 5's fellow villagers in everyday life, for example looked after an injured person, gave some spare grass to a family for its rabbits, patched up a family quarrel. She said she did this without any clear instrumental concern as it was for guarding her nephews in the adjacent Group 7. This appears to be the formation of a horizontal expressive *wanglai* with the group 5 villagers. For example, when a villager asked somebody for something, for example cutting rabbits' hair, and gave them a tea party afterwards, this appears to be an instrumental purpose. But Zhou couldn't randomly choose people that she would help. The help must be given within a context of expressive *wanglai*. In this case villagers from group 5 visited Zhou to either repay many different kinds of help she had given them over a long period in the past, or to ensure her help in the future. Either way, the motivation was not purely generous. The group 5's villagers' action shows that both they and Zhou accepted each other in horizontal expressive *wanglai*, although in a marginal position at the edge of their *lishang-wanglai* networks. Their reciprocal actions were according to the local custom.

There is finally a hidden aspect of visits to patients (*wangxin*) which relates to a religious sense. I asked a number of villagers for the meaning of *wangxin*. They told me that it is a traditional way for villagers to bring proper gifts to visit someone who has had serious illness, an accident causing a serious injury, a hospital operation, or has given birth. In such circumstances, extra money is needed for treatment, medicines, transport, nourishing food and so on, and also this person and his or her household needs more care and attention. According to the village custom, relatives, neighbours, friends and fellow villagers should all be involved, each in the appropriate degree. In particular, the villagers believe a Chinese saying *sanfen bing qifen yang*, literally, the illness involves three parts physical treatment, seven parts caring and spirituality. They think that the more people come to see a sick person, the better they will get over their illness, because the visitors are all on the side of his or her yang and against his or her *bing*.

3. Individuals' vertical *wanglai* with different institutions

Public support can be of different types: finance, information, organisation for related activities and so on. The financial resources can be requested from official sources (bank or village collective or state or collective work unit) or unofficial sources (usury and mutual savings), or others (see Table IX.I). The village collective played an important role in public support. Over the past 25 years in Kaixiangong Village public support usually applied to either a single person, or households (*tekun hu*)[45] in difficulty from serious illness or injury. Outcomes and criteria have both varied from time to time, as can see from looking at uses of the village clinic, medical insurance, disabled living allowances and funerals for the poor and so on (see Chapter III.IV).

Chapter III.IV shows cases involving different types of top-down vertical *wanglai*. They were that of a village doctor and villagers, a village head and a group head, a few village cadres and a nearly disabled villager, a Director of the Village Committee and a poor villager. Normally these relationships would be counted as institutional relationships because they were work-related. However, the relationships were personalised by both sides, in particular in a top-down vertical direction. For example, the relationship between medical insurance and villagers is not a matter of *lishang-wanglai*, but when it was first introduced to the village the villagers were forced to pay for it and *lishang-wanglai* did become involved. It was a mixed vertical, instrumental and expressive *wanglai* between the local government and the villagers via the village collective, through village cadres, that personalised the relationship, as in the case of medical insurance. It was the village cadres' job to complete the transition from the rural co-operative medical system to a commercial medical insurance system. The former head of the village said that the main problem with medical insurance was that most villagers did not want to

---

[45] *Tekunhu* is a technical term used by local officials for households in extreme difficulty, mainly caused by illness and injured persons.

pay for it. They didn't see its relevance and believed the village collective or the township government should help with some of their expenses if they became sick. It was necessary to persuade them, and this persuasion had an instrumental purpose. But nobody could get money out of the villagers without engaging their feelings (*yi qing dong ren*). The village cadres asked villagers, one household by one (*yijia yihu*), to imagine themselves in Han's situation (see the above household No. 7's case) to show how important the medical insurance was. Eventually the majority of the villagers joined the medical insurance system. The transition was largely accomplished by the use of expressive *wanglai* between the village cadres and villagers. Thus the relationship between the medical insurance scheme and the villagers took on an element of *lishang-wanglai*.

The case of No. 5, the Tan family who borrowed money from the village collective, involved a top-down vertical expressive *wanglai* between a village head and a group head. This appears similar to the instrumental *wanglai* when JG Wang borrowed money for his daughter's wedding from the village collective (see Chapter III.IV). However, Tan insisted his own case was different and should be treated as expressive *wanglai*.

(i)   Morally, such a serious illness of his son entitled him to ask for financial support in any way possible. Support from private sources and the township still left him needing 6,500 *yuan* to balance the hospital expenditure. He was told that he was allowed to borrow 2,000 *yuan* from a bank, with interest and complicated formalities. This is, of course, had nothing to do with *lishang-wanglai*. However, Shen, who was then village head, offered to loan him the full sum with simplified formalities and without interest.

(ii) Tan said he was very grateful and was moved that Shen was so concerned and cared about his family's situation. The villagers showed their understanding of it with great sympathy. For them, JG's daughter's wedding was a direct reason, and his mother's operation an indirect reason, to cause him to borrow money from the village collective. Tan's son's operation was a direct reason.

(iii) Tan admitted that he gained resources from the village collective and Shen gained a credit from him, which involved rational calculation. But he pointed out that the main reason he borrowed money from the village collective wasn't *guanxi* between him and the head of the village, although as a group head it did smooth it a bit, due to not requiring him to go through complicated formalities. According to Tan, both he and Shen could leave their posts, but one factor would stay the same. If a village head takes care of a head of group, the group head will work hard for him as well as for people of his own group.

(iv) Recently I asked Tan's son, who suffered blood poisoning 10 years ago, what he thought about his illness and his health and family life in general. He said he was luckily fully recovered from the illness. He was grateful to the village collective which arranged work for him in a village enterprise after he recovered from his illness. He became a culturist in aquiculture after the enterprise went bankrupt. His family repaid all the debt two years ago. His son was sixteen years old and had just performed a ritual of worship for both a life goddess (*ataimo*) and a medical goddess (*xinganmo*). He himself was not interested in gods, but his mother took part in all the spiritual events, which she believed would benefit her family members.

Chapter III.IV shows that the relationship between a doctor at the village clinic and the villagers is a mixed institutional and commercial relationship. The difference between the two rural Chinese medical systems is it contains a higher commercial element now than it did under the rural co-operation medical system. *Lishang-wanglai* took place during the period of transition between the systems.

(i) Dr Ni thought it was morally wrong to charge villagers much higher payments for home visits from 1992, a few years before the new system took over. According to the new regulations, from 1992 onwards he was allowed to charge 50 *fen* registration fee per visit from every patient who visited the clinic, 3 *yuan* in daytime and 5 *yuan* for an evening home visit. However, Ni thought 3 *yuan* was too much for the villagers to pay, when converted to an annual payment per person under the co-operative medical system. Besides, it was a double charge on the villagers because he already received income from the village collective, which originally came from the villagers. So he decided to charge a rate much lower than the regulation rate for the first four years.

(ii) Ni told me that he also felt embarrassed to charge his fellow villagers up to 10 times the normal registration fee, especially when they had an emergency. This is a typical human feeling of sympathy. So during the four years of the transition period Ni adapted the new regulations for the villagers. For example, he always charged a 50 *fen* registration fee per visit, whether a patient visited the clinic or he visited them at home. If a treatment involved having intravenous drips he then charged 2 or 3 *yuan,* including the registration fee. He explained his adaptations to his patients whenever he visited them and gained better understanding from them. This is how Ni mixed an expressive *wanglai* with the institutional relationship between a village doctor and the villagers. Ni told me that if he had suddenly charged high rates according to the regulations he would have earned lots more money, but would also have lost many of the villagers as friendly patients. This is why the villagers liked to make a comparison between the village doctor Ni and the village vet. They said the former had more human feelings (*renqingwei*) than the latter in dealing with the changing situation with villagers.

(iii) From 1996 onwards, after the villagers stopped paying for the rural co-operative system in the village, Ni started to charge fees from the villagers according to the new regulations issued four years previously. His income then increased up to 10,000 *yuan* per year, which is triple what it was before. Ni thought it was fair for the villagers, which accords with rational calculation. I interviewed a household without a serious illness or injured person or disabled person and asked for their yearly medical expenditure. It included registration fees per visit to the village clinic (*weishengshi*), doctor's home visits, and costs for medicine. The medical expense of the household was about 150 *yuan* per year. Interestingly enough, when the informant Ding listed his family's annual expenditure he said his "family spend more or less the same amount, about 150 *yuan*, on farm animals, agricultural plants, and medical expenditure for family members".

(iv) In contrast to the many villagers who praised Ni as a nice doctor, full of human feelings, his father-in-law became a Christian because he believed his son-in-law lacked human feelings. Ni was a man who married into the family as a son-in-law (*zhaonuxu*). His parents-in-law lived in a neighbouring house separately as two households. After Ni's mother-in-law passed away the two households continued the same relationship as neighbours to each other. This is different from most households' family arrangements and the local custom of the village. I suggested it might be because Ni grew up outside the village with professional skills. But the father-in-law insisted that Ni had lack of *renqing* and kept distant *ganqing* (human feeling) from him, which was determined by their fates. The father-in-law suffered heart disease, but he didn't even believe that his son-in-law could cure it with his profession. So he disengaged himself from a situation he didn't understand, by becoming a Christian and getting help from God.

4. Individuals' vertical *wanglai* with spiritual beings

Support from spiritual beings wasn't on the original study of the ESRC social support project. I added this, based on my own findings from my fieldwork in Kaixiangong Village. There has always been an informal system in the village for protection against illness or help with coping with long-term chronic disease, *baifo,* which means worship of Buddha. The reason

I chose the phrase "spiritual beings" rather than a particular god or goddess is because the villagers had different religions. In particular, they mixed Buddhism (*xinfo*) and Taoism (*xinshen*) together. Of the sampled households, 75 per cent said that they worshipped Buddha for health. The most popular way was to go to temples for such worship. However, there were two more kinds of worship which became more popular over the past two decades. One was worship of a "heart and liver" goddess, or medical goddess (*bai xinganmo*), and the other was belief in Christianity (*xinyesu*).

To worship Buddha is a traditional way of praying for relief or cure from illness. It has always been and still remains an active village custom. Such worship can be carried out at home or at a temple, or mixed with everyday religious life. However, the worship of a heart and liver goddess or medical goddess (*bai xinganmo*) was a relatively new phenomenon in Kaixiangong Village. The numbers of villagers who worship *xinganmo* increased since it was introduced in the village from Hehuawan village in the 1980s,[46] and their customs influenced each other.

When I started my fieldwork there were three small temples in the village. However, the local government sent some people to destroy all three in April 1996, one month before I left. The villagers were not very much shocked. A woman, Jin, who I met on the lunar New Year's day when she was looking after the temple, told me that villagers had got used to the fact that different disasters would happen to the temples from time to time, and they were rebuilt again afterwards. For example, East Temple, the main temple in the village, was destroyed completely during the Cultural Revolution and was rebuilt in 1993. It was destroyed again in 1996 and rebuilt again in 2000. In 2003 the temple was closed again due to application of a rule against feudal superstition. Therefore, to worship the heart and liver goddess at home became a necessary supplement to the villagers' religious life.

I attended such an occasion in the Ding family. The paper inscription of the *xinganmo* was presented in the middle of the back table. Ding presented eight plates of sacrifices in front of the paper inscription: peach-shaped cakes, noodles, oranges, apples, a whole fish, a big piece of pork, a whole chicken, and eggs. Six small handleless wine cups lay in line on the back of the table and one candle and one incense-burner were placed in front of the offerings. A metal pail stood by the table for burning money paper. She then made a bow with her knees bent to the paper inscription of *xinganmo*. At the end she burnt it and lit six strings of firecrackers.

---

[46] It was a neighbouring village including four groups when Fei conducted his fieldwork in 1936. It joined Kaixiangong Village in 1982.

Ding told me that she arranged this worship at her mother-in-law's request. Her mother-in-law had suffered gastropathy for more than 20 years and took pain-killers whenever she was in pain. Although she tried different medical treatments, they did not cure the root problem. This time she felt a great deal of pain from her gastric disease and accepted one of her friends' advice to worship the heart and liver goddess (*xinganmo*).

For Ding the worship of the heart and liver goddess was similar to the worship of another goddess (*ataimo*) for celebrations of a one-month-old birthday and sixteenth birthday. The differences were: only people above 16 years old were allowed to worship the *xinganmo*; if a mother got ill her son should worship the *xinganmo* for her and if a father got ill then his daughter should worship for him. However, in Ding's case, her husband was doing business outside of the township. Ding's mother-in-law suggested that her daughter-in-law carry out the worship in her son's absence. This adaptation of the custom was purely for practical concerns, as the worship itself was convenient and easy to perform at home.

To have Christianity as a religion in Kaixiangong villagers' words was *xinyesu*. Although the villagers clearly distinguished Christianity from the different spiritual beings of Buddhism and Taoism, they did not distinguish between the different schools of Christianity. The Chinese characters of *xinyesu* are to believe or to be believers of (*xin*) Jesus (*yesu* – Chinese pinyin for Jesus). So the villagers call it *yesujiao,* which doesn't mean Protestantism. To me their performance and worship looked more like Catholicism (*tianzhujiao*), but it was registered as Christianity (*jidujiao*) with the local government. Here and after I will describe this as Christianity.

I found there were Christian believers in the village from my interviews with my sampled households. Zhu first answered "Yes" to my question of "general belief in spirits", but she then answered "No" to questions on worship of local gods and ancestors. She explained to me that she worshipped local gods and ancestors before she became a believer of Christianity in 1994. She told me that there were 14 such believers by 1996, 4 male and 10 female, in the village. I interviewed all of them. Among them 10 families were recorded by Geddes (in Fei, 1986) and are still Christian believers after 40 years. The oldest one, Xie, was 82 years old. He told me that he became a Christian in 1931, influenced by his uncle (mother's brother). Although there had been several political campaigns over the last half of the century, his family members never stopped praying to Jesus at home and gained benefit from it. Xie also told me that he and his wife had one daughter and brought a man as a son-in-law (*zhao nuxu*), who became a believer. They had three children: one son and two daughters. After the son got married his wife became a believer in Christianity, but the two daughters were no longer believers after they married into non-Christian families. The numbers of believers in his family increased and decreased over generations and marriage, but in the end it more or less balanced.

I've discussed some elements of Christian practice in the village in Village Portraiture. The Christians went to two places for services. One was called *difang jiaohui* – the word-for-word translation being "local church", which meant a fixed meeting place without a church building and no registration with the local government (see Chapter I.IV).

Another place was called *guojia jiaohui* – word-for-word translation being "the state church". This meant a real church building and it was registered with the local government. I went to such a church in Zhenze Township with some believers on a Sunday by public transport. Sun, a pastor, told me that the church was built in 1915. It was taken over by a school to use as a warehouse in 1958 and returned to the church people in 1989. From the early 1980s, before the church was returned to them, they carried out services in private houses. This is very much what I had seen Miaogang Township. However, instead of *difang jiaohui* (a place without church building and non-registered) they called it *dixia jiaohui* (underground church service because it was not registered). Up until 1996 there were about 2,000 people who attended the church for services, 400 of whom were baptised.

Before the service started I found people praying by themselves in waiting rooms. The procedure of the service looked more or less the same as what I have observed in Western churches, although there were small differences. After the service I noticed a little blackboard with a title of "pray for others" (*daidao*) in the church hall (see photo VII-1).

The contents were "for xx village xx and xx the mother and daughter to be converted; For xx village xx's sister's family who are having a difficult time; for xx village xxx's eye disease; for xx village sister xx recovering from her broken leg; for recovery of xx village sister xx from depression; for regaining sister xx village xx's loving heart to her husband; for xx village brother xxx recovering from hepatitis; and for xx village xx to become stronger after an illness." The titles "sister" or "brother" denote believers, so it can be seen that the prayers asked specific help for prayer group members, as well as others. Such requests for prayer are also seen in the UK, where praying for others, both inside and outside their own Christian community, is known as "Intercession." I do not know whether it is a world-wide Christian practice or not, but it is strongly similar to my observations of other religious practices in Kaixiangong, for example where family members pray to obtain specific help for others in the same family: the son worships the heart and liver goddess for his mother or a daughter for her father; a wife worships local gods in a temple for her husband or a mother for her son, and so on. I will come back to this topic in the section of "Implications of *lishang*" below.

The relationship between spiritual beings and villagers involves top-down and bottom-up reciprocal vertical expressive *wanglai*. As I pointed out in Chapter IV.III, the reciprocal *wanglai* is formed by the actions of villagers themselves and the imaginary reactions of spiritual beings. The two-way nature of this vertical *wanglai* can be seen from the two rebuilds of the East temple. The first time was in 1993. Jin, one of the organisers of rebuilding the temple, told me how the East Temple was rebuilt. After she had been suffering illness for some years she saw a fortune-teller (*dalaoye*) outside of

Photo VII-1. "Pray for others" (*daidao*) in the church hall of Zhenze Township

the township. He told her "*qimiao*" (build a temple). She and her friends used the extension of a warehouse which was located in the original temple site as the temple building. They collected about 500 *yuan* from villagers whom she knew were interested in this issue. They then bought *longmen* (a dragon door – a kind of curtains with some decorations), big metal pails, table and so on. Two original big candlesticks were returned by a "workpoint keeper"[47] (*jigongyuan*) who had been keeping them since the Cultural Revolution.

After the temple was destroyed in 1996 the villagers rebuilt it in 2000. Fang told me that a few weeks before the temple was rebuilt a spiritual being appeared in her dream and made a request (*tuomeng*) for her to organise the rebuilding work. It also gave her some details of how the temple should be arranged, such as that it should have two statues, who were of *Caodaren*, a loyal official in ancient China, and his wife. Fang and her friends soon raised more than 8,000 *yuan* donation from the villagers and asked a master to carve two marble statues of two metres high to be placed in the temple.

---

[47] During the Cultural Revolution period villagers worked for collective. Their work was kept by points which can be turned into income at the end of a year.

Motivation for the first rebuild of the Temple came from a villager who believed it would help her with her illness. The second time the driving force came from a villager who was given instructions in a dream. Both cases can be interpreted with *lishang* criteria.

(i)   Morally great merit (*ji da de*) is given to those who organise a rebuild of the temple. The villagers would always remember them. Whoever contributed would also be remembered. For example, they remember the bookkeeper who returned the two original big candlesticks to the East Temple in 1993, and three copies of a record of merits and virtues (*gongde bu*), written by pen brush on a big red paper, published all the people's names and amounts of donations for rebuilding the temple in 2000.

(ii) Human feelings are also in evidence. In the first case, the sick person who organised the rebuild gained great sympathy from the other villagers. But the second rebuild also led to a feeling of fear for the organiser. I tried to contact Fang again for more details of the temple, but her son refused to let me talk to her. I then asked one of her neighbours to see her. He told me that she and her family were afraid of being marked out by a researcher from England as a tall tree catches the wind (*shu da zhaofeng*). I can understand this feeling. It also shows the limitation of telephone interview methods.

(iii) The temple rebuild needed a site, ideas, money and materials. Rational calculation comes into the relationship of the organisers with the private sources from whom they sought financial and labour support, neighbours, friends, and fellow villagers; information support from other temples outside the village; as well as a market for specialised carpenters and sculptors

(iv) The ritual of the record of merits and virtues (*gongde bu*) was a typical way for the villagers to communicate with spiritual beings. As I mentioned earlier, there were three copies of the record of merits and virtues (*gongde bu*). One was burned in the opening ceremony of the temple to show the Heavenly gods (*laotian*) everybody's contribution. Another was put up on the temple wall as a poster, and the final one was kept for a record in the same way in which people keep gift lists (*renqing bu*).

Thinking about the difference between instrumental *wanglai* and expressive *wanglai,* a conversation in the West Temple with Xu, a male villager, enlightened me. Xu was one of two men whom I met in the West Temple. He told me that he went to the temple to worship Buddha for his heart disease (*xinji*). I asked him why so few men visited temples except in the lunar New Year's Eve. He told me that according to village custom, worship for health doesn't have to be carried out by the person who is sick. When he was busy with his work his mother and wife usually did it for him. However, for best results the person who had the illness should go themselves to pray devoutly to the gods in person (*jingchang baibai*). Moreover, if one's prayer was just for the sake of curing illness it wouldn't be effective enough. Xu's opinion can also be interpreted with *lishang* criteria.

(i) Morally, one should be a true believer in a spiritual being rather than using it for a particular purpose; then one could expect a blessing from it. Ding's mother-in-law said that her worship of the heart and liver goddess was simply an addition to her usual worship of a specialist goddess to help her to recover from the illness. Instead of confining her worship gods or goddesses in general, on every 1st or 15th of the lunar month she also read silently the name of *xinganmo*.

(ii) If one worked hard enough by praying to the spiritual being regularly one could awake its sympathy and receive blessings from it. As Ding's mother-in-law said, once she became a believer of the *xinganmo* she would pray sincerely to her over the years and eventually the goddess would be touched by her.

(iii) If one truly believed in the spiritual being but was too busy to worship it oneself, one's close relatives were allowed to do it for one. When I asked Ding's mother-in-law how effective the worship of *xinganmo* was for her illness she said that a one-off worship for a particular purpose would never have an effect. She even quoted a Chinese saying about people who *pingshi bu shaoxiang, linshi bao fojiao* (never burn incense when all is well but clasp Buddha's feet when in distress).

(iv) A Chinese saying embodying a religious sense is that worship would be effective if you truly believed it (*xin ze ling*).

I was surprised by the huge difference between the two neighbouring townships of Miaogang and Zhenze. In Zhenze Township Christianity flourished, and Buddhism seemed very unpopular. After I visited the church I went to all the main places where there had been temples in the past in the township, including three of them in Jinxing village, another fieldwork village of the ESRC social support project, which was located by the township. I found there was no temple anywhere at all in Zhenze Township. It was clear that Christianity was much more popular than Buddhism. I asked some sampled households in Jinxing village why Buddhism had declined and Christianity had increased. Their answers can be predicted from the implications of *lishang* below.

(i) Villagers in Kaixiangong Village or surrounding areas worshipped spiritual beings for curing illness because morally they thought they were right (*dui*) to choose any way they liked for their own bodies and mind, according to their own situation. They used the word of "right" to mean *dui* (opposed to wrong – *cuo*), which has a strong moral sense, rather than the political term (*quanli*). It was important for the local people to have a religious existence, no matter which it was. They told me that Zhenze was a Socialist Spiritual Civilization township (*shehuizhuyi jingshen wenming zhen*). All the temples were destroyed by the local government, which was similar to Miaogang's situation in 1996. According to the local government, a belief in Buddhism was treated as superstition in Miaogang. It was an underground activity, just as Christians carried out "underground" services in private houses before the early 1980s. The increase in the numbers of Christian believers was one way to demonstrate against the government's interference with their spiritual world. But it was also a true religion for some villagers in Miaogang. Zhu told me that she became a believer of Christianity to change her fate and protect against illness. She said her husband served in the army for seven years during the Cultural Revolution. During this difficult period her older son dropped out from primary school because he had to work on the land and her younger son died from intestinal cancer when he was 11 years old. After several visits to a church in Zhenze Township she placed the hopes of her family on Christianity. The change of her belief from "general belief in spirits" to Christianity shows that she had found a new spiritual sustenance that replaced the old one.

(ii) The increasing worship of Christianity and decreasing worship of Buddhism in Zhenze can be partly accounted for by the human feeling of fear of repression by the government, Christian worship being legal and Buddhist worship banned. People who converted believed that as a result their illnesses were cured, or they felt healthier. Local people were tolerant of these conversions out of sympathy, knowing people need for a substitute worship that offered help with their health rather than merely a rational belief that Christianity has some medical power. Most of the requests for group prayer on the blackboard in the church hall were about health and illness. Even those people who gave other reasons for their Christianity, such as changing of fate, bad temper (*piqi*), wanting life in heaven after death, wanting something religious other than Buddhism, also wanted to recover or be protected from illness. They also used two Chinese phrases *wuke jiuyao* and *wuwei erzhi*, with their interpretations modified from common usage. The former used to be used in the sense of "Everyone makes mistakes, but few are incorrigible", but now means that if one is too ill to be cured by medicine one shouldn't ask god for a cure. The latter means: "don't ask god to cure your illness, if you pray to god devoutly enough it will go". This was a basic concept in Taoism, literally, do nothing and everything is done. The above two phrases, for both the villagers and people in Zhenze, imply that their devout prayers will eventually influence the gods. This means one should never become a religious believer for the instrumental purpose of curing illness rather than to express one's feelings to move the god (*gandong shangdi*). The former motivation would make praying to spiritual beings instrumental *wanglai*, and the latter expressive *wanglai*. The distinction is subtle but real, in that the hopes are the same and the actions are the same, but the actions are performed in a different spirit.

(iii) One of the villagers in Jinxing village gave me an answer using rational choice. He said conversion to Christianity was allowed in Zhenze because the church was registered with the local government. This was also the case in Miaogang Township. In order to avoid the matter of superstition, as soon as the biggest temple, *laotai* temple in Miaogang, was properly rebuilt again in 2000 it was registered with the local government. But it was registered into another category as a Tourism Development Scheme. After the temple was rebuilt it attracted a large number of worshipers (*xianghuo hen wang*). The revival of Christianity in Zhenze Township in 1996 and Buddhism in Miaogang Township in 2000 shows that local people's religious sense never goes away. The shifts between Buddhism and Christianity in the two townships can be seen as a rational adaptation to the political changes.

Practicality was also an important reason for worshipping the heart and liver goddess and Christianity's spread in the village. As I mention at the end of Chapter IX.III, Tan, Ni's father-in-law, became a Christian to change his fate and guard against illness. He also said he didn't want to spend more on medicine because he was getting older and couldn't get more income from working on the land. He found that to be a Christian was just what he needed because he understood his illness well, just like the common saying that prolonged illness makes a doctor of a patient (*jiu bing cheng yi*) and he also wanted to understand his life with help from God. Furthermore, Xie, the oldest Christian believer, told me that "Relying on Jesus' direction (*kao ta zhidian*), I can cure disease for both human beings and animals with Western medicine, although I am an illiterate person. I remembered lots of medical names and understood which illness needs which medicine and quantity and never went wrong. Thanks to Jesus."

Let's come back to the Zhenze Church. Sun, a pastor of the Zhenze Church, said that there were three methods of prayer which were called pray together in church service (*daodao*), pray by oneself anywhere (*zidao*), and individual or group pray for others (*daidao*). This reminded me that the oldest believer in Kaixiangong Village mentioned the word "*zidao*" (self pray)", as how his family members prayed by themselves during the Cultural Revolution. Sun agreed that self prayer was a very convenient way for people to practice Christianity without interference, whenever outside situations made it difficult. Referring to the group prayer Notice in the church hall, Sun continued that it has been interpreted in two ways. One is that a person prays for the closest members of his or her family. Another is an extension of this way, namely, the person through a group of people prays for his or her closest member of family, because they believe one person has limited energy and if many people work together it will produce more power. In return the person also joins such a group to pray for others.

(iv) The way in which some Kaixiangong villagers and local people sought support from spiritual beings for curing their illnesses is of course a manifestation of religious sense. Villagers believed that sometimes a god could show its presence or power (*xianling*). I heard a story that in 1993 when the East temple was being rebuilt the bookkeeper recognised subconsciously that it might be the time to return the two candlesticks he had appropriated. After he did it his family members' illnesses were all cured. On the other hand, Xu, the man I met in the West Temple, told me that "it does not matter which Buddha (*fo*), god (*shen*) you worship, and where they are located – local or national, east or west. The important thing is that if one truly believes in the Heavenly gods (*laotain*, or spiritual beings) one can be helped." Geddes noticed the ten households of Christian believers still existed in 1956. He thought the villagers' religious sense was quite unaffected the Communist Party's advocating atheism after 1949 (in Fei, 1986).

Chapter VIII

Instrumental and negative *wanglai*

Having introduced generous and expressive *wanglai,* I now move to the remaining types: instrumental and negative *wanglai.* Instrumental *wanglai* would seem to correspond with "*guanxi*", a much-studied concept in popular usage inside and outside China (see Chapter X.VI). Here I intend to be guided by what I've learnt from Kaixiangong villagers, who regard instrumental *wanglai* as reciprocal action for material gain or utilitarian purpose. This is not at all the same as the negative end of *bao* that Lien-sheng Yang described in 1957 (see Chapter X.IV), which can be seen as negative *wanglai.* In Kaixiangong village both instrumental and negative *wanglai* played only a small part in the totality of activities in social support arrangements, 20 per cent and 10 per cent respectively.

The fact that the proportion of resources-seeking activities involving instrumental *wanglai* in Kaixiangong is relatively small should not obscure its importance, any more than the small role played by the state in social security and welfare resources in rural areas (see table 0-1) affects its huge influence in control of rural people and their lives. In villagers' words, "government manage the big family of the country, women manage our own small families". But the way in which government controls the country is unpredictable. From one time to another villagers need to adapt their behaviour ands customs to meet so much change. Instrumental *wanglai* between individuals and institutions occurred when villagers were seeking "public support". My focus extended from relationships between individuals to those between individuals and "institutions". Whether or not it is possible to "personalise institutions" is a large topic, and I will introduce briefly Polanyi's (1957) and Parsons's (1937/1949) theories after my discussion of Sahlins' (1972) reciprocity including negative reciprocity in Chapter IX. Meanwhile I will use this chapter to discuss both "instrumental *wanglai*" and "negative *wanglai*", comparing their similarities and differences, and also demonstrating the ways in which they can change. This may go some way towards answering to the question "How institutions can be personalised"?

VIII.I. Instrumental *wanglai*: top down and bottom up

As I mentioned in the introduction in Part One, instrumental *wanglai* is very close to *guanxi* (see Chapter X.VI). Kaixiangong villagers use *tuo renqing* (looking for different resources through personal links for benefiting everyday life or emergency with their own resources) for instrumental *wanglai*; whereas *guanxi* refers to negative *wanglai* (see Chapter VIII.II). I divided this common usage of *guanxi* into two parts: instrumental and negative *wanglai*. According to the villagers' standards instrumental *wanglai* relates to people giving something (e.g. loaning money, providing materials, information, emotional or spiritual help, offering special skills or ability, introducing a personal link, etc.) to others for direct gains or long-term benefits in horizontal and vertical ways. Both the horizontal and vertical instrumental *wanglai* relate to individual or groups using their own resources to meet their own interests. Horizontal instrumental *wanglai* normally happened between the same generational members of a family with their personal networks, or a family as a whole with its networks including relatives, neighbours, friends and other personal relations. Kaixiangong villagers use examples such as asking help to get somebody into hospital earlier, or finding better decorators. In contrast to Yan's bottom up instrumental gift exchange (1996b: 21 and its chapter 7), I will stress a bidirectional vertical instrumental *wanglai*. It can be mobilised bottom up (e.g. villagers seek spiritual support - blessings or protection from ancestors or gods) and top down (e.g. from a local official to village cadres, or a village cadre to villagers) directions.

1. Bottom up vertical instrumental *wanglai*

The previous examples in Chapter IV have illustrated how villagers had generous *wanglai* with ancestors and gods: the next chapters will similarly deal with expressive *wanglai*. The following example illustrates a bottom up vertical instrumental *wanglai* between a family and goddesses. Normally when a family held a ceremony for a child's sixteenth birthday they presented offerings to *ataimo* (a life goddess). However, if the child had an illness the *xinganmo* (a medical goddess) should also be prayed to. The villagers consider that praying to *ataimo* on this occasion can be counted as expressive *wanglai*, whereas praying to *xinganmo* is instrumental *wanglai*. As well as individuals who uses their own resources to gain spiritual support (e.g. blessing or protection from ancestors or gods) such vertical instrumental *wanglai* also involves groups. The most obviously instrumental *wanglai* between the villagers and spiritual beings can be seen from religious activities in the township for protecting against drought, locusts or flood before 1949 (Fei 1939:103). It can still be seen in other parts of China (e.g. praying to the dragon king or water god for water, Luo 1997, 2000).

Behind this kind of bottom up vertical instrumental *wanglai* are *lishang* criteria.

(i)   Morally, praying to *xinganmo* may be expressing a general respect for spiritual beings rather than just asking for cures for illness. There is a cautionary Chinese saying about never burning incense when all is well but clasping Buddha's feet when in distress (*pingshi bu shaoxiang, linshi bao fojiao*).

(ii) Sympathy and comfort is another reason for villagers to carry on *wanglai* with spiritual beings. Many villagers told me that the local temples are rebuilt again and again because some villagers insist that they need them to cure illness. This excuse gained a wide range of sympathy from local officials and other villagers.

(iii) The direct purpose of asking spiritual beings to cure illness is obviously rational choice. There was a custom in the village that if a father got ill then his daughter should pray to *xinganmo* for him, whereas if a mother got ill then her son should pray to *xinganmo* for her. With the one child policy, from the 1990s this custom became less practical and needed to be evolved. Xu told me that if a family only has one son or one daughter the son-in-law or the daughter-in-law should pray to *xinganmo* for their mother-in-law or father-in-law.

(iv) The villagers' answer as to whether praying to spiritual beings to cure illness actually works is definitely imbued with religious sense. They told me that prayer would only be effective if one truly believed (*xin ze ling*). There are common Chinese sayings relating to instrumental *wanglai* in religious life that point out its unacceptability − *wu shi bu deng sanbaodian* (one does not go to the temple for no reason, or I wouldn't come to you if I haven't got something to ask of you). Another circumstance that involves bottom up vertical instrumental *wanglai* is when villagers seek resources from the rather meagre public sources for financial support (constituting only 12 percent of such activity, compared with 82 per cent for household and private sources.)[48] I found one instance, JG Wang's family, who borrowed money for a wedding from the Village Collective, whereas normally Kaixiangong villagers finance their weddings through expressive *wanglai* with private sources. Wang and other villagers agreed that this case can be interpreted as instrumental *wanglai*.

---

[48] See "All villages social support summary" pp10, in *Social support in rural China (1979-1991): A statistical report on ten villagers*, by Chang and Feuchtwang, London: City University, 1996.

(v)   It was proper that JG Wang should ask for help from the Village Collective because he was a head of one of the village groups and worked very hard for both the Village Collective and the group's villagers.

(vi) Villagers had sympathy with Wang because his mother had had a major operation a few months before the wedding so they didn't mind the Village Collective lending him money.

(vii) JG Wang's case didn't fit into the existing category of "special difficulty subsidies (*tekun buzhu*)". The way in which the Village Collective sorted out the problem was by creating a new category of "reimbursable assistance". On the one hand this kept the account book clear, on the other hand it didn't set a precedent for other villagers because there were only a limited number of families in the village who could meet the criteria.

(viii) It was bad luck that Wang's family had to spend a lot of money on his mother's operation. However, she believed that "there is always a way out with god's help (*tian wu jue ren zhi lu*)".

The following case can be counted as negatively valued bottom up vertical instrumental *wanglai*. When I was in the village many villagers complained that the Party Secretary Shen favoured his relatives and relations in allotting jobs in village enterprises. I describe the relationship between Shen and the relatives who benefited as negatively valued instrumental *wanglai*, while that between Shen and the villagers, especially the villagers who lost their chances of gaining jobs in the village enterprises, is negative *wanglai* (see next section). Although close, these two types of relationship are distinct. Some villagers thought it was morally wrong for people to obtain posts in village enterprises by giving gifts to Shen. Shen's allotment of posts to those who gave him gifts was an unfair use of power. But villagers interpreted his behaviour in different ways. Some saw themselves as having lost their rightful chance of working in a village enterprise, and their relationship with Shen was one of negative *wanglai*. Others told me that to get a job in a village enterprise was not a big deal (*mei shenme liaobuqi*) and Shen could not yet be rated a corrupt cadre because he did not bribe, embezzle or act villainously. This interpretation led them to the idea that the relationship was a kind of negatively valued bottom up vertical instrumental *wanglai*. Shen's own understanding was quite different. As a successful entrepreneur, he managed the village in the same way as he ran his business. He couldn't keep everybody happy, but generally he maintained expressive *wanglai* with as many people as he could. From my observation this was largely true.

Bribery is a complicated matter in China. The previous head of the village Zhou distinguished between bribery and necessary expenditure on business. He told me that in 2002 Kaixiangong Village spent 40,000 *yuan* on communications, sales promotions, or intercourse with others in order to carry on trade or other business dealings. Instead of the commonly used term *guanxi* fee, Zhou used the term *jiaowang* fee because he thought it sounds less negative, since it means necessary expenditure on business *wanglai* with others. So a *jiaowang* fee can be considered a token of instrumental *wanglai*, whereas a *guanxi* fee denotes negative *wanglai*.[49] Zhou agreed with this clarification of the difference between instrumental *wanglai* and negative *wanglai* (see Chapter XI.V).

2. Top down vertical instrumental *wanglai*

The following case of house construction involved a top down vertical instrumental *wanglai* between local officials with a village cadre, and the village cadre with villagers. House construction requires certain administrative formalities. This is an administrative relationship between villagers and the Township Land Bureau (TLB) and as such is not a case for *lishang-wanglai*. However, the vice Party Secretary of the village, JM Wang, told me that the conduct of this relationship had in this instance required the use of *guanxi*,or instrumental *wanglai*. In 1982 the TLB published a regulation that an application form with a plan should be signed by surrounding neighbours, and approved by the head of a group, village collective, and the Township Land Bureau. Fees were also stated quite clearly, i.e. building control fee, security fee, land occupancy fee, and a deposit of 1,000 to 2,000 *yuan* for a domestic house dependent on land size, or some amount up to 30,000 *yuan* for a workshop of a private industry enterprise. However, for the first few years a couple of dozen villagers ignored the regulations when they built new houses. Officials of the TLB asked JM Wang to rectify this problem on the grounds that he had "a good *guanxi* with your fellow villagers". Although it was not a part of Wang's job − or indeed anybody's, being a new phenomenon− he used his *guanxi* (instrumental *wanglai*) between local officials and villagers to make the regulations workable for about 14 years, until a new version of the regulation was issued in 1996.

Let us use *lishang* to find out how this worked.

(i) The officials of TLB needed JM Wang to do ideological work with the villagers. Wang found the villagers believed that it was wrong morally to have to ask permission and pay a

---

[49] Please note in this thesis I have no intention to treat business relationships with *lishang-wanglai*.

fee for their efforts in rebuilding a house where they had lived for generations. This was the main reason they ignored the regulation. The villagers praised Wang for helping many villagers go though the regulations and for bringing villagers' concerns to the township and eventually getting the regulation modified.

(ii) The villagers who went to the TLB for the administrative formalities with Wang did so partly to give him face (*gei mianzi*), because they were either old friends, family or personal relations. This kind of human feeling played a vital role in establishing the administrative relationship between the TLB and villagers.

(iii) A further reason the villagers refused to meet the TLB's regulation was that its figures for house size, dimensions, directions of location, and so on were unsuited to the village's location along the lakeside and river rather than on a plain. They wanted a more practical version, i.e. a proportion of foundation, house, courtyard, place for livestock, etc., rather than exact dimensions. Wang understood this kind of rational calculation, which is why he did not enforce fines against the households which exceeded the foundation site, or destroy the overstepped houses, but bargained for latitude by bringing many villagers to the TLB to go through administrative formalities and related payments. He believed that the more villagers he brought the more credit he could gain with local officials and the easier it would be for him to take part in policy making. In this he was correct. The adapted regulation was issued in 1985 and it worked well until 1996. Wang also won credit from his fellow villagers. Thus the administrative relationship between the TLB and villagers was fully established and he was no longer needed to do favours for either side.

Here is another case involving top down vertical instrumental *wanglai* from the village cadres to the villagers. Entering the Army through the back door (*zou houmen*) used to be a typical example of *guanxi* before the Social Reform (1970s). However, from the late 1990s onwards this situation was reversed, and it was the Village Collective that had to use *guanxi* to persuade reluctant villagers join the Army. The local township asks the village to choose one person a year to enter the army. A person selected to enter the Army fulfils his or her obligation to the state, but nobody would choose to do so due to loss of income or chances of other benefits, so selecting the candidate from among 20 or so villagers of the appropriate age involved *guanxi*. Normally, according to Zhou, a previous head of the village, physical exams would eliminate some candidates. The most difficult thing then was to draw on (*dongyong*) all kinds of *guanxi*, i.e. relatives and friends of the candidates and their families in the village or township to do "ideological work" (*sixiang gongzuo*) to intercede (*shuoqing*) on behalf of the village collective.

(i) "Ideological work" in this instance can be seen as engaging in a moral judgement as to "soft" and "hard" methods of persuasion. The hard way was to tell the candidate that on the call-up day two cars would come to collect him. One was a specially decorated "glory car (*guangrong che*)" to take the candidate to the Conscription Station at Wujiang City. The other would be a police car to take him to a police station.

(ii) The soft way was an intercession (*shuoqing*) by the village collective. The people who were village cadres or representative of the village collective would express deep concern for the candidate and his or her family and find out and sympathise with their particular reasons for not wanting to go. Moreover, the village collective would spend 500 or 1,000 *yuan* for the candidate's family's seeing-off feast. If a village cadre was invited for the feast he should bring a red bag of 1,000 *yuan* to attend it. If the family did not invite a village cadre for the feast, the village collective still needed to give a red bag of 500 *yuan* to the family to express its greeting.

(iii) Normally if a candidate went into the Army his or her family would receive an allowance of 4,200 or 4,500 *yuan* per year, the village enterprises would recompense the family by employing a member of it, or waiving fees, or making a special allowance for sick members it, and so on. Furthermore, the village collective made more offers to the candidates' families. If the person behaved very well in the Army and gained a title of "excellent soldier (*youdeng shibing*)", the allowance was increased by 10 per cent. If he kept the title for three years the allowance was increased by another 10 per cent. The village collective adjusted their offers according to the problems raised by a candidate's family, but did not accept all the offered bargains. For example, they agreed to repair a road to one candidate's house for free, which could cost a couple of thousand *yuan*, but a family which asked the collective to buy its newly bought motorcycle (about 10,000 *yuan*) on the grounds that it couldn't be used for three years while the candidate was in the Army, was refused. Based on criteria of rational choice the village collective refused this family because they didn't want to set a precedent for the future (*bukai xianli*).

(iv) The religious sense of *lishang* criteria can also be seen in this situation. Some families did not invite a village cadre to the seeing-off feast is because they believed this would bring even more bad luck to the family, even though this means they receive 500 *yuan* less from the village collective. Instead of saying "lucky" as they did in the past, nowadays the villagers think it is unlucky (*daomei*) that somebody has to go into the Army.

3. Bidirectional vertical instrumental *wanglai*

The bottom up and top down vertical instrumental *wanglai* always work reciprocally and can start from either direction. Here I will demonstrate a case which involved bidirectional vertical instrumental *wanglai* between local and senior officials and the village cadres. In 1996 all Kaixiangong Villages' Collective Enterprises were bankrupted with a total debt of nearly 10 million *yuan*. It was equivalent to 18,000 *yuan* of debt per household. Normally the relationship between the village collective enterprises and its lenders, such as a bank, credit union, local government and other enterprises, is a financial and business relationship. However, the process of borrowing and repayment to all parties involved bidirectional vertical instrumental *wanglai* with local or senior officials' personal relations.

The bankruptcy was occasioned when the heavily indebted collective village enterprises were privatised (*gaizhi* or *qiye zhuanzi*). By 2004 the debt was almost cleared. Initially a village cadre told me that they repaid 67% and avoided 33% of it. However, when I went through the details I found there were two tables. Table VIII-1 is an external table which can be provided to outsiders. It divided the debt into four categories: repaid (*huandiao*) 7.5%, mortgaged (*didiao*) 59.5%, avoided (*miandiao*) 23% and repudiated (*laidiao*) 10%. Table VIII-2 is for internal use because it was a true record but looks embarrassing (*bu guangcai*). It shows they only repaid 7.5%, mortgaged land, workshop and equivalents for 46% and repudiated the debt up to 46.5%.

Let's use *lishang* to demonstrate the case as a whole.

(i) A village cadre said they repaid 67% and avoided 33% of the debt because he believed the basic moral principle that a debt should be paid. For the village cadres the more debt that was paid and the less debt that was repudiated the better it sounded. So they made Table VIII-1. However, the 1,300,000 *yuan* in the "mortgages" column was actually repudiated, because the village collective mortgaged two dynamotors to the Shengze factory. The mortgaging was more symbolic than real the dynamotors were not worth more than 20,000 *yuan*. The Shengze factory eventually gave up the 1,300,000 *yuan*, for two rather different reasons, one a question of human feeling, in that the original investment in the Kaixiangong Village silk enterprise had been the achievement of a senior official in his post (*zhengji*) in Wujiang City, and it would be nice for him not to be worried by the outstanding debt. The other was that the Shengze factory had already gained back far more money than its original investment in 1988. Furthermore, this part of the debt should really be counted as repudiated because the village cadres had been asking the township and other sources under the control of the township government to waive it. So these two items went into the category of repudiated in Table VIII-2.

Table VIII-1 Kaixiangong cleared debt for the village enterprises (1996 – 2004) – external version (10,000 *yuan*)

Source 債源	Repay 還掉	Mortgaged 抵掉	Waived 免掉	Repudiated "賴掉"	Total 總計
Township Credit Union		440			440
Agricultural Bank	12			36	48
Shengze Silk Weaving Factory		130			130
Wuxi Light Industrial Products Factory				30	30
Miaogang Alcohol Factory				30	30
Miaogang Township Government			160		160
Others	60		60		120
Total %	72 (7.5%)	570 (59.5%)	220 (23%)	96 (10%)	958 (100%)

Table VIII-2 Kaixiangong cleared debt for the village enterprises (1996 – 2004) – internal version (10,000 *yuan*)

Source 債源	Repay 還掉	Mortgaged 抵掉	Repudiated "賴掉"	Total 總計
Township Credit Union		440		440
Agricultural Bank	12		36	48
Shengze Silk Weaving Factory			130	130
Wuxi Light Industrial Products Factory			30	30
Miaogang Alcohol Factory			30	30
Miaogang Township Government			160	160
Others	60		60	120
Total %	72 (7.5%)	440 (46%)	446 (46.5%)	958 (100%)

(ii) The village cadres expected the township government to be influenced by a common human feeling of sympathy towards the weak, which would lead them to allow the 23% debt owed to its various departments to be repudiated. After the village collective enterprises became bankrupt the redundant workers asked them to repay the account payable (*yingfu kuan*). The collective sold a plot of land to a private enterprise and paid off all the debt to the unemployed. It also fulfilled the debt of fund raising (*jizi kuan*) for the township hospital. The village cadres made the same case to the township officials and Wujiang City officials as the unemployed, explaining that the village was in too much difficulty to repay the debt, i.e.

300,000 *yuan* road work project loan to the Financial Bureau of Wujiang City, 150,000 *yuan* fee to Grain Management Institution of the township, 50,000 *yuan* construction arrears to the Construction Company of the township, 30,000 *yuan* fee to the Institution of Land Management. Both Wujiang City and Miaogang Township accepted the village's proposal and the 23% of debt was waived. The parlance (*shuofa*) behind the proposal was a Chinese character *kunnan* (difficulty). The *kun* of *kunnan* is the same character as the *kun* of *pinkun* (poor). The village cadres linked the debt with the aid-the-poor programme. Kaixiangong is certainly not a poor village (*pinkun cun*), but it was a village with a particular financial difficulty (*kunnan cun*). Every department of Wujiang City and Miaogang Township has its own quota of aid-the-poor expenditure, varying from around 20,000 *yuan* to 100,000 *yuan*, so Kaixiangong's debt could all be covered. This is how the village cadres argued, with eventual success.

(iii) Rational calculation was an important way for the village cadres to work out how to clear the debt. In China there were no laws or regulations related to bankruptcy of an enterprise run by a township or village (*xiangzhen qiye pochan fa*). However, there was a regulation that debt can be dismissed (*buyu duizhang*) two years after the legal procedure of bankruptcy. The village had in total 1,900,000 *yuan* of debt from three factories. By law, the debt could all have been dismissed. For the reason shown in i) the village only let 600,000 *yuan* of debt be dismissed in this way in order to keep the senior official's face. For the village the real problem was the biggest debt, of 4,400,000 *yuan* from the Credit Union of the Miaogang Township, which there was no way to avoid. The village mortgaged a large plot of land and a workshop to the Credit Union. At the same time it asked the township government to waive other debts instead (see last point ii)). As a village cadre pointed out, why should Kaixiangong Village take responsibility for the 4,400,000 *yuan* debt when it came about as a result of some senior officials of Wujiang City's informal notifications (*shangji lingdao da zhaohu*) to both the Credit Union and the village for its special situation.

(iv) During the seven years from 1997 to 2004 the village cadres had both good and bad luck over the matter of the debt. YG Zhou told me it was unfortunate that the village enterprises were bankrupted with a large amount of debt. Luckily the debt is now more or less cleared. A village cadre Yao told me the village was lucky to have had YG Zhou, the successful manager of a private company, as its head when all of the village enterprises were bankrupted. Unfortunately as soon as Zhou sorted out all the worst problems he lost his post. Zhou said a new policy of state banks cleaning up bad capital (*qingli buliang zichan*) came out in 2002, which enabled him to clean up the 480,000 *yuan* debt with a bank before he stepped out of the post. The village paid 120,000 *yuan* and the bank waived 360,000 *yuan*. Zhou said, one of his personal achievements as a head of the village for seven years was clearing the debt and clarifying procedures between village cadres and different officials. Institutions had wasted a lot of money, he would say, but the relationship between the officials concerned is mainly instrumental *wanglai*. They did not put the money into their own pockets, but they were promoted for using public resources inefficiently.

Furthermore, before I left the village a village cadre told me that thanks to Fei (*tuo Feilao de fu*) the village enterprises got 4,400,000 *yuan* loan from the local Credit Union. A few months later they said it was unfortunate the village was suffering such a big debt. The background to this change of attitude is that Kaixiangong was a fine example of the "Sunan model (successful enterprises of villages and towns of Southern Jiangsu Province)" advocated by Fei Xiaotong. Local officials thought a large loan would help them implement the model. And the timing had been good. Fei Xiaotong's 60 years' academic career conference was held in the village, which seemed auspicious for asking the local Credit Union and the village for such a big loan. A village cadre even said that Fei [*lao*] had an indissoluble bond (*bujie zhi yuan*) with Kaixiangong, having experienced a cycle of sixty years (*huajia*) in the village. Fei's first fieldwork, conducted in the village, had led to an internationally renowned book *Peasant Life in China* (1939). Now he got the privatisation of the collective enterprises off the ground by admitting that the South Jiangsu model was no longer suitable for the development of this area, winning over villagers who had complained about him. They were still proud of him.

Throughout these events, recurring ideas of lucky and unlucky, fortunate and unfortunate, *fu* and *yuan* embodied a religious sense.

VIII.II. Negative *wanglai*: vertical and horizontal *wanglai*

Instrumental *wanglai* was understood in Kaixiangong to be a relationship based on people's own skills and resources and ability to gain benefit for everyday life or emergencies. However if people use public resources to gain their personal benefits or mis-use materials or use other ways to gain a high status or control more resources, this should be counted as negative *wanglai*. As I mentioned in the case of Party Secretary Shen, the way he recruited workers was a case of instrumental *wanglai*. But if as a result the workers' social status was higher with more benefits, and Shen himself gained material benefit from distributing the posts, then the relationship between them was a case of negative *wanglai*.

Negative *wanglai* refers to three kinds of negative transactions: i) getting something for nothing, or taking much more and giving much less or return nothing, which is Sahlins's main usage[50]. This kind of horizontal relationship involves negative value (*guanxi jinzhang*). ii) Getting something for personal interests (such as a promotion by the back door), using public resources (from higher status people) or bribes of money or services (from lower status people), is a kind of vertical negatively valued relationship (*bu zhengchang guanxi*). iii) Getting something one wants by losing kinship, friendship or even life, which appears as a broken down relationship (*guanxi polie*). This can lead to extreme results: court proceedings for family abuse, estrangement between family members, or even suicide used as a method of revenge. I will omit previous researchers' related work (e.g. Sahlins 1972; Guo, 2001; Yan 1996b and 2003) and proceed to analyse vertical and horizontal negative valued relationships and broken down relationships.

1. A vertical negatively valued relationship

I've described the instrumental *wanglai* of a previous Party Secretary Shen who recruited workers from among his relatives and relations. It caused a negative *wanglai* between him and the villagers vertically, especially those villagers who lost their chances of gaining posts in the village enterprises. Although Shen gained material benefits from his mis-use of power, he lost trust from the majority of the villagers and eventually his post. This kind of negative *wanglai* is a negative value relationship, which appears in a hidden way. The villagers' complaints accorded with *lishang* criteria. i) Morally it is wrong that Shen gave certain positions in the

---

[50] See related review of Sahlins' negative reciprocity in Chapters VIII.II and IX.I.

village enterprises to people who sent him gifts. In Xiajia villagers also look down on such behaviour (Yan 1996b: 69-70). Shen lost trust from the villagers, especially those who lost opportunities unfairly. In return they did not support his work as they did with other village cadres such as Wang, Yao and Zhou. If a democratic system had been in place, the villagers would not have voted for Shen. ii) Many village girls told me that they were hurt that they didn't get places in the village enterprises because they didn't have good *guanxi* relations (*guanxi buhao*) with Shen. Instead of making a good showing (*zhengqi*) to Shen they went to far away places to earn bigger salaries. They laughed about this because they felt they had beaten Shen. iii) The girls told me that there were some criteria for getting into the village enterprises, such as a quota of one per household, disqualification of those with poor eyesight, priority for someone with a family member in the Army, and priority for those with a high school qualification. This is a rational way to judge different applicants. However, the redistribution of limited public resources is determined by local cadres. This provides space for some to pull *guanxi* or use bribery. iv) Many villagers told me that Shen wouldn't stay in power long. A few months after I left the village Shen did indeed lose his post as the Party Secretary of the village. During telephone conversations two villagers said this was god's will or providence (*tianyi*), which obviously involves their religious sense.

Based on villagers' discussions about the *lishang* criteria involved in the negative *wanglai* between Shen and the villagers, moral judgment and rational choice weighed most heavily. There are two sayings used by the villagers to judge a cadre or official in the village: they may have both ability and moral integrity (*de cai jianbei*) or corruption and incapacity (*fubai wuneng*). The villagers told me that Shen was not actually a corrupt cadre, but morally he was not very respectable and he was not able to do his job because he hired incompetent persons (*wuneng de ren*) for his own reasons, who managed the enterprises badly. After Shen left his post, Kaixiangong villagers enjoyed quoting the saying that if the economy did not go up then cadres must go down (*jingji shang buqu, ren jiuyao xialai*).[51] However, Shen said that he had been made a scapegoat for the village-run enterprises' failures. He asked how he could possibly be capable of saving such a desperate situation when the historical trend was against it. To prove

---

[51] According to a fieldwork report in a conference on the ESRC social support project (City University, London, 1993), there was a different situation in Heming village, Anhui Province where Zhu Weimin did his fieldwork in the ESRC social support project. Zhu found *guanxi* didn't work in Heming because the head of the village enterprise preferred to use able people (*nengren*), rather than relatives, to work for the enterprise.

his ability, Shen established his own business making silk and textile products. It was very successful, even though he still hired relatives.

This case involved vertical negative *wanglai* between a village cadre and the villagers. However, in real life there are many horizontal negative *wanglai* which exist in ordinary people's lives (Y. Yan 2003: 126 and 129). Here I will show a relationship between HW Zhou's family and her husband's sister's family, which involved a hidden, lifelong negative *wanglai*. Before I go ahead with the case I should point out that this family does not have any particular difficulty in making relationships. There are other types of *wanglai* that co-exist in the family, e.g. generous *wanglai* and expressive *wanglai* with their many close relatives.

2. A horizontal negative valued relationship

To clarify the relationships involved in the case I will provide two diagrams: the Zhao family and their relatives (Figure VIII-1)[52], and the Zhao family's non-agnatic kin (Figure VIII-2). I will then mark which relationships are involved in negative *wanglai* on Figure VIII-2.

Figure VIII-1   FL Zhou family tree

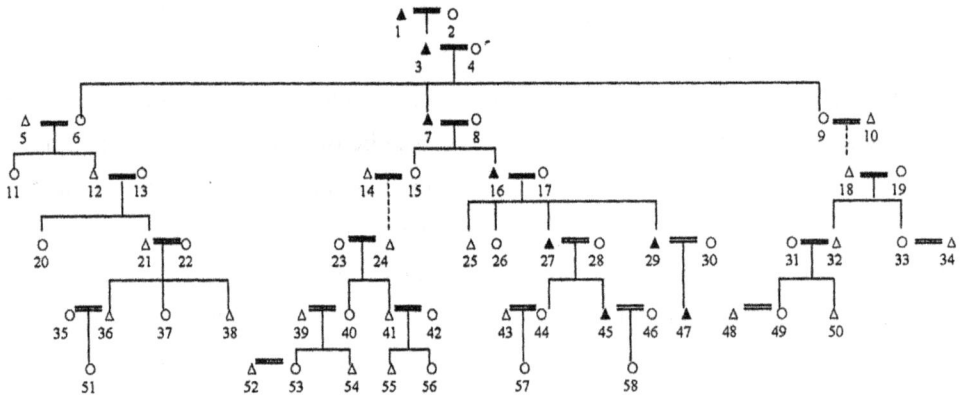

Interviewees: FL Zhou (No.16), HW Zhou (No.17) and XG Zhou (No 27)

Interviewers: Yinghao Lu (September 1991), Xiangqun Chang (Feb-May 1996 and October 2002)

---

[52] FL's story is quoted from Lu Yinghao's fieldwork notes.

The blackened code of ▲ means male head of the Zhou family; the empty codes of O △ means the rest of the members of the extended family came from the same clan.

1—HM Zhou; 2—XX Lu; 3—HR Zhou; 4—XX Zhang; 5—TQ Zhou; 6—AD Zhou; 7—RB Zhou; 8—AS Chen; 9—AN Zhou; 10—JR Chen; 11—XX Zhou; 12—SB Zhou; 13—AW Zhou; 14—RS Zhang; 15—AhN Zhou; 16—FL Zhou; 17—HW Zhou; 18—DB Chen; 19—XX Li; 20—XX Zhou; 21—YF Zhou; 22—YN Jin; 23—BN Zhang; 24—XQ Zhang; 25—XF Zhou; 26—XX Zhou; 27—XG Zhou; 28—MY Yao; 29—FS Zhou; 30—SZ Xu; 31—XX Chen; 32—JM Chen; 33—XX Chen; 34—XXX;

35—SB Zhou; 36—PG Zhou; 37—PY Zhou; 38—PQ Zhou; 39—XX Pan; 40—YN Zhang; 41—YH Zhang; 42—XXX; 43—RG Zhou; 44—XF Zhou; 45—YF Zhou; 46—LJ Chen; 47—ZF Zhou; 48—XXX; 49—XX Chen; 50—XX Chen; 51 to 56 –don't know; 57—CY Zhou; 58—MQ Zhou.

Background information for Figure VIII-1

FL Zhou's family tree includes 58 people and 7 generations. No. 16, FL, was the interviewee. He started the family tree with his great grandparents and grandparents. According to FL, his grandparents (No. 3 and 4) had three children, his father (No. 7) and two aunts (No 6 and 9). The old aunt (*da gugu* No. 6) married a farmer in Kaixiangong village. They have one daughter and one son (No. 11 and 12). Their son's family also has one daughter and one son (No. 20 and 21). Their son's family had two sons and one daughter (No. 36, 37, and 38). The older son's (No. 36) family had a daughter (No. 51). FL's younger aunt (*xiao gugu*, No.9) married a rich person in the other village of the same township. They didn't have a child and adopted a son (No. 18). The adopted son had one son and one daughter (No. 32 and 33). His son also had one son and daughter (No. 49 and 50).

FL's parents (No. 7 and 8) had one daughter and one son (No. 15 and 16). FL's sister (No. 15) married a man in the other village of the same township. They did not have their own child but adopted a son (No. 24). After the adopted son married he had one daughter and one son (No. 40 and 41). The daughter's family also had one daughter and one son (No 53 and 54). The son's family had twins, a son and daughter (No 55 and 56).

FL and his wife (No. 17), HW, had four children in total. The first boy (No. 25) died of dysentery when he was one year old and the second child, a girl (No. 26), died at birth. The third child, a son, was born in 1944. This older surviving son (No. 27), XG, married a village girl, MY (No.28), in 1964. They had a daughter and son (No. 44 and 45). The daughter XF (No.44) married out from the family in 1986 and the son YF (No. 45) married in 1990 and lived in the family. FL (no 17) and HW (No. 18) had their youngest child, a son (No. 29), FS, in 1953. After FS got married and had a baby in 1978 the Zhou family divided into three families: the old couple FL and HW as one family, XG's family and FS's family.

Figure VIII-2 XG Zhou's family non-agnatic kin

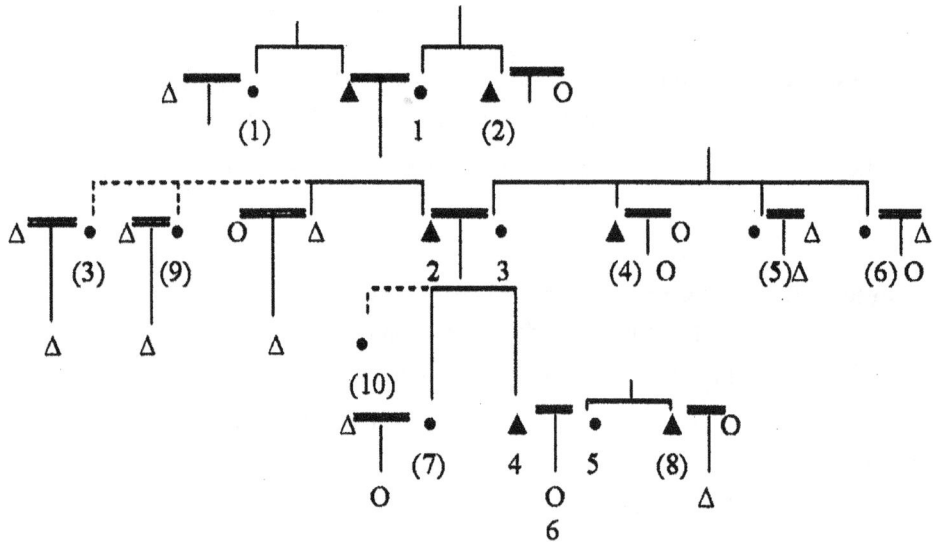

Members of family:

1—HM Zhou: XG's mother;

2—XG Zhou: XG;

3—MY Yao: XG's wife;

4—YF Zhou: XG's son;

5—LJ Chen: XG's daughter-in-law;

6—XX Zhou: XG's son's daughter.

Close kin (mainly non-agnatic kin):

(1)—XG's father's sister's family;

(2)—XG's mother's brother's family;

(3)—XG's mother's adopted daughter's family;

(4)—XG's wife's brother's family;

(5)—XG's wife's sister's family;

(6)—XG's wife's sister's family;

(7)—XG's married out daughter's family;

(8)—XG's son's wife's brother's family;

(9)—XG's married out daughter's quasi mother;

(10)—XG's daughter's quasi mother.

Interviewees: HW Zhou (No.1 of Chart 2) and XG Zhou (No. 2 of Chart 2 or 1 of Chart 3)

Interviewers: Xiangqun Chang (Feb-May 1996 and October 2002)

Notes:

- The blackened code of ▲ ● with numbers without ( ) means members of the given Zhou family;
- The blackened code of ▲ ● with numbers in ( ) shows how each non-agnatic kin was related the given Zhou family;
- The empty codes of △ ○ mean the remaining members of agnatic families.

This case, as told to me by HW Zhou (No 17 of Figure VIII-1 and No 1 of Figure VIII-2) involved horizontal negative *wanglai* between her family and her husband FL's father's younger sister AN's (No 9 of Figure VIII-1 and No1 of Figure VIII-2) family. AN asked FL's mother for her adopted son DB's wedding presents, in the full quantity expected from a *jiujiu* (mother's brother), just after FL's father had died and left two little boys. FL's mother complied but was reduced to poverty and ruin. Later, AN refused a bowl of rice to FL when he was very hungry and passing her door on a business trip. At the time, she was entertaining the head of the township (*wei xiangzhang*) with a grand feast for DB who was head of the village (*wei baozhang*) during the Japanese War period.[53]

In this case, one would think FL's mother was unwise to give away a family fortune in order to present grand wedding presents to her husband's nephew, AN's son. However, what FL's mother did can be understood with *lishang* criteria.

(i) Morally it was FL's mother's duty to provide grand presents for AN's son's wedding. She couldn't break the local custom, especially just after her husband died. The villagers kept different lists for major family events which recorded obligations, regarded as a special kind of debt. In order to keep the Zhou family's face and establish a good reputation as a new widow, FL's mother had to carry out the *jiujiu*'s family's duty for the nephew's wedding with most of the family property (see Chapter IV.I). This behaviour can be described with a Chinese saying "slap one's face until it's swollen in an effort to look imposing (*da zhong lian chong pangzi*)".

(ii) However her motivation can be described with some Chinese sayings related to feelings of the human heart, such as "poverty can't chill one's vital energy of ambition (*ren qiong*

---

[53] *Bao* is an old administrative system organised on the basis of households. It is equivalent to a village.

zhi bu duan)", "try to make a good show with vital energy (*zhengqi*)", be swayed by personal feelings (*yiqi yongshi*), etc.

(iii) Although AN seems greedy, and indeed was, depending on one's point of view, she only claimed for a *jiujiu*'s (mother's brother) family's share for DB's wedding presents. The major gifts are a huge wedding cake equivalent to 150kg rice, a special hat like an official's hat in Qing dynasty and a big envelope with gift money, etc. They were equivalent to the family's expenditure for one whole year. They were in line with the local custom, and to comply with this custom can be seen as a rational choice.

(iv) HW told me that AN received fair retribution (*baoying*), which determined her fate (*ming*). She was a greedy person. She desired to be a rich lady and married a rich man, JR Chen, in another village of the same township. After JR's elder brother and his wife died, AN and JR adopted their son, DB Chen, and inherited their property. Their family became a big landlord. After her husband died AN controlled all the Chen family's property. However, AN could not save herself from misfortune. Firstly, she could not have her own child, commonly agreed to be one of the biggest misfortunes possible. Secondly, she became a widow while she was still middle-aged. She then lost most of her property before the Liberation in 1949 because her adopted son DB was not good at managing, but her family was still tarnished with the classification as landlord class during land reform. Consequently her grandson's fiancée's family broke off the engagement that had been made before the Liberation. Finally, she died a few years after the Liberation. HW, who told me this story, believed out of her own experience that sweetness and bitterness moved in cycles in AN's life. That is to say her life mixed happy times and hardships at different stages of her life journey, but no-one, said HW, could be either happy all their lives, or unhappy.

Although HW was quite clear that the relationship between the Zhou family and AN's family was mainly negative *wanglai*, she agreed it was not absolutely fixed. At times it became instrumental *wanglai*. HW told me that both AN and DB had contacts with FL's family before the Liberation in 1949, although FL's family was poor. When FL needed money for an emergency he borrowed some money from his aunt, although AN charged him usurious interest. At this period the relationship between these two families can be seen as instrumental *wanglai*. However, after the Liberation AN's family were classified as of the landlord class and FL stopped the physical *wanglai* with the family because it would have affected his political career, as he was the second member of the Communist Party and one of the heads of Kaixiangong

Village. But the negative *wanglai* remained because the negative feelings were still there.

3. A rupture case in a broken down relationship

In written Chinese a broken down relationship is called *guanxi polie*, whereas orally people describe such negative *wanglai* with *si po lian* (literally, put aside all considerations of face or not spare somebody's sensibilities). I recognised one Chinese characteristic is to be allusive (*hanxu*), not liking to "poke a hole in the window paper", which allows a safe space for people to work out different types or qualities of personal relationships (see Chapter IX.III). Normally, in a relationship of "face society" (Hu's term, 1944) if one's face is not cared for in public the relationship can be counted as a broken down relationship in a negative *wanglai*. It might be repaired, though that would be very difficult. More probably it more likely leads to its extreme end: court proceedings for family abuse (Y. Guo 2001; Y. Yan 2003: 168), long-term estrangement, or even one party taking revenge against another by committing suicide (Y. Yan 2003: 86 & 162).

I interviewed HW Zhou in 1996 and found a case of negative *wanglai* involving rupture. Figure VIII-3 will show the relationships between the two brothers and the relationship between the younger son's family and his parents.

Figure VIII-3 XG Zhou family's close kin list

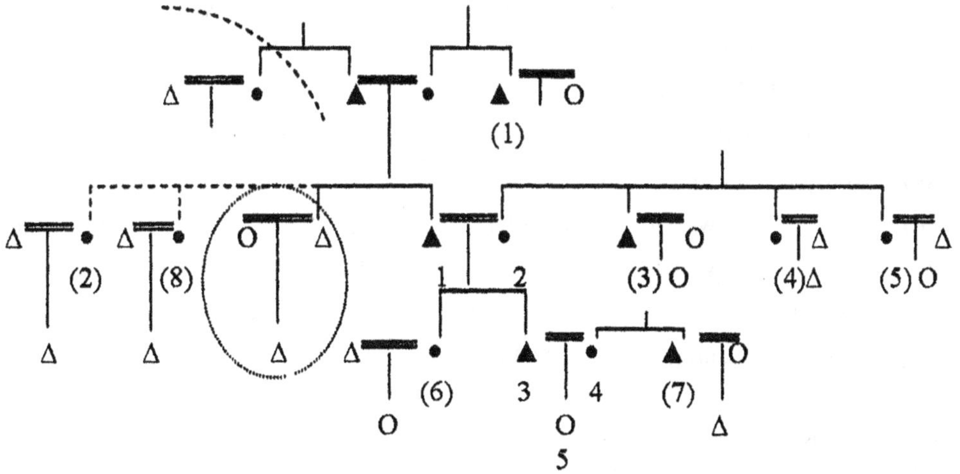

Members of family: Close kin (non-agnatic kin):

1—XG Zhou: XG;

2—MY Yao: XG's wife;

3—YF Zhou: XG's son;

4—LJ Chen: XG's daughter-in-law;

5—XX Zhou: XG's son's daughter

(1)—XG's mother's brother's family;

(2)—XG's mother's adopted daughter's family;

(3)—XG's wife's brother's family;

(4)—XG's wife's sister's family;

(5)—XG's wife's sister's family;

(6)—XG's married out daughter's family;

(7)—XG's son's wife's brother's family;

(8)—XG's married out daughter's quasi mother.

Interviewees: HW Zhou (No.1 of Chart 2) and XG Zhou (No. 2 of Chart 1 or 2 of Chart 3)

Interviewers: Xiangqun Chang (Feb-May 1996 and October 2002)

Notes:

- The blackened code of ▲ ● with numbers without ( ) means members of the given Zhou family;

- The blackened code of ▲ ● with numbers in ( ) shows how each non-agnatic kin is related to the given Zhou family;

- The empty codes of △ ○ means the rest of members of agnatic families.

- Outside the dotted arc is XG's father's sister's family which should be on XG's family's close kin list. However XG's family stopped *wanglai* with it due to a negative relationship between the two families (see Chapter VIII.II).

- Inside the oval is FS's family, which should be agnatic kin of XG's family. Since the brothers' families broke up, FS's family has had no relationship with XG's family (also see Chapter VIII.II).

HW Zhou told me that in 1978 the Zhou family divided into three nuclear families: she and her husband were one, her older son and younger son's families were the other two.[54] Ever since her husband passed away in 1995, she has been living with her older son, XG's family, which became a stem family. It is unusual for a mother to live with her older son's family and contra to local tradition.[55] This drew my attention to an example of negative *wanglai* between a son / younger brother and a mother / older brother's families.

---

[54] HW is No 17, XG is No. 27 and FS is 29 in Figure 5; HW is No1, XG is No.2 in Figure 6.

[55] It says that a mother should always live with a younger son because normally an older son marries and separates from the joint family earlier. Moreover, it is a mother's job to look after the younger son's child and in return it is mainly the younger son's job to look after the aged mother.

The Zhou family made a family division in 1978, and the younger son, FS, was involved in a big scandal with his parents and brother's family in 1986. The incident that touched off a family war was the quota for transferring a rural registered resident to a much-sought-after urban registration (*nong zhuan fei zhibiao*). A new policy procured this privilege for HW.[56] Since she was then 70, she and her husband decided to give the opportunity to XG's son, their oldest grandson, YF, who was serving in the Army. FS thought this decision was unfair and had a row with his parents, shouting that he would stop providing them with his share of grain ration, 500 *jin* per year. Afterwards, HW went to see FS wanting to make up with him but instead was involved with him in physical violence. FS hit her on the head several times. The fight was stopped, but the dispute hardened the relationship between FS and his parents. The village collective and even the court in the township could not mediate the family quarrel. Finally, FS broke with his parents by announcing that he would never take any responsibility for his parents from life to death (*yeniang shengsi buguan*). Even when his parents passed away in 1995 and 2000 he remained untouched. By 2004 the two brothers' families' relationship still remained negative. Although the relationship between FS and his parents and brother's families seemed to have stopped after the serious family quarrel, it can actually be categorised as a negative *wanglai* because their enmity kept the relationship active. They were still thinking of each other, in a negative way.

This case involved a mixed vertical negative *wanglai* between HW and FS, and horizontal *wanglai* between XG and FS's families. Let me first use *lishang* criteria to illustrate the vertical negative *wanglai* between the mother HW and the younger son FS.

(i) On the one hand, some old villagers told me that FS's case was a typical example of returning kindness with enmity (*en jiang chou bao*) and he was a non-filial son (*buxiao*), because he grew up during the Cultural Revolution when traditional moral codes were destroyed. On the other hand, FS insisted he was morally right that his parents should have consulted him about such an important family matter. FS has also kept his promise and has had nothing to do with the Zhou family since the serious family quarrel, because it is morally right to be true to one's word.

---

[56] HW was a child labourer in the silk factory established by Fei Dasheng (Fei Xiaotong's sister) when she was 13 years old until the Japanese War broke out. After the war she worked in different silk factories in Suzhou City and Zhenze Township. Like many people in the special difficult period after three years of natural disasters in 1962, HW lost her urban registered residence and was sent back to her hometown, Kaixiangong Village. To rectify this, under the new policy HW could be transferred from a rural registered resident to urban.

(ii) The major cause of the expressive *wanglai* between FS's family and his parents turning into a negative *wanglai* is that FS acted impetuously. FS told me that although he said he would never look after his parents' later life, it was said in a fit of rage. After the fight with his mother he still prepared a big gunnysack of unhusked rice for his parents as usual. But instead of sending it to their house he expected one of them to collect it because he felt embarrassed to face them. However, this did not happen. FS told me that he always wanted to make up with his parents and brother's families after the fights, if only they would forgive him.

(iii) FS's rational judgement was that the opportunity of transferring to an urban registered residency would have taken him "from hell into Heaven"[57]. He was 33 years old with little hope of escaping from a rural area, whereas YF was just 20 years old with a bright future in the Army.[58]

(iv) Religious sense is the fourth criterion. HW told me, from her point of view, the most convincing explanation for the negative *wanglai* between her family and her younger son's family is fate. She didn't think she could change it. When I asked HW whether or not FS would receive retribution (*baoying*) for treating his parents badly she choked down her tears and repeated, perhaps, it was a retribution (*baoying*) for her own sin (*zuonie*) in giving birth to FS and then not bringing him up properly herself. She told me that she worked in the Town from FS's birth until he was 9 years old. She also told me that for an aged person there were two "door steps" to the other world, which were called seventy three and eighty four (*qishisan bashisi*). It meant that if one had enough *fu* one's life could last for seventy-three years, or even eighty-four. HW said she had passed the milestone of seventy-three years and was content with her life. But she would not pass the milestone of eighty-four because she was partly responsible for the great misfortune of the broken relationship with FS and his family[59]. In the end HW told me that she forgave FS and would pray for him not to receive retribution (*baoying*) for what he did to his parents. Later I heard that HW Zhou died in 2000, just 84 years old.

I will now show a horizontal negative *wanglai* between the older brother XG and the younger brother FS's families with *lishang* criteria. (i) XG is a model example of paying a debt

---

[57] This was true enough until privatisation. But from the late 1990s it was no longer such a privilege to be an urban registered resident. YF even returned to the village from the town to work in the family business.

[58] YF was just 3 marks below the pass mark for an army college and was promised by his company commander that he could try again the following year. According the then current State policy if YF graduated college he was a life in an urban area with a white collar job, which was a dream for a villager.

[59] HW died in 2000 when she was aged eighty-four.

of gratitude (*bao'en*) to his parents in the village. Although his parents lived apart as a separate household after the family division, they were well looked after from their later years to death and burial by XG and his wife. Normally, a relationship between parents and grown up children is categorised as expressive *wanglai*. Only when grown up children treat their elderly parents extremely well, as did XG, will they be praised as a filial or dutiful son or daughter (*xiaozi or xiaoshun nu'er*) by the villagers. Their relationship was one of generous *wanglai*. After the split between FS's family's and his parents and brother's families, XG claims that FS returned his parents' kindness with enmity. It was unforgivable that FS remained untouched when their parents passed away in 1995 and 2000. From XG's point of view, FS lost the chance ever to reunite with his family after their mother died. But, from FS's point of view, it was XG who took away his chance of returning kindness to his parents forever as a punishment for the family dispute. XG's son, YF, confirmed that punishment of his un-filial uncle was part of his parents' filial duty to their grandparents. In this case punishment meant the exclusion of FS from the Zhou family. XG's determination to punish his brother is the main reason why the rift between his parents and his brother's family could not be healed. But YF suggested that he could perhaps reinterpret the moral code to mean that the Zhou family should be reunited to comfort the soul of his grandparents. YF said that he might find a gap (*tupokou*) to turn the hidden negative *wanglai* into a visible expressive *wanglai*, but it would take time.

(ii) From FS's side, the main reason he did not turn the negative *wanglai* into an expressive *wanglai* is emotional. He eventually gave up all hope that his parents or brother would forgive him and felt deeply hurt. He thought he had been punished and abandoned by all of them. He was swayed by his emotions and developed feelings of hate that prevented him from mending the relationship when it might have been possible, during the periods when his parents were ill and passed away. I asked him why he was unaffected by his parents deaths? He explained that he had been excluded from the Zhou family, so he had had no chance to express himself. If his brother had come to his house and told him the sad news of his father or mother's death he would have definitely done his duty and attended the funeral. In 1993 YF told me that the reason his generation still did not *wanglai* with each other was because both sides felt too embarrassed to make it up first (*buhao yisi xian kaikou*). It was a kind of human feeling which has to do with face. FS's son had graduated from Tianjin University and worked in Wujiang City and recognised his father's desire to be an urban resident. YF did not want to get close to FS's son because he did not want to be thought to be flattering him someone whose social status was higher than his own, in that he had graduated from university and got a good job in Suzou City.

(iii) Rational calculation is the third criterion. XG explained that according to a local custom regarding illness (*wangxin*), the relatives, neighbours and fellow villagers were supposed to have informed FS on their own initiative. So he did not go to his brother's house to tell him about his parents' illness personally. But FS quoted a different local custom according to which it was XG's duty to inform him about his parents' death (*baosang*). These two pairs of reasons appear to be based entirely on rational calculation. But they could not stop things getting worse.

(iv) There did not seem to be any religious feeling behind the brothers' relationship. However, I found that XG still held by his duty to his parents to never *wanglai* with FS, which affected religious activities. After I finished the "funeral section" of the dissertation on which this book is based I rang XG to test whether or not he still qualifies to be a filial or dutiful son.[60] I asked him the dates of the anniversaries of his parents' deaths (*jiri*). He told me emotionally "My father's is on the third day of the fifth lunar month, and mother's is on the second day of the eleventh lunar month". He had been holding a memorial ceremony once a year for each of them and would continue to do so until the end of his life. Whenever he worshipped them he told them that he would not forgive FS. But he would not stop the younger generation from sorting out the remaining family matters in their own way.

4. A suicide case in a broken down relationship

BY Zhou told me of a case which involved the suicide of her sister and negative *wanglai* between families horizontally and generations vertically. BY's older sister BZ married RF Rao in 1964 when they were both 22 years old. After they got married they had two boys, but the marriage was not a happy one. Moreover BZ's parents-in-law treated her badly. She committed suicide by drinking a large quantity of pesticide in 1972.

This suicide turned an expressive *wanglai* into negative *wanglai* between the Zhou and Rao families horizontally, which can be understood with *lishang* criteria as follows. (i) BZ's suicide can be explained as retaliation (*baofu*) against her mother-in-law which morally counted as the righteous act of objecting to an oppressor (*yiju*). BZ was generally unhappy with her marriage, but her suicide was immediately after she had a big row with her mother-in-law. BZ's suicide roused BY's family and her mother's relatives to great indignation. Dozens of people were organised immediately and went to the Rao family to avenge (*baochou*) BZ's death. They said

---

[60] I learned this way from a villager at a late stage of my writing when I looked at my fieldwork notes about funerals.

they wanted to kill BZ's husband RF and put him at the bottom of her coffin to accompany his wife (*peizang*). This was allowable according to a very old village custom., which also sanctioned the tearing off of rooftiles from the Rao family's house.[61] BZ would be satisfied if she could watch it from the nether world, BY said.

(ii) The extremes of attitude and behaviour shown by this revenge (*baochou*) were caused by human feelings. The relatives were truly filled with grief and indignation and expressed their anger to the Rao family for their treatment of BZ. They then expressed these feelings in extreme ways, rather similar to "embodying *ganqing*" (Kipnis's term, 1997).

(iii) The final outcome of the suicide was settled on the basis of rational choice. According to local custom, RF should die with his wife by lying on the bottom of her coffin to accompany her (*peizang*) and the Rao family's house should be demolished. However, in Kaixiangong Village there had not been a case of suicide for decades. BY's had family moved into the village from a fishing village in the Zhenze Township in 1955. After the suicide all the relatives came from Zhenze and heard about this custom from Kaixiangong villagers. The outward expression of feeling gave BY the opportunity to work hard and stop her relatives from settling the score in this drastic fashion. In reality if they killed RF it might get BY's family into trouble because the custom had been disused for a very long time. If they destroyed the Rao family house they would probably get away with it, according to the local custom, but then where would the two little boys have lived? BY believed the boys should be considered the top priority. So she made a proposal that the Rao family bury BZ with full honours (*houzang*) and give assurances that the orphan boys would grow up in the Rao family meaning that theywere not to be adopted by other people under any circumstances. Her proposal was accepted and agreement reached between the two families, avoiding a vicious circle of revenge between them. BY's creativity in working out a solution to the conflict between tradition and the present actuality allowed a rational and sensible solution.

(iv) I mentioned earlier that BZ's act of suicide could be seen as a kind of revenge (*baofu*), and the villagers described its negative effect on the Rao family as retribution (*baoying*), which embodied a religious sense. BZ believed her death could be used to call on her natal family's resources to punish her married family. And she also hoped to turn into a ghost to frighten her

---

[61] This is mentioned in Fei Xiatong's first monograph. If the daughter-in-law committed suicide her own parents and brothers will seek redress, even destroying her husband's house and she will become a spirit and is able to revenge herself (1939:49).

mother-in-law.

This suicide also exposed a vertical negative *wanglai* between BZ and her mother. There is no doubt that BZ had a negative *wanglai* with her parents-in-law. Thus one of the main reasons for her suicide was to take revenge on them. It was the most difficult thing for BY to admit that BZ's suicide was also retribution for her beloved mother's marriage arrangements for BZ. I could not interview BZ to verify this, but I showed BY interview notes, by Lu Feiyun of the ESRC project. She agreed with my explanation with the *lishang* criteria.

(i) BZ twice obeyed her mother's marriage arrangements for her because she thought morally it was her obligation to repay her mother for the great debt of her mother's upbringing of her. The first time was when she married her adopted brother, AM, who was two years older than her, when she was 14 years old. After they got married they didn't get on well and had a difficult time for years. The second marriage was eight years later when she married her younger sister BY's boyfriend RF, and BY married her ex-husband AM. BY told me that by then both she and her sister had escaped from their mother's morality. BY's mother had married a man whom she did not love, as arranged by her family. Then BY's father became disabled physically and her mother had to look after him until his death, when BY was aged 13. Her mother had also worked very hard to bring up four children after her husband passed away.

(ii) BZ thought her mother didn't care for her feelings when she arranged marriages for her, one after the other. BY also told me that her mother ignored BZ's happiness. BZ's suicide was an extreme way of expressing her feelings.

(iii) BY admitted that her mother's series of mistakes over her and her sister's marriage arrangements caused her sister's tragedy, even though they were based on rational choice. When she was born in 1948 she had an 8-year-old adopted brother AM and a 6-year-old sister BZ. When BY was 4 years old her mother adopted a 7-year-old boy BX as a son-in-law-to-be (*tongyangxu*) for her. Her mother's plan was to get the two daughters to marry the two adopted boys. Such marriage plans were in line with a popular Chinese saying, get married first and then be in love (*xian jiehun hou lianai*). BY's mother's change of the plan of marrying BY and BX was also a rational choice because she could see that they didn't love each other. She then accepted RF Rao's family's marriage proposal for her daughter BY. However, after BZ and AM's marriage failed, she became aware that AM was in love with BY and rational choice again changed her mind. She swapped the marriage arrangements that BY should marry AM and BZ marry RF Rao, although BZ was not happy with it.

(iv) BY told me that her mother regretted the swap of her two daughters' marriages before her death. She repeated the word of *baoying* (retribution), which has quite a strong religious sense, about her behaviour in making BZ marry RF. She experienced one of the commonly agreed worst misfortunes in life, that her daughter died much earlier than her, a situation described in a Chinese saying, "people with white hair attended the funeral of a person with black hair" (*baifaren song heifaren*).

This case shows the *wanglai* between the two families changing from expressive *wanglai* down to negative *wanglai*, and from negative *wanglai* up to expressive *wanglai* again. After BZ was buried with full honours (*houzang*) the two families' relationship became one of instrumental *wanglai* occasioned by necessary contact with each other about the two orphan boys. Although it was very hard for BY's family to forgive the Rao family, the relationship between her family and the two Rao surnamed boys increased to the expressive *wanglai* of close relatives (*jinqin*). I saw the boys when I was there. They have become fathers now, with their wives and children attending a feast on the lunar New Years Day in BY's house. When BY's son got married in 2002 these two cousins' families loaned 20,000 *yuan* to him, which were his biggest sources of financial support. Their *wanglai* was the same as before BZ's death.

To sum up, the above cases show that negative *wanglai* does not always take place at a distance, just as a generous *wanglai* does not necessarily come from close kin. These findings differ from Fei's (1947) *chaxugeju* and Sahlins's (1972) reciprocity model of close kin, which assume generalised reciprocity (199) (see my discussion of Sahlins' ideas in IX.I). Revenge (*baochou*) is the "extreme end" embodying discontinuity: a repayment that terminates the exchange behaviour. For an example, it was a kind of revenge when JR, who had been adopted out of his natal family many years before, refused his brother's proposal of reunion. But his hostility gradually diminished. BY Zhou's family also gave up their revenge on the Rao family after BY's settlements were realised. Once an action of revenge was finished a new kind of *wanglai* could take a place between the two parties. Yan's (1996b) finding in Xiajia also supports this (143-144). Both *baoying* (retribution) and *lishang-wanglai* have the character of moving in cycles of endless repetition. It can be in one's own life, i.e. FY or in one's family as in the Tan Family (see Chapter VIII.II). This kind of movement can be seen in different ways, i.e. fortune and misfortune can take turns in one's life cycle, or through a family's generations. *Lishang-wanglai* networks can be changed in different ways (see Chapter IX.II). As we have seen earlier anybody can have any one of generous, expressive, instrumental and negative *wanglai*, or all of them at the same time with others, or have one type of *wanglai* at one time and other *wanglai* at another time with the same relation. The changes of different types of *wanglai*, or updating *lishang-wanglai* networks, can be natural, or deliberately made through social creativity. Analysing the modification of *wanglai* between close relatives requires much understanding of *lishang*. Any such change or adaptation, however big or small, can be seen as a reaction to local customs, demanding coherent reasons (*lishang*).

PART THREE

"LISHANG-WANGLAI" MODEL

Part Three consists of four chapters. Chapter IX reviews theories of reciprocity, social support and social creativity. Firstly, it reviews Marshall Sahlins's theory of reciprocity in great detail, follows with Karl Polanyi's notion of redistribution and Talcott Parsons's personalized relations Then, in sequence with social support and network theory, the *lishang-wanglai* network is introduced and used to demonstrate how resources (money, goods, information) flow via different types of *wanglai*, with causes or reasons for change of type. Finally, social creativity theory is introduced, which provides a tool for further understanding the mechanisms of *lishang-wanglai*. Through discussion the author reaches the conclusion that social creativity is the driving force of the ego-centred *lishang-wanglai* networks.

Chapter X reviews a number of China-related terms, *mianzi* (face), *chaxukeju* (social egoism), *yuan*, *bao*, *huhui*, *guanxi*, *renqing*, *ganqing*, *yang* and *laiwang*. Scholars from mainland China, Hong Kong, Taiwan and overseas have successfully forged concepts from social and cultural matrices for use in their study of Chinese society. Studies on China produced by non-Chinese scholars based on methodologies of social science are equally valuable. Both Chinese and non Chinese scholars' efforts play an active role in promoting the integration of Chinese scholarship into the world of global social science research. Discussion of the different types of relationships in China and their corresponding principles will lead to the concept I then introduce, the core concept of this book: *"lishang-wanglai"*, which runs through the book from beginning to end.

After descriptions of the fieldwork site and analysis of empirical data in the eight chapters of Part One and Two, and studies on both Western and Chinese literatures in chapter IX and X of Part Three, chapter XI concentrates on the concept of *lishang-wanglai* itself. This enlarges on the material in section II of chapter IX and continues with an introduction of the origin of *"li shang wanglai"*, a separation of *lishang-wanglai* into its parts *"lishang"* and *"wanglai"* and a refinement of their contents. It then moves on to demonstrate how instrumental *wanglai* turns to negative *wanglai* via a kind of negative-valued instrumental *wanglai*. Finally, this chapter points out that *"lishang-wanglai"* model has methodological implications.

Chapter XII further demonstrates the concept of *"lishang-wanglai"* and discusses the model's methodological implications, apparent even though *"Lishang-wanglai"* itself is not a method. Whether or not *"lishang-wanglai"* can be developed as a general analytic concept still needs much testing. Although in the 1980s Chinese intelligentsia were aware of the importance of forging conceptual tools with Chinese characteristics based on empirical research (Chang 1992:546), much of this work is still immature and still challenges Chinese scholars after three decades. Stephan Feuchtwang always encourages Chinese colleagues to make contributions to world anthropological theory using conceptualization based on China studies (Feuchtwang, 2001:57). In this chapter I will try to use myself as an object of study, to analysis my own fieldwork experiences with *"lishang-wanglai"*, and extend this attempt to Feuchtwang, my supervisor, based on his experiences on a field visit in Kaixiangong and Wujiang County − hoping to use the relationships between local officials and a foreign professor and the subtle changes of types of *wanglai* involved in them to further elucidate the operating mechanism of *lishang-wanglai.*

Chapter IX

Theoretical approaches and exploration of

"lishang-wanglai"

The ESRC project and my fieldwork show that resource exchanges, in which reciprocity is central, play a leading role in the arrangement of social support among rural Chinese people. This confirms previous researchers' studies on social support related reciprocity[1]. To help readers understand the villagers' reciprocal relationships that I have described in the previous chapters, this chapter will review related theories on reciprocity, social support networks and social creativities. Section 1 will review Sahlins (1972)'s theory on reciprocity in considerable detail, and briefly introduce Polanyi's (1944) thoughts on different kinds of exchange and Parsons's (1939) personalised relations. Section 2 will review social support network studies through which the *"lishang-wanglai* network" is introduced. It will also show how resources, such as money, gifts and information, are transferred between an individual or family and their networks, and how *lishang-wanglai* networks function. Finally, in section 3 the theory of social creativity is introduced from Chinese and Western perspectives. It will further explore the motivation of ego-centred *lishang-wanglai* networks and draw the conclusion that social creativity is the driving force of *lishang-wanglai*.

IX.I. Sahlins's reciprocity, Polanyi's redistribution and Parsons's personalised relations

Reciprocity, as a principle, was first introduced by Mauss in his (1925) "the spirit of the gift" (1967:8-9). Instead of his earlier categories of the "pure gift" and "real barter" (1922), Malinowski (1926) articulates the principle of reciprocity and concludes "the principle of give-and-take" is the foundation of Melanesian social order (chapters 3, 4, 8, and 9). Levi-Strauss (1949) believes the principle of reciprocity can be the foundation of all social relations (1969:84). Meanwhile other researchers challenged Mauss' views of *hao* of the Maori.

---

[1] e.g. Cobb 1976, Dunkel-Schetter, 1984, Gouldner 1960, Greenberg 1980, Shumaker, 1983, G. J. Wentowski 1981.

Firth (1959) argues about the importance of the Maori's *utu* to the notion of "compensation" or "equivalent return" (12ff.). Marshall Sahlins's (1965a and b, 1972/74) elaboration of reciprocity and the links between material flow and social relations in primitive economies particularly interests me. Sahlins's reciprocal theory is based on a 'primitive' economical society. When introduced into China, a highly complex and advanced country, this caused much confusion. Amongst many studies on reciprocity, in this section, I will first focus on Sahlins's work within the context of the related studies in China. I then briefly introduce Polanyi's thoughts about redistribution because they are both close to my study.

1. A review of Sahlins's reciprocity

I will summarise Sahlins's ideas first. He proposed the use of reciprocity in anthropology to define a set of exchange relationships among individuals and groups. He suggests that these types of reciprocity form a continuum, which correlates with kinship and social distance. He identifies three variables as critical to determining the general nature of gift giving and exchange: kinship distance, sociability, and generosity. He also introduces a tripartite division of exchange phenomena to demonstrate the universality of reciprocity: generalized reciprocity, balanced reciprocity and negative reciprocity. Generalized reciprocity, as posited by Sahlins, is the solidary extreme and characterises interactions between close kinsmen or within a restricted and intimate social group. "Generalized reciprocity" refers to transactions that are putatively altruistic, transactions on the lines of assistance given and, if possible and necessary, assistance returned. The ideal type is Malinowski's "pure gift." Other indicative ethnographic formulas are "sharing," "hospitality," "free gift," "help," and "generosity". The free gift or the sharing of resources without strict measurement or obligation to repay is the norm. Thus close kinsmen often assist one another and interchange food and other goods without any strict expectation of return, other than the existence of a diffuse obligation of a moral rather than economic nature to reciprocate or to assist when needed. Examples include parents housing and feeding children or paying for their education. "Balanced reciprocity" refers to direct exchange. In precise balance, the reciprocation is the customary equivalent of the thing received and is immediate. It is the midpoint and is the form of exchange between structural equals who trade or exchange goods or services. Balanced reciprocity is less personal and moral, and more economic in type. "Negative reciprocity" is the attempt to get something for nothing with impunity. It is characteristic of interactions between enemy or distant groups and is the attempt to maximise utility at the expense of the other party. Negative reciprocity ranges from haggling to theft and raiding or warfare. It is the most impersonal sort of exchange. In the end Sahlins shows reciprocity is a measure of social distance, on a scale from very close: close kinship, marriage, to very far: trade and war. The greater the social distance, the closer to negative reciprocity, like war (1972:185-230).

Among the above three reciprocities the different uses of "balance" must be noted. The whole point of gift exchange is that "balance" is always deferred in every exchange except market exchange. Only in market or barter exchange is the balance completed in the single act of exchange. Market exchange is a separate category. Many researchers have used Sahlins's model of reciprocity as a framework for analysis of their data.[2] My fieldwork experiences verify the widespread existence of a combination of Sahlins's three types of reciprocity. However, this generalised concept of reciprocity has many drawbacks.

(1) Sahlins's typology of reciprocity is not enough to describe my fieldwork in Kaixiangong. Based on my fieldwork I proposed a *wanglai* typology (see Chapter XI.V)[3] by combining Sahlins's (1965) typology of reciprocity and Befu (1966-67) or Yan's (1996b) categories of expressive exchange and instrumental exchange. I did not use Sahlins's notion of balanced reciprocity because both expressive and instrumental exchanges normally are balanced, otherwise they can be counted as generous or negative *wanglai*. I use Sahlins's category of generalized reciprocity but describe it less ambiguously as "generous *wanglai*" to highlight its character of "pure gift", "free gift", and "generosity". I also have included the negative reciprocity as negative *wanglai*.

However, my use of the term negative *wanglai* differs from Sahlins'. It is not clear why the two extremes, altruism and theft, are to be called reciprocity, since no reciprocal transfer is involved. Also, Sahlins did not make a distinction between terminating a relationship and turning one type of exchange relationship into another. For me, ending a relationship "naturally" won't affect the parties emotionally, for instance Kaixiangong villagers normally would end a relationship with one or more of their distant old-generational relatives (*laoqin*) after the marriage of a son because of their involvement with a new generational relative (*xinqin*), and this is expected. But turning one type of exchange relationship into another would continue to

---

[2] e.g. Befu 1967, 1968, 1974, Davis 1973, Hostetler & Huntington 1967, Johnson 1974, Paine 1971; or to test it with their own field data, e.g. Brady 1972, Damas 1973.
[3] I use different types of *wanglai* instead of reciprocity because I am using it to distinguish the action part of reciprocity from its principle.

affect both parties for a certain period. For instance, if a son stopped a relationship with his parents he would turn an expressive *wanglai* into a negative *wanglai*. It looks as if they have no relationship but they never stop thinking of each other. One day it might turn back to expressive *wanglai*. Stopping one kind of relationship with somebody can mean starting another kind of relationship with the same person. For example, to turn an expressive *wanglai* into an instrumental *wanglai* between the same persons means the relationship is still there but with a different nature. Such phenomena of different types of relationships co-existing between two persons or groups are quite common in rural China. Based on Sahlins's negative reciprocity and other related work I made further divisions within the type of negative *wanglai* (see "Negative *wanglai*" in Chapters XIII.II; XI.V).

(2) Sahlins's definition of social distance, paying regard to closeness of kinship or geography, is not appropriate to Chinese culture. Chinese people have their own ways to calculate kinship or friendship distance, which are less affected by geography. For example, at a funeral mourners within *wufu*[4] of patrilineal descent may never have met but if they are mourning together for a common ancestor, they are close in the sense that they are related to the person who has died. There is also the calculation of relationships through affinity, through women, and through marriage. Among kin one may be closely related in kinship or live geographically close but not feel close. One can also have close feeling among non-kin, as in the popular Chinese sayings that within the four seas all men are brothers (*sihai zhi nei jie xiongdi ye*) or a relative far off is less help than a neighbour close by (*yuanqin buru jinlin*). I found that rural people who live in the same place and feel close to each other do not apply generalized reciprocities in all their contacts. Balanced or even negative reciprocities can occur quite often, but this does not mean that they are distant to each other. I have also found a simpler measure of social distance to be more useful when considering social support in my research work. Yan also noticed that "kinship proximity does not always necessarily result in generosity; and under certain circumstances extraordinary hospitality is displayed to guests, strangers, or potential enemies" (1996b:100).

So instead of Sahlins's statement that the closer the social distance, the greater the generalized reciprocity, and vice versa (1972: 203), I propose a statement: the better *lishang* the

---

[4] *Wufu* of one family is a measure of close kin by five generations of a family's agnatic kin as distinguished from the other, more distant agnatic kin and all the non agnatic kin. The 1st *wu* is oneself (male), the 2nd *fu* is brothers (same father), the 3rd *fu* is cousins (same grandfather), the 4th *fu* is second cousins (same great grandfather), and the 5th *fu* is the third cousin (same great great grandfather).

more likely *wanglai*, the more frequent the *wanglai* the closer the social distance, and therefore, the greater the generous *wanglai*, and vice versa. For me closeness or distance is not fixed. To make or maintain relationships creates closeness, and to stop or cut off relationships with others creates distance. It is *lishang* which determines the degree of closeness and distance of a relationship through different types of *wanglai*. The more one understands the *lishang* of the relationship, the greater one's ability to use the particularistic component of the relationship, opposite to universalistic criteria used in modern society.

This greater understanding has a positive moral value, relating to the enjoyment of mutual interaction and respect, and the shared liking which these engender. Like Sahlins, the moral value of the exchanges has generalized reciprocity at the "highest" level, with balanced and negative reciprocities decreasing by degree in their order. Amongst the categories of generous, expressive, instrumental and negative *wanglai*, Chinese people also consider the higher levels to have greater moral value than the lower levels. My contribution to the discussion is to lay importance on the innate variability of each type of *wanglai*, which can be transformed into another at any time within one particular relationship according to *lishang* criteria: moral judgment, human feeling, rational calculation and religious sense (see *lishang* in Chapter XI.III). Consideration of the change in moral values and how this is accomplished is central to the study of *lishang-wanglai*. Moral scaling may differ when comparing *lishang-wanglai* in different cultures or different historical periods within one culture.

I also consider it more appropriate to measure social distance by frequency of *wanglai*. For me, social distance, as the opposite of social closeness, is a measurement of social relationships determined by frequency or infrequency of contacts (*wanglai*). This is similar to Stafford's (2000a) idea that social distance follows the term relatedness, which includes the feeling of closeness and contacts (*laiwang*). The term *wanglai* in *lishang-wanglai* enlarges the meaning of the Chinese version of reciprocity and includes exchange relationships and connections. This means one can make a relationship by personalising any individual or group in any place at any time through contacts (*wanglai*). This is more important than kinship relationships, geographical distance, and closeness of human feeling. According to this measurement, no matter where you live or whom you live with, if you contact each other frequently you have a close relationship. Otherwise, even two brothers who used to live in the same family, and still live in the same village after they have divided into two families, have different kinds of contact and are likely to become more distant (see Chapter VIII.II). I differentiate contacts by resources and size of resource exchanged. The closeness is also measurable in the generosity as distinct from the frequency of gifts.

(3) Another difference between Sahlins's work and mine is that Sahlins's writing is about social relationships, whether made or inherited, as static. Sahlins rather incidentally introduces the possibility of change by mentioning that balanced reciprocity is inherently unstable. On theoretical grounds, it would seem either to tend to closer relations, towards a generalized reciprocity or to less close relations, to a negative reciprocity (1972:223). However, he gives no evidence for this useful speculation. Based on his fieldwork Kipnis (1997) made clearer statements. According to Kipnis, "human relationships are the by-products of neither biological generation, a Confucian worldview, nor any sort of abstract 'social structure' that works outside of or above human subjects; they are the results of purposeful human efforts, of a type of practice". This kind of practice is dependent upon the human actors' continuing work, which is not merely "remnants" of tradition, but rather is activated or vitalised in present village life (1997:7). I agree with this and will support it by showing the dynamic flux in exchange relationships. I am going to emphasise a particular aspect in which relationships are dynamic, flowing and variable, and so are changed by people according to *lishang-wanglai*. I am also interested in how exchange relationships work among rural people and affect their lives, and its changing process. For me, relationships are not fixed things, and to decide to make a new relationship or to discontinue social relationships is a creative process.

Compared with the previous researchers, I will be concerned much more with the making of social relationships, with their changes and with the activity of keeping them, because my fieldwork material provides more information about this. I am doing an analysis in which the change or creation of social relationships is very central. Chapters IV to VIII show how I looked at the whole process of making, maintaining, altering, and stopping social relationships when I analysed social support in Kaixiangong Village. Furthermore, *wanglai* (contacts) are signs which give information about relationships. The way in which a person would choose a relationship is through changing contacts or through using existing contacts in different ways. Existing relationships are partly spontaneous, and partly chosen on purpose (when the wish to make closer relationships results in actions which achieve this). In other words, relationships are continually redefined by people.

2. "Personalised institutional *wanglai*" is inspired by Polanyi's redistribution and Parsons's personalised relationships

The previous ESRC social support project shows "public support" provided support for finance and information for major family events and emergency. Chapters IV to VIII also demonstrated the indispensability of public support. In particular instrumental *wanglai* (Chapter VIII.I) is more likely to engage "institutions" simply because they control resources. This led me to look at this area by going beyond different type of reciprocities amongst individuals (e.g. Sahlins's work). In this subsection I will borrow references from both Polanyi (1957) and Parsons (1937/49) to expand instrumental *wanglai* covering both personal relationships, as well as personalised institutional relationships, or "personalised institutional *wanglai*".

(1) Polanyi's Redistribution

The idea of an institutional relationship comes from Karl Polanyi's (1944) typology of exchange. He drew heavily on Malinowski's work in the Trobriand Islands. In his discussion of anthropological economics Polanyi divided all economies into three types according to the dominant mode of distribution: reciprocity, redistribution, or market exchange. He proposed that there were radical differences between capitalist economies dominated by market exchange, and pre-capitalist ones where gifts or ceremonial exchange predominated (1957:43). Interestingly, Polanyi thought the "great transformation" of the industrial revolution to capitalism defined social relations by economic relations which build on self-interest and rational calculation, whereas in previous societies economic arrangements were "embedded" in social relations which ruled by reciprocity (kindness and generosity) or communal obligations, and redistribution, but he didn't say much about motives associated with redistribution. Although his argument as to the great transformation of history from pre-capitalist to capitalist society and the emergence of market exchange as the dominant economy in the 20th Century received many criticisms, the quarterly journal *Co-existence* (edited by the Marxist Rudolf Schlesinger) that he founded offers food for thought.

I found strong evidence from my fieldwork experiences that a combination of reciprocity, redistribution, and market exchange exists widely in rural China. The way in which Polanyi uses redistribution as a new concept of exchange to contrast with anthropological reciprocity and economic market exchange persuaded me to go further into this topic with my fieldwork data. As Polanyi explained, redistributive systems can be as small as a band of Kung bushmen or as large as Hammurabi's empire, or even as large as the planned economy of the Soviet Union. I too found the redistributive system can be seen in "Kula Ring" in a primary society, or Kaixiangong Village collective's redistribution, or indeed that of any kind of resource owner, such as an institution's redistribution in rural or urban areas of socialist China. Even the term "co-existence " that I use in my study is directly borrowed from the name of the journal that Polanyi founded in his later life.

(2) Parsons's personalised relationships

In this small section I am not going to introduce the great sociologist Talcott Parsons's grand theories, but rather simply highlight those parts of his work which are close to my research. Parsons founded the Harvard Department of Social Relations to encourage interdisciplinary collaboration on relationship research between anthropologists, sociologists and psychologists.[5] He observed that people develop two types of relationship: personalized (e.g. families, clubs, small social settings) in expressive societies, and social relationships based on roles (e.g. bureaucracies and markets) in instrumental societies. He described Chinese society as forming particularistic relationships in contrast with the universalistic impersonality of the West, an idea broadly accepted (1947/49).

Building upon Polanyi's redistributive exchange system I borrowed Parsons's term of "personalised relationships" to make my term "personalised institutional relationships" in the social setting of a Chinese village. A Chinese village collective is an administrative body of the village community, not a part of the governmental system. In Kaixiangong , as an institute the village collective uses its various resources to work for local government and villagers (see Chapter I.II). This institute can be personalized by persons (villagers) because it is operated by village cadres who are human beings. Individuals outside the institute can find different ways to engage with the people who work within it, making relationships with them. The process of redistribution of resources can be flexible, dependent on types of relationship and situations. Four different types of *wanglai* are in theory possible in any combination in these relationships. This is why, for instance, "*guanxi*" takes place in institutions everywhere (see Chapters VIII.I and X.VI). Types of *wanglai* can also be changed according to the associated four criteria (*lishang*).

I use the term personalised relationship to refer to any relationship in which people act purposefully according to a set of criteria (*lishang*) through personal sources and personal resources to directly turn any kind of social relationship into a personalised relationship (*wanglai*), e.g. turn institutional relationships into personalised institutional relationships. All

---

[5] Parsons acted as chair of the department from 1946 to 1973 when he retired. The Department of Social Relations then became a library only.

personal direct contacts can be counted as ways of personalising relationships, whereas other contacts such as formal complaints made by writing to a newspaper or writing a letter to officials, via indirect contacts, are not. It is easy to understand that for local officials it is important to have a good long-term relationship with local people, since even when they retire they still live in the area. But for more distant officials there is no continuing potential cycle of personalised relationship, so why do they need to build such long-term relationships with local people? For over two thousand years Chinese people have always had access to contact their institutions – whether or not this contact can involve personalisation, or how much, is another matter. What I look at are personalised relationships in which the *wanglai* element is essential and *lishang* is the calculation of *wanglai*. Chinese people believe that to contact someone in person (*wanglai*) is not only (i) effective (rational choice) but could (ii) help the institution to work better (moral judgement). By my definition, which I believe to be appropriate, when villagers personalise local officials they actually personalise the institution where the officials work, and it doesn't matter where the officials come from – local or distant.

Lishang-wanglai can describe personalised relationships by specifying the way they are calculated and the principles according to which they are created and maintained. Each of these terms can be expanded: how relationships are made personal, how personal relationships are recreated, changed and maintained, and how they are ended, an on-going creative process. The way of personalizing an institution operates in terms of long term cycles extended over generations in which both the vertical and horizontal are involved. Of the *lishang* criteria human feelings is the most important, co-existing with all the other criteria, and being the root cause of *lishang-wanglai* personalised relationships.

How is social justice or rational calculation different as between personal relationships and impersonal relationships? Although social justice or rational calculation can be applied to impersonal relationships as much as to personal relationships, when they are used in the presence of human feelings, impersonal relationships can become personalised. Once the "personalised institutional relationships" have been established the relationship between institute and persons cannot be treated as purely bureaucratic.

What is involved when a relationship becomes personalised? Three factors are at work: the sharing of common interests, personal recognition of the other and memory. Sharing common interests is important in evolving a new personal relationship and recognition and memory are important in developing existing sources. For example, when A reminds B about some links between them in making a personalised relationship, B recognises something about A, remembers how A is and the history of relationships between them. *Lishang-wanglai* can be used to personalise different kinds of relationship, and people act according to *lishang* to personalise relationships, which can be maintained, and changed, with different types of *wanglai*.

Personal relationships and personalized institutional relationships work bidirectionally. If someone entered a new place and met an old classmate who works in an institute, this personal relationship could be turned into a personalized institutional relationship. The other way round, universities normally use alumni for seeking resources. Their personal or institutional resources can be mobilized by another institute, in this case, the Alma Mater's, "personalization".

3. State and personal interventions of the market

When discussing market exchange relationships Polanyi discriminated between market and market economics and said that domestic trade can be created by state intervention (1957: 63). Compared with large literatures on state intervention on markets (e.g. Nee and Stark 1989; Szyszczak 2004) no literature seems to have shown whether or not, and how, individuals or persons have intervened in market economics.

In Kaixiangong ordinary market relationships can be partly personalised, very commonly for instance in village shops. A shopkeeper in the village talks to people by sitting in a little chair next to the cash desk, rather than standing behind it. This is a way to make personal relationships with customers. Once he has established special relationships with them then their relationship has become a personalised relationship. Although by doing this the shopkeeper gains more customers and the customers gain various items in what looks like a market relationship, in fact only some villagers, those who choose to be his customers, and acknowledge his friendly pose, are part of it. This therefore has all the elements of a personalised market relationship. In my study such a personalised market relationship, together with a personalised institutional relationship, can be seen as a part of instrumental *wanglai*, which is identical to *guanxi* in other researchers' studies (Yang M.1994, Yan 1996b).

Once a person is involved in such a relationship by personalising it to gain resources from it, the relationship becomes a personalised institutional relationship or instrumental *wanglai*. *Lishang-wanglai* involves mutual respect or etiquette through the process of personalising relationships. If one of the participants is a website or automatic information system, the relationship is totally based on universalistic criteria. If, however, it involve people's feelings, even via an exchange of letters, it becomes partly particularistic. For example, I had such a relationship when buying a thirty-five year old model of Ian Fleming's Chitty Chitty Bang Bang magic car for my son from the online auction site eBay. The cost varied from a few pounds up to £300 each, depending on condition. One can't always rely on the photos or description of what one might want to bid for. In the end I kept one of a few I bought, and sold or exchanged the rest of them with other fans. It looked like a pure market relationship, but the system allows bidders to contact each other through email, which means personalised relationships can be involved. I collected many moving stories from this experience but won't show them here due to lack of space. My point is that even in the virtual market, like internet shopping, market relationships can be personalised.

In summary: although I based the *wanglai* typology mainly on Sahlins's (1965/72) work on a reciprocity typology which can be used as an analytic tool, I introduced "personalised institutional relationship" as a version of the exchange relationships I found in my fieldwork. Setting up the boundary of *lishang-wanglai* distinguishes all the other social relationships outside of *lishang-wanglai* from *lishang-wanglai* relations. I do this by borrowing Parsons's term "personalised relations" (1937/49) and Polanyi's (1957) idea on exchange relationships and creating the term "personalised institutional relations". Thus Polanyi's redistribution and market exchanges have been treated as part of instrumental *wanglai* when they are personalised. Instrumental *wanglai* (see Chapter VIII.I) include both personalised *wanglai* and personalised institutional *wanglai*. Basically, people can personalise almost any relationship subjectively, but not every relationship actually can be personalised, for example, the international trading market or legal systems (in some countries).

IX.II. Social support networks and *"lishang-wanglai"* networks

The study of social support is spread across a range of disciplines including sociology, social psychology and social anthropology. Initially social support study came from studies by the Chicago school on urban life, which served as a major foundation for social support study. But it was not until the 1970s that social support became a serious topic.[6] Since then social support has covered a very wide range: some researchers have used it in the study of human

---

[6] See *Journal of Social Issues*, Vol. 40, No. 4, 1984 & Vol. 41, No.1, 1985, and 2,693 entries in *Social support networks — A bibliography, 1983-87*, Compiled by D. Biegel, K. Farkas, N. Abell, J. Goodin, New York/London: Greenwood Press, 1989. One can also find 3,506 items of "social support" in the databases of Sociological Abstracts and Econlit (1969-1998/12).

personality, e.g. from behavioural scientists (Homans 1961; Bergess & Huston 1979; Foa & Foa, 1980; Sarason, Sarason & Pierce, 1990), "[To] the social scientist, it represents a focal point around which social ecological models of distress can be developed (Cassel, 1974a, 1974b, 1976), [to] the interventionist, it promises powerful techniques for the amelioration and prevention of psychological problems (Caplan, 1974; Cobb, 1976)"[7]. Others have used it in human / social services (Cook 1979, Gottlieb 1981, Whittaker, Garbarino et al. 1983, Naran 1991) or elderly care (Wentowski 1981, Sauer & Coward 1985, Yang H. 1990, Kallgren 1992, Wenger 1992 and 1994). They have used it in the study of poverty (The world bank 1988, Ellwood 1988), in relation to social policing (Netzer 1978, Sandison & Williams 1981, Orcutt, Merz & Quinke 1986 Hill et al. 1989), and even in studies of decision making in information sciences (Zhang 1990), etc. Although initial excitement in the topic of social support gave rise to a flood of empirical studies, the term social support still has not been included in either general sociological or social work textbooks or dictionaries.[8] By the early 1990s social support study became more focused, i.e. Sarason, et al., (1990: 2) emphasised its aspects, as: (i) the conceptualisation of social support, e.g. the network model, the received support model and the perceived support model; (ii) social support in ongoing personal relationships; (iii) the role of social support in coping with stress, and (iv) applications of social support in clinical and community interventions.

Generally speaking, social support has been defined as the benefits that can be gained through interaction with others (Deaux & Wrightsman, 1988: 245). As it will be used in this book, social support is about how people use different sources to get help to either cope with life events, or buffer stress, or meet social needs. They can be seen as seeking resources through social support. Table IX-1 shows there are more than 40 different kinds of resources that people are looking for through social support since the 1970s: goods, service, information, love, status, concrete aid, practical service, information, problem solving, emotional mastery, feedback, rest

---

[7] This quotation comes from Alan Vaux's preface to his book *Social support: theory, research, and intervention*, New York/London, etc.: Praeger Publishers, 1988.

[8] See Ritzer, George, 1996 (fourth edition), Sociological theory, New York, etc.: The Mcgraw-Hill Companies, inc. Giddens, Anthony, 1993 (second edition), Sociology, Cambridge: Polity Press. Haralambos, Michael, ed. 1994 (second edition), Sociology: a new approach, Ormskirk: Causeway Press Ltd. Jary, David & Julia, 1991, Collins Dictionary of Sociology, Glasgow, Harper Collins Publishers. Marshall, Gordon, ed. 1994, The Concise Oxford Dictionary of Sociology, Oxford/New York: Oxford University Press. Even in sociology for social work (Dominelli, 1997), the terms of support, and support network have been mentioned a lot, but social support still wasn't discussed.

Table IX-1 Social support resources

Foa	1971	Goods	Service	Information	Love	Status	-
Caplan	1974	Concrete aid	Practical service	Information prob. solving	Emotional mastery	Feedback	Rest & recuperation
Weiss	1974	-	Social integration	Guidance	Attachment	Reassurance of worth	Social integration
Cobb	1976	-	-	-	Love	Esteem	Belonging
Tolsdorf	1976	Tangible	assistance	Advice	Intangible	Feedback	-
Pattison	1977	Instrumental			Affective		
Gottlieb	1978	Problem solving			Emotional sustenance	-	-
Hirsch	1980	Tangible assistance		Cognitive guidance	Emotional support	Social reinf.	Socialising
House	1980	Instrumental		Information (environ-ment)	Emotional	Information (self-eval.)	-
Mitchell & Trickett	1980	Task-oriented assistance	Communi-cation of expectations	Information & social contacts	Emotional support	Evaluation & a shared world view	
Vaux	1982	Financial assistance	Practical assistance	Advice / guidance	Emotional support	-	Socialising
Barrera and Ainlay	1983	Material aid	Behavioural assistance	Guidance	Intimate interaction	Feedback	Positive social interaction
Wills	1985	Instrumental		Information	Motivation	Esteem	Social comparison
Lin, Dean, and Ensel	1986	Instrumental			Expressive		
Chang & Feuchtwang	1996	Financial support	Labour support	Information support	-	-	-
Chang	2004	Financial support	Labour support	Information support	Materials	Human feeling	Religion

& recuperation, social integration, guidance, attachment, reassurance of worth, social integration, esteem, belonging, tangible, assistance, advice, intangible, instrumental, affective, emotional sustenance, tangible assistance, cognitive guidance, emotional support, social reinforcement, socializing, task-oriented assistance, communication of expectations, social contacts, evaluation and shared world view, financial assistance, material aid, behavioural assistance, intimate interaction, positive social interaction, motivation, social comparison, expressive exchange, labour support, human feeling and religion. But no individual study covers more than six types of resource, determined by the focus of the project the researchers have undertaken. In the ESRC social support project three kinds of resources were looked at, financial support, labour support and information. In my own study three more resources were added, material, human feelings and spiritual beliefs.

The ESRC project on social support examined how rural Chinese people arranged resources from different sources for their everyday life (see Introduction). It provides important data for this book based on a framework related to social support networks. Apart from resources (or nature of the benefits) it is necessary to consider the *source* of the benefits and *purpose* to which the benefits are put in an examination of social support. In this section I will show how the social support networks based on the ESRC project were developed by reviewing related work; introduce the *lishang-wanglai* model into the ESRC related social support networks and turn them into *lishang-wanglai* networks. At the same time a framework of *lishang-wanglai* networks will be presented; and finally I will demonstrate how the *lishang-wanglai* framework functions.

1. Social support networks

Social network study can be traced back to the Chicago school. The development of social network analysis has been complex. One tradition, called sociometry, coined by J. L. Moreno (1934), uses mathematics to develop formal models of the links and topology of social networks. Another tradition explores patterns of interpersonal relations and the formation of cliques. In this tradition, the psychologist Elton Mayo (1933) and the anthropologist W. Lloyd Warner (1937, 1941) worked together and applied Radcliffe-Brown's (1930-31, 1940) structural concerns to their investigations of American factory and community life.[9] The third tradition is based on the works of the Manchester anthropologists (e.g. John Barnes 1954, Elizabeth Bott 1956-57 and

---

[9] See John Scott 1991:16-23.

Clyde Mitchell 1969). They are also influenced by Radcliffe-Brown, but are interested in conflict and change in investigating the structure of community relations in tribal and village societies. From the 1960s onwards the crucial breakthroughs in social network analysis occurred at Harvard. Harvard structuralists (e.g. White 1963, Boyd 1969, Lorrain and White 1971) carried on from the above traditions and pushed network analysis into much more highly theoretical and technical areas. They even established their own journal: *Social Networks*, an interdisciplinary and international quarterly.

Although social network theory has been incorporated further in studies of social support by several researchers,[10] some researchers have diverted their interests toward other ways of using networks as an analytical tool, because many social phenomena cannot be quantitatively measured. For example, Lommnitz (1977) examined life in a Mexican town, Hannerz (1980) explored city life in America, and Wallman (1984) studied eight London households.

My exploration of social support networks and reciprocity is mainly based on ego-centred social network analysis. According to Wasserman and Faust (1994:42), ego-centred networks have been widely used by anthropologists to study the social environment surrounding individuals (Boissevain 1973), families (Bott 1957) or households (Wallman 1984). Social psychologists and sociologists have often used ego-centred networks in the study of social support, which refers to social relationships that aid the health or well-being of an individual, (e.g. Hammer 1983, Cohen and Syme 1985, Seed 1990). The emphasis on relationships has allowed researchers to study support using social networks.

Amongst the anthropological studies Sandra Wallman's (1984) work on eight London households is close to mine. Wallman combined a total social field network and ego-centred social field network together, and used two network maps. One situates its contacts in relation to the local context and records the geographic distance of people in the household network. The other classifies these contacts in term of their practical or emotional resource value and also records the affective distance of people in the household network. According to Wallman, the latter is adapted from a family therapy model (Speck and Attneave 1974). Wallman also divided the rings of increasing distance into three parts. *Kin* go in the central circle, then *non-kin* form a ring, and *uncomfortable people* form an outer circle. This allows more detail in the closeness of

---

[10] e.g. Tolsdorf 1976, Craven & Wellman 1974, Hirsch 1979, Mitchell and Trickett, 1980, Barrera, 1981, Vaux and Harrison, 1985, Cochran and Brassard 1979; Wellman, 1981, Nan Lin 1979 et al., 1986a, G. J. Wentowski 1981, Whittaker 1983, Hooyman 1983, Wellman 1981, Garbarino 1983, Cohen and Syme 1985, Seed 1990, etc.

contacts to be illustrated.

Wallman's ego-centered network study has influenced the ESRC social support project in two ways. (i) She looked at the geographic distance of people in the household network, whereas we looked at ranges of geographical distance in order to see how far the different supporters who feature in the ego's network are from the ego. (ii) She divided people within the network into kin, non-kin and uncomfortable people, whereas we distinguished social support sources as households themselves, neighbours, friends and others. However, Wallman looked at how people in the ego's networks interrelate with each other by providing a chart of the density interactions between people who are in ego-centered networks. I have noticed such linkage between people within an ego-centered network, but I did not study them because my purpose is not to compare egos in more dense networks with egos in less dense ones, but rather to establish other variations of ego-centred networks. I look at all the relationships an ego, e.g. one household, has and find out how different relationships relate to the ego and what kind of resources and quantity of support they provide to the ego, and how the ego maintains the different relationships within the ego-centered networks.

It is worth mentioning another anthropologist Yan Yunxiang's (1996b) *guanxi* network, which is also close to mine, because we are both concerned with the topic of reciprocity in a rural Chinese village. Yan examined both the dynamic process of cultivation of *guanxi* networks and their functions in everyday life, and the structure of *guanxi* networks with metaphorical and analytic uses. Yan analysed patterns of gift lists in the structure of *guanxi* networks, which are formed from a core zone, reliable zone, effective zone, village society, and beyond the village society, in all five categories of a donor's relationships. He distinguished inherited from created relations, and degrees of closeness between donor and recipient. Yan states "the closer to the centre in a given *guanxi* network, the more gift-giving relations are involved (101);" "all instrumental gift-giving relations go beyond the village boundary (102)." However, the nature of Yan's structure of *guanxi* network is not significantly different from Wallman's (1984) geographic and affective distance in the study of relationships or networks and Sahlins's (1965/72) reciprocity and kinship distance (see section Chapter IX.I).

Philip Seed's (1990) study on social network analysis in the social work field also helped me in sorting out contents of social support networks based on materials of the ESRC social support project. According to Seed, 'social network analysis is all about making connections between different kinds of network features, types and relationship qualities' (1990: 45). Figure IX-1 shows how the structure of the social support network is formed.

As I mentioned in the Introduction, the ESRC project on social support was designed to provide further insights into resource exchanges among rural people in the Post-Mao era. The assumption of the exploratory survey on the above project was that there is a large, informal and family-based fabric of social support network performing the function of social security in rural

Figure IX-1 A framework for social support networks

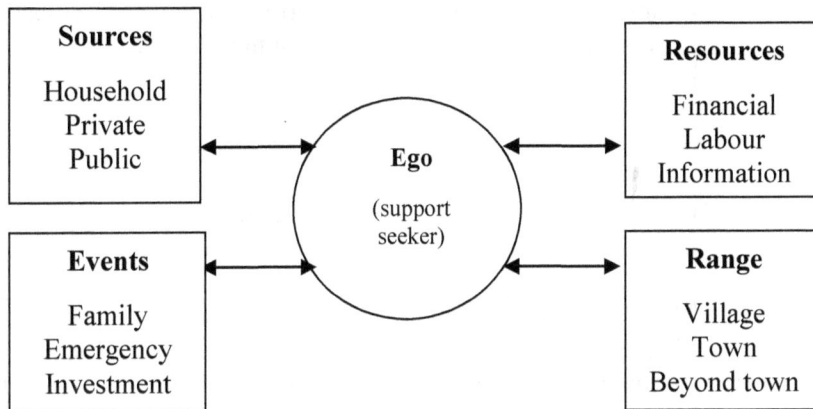

China. In rural China "social support network features" include *sources* for support (family, kinship, friends, neighbours, and other institutions), *resources* (financial, labour, and information), *events* (family, emergency, and investment), and *range* (village, town, and beyond town). See Table IX-2. Seed divided "network types" into dense, self-contained, and embracing categories, which I do not use. I am not going to measure the density of the network and its other structural properties because I am not applying a structural network analysis. For "relationship qualities", Seed made a comparison between the sociological view and that of social work.

According to Seed, from the sociologists' (Knoke and Kuklinski 1982) viewpoint, the relationship qualities include transaction, communication, boundary penetration, instrumental relations, sentiment, authority power, and kinship and descent relations. For Seed, based on social work studies, relationship qualities concern communication and access, instrumental qualities, sentimental qualities, influence, esteem, and reciprocity qualities.

I am looking at different kinds of exchange relations which are based on my informants' own perceptions, namely, generous *wanglai*, expressive *wanglai*, instrumental *wanglai*, and negative *wanglai* (see *wanglai* typology in Chapter XI.V). "Relationship qualities" are very

Table IX-2 Contents of social support networks

Source	Resource	Event	Range
Household support is working members of household's resources which are used or requested.	**Financial support** quantified in two different ways: the amount of money and the number of transactions which we call contacts.	**Family events** include funerals, engagements, weddings, birthdays (e.g. first month after birth, anniversary, reaching an old age), feasts or other means of maintaining good relations.	**Village** support from within the administrative village.
Private support is resources used or requested from other households. Those of kin, neighbours, and friends, given as part of a reciprocal relationships.	**Labour support** include hands for building, cooking a banquet, peak harvest, repair of furniture, cementing ground, transport, and others.	**Emergency events** include illness or injury, natural disasters, market collapses.	**Town** support from beyond the village but within the township (*xiang* or *zhen*)
Public support is resources, especially financial resources, used or requested from official sources (bank or village collective or state or collective work unit) or unofficial sources (usury and mutual savings), or others.	**Information support** The questionnaire suggested no categories of information, but it was assumed that information includes influential advice, and so the status of the person providing it was coded: official beyond village, official in village, enterprise agent, enterprise manager, specially skilled person, popular person and others	**Investment events** related to those in housing or production (e.g. new equipment, new crop, or a new line of work)	**Beyond town** support from beyond township

important to my research because maintaining good relationships stand families in good stead for various eventualities, and in the course of so doing there are continuous benefits, as in the fattening of pigs or *lishang-wanglai* (villagers' terms, see Introduction). I initially applied social support network theory in a restudy of the ESRC social support project in Neiguan Village, Gansu Province in 1996. In the next section I show why this was not sufficient to explain my results and how I expanded the social support networks into *lishang-wanglai* networks

2. *Lishang-wanglai* networks

I developed the notion of *lishang-wanglai* networks because of the problems I encountered, listed below, in using social support networks to analyse social support in Kaixiangong Village. (i) Social support is very little to do with generous *wanglai*, although it is an outcome of generous *wanglai* from Kaixiangong villagers' point of view. As I will show in Chapter X, the villagers hardly ever use *bao* or *huibao* (repay, reciprocity) for social support issues. They told me that they won't say *huibao* (repay with gratefulness) because that would finish a *wanglai* relationship. (ii) According to the ESRC project report the *renqing* kind of expressive *wanglai* was mainly based in the village, whereas the *guanxi* kind of instrumental *wanglai* was more likely to come from outside the village. In other words, social support networks mainly work in expressive *wanglai* within a village. (iii) The villagers didn't consider the *guanxi* kind of instrumental *wanglai* or negative *wanglai* as social support, although social support have an element of instrumental *wanglai* (see section 1.2). They also asked me to move investment, one of the possible family events in the ESRC project's social support classification, into a different category. From their point of view, to invest in new equipment, and new corporation or a new line of work etc. should be regarded as instrumental *wanglai*, which is more likely to involve *guanxi*. (iv) Social support resources (see Table IX-1) are to do with human beings, but the villagers also view gods and spiritual beings and spirituality as an important source of resources. In this case geographical range is not relevant. (v) Social support networks consider geographical range, but the villagers also consider time and space in vertical and horizontal ways (which I will define later in this section) when they arrange resources.

(1). "*Lishang-wanglai*" framework

Bearing in mind these difficulties with the social support networks that I was using, I expanded social support networks into *lishang-wanglai* networks (see "*Lishang-wanglai* framework" in Figure IX-2). To begin with I had to specify a *lishang-wanglai* framework (see

Table IX-3). It was derived from the Kaixiangong villagers' practice in their everyday life which I have described in Chapters IV to VIII, with their assistance. I showed how the four types of *wanglai* worked and demonstrated the four criteria embedded in each type of *wanglai*. Chapter XI will further discuss their meanings and boundaries of implication.

Table IX-3 *Lishang-wanglai* framework

Lishang criteria	*Wanglai* typology
Moral judgment	Generous *wanglai*
Human feelings	Expressive *wanglai*
Rational calculation	Instrumental *wanglai*
Spiritual beliefs	Negative *wanglai*

(2). "*Lishang-wanglai* network"

The *lishang-wanglai* networks are enlargements of each element of the social support network (see Chapter IX.II), whereas the *lishang-wanglai* framework is a diagram which includes how the *lishang-wanglai* networks are structured and how they work (see chapter IX.II and III). Figure IX-2 shows the expanded *lishang-wanglai* networks and includes the following elements.

(i) Under "sources", in the ESRC social support project, 'household' means members of family, 'private' includes relatives, neighbours and friends, 'public' includes the village collective and other institutions. To these I added 'fellow villagers', 'ancestors', and 'local gods and goddesses'. All the above items together form the sources of *lishang-wanglai* networks. This goes beyond "social relationships" for social support because ancestors and local gods and goddesses are spiritual beings. This idea was confirmed by all my informants.

(ii) The "resources" in *lishang-wanglai* networks' include not only the finance, labour, and information that the ESRC project looked at, but also materials, human feelings, and religious aims and categories because their range of exchange is much broader.

(iii) Apart from the family events, emergencies and investment in the ESRC social support project, the "events" in *lishang-wanglai* networks also include 'family division', 'house construction', 'annual cycle events' and 'lifecycle events'.

To supplement the "range" of 'village', 'town' and 'beyond town' in the ESRC project, I have added four more dimensions to the geographical element. They are time / space, vertical / horizontal, real / imaginary and *yin* / *yang*. Thus the "*lishang-wanglai* networks" constitute the dynamic part of the concept of *lishang-wanglai*.

Figure IX-2 shows that the *lishang-wanglai* model is dynamic. Yan Yunxiaong's "flow of gifts" (1996) has been expanded into a "flow of resources", the sources and ranges of flow have also been maximally expanded to include the nether world as well as this one. Villagers mobilise resources for different events and these are always accompanied by rituals. Through these rituals individual or family based ego-centred networks are established, and sources and ranges for seeking resources are determined. The flow of resources in every pair of relationships is always interactive and bi-directional. The directions can be top down or bottom up vertically, and inwards or outwards horizontally. Each relationship can have up to four types of *wanglai* existing at the same time, and they can be explained with a set of four criteria (*lishang*) or found through analysis with them.

Figure IX-2 *Lishang-wanglai* framework

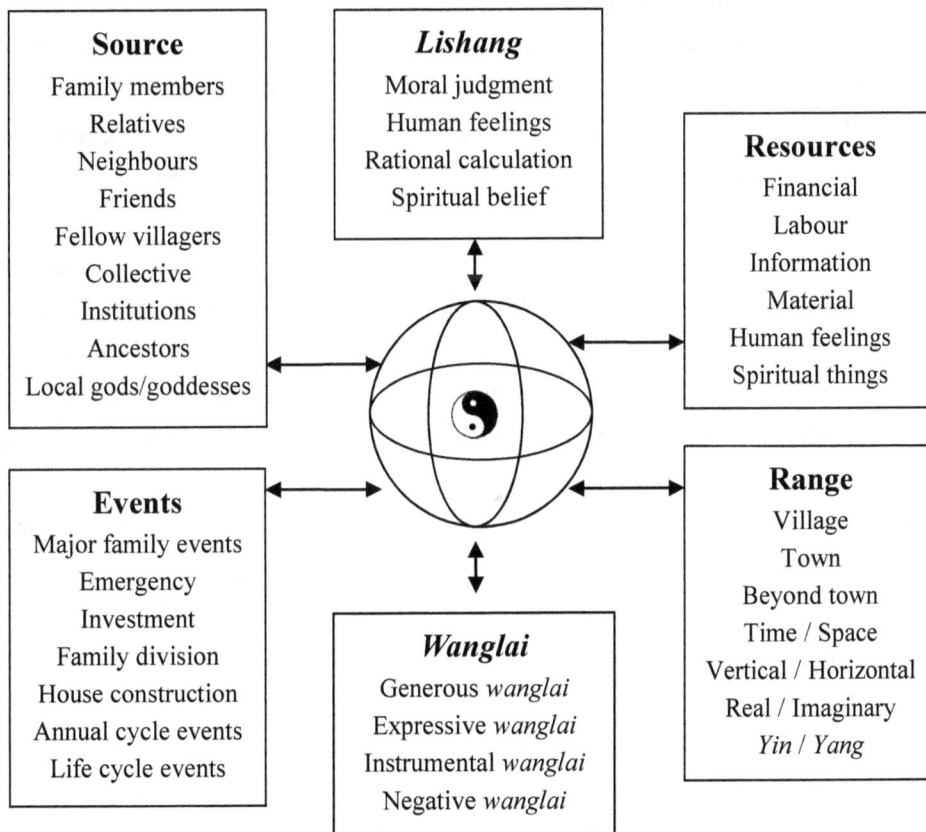

Source
Family members
Relatives
Neighbours
Friends
Fellow villagers
Collective
Institutions
Ancestors
Local gods/goddesses

Lishang
Moral judgment
Human feelings
Rational calculation
Spiritual belief

Resources
Financial
Labour
Information
Material
Human feelings
Spiritual things

Events
Major family events
Emergency
Investment
Family division
House construction
Annual cycle events
Life cycle events

Wanglai
Generous *wanglai*
Expressive *wanglai*
Instrumental *wanglai*
Negative *wanglai*

Range
Village
Town
Beyond town
Time / Space
Vertical / Horizontal
Real / Imaginary
Yin / Yang

I will now consider previous researchers' work to show how the additions to the categories of "events", "resources" and "sources" of the social support networks are influenced by them. The idea of linking a time dimension to ego-centred family network benefits is from He Ruifu's (1992) work. Based on a field study on family life and networks in his hometown, a Southern Chinese village, he defined a family network "as the social phenomenon formed by a group of families that are directly linked by kinship, friendship or other relationships and frequently interact (*laiwang*) in daily life with the ego family (25)." He believed family networks are made up of separate individual networks and distinguished his network analysis by putting a family network in the time dimension, and viewing the relations of network structure and people's behaviour dialectically (27). His idea of time dimension in dyadic ties of *laiwang* (the same as Stafford's term *laiwang*) is particularly important for me. For me, an ego can be involved in different types of *wanglai* with one or more relationships at different times or even at the same time.

(i) **At the same time,** the ego can have a relationship with **a particular person or object** with one or more than one type of *wanglai*, e.g. the Chinese famous story of the Hongmen feast (*Hongmen yan*). This told of a feast held at Hongmeng by Xiang Yu for his rival Liu Bang in the Three Kingdom time, at which an attempt was made on Liu's life. Here inviting someone for a feast sounds like an expressive *wanglai*, but the attempted assassination turned it into a negative *wanglai*.

(ii) **At different times,** the ego can have a relationship with **a particular person or object** with one or more than one type of *wanglai*. For example, a friend of the given family (ego) attended its son's wedding in which the *wanglai* of gift and banquet between them can be expressive *wanglai*. A few days later the same friend came to the family asking to borrow its truck. The family interpreted this as instrumental *wanglai* because it went beyond their understanding of mutual help between friends.

(iii) **At the same time,** the ego can have a relationship with **a different person or object** with one or more than one types of *wanglai*. It was common for beggars to perform a greeting song whenever an ego family held a wedding banquet. The given family always gave them some food and sent them off quickly, which can be seen as mixed generous *wanglai* and instrumental *wanglai*, whereas its relationship with all the guests is expressive *wanglai*.

(iv) **At different times** the ego can have a relationship with **a different person or object** with one or more than one types of *wanglai*. This can be seen from how an ego centred family maintains its networks. An ego-centered family's networks are not fixed. They increase and decrease because the family adjusts their lists according to changing times and situations (see

Chapters IV to VIII). The important thing is that different types of *wanglai* can be created, improved, decreased or destroyed by people at any time.

Charles Stafford's (1995, 2000a and c) cycle of *yang* encouraged me to use a similar spatial analogy in which links can be either vertical or horizontal. Compared with Stafford's *laiwang* cycle, which indicates a kind of latitudinal circle between an ego and its neighbours and friends, the *yang* cycle indicates to me a kind of longitudinal cycle between parents and children. According to Stafford, alongside patriliny and affinity the *yang* cycle is equally forceful and a relatively incorporative Chinese kinship system (2000a: 38). The way in which the *yang* cycle looks at parent-child relationships within a family is similar to the way we looked at household support[11] in the ESRC social support project. It showed that 70 per cent of the "contents" in social support came from members of households (household support) from 10 villagers (Chang and Feuchtwang 1997). Stafford's finding and the above data back up each other when it comes to relationships inside a family rather than those outside of the family. Although I would not think it appropriate to treat a married daughter's family who lived in a different place from the given family as a part of the *yang* cycle, I agree with the idea of a *yang* cycle as a generational relationship between members of the family (ego), which can be seen as vertical *wanglai*. My addition to Stafford's work on the *yang* cycle is to insist on a generational cycle, and to include his *laiwang* cycle as a part of the horizontal *wanglai* including *wanglai* with the married out daughters' families (see chapters 3 and 4). For me, the family based *lishang-wanglai* networks can be inherited. I have shown, in Chapters 3 and 4, how children can be brought into a set of family *lishang-wanglai* networks, how they inherit their family's relatives and neighbours, how they make their own friends, etc., and how *lishang-wanglai* networks work continuously over generations.

Yan Yunxiang's (1996b) division of horizontal and vertical social relations (169) helps me directly in joining horizontal and vertical *wanglai* together in the family (ego) based *lishang-wanglai* networks. By using this we can see that the gift exchange of previous researchers includes mixed vertical and horizontal exchanges (Malinowski Kula 1922, Mauss's give-receive-repay circle 1925, etc.), or sometimes divided as either vertical exchange (Polanyi's redistribution 1957, Stafford's *yang* cycle 1995 and 2000a, etc.), or horizontal exchange (Fei's "ego centred ripples in a pond" 1947), Sahlins's "reciprocity and kinship residential sectors"

---

[11] The household support considered members of a household, e.g. grandparents, parents, adult children, etc. who live in one household (see table 4).

1965/1972:199 and Stafford's *laiwang* circles 1995 and 2000a, etc.). For me, the ego (family) based *lishang-wanglai* networks look like a globe formed by crisscrossing circles (like lines of latitude and longitude). Here a vertical relationship indicates that one side's status or position is higher than the other, whereas a horizontal relationship indicates an equal rank between the two sides. Thus one can have longitudinal or vertical *wanglai* with one's ancestors, or local officials. One can also have latitudinal or horizontal *wanglai* with different people, between fellow villagers, or colleagues. In my study I will use the terms *vertical* and *horizontal* to describe the longitudinal and latitudinal mobility of *lishang-wanglai*.

The dimension of real / imaginary came from Kaixiangong villagers' practices on social support and *lishang-wanglai*. I mentioned earlier in this section that Kaixiangong villagers considered ancestors and local gods as part of their sources for seeking support and general religious beliefs as part of their resources. This is to say that the imaginary world co-exists with the villagers' real life. The villagers categorised their relationships with their ancestors and local gods as vertical *wanglai*, whereas those with other spiritual beings, such as ghosts, were horizontal *wanglai*. Various examples can be seen from the villagers' related practices throughout this book whenever I described or analysed cases with the religious sense of *lishang* criterion. Moreover, imaginary time or space can also be used in real life in this world, such as the villagers' memory of the past and wishes for the future vertically, and imaginary closeness with different relations horizontally.

3. The overlapping of *"lishang-wanglai* network" and *"lishang-wanglai* model"

I added the dimension of *yin / yang* based on my understanding of Kaixiangong villagers' practice of *lishang-wanglai* and the Chinese classics. Figure 2 shows a Taiji Diagram (Tai-chi Tu diagram) in the middle of the framework of *lishang-wanglai* networks, creating a *"lishang-wanglai* model". In Chapter XI I will show further the construction of the *lishang-wanglai* model.

I shall point out that amongst many studies on the Taiji Diagram my usage of it is based on the natural humanism of Taoism rather than the I-Ching. According to Shu Jingnan (1994) the former is the origin of the Taiji Diagram and the latter is an annotation of the Taiji Diagram. In ancient Chinese philosophy, the rhythm of life, which pulsates through the universe, is the action of complementary principles. The Taiji Diagram illustrates this principle with *yin* and *yang*. The symmetrical disposition of the black *yin* and the white *yang* suggests cyclical changes. When *yin* reaches its climax, it recedes in favour of *yang*, then after *yang* reaches its climax it recedes in favour of *yin*. This is the eternal cycle. The dots inside the white and black halves indicate that within each is the seed of the other. *Yin* cannot exist without *yang* and vice versa. Although the dots are very important, they are so small that they may be ignored. Even the Chinese – English Dictionary (Revised edition, Cidianzu, 1995) ignores the spots in the Diagram. It says the Diagram "consists of a wavy or double curved line bisecting a circle, one half of which is white and the other black (973)." But the white-on-black or black-on-white dots are the seed that can turn the black half into white or the white into black. The ideal state of things in the physical universe, as well as in the world of humans, is a state of harmony represented by the balance of *yin* and *yang* in body and mind.

The main reason I replaced the word "ego" on the framework of the social support network with the Taiji Diagram in the middle of the crisscrossing globe of the framework of the *lishang-wanglai* networks, is that it depicts a pair of basic dialectic changes as a single unit. It can be an ego, i.e. individual or a family, or one pair of relationships (two sides). For example, the relationship between commoners and an emperor can be a pair of relationships formed by the commoners (*yin*) and an emperor (*yang*). According to a Chinese saying: the water can bear the boat as well as sink it (*shui neng zai zhou, yi neng fu zhou*). This is to say that if the emperor is a boat, then the people are the waters of the river and the inalienable water (people) can bear the emperor's ruling as well as overthrow the ruler. The above two outcomes can be seen as a kind of vertical interaction on the globe shaped *lishang-wanglai* framework: bottom up or top down. The idea of a *yin-yang* dialectic relationship provides another dimension for analysing how the two directions are exchanges (see Conclusion I).

Figure 2 also shows how both the *lishang* criteria and the *wanglai* typology were expanded. To add the *lishang-wanglai* model to the framework of the *lishang-wanglai* networks is not only for categorising different kinds of relationships statically or explaining reasons for the differences mechanically, but also providing certain patterns for changing of relationships dynamically and a set of criteria for illustrating the orderliness of changes. For example, *wanglai* has four types: generous *wanglai*, expressive *wanglai*, instrumental *wanglai* and negative *wanglai* (see Chapter XI.V). By involving vertical and horizontal directions the types of *wanglai* can be further divided as vertical generous *wanglai*, vertical expressive *wanglai*, vertical instrumental *wanglai* and vertical negative *wanglai*; horizontal generous *wanglai*, horizontal expressive *wanglai*, horizontal instrumental *wanglai* and horizontal negative *wanglai*. Unlike in Xiajia (Yan 1996b), where the relationship between village cadres and villagers was always based on an instrumental or negative *wanglai*, Kaixiangong shows that sometimes village cadres also engaged in expressive *wanglai* with the villagers. *Lishang* criteria explained the reasons and illustrated how the different kinds of *wanglai* between village cadres and villagers had been made close or distant (see Chapter VII.II and III). Horizontally, a large number of cases in Chapters IV to VIII illustrate *lishang* through the flow of different resources (*wanglai*) between an ego (family or family based individual) and its sources (networks) of neighbours, friends, and fellow villagers, and how the networks were maintained.

4. *Lishang-wanglai* mechanism

The above section "*lishang-wanglai* networks" shows how the social support networks in the ESRC project were enlarged and how the four dimensions were added to my ethnographical materials and previous researchers' work. The *lishang-wanglai* framework (Figure IX-2) looks very complicated. It is actually simple to use because it can be treated as a toolbox which contains many different dimensions for analysing different relationships. One can have them ready whenever one needs to apply them, but need not use all of them for every single piece of work at once. In the previous section, although I have shown there are four dimensions and many different possibilities of changes in a *lishang-wanglai* framework, they can be generalised as four basic changing patterns. In this section I will explain how *lishang-wanglai* networks work, based on the diagram of the *lishang-wanglai* framework.

(1) The idea of ego-centred globe shaped *lishang-wanglai* networks suggests the mobility of *wanglai* typology flowing upwards or downwards vertically, as well as inwards or outwards horizontally. Networks always include symmetrical and asymmetrical relations or latitudinal and longitudinal relations. The ego can be an individual, a focal family or an institution. Based on this, one can see how resource exchanges via different kinds of relationships or different types of *wanglai* flow in horizontal or vertical ways. For example, Yan Yunxiang was interested in bottom up vertical relationships. According to Yan (1996b), most previous researchers[12] arrived at the conclusion that it was the donors who gain prestige and power in unbalanced transfers downwards to a debtor in the social hierarchy, whereas in Xiajia and even in China gift receiving is regarded as a symbol of prestige which motivates villagers to give. It is clear that Yan is interested in forming a sharp contrast with earlier generalisations within vertical contexts

---

[12] e.g. Malinowski 1922/1984, Mauss, 1950/1990, Sahlins 1965/72, Befu 1966-67, A. Strathern 1971, Vatuk and Vatuk 1971, and Raheja 1988, etc.

(147-48). In addition to this I am interested in both directions of gift flow: *wang* and *lai* (come and go). Kaixiangong's cases will show that both downward and upward gift flow co-existed in the villagers' everyday life (Chapters IV to VIII). This happened in Yan's Xiajia too. On the one hand, Yan shows that in Xiajia there was a kind of *xiaojing* gift given by the younger to senior generations, with no expectation of a return gift. This indicates an upward direction of gift flow in a hierarchical context (63, 151). On the other hand, he suggests that in Xiajia the system of marriage transaction is no longer a circle of gift exchange between two families. It is a new form of premortem inheritance for a marrying son or a way of distributing wealth from older generations to younger generations (206). My understanding of the above two directions of gift giving is that they formed actually one reciprocal process of vertical expressive *wanglai* between two generations. The reason elder generations received gifts from the younger generations can be seen as part of the repayment from the younger generations. A Chinese saying that one rears children against old age (*yang er fang lao*) is another such a reciprocal circle of expressive *wanglai*. Thus marriage transactions, *xiaojing* gifts, and *yang er fang lao* form a vertical circle of gift exchange between two generations (see chapters V to VII).

(2) The addition of the time / space dimension allows us to see the changes of *wanglai* or reciprocity over time and across space with vertical / horizontal dimensions. As I have shown in the previous section, horizontally there are four possibilities for the time dimension, e.g. **at the same time** the ego can have a relationship with **a particular person or different person** with one or more than one type of *wanglai*; **at different times** the ego can have a relationship with **a particular person or a different person** with one or more than one types of *wanglai*. From the **time vertical** way, *wanglai* (activities of exchange or reciprocity) can be seen as real vertical relationships, e.g. different generations or social status; imaginary time can be seen from historical evolution, e.g. looking back to the past or forward to the future. *Lishang-wanglai* between an individual or group and institutions, used in a time dimension, can be seen over different historical periods. In the *lishang-wanglai* model the classification of a relationship can be altered over time. Thus a relationship can move from expressive to instrumental and back again to expressive through the actions of *wanglai*. The effect of a particular action (*wanglai*) on a relationship is determined by the existing *lishang* of the relationship. For example, it can be a reduction of institutional exchange in favour of market exchange, or market exchange can be used to reduce the amount of obligation to the party and the state, which is under expressive exchange. In this sense Polanyi's notion of redistribution is applicable to China as a communist society and in a transition period. Under Mao there was a dominant redistribution system. Then from 1974 in Anhui and

Sichuan, where the Household Responsibility System was first introduced, and then in the rest of China, there has been much change. A mixture of market and the command economy was in Polanyi's Soviet Union and China, although China is no longer now a command economy. But it is ruled by a one party government with quite strong economic powers. All the economic levels are indirect not direct and more work units (*danwei*) are released from their welfare responsibility in urban areas, although this has been changing rapidly only since the 1990s. The rural economy in China was the first to become marketized. To see the relationship of reciprocity in the long term and the way in which this forms cycles or criss-cross circles in which the exchange of reciprocal gifts or obligations can operate over several generations requires longitudinal study. This I was able to do in Kaixiangong (Chapters IV to VIII).

(3) Apart from a real life in the real world there is also, from the villagers' point of view, an imaginary life in the imaginary world. As a copy of real life the relations with ancestors or gods are always vertical imaginary because they are more powerful than the living, whereas relations with ghosts, who could be souls of dead relatives or friends, can be horizontal imaginary. Moreover, real life and imaginary worlds can also be seen from the space dimension in which *wanglai* (exchange or reciprocity) can be seen from geographical distance, e.g. from family, neighbours, village to outside village or even abroad, etc. as well as imaginary distance or space. FY Tan never thought her adopted son was distant from her even when he hated her (see chapter VIII.II).

Lishang-wanglai can be also used to understand the real world with the imaginary time / space dimension because personal participation and experiences (*wanglai* with a real world in time / space vertically and horizontally) are very helpful. Serge Moscovici, the originator of "social representations", said that he gained an inductive radar through his unconventional life experiences, and therefore, was more sensitive in touching the pulse of the world. In her interview with the Romanian-Parisian Serge Moscovici, Yu Shou (Preface, 2004) told us that he thought that the logic of history has a law of its own: from Communist Romania to Red China, from the French Revolution to the Cultural Revolution in China, from Hitler's genocide of Jews to Mao's "brain washing" of all Chinese people, from the Industrial Revolution to the Chinese centralized industrial development model, from globalising into a single world market to the Chinese complex "going abroad" strategy. All these similar historical events happened haphazardly in different places and at different times, but they were determined by an invisible historical rule, even if any individual incident is unexpected. In addition, Moscovici recognised that the Chinese characteristic of indirectness or allusion (*hanxu*) is likely to be found more often in times of unexpected or uncertain social change. Moscovici is convinced that rational choice is powerless with the above phenomena. As a natural humanist Moscovici appropriated much of Taoism's outlook on nature. He believed Taoism is not only a philosophy on the origin of life and source of metaphysics, it also offers great wisdom for the practice of human beings' self cultivation (2004). Kaixiangong's case very much suggests that the Chinese characteristic of indirection or allusion (*hanxu*) and the uncertainty of the environment stimulated creativity in the practices of *lishang-wanglai*. Borrowing Taoist philosophy in studying *lishang-wanglai* reaches the same goal by different routes as Serge Moscovici's concern for the world.

(4) Adding the dimension of *yin / yang* to the *lishang-wanglai* framework is illustrated by Kaixiangong villagers' everyday life. In Kaixiangong there are many things related to a circle or cycle (*yuan*), e.g. *yuanzi* or *tuanzi* (different kinds of rice balls); and they used many suggestive Chinese terms relating to reciprocity, e.g. *yuanhua* (smooth and evasive; slick and sly), *yuanhuo* (be flexible in handling a matter), *yuanman* (satisfactory), *yuanmeng* (dream become true or oneiromancy), *yuanshu* (dexterous), *yuantong* (accommodating), etc. For them the nature of dynamic change in *lishang-wanglai* networks can be represented by the eternal cycle of the Taiji Diagram.

I will now use the Taiji Diagram, the Taoism Symbol, to demonstrate that particularism and universalism co-exist in Chinese society. Chinese society has been labelled as a particularist society for more than half a century. This notion originally came from Parsons (1937/49). I will omit an academic debate that China is mainly a particularistic society compared to the Western universalistic society. I shall point out that some Chinese scholars[13] using this idea (e.g. Fei 1947, Skinner 1971, King 1986, Yu 1987a, Zheng 1995a, Bian 1997a and b, Zhai 1997, and Yang and Peng 1998/99) have not made clear *how* particularism and universalism co-exist in Chinese society. For me, universalism can be seen as a white dot in the black half of the *yin-yang* diagram where Chinese society is concerned, whereas particularism is a black dot in the white half of the diagram where Western countries are concerned.

But how have the dots moved? 10 years ago, I heard a Chinese businessman say "whether USA trained Taiwan businessmen or UK trained Hong Kong businessmen, when they come to mainland China for business we are going to turn all of them black (*women hui ba tamen quandou bianhei*)". This means that universalism won't work in China because particularism will melt it down. Looking back at the last ten years of development in China I can recognise only a partial truth in his words. With the development of the concept of *lishang-wanglai* I

---

[13] For example, Fei 1947, Skinner 1971, King 1986, Yu 1987a, Zheng 1995a, Bian 1997a and b, Zhai 1997, and Yang and Peng 1998/99.

understand now that there is a different way to understand and analyse Chinese society.

To do business involves a market relationship which is pushed by an invisible hand – universalism. Particularism relates to personalised relationships everywhere in the world. In theory people can personalise all sorts of relationship including even the market relationship itself. In practice, some relationships can't be personalised, e.g. the international standard market system or the legal system. However, in China there is a problem as to which is more powerful: law or political power (*fa da haishi quan da*) because the Chinese legal system has never been separate from political power. Individuals can be personalised by Chinese particularism, but international systems act as a necessarily universalistic restraint on this. China is a part of the world so processes of sinicization (*zhongguohua*) and globalisation (*quanqiuhua*) are happening at the same time. *Lishang-wanglai* delineates the boundary between what is non-personalised or personalised in complicated relationships and further categorises the four different types of personalised relationships (*wanglai*). According to the *lishang-wanglai* model, apart from the different types of *wanglai* there are different *lishang* criteria (see Chapter XI) which can help people to distinguish different *wanglai*, improve the quality of *wanglai*, maintain or update *lishang-wanglai* networks, etc.

Lishang-wanglai provides a way to understand Chinese society and could in principle be applied to the rest of the world, although its effects might be less obvious in Western countries. The key is that in China universalistic exchange relationships may be, but do not have to be, turned into personalised relationships, and vice versa. When this happens relationships become partly particularist or partly universalised. But the co-existence of particularism and universalism is not static. My examination of possibilities and changes between particularistic and universalistic relationships sets my work apart from that of other researchers. In this book I have shown that by empirical investigation with help from *lishang-wanglai* it is possible to discern how in Kaixiangong people use a set of principles to act on social relationships and to make them personal.

In order to show how the globe shaped ego-centered *lishang-wanglai* networks spin, I will now discuss the motivation for conceptualised *lishang-wanglai* in Chapter IX.III.

IX.III. Social creativity as motivation behind *"lishang-wanglai"*

When I mentioned creativity my English husband said that Chinese people are generally less good at scientific creativity than English. He formed this view from his teaching experiences over many years at Imperial College of London University, where Chinese students (including those who come from Hong Kong, Taiwan, Malaysia and Singapore, overseas) lead where passing examinations are concerned but often perform less well doing project work. However, he and many like-minded Europeans have been similarly categorised as simple-minded or scatter-brained (*que xinyanr*) by Chinese people because they are not good at working out complicated human relationships in everyday life. Here the Chinese character of *xin* (heart) has been translated as mind or brain. Half a century ago Liang Suming (1949, 1975) believed that the human heart is different from the human mind. He said non-Chinese scholars have not yet acknowledged the importance of study related to a human being's "heart" as opposed to psychology which is concerned with the mind [14], and is so advanced in Chinese culture that it is impossible to have an equal dialogue with the West in this field (132, 280). However, towards the end of the twentieth Century a Chinese woman's American husband Kipnis (1997) conceptualised a kind of *ganqing* which touches upon Liang's "human heart" in its understanding of Chinese people and culture. Liang's notion can also be linked to social creativity in the Western social sciences.

1. Kipnis's *ganqing* and Liang's *qingli*

I will consider Kipnis's study on *ganqing* first and extend it to Liang's study on the human heart. Apart from embodying *ganqing* (see *ganqing* in Chapter X.VII) Kipnis's study of *ganqing* also touches upon its psychological effects and cultural aspects (111 and 195, n.2). In Fengjia village clinic a four-year-old boy was crying for fear of an injection and his mother told him that "[There] won't be a shot (*bu dazhen*)" or "[No] more shots (*bu dazhen le*)" before and after the injection. Kipnis thought this way of handling children would normally be considered as lying or dishonest by the Western standard or at least "white lies" (111-115) and explained this kind of *ganqing* with "nonrepresentational ethics". However, in China it is considered as comforting or soothing for the boy because the mother shared the boy's pain with her heart (*ganqing*) and encouraged the boy with "It's OK" (*renqing*) – an interpretation of "There won't be a shot" and "No more shots". By contrast, it would be considered that the mother was too cruel (no *ganqing*) with her son if she told him the truth. Let's move to another common case in China. A warm-hearted host offered to share her favourite hot dish with a guest and told him "It is not hot (*bula bula)* and have some (*chang yi chang*)". This is considered as perfect manners (*renqing*)

---

[14] Liang didn't mention psychoanalysis, and especially did not follow the development of psychoanalysis after Freud's original work. I will exclude the discipline of psychoanalysis, although it may have some bearing.

for the host because she believed that if your mind thinks "it's not hot" your body would feel "it's not hot" and therefore you would enjoy the food well. In contrast, it would be impolite or rude if the guest refused her (*renqing*) because it would hurt her feelings (*ganqing*).

In China this effect of *ganqing* is very powerful. For example, there is a pair of sayings representing two extremes of how the contemporary Chinese government controls its people. One is "A fine example has boundless power (*bangyang de liliang shi wuqiong de*)" meaning that to make a model of a positive character, like Lei Feng in 1960s or models of patriotism nowadays, could gain endless benefits. Another saying refers to "killing a chicken in front of monkeys", or "to punish someone as a warning to others" (*sha ji jing hou*) which is also very effective, examples of its use being action against counterrevolutionaries in the Cultural Revolution or the Chinese democrats or Falungong practitioners. This kind of *ganqing* can also be used by an elite to encourage the young. A successful Chinese writer, Liang Xiaosheng, said that all his achievements were inspired by a single sentence about him from a famous writer, Ru Zhijuan, who had said "Xiaosheng is a good young man (*Xiaosheng shi ge hao qingnian*)" in a symposium when he was an undergraduate. There is another saying which appeared in 1989 and is still quite popular: "You will be fine if you are told you should be, even you are not. You won't be good if you are told you aren't, even if you really are. (*Shuo ni xing ni jiu xing buxing yexing, shuo ni buxing ni jiu buxing xing ye buxing*)". This gives rise to several questions: Who said that to whom? And, what is the real power that determined a person's fate?

I will now invoke a Chinese sinologist Liang Shumin's (1949/84) *qingli* (reason, sense, code of human conduct) which is central to Liang's notion of human heart. Here the *qing* of *qingli* relates to human feelings. According to Liang, *qingli* includes external and internal feelings, such as to be a kindly and loving father, to be a filial and dutiful son, to love people, fairness, a sense of justice. This kind of *qingli* comes from the human heart (129, 134) and relates to Kipnis's very different examples of *ganqing*: one person's anger at another (a woman shouted at a watermelon seller, 28), informal group *ganqing* (a women yelled at birth control officials, 107), collective *ganqing* (28), and class *ganqing* (104-10, 185-86). In China there is also patriotic *ganqing*, nationalist *ganqing* and religious *ganqing*, all of which can grow into *reqing* (a strong warm feeling, ardour, glow, enthusiasm) or even *kuangre* (excessive, irrational zeal, fanaticism and craze). Where does the re of *reqing* or *kuangre* come from? According to Liang (1975) it might be driven by "*qi* (spirit, morale, anger, rage, insult, vital energy, energy of life)". For Liang, the human heart is formed by *zhudongxing* (go-aheadism), *linghuoxing* (flexibility) and *jihuaxing* (plan, arrangement) (16). The character of the human heart is *jing* (stillness) of *xinqi* (heart and *qi*) (40-41). It sounds like psychology, religion, or something beyond human knowledge. There are some *ganqing* related Chinese phrases involving "*qi*": "acting impetuously (*ganqing yongshi*)", "be swayed by personal feelings (*yiqi yongshi*)", "get angry (*shengqi*)", "try to make a good show or win something (*zhengqi*)", "with justice on one's side, one is bold and assured (*lizhi qizhuang*)", "full of vigour and vitality or sap or animal spirits (*xueqi fanggang*)".[15] The translations of these phrases lose some of the original meanings because "*qi*" is virtually impossible to translate. "*Qi*" can be traced back to Taoist philosophy on the origin of human life. It might be helpful if we use some concrete examples. Why do the peasants shout at each other in villages in rural China, or in urban China professors shout at each other in top institutions, or doctors fight each other physically in a top university not only during the Cultural Revolution but in ordinary times in the twenty-first century? Why did the Chinese people climb Everest from the North side in 1960 without having the technology, advanced requirements and traditional interests of the British mountaineers who failed on the same route?[16] What are the different motivations behind Mao Zedong starting up the Cultural Revolution? Solutions to this kind of question might come from the "human heart" that Liang (1949/84, 1975) proposed.

According to Liang (1949/84) the *li* of *qingli* relates to *lixing* (理性) which came from Confucius *lunli* (ethic) and its core *li* (Confucian theory). Liang divided *li* into *liyue* (religion and moral rites, 108) and *lisu* (customary rites) based on his human heart theory and the idea of Chinese society formed with Confucius *lunli*. For Liang, *liyue* relates to religion, ideology and morality, which means people can cultivate themselves with *li* through enjoying activities such as music, poems, songs, and dance (109-113). Here the *yue* of *liyue* is the same character and a synonym of the *le* (happiness and enjoyment) but with different pronunciations. *Lisu* refers to customary rites and can also be understood as a kind of popularised morality (*daode*) which is much more flexible than law (118-120). Thus over two thousand years Chinese people actions have been based on the understanding of *qingli* (human feelings with moral judgement) shown above to be implicit in their language and *lixing* (clear, bright, still and harmonious heart) traditionally idealised in their culture, and consequently forming the corresponding structure of Chinese society (128-41).

---

[15] A Chinese-English Dictionary (Revised Edition), Beijing: Foreign Language Teaching and Research Press, 1995.

[16] See: http://www.everesthistory.com

Many popular Chinese usages in everyday life show the relevance of Liang's idea of human heart. For instance, when children do homework their parents often encourage them with the characters of *yonggong* (use your energy for working hard), *yongnao* (use your brain and mind to get the correct answers – good results depend on the intelligence of the child), *yongxin* (use your heart for willing to do it well – it depends on an attitude of trying) and *zhuanxin* or *zhuanxin zhizhi* (concentrate your attention on the work with your heart or with single hearted devotion – if you concentrate the *qi* will push you to finish the work easily). Apart from the Chinese saying I quoted at the beginning of this section that *que xinyanr* (literally, lack of a hole at the right place in the heart is blocking spirit *qi* from getting through) inaccurately translated as simple-minded or scatter-brained[17]), there is another popular Chinese saying that "there is no grief greater than the death of the heart, and no anxiety greater than the loss of aspiration (*ai modayu xinsi chou moguoyu wuzhi*)". Here the death of heart is not a medical term, but explained by loss of aspirations (*zhiqi*), in which *qi* is again involved. Yan Yunxiang also found Xiajia villagers used "heart" in this way, e.g. *mei liangxin* which was translated as "no conscience" (1996b:70). This should be "heartless" which is opposite to "good-hearted" according to the context, and *fumuxin* (heart of parents) which means the parents' limitless benevolence and love of the children, though Yan explained it as a psychological factor (2003:181). Similarly, Kaixiangong villagers always spoke of *xiaoxin* (filial heart or sentiments) rather than *xiaodao* (filial duty or obligation), *xiaojing* (filial respect) or *xiaoshun* (filial obedience) in talking about elderly care (see Chapter VI.II).

Therefore, as I said earlier, based on *jing* (stillness) of *xinqi* (heart and *qi*), Liang (1975) claimed the human heart was formed with three *xing* (nature or character): *zhudongxing* - go-aheadism, *linghuoxing* - flexibility and *jihuaxing* - plan or arrangement (16-41). To a certain extent, the above three *xing*s of a human heart can be generalized with Mao Zedong's one *xing*: *chuangzaoxing* – creativity, and interpreted with Mao's famous slogans. "[People], only people are a real force of creating world history (*renmin, zhiyou renmin caishi chuangzao shijie lishi de zhenzheng dongli*)", "[Only] human beings can create whatever wonder in the world (*zhiyao you le ren shenme renjian qiji dou keyi chuangzao chulai*)"; "[Fighting] with the Heavenly gods and the earth (nature) and creating a new world (*zhantian doudi chuangzao xin shijie*)" and "[It] is endless enjoyment of fighting with the Heavenly gods, the earth (nature) and human beings (*yu*

---

[17] Same as note 75.

tian fendou qi le wuqiong, yu di fendou qi le wuqiong, yu ren fendou qi le wuqiong)".[18]

Watching Kaixiangong villagers evident enjoyment at working on their *lishang-wanglai* networks, I was struck by the similarity of spirit between these heroic slogans of Mao and the creativity daily expressed in villagers' ordinary lives. This kind of creativity with enjoyment might describe Chinese people's social creativity in the process of people making, maintaining, or stopping relationships with *lishang-wanglai*.

2. Social creativity and a case study

In rural China the real work in managing family social support comes from decisions to alter exchange relationships by developing some, or dropping others. Chapters IV to IIIV have shown how the dynamics of *lishang-wanglai* can be considered a socially creative process. I am finally moving onto a relatively new theory of social creativity as a driving force for *lishang-wanglai,* which is a combination of principle, criteria and motivation, etc.

Social creativity was a quite commonly recurring phrase in the 1960s, according to John Davis, former President of the Royal Anthropological Institute (1997-2001). Here I would like to omit a full literature review in the field of social creativity and instead quote some statements directly from John Davis (1994). After reviewing other researchers' work, Davis came to his conclusions: "social order we seek to create is in fact not a system, nor a structure, nor an organic functioning whole nor a necessary and inevitable evolutionary track, but a series of ramshackle contraptions which serve to get us through from one day to the next. They are ingenious, clever, often pleasing to contemplate, but they are inherently unstable and need continual affirmative re-creation and maintenance" (1994:107-108). "People use their given sociability to create agreements about actions" (97). "Every action and thought which involves other people is creative sociability, attempting to make a social world which is secure and stable to live in... This is a universal, popular and irrepressible activity: everyone is creating most of the time" (98). Therefore, "social creativity is purposeful action aimed at routinising and ordering life to make shared existence predictable from one day to the next; and is in fact a universal, continuous activity"(99). He suggested that social organisation is the product of humans using their imagination and social creativity to work on raw materials, rather than an organic growth of some systemic kind or spontaneous product of society itself. He also suggested that "social

---

[18] Chinese people of my age grew up with endless repeating of Mao's famous slogans in primary schools. They are rooted in our hearts, although my mind can't remember references, which can be found if necessary.

creativity is part and parcel of human creativity as a whole, and that the principles and procedures for studying it are those we use when trying to understand the production of music and pottery, songs and dances, houses and cathedrals. In this sense we are all authors of our social worlds, engaged in continuous creative activity" (103).

My understanding of Davis' idea of social creativity is that people are always creating in order to maintain. In order to make it as it always has been, they are actually always changing things. Based on my empirical study and Chinese literature study I join Kipnis's notion of "nonrepresentational ethics," and Liang's idea of "human heart" to Davis's social creativity and make it the fundamental motivation of *lishang-wanglai*. Liang's human heart includes *qingli* (positive human feelings), *lixing* (clear, bright, still & harmonious heart), and three *xing*s (social creativity –go-aheadism, flexibility and planning, p100). Liang's idea of three *xing*s related to the human heart is congruent with one of my own important findings that *lishang-wanglai* is the way in which participants enjoy balancing the multiple criteria in personalising different relationships. Therefore, Davis' idea of social creativity[19] has reached the same goal as Liang's three *xing*s by a different route. To summarise, we can see that for Davis social creativity is **purposeful action** because the social order people sought is a series of **ramshackle contraptions** which are **ingenious, clever, pleasing to contemplate, inherently unstable,** and need continual **affirmative** re-creation and maintenance.

Davis also classified social creativity into two kinds. One kind of social creativity "implies centres of power", namely it is a top down type, e.g. Thatcher's programme of social engineering. Another is "populist sociability - a form of diffuse power". For me both these types of "implied centres of power" and "populist sociability" can be understood as vertical and horizontal forms, respectively, of social creativity. They are thus highly appropriate to be used with *lishang-wanglai* and social support in rural China.

Finally, I will analyse a small case with *lishang-wanglai* as an example of social creativity. In Kaixiangong Village there are many events on the 5th day of the 5th lunar month, the traditional Chinese Dragon Boat Festival (*duanwu jie*). At one of these, according to the villagers, children less than one year old should wear tiger hats, clothes, and shoes. The tiger suit is for health and luck, because villagers believe it can keep mosquitoes and evil away from the

---

[19] On 15th December 2003 City University organised a workshop on the theme of "Creativity" which encouraged new multi-disciplinary research initiatives in creativity. More details see: http://www.city.ac.uk/researchdevelopment/creativity.htm .

child. A working mother told me a story of how she created a new way for getting the tiger suit (see Photos III-40 and 41) for her son. In the past mothers gathered together to help each other make different parts of the tiger suit because they enjoyed working together to discuss fashions. However, this mother had a job in the township and could not go about getting a tiger suit in the same way. Eventually, to her evident satisfaction, she worked out an alternative.

This case illustrates many points. The working mother created a new way of maintaining the customs of a tiger suit; she did it based on local custom and through her brother (*lishang*); she altered the custom a little to fit into her change of situation; she enjoyed both her creation of a suitable new solution and the allusive way of ending a labour support relationship with neighbours and friends. Different types of *wanglai* can be changed between the same people or different people over time, i.e. expressive *wanglai* to a market relationship; different types of *wanglai* can be changed with space, i.e. geographical / social distance or closeness; the tiger suit case illustrates how *lishang-wanglai* worked in a social support arrangement in which the relationship can be maintained and ended. Below are detailed analyses of the case.

(1) The tiger suit involves both *lishang-wanglai* and non-*lishang-wanglai* relations, and indicates how it is necessary to be continually creative to maintain existing relationships. The working mother had several possibilities to obtain the tiger suit. The simplest way would be to buy one from a shop in the township where she worked, which wouldn't involve *lishang-wanglai*. However, according to local custom, the material should be given by her brother, which involved an expressive *wanglai* between non-agnatic kin. If her brother noticed that the tiger suit was not made from the materials given by him, then he would feel hurt (*ganqing*). If she followed the local custom, she would have had to ask somebody to make it for her because she couldn't do all of it by herself, which would involve them in an instrumental *wanglai*. In the end, she asked her brother to give her some money before he or his wife purchased the materials. She then used the money to buy the outfit from a shop. The idea of buying a tiger suit, and asking her brother for the money, without bothering another person to make it, was creative.

(2) The effect of a particular *wanglai* on a relationship is determined by the existing *lishang* of the relationship. In the relations with her brother, the working mother thought she should keep in with the local custom to let him express himself on that occasion. This can be counted as a moral judgement. She should also care for his feelings and allow him to keep face by letting him take part in the event. This counts as human feelings. She asked for money to buy the suit because she did not want to waste the materials, which is a rational calculation. Although the

tiger suit was not obligatory but optional on the Dragon Boat Festival, it was important to her because she believed it would bring her baby double luck because he was 100 days old at about that time. This is a religious concern. However, these reasons differed in importance. She agreed that human feelings and religious sense weighed more than other reasons. This example shows how *lishang* cause the making, maintaining, altering, and stopping of relationships. They can explain why and how people use their *wanglai* in different ways. What a particular contact or lack of contact means depends on the reason for it. *Wanglai* are the actions of people making relationships. The ways in which people, through contacts (*wanglai*), exchange resources are according to different reasons and principles (*lishang*). The real reasons behind the *wanglai* by which people seek different resources are different criteria of *lishang*. Thus an observation of *wanglai* gives a superficial view of social contacts, whereas determinations of *lishang* allow the overall effect of the contacts to be evaluated.

(3) The tiger suit example illustrates that the local custom can be adapted in changing situations, although customs normally determine what a *wanglai* means. Yan also noticed this (1996b:230-32). Local customs involve *lishang*'s aspects of morality: human feelings, rational choice, and religious sense. Traditionally, good luck (*tu jili*) required that the tiger suit be made by oneself, or any other personal connection. This led to the enjoyment of making it being an expressive *wanglai* with others. This local custom was adapted by the people who bought a tiger suit instead of making one. The working mother was one of the first people who did this. Nowadays, villagers accept the idea of buying a tiger suit for practical reasons. *Lishang* is also intimately related to local customs for annual and life cycle ceremonies. These customs are used by villagers to make *wanglai* – and the *lishang* is affected by the local traditions, as shown by commonly understood customs. Kaixiangong's villagers created their customs while they were using them to support each other. On the one hand, they can meet all changes by remaining unchanged - coping with a constantly changing situation by sticking to a fixed principle (*yi bubian ying wan bian*), which can be understood as *lishang*, even though the contents of the *lishang* could change. On the other hand, they keep a principle of adaptability for survival (*shizhe shengcun*) to adapt themselves to all change. From this point of view, customs live. I think sometimes people want to *zao shi* (create something new), but they always like to have excuses to support their ideas. They make changes, but only for adaptation. They explain that other people always do this, or people already have done something. Their changes may be similar or close to what other people have done, but this is creativity. In other words, the villagers count adapting customs as being socially creative or acting to foster creativity, and no

less so because customs act as external constraints on what is possible. The most significant observation from my fieldwork relates to the way in which customs are modified by villagers when necessary, in order to get the right *lishang* for *wanglai* and so maintain or alter *lishang-wanglai* networks.

(4) In the village the ability to work out *lishang-wanglai* in creative ways for resources is valued and enjoyed. Among the above *lishang* criteria I will concentrate on the meaning of human feelings, which the working mother weighted importantly, by stressing the element of enjoyment. The way in which she worked out an appropriate series of actions without speaking to others, to balance and maintain different *wanglai,* gave her even more enjoyment than working with others in making the tiger suit. This tallies with the nature of Chinese people who prefer to do things in a way that is indirect: "hazy, dim, or allusive" (Smith, 1894: chapter 8). It also conforms to Chinese academic habits, which are also said to be similarly allusive (*hanxu*) or imaginative (*xiangxiang*) in (Gao, 1994:167-205). This can be seen from an old Chinese saying *buyao tongpo chuanghu zhi* (don't poke a hole in the window paper - there was no glass in ancient China). This is a single phrase with a double meaning. On the one hand, the obvious meaning of poking a hole in the window paper is that it causes broken property and lets wind through, and looks nasty even after repair. This is why adults stop children from doing naughty things to the window paper. On the other hand, the real meaning behind the saying is usually used among adults, especially for educated Chinese people. It would be considered too foolish to point out why or to ask why one shouldn't poke a hole in the window paper. The philosophy behind it is to let the audience or reader understand (*wu*) and enjoy the taste (*wanwei*) of it. For them an educated Chinese should be able to understand that poking a hole in the window paper would give a clearer view and at the same time destroy the enjoyment of a hazy view. Since the window paper is too ancient for modern people there are some common sayings developed from it meaning the same thing, such as "*buyao tongpo* (don't poke through)", "*diandao weizhi* (don't mention more than a little touch)", *yidian jiutou* (someone understood it as soon as one touched it a bit). There is an essential difference between "don't poke a hole in the window paper" and "don't give him or her all the answers", a Western principle of education. The former wants to keep a thing unclear because if it is obvious it would be tasteless (*meiyou yisi* or *weidao*). The latter wants to encourage others to think for themselves and it doesn't matter whether the answer is superficial or not. This explains the non-explicit nature of Chinese people's actions in personalised relationships and Chinese social studies in which the method of allusion has often been used. I assume this is why people enjoy the maintenance of different *wanglai*, even if

allusiveness sometimes causes misunderstandings (see Chapter XII.III) or goes completely wrong.

(5) The creation and change of *lishang-wanglai* between individuals or groups and institutions can be seen at work over time. As the working mother said, traditionally women made tiger suits together, and this can be counted as expressive *wanglai* because they enjoyed themselves. She has had such expressive *wanglai* in many ways with her relatives, neighbours, and friends. She did not want the business of the tiger suit to reduce her relations with them from expressive *wanglai* to instrumental *wanglai*. Her asking her brother for money to buy the tiger suit could have dropped her expressive *wanglai* with him into instrumental *wanglai,* because the local custom was designed for a son who inherited a family's wealth to support his married out sister, effectively sharing the inheritance with her, by giving gifts on different occasions. However, the tactful way she did it enabled her brother to keep his *mianzi* (face) and *ganqing* (human feeling) so that expressive *wanglai* remained. The working mother's purchase of a tiger suit can also be seen as a market exchange, which is not *lishang-wanglai*. This case also shows the time dimension of *lishang-wanglai* can be a reduction of expressive *wanglai* in favour of market exchange, in tune with the growth of the market economy in rural China. In other words, market exchange can be used to reduce the amount of obligation which occurs under expressive *wanglai*.

(6) The case of the tiger suit shows *lishang-wanglai* can be changed with space. The way in which the working mother did not want to bother others for the tiger suit is one type of changing relationships with space. It can be seen from a close distance geographically. On the one hand, she and her neighbour are neighbours and friends to each other and might have a business relationship at the same time. If the neighbour provides labour support for her the relationship this time between them is more instrumental *wanglai* than expressive *wanglai*. On the other hand, they invite each other for meals, or see each other often socially. In this way they can be close to each other with no or small gifts. Contacts of this kind are more generous *wanglai* or expressive *wanglai* than instrumental *wanglai*, because they involve emotion and enjoyment. There is another type of changing relationships with space that can be seen from the quality of relationships. This is similar to the above point (2) but from the angle of space rather than time. People can convert a relationship into a better or worse relationship by moving to exchanges of higher or lower types. For example, suppose household A was normally engaged in an expressive *wanglai* relationship with household B. A for some reason rejected that kind of relationship, by going down to the next lower type of *wanglai* with B, namely instrumental

wanglai. This was a visible sign that A no longer wanted to have the better (expressive) relationship with B. By doing this A was increasing his social distance from B. Under this circumstance B would stop expecting to have expressive *wanglai* with A, without a word having been said. Thus, *lishang-wanglai* allows some space for people to apply all levels of *wanglai* relationship into their relationships. Even one relationship can have different types of *wanglai* at the same time.

(7) The case of the tiger suit shows how *lishang-wanglai* networks operate, although it is a very small example from everyday life. Household events, whether a tiger suit or a wedding, make variable demands on resources. Resources normally include material, financial, labour, information, technological, emotional, sociability, enjoyment and others. Different people are dependent on different sources with different resources – one can have emotional closeness without relying on the other for information resources, or one can rely on each other, for finance or professional advice, but not for emotional resources. It is these demands, particularly, which require villagers to make creative use of *wanglai* based on *lishang* and hence get the required resources. According to what the resources are, social distance may be much more connected with relationships of interdependence and sharing, including sharing emotional resources and several others. The closer you are the more different kinds of resources you share. The greater the mixture of resources, the more close they are. The tiger suit case involved financial support from the baby's uncle and the possibility of labour support for making the tiger suit. *Lishang* will determine to what extent a particular relationship can be used, currently and in the future, to provide social support. *Lishang* will also determine, for a particular relationship in a given circumstance, what is the appropriate type and quantity of social resource to provide. This use of *lishang* is regarded by the villagers as important both for reasons of utility, to manage household resources, but also as an expressive and enjoyable exercise. Thus, relationships can be made, maintained, altered, and ended through contacts of resource exchange.

The *wanglai* of *lishang-wanglai* are practices including social support in which different types of relationships can be altered based on *lishang*. *Wanglai* can be held with a great variety of contacts. In the tiger suit example, the woman could have asked relatives, neighbours, friends or fellow villagers to make the suit. In both the ESRC project and my study, to deal with different relationships means to connect with different contacts or sources. For major events, contacts or sources include personal sources like kin, neighbours, and friends, and impersonal sources like the collective, government, markets and other institutions. *Wanglai* describe how individuals or groups use different sources and ways at different times to keep in touch with others. It is typical of geographically (but not necessarily socially) close relationships and not identical with physical contacts. It may alternatively be made spontaneously without deliberate intent. The essential difference is that a social contact will have some deliberate effect on exchange relationships. There are a number of ways for new and old contacts to change relationships. Firstly, a new relationship can be promoted, by e.g. making a marriage relationship between two families. Secondly, contacts can maintain or alter exchange relationships. In Kaixiangong, families would update their list of different relationships by adding new or removing old. Thirdly, people can discontinue an old, no longer desired relationship. Relationships can end gradually or suddenly. When relationships change suddenly it affects people more. People are not so affected by a gradual ending, such as the married out woman's discontinuance of the relationship with her father's father's brother's grandson's family in Chapter V, which took place gradually over a period of several years between the girl's first engagement with her fiancé and the marriage, a process also involving the establishment of new relationships between two families and their relatives. According to local custom, everybody who is related to these two families would update their relatives' lists, without involving any words. Thus the married out woman's great-uncle's grandson's family wouldn't feel shocked if they didn't receive an invitation from her.

To sum up, my argument is that to deal with different personal or personalised relationships in different ways (*lishang-wanglai*) is a creative process, and the creativity of people in making and maintaining their relationships is an operation of *lishang-wanglai*. Just as Yan attempts to use *renqing* and *guanxi* as conceptual instruments in social analysis of China (1996b:123), I suggest that *lishang-wanglai* as a whole can be such a concept, its framework serving both principle and action functions of reciprocity. For the purpose of analysis, *lishang-wanglai* is separated into its two constituent parts, *lishang* and *wanglai*. There are also different dimensions of social closeness and social distance. I observed practices (*wanglai*) and look separately at what contacts are and what the principles (*lishang*) for the practices are. I also use *lishang-wanglai* networks to show how people change, start, maintain, alter, and stop their social relationships, and how social support resources are transferred. I have shown how social creativity works with *lishang-wanglai* in making personal or personalised relationships throughout the book.

Chapter IX.I has reviewed how within Chinese culture there are a variety of terms describing the principles behind social relationships. I have already shown that these terms have been the subject of much debate among anthropologists and sociologists inside and outside

China. From these ideas in Chapter XI I will further develop the *lishang-wanglai* model, which is crucial to the concept of *lishang-wanglai*.

In Chapter IX.II a brief review was undertaken of the large field of social support and particularly social support networks. From this the concept of *lishang-wanglai* networks is developed. In this book I am emphasising the dynamic nature of exchange relationships. In rural China the real work in managing family social support comes from decisions to change exchange relationships by developing some, or dropping others. Chapters IV to VIII looked at how the theoretical ideas developed here were applied to analyse fieldwork materials.

Finally, Chapter IX.III reviewed Kipnis's *ganqing*, Liang Shumin's *qingli* and especially Davis' work on social creativity and showed how they can be fitted together. I highlighted that enjoyment of social creativity can be a motivation of conceptualised *lishang-wanglai* and showed how the dynamics of social exchange relationships can be considered a socially creative process.

Chapter X **Review of related Chinese notions**

Chinese scholars from mainland China, Hong Kong, Taiwan and overseas[20] have been able to use concepts from the Chinese socio-cultural matrix to examine Chinese society successfully. The greater objectivity possible from an external observer is equally valuable[21]. This section will attempt to appraise critically Chinese notions relating to reciprocity from both perspectives. In this subsection I will review each of these: *mianzi, chaxugeju, yuan, fu, bao, huhui, guanxi, renqing, ganqing, yang* and *laiwang*. This review will lay the groundwork for my introduction of *lishang-wanglai*, as a key concept with unifying framework in Chapter XI.

X.I. *Mianzi (mien-tzu)*[22]

Mianzi (face) is the first Chinese notion in the area of interpersonal relationships to gain the attention of non-Chinese writers and scholars. Arthur Smith (1894) began his description of the Chinese character in the late nineteenth century with a discussion of face. Lin Yutang (1935/95) summarised "three immutable laws" of a Chinese universe: face (*mianzi*), fate (*mingyun*), and favour (*enhui* part of *bao*), as early as 1935. Hu Hsien Chin (1944) was the earliest researcher to study Chinese face systematically. She divided Chinese face into *lian* (*lien*) and *mianzi* (*mien-tzu*) with a list of five different uses of *lian* and twenty-one of *mianzi* (45-60). According to Hu, "The importance of *lien* and *mien-tzu* varies with the social circumstances of ego. All persons growing up in any community have the same claim to *lien*, an honest, decent 'face'; but their *mien-tzu* will differ with the status of the family, personal ties, ego's ability to impress people, etc. In a tightly knit community the minimum requirements for the status of each person are well recognised. Anyone who does not fulfil the responsibilities associated with his roles will throw out of gear some part of the mechanism of well-ordered social life."(62).

All subsequent discussions retain Hu's distinction between *mianzi* and *lian*, but each elaborates one or the other's importance. They also refer to Erving Goffman's work on face

---

[20] Hu 1944, Fei 1947, Yang L. 1957, Yang G. 1982, Qiao J. 1982, King 1980, Hwang 1985, Zhai 1993, Yang M 1994, and Yan 1996, etc.

[21] e.g. Arthur Smith, Kipnis, Stafford, etc.

[22] *Mien-tzu, pao*, etc. in brackets are older Romanization. I here follow consistently the modern pinyin transliteration, and write mianzi, bao instead.

(1959), which cites Hwang's (1985/87) use of the concept in a study of Chinese power games. As a micro-sociologist Goffman analyses everyday life and is concerned with the ways in which people play roles, and manage the impressions they present to each other in different settings, showing that societies are ordered through a multiplicity of human interactions. In short, Goffman conceptualises "face work" as being about the maintenance and the disturbance of the surface. The key difference between Goffman and Hwang's face studies and the Chinese version of face is that Chinese face has a much richer and more positive concept to do with one's reputation, respect, dignity, prestige, status, feeling, sensibilities, self-respect, and whole concept of selfhood. Thus Chinese face can serve the positive role of keeping society in harmony as well as having adverse effects for certain individuals, e.g. forcing people to commit suicide.

It's useful to make distinctions between *mianzi* and *lian* (Hu 1944), ascribed and achieved status (Ho 1976), social and moral face (King and Myers 1977, Cheng 1986, Chen 1989, Zhu 1989, Yang M.[23] 1994, Yan 1996b). It's also helpful that previous researchers have identified *li* or *liyi* (propriety) and *de* (morality) as respectively the social and moral roots of Chinese face (Cheng, King and Myers, Zhu). Yang M. (1994), Yan (1996b) and Kipnis's (1997) empirical studies have shown how *mianzi*, *guanxi*, *renqing* and *ganqing* work together in Chinese society. In contrast to these writers, I am particularly interested in the principles of high regard and the maintenance of good social relations. For me, both *mianzi* and *lian* or *lianmian* (Kaixiangong's term: *lian* + *mianzi*, cheek and face) touch upon two principles in maintaining reciprocal personal relationships. They are moral constraint (Yan's term) and social embarrassment, which can be seen as part of the *lishang* criteria. In the villagers' words "face is important for man as the bark is to the tree (*ren yao lian shu yao pi*)". In Kaixiangong, villagers use the term *buhao yisi* (to feel shy, ashamed, embarrassed, or humiliated) to describe the feelings involved in situations such as asking for help in return from those people they have helped, or refusing those people who are asking for help even though they would really like to help, or delaying returning a favour. M. Yang's finding in her fieldwork also supports this idea (1994: 141, 196). A villager explained to me that this kind of *buhao yisi* is complex. It includes their own feeling of embarrassment at not being able to live up to the expectations of the others, who might feel resentment, disappointment or disapproval. I confirmed this with my English friends who said

---

[23] This chapter involved six researchers whose surnames are Yang, e.g. Yang Guoshu, Yang Haiou Yang Liansheng, Yang Meihui, Yang Yinyi and Yang Zhongfang. In order to distinguish who is who whenever I mention them I will put their middle initial after the surname.

they would normally feel *buhao yisi* to ask their friends financial questions, invade their privacy, or take advantage of them. In addition, a villager told me that the idea behind the feelings of *buhao yisi* is a set of moral judgments distinct from formal politeness. There are some relevant Chinese sayings consciously held by the villagers: one ought to repay debt (*qianzhai yao huan*), one would feel light without debt's pressure (*wuzhai yishen qing*), the better the returned credit the easier it is to borrow (*you jie you huan zai jie bunan*), never becomes a "debt-asking ghost" (*bu zuo taozhaigui*).

X.II. *Chaxugeju*[24]

Based on Chinese classic texts and villagers' everyday life in Yunnan Province, Fei Xiaotong (1947) defined the ego-centered social relationships of *chaxugeju*. He used the notion of a "differential mode of association" to describe Chinese social structure, involving certain principles. Fei explains Chinese social structure with an image of the effects of throwing a stone into a pond. An individual's ego is at the centre of his social world, and all other people have different distances around him. Social relationships (*shehui guanxi*) are a network (*wangluo*) formed by increasable personal connections (*siren lianxi*) (21-28). On the other hand, Fei (1947) explains that the *xu* of *chaxugeju* is based on Confucius's *lun*, which relates to ten types of relationships (25).[25] Fei claims the starting point of a moral system in *chaxugeju* is to cultivate oneself according to *li* and the whole set of personal relationships[26] maintained by *de* (29-35). In other words, restraint, by self-cultivation (*keji xiushen*) based on *li*, is the most important factor in building personal networks (*siren guanxi*) (25-26). Fei also compared *li*, *de* and law in people's lives. He said *li* is the most important element, maintained by internalised customs, *de* is maintained by public opinion, and law is a restraint on people from outside. So rural society is a *lizhi* (rule by rites), a society which is ruled mainly by *li*, not by law (48-59). Although the contents of *li* are sometimes cruel, they are maintained as traditional customs revered from

---

[24] While writing a book *Study of Fei Xiaotong's theories and Restudies of Kaixiangong Village*, will be published in October 2010 by the Foreign Language and Teaching Research Press, I reread the book *From the Soil* (1992), a translation of Fei xiaotong's *Xiangtu Zhongguo*, by Gary G. Hamilton and Wang Zheng. I found the introduction, Epilogue and notes extremely helpful for learning Western opinions of the same subject matter.

[25] They are relationshi0ps to ghosts and gods, between a monarch and his subjects, father and sons, husband and wife, noble and commoner, close and distant, near and far, and so on.

[26] This is the first time Fei broadened his term of *shehui guanxi* (social relationships) from the previous paper instead of *siren guanxi* (personal relationships) (1947:33).

inside. Fei pointed out that rural Chinese people live one small area with close relationships that limit some social activities. For example, due to strong senses of *renqing* and *mianzi* (face), some villagers go to a market a long way away from the village to trade, to avoid a conflicts of principle within the village (75-77).

The idea of *chaxugeju* has influenced many researchers. For example, Lau (1982) divided kinship into the three categories of family, close-kin, and other kin in 1977 Hong Kong. He found that *chaxugeju* existed in emotional support, financial support, and in the resolution of problems. Both Yang Yinyi (1995, 1999) and Chen Junjie (1996/98) suggested that *lunli* (Fei's *chaxugeju*-based Confucian basic relationships) should be one of three basic dimensions of *guanxi* structure. Yan (1996b) also mentioned *chaxugeju* related to *guanxi* (228). From my point of view the structure of *chaxugeju* looks similar to Sahlins's model of reciprocity (see Chapter XI.I). Fei touched upon principles of moral judgment, human feelings, rational calculation and religious sense. However, over half a century later Fei's *chaxugeju* is still regarded as debatable. Its main drawback is a lack of testing in empirical studies and refinement through studying related theories. Fei's ideas chiefly came from Confucius's classic texts, but there were other related social theories in ancient China. Fei's understanding of Confucius's morality needs to be justified in people's real lives. How I see *li*, *de*, and law working now are quite different from what they were either in ancient times or when Fei wrote his work because situations in my fieldwork villages have changed. Although Fei noticed changes in relations, more work needs to be done to understand the process of changing personal relationships.

X.III. *Yuan* and *fu*

Fei (1947) introduced two related terms *xueyuan* (ties of blood, consanguinity and blood relationships) and *diyuan* (people born in the same land) in studying rural Chinese society. They correspond to *xueyuan shehui* (blood and marriage tied society) and *xiangtu shehui* (native and popular society). In mainland China from the 1980s onwards some *yuan* related terms appeared in Chinese sociological textbooks.[27] They formed personal networks: *xueyuan* for relationships based on ties of blood, *qinyuan* for kinship relationships, *diyuan* for fellow-townsmen relationships, *yeyuan* for colleagues' relationships and *youyuan* for friendship. Many researchers

---

[27] e.g. *Shehuixue Gailun* (*An introduction to Sociology*), Fei Xiaotong, eds. 1984, Tianjin: Tianjin People's Publishing House.

have carried out empirical studies with the above "*yuan*" related relationships in different subject areas, e.g. Wang Xiaoyi (1993) from sociology and Zhai Xuewei (1993) from social psychology.

Commonly *yuan* is used to mean a predestined relationship, luck or fate by which people are brought together (Cudianzu 1995:1262). It originates in Buddhism. According to Sun Shangyang (1994), Buddhism was successfully brought to China by eminent monks who interpreted Buddhist doctrine as in sympathy with Confucian and Taoist beliefs. The Chinese version of Buddhism accepted the idea that people should deal with relationships according to *lunli*. For example, people linked by marriage are called *yinyuan*, and by blood as *xueyuan*, and by the same place are *diyuan*.

Yuan became an object of study in its religious sense starting with Yang Guoshu (1982/89) in Taiwan. He claims that the Chinese have a strong sense of fatalism, which is expressed as *yuan* in interpersonal relationships. According to Yang G., there are five direct sources of *yuan* in people's everyday life in traditional society: gods or immortals descending to the world, the transfer of evil spirit and fraud, reincarnation and transmigration, retribution of good and evil, and design by the nether world. Yang G. lists 17 types of *yuan* and divides them by time (long term or short term) and moral judgement (good, bad, and normal). He also lists 30 popular phrases about *yuan* and divides them into different groups. 70 percent derive from marriage relationships, either good or bad, long term or short term. Based on his initial results of an empirical study in university students in 1980 he believes *yuan*'s basic function is to maintain harmonious interpersonal and social relationships. Yang G. related five functions of *yuan* to psychologists' (e.g. Weiner, B. 1979) work on the process of establishing, making and maintaining social and interpersonal relationships. They are an attributional process in establishing relationships, an acquaintance process as soon as there is contact, defence mechanism after the relationship fails, defensive rationalisation in maintaining relationships, and self-fulfilling prophecy. Some empirical studies also proved the importance of *yuan* in social or personal relationship, e.g. Zhai Xuewei (1993) and Yang Yinyi (1995). I too use *yuan* in the analysis of my fieldwork, e.g. I use the common term of *xueyuan* (tie by blood or relationship by blood) to distinguish family relationships from other types. However, I do not use the terms of blood for the male line and flesh for female care and reproduction, which tends to be patriarchal and marginalising towards women. I found in Kaixiangong Village that it is quite common for married couples who have difficulties in working together to blame the marriage itself, as *mei yuanfen* (not a predestined relationship). This belief in destiny focussed my attention on the "religious sense" of *lishang*.

Religious sense can also be seen from Fei's (1947) earlier work on *fu*. When Fei introduced the terms *xueyuan* and *diyuan* he was not thinking of involving a religious sense in social relationships. However, when he described the power of tradition with the term *fu*, he was clearly referring to a kind of religious sense. Fei tells us that some traditional treatments for curing illness are highly effective (*lingyan* - work magically). Such things are not easy to understand, and the villagers do not bother to ask questions about them. They simply believe that to follow the traditions will bring *fu* for them and there will otherwise be endless problems (52-53).

Fu is a general term for blessing, benediction, happiness, good luck, and good fortune. There are many terms related to *fu* in Chinese everyday life. For example, *fuqi* or *fufen* (good luck, good fortune), *fuxiang* (a face showing good fortune), *fuxing* (lucky star), *fuzhi* (happiness, blessedness), *fuli* (welfare, well being), *xiangfu* (enjoy a happy life, live in ease and comfort) or *xiangqingfu* (a peaceful, quiet and easy life), *xingfu* (happiness), *zhufu* (blessing, benediction). Gou Chengyi (1994) carried out a literature study especially on the topic of *fu*. He summed up the traditional meanings of the term based on *wufu* (five good things) in the traditional Chinese culture of *jixiang* (lucky, auspicious, and propitious). *Fu* is the first word of the five *fus* (*fu-lu-shou-xi-cai*). The rest includes *lu* (official's rank and salary in feudal China), *shou* (long life), *xi* (happy, joyous, delighted), and *cai* (wealth, money). However, ordinary people's understanding of *fu* is concrete. For them, *fu* means to be well-fed and well-clothed, all is well, calm and peace, have a long life and many sons, no misfortune and disaster.(5-66). Gou also described different ways to reach *fu* in Confucius, Taoism, and popular culture. According to Gou, Confucius's ways include "*li* (morality, etiquette, manners, rituals)", "*xiao* (filial sentiments and behaviour)", "*ren* (kindheartedness, benevolence, humanity)", "*shun tianming* (acceptance of destiny and cultivating oneself)", "*zhongyong* (opt for the golden mean)" (124-164). Gou continues that the Taoist ways to reach *fu* are "*zhizu* (be content with one's lot)", "*ziran* (conform to natural trend)", "*wuyu* (constrain one's desire)", "*wuzhi* (humble)", "*xiaoyao* (free and unfettered)" (165-194). However, Gou found that in ordinary people's life and popular culture there are other ways to reach *fu*, not covered by the classics − hard work and frugality, modesty, tolerance and forgiveness, accumulating merit for both this and the other world. Gou then listed twenty customs of praying for *fu* (78-123, 196-252) and distinguished *zhifu* (reaching *fu*) and *qifu* (praying for *fu*) .

This was endorsed by Wang Mingming in an empirical study (1998), but Wang overlooked the main meaning of *fu* (good fortune) in assessing his fieldwork materials, mechanically using "practice" (Bourdieu's term) to analyse rituals, and treating *fu* as "social ontology" (24-25). This is of little help in understanding rural Chinese people's life because it omits religious sense. Kaixiangong villagers who were very poor or ill always talk of their *ming buhao* (bad fate) or *mei fuqi* (misfortune). The villagers also often use *you fuqi* (good fortune) to describe people with long and happy lives. I will use *fu* as a part of the religious sense of *lishang* and show how it affects rural Chinese people's life and their personal relationships. This way of treating *fu* is similar to Fei's (1947) and Yang M.'s (1994). In her fieldwork she also found people often use the term *youfu* for having good fortune (1994: 332).

These usages of *yuan* and *fu* by the villagers are what drew my attention to the existence of a religious sense in the first place. This sense is classified as one of the four criteria of *lishang* (see Chapter X.III) in my study. My fieldwork materials will show that religious sense is very important in making, maintaining and leaving off personal relationships in rural China (see chapters IV to VIII).

X.IV. *Bao (pao)*

Yang Liansheng (Yang Lien-sheng 1957) is one of the first scholars to study *bao (pao)*[28] related to social exchange and social relations in the 1950s. Yang L. found a good starting point for understanding the Chinese meaning of reciprocity from the Confucian classic the *Book of Rites*, and in common sayings. Both sources touch upon the *quality* of return, e.g. to recompense injury with kindness or injury, and *quantity* in exchange relationships, e.g. a person should return either lots more or nothing, or a little bit more, or the same amount of things to those people who have helped or presented gifts to him. This treatment of exchange relationships fits fairly well with Sahlins's reciprocity typology (see Chapter IX.I). Yang L. lists *bao*'s wide range of meanings: report, respond, repay, retaliate, and retribution, response, return, and claims that *bao* as a verb refers to the action of exchange, and that *bao* is also a basis of social relations and principle of reciprocity (1957: 291). Yang L.'s idea of *bao* as the Chinese version of reciprocity has been accepted by a number of other researchers (King A. 1977, Yang M. 1994, Yan Y. 1996b, Guo 1998, etc.) However, I will argue that *bao* is not a proper Chinese term for reciprocity.

---

[28] In his paper Yang uses the term *pao* in an older Romanization. I here follow consistently the modern *pinyin* transliteration, and write *bao* instead.

1. *Bao*'s two extreme ends

Yang L.'s discussion of different kinds of *bao* (see Table 3) from Confucius leads to two extreme ends. One is *bao'en* (pay a debt of gratitude) to the five most respectable persons, which are heaven (*tian*), earth (*di*), one's Lord (*jun*), one's parents (*qin*) and one's master (*shi*); because one owes them so much that it is beyond one's power to return it, so one is obligated to be respectful and grateful to them (291-304). The other is *baochou* (revenge, avenge) for the above special relations. Apart from Confucian social ethics Yang L. introduced another traditional use for *bao*, namely *xia* or *youxia* (*hsia* or *yu-hsia*, knights-errant).[29] According to Yang L., knights-errant distinguished themselves as *xia* (*hsia*) and *yi* (*i*, rightness) who were extraordinarily gifted in personality and talent. They would not expect any reward, and would even reject such a reward when they did favours for others. They wanted to behave ultra morally on a level even higher than that of the sages and the wise, who took pleasure in treading comfortably the moral middle way (294-96). Obviously, this tradition of knights-errant (*youxia*) is even more extreme in terms of exchange behaviour and relationships.

The importance of the two extremes is also apparent from Wen Chang-I's (1982) literature study on *bao*. He found 145 cases referring to *bao* in classical historical literature from Zhanguo, Qin, Han, Wei, Jin, Nanbeichao, to Sui, Tang, Song and Ming Dynasties. 84 per cent of them related to the extreme ends of paying a debt of gratitude (*bao'en*) or revenge (*baochou*).[30] Wen's work is helpful, although the cases are not representative of everybody's views because the sources themselves are an official perspective. The officials writing the literature wrote little about commoners and so the cases involved many more officials than commoners. If something happened to a commoner it would have to be exceptional for anyone to be bothered to include it. My empirical study will show that the rare phenomena of *bao'en* (pay a debt of gratitude) and *baochou* (revenge) don't represent ordinary Chinese people's relationships in daily life (see Chapters IV and VIII.II). I find that *bao* types of reciprocity are identified with generous and negative *wanglai* (see Chapter X.IV) in the villagers' everyday life and religious life.

---

[29] These people were first recognised as a group during the period of the Warring States. During that time some people lost their positions, titles, and became knights-errant. They sought to right wrongs, and were distinguished by their reliability, which was their professional virtue. They proved most helpful to people who desired to secure revenge.

[30] According to the values of those days revenge for one's parents also had positive moral standing.

2. *Bao* is unclear when type and principle are confused

It is confusing to use *bao* for a type as well as a principle in personal exchange relationships. Guo Ying (1998) replaced Yang L.'s *i-yuan pao-te* (*yi yuan baode*, to recompense kindness with injury) with *lishang-wanglai* as one type of *bao* relationship, whereas Wen stated that *lishang-wanglai* is a basic principle of *bao* exchange (1989: 374).[31] (Note that I will provide my own different definition of *lishang-wanglai* in Chapters IX.II and XI.I). For Yang L, *bao*'s two traditions, Confucius's classic and the spirit of knight-errantry, provide a common ground (the principle of reciprocity) for the whole of society (309). Conversely, it is not clear how *bao* based on Confucius's dual standard of ethics (gentlemen and small men), works in the relationships of a commoner's daily life. According to Confucius a society is formed from two classes: the *chun-tzu* (*junzi*, gentlemen) and the *hsiao-jen* (*xiaoren*, small men)[32]. Yang L. explained that gentlemen prefer to discuss and deliberate and find out *yi* (righteousness or the right decision after deliberation) rather than to fight against an unreasonable person - the latter is a mere brute according to Confucius. In this case the knight-errant – Yang L.'s other ethical code of *bao* – would have to be categorized as a small man. Yang L. argues that gentlemen extend their help without seeking reward because their mind is conversant with *yi* (righteousness), whereas small men extend their help seeking reward because their mind is conversant with *li* (gain) (305-306). I, therefore, will treat *yi* (righteousness) and *li* (gain), etc. as part of the criteria of *lishang* and make justifications for how I apply them in common people's everyday life (see Chapter X).

3. Discontinuity is a characteristic of *bao* types of exchange.

As Wen pointed out, the exchange behaviour is finished after repayment (1989:347-382).[33] Among Yang L.'s complicated list of *bao* it would appear that only *huibao* (repay, reciprocity) can be used for ordinary people's reciprocal exchange. However, I found that Kaixiangong villagers hardly ever use this sense of *bao* in everyday practice. I used *huibao*, the term used in our questionnaire[34] to ask the villagers whether or not they support each other using a *bao* kind of

---

[31] Wen didn't use the term *lishang-wanglai*. Instead, his quotation is *lai er bu wang fei li ye, ci chou bu bao fei junzi* (1989:374). The way in which he uses the Confucian passage means the same thing.

[32] Confucius classifies people into *junzi* (gentlemen), *xiaoren* (small men), and *shumin* (commoners). Sometimes *xiaoren* and *shumin* are interchangeable, e.g. *li buxia shumin, xing bushing dafu*.

[33] This paper was first published in 1982. It has been collected in Guoshu Yang, ed. *Zhongguoren de xinli* (The psychology of the Chinese) which was published in 1989, Taipei: Guiguan Press. The pages which I cite are from the latter.

[34] See question number 56 and 59 of questionnaire in the ESRC project, as Appendix A, in Chang and

return. The answer is "No". They explained to me that they always expect a little bit more in return from those people who accepted help from them, and they would also give more in return when they asked others for help. The amount of return to other people should be slightly more than they received, both in principle and in practice. They said this is *renqing* rather than *bao* because they want to keep the balance of reciprocity in the long run. They only use *bao* in the sense of *bao'en* (to pay debt of gratitude) for looking after their parents in their old age and giving them a proper funeral after their death (*yanglao songzhong*). This kind of *bao* is a one-off behaviour which will be finished after they have fulfilled their duty. After that their relationship with their passed away parents will continue in a different form (see Chapter VI.II), but it is not *bao*.

X.V. *Huhui*

Reciprocity is a very unclear concept in mainland China. It became well known as *huhui* (mutually beneficial) from the 1980s when the subjects of anthropology and sociology reappeared in socialist society.[35] There are six different translations for reciprocity in a Chinese version of the *Anthropological Dictionary* (1991), edited by Wu Zelin et al., based on the *Anthropological Dictionary* by Charles Winick (1956/80). They are *huizeng* (return), *yibei hucheng* (address to each other between different generations), *quanli yiwu duideng guanxi* (rights and obligations on a reciprocal basis), *pingdeng huhui* (balanced reciprocity), *yuanshishi wuwu jiaohuan* (generalised reciprocity), and *budengjia jiaohuan* (negative reciprocity) (Wu 1991:576). "*Budengjia jiaohuan* (negative reciprocity)" is one of Sahlins's reciprocities (see Chapter IX.I), which has been translated back into English as "exchange of unequal values" by Luo Hongguang (2000), who actually meant negative reciprocity and unbalanced reciprocity. Instead of *huhui*, Wang Mingming also uses *huhui jiaohuan* for reciprocity (1997a: 133) and *gaihua jiaohuan* for Mauss's generalised exchange (1997a: 175). However, Wang made no mention of Sahlins's different types of reciprocity in his general introductions to anthropology

---

Feuchtwang, *Social support in rural China (1979-1991),* City Uinversity, 1996. Recompense in the Chinese version of the questionnaire has been translated in Chinese as *huibao*.

[35] The subject, together with sociology, etc. was banned in the 1950s, both being treated as bourgeois pseudoscience in China. Scholars introduced the concept from the West, e.g. in William A. Haviland, *Anthropology*, CBS College Publishing, 1982, trans. by Wang Mingming et el., *Dangdai renleixue*, Shanghai: Shanghai People's Publishing House, 1987; Marvin Harris, *Cultural anthropology*, Harper and Row publishers, 1983, trans. by Li Peizhu and Gao Di, *Wenhua renleixue*, Beijing: Dongfang publishing House, 1988.

and his related studies of social support (1997a and b). In Yan Yunxiang's Chinese version of *The flow of gifts* (2000), reciprocity was used in two ways. Firstly, it has been translated as *huhuan* or *huhui* when it was associated with *bao* (14, 18, 142, and 170), which is consistent with Yan's understanding that *bao* is the Chinese expression for reciprocity. Secondly, Sahlins's generalised reciprocity, balanced reciprocity, and negative reciprocity have been translated as *yiban huhui, junheng huhui*, and *foudingxing huhui* (98), and the unbalanced reciprocity as *feijunheng huhui* (155).

Huhui (mutually beneficial) is still a Chinese expression for reciprocity in exchange relationships. Compared with "*huhuan* (exchange or mutual exchange)", commonly used as an economical or sociological concept of "exchange", *huhui* seems to include the character of reciprocity - a long term return without exact equivalence. However, I don't think *huhui* can be an appropriate Chinese term for reciprocity because it excludes "unbalanced reciprocity" and "negative reciprocity". I checked the term *huhui* with Kaixiangong villagers. They always say "*huli huhui*". The *li* of *huli* is the same as the *li* of *liyi*, meaning "interest", "benefit", "profit" or "advantage". The *hui* of *huhui* has a similar meaning to the *yi* of *liyi*, namely, direct gain and long term benefit. *Liyi* was given by an old villager in Kaixiangong Village to show the difference between the direct gain exchange and strategic exchange. I found that *liyi* is a very interesting concept, which can help in understanding social support resources exchanges in rural China. In common usage, *liyi* can be translated into English as the following: "interest", "benefit", "profit" or "advantage". None of these translations can express accurately the intention of *liyi*. They explain half the meaning of *liyi*, namely "*li*". The old villager said people understand *li* as representing the basic needs for their life, as the old saying "*ren wei cai si, niao wei shi wang*" (literally, people die for seeking wealth, birds die for seeking food). He also understood they can't always get *li* by doing something for somebody. This is why sometimes people use *liyi* as separate words, like *youyi wuli* (literally, "get long term benefit but didn't get direct gain").

Yi is one part of *liyi* and itself is a useful word to understand strategic exchange. I couldn't find the right English word for it. I think *yi* is best explained in English as "long term benefit". A villager who gave me the word *liyi* told me the villagers understand that one can't always get direct benefit by doing something, but one might get something useful (*youyong* or *haochu*, literally, "a good thing") in the future when one is in a difficult situation. He even knew the famous Taoist saying *youweili wuweiyong* (literally, "full is gain, empty is benefit", meaning one can see the gain in one's basket which has been filled by gifts, one can also in the empty basket see the long run benefit", in short *youyong*). This is at the core of Taoist social theory. It is the same as Yan's finding in Xiajia: "Within the boundaries of this local moral world, the pursuit of personal interest mingles with the fulfilment of moral obligations, and the value of a gift lies mainly in its role to sustain a long-term order of social life rather than a short-term personal benefit" (Yan, 1996b:226). It is also confirmed from Chen Junjie's (1996/98) fieldwork in which he considered *liyi* (gain, benefit, interests) as one of three dimensions of his *guanxi* structure. For me, *li* and *yi* is a pair of terms related to the reason for producing social exchange relationships. As immediate gain, *li* can figure in market exchange, instrumental exchange, and negative exchange. As long term benefit *yi* can be involved in almost all kinds of exchange relationships except market exchange. In particular *yi* is a strategy for instrumental exchange. Even to cut off a relationship with somebody which could cause harm to oneself would be of benefit. This kind of exchange relationship can be classified as Sahlins's negative reciprocity (see Chapter IX.I).

I found another use of *yi* when I discussed the term *liyi* with other villagers. They gave me the pair of related terms: *jianlisiyi* or *jianliwangyi*. This *yi* is derived from Confucian *renyilizhixin* (i.e. benevolence, righteousness, propriety, wisdom and fidelity). When villagers used this kind of *yi* they linked it with *dao*. The *dao* of *daoyi* can be translated into English as Taoism, doctrine, morals, morality, ethics etc. *Yi* has an original complex form, which is formed by *yang* (sheep) and *wo* (me). Sheep symbolise kindness and happiness, literally one should have or ought to do something leading to perfect satisfaction. In common usage, the *yi* can be translated into English as justice, righteousness, personal loyalty (*yiqi*), and human ties or relationship (*qingyi*), which is similar to *renqing*. In this sense the *yi* is a very important and practical term in particular in personal relationships. *Daoyi* means morality and justice. It is a moral constraint in the exchange relationship. Thus the meaning of *huhui* (mutually beneficial) has been enlarged by the villagers' interpretations from rational calculation (*liyi*) to moral constraint (*daoyi*) in maintaining long term personal relationships. Both rational calculation and moral constraint are components of *lishang* criteria.

X.VI. *Guanxi (kuan-hsi)*

A study of *guanxi* can be traced back to Fei (1947) in the 1940s. Since the late 1970s a number of scholars have made efforts to bring to light the leading role of gifts and other exchange relations in Chinese social life, which relate to *guanxi*.[36] *Guanxi* seems to have

---

[36] e.g., Chen 1996/98; Gold 1985; Ho 1976; Hwang 1985, 1987; Jacobs 1979; King 1988, 1991; King & J. T.

become an important notion and a general analytic concept for the understanding of social exchange and relationships in Chinese society. I will first summarise related work and then provide my arguments.

Qiao Jian (Chiao Chien 1982)[37] is perhaps the first researcher who suggested that *guanxi* should be a general concept for studying complex society. He claims *guanxi* to be characteristic of personal networks and refers to J.C. Mitchell's word (1969: 13) reticulum, (also used by B. Kapferer (1969: 182)), and Jacobs's 1979 phrase, particularistic tie, and proposes *guanxi* as a basic concept for the study of complex societies. Qiao defines *guanxi* as a situation of mutual effect between individuals and groups (1989:105-122). He classifies *guanxi* itself as a common people's saying because he could not find it as a proper term in the formal dictionaries of *Cihai* and *Ciyuan*. He listed twelve uses of *guanxi* (kin, classmate, colleague, friend, etc.), six ways of maintaining *guanxi* (heredity, adoption or entry into a certain relationship with somebody, pull, currying favour with somebody in authority for personal gain, trying to get on well with somebody, strengthening the bonds of friendship), and fourteen functions of *guanxi*.

Huang Guangguo (Hwang Kwang-kuo 1987) provides a complex framework in which he links the notions of *guanxi*, *renqing*, and *mianzi* together. In this framework *guanxi* has been divided into three types of relationships: the expressive tie, the instrumental tie, and the mixed tie (see Table 3). The related rules of the three ties are respectively need, equity, and *renqing*. According to Huang, the expressive tie is generally a relatively permanent and stable social relationship, which characterises family relationships in China in particular. A typical Chinese family is governed by the rule of need since it can meet almost all the needs that its members have, although interpersonal conflict can occur. The relationship in instrumental ties serves only as a means or an instrument to attain other goals. Such relationships between salesmen and customers, bus drivers and passengers, nurses and outpatients are basically unstable and temporary since both parties consider this kind of social interaction solely as a means to achieve their own purposes, and equity rules can be applied. The mixed tie is the most popular kind of

---

Myers 1977; Kipnis 1997; Oi, 1989; Peng 1998/99; Qiao 1981; Sun 1996; Walder, 1986; Yan 1996; Z. Yang 1989; and M. Yang 1989/94, Y. Yang 1999; Zhai 1993/96, Zheng 1984/96, etc.

[37] The name in square brackets is a modern *pinyin* which looks and sounds completely different from the older Romanization. I will apply this to what follows. The paper was originally published in K.S. Yang and C.I. Wen, eds., *Shehui ji xingwei kexue yanjiu de zhongguohua* (The sinicization of social and behavioral science research in China), Academia Sinica, Taipei, pp345-60. It has been collected in Guoshu Yang, ed. *Zhongguoren de xinli* (The psychology of the Chinese), 1989, Taipei, Guiguan Press.

relationship in China in which *renqing* rules are applied. Both sides of a mixed tie know each other well, have some connections or interests in common, thus forming complex networks, with relatives, neighbours, classmates, colleagues, teachers and students, people sharing a natal area, and so forth. The mixed tie can last as long as both parties see each other frequently following the *renqing* rule (1987: 947-953 or 1989: 294-298[38]).

Ambrose King (Jin Yaoji, 1989a, 1989b, and 1994)[39] offers an elaborate interpretation of *guanxi* in Chinese society. He believes there are two basic types of interpersonal relationships or *guanxi*: social exchange (social *guanxi*) and economic exchange (economic *guanxi*) (see Table 3). "In a strict sense *jen-ching* hardly enters into economic *kuan-hsi* since economic exchange is dictated by impersonal market rationality" (1994:120). For King, in social *guanxi*, which is by contrast diffuse, unspecific, and ruled by the principle of reciprocity, *renqing* plays a central role. Furthermore, King claims the focus of the Confucian relation-based social system is fixed on the particular nature of the *guanxi* relation between individuals. Thus *guanxi* is established through social interaction between two or more individuals. The existence of *guanxi* depends on the existence of the attributes (Nakane's term, 1970) shared by the individuals concerned. In Chinese society the most common shared attributes for building networks are locality (native place), kinship, workplace, being classmates, sworn brotherhood, a common surname, and a teacher-student relationship. *Guanxi* building is a work of social engineering through which the individual establishes his personal network. Chinese individuals have commonly utilised this kind of highly personal relation construction as a cultural strategy for securing social resources toward goal attainment, which is usually denied them through normal channels in Communist China. King points out that economic *guanxi*, on the other hand, is dictated by impersonal market rationality. As he states: "the widely cursed phenomenon" of "going through the back door" "will not go away easily, not until the day when market rationality is fully operational, and law becomes the rule of everyday political life" (1994: 109-126, 126).

---

[38] The later reference is written in Chinese and was first published in 1985. It has been collected in Guoshu Yang, ed. *Zhongguoren de xinli* (The psychology of the Chinese), 1989, Taipei: Guiguan Press.

[39] The first two papers (1989a and 1989b) have been selected in Guoshu Yang, ed. *Zhongguoren de xinli* (The psychology of the Chinese) which was published in 1989, Taipei: Guiguan Press, pp75-104 and 319-345. The paper 1989a was originally published in *Collected Papers of the first international Sinological Conference*, Taipei: Academia Sinica, 1980, pp.413-42. The paper 1989b was originally published in *Collected Papers of the second international Sinological Conference*, Taipei: Academia Sinica, pp.39-54. The third paper was originally published in Daedalus 120 (2): 63-84. It has been collected in Tu Wei-ming, ed., *The Living Tree*, Stanford: Stanford University Press, 1994, pp.109-126.

Yang Zhongfang (1991) divided *guanxi* into four types based on *zhenqing* (psychological feeling) and *yingyou zhiqing* (social moral feeling): namely *qinqing* (intimate feeling), *youqing* (friendly feeling), *renqing* (human feeling), and market exchange relationships. She (1998) defined another typology of interpersonal relationships, which are: ascribed relationships (members of family, classmates, etc.), instrumental relationships, and expressive relationships. She (1999) then turned to develop three stages of the dynamic process of building a relationship, starting from courteous reception, to instrumental, then to the expressive stage.

Basing empirical studies on *guanxi,* some Chinese researchers concentrated on the principles in social or personal relationships. Zhai Xuewei (1993) suggested that three Chinese characters *yuan* (predestined relationship), *qing* (human feelings), and *lun* (Confucian relationships) form a Chinese style of interpersonal relationships (*renji guanxi*). The three characters correspond to God, rulers, and laws in the West. He explained the three backgrounds for each of them. *Yuan* is an idea of destiny (*tianming guan*), which provides the root cause of people's relationships. *Qing* tells what kinds of conduct should be followed in these relationships. *Lun* is Confucian centered *lunli* thoughts, which tell people how to keep relationships.[40] Correspondingly, there are religious ideas, individualism, and social contracts in the West. Thus, Zhai concludes that Chinese interpersonal relationships are more likely to be stable, to give more than to receive, dependent, thinking for others, law-abiding, while the Westerner is more likely to move, reciprocate exactly, be independent, think for himself, cherish freedom. Similarly, Yang Yinyi (1995) also claims that in Chinese logic the starting point in making a relationship is the family oriented self rather than the individual self as in the West. So Chinese relationships involve *lunli* (Confucius basic relationships), *renqing* and *yuan* (predestined relationship). Chen Junjie (1996/98) suggested that *guanxi* structure has three dimensions: *lunli* (Confucius basic relationships), *ganqing* (human feelings), and *liyi* (gain, benefit, interests). His fieldwork materials in Yue village, Zhejiang Province, show *ganqing* to be a kind of pure human feeling, sometimes beyond kinship feeling. He also showed how brothers' relationships can turn to enmity to prove the importance of *liyi* in maintaining relationships.

Yang Meihui (1994) offers a systematic study of gift exchange and personal relations in urban China. For Yang M, *guanxi* refers to an interpersonal relationship or personalistic

---

[40] I reviewed Zhai's explanations of *yuan, qing*, and *lun* in X.III and X.VII.

relationship (151), whereas *guanxixue* refers to the art of social relationships, which has elements of ethics, tactics and etiquette (109). Yang M. then shows how *guanxixue* worked in different kinds of *guanxi* through his three elements. *Guanxixue* are embedded in interpersonal exchanges and reciprocal commitments in which *ganqing* (human feelings) or *yiqi* (loyalty)[41] ethics are involved. On the other hand, *guanxixue*'s tactical instrumental dimension links it to impersonal money relations and bribery, in which ethics do not play a role (122-23). Yang M. applies both *guanxi* and *guanxixue* as general concepts in a very wide scope of social relationships in urban China. She also provides many details to show how they emerged in the different periods of socialist China. In particular, Yang M. sees that *guanxi* and *guanxixue* can form a *minjian* (society of people), and become an "oppositional power" to contend with the "administrative power" in China.

Compared with research based on general studies, or observations of urban life, Yan Yunxiang's (1996b) analysis is a case study based on observations of rural life. Yan presented a new interpretation of *guanxi*, giving two chapters of his book to analyse it in emic and etic views. He explored the interlocking relationship between gift giving and network building, and how *guanxi* networks behave in action (20, 75-97). He defined a *guanxi* network's structure which includes personal core, reliable zone and effective zone, based on the local definitions (105-114). He drew three ethics of *renqing* (rational calculation, moral obligation and emotional attachment) as principles of *guanxi* networks (146). For Yan, *guanxi* is the operation of *renqing*, and *renqing* is the deeper level of *guanxi*. In other words the higher the *guanxi* relations the deeper the consideration of *renqing*.

Instead of *guanxi* and *guanxixue* (Yang M., 1994), *guanxi* and *renqing* (Yan, 1996b), A. Kipnis (1997) uses a pair of terms *guanxi* and *ganqing* to analyse human relationships in peasants' village life. For Kipnis, *guanxi* refers to different types of interpersonal relationships (25, 224-25). The reference of *guanxi* is "self". Influenced by Pierre Bourdieu, Kipnis's 'self' is broad. It is not an internal one, but a place in the social hierarchy and an association with appropriate feelings (*ganqing*). "[When] Fengjia villagers re-create their networks of relationships, they also re-create themselves. If one considers the self to be socially determined…, then one's relationships in fact constitute one's self" (8). Thus according to Kipnis, *guanxi* stands for making relationships and associations, and therefore for the creativity

---

[41] I will explain the terms *yiqi*, *daoyi*, and *yi* in 6.2.

of social actors in contracting themselves in terms of relationships. He demonstrated how *guanxi* is produced by examining how *ganqing* is embodied over different events and rituals with a broader sense, what the cultural logics of *guanxi* production reveal about the kinship, gender, local patterns of subjectivity, and Fengjia political economic evolution, and how Fengjia people are 'subjects' producing *guanxi* through gift giving, banquets, *kowtowing* in everyday life, weddings, funerals and other occasions to constitute their 'self' and 'subculture'.

The above researchers' efforts to conceptualise *guanxi* shows, on the one hand, *guanxi* is a structure of networks (Qiao, Hwang, King, Yang Z.) as well as principles (Hwang, King). On the other hand, while Zhai, Yang Y., Chen draw principles for *guanxi,* Yang M., Yan and Kipnis used other concepts (*guanxixue, renqing* and *ganqing*) to pair with it. However, my understanding of *guanxi* and my fieldwork findings are not consistent with them. Here I would like to argue that *guanxi* is no longer a useful general analytic concept in the study of ordinary people's personalised relationships and reciprocity. My reasons are as follows:

1. *Guanxi* is over-extended and imprecisely used by earlier researchers

Some researchers use it in the narrow sense of personal relationships (King, Huang), and some researchers use it in the broad sense of social relationships (Yang M., Chen) or human relationships (Kipnis). Some researchers use it with a negative connotation (Gold, Oi, Huang), and some researchers use it with a positive connotation (Yang M.). Some researchers use it as a descriptive term (Jacobs, Walder); some researchers use it as a general analytic term (Qiao, Huang, King, Yang M, Yan, Kipnis and Chen). I have no problem in using *guanxi* as a descriptive term and to classify different types of relationships, although there is perhaps a difference in usage within rural China, or between rural usage and the generalisation of the concepts of Kipnis and others. *Guanxi* is more likely to be used in a negative sense in Kaixiangong Village. For them, *guanxi* refers to a specific kind of exchange relationship applicable only to special or important people. In this sense *guanxi* in rural China does not accord with that assumed by Yang M. and Kipnis. Kaixiangong villagers told me that most people are ordinary people (*putong ren*) who haven't got *guanxi*, there are only a few special people who have *guanxi*. Those people are either themselves local cadres, or have important kin. Villagers also told me that their households could become upstart households (*baofa hu*), if they had *guanxi*, as Yan found from Xiajia village "rural cadres can absorb more non-kin ties into their personal networks and build larger networks" (1996b: 119). Since *guanxi* appears as a one way flow and unbalanced and unequal relationship in China, it always demands that people of lower social status give more to those of higher status in order to obtain some kind of resource controlled by the latter, as Yan described in his book (1996b: 147-75). Oi also shows that a few succeeded in using personal connections (*gao guanxi*) for better jobs or to receive special favours from leaders (1986/9:146). In Kaixiangong, the villagers value working ability more than the ability to make *guanxi,* due to *guanxi*'s strong instrumental flavour and negative sense. In the past the term of "ability" was never used in connection with *guanxi*. An elderly villager told me that decent people rely on ability rather than *guanxi* to live (*kao benshi er bushi kao guanxi chifan*). Here ability refers to working ability rather than *guanxi* (making and maintaining special relationships) for their households. Like the shop owner in Fengjia (Kipnis, 1997), Kaixiangong people also believe that they do not want to rely on *guanxi* or make *guanxi* in their business. They don't feel shamed to be without *guanxi* or not being good at *gao guanxi* (to make *guanxi*). This is why to make *guanxi* is a rare phenomenon in ordinary people's everyday life in Kaixiangong Village. Although some young people agreed that making *guanxi* for special relationships is a kind of skill nowadays in Kaixiangong, it does not alter their behaviour much. I invited 14 women for a group interview in Qiu's house in April 1996. They all agreed that they would rather work hard outside the village than get a job in the village through making *guanxi* with village cadres.

2. *Guanxi* only represents a particular historical period of China

Qiao Jian (1982) found *guanxi* does not appear in the formal dictionaries of *Cihai* (the sea of the word) and *Ciyuan* (the sources of the word). Nor does it seem to be part of everyday speech in Taiwan (Yang M. 1994) and she surmises that *guanxixue* emerged in socialist China (49). This agreed with Zheng Yefu's (1996) explanations that *guanxixue* became an important behavioural art of particularism in contemporary China because the Imperial examination system was abolished at the beginning of this century, and the market system was abrogated in the middle of the century (55). Sun Liping (1996) even made a structural analysis of it by comparing changes in social relationships before and after social reform at the end of the 1970s. Based on Parsons's general system of action, Sun also provided a typology of *guanxi,* which mixes particularism with universalism and correspondingly expressive and instrumental functions. His document-based analysis showed how particularism worked in different periods of new China. This theoretical exercise is helpful for Chinese in their use of ideas from the West. G*uanxi* and *guanxixue* might be useful descriptive terms to describe phenomena in socialist China, in urban areas, and only some phenomena in rural areas.

3. *Guanxi* attaches to urban areas, but does not generalise to rural personalised relationships

I would like to quote a conversation between Kipnis and a shop owner in Fengjia. When a woman's shop opened for business she received lots of "congratulatory gifts". Kipnis "took the giving of such gifts by the shop owner's friends and relatives and her own prominent display of them to be archetypal *guanxi*-building activities."

> "I asked if these gift givers were also regular customers. She replied 'yes' and I thought to pay her a compliment by saying: 'Your skill at forming *guanxi* has helped speed your success' (*guanxi gao de hao shi ni chenggong de kuai*).
>
> I was surprised when she replied, '*Guanxi* has nothing to do with it. I rely entirely on myself.'
>
> 'But aren't your best customers also the friends and relatives who gave you these decorations'? I asked.
>
> 'Yes,' she said, 'but I charge everyone the same price, so *guanxi* has nothing to do with it.'
>
> 'What about your business license?' I asked.
>
> 'Party Secretary Feng helped me get that, and he's my nephew, so that doesn't involve *guanxi* either' " (183).

For Kipnis, *guanxi* is a concept which covers all personalised relationships in rural areas. But this story shows it is not. Normally I would count the relationship between the shop owner and the Party Secretary Feng as *guanxi*. However, in this case I believe the woman "that doesn't involve *guanxi* either", because Party Secretary Feng himself is a special case. He took this post from 1964, after the old Party Secretary died, until Kipnis left Fengjia. He was a representative to the National People's Congress from 1978 to 1987. He was on the standing committee of the Shandong Province People's Congress and the only "peasant" member of it from 1980 until Kipnis left Fengjia (127, 129). As a local cadre, if he had not treated his relatives and fellow villagers equally, he would have lost his post by the end of the Cultural Revolution in 1976. All of this adds up to a picture of Party Secretary Feng as a local *qingguan* (honest and upright official). It's his job to deal equally and kindly with anyone in the village. The relationship of the Party Secretary with his aunt, in which he gave her a license, is not a personal relationship and would not be covered by *guanxi*.

4. The character of *guanxi* itself cannot be a general analytical concept

The common usage of *guanxi* has been translated to be connections, relations, and relationship (Cidianzu 1995:354). They are nouns which always require working with a verb, e.g. *gao* or *la guanxi* (making relationships), or cultivate *guanxi* (Yan's term), or manipulate *guanxi* (Kipnis's term). To a certain extent, Fei's term of *lianxi* (1947) is even better than *guanxi* because *lianxi* combines *lian* (verb) for making *guanxi* and *xi* (noun) for *guanxi*. The mixture of structure or networks and principles of *guanxi* always causes difficulties in study. On the one hand, as Yan found in Xiajia, villagers "may talk about how much *renqing* they possess when in fact they are referring to the size of their *guanxi* networks (122-123)". The same happened in Kaixiangong. When I asked the villagers "How much *guanxi* have you got?" they always replied "None" because they categorized it as a kind of negative relationship. On the other hand, when *guanxi* is used as a principle for analysis it always requires longer or different phrases, e.g. *guanxixue* (principles, or the art of cultivating good personal relations), *renqing* or *ganqing*.

In sum, the character and the meanings of *guanxi* are too confused for it to be an appropriate general analytical concept. *Guanxi* is not a powerful enough term to cover people's relationships in the wide range of China and the change in different historical periods. *Guanxi* belongs to a particular historical period. Even within that historical period *guanxi* is only true of the cities and not of all the countryside. More crucially for my argument, *guanxi* doesn't cover all personalised relationships for the villagers. Thus *guanxi*'s utility in my own work is limited. Since there are no Chinese characters accurate enough to interpret the Western sense of reciprocity and at the same time analyse how Chinese people perceive the making and maintaining of personal relationships, I borrowed my villagers' usage of *li shang wanglai* (see Chapter XI.I) in my study. In China its use is common, with a long history, and it is still a concept for related phenomena of *guanxi* and *guanxixue*. My use of it is to show how particularism and universalism co-exist in China, as I have shown how expressive, instrumental, and other types of exchange relationships operate under the influence of a set of principles or criteria in making and maintaining personal relationships, basing this work on my fieldwork materials (see chapters IV to VIII).

X.VII. *Renqing (jen-ch'ing)* and *ganqing (kan-ch'ing)*

Renqing is commonly used with the following meanings: (i) human feelings, human sympathy, sensibilities; (ii) natural and normal human relationships; (iii) etiquette, customs, propriety and courtesy; (iv) favour; (v) gifts, presents.[42] *Renqing* used as a principle of social relationship can be traced back to Fei (1947). Based on his fieldwork in Yunnan Province Fei found that people who lived in the same community liked to keep their relationships going with *renqing*. They made sure they were never in debt (*bu qianqing*) overall but in any individual relationship never cleared their accounts (*bu qingzhang*) − so that that balanced relationships can only be seen over a long term (75-77). Yang Liansheng (1957) simply suggested *renqing* could be termed 'social investment' (291). In this case the materialised *renqing* investment is always linked with *ganqing* investment. However, others (King 1980/89, Hwang 1985/89 & 1987[43]) noticed there are always problems in *renqing* practices. Hwang points out the dilemma of *renqing* clearly: the high price of accepting *renqing* from others; the low guarantee of receiving an offering back from others; the risk of feelings and emotions being hurt. Especially when those who lack resources, power, or good *guanxi* face adversity, there is a change in warmth or coolness in the attitudes of their associates following on their success or failure. *Renqing* is as thin as a piece of paper (957-59).

In order to enquire how such investment may be guaranteed previous researchers explored *renqing* as a system. Ambrose King (1980/1989)[44] is one of the first scholars to introduce the notion of *renqing* as a main conceptual tool in the study patterns of personal relations. Based on his study on Chinese ancient literature, King shows the three meanings of *renqing* to be human feelings, resources, and *shigu* (the ways of the world, worldly-wise) (77-83). Hwang (1985/89 & 1987) elaborates the contents of *renqing,* which include human feelings or emotional responses,

---

[42] For points number 1, 2, 4, and 5 see *Han ying ci dian* (A Chinese-English Dictionary), Beijing: Foreign Language Teaching and Research Press, 1995, pp836. For all the five points see *Xiandai Hanyu Cidian* (Modern Chinese Dictionary), Beijing: Shangwu Yinshuguan, 1983, p961.

[43] I have two papers in both Chinese and English written by Hwang. The Chinese one which I have was originally published in 1995. It was then published in Guoshu Yang, ed. *Zhongguoren de xinli* (The psychology of the Chinese) in 1989, Taipei, Taiwan: Guiguan Press, pp289-317. The English one was published in 1997. The page number which I gave comes from the latter.

[44] The paper is written in Chinese. The English text here is translated by me. It was originally published in *Collected Papers of the first international Sinological Conference*, Taipei: Academia Sinica, 1980, p413-42. It was later published in Guoshu Yang, ed. *Zhongguoren de xinli* (The psychology of the Chinese) in 1989, Taipei, Taiwan: Guiguan Press, p75-104. The pages I give come from the latter.

a kind of resource which can be used as a medium of social change, and a set of social norms and moral obligations (953-54). Based on their fieldwork some researchers reached a similar conclusion. For Yang Meihui (1994), "*renqing* is part of the intrinsic character of human nature..., ...the proper way of conducting oneself in social relationships, ...refer to the bond of reciprocity and mutual aid between two people, based on emotional attachment or the sense of obligation and indebtedness" (67-68). And one meaning of *renqing* together with *ganqing* (human feelings) and *yiqi* (personal loyalty) is as the affective sentiments of *guanxixue* (109-145). Unlike King and Hwang, who treated *renqing* with different elements as a part of the *guanxi* principles, Yang Yinyi (1995) simply used *renqing* together with *lunli* (Confucius's basic relationships) and *yuan* (predestined relationship) as the principle of the *guanxi* concept. Yan Yunxiang (1996b) treated *renqing* as a synonym for *guanxi* as a type of exchange relationship (122-23) and emphasises "the system of *renqing* has three structural dimensions: rational calculation, moral obligation, and emotional attachment" (145-146).

Ganqing can be summed up using its definition in Chinese dictionaries: (1) a strong psychological response to a stimulus from outside; emotion, feelings, sentiment; (2) affection, attachment, love of somebody or something, i.e. *lianluo ganqing* (to make human feelings or close relationship with somebody).[45] *Ganqing* (human feelings) studies can also be traced back half a century by non-Chinese scholars (i.e. Fried 1953, Gallin 1966). Since the late 1970s the meaning of *ganqing* has been broadened by some researchers (De Glopper (1978, Jacobs 1979, Oi 1989 and Potters, 1990). Sun Longji (Sun Lung-kee 1987) perhaps is the first Chinese scholar who used *ganqing* as a key term to analyse the deep structure of Chinese culture. Chen Junjie (1996/98) suggested that *ganqing* (human feelings) together with *lunli* (Confucius basic relationships) and *liyi* (gain, benefit and interests) can be seen as the three dimensions of *guanxi* structure. Influenced by Sun's (1987, 1991) work on *ganqing,* Kipnis (1997) argues that *ganqing,* through the processes of gift giving, ritual, and emotional interaction, "simultaneously define (sic) the individual and the social. Through the managing of *ganqing*, villagers create and are created as subjects" within their society (10-11). He also introduced the interesting term "embodying *ganqing*" (27). For him the process of drinking in a banquet (53-54, 56), gift giving (58, 72), weddings (89-96), funerals (97-97, 103), rituals and ritualised decorums such as toasting, bows and kowtow, are discernible forms or methods of materialising *ganqing* (27).

---

[45] Idem. see note 25, Yang 1989.

Furthermore, "*guanxi* unite material obligation and *ganqing*" (72), "*ganqing* is a central component of *guanxi*" (105), and it "must be conceived of more socially rather than psychologically", whereas sincerity, a kind of "inner" feelings of one's heart, is usually absent from *ganqing* (108).

It would seem that Kipnis's usage of *ganqing*[46] is no different from previous researchers' use of *renqing* relating to *guanxi*. More exactly, almost all Kipnis's examples of embodying *ganqing* appear to be describing what others (e.g. King 1986, Yang M. 1994 and Yan 1996b, etc.) called *renqing*.[47] This is also the case with Kipnis's citations of Sun's "magnetic field of human feeling (*renqing de cilichang*)" (9-10) and Fengjia villagers' saying "*zou ge renqing* (to make human feelings)" (58). Previous researchers' *renqing* and Kipnis's *renqing* related *ganqing* can be understood as the same issue. For me Kipnis's embodying *ganqing* (*biaoda ganqing*) or embodiment of *ganqing* can be interchanged with expressing *renqing* (see Chapters V and VI).

Since *renqing* and *ganqing* are so easily confused Zhai Xuewei (1993) suggested neither *renqing* nor *ganqing* but *qing* (human feelings), together with *yuan* (predestined relationship) and *lun* (Confucius's relationships) form the Chinese style of interpersonal relationships. Yan (1996b) makes a good distinction between *ganqing* and *renqing* by borrowing an educated villager's explanation "*ren* stands for personal relations here, like the relationship between you and me. And *qing* is an abbreviation for *ganqing*. So, the term *renqing* should be understood as personal relations based on good feelings" (139). Here Zhai's *qing* is too broad and Yan's "good feelings" is too narrow. From my point of view *renqing* and *ganqing* are useful terms for understanding norms of exchange relations, but they need to be further differentiated.

Based on my fieldwork I define *renqing* as a type of exchange relationship, whereas *ganqing* is a kind of principle or criterion in a relationship. Discovering *renqing* as a type of exchange relationship came from conducting a questionnaire in the ESRC social support project.[48] I found when I asked the villagers "how many *renqing* have you had?" it worked much better than when I asked them about *guanxi* or *huibao* (repayment, reciprocity). The villagers immediately gave me a full list of their relationships. The whole study on

---

[46] Kipnis's other way of using *ganqing*, which touched upon psychological effects and culture aspects, will be reviewed in Chapter IX.III.

[47] See Kipnis's other part of *ganqing* (psychological and cultural aspects of human feeling) in 6.3.

[48] See question number 56 and 59 of questionnaire in the ESRC project, as Appendix A, in Chang and Feuchtwang, *Social support in rural China (1979-1991)*, City Uinversity, 1996. Recompense in the Chinese version of the questionnaire has been translated in Chinese as *huibao*.

lishang-wanglai stems from this finding, which is confirmed by Yan's (1996b) fieldwork finding. Yan perhaps is the first researcher to come upon this phenomenon − when Xiajia villagers talked about how much *renqing* they possess, in fact they were referring to the size of their *guanxi* networks (122-23). However, he overlooked his own finding when he developed his *renqing* system, choosing instead to rely on a literature study of previous researchers (245, n.1 of Reciprocity and *Renqing*).

A full account of the *lishang-wanglai* concept is given in Chapter IX.II and XI. Although I mainly use *renqing* in the sense of expressive *wanglai*, I will also sometimes use it and *ganqing* as descriptive terms like the villagers. I will use the *lishang-wanglai model* to argue that neither *renqing* nor *ganqing* can be general concepts for the analysis of Chinese personal relationships and reciprocity:

1. *Renqing* and *ganqing* cannot analyse a specific type of personal relationship

Renqing and *ganqing* do not help understanding of Yan's finding that rural cadres can absorb more non-kin ties into their personal networks and build larger networks (119) than ordinary villagers. Yet analyses of other kinds of exchange such as instrumental *wanglai* or negative *wanglai* (see Chapter XI) have been successful. My own fieldwork findings agreed with earlier researchers about *renqing*, which accords to four types of *wanglai*. The villagers used three pairs of Chinese characters to describe *renqing*. These are *duo* and *shao* (more and less), *qing* and *zhong* (light and heavy), and *bo* and *hou* (thin and thick). However, when I asked them to explain these characters I received many different answers.

(i) Some people said having more or less *renqing* means more or fewer connections with other people. This agrees with Yan's fourth itemisation of *renqing*, to mean a large or small *guanxi* network, whether expressive or instrumental *wanglai*.

(ii) Others said that more, or heavy, *renqing* means the gifts of *renqing* cost too much to endure (*renqing ya si ren*). Equally, too much or heavy *renqing* means loving-kindness (*enqing*) or owing a great debt of gratitude (*qian renqing zhai*). This kind of *renqing* has more to do with emotional attachment. Extremes of this phenomenon are apparent as negative *wanglai* and generous *wanglai*. Ordinary people tend to "escape" from such a heavy *renqing* situation (King, 1987) and try to keep their relationships more balanced.

(iii) For thin, less, or light *renqing*, some people said this means lack of truthful feeling and shallow *ganqing*. This accords with King and Hwang's description of how some people treat others badly because the latter have lost their resources or power. This kind of *renqing* is more like *guanxi* as a negative *wanglai* rather than instrumental *wanglai*.

(iv) Others thought less *renqing* also means *boli*, which literally means that the gift carries not enough value, or it is a 'small' gift in a self-deprecating remark made as a gesture of politeness. A more popular saying is *li qing qingyi zhong* (literally, the gift is trifling but the feeling is profound). For example, when I presented a small gift[49] to the sampled households where I conducted my interview, I always said it was a *boli* or *xiao yisi*, which I had learnt to do from them. The villagers' reply always was either *qianli song emao* or *li qing qingyi zhong*. (The original saying puts these two sentences together, and means that the gift may be light as a swan's feather, but sent from a thousand miles away, it conveys deep feeling). An informant told me that he appreciated my gift very much because it was I who had chosen, bought, and carried it all the way to them from England. This is an indication of villagers' moral norms for judging other people's behaviour. This kind of *renqing* is more like the system of etiquette, customs, propriety, and courtesy which Chinese people commonly used. It can be understood as expressive *wanglai*, but the relationship can be short or last longer, dependent on maintenance between the two parties.

2. Both the characters of *renqing* and *ganqing* are not simple enough to be general analytic concepts

On the one hand, they are both nouns and have to be used with verbs: "*zou renqing*" in Kaixiangong or "*zou ge renqing*" in Fengjia; "*lianluo ganqing* (to make human feelings)" or "*shenhua ganqing* (to deepen human feelings)". On the other hand they are mixed up with human feelings, exchange principles, resources, a type of exchange relationship. With *lishang-wanglai*, once a specific type of *wanglai* has been judged the criteria of *lishang* can be easily applied. For example, a London-based Chinese woman told me that she had a headache from a gang of English neighbours' children who played with her children in her house. She and my English husband discussed how to stop them from playing for too long and messing up the house, without hurting their feelings. I found how *renqing* and *ganqing* were mixed in this situation, which can be analysed using the criteria of *lishang*.

---

[49] A mini-torch with the badge of City University on the surface.

(i) Morally the Chinese woman believed that as a host she should restrain herself to be always polite, consider guests' feelings, and never tell guests to go away directly (ethic of *renqing*).

(ii) She believed that if she sent them home untactfully she would hurt those children's feelings (*ganqing*). Deep inside she worried (*ganqing*) she might lose potential friendly neighbours (*renqing* network) if she didn't handle the situation well.

(iii) She found that Chinese ways did not work with the English neighbours' children, such as asking them indirect questions: "Are you tired yet"? "Have you done your homework"? "Do you enjoy helping your mum doing housework"? Or even offering them more drinks. Chinese children would understand that it was time to go home without feeling embarrassed (*renqing* practice). She decided to find an English way to deal with the situation. This is a rational choice, like a Chinese saying that wherever you are, follow local customs (*ruxiang suisu*). My husband said that his method of sending them home would be to give the reason that he felt tired and he wanted some peace, in a straightforward and friendly manner, and invite them to come again at some other time. This can be described as saying that: "true politeness is to do with making other people feel comfortable, not following social rules". She told me that although the English saying discourages "following social rules", she would treat the saying as a "social rule" itself or *renqing* principle for dealing with English people.

3. It is too difficult to use *renqing* and *ganqing* as analytic concepts when they are mixed in one relationship at the same time

This can be seen from an example in Kipnis's fieldwork in Shandong. When Kipnis was sick and wanted to rest he received a stream of visitors, but a local person told him that he shouldn't show his irritation to them otherwise he would lose them as friends (27-28). Based on my experience in Kaixiangong Village there might be four reasons for the possibility of losing the villagers as friends, which accord with *lishang*.

(i) It could reduce the villagers' trust of the anthropologist if he behaved strangely, because they expected the specialist on Chinese cultural studies to know the basic ways of the local world (*renqing*). To visit the sick (*tanbing* in Yan's Xiajia and *wangxin* in Kaixiangong) is a quite common custom in China. Not showing one's irritation to the villagers would be can be considered a "white lie" in the West according to Kipnis, whereas in Chinese society a mutually understood code of social behaviour (*renqing*) is considered to be more important than the person's private "true" feelings (*ganqing*).

(ii) Some villagers accepted him for a friend, so it could hurt their feelings (*ganqing*) if he did not appreciate their kindness in paying visits to him (*bu lingqing*). This kindness was not deep, but arose from sympathy with him for being ill and a long way away from his own home. If the villagers felt hurt or embarrassed they would close their hearts towards him. This kind of feeling is *ganqing* rather than *renqing*.

(iii) Other villagers visited Kipnis as a way of following local custom (*renqing*), a rational choice because it was polite for them to do so, although they had not yet developed a friendly feeling (*ganqing*) towards him. In this case they were embodying *ganqing*

(iv) Religious sense can be seen in a Chinese saying that *sanfen bing qifen yang*, literally, the illness is three parts physical, seven parts spiritual. Kaixiangong villagers had a general belief that a sick person would recover more quickly if many people were on his side of *yang* (spirit) and against his *bing* (illness).

These cases show how *ganqing* (human feelings) can be in everybody and everywhere, and *renqing* (tactful ways of dealing with people) also exist everywhere, but operate differently from place to place. The term *renqing* covers a wide variety of meanings: in exchange relationships it partly relates to human feelings, but is also used in the sense of ethic or norm – moral judgment, etiquette, customs, propriety which relate to rational choice, but not to human feelings. I therefore avoid using the term *renqing*, which is insufficiently precise for my purposes. Instead, "human feelings" (*ganqing*) become the second criterion of *lishang*; and I use the term "expressive *wanglai*", rather than *renqing,* as the second type of *wanglai*. *Guanxi*, *renqing* and *ganqing* are thus all incorporated into the *lishang-wanglai model*.

X.VIII. *Yang* and *laiwang*

Finally I will discuss a pair of Chinese notions *yang* and *laiwang*, used in a systematic study of Chinese kinship and related relationships, made by a non-Chinese scholar Charles Stafford (1995, 2000a)[50]. Alongside patriliny and affinity Stafford found two equally forceful, and relatively incorporative, systems of Chinese relatedness, which he called the cycle of *yang* and cycle of *laiwang*. The cycles went beyond earlier anthropologists' (e.g. Freedman 1958, Watson 1982, Faure and Siu 1995) idioms of Chinese kinship and social life with reference to

---

[50] There are some related discussions, e.g. M. Cohen 1976, Chen 1985, Hsieh 1985, J. Watson 1988, Thompson 1988, etc. on *yang*; and Pasternak 1972, Potter and Potter 1990, He 1992, Yang 1994, Yan 1996, etc. on *laiwang*.

patrilineal descent and the kinship system itself (2000a: 38, 52). Furthermore he states that ties are not only based on kinship (2000a: 50) but that "in many Chinese contexts ties based on mutual assistance, co-residence, friendship, and discipleship may be more significant than ties of kinship". This is very true as we have seen from the above discussions of Chinese notions, and will be further substantiated when "*wanglai*" is elaborated in Chapter XI.

To me, Stafford's "cycle of yang and cycle of *laiwang*" can be seen as intergenerational vertical *wanglai* and interpersonal horizontal *wanglai*. From a methodological perspective the cycle of *yang* provides a third dimension in thinking about relationships. Stafford's two cycles came from different routes with the same goal as Yan Yunxiang's directions of flow of gifts: vertical and horizontal (1996b). Furthermore, Stafford also introduced a time dimension, with analyses of separation (*fen*) and reunion (*he*) in the process of people's *wanglai* with each other in their everyday life, both in this world and the nether world. This angle of view is very helpful for looking at dynamic changes of relationships and understanding of *lishang-wanglai* (see Chapter VI.III and later in this section).

However, there are some differences between Stafford's cycles of *yang* and *laiwang* and the conclusions I came to from my study on *lishang-wanglai*, although we both made note of the characters of *laiwang* or *wanglai* from our own fieldwork informants, who used the term of *li shang wang lai* in different areas of China. Stafford interpreted the term as "'ceremonial (*li*) generates back-and-forth (*wanglai*)" (2000a: 47; 2000c:105). According to Stafford "*li*" can be simply understood as ritual/etiquette, such as attending the ceremonial (*ganli* or *suili*), sending-off (*song*), greeting (*ying*), summoning (*qing*), receiving (*jie*), and detaining (*liu*) (2000c: 106). Stafford supposes that "*wang lai*" as the cycle of *laiwang* centres mostly on the relationship between friends, neighbours, and acquaintances (2000a: 38) and uses it as synonym of *guanxi*, i.e. the production of 'social connections' through gifts, favours and banquets as Yan 1996b and Yang M. 1994 have both discussed (2000c: 105). For a different opinion from mine on *guanxi* refer back to the section on the above notion of *guanxi* (see Chapter X.VI). In fact, the starting point of the "cycle of *wanglai*" can be seen from an ego, who builds networks around himself spreading outwards, like the patterns of *chaxugeju* (see chapter X.II). The cycle of *laiwang* is interchangeable with Fei's *chaxugeju*, but unlike Fei's work is based on empirical studies.

Furthermore, Stafford treats the cycle of *laiwang*, between non kin relationships, as "a crucial element in the building up of relatedness between those who are *not* related by kinship" (2000a: 47). He also treats it as an extension of *yang* to the outside world (2000a: 44) or the extension of *yang*-linked reciprocity to the outside world (2000c: 52). However, it is not clear how the two cycles work together with existing systems of patriliny and affinity in Chinese society. Obviously, the cycle of *yang* centres mostly on the parent-child relationship (2000a: 38) which deals with a relationship within a family, whereas previous studies on patriliny and affinity related to kinship or relatives of the given family, and the cycle of *laiwang* has to do with friends, neighbours, and acquaintances of the given family (2000a: 38). Within this framework the two cycles don't answer the following questions: how the cycle of *yang* operates in the respectful care for parents (*yanglao*) in increasingly nuclear families in Xiajia (Yan, 2003) and giving birth for the husband's family (*yang erzi*) in the increasingly frequent marriage pattern of taking a son-in-law into a family (*zhao nuxu*) in Kaixiangong? What is the difference between an affinity relationship and a *yang* cycle of married out daughters and their families to a given family? If the two cycles are to do with **social and personal connections** how can the relationships between a given family member and the dead ancestors be related with the cycle of *yang*, and how can local people be related to local gods with the cycle of *laiwang*? What are the reasons or principles motivating the two cycles' mobility and the social malleability of connections, e.g. reinforced or depleted through successes or failures in the cycle of *yang*, and extended through adoption, or the extension of *yang*-linked reciprocity to the outside world (2000a: 52)?

Let me move now to the key notion of *yang*. Stafford listed its range of meanings: 'to give birth to', 'to cultivate', 'to educate', 'to nourish', and *fengyang* (respectfully care for the elderly), *yang haizi* (raise children), *yang zhu* (raising pigs) and *yang hua* (growing flowers), etc. (1995: 80). He did not delve into the Chinese cultural context to extract the full range of meanings of *yang*, but limited his usage to that to do with "*life*", i.e. human beings, animals and plants. But this meaning of *yang* does not extend to death. The Chinese would have relationships with their ancestors forever, but never accept the concept of *yang* with a dead person or an ancestor (*yang siren* or *zuxian*).

Based on Fei's (1947) ego-centred *chaxugeju* of Chinese social structure, here I will show my understanding of *yang*. The starting point of *yang* is ego.. It extends outwards in the following ways: to cultivate oneself morally, e.g. *yangxing* (nourish one's nature) or *xiushen yangxing* (cultivate one's native sensibility and nourish one's inborn nature, e.g. foster the spirit of nobility by moral cultivation or through a moral life as advocated by Confucianists; conserve one's vital powers by avoiding conflict with the unchangeable laws of nature as practised by Taoists); to cultivate one's spirituality or mould one's temperament, e.g. *yang hua* (growing flowers) *niao* (raising birds) *yu* (feed fish) *chong* (raise insect or worm), *yang mau* or *gou* (keep cat or dog); to take care of one's health and life, e.g. *yangbing* (take rest and nourishment to regain one's health), *yangshen* (rest to attain mental tranquillity), *yangjing xurui* (conserve strength and store up energy), *yangsheng* (care for life or preserve one's health), *yangzun chuyou* (enjoy a high position and live in comfort); to gain material benefits, e.g. *yang zhu yang niu ma* (raise pigs, sheep, cows and horse), or *yang can* (raise silkworms) in Kaixiangong; to maintain or keep in good repair, e.g. *yang di* (increasing soil fertility) or *yang lu* (maintain a road).

The ego of *yang* can be extended to family and country (*guojia*). To provide for a family in a vertical way, e.g. *yanghuo* or *yangjia hukou* (support or feed one's family), *yang erzi* (give birth to), *yang er fang lao* (one rears children against old age), *yanglao songzhong* (look after one's parents in their old age and give them a proper burial after they die), *yang fu mu zi nü* (foster father, mother, son and daughter). To support or serve somebody or something in a horizontal way, e.g. *wei nüzi he xiaoren nan yang ye* (the most difficult thing is to manage one's women – wife, concubine, hetaerae or lover, and to deal with a small man – who is always playing tricks behind one's back), *yanghan* (of a woman having a lover). Examples for *yang* extend to the whole country in vertical and horizontal ways, *yangbing qianri yongbing yishi* (maintain an army for a thousand days to use it for an hour), *jianyi yanglian* or *gaoxin yanglian* (nourish honesty of government officials by living a frugal life or paying high salaries to avoid corruption). My previous work unit refused a person's application for a bigger flat and even skimped part of his salary to punish him for his strong complaints. He angrily left his baby in an office and asked officials: "How can I nurture and educate the revolutionary successor (*peiyang geming jiebanren*) for the party while I can't even survive (*yanghuo*) myself"? Similarly, in Kaixiangong a woman said "I raised sons for the country so the country should support me in my old age" (*wo yang erzi wei guojia guojia wei wo yanglao*), because one of her sons went to University and another went to the Army. In contrast, some Miaogang Township officials received a downwards vertical *yang* from the party and state when it was joined to Qidu Township in 2003. According to the related policy the officials past their 57th birthday should take early retirement. It was called "*li gang tui yang* (to leave their posts and retire with full salary and premium)" which meant the state will take care of (*yang*) their later years. There is also an upwards vertical *yang* between people to the party which is mixed with horizontal *yang*. A popular saying among overseas Chinese goes "I should pay for the great debt to the party and people who raised me" (*wo yinggai baoda dang he renmin de yangyu zhi en*).

Having reviewed the rich meanings of *yang* one can see that the concept of a cycle of *yang* is insufficiently related to their own natural conceptualisations to be understood and accepted by Chinese people. It is also too narrow to cover different social and personal relationships in both vertical and horizontal ways. Even so, the mobility of cycles of *yang* and *laiwang* in vertical and horizontal ways is helpful for understanding the mobilization of *lishang-wanglai* networks (see Chapter IX.II).

Stafford's study on cycles of *yang* and *laiwang* can also help in understanding the *lishang-wanglai model*. Firstly, the study on *yang* and *laiwang* touches upon four basic *lishang* criteria. Stafford said a relatively poor family borrowed 14,000 *yuan* for the son's wedding in order to "look good for the guests" (*mianzi* or face). The reason behind this is complex.

(i) Moral restraint can be one of the reasons. The groom's family provided a grand ceremony to honour the bride and her family. They intended the bride for their hoped-for future, i.e. giving birth to the husband's family and respectfully serving his parents in their old age (2000a: 43, 40-41). At the wedding banquet the guests of relatives, neighbours and friends are monitors for the bride. The bride is under obligation (*yiwu*) to show filial piety or filial obedience (*xiao*) to the groom's parents. The moral idea of *xiao* was transferred through red envelopes from parents to children (1995: 85). If the bride didn't do well in her duty she could receive moral censure from others or self-reproach due to the groom's family's own debt incurred to honour her on the wedding.

(ii)According to Stafford the cycle of *yang* means that parents provide their children with housing, clothing, food, financial support, emotional inclusion and education, and children provide care (*shanyang*) or respectful nurturance (*fengyang*) for their parents in old age, (material assistance, entailing emotional and ritual inclusion, and other things as well (2000a: 42; 2000c: 108)). The contents of the cycle of *yang* obviously include human feelings, i.e. mutual emotional inclusion between both sides. For example, a foster son takes bags of fruit to visit his foster parents, from affection, as married out women do (1995:87).

(iii) The idea that people have relations of *laiwang* with others to provide each other with mutual assistance (2000c: 106) is based on rational choice rather than biological closeness. For example, a foster son, with his wife and children, continued to live at the family home and give almost all of his income to his foster father. He received a larger share of the inheritance, whereas one of the biological sons who moved away from the family and made no contribution to the family wealth was excluded from a share (1995: 88-89).

(iv) Religious sense can be seen in many aspects. There are food-related symbols such as *shoumian* (long-life noodles) or *shoutao* (eternal-life peaches) (1995: 95-96), which loosely relate to a religious sense. This saying embodied religious sense clearly: "Special efforts are made to keep the dead comfortable and well-fed, because it is under-fed spirits who most often become hungry ghosts (*egui*)" (1995: 97). In Angang parents strengthen the bodies/persons (*bushen*) of the children as well as protect them (*hushen*), by giving them expensive magical charms (*fu*) to ward against evil spirits (1995: 97-100). When Angang people celebrate a god's birthday the process of giving and participating relates to a circular logic in which the god's power (*ling*) is produced through the collective efforts of devotees. It shows a strong deity is made strong by his worshippers because a strong god provides protection for all his devotees (2000b: 107).

Secondly, Stafford's study on *yang* and *laiwang* also touches upon four types of *wanglai*.

(i)   It is normal for parents to internalise a popular idea of returning one's parents' great debt of gratitude and loving-kindness for upbringing (*baoda fumu de yangyu zhi en*) through various *yang*. Stafford differentiated the contribution from children to parents into different levels of *baoda* (repay or respond): *yang* (to support) and *fengyang* (to respectfully support). The latter is similar to *bao'en* (pay a great debt to one's parents). This idea is commonly agreed by Kaixiangong villagers to relate to generosity between children and parents.

(ii) Stafford pointed out that when young people are old enough to work and hand over most of their income to their parents this is not "support for parents (*yang*)", but did not try to explain why this behaviour is at the very core of Chinese notions of parent-child reciprocity (2000a: 44). For me, according to the context, it is a kind of bottom up expressive *wanglai* from a child to its parents. It expresses his or her trust and respect for parents, who will keep the money for use on his or her wedding.

(iii) Mr Zhang decided to attend a wedding because he was paying back the groom's father's help for his family. Neighbours and friends came to the wedding as a kind of investment: you give money at the wedding banquet, and then if you later have some 'matter' or 'business', this family will come and help (2000a: 45, 47). It looks like a purely instrumental *wanglai*. But if this is the case why do the rest of the neighbours and friends come to the wedding banquet even when Mr Zhang, who received help from the groom's father, was reluctant to attend the wedding?

(iv) There are extreme *yang*-related Chinese sayings for negative *wanglai*: *yang hu yi huan* (to rear a tiger is to court calamity - appeasement brings disaster) or *yang yong cheng huan* (warm a snake in one's bosom). Stafford describes a case fitting negative *wanglai* when a woman complained bitterly about one of her sons who moved away from Angang and provided the family with no financial support (1995: 86).

This concludes my discussion of Chinese terms that relate to reciprocity. As can be seen, there are a large number of related ideas, in some cases used inconsistently. However there are themes that predominate. *Guanxi* is used, confusingly, to describe a variety of different concepts. It is clearly important. Equally, *renqing / ganqing* and *yang / laiwang* are used to describe Chinese relationships of real importance. I conclude that the confusion arises from any attempt to fit a possible multiplicity of motives (*lishang*) and reciprocity-related relationships (*wanglai*) into a framework that does not explicitly disambiguate them. I have already hinted that *lishang-wanglai* will provide a solution to this ambiguity.

This review of Chinese notions begins to reveal a framework for *lishang-wanglai* . As I mentioned earlier in this chapter, *lishang-wanglai* correlates with reciprocity seen in two ways: as a set of exchange principles (*lishang*) and as a set of exchange relationships (*wanglai*). Here *lishang* includes moral judgement (*de, dao, yi, lunli* or *mianzi*), human feelings (*qing, ganqing* or *mianzi*), rational calculation (*huhui, li* or *liyi*) and a religious sense (*ming, yuan* or *fu*), whereas *wanglai* includes generous *wanglai* (*bao* or *en*), expressive *wanglai* (*renqing*), instrumental *wanglai* (*guanxi*) and negative *wanglai* (*guanxi* or *baochou*). A full account of the *lishang-wanglai* concept is given in Chapter IX.II and XI.

Chapter XI

Construction of the *"Lishang-wanglai"* model

In this book the term *lishang-wanglai* has been used to denote a Chinese model of reciprocity. This theoretical innovation is built on a term deeply rooted in Chinese culture, *li shang wanglai,* first found in a Confucian classic. This chapter will begin with introductions of its origin and adaptation of its usage as *lishang-wanglai*, justifications of *lishang* and its criteria, clarification of *wanglai* and its typology, and methodological implications of *"lishang-wanglai"*. With the introduction of *lishang-wanglai* networks and their driving forces in Chapters IX.II and III, it completes the construction of the *lishang-wanglai* model. This will lead on to initial tests of the application of the *lishang-wanglai* model in the next chapter.

XI.I. *Li shang wanglai* and *"lishang-wanglai"*

Li shang wanglai is a quotation from the Confucian book of *Li Ji* (Book of Rites): "In the highest antiquity they prized (simply conferring) good; in the time next to this, giving and repaying was the thing attended to. And what the rules of propriety value is reciprocity (*bao*). If I give a gift and nothing comes in return, that is contrary to reciprocity; if the thing comes to me, and I give nothing in return, that also is contrary to reciprocity" [*Li Ji* (The book of rites), Legge 1885:65]. In short, *li shang wanglai* can mean "giving and repaying is the thing attended to". This quotation sounds as though it is only to do with etiquette or propriety but the whole of *The book of rites* shows it is applied to almost every aspect of social life. This can also be seen from its use within the wider Chinese socio-cultural context.[51]

Although *li shang wang lai* is a four-character idiom, I noticed in Yan's book (1996b) that he consistently used *li shang wanglai*, as in A Chinese-English Dictionary (Cidianzu 1995:598). It is the standard way of writing the phrase in mainland China. However, in Stafford's books (1995, 2000, etc.) he spelled it *li shang wang lai,* the practice of the Far East Chinese-English Dictionary by Liang Qiushi from Taiwan. The meanings ascribed to the notion as a common

---

[51] On the 60th anniversary Reith Lectures the eminent historian Professor Jonathan Spence gave a lecture on Chinese Vistas in June 2008. The first section "Confucian Ways" will help readers to understand the background of *li shang wanglai*. http://www.bbc.co.uk/radio4/reith2008/ .

usage are slightly different between the two dictionaries. The former explains "courtesy demands reciprocity", "deal with a man as he deals with you", "pay a man back in his own coin", and "give as good as one gets". The latter is translated succinctly as "courtesy emphasizes reciprocity". A less succinct translation would be: "for the sake of propriety/etiquette (*li*), people must engage in *wanglai*". From my understanding the reason *wanglai* in the mainland version doesn't split into *wang lai* is because *wanglai* had already become a free-standing term a long time ago, meaning "come and go", "contact", "dealings", and "intercourse" (Cidiancu 1995: 1043). By extension, the usage of *li shang wanglai* went beyond the literal meaning of *li* (propriety or etiquette), and it is now broadly accepted by mainland Chinese people that *li shang wanglai* is a general method for dealing with relationships. This is indeed the Kaixiangong villagers' usage of *li shang wanglai*. Comparing with *guanxi*, a popular Chinese notion, *li shang wanglai* has a positive connotation which indicates a sense of balance: neither haughty nor humble, neither supercilious nor obsequious, neither overbearing nor servile. My use of this terminology is deliberate – I take a more positive view of personalised relationships in China than M. Yang's (1994) *guanxi,* and different from Kipnis's *qanqing* in which balance is the essential element (1997).

Although *wanglai* is a verb, when it is combined with *li shang* as one phrase it can also be used as a noun and adjective according to Chinese grammar: as a verb, we *li shang wanglai* with each other (*women shuangfang zhengzai lishang wanglai*); as noun, the principle of our contact is *li shang wanglai* (*women jiechu de yuanze shi li shang wanglai*); as an adjective, our relationship is based on the principle of *li shang wanglai* (*women de guanxi shi jianli zai li shang wanglai de yuanze jichu shang de*). *Li shang wanglai* always mixes principles with actions. When *li shang wanglai* is used as a noun the stress is on principle, when it used as a verb the stress is on action and when it used as adjective both aspects are implied.

The problem is *li shang*. Here *li* is a noun which is commonly used to mean ceremony, rite, etiquette, propriety, gift or present. However, in the original Confucian work *li* of *li shang wanglai* represents the whole range of ideas from Confucianism that touch upon thoughts of philosophical and religious ideals: social, political, economical, educational and moral principles, ethics, and courtesy, propriety, rite, etc., as given expression in *The book of rites*, by Confucius. *Shang* can be a noun or adjective but more often a verb. It can be translated as to esteem, to value and to set great store by, but it is hardly ever used in its independent form. The most common terms joined with *shang* are *chongshang* (uphold or advocate), *gaoshang* (noble or lofty) and *shangwu* (encourage a military or martial spirit). Here *chongshang* is a verb, *shangwu* is a noun and *gaoshang* can be an adjective or noun, e.g. He is a noble man can be translated into Chinese as *ta shi yige gaoshang de ren* (adjective) or *ta hen gaoshang* (noun). When *shang* is put at the front, as in *shangwu*, one can make a term *shangli* which can be easily understood as to encourage a ceremonial and appropriate spirit. The popular saying that China has long been known as a "land of ceremony (*liyi zhibang*)" is a case of *shangli*. When *shang* is put at the back, as in *chongshang* or *gaoshang*, one can make a term of *lishang* which means principles based on the valuing of *li*. The meaning of *lishang* is thus broader than that of *shangli*. Both *shangli* and *lishang* can be used as a noun and adjective, i.e. *lishang* indicates a set of principles (noun) or the contents of *lishang* include a set of principles (adjective). The four principles or criteria of *lishang* that I define were part of *li* in the Confucian classics, my definition being much narrower than the richness of the original but easer to use. This is why and how I use *lishang*.

Although there is no free-standing term *lishang* in China, nor the terms *lishanglai* and *lishangwang* in China, this doesn't stop the Taiwanese from using them. There were no such terms as *li gang tui yang* (to leave their posts and retire with full salary and premium) or *qiye zhuanzi* (changing of collective village enterprises into private) a few years ago in China but this didn't stop them from being introduced to Kaixiangong village. There are a couple of dozen terms Kaixiangong people used which can't be found from any dictionary, i.e. *canba*, *chuxing*, *fanyi*, *shengqian*, *wangxin*, *zhoudai*, etc, although these have well-defined bcal meanings.

The way in which I grouped *li shang wanglai* as *lishang wanglai* or, to be more precise, I divided *lishangwanglai* into these two parts, is influenced by Liang Shumin (1949/95). According to Liang, Chinese society is a *lunli* based society. Here *lun* is Confucius's family based relationships,[52] whereas *li* can be interpreted according to another meaning of *li*[53], which includes *qing* (*ganqing*, *renqing* - human feeling, *qingyi* - friendship) and *yi* (*yiwu*, obligations). As defined above *li* and *yi* are basic principles which come from Confucius's *ren* (benevolence) (79-80). For Liang the relationships (*lun*) can be made with anybody anywhere according to principles (*li*), which are lively and can never be fixed (93), whereas I replace *lun* with *wanglai* and *li* with *lishang*. Liang's view that Chinese society is based on *lunli* has remained uncorroborated for more than half a century: the term is widely interpreted as ethics, but its

---

[52] Five basic relationships, which are husband and wife, father and son, brothers then extend to relationships of the monarch and his subjects, friends. 五倫也稱五常或五典。唐孔穎達疏：〝常即五典，謂父義，母慈，兄有，弟恭，子孝；五者，人之常行。〞

[53] See more about this *li* in Chapter XI.I.

pre-eminence has not been validated by empirical study.

In order to distinguish different usages of *li shang wanglai* or *li shang wang lai,* I coined a single hyphenated word *lishang-wanglai.* Although when translated back to Chinese it is still a four-character idiom, the word socialism is also a four-character term but this doesn't stop it being one word *shehuizhuyi* in Chinese *pinyin* (Cudianzu 1995:884). One thing that is not fully worked out in my dissertation, but is nevertheless implied, is that *lishang-wanglai* as a new concept in reciprocity is generally applicable, as is Sahlins' typology of reciprocity. There is therefore an issue of how best to translate the word *lishang-wanglai* in a way that will be easily understood by a non-Chinese audience. (i) *Lishang-wanglai* can also be literally translated as contacts-ethics word to word; (ii) Its meaning can be "the calculus of changing reciprocal relationships", or "reciprocally personalising relationships". (iii) It might be best to simply use *lishang-wanglai,* asking English speakers to accept it as they have accepted *kula* and *guanxi.* *Lishang-wanglai* looks very long but sounds easy, having only 4 syllables compared with the long words particularistic or universalistic which have 8 syllables each. In making this comparison I am of course speaking as someone for whom English is not a first language.

Previous researchers have had varying interpretations of *li shang wanglai* in studying social and personal relationships. Lian-sheng Yang (1957) quoted a famous passage on *li shang wanglai* to show that the concept of *bao* is a basis for social relations in China. Meihui Yang (1994) even puts the original saying of *li shang wanglai* at the beginning of the introduction to her book. She clearly regarded it as a central point of social relationships in China, but she didn't discuss it in her book since her interests are *guanxi* and *guanxixue.* Yan Yunxiang (1996b) quotes it as a principle of reciprocity based on *renqing* ethics. He claims the ancient text is "propriety upholds reciprocal interactions", whereas Xiajia villagers' version of this is "people interact with each other in terms of gift exchange" (14; 16; 124-125). He discovered four operating rules of gift giving which reflect the principle of reciprocity. They are firstly that a good person always interacts with others in a reciprocal way, namely, *li shang wanglai.* Secondly, the offer of a gift should not break the existing hierarchical system of social status in either kinship or social terms. Thirdly, gifts must be made in accordance with previous interactions and fourthly the returning of gifts requires the proper manner (123-127). Thus Yan narrowed *li shang wanglai* to be one of the four rules of reciprocity with his understanding of what Xiajia villagers were doing. Charles Stafford (2000a and c) interpreted *li shang wang lai* as "'ceremonial (*li*) generates back-and-forth (*wang lai*)" (2000a: 47 and 2000c: 105) and from this derived his notion of *yang* and *laiwang* cycles (see *yang* and *laiwang* in 6.1.2). Although Yang

L.'s *bao*, Yang M.'s *guanxi*, Yan's *renqing* and Stafford's cycles of *yang* and *laiwang* all derive from the same famous quotation of Confucius, they carry materially different conceptuality. From my point of view, none of these existing concepts provide a sufficiently general model within which to analyse Chinese complex exchange relationships (see Chapter IX.II). One of my motivations is to provide a coherent general model within which the social exchange interactions in my fieldwork can be described. As the above survey shows, this is necessary because existing notions may cover all the individual elements of social interactions, but they are not consistent with each other and cannot easily be used together to provide a complete descriptive model.

I have, however, also been struck by the way in which many non-Chinese attempts to understand complex Chinese society have been reductionist. They have led to concepts that make Chinese society appear very different from non-Chinese societies. Of course the differences do exist, and are of a natural interest to researchers. However the detailed analysis of my fieldwork results, using the *lishang-wanglai* model, as well as its networks (see Chapter IX.II), allows the complexity of Chinese society to be understood more deeply, by highlighting the way in which universal human motivations, used creatively in the context of Chinese social exchange, can give rise to the observed behaviour. Social artefacts such as expressing *ganqing* (see Chapter X) – very alien to non-Chinese people – become more explicable when considered in the light of the social creativity implicit in *lishang-wanglai*.

These preliminaries motivate my definition of *lishang-wanglai* as a new way of conceptualising personalised relationships. In view of the previous discussion, I use the word *lishang-wanglai* with its grounding in the Chinese socio-cultural matrix. The conceptual basis for *lishang-wanglai* comes partly from my review of Sahlins's work, and the many Chinese concepts relating to reciprocity. I use this notion for a Chinese version of reciprocity which contains a model (see Chapter XI.I) and networks (see Chapter IX.II). In the *lishang-wanglai* model *wanglai* covers different types of reciprocities and *lishang* provides different criteria to judge them. This distinction between type and criteria is necessary to provide an accurate description of the complex relationships found in my fieldwork. As the preceding sections have indicated, it is also motivated by the wish to incorporate existing useful concepts within a single unambiguous framework. Moreover, my purpose is to elaborate a general concept of reciprocity by exploring the richness of meaning contained in the notion of *lishang-wanglai*. This new way of thinking about social exchange relationships is certainly appropriate in rural China and might well be applied to other societies.

My interest, in proposing *lishang-wanglai*, is to provide a tool to examine Chinese personal relationships including personalised institutional relationships that explicitly allows a multiplicity of motives, and does justice to the nature of the interactions found in my fieldwork. One of my key findings is that over and above their material utility, Chinese villagers derive satisfaction from their complex social relations, and prize the ability to create new solutions to social problems. This is an example of social creativity (reviewed in Chapter IX.III). A single social action (*wanglai*) can be interpreted in different ways simultaneously, which explains much of the complexity, and enjoyment, inherent in Chinese social exchange (see Chapter XII.III).

The *lishang-wanglai* model is thus my interpretation of Kaixiangong villagers' social support action patterns (*wanglai*) based on certain implicit cultural models. The *lishang* criteria come from the reasons and explanations given by the informants. They include some Chinese sayings consciously held by the villagers, e.g. *you jie you huan zai jie bunan* (the better the returned credit the easier it is to borrow), *zaijia gao fumu, zaiwai gao pengyou* (at home one can rely on parents, away from home one can rely on friends), and some folk concepts, e.g. *bang qiong bu bang fu* (support for poor people but not for rich) or *jiu ji bu jiu pin* (help for emergency but not for poverty), *zou renqing* but not *zou guanxi* (use expressive *wanglai* rather than via instrumental *wanglai* in everyday life). For the villagers mutual support in everyday life within close relations was considered as expressive rather than instrumental *wanglai* (see Chapters VII.I and X.VI). It was the villagers who drew an explicit distinction between expressive and instrumental *wanglai* with the notions of *renqing* and *guanxi*, although they were unfamiliar with Befu's (1966-67) terms of expressive or instrumental exchange. This kind of distinction can also be seen from Yan's Xiajia (see Chapter X.VII). Based on these observations I intend the *lishang-wanglai* model, which is very close to implicit "Chinese folk models", to describe what the villagers appear to be doing, but not to be a literal rendering of folk models.

The conceptual foundations of the *Lishang-wanglai* model are as I have previously intimated based on the work of other scholars.. For example, the idea of dividing *laiwang* into different types directly came from Sahlins's reciprocity typology and even the term "negative" is borrowed from Sahlins (1972), and "expressive" and "instrumental" from Befu (1966-67). For more details see the subsection "*Wanglai* typology" later in this section and for a comparison of the full list of influential scholars' related work see Table XI-1. The *lishang* criteria directly benefit from Yan's three elements of *renqing* ethics (1996b: 146) which are, however, themselves influenced by previous scholars (1996b: 245, n.1 of the Reciprocity and *Renqing*). More details may be found in my review on related Chinese notions (see section 6.1.2) and the section "*Lishang*" later in this Chapter.

Table XI-1 Social exchange relationships (I give middle initials to distinguish the three Yangs)

Weber	1904	-	Traditional (customary) Affective (emotional)	Value-rational (ultimate values) & or impersonal	End-rational action	-
Parsons	1937 /51		Particularism	Universalism	Particularism	-
Polanyi	1957	reciprocity		Market exchange	Redistribution	-
Yang L.*	1957	To return good for evil; pay a lot more for debt of gratitude (*Yi de bao yuan*; *baoen*)	To return kindness with kindness (*Yi de bao de*)	To return injury with justice (*Yi zhi bao yuan*)	-	To return injury or kindness with injury (*Yi yuan bao yuan* or *yi yuan bao de*)
Sahlins	1965 /71	Generalized reciprocity		Market exchange / Balanced reciprocity		Negative reciprocity
Befu	1966 /67	Expressive exchange		-	Instrumental exchange	-
Mitchell	1969	Communication action		-	Instrumental action	-
Wen	1982	To return good for evil; pay a lot more for debt of gratitude (*Yi de bao yuan*, *baoen*)	-	-	-	To return injury or kindness with injury (*Yi yuan bao de Bubao, Baochou*)
Lin	1986	Expressive support		-	Instrumental support	-
Walder	1986	-	-	-	Instrumental / personal ties: particularism	Instrumental /personal ties: ceremonial-ised bribery
King	1985-94	Social exchange		Economic exchange	Social exchange	-
Hwang	1987	Expressive tie		Instrumental tie	Mixed tie	-

Yang, Z.	1991	Intimate feelings (*Qinqing*)	Friendly / human feelings (*Youqing* / *renqing*	Market exchange	Friendly / human feelings (*Youqing* / *renqing*	-
Yang, M.	1988 /94	Interpersonal exchanges & reciprocal commitments		Impersonal money relations	*Guanxi*	Bribery
Yan	1996	Expressive gift giving		-	Instrumental gift giving / Unbalanced gift giving	
Chang	2004	Generous *wanglai*	Expressive *wanglai*	-	Instrumental *wanglai*	Negative *wanglai*

XI.II. Justification of *lishang*

From the reviews in Chapter X we can see that previous researchers explored many Chinese terms such as *lun* (relationships), *de* (morality), *renqing* (human feelings), *fu* (fortune) and *yuan* (predestination) to examine deep reasons, principles and criteria for making and maintaining personal relationships. The above terms can all be traced back to ancient Chinese philosophers' texts. Justification is necessary here for my use of these texts, which were written a very long time ago. How they are interpreted now may be quite different from how they were understood when they were first written. Also, they have been used in different periods as a means of cultural rule or as a cultural regime. Therefore, one can't assume that they reflect the thoughts of the ruled people. Their popularity relates to their use as an instrument of control, and therefore does not necessarily mean that they epitomise popular ideas. They may reflect something about the way people were ruled, but not necessarily how people rule their own lives. Even in the same historical period the usage of *lishang-wanglai* in Kaixiangong Village may differ from other villages. The following points justify my use of concepts from these ancient texts: they are made here but apply throughout my book.

(1) It needs to be clear that the texts were used as a set of cultural rules and may not reflect what the "ruled" people think. I found a traceable source through a set of steps. For instance, the term of *lishang-wanglai* was given by a villager verbally. He referred it to another villager who had a better education than him. The latter also confirmed it verbally by saying it came from Confucius, which he had been taught in school, although he had not read the original text. As can be seen, villagers sometimes refer to others for knowledge which is then transmitted to them,

or to which they defer, in the belief that the people concerned have better knowledge and can provide explanations (See Jing Jun 1996). If a person cannot explain something himself, he will enquire of other people better read than he is. For example, the chef of the Village Committee, who was employed by the collective, recommended an old Kaixiangong villager to me as an interviewee about rituals in the village. He then asked me for a copy of my notes on the interview. He told me that he needed them because he wanted to establish his own business doing proper banquets for villagers. I asked him why didn't he simply buy a book about it. He said that information from books did not necessarily tally with the actual situation in the village. So I will use educated or old villagers as points of reference, just as the villagers do themselves.

(2) The texts to which I will refer are read in the light of my understanding of villagers' explanations of their meanings – even though they haven't read them. It is normal for educated Chinese people, including myself, automatically to associate what is said with these texts, which we have read as classics. For example, in the film *The Story of Qiuju* [54] Qiuju wants to *"tao ge shuofa"* for her husband after he is hit by the village cadre. Some educated Chinese would use terms like *pingli* (reason things out), *shenzhang zhengyi* (uphold justice) to describe it, which involve the ancient terms *li* (reasonable, sensible) and *yi* (justice). This kind of understanding is quite accurate for *"tao ge shuofa"* which means that she wants to ask for justice.

(3) I understand that people's use of the same texts or terms may differ from place to place. For example, villagers in Yan's Xiajia village wrote *lishang* like 禮上 and simply meant gift-flowing. This *shang* is different from the textual characters *lishang* and so the common usage meant that the system of propriety upholds the reciprocal interaction among people (1996b:123-24). This happened in Kaixiangong Village too. Although many villagers did not know how to write *shang* of *lishang* (禮尚), they were quite clear that the meaning of *lishang* in their everyday life is not limited to gifts or rituals. According to their understanding, the *li* of *lishang-wanglai* has a very wide range of meanings. I learned many related terms and associations in Kaixiangong, starting with *liwu* or *liping* (gift), *liqing* (a gift of money), *lidan* or *renqingbu* (a list of gifts). They told me that when you *zuoke* (be a guest) or *daike* (be a host) you should understand *limao* (courtesy, politeness, manners), *lijie* (courtesy, etiquette, protocol, ceremony), *lisu* (etiquette and custom), *liyi* (ceremony and propriety), *lifa* (rules of etiquette, the priorities), *lishu* (courtesy, etiquette). They care about *liyu* (courteous reception) -- how the host

---

[54] *Qiuju da guansi*, directed by Zhang Yimou, 1993.

treats them, i.e. when a newborn baby with its mother arrives at her natal family as the first visit *lipao* (gun salutes – firecrackers) should be fired. They have complicated *lifu* (ceremonial robe or dress) especially for weddings and funerals. These usages are more concrete than the more philosophical interpretations of the classical *lishang*.

XI.III. *Lishang* criteria

As I have shown in Chapter X, previous researchers highlighting the making and maintaining of reciprocal social or personal relationships in China discuss many motivations and criteria, and in particular: moral judgement, human feelings, rational calculation, religious sense. These four elements also make up the Confucian *li* or *lishang-wanglai*. The term relates to many forms of social behaviour in ancient China. I therefore use these four motivating principles to form my *lishang* criteria, and discuss each individually below.

1. Moral judgement

Moral judgement as to the making and maintaining personal relationships comes into play with terms such as *gou yisi* (honourable, loyal), *jin yiwu* (fulfil obligation), *jiang daoli* (fair, sensible, reasonable, rational, equitable), and *you liangxin* (have a conscience, be good-hearted). For example, Yan's (1996b) *zhanguang* (sharing) functions as a moral constraint for both the helper and the helped because they are obligated (*yiwu*) to each other in sharing resources (130). The idea of sharing is also used in Kaixiangong Village and is expressed as *gou* or *bugou yisi* (honourable or loyal). The villagers explained this using the following examples related to Fei Xiaotong (hereafter XF).

According to the villagers, XF's academic and political success was helped by some villagers individually and also the village as a whole. Of the villagers who helped him more than half a century ago, many have died. However, their accumulated merit (*jide*) in helping XF can be passed on to younger generations. The principle is the same as keeping a family gift list in order to repay it from the next generation in case the current generation has not done so. The villagers thought that XF was obligated to them and it was morally right that they should share in his success. So when XF became an important public figure (*dang he guojia lingdaoren* – beyond a Minister of any Ministry of the state) at the end of the 1970s they expected him to express his gratitude by supporting the development of the village. Over a twenty year period Fei twice expressed this kind of *yisi* via local government: his actions can be categorised as expressive *wanglai*. Firstly he made Kaixiangong Village a part of the "Southern Jiangsu model (*sunan moshi*)" from the middle of the 1980s to 1996. He also helped the village to gain a 4 million *yuan* loan from the township Credit Corporation (*xinyongshe*) at the time of the 1996 ceremony to celebrate his 60 years in academia. It appears that XF was indeed *gou yisi* (honourable, loyal) to the villagers. However, villagers told me that in fact XF lacks *yisi* with them because both these benevolent acts went wrong. The first one delayed the village's economic development and the second case caused the village to be involved in heavy debt from 1996 to right up to 2004 (see section Kaixiangong Village in the Introduction).

Moral judgement is central to people's actions but differs in different places and among different peoples. For instance, to kill someone who killed your father (*baochou*), or to kill oneself for *mianzi* because of unpleasant gossip, to obey absolutely one's ruler, father, husband, older brother etc. used to be classified in the highest rank of moral valuation. Conversely, to do business, to have a daughter rather than a son etc. used to be classified in a low rank of moral valuations. But not everyone now agrees with all of these ideas, and some have become wholly obsolete. For the villagers, everybody has a steelyard in their heart (*renren xin zhong you yi gan cheng*). This means that moral judgement can always change with changing times, but they measure their actions with the steelyard in their hearts, which will live in their hearts throughout their lives.

2. Human feelings

Human feelings, as one of the *lishang* criteria, can be translated into Chinese as *renlei zhi qing* (feelings of human being), *ganqing*, and *renqing*. Here *qing* can be translated into English as emotion, feeling, sentiment, affection, attachment, and love. I use "human feelings" to describe this motivation since I am concerned with personal relations. In Chinese *qing* is a root which can produce a few dozen related terms including *renqing* and *ganqing*. *Qing* can be traced back to Confucius. He concludes that human feelings *(renqing)* are of seven kinds (*qiqing*), joy, anger, sorrow, fear, love, hate, and desire.[55] Yan (1996b) finds that village people also count enjoyment as an aspect of their exchanges. "There are two kinds of gift giving: one is joy and another is suffering. For those with whom I have good feelings, I am very happy to present gifts when they host ceremonies, because the gifts come from my heart. But, I often have to attend

---

[55] "何謂人情？喜怒哀懼愛惡欲，七者弗學而能"《禮記。禮運》。

rituals and offer gifts to people with whom I have no good feelings, and that is really awful"
(141).

My fieldwork material forced me to pay attention to a particular kind of positive feeling - enjoyment in making and maintaining personal relationships, although enjoyment in general can be for good or bad reasons. In a previous paper (Chang, 1999), I mentioned women who maintained social relationships for their own sake. The enjoyment came from making personal relationships just to have the relationships, not for any instrumental reasons or for any moral reason of obligation to maintain sociability. This kind of motivation is visible in reciprocal social support and *lishang-wanglai* in many ways. The most obvious example is that people so often say *tianlun zhile* (enjoying family happiness together is the highest rule). This is the same for males and females, older generations and younger generations. When I asked some women why they spent so much energy in preparation, doing ritual events, and gift giving, the answers were more or less the same, that it is *hao baixiang* (have fun, play, joy, cheerful), or *you yisi* (interesting, enjoyment). The meaning of *yisi* here is quite different from when it is used in *bu gou yisi*. I also found that people will sometimes do "something for nothing", This kind of behaviour looks like altruism, but could at the same time be for the sheer enjoyment of the sociability. Some Chinese scholars (Chen J. 1996/98, Chen W. 1997, Xiang 1999 and Zhai 1998) also noted the occurrence of enjoyment and creativity in making and maintaining social or personal relationships. I have given more examples of this in chapters IV to VIII.

3. Rational calculation

The idea of rational calculation is used in rational choice theory, exchange theory, strategic interaction, which have been relatively fully studied and developed. It has been accepted as a universal truth that individuals always seek to maximise rewards from their interactions with others (i.e. Blau, Homans, etc.). In studies of *guanxi* and *renqing*, King, Huang, Yang M., Yang Y., and Chen all took Chinese *liyi* (advantage, benefit, profit, interest) as an important reason to make social or human relationships. Yan (1996b) simply used the Western term of rational calculation for it (146). This is initially proper because the sense of the villagers' *liyi* is identical with what in theory is called rational choice. It is also true in Kaixiangong Village. When I discussed this issue with villagers an old villager told me an old saying "people die for seeking wealth, birds die for seeking food" (*ren wei cai si, niao wei shi wang*), implying that seeking *li* (profit, money) is a basic human need. This idea of *li* fits well into Western ideas of rational choice, and I do not need to go any further into the huge literature on the subject.

4. Spiritual beliefs

Before I went to China for my fieldwork I did not quite understand why the question "Do you have any religious beliefs?" was included in the questionnaire of the ESRC social support project (see Introduction). When I finished collating the results I had no doubt about the validity of the answer that 95 per cent of informants had a "general belief in spirits".[56] This kind of "general belief in spirits" is mixed with popular religious practices in everyday life, as Smart puts it: "meaning the general and usually very localised religion of the people, which also is sometimes loosely referred to as Confucianism, but is actually a set of practices and ideas which draws on various aspects and institutions of Taoism, Buddhism and the state religion. From a Western angle, this is all rather messy and muddled" (1989/95:103). I am mindful that if I get involved in such a "messy and muddled" situation it will make this dissertation too complicated. However, no work has yet examined the role that spiritual belief plays in issues of social support, although there are many studies and discussions on the Chinese "general belief in spirits" by sinologists, anthropologists, and sociologists in both Chinese and English.[57]

I noted two ways in particular that this kind of "general belief in spirits" is important in the villagers' everyday lives. Firstly, it is quite common for villagers to explain something as due to *ming* (fate), *yuan* (a predestined relationship) and *fu* (good fortune), etc. (See *Yuan* and *fu* in Chapter X). Secondly, ancestors and the local gods are included in the *lishang-wanglai* networks (see Chapter XI.II) which comprise almost all the ceremonies and rituals in the villagers' everyday life. For the villagers, human relationships and personalised institutional relationships can be made and maintained in different ways, whereas relationships between villagers and

---

[56] See our questionnaire number 107 in Chang and Feuchtwang, 1996. The choices are none, Taoist, Buddhist, Christian, Muslim, general belief in spirits, others. The answers are unclear because most of them told me that they have no religious beliefs because they do not like the word religion. However, they told me that they believe a bit of this, and a bit of that, and so on. In the end they agreed that these kinds of belief can be classified as "general belief in spirits".

[57] For example, Emily Ahern, 1973, *The cult of the dead in a Chinese village*; Clarence Burton Day, 1969, *Chinese peasant cults*; De Groot, 1892-1910, *The religious system of China*, Vols.I-VI, Leiden; Stephan Feuchtwang, 1992, *The imperial metaphor - popular religion in China* and its new edition of *Popular religion in China – the imperial metaphor* in 2003; Maurice Freedman, 1974, "On the sociological study of Chinese religion"; Marcel Granet, 1936; Max Weber, 1915, *Chinese religion*; Arthur Wolf, 1974, *Religion and ritual in Chinese society*, etc. Chang Yansheng, "*Zhongguo minzu zenyang shengcun dao xianzai*", *Guolun*, Vol 3 (No. 12,13,14 in one volume); Wang Mingming, 1997, "*Shenling, Xiangzheng yu yishi: minjian zongjiao de wenhua lijie*"; Wang Zhixin, *Zhongguo zongjiao sixiang shi dagang*; Xu Siyuan, 1949, "*Lun zongjiao zai zhongguo bu fada zhi yuanyin*", *Dongfang yu xifang*, No.1; Zhang Zichen, 1990, *Zhongguo wushu*; Zhu Tianshun, 1982, *Zhongguo gudai zongjiao chutan*, etc.

ancestors or local gods can only be practised through the praying for *fu* (see more discussion below) which occurs in almost all ceremonies and rituals. In fact, the relationship between the villagers and ancestors or local gods is a very complex exchange relationship. When there is a ritual or celebration it involves a three-way relationship. People share a meal, and therefore maintain relationships between each other, through reference to the ancestor or the god. So three distinct relationships need to be considered. The way in which a god or ancestor is honoured in ceremonies involves not only food but also incense. The god or ancestors become representations of how the people who come together consider themselves to be related to each other, so the ancestor represents the relationships of the people who come to worship the ancestor together. The ancestor is the point of reference to show that we are all related to each other through the ancestor. Or to phrase it differently, we come together in worship of the ancestor or god because we belong to the same kind of world (*quyuan*, share the same interests) or the same locality or we all come from the same place (*diyuan*), etc.

The villagers gain pleasure from praying for *fu* through rituals or ceremonies. Luo Hongguang (1995 and 1997) found, in Yangjiagou and Heilongtai villages in the north west of China, that the richer people were the greater their expenditure on ritual activities, and the more spending on ritual activities, the more prestige they could gain. This is because the local people enjoy accumulating merits and virtues from the nether world which will reward them with good fortune (*ji yingong*). Luo calls this kind of exchange that of moral-soul (1995:445-475; 1997: 689-705). Stafford (1995, 20001a and c) provides many cases of how Angang people and Dragon-head villagers enjoyed the everyday practices, in particular as to separation and reunion, which related them to their ancestors and the local gods for protection and good fortune.

XI.IV. Clarification of *wanglai*

Wanglai, as part of *lishang-wanglai*, has its own meanings: come and go, contact, dealings, intercourse, or back-and-forth (Stafford's term). These meanings can be extended to include a Taiwanese saying that *lishang wang* and *lishang lai*.[58] This is a way to see an exchange relation on both sides according to its own *lishang* criteria. Chapter XI.II will show *wanglai* can also be displayed in both horizontal and vertical ways. Fei's (1947) *chaxugeju*, Sahlins's typology of

---

[58] It was one of Taiwanese usages offered by Shih Fang-long, a Taiwanese scholar, in a seminar in 2000 at LSE.

reciprocity (1965/72) and Stafford's *laiwang* circle (2000a and c), can be categorised as horizontal *wanglai*. Other relationships e.g. Polanyi's redistribution (1957), Stafford's *yang* circle (2000a and c), worship of ancestors and local gods (Luo 1997; Wang 1997c), people carrying on traditions or customs in making and maintaining relationships, and a Chinese saying *jiwangkailai* (carry forward the cause and forge ahead into the future) can be categorised as vertical *wanglai*. *Lishang-wanglai* networks are formed by criss-cross horizontal and vertical connections circles like lines of latitude and longitude on a globe (see Chapter XI.II). My use of the term *wanglai* differs from that of previous related studies and there are a number of points that need to be clarified.

1. The implications of Polanyi's and Sahlins's references to 'primitive' economics are in one crucial sense not acceptable

I will show how 'primitive' reciprocity and redistribution exist in the highly complex and developed economy of China. Mauss (1925/50) in the last chapter of *the Gift* shows how they co-exist within the capitalist society of France. In Mauss's study what might be understood as 'stages' actually co-exist. John Davis (1994) showed that large gifts can be made at Christmas and various other times in a developed capitalist economy in Britain. When talking about different principles of market exchange, he and others showed that in the same society you have a coexistence of highly industrialised market exchange, production for exchange, plus all these other things which have been called redistributive, or dyadic reciprocity. There have been a lot of recent discussions as to whether or not it makes any sense to distinguish between consumption of commodities and consumption in other ways to create a self in a set of relationships. It plainly has a social meaning. The social meaning of the use of commodities or anything produced for exchange has been a major object of study in many mainstream theoretical and empirical studies e.g. by Daniel Miller et al (1998). However, I am making no assumption about the question of evolutionary stages from Mauss onwards, I merely show that different kinds of relationship do co-exist in China.

2. Parsons's (1937/49) generalisation of Chinese society as particularistic relationships is incorrect

According to Parsons, in contrast with the impersonality of the West, the whole Chinese social structure accepted and sanctioned by the Confucian ethic was a predominantly 'particularistic' structure of relationships (550-51). Yang Liansheng (1957) accepted Parsons's idea and claimed that "personalised relations have a tendency to particularise even institutions which were intended to apply in a universalistic manner (303)". However, some scholars have noticed that different types of relationships co-existed in China. Fei (1947) wondered why villagers carry goods to a market more than ten miles away from the village, rather than sell or exchange them within the village. The villagers told him that this is so as to keep a distance from other villagers. In the market no *mianzi* (face) relationships are involved in exchange relations, and people behave as strangers to each other (77). G. W. Skinner (1971) found that in traditional Chinese society there were two ways to escape from the dilemmas of *renqing*: a person who was born locally was not allowed to be a county magistrate; and businessmen preferred to do business outside their hometown (277). This shows traditional China to have had a meritocratic political system, and the idea of an impersonal market. There are also ways to escape from *renqing* into negative exchange, which is neither *renqing*, nor meritocratic, nor market. Yu Yingshi (1987) argues that particularism and universalism actually co-exist in all societies. There are some cases in which personal relationships play important roles in America and England. In terms of cultural values, the highest principle in the West is justice, whereas in China it is *ren* (later called *li*). King (1986) has a clear sense that Chinese people act always both in particularistic and meritocratic ways. According to King, meritocratic, namely, universalistic, legal and rational relations are ways established to keep a balanced and harmonious society. Zheng Yefu (1995) claims that universalism and particularism have always co-existed and conflicted with each other in human society (47). The imperial examination system is such an example. Zheng quoted a figure from Ho, which shows that in the early Ming dynasty commoners made up 60% of the successful candidates in the imperial examinations at the provincial level (1962:49), although there were problems involving particularism in the final stages of different dynasties (54). This figure shows the imperial examination system was fair in a universalistic way for people from different social backgrounds. The differences between early and late periods of different dynasties show particularism gradually filling and growing in the system. Zheng points out that particularism does not easily disappear and it is most important to study how to deal with the relationship between universalism and particularism (43-47). Zhai Xuewei (1997) examines particularism and universalism with an analysis of local policies (*tu zhengce*). According to Zhai, neither particularism nor universalism can be called local. Both characteristics are included in the process of policy making. The starting point is universalism (from central government) to particularism (local characteristics), then back to universalism (looks fair to local people). Peng Siqing (1998/99) explored *guanxi* in Chinese interpersonal trust relations and showed, from his fieldwork findings, that the *guanxi* operation establishes and develops interpersonal trust and can co-exist with the legal system in China.

I find these arguments that Parsons's notion of the wholly particularistic structure of relationships in Chinese society is too simplistic convincing, and believe that China is a particularistic society as well as a universalistic, meritocratic, market, and exploitative society. It is important to recognise the co-existence of universalism and particularism in Chinese society, which is characterised by mixed reciprocity, redistribution, market, and other kinds of exchanges and relations. *Lishang-wanglai* therefore, which provides a way of understanding Chinese society, could in principle also be applied to Western societies, though possibly its effects will be less obvious. A key idea is that in China universalistic exchange relationships may at choice be turned into personalised relationships, and vice versa. Such relationships then become partly particularist or partly universalist. Analysis of the possibilities and ways of changing between particularistic and universalistic relationships distinguishes my work from that of other researchers.

3. Previous researchers' related work has always mixed up different kinds of relationship which cannot be covered by *wanglai*

We have seen the development of theories of social relationships (e.g. Huang 1986; King 1989; Yang M.1994), interpersonal relationships (e.g. King 1987/89; Zhai 1993), human relationships (Kipnis 1997), and personal relationships (Fei 1947; Zhai 1999). I will omit discussion of them for the following reasons. (i) Social relationship is too wide. In its broadest sense, it could cover every relationship in society, such as rational choice transactions, bureaucratic relationships, public service relationships involving justice, marital relationships, purely instrumental and personalised relationships, etc. Many of these social relationships are not characterised by *wanglai*. For example, China is in a social formation. A whole social system can be a global social system or a social formation, defined by a division of labour, or other aspects of culture, considerations more abstract or general than those concerning people entering into relationships. *Wanglai* is nothing to do with such interdependence as a division of labour, or public transport, on which people's lives are generally dependent but which are not personal relationships. Other sets of relationship not characterised by *wanglai* are for instance a system of domination of power / governmental power or economic power, and relationships of knowledge which authorise who is to say what is truth or what is not truth. (ii) The objects of Kipnis's human relationships are friends, lovers, and members of family relationships. This in turn is too narrow. Anthropologists tend to explore cultural explanations and psychologists tend to look for internal reasons for difficulties and ways to deal with them. I will touch upon both but will place more weight on cultural explanation. (iii) Equally I am not using the term "interpersonal relationships", since I do not want to be involved in interaction theory.

4. Ego or family based *lishang-wanglai* networks do not conform to the idea that Chinese social structure is an enlargement of family relationships

According to Confucian philosophy, the society and family should be structured in the same way, based on three principles and five relationships (*sangang* and *wuchang*). This idea has influenced China in different ways over two thousand years because the Confucian philosophy became orthodox. It provides a powerful ideal that the family should be the model for the whole of society and the ideals of family relationships should be ideals of all other social relationships. However, the Confucian ideal is not universally accepted, not even in his own time, when it was in competition with the ideas of legalists. In today's China we find a bureaucratic official's ideal applied in the organisation of government or public works, and ideals of official social relationships, market social relationships, even of ruthlessness (pure self-interest), and of course of friendship. All these differently situated relationships are equally idealised and do not conform to the patterns of the family. Furthermore, people may be expected to act according to ideals but they cannot always do this well. For example, the head of a *danwei* (work place) may claim that he is head of a big family, but he can't treat everybody as well as he should do as a head of a big family. Other ideals are political ideals of equality, *chaxugeju* (Fei, 1947), *yang* and *laiwang* circles relationships (Stafford, 1995 and 2000c), or the ideal of women's relationships which involved mutual help, enjoyment of each others' company and making things for different events or rituals in Kaixiangong Village.

5. In order accurately to model the exchange relationships it is necessary to make a clear boundary for my research

My own use of the term "personal relationship" derives from my fieldwork. "Relationships" for the villagers applies without distinction to any relationship which a person can possibly have. The term covers personal relationships, interpersonal relationships, market relationships, and institutional relationships. For example, before the Jinfeng silk factory (Photo I-7) was taken over from Kaixiangong Village by the township, it had an instrumental relationship with the villagers. However, the relationship deteriorated to a negative one because the villagers judged there was an unfair exchange. The main problem was that the factory caused environmental pollution in the village but paid nothing to bring it under control. The village cadres formally reported this many times to the township government but nothing happened. They then explained this to their villagers and complained with them to anybody who visited the village, officials from the township and above, related higher authorities, i.e. bureaux of industry, commerce, tax, electric power, water, health, public security, and journalists and researchers from the locality or outside. To mitigate the perceived inequality they made an infomal rule that researchers must be lodged not in the village but at the factory.[59] For the villagers, this was their way to use *lishang-wanglai* in the furtherance of an institutional relationship. They believed that if they kept complaining to all these people then one day the problem would be solved. By treating a problem as soluble by *lishang-wanglai* the nature of other relationships of government administration or general economic interdependence are affected. The whole way in which government administration is held to account can therefore be analysed according to *lishang-wanglai*. So the relationship between the villagers and the local government in controlling environmental pollution became part of a negative relationship because it received financial benefit from the factory. I read on the internet that in another part of China under the same circumstance villagers actually blew up part of a factory to express their complaint.

The negative *wanglai* between Kaixiangong Village and the Jinfeng Factory or local government returned to instrumental *wanglai* from 1997 with privatisation (known as *gaizhi,* "changing of the system". For the villagers, the new policy of changing the whole system from collective to private ownership was exactly what they wanted. It came about as a result of their continuously personalising relationships with different kinds of visitors including local officials and researchers. We see that government relationships, economic relationships, and knowledge relationships, none of them intrinsically characterised by *lishang-wanglai*, were all involved in the relationship between the Jinfeng Factory and Kaixiangong, and that they could be changed by being treated by villagers and village cadres according to *lishang-wanglai* principles. The concept of *Lishang-wanglai* can be applied to any social relationship, from relationships with parents to those with enemies, or any other groups anywhere at any time, provided that *lishang-wanglai* activities affect the participants' relationships in a personalising way.

Hence my inclusion of "personalised institutional relationships" in the notion of general reciprocity, bringing together all the relationships to be studied under the single topic of *lishang-wanglai* (see Chapter IX.I.2).

---

[59] I was told any researcher should live in the Jinfeng factory, which is located in the village but belongs to the township. Details see Chapter XII.II.

XI.V. *Wanglai* typology

Table XI-1 shows a comparison of typologies for social exchange relationships and reciprocity taken from the work of earlier sociologists and anthropologists – Weber, Parsons, Polanyi, Yang L., Sahlins, Befu, Mitchell, Wen, Lin, Walder, King, Hwang, Yang Z., Yang M., Yan – with my own *wanglai* typology. The table has five columns which contain four types *wanglai*: generous *wanglai*, expressive *wanglai*, instrumental *wanglai* and negative *wanglai*. I will show what each type has inherited from previous researchers and how I use them.

1. Generous *wanglai*

Generous *wanglai* relates to people giving without expecting any kind of exchange in return: to do something for nothing, for no obvious reason, or for an immaterial gain, like enjoyment. This kind of exchange also includes what Chinese scholars called 'moral or soul exchange' (Luo 1996, Wang 1998, see Chapter XI.I). I replace Sahlins's (1965) term "generalized reciprocity" with the term "generous *wanglai*", referring to the same phenomena as Sahlins but highlighting the sense of "pure gift", "free gift", and "generosity". Yang L.'s (1957) and Wen's (1982*) yi de bao yuan* (return good for evil) is one extreme such case. Most scholars' related categories contain the meaning of *bao'en* (repay a debt of gratitude without interest), e.g. Polanyi (1957) reciprocity, Yang L.'s (1957) and Wen's (1982*) bao'en*, Mitchell (1969) communication, Lin's (1986) expressive support, King's (1985) social exchange, Hwang's (1987) expressive tie, Yang Z.'s (1991) *qinqing* (family and relatives' relationships), Yang M.'s (1994) interpersonal exchange and reciprocal commitments, Yan's (1996b) expressive gift giving.

2. Expressive *wanglai*

Expressive *wanglai* is the term I choose for relationships in which sincere human feeling is mixed with mutual obligation in the creation of long-term bonds. This is almost synonymous with the kind of exchange relationship denoted by *renqing*. Table XI-1 shows the following researchers' related work is a direct source for the expressive *wanglai*. They are Weber (1904) traditional (customary) and affective (emotional) categories, Parsons's (1937) particularism, Polanyi's (1957) reciprocity, Yang L.'s (1957) *yi de bao de* (return good for good), Sahlins's (1965) generalised reciprocity, Befu's (1967) expressive exchange, Mitchell's (1969) communication action, Lin's (1986) expressive support, King's (1985) social exchange, Hwang's (1987) mixed tie, Yang Z.'s (1991) *youqing* (friendship) and *renqing*, Yang M.'s (1994) interpersonal exchanges and reciprocal commitments and Yan's (1996b) expressive gift giving.

However, I find the distinctions Yan makes between different kinds of expressive gift giving misleading. Yan (1996b) used Bafu's expressive and instrumental exchanges and divided gift giving into two types, expressive gift giving and instrumental gift giving (52-73). Based on Xiajia villagers' practice of *dashi* and *xiaoqing,* Yan (1996b) made further classifications of expressive gift giving into giving on ceremonial occasions and giving in non-ritualised situations (1996b:52-67). This distinction breaks the links between small events and big occasions. For Kaixiangong villagers, *dashi* and *xiaoqing* can be seen as the knot and string which knit *lishang-wanglai* networks. For example, a wedding is a big event which involves different steps, such as asking for red paper from a fiancée's family, engagement with several gifts of bridewealth, leaving feasts for a fiancée from her family's agnatic kin, the ceremony from the natal family, the wedding, the new wife's natal family's visit, welcome feasts for a new wife from agnatic kin, welcome feasts for a new groom from the wife's natal family's agnatic kin, post wedding tea party with the groom's neighbours and fellow villagers families. *Dashi* and *xiaoqing* can be seen as inputs and outcomes, in the process of knitting *lishang-wanglai* networks, because each knot is tangled by the string. The whole process of establishing a marriage relationship included both *dashi* (wedding) and a number of *xiaoqing*. It would be difficult to understand how the marriage relationship is established without following the whole process (see Chapter V.II). In villagers' own words, suppose the wedding is a pig, then the whole process of getting married is like fattening the pig and needs a long time of preparation and maintenance before and afterwards.

3. Instrumental *wanglai*

Instrumental *wanglai* relates to people giving something (e.g. loaning money, providing materials, information, emotional or spiritual help, offering special skills or abilities, introducing personal links) to others solely for the purpose of direct gain or long-term benefit, whether in horizontal and vertical ways. Both horizontal and vertical instrumental *wanglai* relate to individuals or groups using their resources to meet their own interests. The vertical instrumental *wanglai* can be mobilised from bottom up (e.g. villagers seek spiritual support - blessings or protection from ancestors or gods) or top down (e.g. from a local official to village cadres, or a village cadre to villagers) directions. The theoretical source of the term instrumental *wanglai* can be traced back to Weber's (1904) category of end-rational (instrumental) action. A part of Parsons's (1937) particularism, Polanyi's (1957) redistribution, Sahlins's (1965) reciprocity, King's (1985) social exchange, Hwang's (1987) mixed tie, Yang Z.'s (1991) friendly / human feelings can also be categorised as instrumental *wanglai*. Befu's (1966-67) instrumental exchange, Mitchell's (1969) instrumental action, Lin's (1986) instrumental support, Walder's (1986) instrumental / personal tie and particularism, Yang M.'s (1994), Yan's (1996b) instrumental gift giving are identical with instrumental *wanglai*. However, Yan's categories of instrumental gift giving and unbalanced reciprocity seem to me rather confusing. Yan's instrumental gift giving includes indirect payment, flattery gifts and gifts of lubrication (68-73). According to Xiajia villagers, gift giving for daily life help, for the public interest of the entire community, gaining access to buy state-controlled industrial products for village collective or buying house building materials for villagers, or entering a hospital for earlier treatment, can all be accepted as instrumental gift giving. But, when Yan discusses a kind of gift giving in imbalanced gift exchange (Yan 1996b: chapter 7) he used another category of "unbalanced reciprocity". This kind of imbalanced gift exchange refers to people of lower status who give gifts upwards for direct or indirect instrumental purpose, while people of higher status accumulate monetary gifts and make a show by using their prestige. However my understanding of this kind of exchange in Kaixiangong and my own understanding of that in Xiajia have led me to further divide Yan's instrumental gift giving into two types of *wanglai*: instrumental *wanglai* and negative *wanglai*. A part of Yan's (1996b) "unbalanced reciprocity" relates to the developmental cycle of the family and can be counted as instrumental *wanglai*, and another part relates to a gap in social status and can be counted as negative *wanglai* (148). Amongst Yan's instrumental gift giving, which includes indirect payment and flattery gifts and gifts of lubrication (68-73), the indirect payment and part of the flattery gifts and gifts of lubrication can be seen as instrumental *wanglai*, and the rest relating to bribery are better understood in terms of "negative *wanglai*" (see next point).

4. Negative *wanglai*

Negative *wanglai* is a more complicated category. The category of negative *wanglai* is taken from Sahlins's (1965/72) negative reciprocity which refers to getting something for nothing, or to taking much more and giving much less, or returning nothing. I also take the following related work into consideration: Yang L.'s (1957) *yi yuan bao yuan* (to return injury with injury) and *yi de bao yuan* (return good with injury), Wen's (1982) *bu bao* (never return), *bao chou* (take revenge or make reprisals in an extreme way), and *yi yuan bao de* (return of evil for good), Walder's (1986) instrumental / personal ties (the ceremonialised bribery attached to the ties), Yang M.'s (1994) bribery, and one part of Yan's (1996b) instrumental and unbalanced gift giving, are all sources for negative *wanglai*.

My own work leads me to divide negative *wanglai* into three distinct subtypes: a) Sahlins's usage: getting something for nothing or taking much more and giving much less or returning nothing. This is a kind of horizontal negative valued relationship (*guanxi jinzhang*). b) Getting something for personal interests (bribe with a gift and/or loyalty, for instance in the case of someone getting promotion by the back door), using public resources if a higher status person, or if of lower status getting permits, protection or promotion with materials or in other ways, rather than through ability or hard work. This is a vertical negatively valued relationship (*bu zhengchang guanxi*, i.e. nepotism, jobbery or bribery which can be either top down or bottom up). c) Getting something one wants at sacrificial cost, for instance the loss of kinship, friendship or even life, which appears as a broken down relationship (*guanxi polie*), very difficult to repair. At its extreme end are abuse followed by going to court (e.g. Y. Guo 2001; Y. Yan 2003: 168), a long period of estrangement, or even one party's revenge against another by committing suicide (Y. Yan 2003: 86 & 162).

The key issue in distinguishing negatively valued instrumental *wanglai* from vertical negative *wanglai* is to understand the meaning of nepotism, jobbery and bribery in China. (a) Nepotism or jobbery normally applies to a kind of top down negative *wanglai* from an official who uses public resources through his or her power to gain his or her personal benefit, whether material or non-material. Although it appears to be a kind of negatively valued instrumental *wanglai* to begin with, it is more likely to be vertical negative *wanglai*. The negative *wanglai* of condemnation and sometimes of eventual dismissal or demotion comes later. Condemnatory terms used include: *qundai guan* (an official who owes his position to petticoat influence); *yi quan mou si* (abuse power for personal gain), *jia gong ji si* (use public office for private gain), *fubai duoluo* (corrupt, embezzle, degenerate and villainous). (b) Bribery is a negatively valued word in both moral and legal senses under any circumstances. It normally applies to a kind of bottom up negative *wanglai* between people of lower and higher status. In Yan's (1996) Xiajia, villagers looked down on people who bribed those in higher positions to gain a post of village cadre or get a place in higher education, including cases of upwards gift giving that Yan sees as "unbalanced reciprocity". For them it is morally wrong and they regarded it as "no conscience" (*mei liangxin*), "conscience" referring to the fundamental self-restraint that should be obeyed (70). Strictly speaking, to bribe somebody or be bribed by somebody are serious matters which count as a breach of criminal not civil law. In an exchange relationship, once bribery is involved, it would never be an equivalent exchange according to the Chinese usage I described earlier. For one side the cost is quantifiable with money, whereas for the other side it cannot be quantified since it involves a loss of high position or even life. This is why in Xiajia's case the word bribery is used very cautiously (Yan 1996b: 70, 72). So, in theory, the involvement of bribery distinguishes negative *wanglai* from Yan's flattery gifts and gifts of lubrication of instrumental gift giving and from cases of Yan's "unbalanced reciprocity", an upwards gift giving. However, in practice it is still not an easy thing to distinguish between vertical negative valued instrumental *wanglai* and negative *wanglai*.

I defined a typology of *wanglai* both capable of adequately categorising my fieldwork observations, and related to existing classifications used by other researchers. Its four categories can be seen as ranking in four levels arranged on the basis of moral valuation from higher to lower. The levels are generous, expressive, instrumental and negative *wanglai*. The frequency of *wanglai* in *wanglai* typology can be illustrated as the shape of a rugby ball standing on a pointed end: generous *wanglai* and negative *wanglai* are two small ends on top and bottom, and expressive *wanglai* and instrumental *wanglai* are two big sections in the middle. In Chapters IV and VIII I deal with these two relatively infrequent ends, and also cover instrumental *wanglai,* which although very important has been thoroughly studied and developed by others (Yang M. 1994, Yan 1996b, Kipnis 1997, etc.). Chapters V to VII will concentrate on the manifold varieties of expressive *wanglai*.

Looking at how Chinese people make and maintain social or personal relations, the *lishang-wanglai* model demonstrates four distinct criteria and four distinct types of relationship. In practice, however, they can and do co-exist. Criteria called into play can be mixed moral obligation, enjoyment of sociability or emotional attachment or greed, rational choice or utility, and religious sense in combination. The different types of *wanglai* can also be mixed. When I talk about *bao* or *mianzi* I look at generous *wanglai* or negative *wanglai* with the criteria of moral and human feelings. When I talk about *renqing* or *ganqing* I look at expressive *wanglai* with a combination of the emotional and the enjoyable criterion. When I talk about *guanxi* I mean instrumental or negative *wanglai* depending on moral judgment. The *lishang* criteria can also weigh differently, more instrumental in some cases or more to do with enjoyment in others. When I talk about *huhui* or *liyi* (long term benefit or short-term gain) I place more weight on the instrumental than the moral aspect. When I mention *yuan* or *fu* I place more weight on the religious sense than other aspects in different *wanglai*. And so on and so forth.

XI.VI. Methodological implications of *"Lishang-wanglai"*

This book has contributed to empirical knowledge about Kaixiangong Village, which was introduced to the anthropological field by Fei Xiaotong in the 1930s. It is the most up-to-date and thorough ethnography of the village since that time. It also provides a fuller range of personalised relationships in annual and life cycle events with a highly detailed empirical study. The related ethnographical materials of the village amount to 150,000 words. They are in sections "Kaixiangong Village" and "The villagers' usage of *li shang wanglai*" of the Introduction, Chapters IV to VIII and Chapters XII.I and II. My personal use of *lishang-wanglai* no doubt helped methodologically to gain this material in many ways.

Lishang-wanglai is not a research method, but it has methodological implications in fieldwork (see Chapters XII.I and II). Looking back on my experiences whether in gaining access to field sites or during the process of the research, I see them in terms of different types of *wanglai* and varied criteria of *lishang,* as described in Chapter XII. For example, the Wang Family's sympathy for me made them decide to provide accommodation for me and the policeman's rational calculation led him to help me indirectly through a friend of his rather than in a direct way (Chapter XII) The application of *lishang-wanglai* demonstrated self-reflection of my fieldwork experiences with *lishang-wanglai* (see section XII.I and II). Obviously, *lishang-wanglai* is a topic for all fieldworkers because they have to establish personal relationships in doing any fieldwork, which will in general be different in every new piece of fieldwork. Fieldworkers must necessarily learn how to relate to the people in their places of investigation. They need to learn the principles of personalised relationships and the local system for establishing trust. *Lishang-wanglai* can be helpful in the learning process during periods of conducting fieldwork and post-fieldwork.

The post-fieldwork method (see section "General methods and the scope of the research" in Introduction), which I innovated while developing the *lishang-wanglai* concept, benefits from application of *lishang-wanglai*. My post-fieldwork experiences and the huge amount of additional empirical data showed how helpful the post-fieldwork method is for a longitudinal study. I mentioned in the introduction of Part Two that I went to Neiguan in 1995 and Kaixiangong in 1996. I split the two periods of six months' fieldwork because I had become very interested in some of the implications of the research, and I wanted to adapt the ESRC project questionnaire to follow them up. After careful consideration of the fieldwork materials I added more questions to the questionnaire and then went back to Kaixiangong. I spent three months there in total, one month longer than Fei[60] when he was doing his fieldwork for *Peasant life in China* (1936). Based on the newly adapted project guide and additions to the questionnaire I collected as much information in the village as possible, though of course it was not yet fully related to the *lishang-wanglai* model, which I developed after my literature review and re-interviews though the "post-fieldwork" method. In this book I dated the additional empirical data via post-fieldwork (1997 – 2004) whenever I used them. They strengthen the *lishang-wanglai* model by providing complete cases for the change in types of *wanglai* from one to another over a lengthy period (Chapter IV), and very much increasing my understanding of the reasons (principles or criteria -- *lishang*) for the villagers' actions (*wanglai*). I will omit almost all the details of how *lishang-wanglai* worked between me and my informants during the post-fieldwork period. I paid a thank you visit to my informants, with gifts brought from the UK, immediately after I submitted my dissertation, as they themselves had taught me. When I asked them "How can I thank you?" they replied "Don't forget us" or "Come and see us" (*lai kankan*), or "Visit us and share the enjoyment with us" (*lai wanwan*). Amongst many reasons for their friendly attitude the most important is that they believed I respected them, because I continued physical *wanglai* with them.

The implication of *lishang-wanglai* indicates fieldwork is a process of two-way communication[61] between fieldworkers and informants.[62] In Chapter XII I show a fuller account of interviews between myself, the researcher, and the villagers, the informants. The whole process was full of questions, answers, queries, explanations, blame, feedback, etc. between the two sides. Such a *wanglai* indicates that in rural China a researcher may gain a cordial and relaxed fieldwork atmosphere if she/he knows how to develop *wanglai* with

---

[60] In the Introduction of the Chinese version of Fei's *Peasants life in China* (1986) Fei said he conducted fieldwork in Kaixingong for one month or so (*yige duo yue*) (1986:1), although in the main text he said it was two months (1939:26). The Chinese version of the book said it was sometime between July and August (1986:19).

[61] In a globalising world, "communication" is becoming increasingly important in shaping both our institutions and everyday lives. The BACS's (British Association for Chinese Studies) Annual Conference "Goutong: Communicating", January 2004, Durham involved sinological aspects in this topic. City University held a workshop on the theme of communication on 2 June 2004, which brought together researchers with research interests in an open-ended view of "communication" to encourage multi-disciplinary research initiatives.

[62] I showed this in a postgraduate workshop on fieldwork research methods in contemporary Chinese Studies, Oxford on 19-21 September, 2000. The title of the paper is "Importance of intermediaries in gaining access to a Chinese village with *lishang-wanglai*".

informants based on understanding of their *lishang*. This would be very useful for external researchers. I should point out here that to understand *lishang-wanglai* and to understand a specific fieldwork site with *lishang-wanglai* is not the same as knowing how to put *lishang-wanglai* into practice. This would take a long time to learn and might be impossible for external researchers or even many Chinese.

The process of developing *lishang-wanglai* as a general analytic concept requires engagement of a two-way communication between nativization and globalization. I reviewed the related Chinese notions in Chapter X. They are *mianzi, chaxugeju, yuan, fu, bao, huhui, guanxi, renqing, ganqing, yang* and *laiwang*. I have tried to profit from an enormous amount of previous writing, in both Chinese and English, on personalised relationships by using my field study as an illustration. I have been able to show from previous studies of *mianzi, bao, chaxugeju, yuan, fu* that what previous researchers considered as quite separate ideas can be brought together. My attempt at synthesis brought this: (i) I developed a much larger sense of the nature of personalised relationships. For example, the fourth criterion of *lishang* – religious sense – was added naturally to Yan's (1996b) three *renqing* ethics. It is especially useful for understanding Chinese society because China is a non-religious society with a religious sense deeply rooted in people's hearts. (ii) I unified all the Chinese notions with a single notion of *lishang-wanglai,* as a way of seeing how the numerous different Chinese terms of operation about human conduct or social conduct fit in together. *Lishang-wanglai* does not have the negative and predominately particularistic connotation of *bao* and *guanxi*. It also conveys a more general notion of social relationships than *renqing* or *ganqing*. It is an appropriate term and an important key to understanding reciprocity among Chinese people and society. (iii) More importantly, the process of synthesis allowed me to develop *lishang-wanglai* as a general concept forged from Chinese culture[63] to analyse personalised relationships, just as Yang Meihui (1994) did with *guanxi* and *guanxixue*, Yan Yunxiang (1996b) did with *guanxi* and *renqing*, Andrew Kipnis (1997) did with *guanxi* and *renqing*, and Charles Stafford (1995, 2000a and c) did with cycles of *yang* and *laiwang*. I believe the process of developing *lishang-wanglai* until it becomes a general conceptual tool is one way of globalizing from Chinese culture to general knowledge.

---

[63] My ideas of hammering a conceptual tool from Chinese culture and the trend of internationalization and nativization between China and the rest of world can be seen from my book in Chinese (1992: 545-47).

Chapter XII

Tests and applications of the *"lishang-wanglai"* model

Although *lishang-wanglai* itself is not a method or methodology in anthropological or social science studies, it has methodological implications for fieldwork research. The first two sections of chapter XII will illustrate the fieldwork implications of *lishang-wanglai* with my own fieldwork experiences in two villages. Section XII.III will then extend the focus to a case I observed during my fieldwork period in which the practice of *lishang-wanglai* went beyond Kaixiangong village.

XII.I. Gaining access and getting to know informants

According to books on fieldwork methodology, it is important to let both institutional and informal gatekeepers understand the goals of a research study, since their power over processes of gaining entry continues throughout the research process (Bailey 1996, Burgess 1991). However, my own unusual experience of gaining access to a Chinese village fell into two stages: first finding intermediaries, then gaining permission. In this context intermediaries are those who can provide introduction to the fieldwork site. Permission from the fieldwork site itself largely depends on the importance of a researcher's intermediaries. In rural China "permission" is most clearly seen as the process of arranging accommodation, since without this fieldwork cannot be done. I will now illustrate how *lishang-wanglai* works by showing the establishment of relationships at this stage of my fieldwork.

1. Importance of intermediaries

Many Chinese anthropologists carried out their fieldwork in places with which they were familiar. For example, Yan Yunxiang, the author of *The Flow of Gifts*, did his in the village he had lived in for many years as a school graduate (*zhiqing*) during the period of the Cultural Revolution. Gao Mobo, the author of *The Gao Village*, carried out fieldwork in his own hometown. In China an individual researcher carrying out fieldwork in a strange place is a relatively new phenomenon. Chinese people are more familiar with social surveys or social investigations (*shehui diaocha*), rather than qualitative fieldwork (*tianye zuoye*). It therefore seems normal to Chinese people that social investigation involves a group of people from a university or research institution for a short period (one week or ten days). It is also not unusual for an individual fieldwork researcher to be a foreigner, his visit being specially arranged by a university or research institution. However, it is uncommon for a mainland Chinese researcher to carry out fieldwork in any one place for three months. It is even unusual for an individual Chinese based overseas to do fieldwork in a place in China with which they are unfamiliar. An exception is Liu Xin, the author of *In One's Own Shadow*, who found his fieldwork village after three failed attempts through respectively a friend, colleagues, and former university links. Either villagers had an open expectation of potential business benefits from him, clearly an impossible situation, or there was too much intervention from local officials. Eventually he found his fieldwork village through a postgraduate student of the university where he used to teach. Liu lived with the student's family in a village in Shanxi Province (Liu 1995: 23-24)..

My situation and experience were similar to Liu's, but with one advantage, and some disadvantages, in terms of entry to a fieldwork site. The advantage is that I was to do a restudy in Neiguan and Kaixiangong Villages, where the ESRC project researchers had already conducted fieldwork. My choice was made for me. The concomitant disadvantage is that I had no resources for contact with the villages, the resources I had only being useful elsewhere. In the ESRC project these two villages were selected because of special links with Shanghai University, which organised five researchers to go to the villages more or less at the same time. But I have no special link with Shanghai University other than through the ESRC project. As a favour, Shen Guanbao, the Chinese supervisor of the project, said he would take me to Kaixiangong Village himself personally, and wrote me a personal letter to a researcher who worked in Neiguan Policy Study Institution. It is obvious that Shen did not want to introduce me to the two villages officially through Shanghai University, because my fieldwork was not part of his job. That was all I had before I set off to China.

I had to ask myself many questions. Would Shen's letter be enough? Who else should I contact as intermediaries? How could I introduce myself to them? What kind of help did I need? Who would be able to help me? How could I get to know them? How could they accept me? Where could I sleep? Where could I eat? It was necessary to seek different kinds of resource to answer these questions and gain access smoothly. I had the same problems to solve for both my fieldwork villages. Although they were very different, I found before I started fieldwork that the gatekeepers and villagers summarised my study with one term, mutual help (*xiangbang* in

Neiguan, and *huxiang bangzhu* in Kaixiangong), and had their own questions for me: Who are you? What do you do here? What should we do for you? How long are you staying? How should we treat you? What can you do for us?

Initially I thought that when I arrived in China I might go to Kaixiangong Village first, because the women's issues in that village interested me more. However, the first intermediaries I found led me to Neiguan Village. I will now describe the process. (i) A friend told me that he could introduce me to local officers in Dingxi County while he visited Dingxi Prefecture, where Neiguan Village belongs, in Gansu Province, with Fei Xiaotong in August 1995. However, he was not sure how long they would be staying there. I went to Dingxi as soon as the NGO Forum of the Fourth World Women's Conference in Beijing[64] finished. Luckily, I was able to meet my friend in Dingxi Hotel. He was still doing investigations for a few more days after Fei left, and introduced me to the county officials. This was very helpful. (ii) I got a very nice letter of introduction to one of the vice-directors of Dingxi Prefecture from Han Xiangjing, a vice Chief Editor of *Chinese Women's Newspaper*. I found this link accidentally. I had been invited for a meeting by a rural women's magazine while I attended the NGO Forum. The editor introduced me to Han after she knew I would be going to Dingxi for my fieldwork, because Han came from there. Han then happily offered me the vital letter of introduction. It was addressed to the vice-director, a female head of a county in the prefecture, who was also a "model head" among the one hundred female heads of county in China. In this letter Han asked the vice-director to look after me, a female comrade (*yige nutongzhi*), while I was there, a typical female's approach −in this case looking after me entailed helping me sort out every problem, including the provision of accommodation. I was indeed helped in such a way. I will say more about this in the section on accommodation. (iii) I also brought a letter of introduction from my former University, the Chinese People's Public Security University, with me. I had asked for this letter when I gave a talk there. The letter did not directly help my fieldwork because it named me as a visiting fellow of the University, and officials in Dingxi thought it improper that I should be introduced by the Public Security Bureau when I had no position there, by their way of thinking. Maybe they also thought my research object was nothing to do with public security. However,

---

[64] I attended the NGO Forum of the Fourth World Women's Conference in Beijing as a UK based female Chinese scholar whose research involved gender issues. The direct reason for my gaining the chance to go to the NGO Forum was because I was also one of the organisers of a conference on Social-economic Transformation and Women in China in SOAS, June 1995, and a co-editor of the proceedings from the conference, (West, Zhao, Chang, and Cheng, 1999, Macmillan).

the letter was useful in terms of proving that I was a trusted person politically, although I came from a university in England. (iv) The only letter I brought with me from the UK was from Shen Guanbao (hereafter "GS", Shanghai University). GS was the Chinese research adviser of the ESRC project. His university has had a special link with Dingxi, which was how the original study took place there. The letter was addressed to researchers working in the Policy Research Office of Dingxi Prefecture, which is in charge of Neiguan Village. This was also helpful. I would say all the above introductions worked together and made my entry to the fieldwork site much easier.

Events then took a series of dramatic turns. Although I did not know when I would be able to go to Kaixiangong Village, I was much more confident about doing fieldwork there because GS had promised he would sort everything out before I got there. He also offered to take me there since it was only eighty miles away from Shanghai. After I finished the fieldwork in Neiguan Village in November 1995 I decided to carry out my fieldwork in Kaixiangong Village from February to May 1996. I contacted GS two months in advance. I was told that everything had been arranged and he would meet me at the airport in Shanghai and take me to the village. However, just three days before my departure I received a fax in which GS told me there had been an accident in his wife's natal family and he and his family had to visit them. He gave me the names of several cadres and explained how to get to the village (a two-hour taxi-ride from the airport). Thus, at the last moment, I suddenly lost the only connection I had with the village.

It sounds foolish of me not to have asked for more details about the arrangement in advance, or even asked for a letter of introduction from GS. But it is perfectly explicable according to Chinese common knowledge about interpersonal relationships. It would have been impolite to ask GS for such details when he had told me that everything was OK. It would also have meant that I did not trust him. I trusted his promise based on my understanding of Chinese ways of making and maintaining personal relationships. Over the past few years I had put much work into different ways of helping him at his request, before, during and after he himself came to England, or brought his colleagues to visit England. I did not do this to get help for my fieldwork in Kaixiangong Village, because when I started this I had no plans to go there.

After GS's wife's natal family's accident, I recognised that my situation in entering Kaixiangong Village had suddenly become very bad. To my knowledge there are many ways to enter field sites in China, excluding cases of researchers who return to their hometowns (i.e. Gao Mobo, 1999) or places where they had once lived (i.e. Yan Yunxiang, 1996b). (i) The worst way would be if I had no information about the site and no formal letter of introduction from any institution to prove who I was. Under these circumstances it was known that as a lone female I could even be abducted and sold as a wife. A French anthropologist told me that she had carried out her fieldwork in a part of China without the benefit of any such letter, but she would not be in danger in the same way as female Chinese researchers because rural males would not risk their lives to marry a "non-Chinese face (*yizhang waiguo miankong*)". (ii) I had no letter of introduction but knew some names in the village and had information from the original study of the ESRC project. That was all. I recognised that I had to create more links to gain access. (iii) A normal way would be to bring a formal letter from one's work place or a personal letter from a friend or relative. It is not necessary to show the formal letter to a fieldwork site if one's arrangement is through the institution rather than made privately. When I was a postgraduate student in 1986 I carried out fieldwork for a few weeks in an area inhabited by the Jinos[65], in Xishuangbanna Autonomous Prefecture, Yunnan Province. The only letter I took with me was a formal letter of introduction from my former University in Northeast China: I used it to go to Yunnan University and the Yunnan Academy of Social Sciences, which gave me many personal links to the site. (iv) A better way would be to have a formal letter from any institution plus one or two personal letters. If the personal letter came from an important person, or a person who worked in an important institution, then things would be much easier. This was my situation for Neiguan. (v) An alternative could be attachment to a project which belongs to an institution. It is much easier to enter a field site with a group of people, as my other experiences in China show. In 1993 I had spent two weeks on surveys in Sichuan and Shandong Provinces with a group from the Chinese Academy of Social Sciences. It was much more difficult to do fieldwork alone because in both Neiguan and Kaixiangong informants would keep asking questions, such as "whom are you working with?" and "why do you come here alone?" (vi) A slightly better way is to enter a fieldwork station which has a strong link with a University or institution. It would be very easy for anyone to enter if the key person brought him or her. This was what I had expected in Kaixiangong. (vii) The most comfortable way to enter a site is through administrative links from top to bottom. "Top" in this case can mean several levels higher than the field site or only one level higher. For example, the Public Security University, where I worked, belongs to the Public Security Ministry. If staff who worked in this university do research work anywhere, their accommodation and so on can all be arranged through the Ministry to the Public Security Bureau

---

[65] The last minority people of the 56 minorities in China.

of province, cities, and counties. However, the most comfortable way to enter the site is not the best way for the purpose of research because it could rouse suspicion and potential informants would hold back. There are stories even in ancient China about how senior officials from the centre visited local places incognito (*weifu sifang*), in order to gain true information.

Pursuant to the above categories my situation had changed from comfort level (vii) to barely viable level (ii), when I suddenly lost my link to Kaixiangong. I then, in the space of three days, managed to improve my situation from the (ii) to (iv). I knew I had to go to the village during the Chinese New Year's period because it was particularly important for my study and anyway my tickets were all booked. Since I had no way at all to contact GS I had to arrange everything by myself from scratch. My arrangements were as follows. (i) I rang a friend of mine who was an assistant of Fei Xiaotong in Beijing University. He told me that he would write me a personal letter to a senior official in Wujiang City (county equivalent) to which Kaixiangong belongs. But he couldn't give it to me personally because he had already booked tickets to his hometown for Chinese New Year. (ii) I rang another friend, who was doing a Postdoctoral Program in Beijing University, to collect the first friend's letter. He would meet me anyway because I had bought him many academic books in the UK at his request and brought them with me. He collected the letter, together with two bottles of liquor (*erguotou*)[66], from his colleague and brought them to me. The two bottles of liquor (*erguotou*) were a present from the letter writer to the letter receiver. (iii) I rang a former colleague and asked him to provide a letter of introduction from my former University, similar to the one I had to Neiguan Village.

I arrived at Beijing in the middle of the day. I collected the letters and changed some currency with friends in my former university. I went back to the airport, departure being at six p.m. from Beijing with arrival in Shanghai at nine. But the aeroplane was delayed for two hours due to bad weather. I took a taxi to the village straightaway. It was a dark, rainy night and on the way our car collided with another. At that time cars did not have seatbelts in China. My head broke the windscreen, my forehead was scratched, I had bruises on both my knees, and my back and neck were sprained. The car which caused the accident drove off. After we got police to sort out the accident I found another car and got to the village at three o'clock in the early morning. It was Chinese New Year's Eve. The only light on was a guard's room in the town silkworm enterprise, which is located in the village. I knocked at the door and showed my letter from my

---

[66] A Beijing traditional liquor with a strong taste but colourless, which is distilled twice from sorghum.

former University to him. The guard, Wang, immediately contacted the managers of the enterprise and the head of the village for me. The enterprise managers told me to go back to Shanghai for a few days and come back if I needed any help after the holiday had ended. But the head of the village, ZR Shen, agreed to see me at nine o'clock. A few hours later I met him, and he arranged for me to meet BY Zhou, the director of the Village Women's Federation. Now I could start my fieldwork.

I should say more about where I lived during the holiday period while I was doing my fieldwork there. Although the following section is about accommodation, this relates to another "intermediary" which allowed me to carry out my fieldwork. This intermediary was my battered appearance! As soon as Wang, the guard, found out about the refusal of the enterprise managers to help until after the holiday he started to complain. "How could they let an injured woman who came all the way from England go away on the Chinese New Year's Eve?" "Their sympathy must have been eaten by a dog." I asked for information about possibilities for eating and sleeping. He told me that the enterprise has a luxury hotel (*bieshu*) with lots of suites and some modest guest rooms in a different building, but they were all closed and sealed with stamped paper during the New Year's holiday. There was no B & B or other accommodation run as a private business in the village at all. No shops and restaurants would be open during that time either. There was even no transport to go to the township. So he took me to his own home. He lived in one room with his wife and a few months old baby. They had borrowed another room from their neighbours next door during the holiday because they needed more space. This room was a shared bedroom for two female workers. I lived in that room and shared everything with this family for the first week of my fieldwork.

2. Permission and accommodation

In rural China to enter a field site means more than gaining permission to do fieldwork. Permission from the fieldwork site largely depends on the importance of a researcher's intermediaries, and accommodation arrangements are a crucial part of that permission. I have shown that *lishang-wanglai* is useful in this step of gaining access. Before I start to demonstrate my case I would like to make it clear again that *lishang-wanglai* can be involved in relationships between individuals, an individual and institutions (personalised institutions), and among institutions. Before I went to China I thought I could simply stay with a suitable family by paying for my accommodation, so that the relationship between us would be a mixture of expressive *wanglai* and instrumental *wanglai* (personalised market exchange). If this were the case, living together for several months could make our expressive *wanglai* very close. However, I failed in such arrangements in both Neiguan and Kaixiangong at that time (I will explain this later in Chapter XII.II). If researchers come to a village with a group or with a formal institutional introduction, like Shanghai University, the relationship can be counted as institutional reciprocity. A member of the group does not need to do anything because everything is arranged by the institution(s). In this case the relationship between researchers and the village can be institutional exchange, which may or may not involve *lishang-wanglai* (instrumental *wanglai* or *guanxi*). In my case, food and accommodation, local guides, etc. were all arranged (*anpai*) for me by local officials through my personal links. Such a case can be counted as a personalised institutional *wanglai* because I am an individual and the village cadres and local officials were representative of different institutions. Basically, there were two types of reciprocity involved in this stage of my fieldwork: market exchange and instrumental *wanglai* (personalised institutional exchange).

Firstly I will describe the aspect of market exchange (in which of course *lishang-wanglai* plays no part) in my case. My accommodation in both Neiguan and Kaixiangong Village was arranged by local officials for free. Kaixiangong Village even offered me catering for free (see instrumental *wanglai*). The only arrangements involving market exchange were catering in Neiguan and eventually in part in Kaixiangong.

In Neiguan Village the food which I arranged for myself can be counted as pure market exchange. At first I ate in a canteen (*shitang*) which was located in the township court. The food and service were poor, although it was run by a private business under a contract which was supposedly better than the one run by the township itself. However, the local cadres told me that the canteen reform made it even worse than it was before, because it became less flexible in service times and more expensive. But I then found many different sources for eating because there were restaurants and shops in the township. I sometimes ate in restaurants and sometimes bought canned food from the shops.[67] Obtaining food was simply a question of paying for it.

However, in Kaixiangong Village the whole business of my catering was much more complicated. I was given a kitchen key and told that I should eat in a kitchen shared with three

---

[67] Sometimes I ate at food-stalls on the street on market days (twice a week). There were also different types of fresh fruit and vegetables which could be eaten without cooking, e.g. a big white radish which was especially delicious. For breakfast I always bought some fresh made deep-fried twisted dough sticks (*youtiao*) and soymilk from a stall at the street. This kind of traditional popular way of eating breakfast was newly introduced to the town.

technicians of the village enterprise. They came from Shanghai and shared the only guest suite in the village. I will demonstrate this arrangement in the next section. So I sometimes cooked something which I bought from the open market for myself in the kitchen. Occasionally I ate in one or other of the village's two restaurants. Sometimes I ate with my informants when the interview lasted through a mealtime or when I took part in events with feasts. I normally made breakfast for myself. I had bought a cup with a built-in heater (*dianrebei*). It was only 800W because if the heater were larger than this the fuse would blow. I used it to infuse instant noodles, boil eggs, etc. I also used it to boil water to make tea because there was no electric kettle available.

In sum, 45 per cent of my food consisted of free meals arranged by the village. Ingredients I bought directly for my own catering accounted for about 40 per cent of my food and can be counted as pure market exchange. What I paid for indirectly, by giving extra gifts to my informants when I ate with them, comprised 15 per cent of the total. Eating with my informants in both villages should also be counted as expressive *wanglai* because we all enjoyed the mealtimes and my extra gifts to them, which were more or less equivalent to the value of the food.

Secondly I will describe the instrumental *wanglai* (personalised institutional *wanglai* or *guanxi*). The way in which I used this in Dingxi was as follows. I showed different letters to different people in Dingxi County, as I mentioned in the section on intermediaries.   A friend introduced me to the county official, Mr Yan. I gave Mr Yan my book on *Marxist Sociology*[68] and a little present brought from the UK. Mr Yan told me that it was all arranged that during my village fieldwork I would share with a female cadre and live at the Women's Federation of Neiguan Township, which is located by Neiguan Village. This arrangement was largely due to the influence of the female vice-director of Dingxi Province. As well as this, Yan offered me accommodation in a grand hotel (*binguan*) for refreshment, so that I could go back there once a week to have a bath and a nice meal, free of charge. (I was too busy in the village to take this offer up). When I was in the county again after finishing my fieldwork Yan invited me to a banquet with senior officials of Dingxi Prefecture and the county, who asked me many questions about the village. They told me they were very satisfied with my answers and felt my

---

[68] The book is published by Henan people's Publishing house, 1993. It was unusual to give such an academic book to local officials. However, it did work.

information was very useful.[69] They then arranged a free tour for me to visit otherwise inaccessible villages by jeep for a few days before I left the Province. All of this was due to my input and the outcome of instrumental *wanglai* (*guanxi*) with officials of the Dingxi Prefecture and the county, because both sides gained information in which we were interested. This kind of instrumental *wanglai* has no negative implication, such as is the case with *guanxi*. It extends over a longer time period, and a re-entry to the site is much easier.

My experience in Kaixiangong Village was again more complicated. On the third day after I arrived in the village I contacted the senior official, Mr Yu of Wujiang City. He came to see me immediately and I gave him the letter and the two bottles of liquor from my friend. I also gave Mr Yu my book on *Marxist Sociology* and a little present I brought from the UK. He then called a meeting with the managers of the town enterprise and the head of the village. They discussed my situation and decided that (i) the town enterprise should open one of the guestrooms for me as soon as the holiday ended. (ii) The village collective should sort out my catering problem. These decisions could be interpreted in different ways, because they did not refer to the question of payment. The matter was a simple one for the enterprise, which arranged for me to live in an en-suite guestroom located in a modest building. I will come back to this in Chapter XII.II.

My catering problem is more interesting. The kitchen where I ate belonged to the village collective. Apart from supplying food for the village enterprise technicians, it also provided feasts for higher authorities such as bureaux of industry, commerce, tax, electric power, water, health, public security, and other links. According to my fieldwork notes there was a feast on average every three days. So I ate sometimes with the technicians, sometimes in the different dining rooms with the guests, sometimes I cooked something for myself in the kitchen when it was free after normal mealtimes. When I asked Mr Shen, the head of the village, how much I should pay for my food, he told me not to feel embarrassed (*buyao buhao yisi*) to eat with them. He explained that they would be cooking food for their guests including the technicians anyway, and that to add one extra person was as simple as adding one pair of chopsticks (*jia yishuang kuaizi*).

This was easy for Shen to say, but it was not easy for me to be "a pair of chopsticks". Although physically I settled down, I felt uneasy inside at accepting their arrangements. It did not seem right to live there without paying properly for my accommodation. Apart from asking

---

[69] A similar thing happened again in Kaixiangong Village (see Chapter XII.II). However, I do not know whether the local officials interested in my information affected local officials' decision making.

Mr Shen about paying for food in Kaixiangong, I did not raise the question of payment until just before I left, in either site. The reasons were (i) I did not want to interfere with the arrangements they had made for me; (ii) I wanted to find out how the institutional system works and why. However, I was not sure whether this kind of arrangement for me in both the villages could be counted as taking advantage or even corruption[70]. If it was, then why did they do this for me? If it was not, then how was I to understand this kind of relationship between them and myself? What was the way in which they normally treat other researchers and what did other researchers do? What would the villagers think about this? I will leave these questions until the next section.

3. A mutual learning process

My understanding of who is a fieldwork informant is very broad. They include people interview, any villagers in the village, local cadres and officials in the village and township, even anybody who I contacted for information around the village. In short, everybody in the field could be my informant. However, a problem in asking information from so many is that I could not always remember informants' names, being either busy taking notes or talking to a group and having no time to identify individuals. In this case I simply say "according to a villager..." in my book. Besides, for me the period of getting to know informants can be counted from the moment of arrival to that of leaving. I was learning all the time. I also learned from my mistakes. I found that getting to know informants was a mutual learning process. To illustrate this I will rely mostly on my fieldwork experiences in Kaixiangong Village.

The following example will show how we learnt about each other. One day I was observing a house completion ceremony. Before the feast started, I told the host that I had a stomach ache and needed to rest, and went away. A few minutes after I got back to my room a villager knocked at the door. He told me that the host had sent him to invite me formally to the feast. I told him again why I could not go. He told me that the host thought I was quibbling about etiquette, or reproaching him with an excuse (*tiaoli*) because he was not treating me warmly enough. I showed him the medication on my desk and said I had been taking it for some time. He was surprised that my stomach ache was real. He then told me what had been said when I left the ceremony. One villager said that I might feel embarrassed at taking part in the feast without a gift. But another said that wherever there was a feast, I took part. A villager even suggested that

---

[70] Note that the word "corruption" has different connotations in China and the West. I am using it here in the normal Western sense, i.e. Charles Stafford 2000b.

the village collective was not giving me enough to eat so I had to eat with the villagers as well.

I cried when I heard this gossip. The catering was a sensitive topic to me because I had accepted the arrangement made by the village collective together with the permission to enter. I had not yet worked out the best way to sort out the problem. Here I was involved in another problem about eating again, although I had been very cautious. I asked him: why should I come here to eat all of your food? It was not comfortable at all for me to eat in the feasts because I would sometimes have to eat things I did not like. I also had to eat food I regarded as unhygienic because it had been put on the table around my bowl when the bowl was full. I learnt from villagers on different occasions that it was the custom for everybody on the same table, normally eight people, to serve a guest by continually putting different food on his or her bowl or on the table around the bowl. The guest should feel honoured and eat all of it – it was rude to refuse. I tried saying no sometimes, but they thought I was merely being polite. Sometimes they asked me why I refused one person and accepted another. It was very difficult to remember which person served which food, because I was talking with people during the mealtime and I ate with different people in different ceremonies. Anyway, to take part in as many ceremonies as possible was part of my fieldwork. To show that the stomach ache story was indeed true I didn't go back to that particular feast. Otherwise they would think that if they tried hard enough to invite me I would accept. The villager who had come to see me had sympathy with me and seemed to understand my awkward situation. He said he would explain it to other villagers. This might be one of the ways that the villagers learned about me.

I am sure there was plenty of gossip about me. Some was good and some bad. Some gossip came directly back to me, like with the feast, and some did not, or might come back to me in other ways. It was always extremely difficult to find out what people said about me. However, I heard much gossip about previous researchers, e.g. a male and a female who slept together when they were not a married couple; and another researcher had told the villagers that his meals, even cigarettes, could be refunded from the project.

I found that the villagers were generally hostile to researchers. They complained about the researchers constantly studying them. They said their research projects were no use at all for village development, quite the reverse: some researchers had told the villagers that the village had to always stay as it was just for the sake of the study. However, as I mentioned in the "moral judgement" Chapter VII.III, the village believed its development had been held back by policy oriented studies. Under all these circumstances I had to work out my situation and ways to gain trust and friendship with all types of informants. I understood that I should not interfere with my field site when I was carrying out my fieldwork. However, in the two-way communication process a fieldwork researcher cannot avoid interfering with local development in many ways. On the one hand, the village and villagers have already been interfered with, directly or indirectly, over several decades by previous researchers' work, because these previous studies were more or less policy oriented, and therefore very close to policy-making from central or local government. On the other hand, both the local officials and the villagers expected any fieldwork researcher and project to be useful in developing the village and improving the villagers' living standards, because they did not know the difference between policy-oriented studies and purely academic studies. Therefore, as soon as a fieldwork researcher entered the site, he or she became involved in a triangular relationship: fieldwork researcher and the local officials, fieldwork researcher and the villagers, and local officials and the villagers. So, it is very important for a fieldwork researcher to make clear what he or she can do with these relationships. What I did was as follows.

(i) I chose gifts and presents to the villagers or informants in a proper way. For example, when I presented a small gift to sample households where I conducted my interview, I always said, with the local term, it was a *xiao yisi* (small gift). The reply from the villagers always was either *qianli song emao* or *li qing qingyi zhong*. The original saying puts these two sentences together, and means that the gift may be light as a swan's feather, but sent from a thousand miles away, it conveys deep feeling. They saw the small gift, a nice shaped mini-torch with the badge of City University on the surface, as an object that I myself had thoughtfully chosen, bought, and carried all the way to them from England. This indicates villagers' moral norms for judging other people's behaviour. I also brought gifts to any household when I attended their events. I bought these gifts from the village shops, i.e. fruit, sweets, cakes, canned food, wine, and stationery, etc. I learnt what and how to buy gifts from the villagers. I bought different things for different people depending on my understanding of what they might like.

(ii) I helped any villagers, not necessarily informants, if I could. Many Kaixiangong villagers called me the "photographer" because I always carried a camera and a video camera recorder with me. According to the local custom, members of a family should have a family feast in the Chinese New Year period. A few people asked me to take a photograph for them on that occasion. Others then thought this was a good idea. So I took photographs, of course for free, for anybody who asked me. I had the films developed and printed in a photo shop in the township as soon as possible and made sure everybody had his or her own. Even the photos from my last film, which was developed after I came back to the UK, went back to the villagers. I never forget a story some villagers told me a few days before I left. An old lady had died and the only photo of her was the one I had taken. They said it would have been a shame if I hadn't helped her, for her family would have had no picture of her at all.

I also took a camcorder to villagers' weddings or funerals. After I had shown them my videos on a TV, some villagers asked me to take videos for them. Mr Tan told me that although he spent 700 *yuan* hiring a photographer to make a video tape for his daughter's wedding, he still wanted to have my version because he thought mine was in some ways better than a real photographer's. They could see everybody who played different roles in the events, rather than boring shows of the bridegroom and bride. Other poorer families asked me to do so because they wanted to save their budget on it. So I went to Shanghai and bought equipment and tapes and made copies for people. The villagers preferred to play and replay the wedding tapes because they could find themselves on the TV and laugh from the beginning to the end. Although they asked for the tapes of funerals, they didn't play them repeatedly because the adults had to stop the children from laughing when they were watching. The funeral tapes were only for keeping memory of the dead people.

There were a few extremely poor families in the village. One of them was a young widow whose husband had died in an accident. She lived with her sick father and two children. I left some money for her, and also for a few other poor people.

(iii) I provided useful information for the local officials and village cadres. As was also the case in Dingxi County, the village cadres, township and county (city) officials in Wujiang asked me for information and my opinion about the village whenever we met. Especially during many mealtimes with the local officials, I tried very hard to show them the villagers real situation and wishes[71]. An editor of *Wujiang Newspaper* invited me to write a paper about Fei's nineteenth's visit[72] to the village. I therefore accompanied the visit and took part in the meeting report. I noticed that Fei himself was confused about what was best for the villagers. On the one hand, the "Southern Jiangsu model" came originally from Fei's own theories and was successful in some villages. On the other hand, Kaixiangong Village was in an undoubtedly depressed situation. He

---

[71] It is debatable whether or not a researcher should take part in any policy making activity in his or her field site, especially in China. Some Chinese researchers, i.e. Li Xiaojiang, Guo Yuhua, etc. told me that it was necessary to do so. My experience shows that whether and how much to take part in policy making activities would depend on how well one understood the site, and can be judged by the corresponding benefit or harm to the local people.

[72] Up to September 2003, Fei Xiaotong had visited Kaixiangong village 25 times since 1936, his first visit to the village. 14th April 1996 was his 19th visit to the village.

asked local officials to show him some private businesses and showed great interest in them. I picked up the topic of private economy and tried to get the newspaper to press for policy change – which it failed to do, since at that time it was not politically sensible to mention the words "private economy".

(iv) I promoted an equal communication between Chinese and Westerners. Before I left the village the local officials asked me to encourage Stephan Feuchtwang (hereafter "SF") to come back for Fei Xiaotong's (hereafter "XF") ceremony for 60 years in academia. Afterwards, SF received XF's paper in which he summarised his lifelong academic achievements[73]. I spent a few days with SF to study XF's paper and helped SF work out XF's position as an anthropologist in his speech (Feuchtwang, 1998). I have also been working hard to be a bridge between Chinese and Westerners, which can be understood as an indirect way to repay the villagers' generosity. I remembered XF's earnest wish in Wujiang Hotel that he hoped Chinese anthropologists should get their work accepted onto the international academic track (*yu guoji jiegui*). Bearing this in mind while I was doing a literature review, I recognised that there is a link between XF's idea of *chaxugeju* and Sahlins's model of reciprocity. This was very helpful in promoting an understanding between China and the West. Furthermore, a characteristic of this book is an interest in Chinese scholars' related work, both materials and ideas. I refer to Chinese scholars' related works as much as possible, as often as I refer to Western scholars'. In a popular Chinese saying this is my way to repay people's loving-kindness in rearing me (*baoda renmin de yangyu zhi en*).

(v) I helped other local researchers to further their careers. As an example, SF and I invited Hui Haiming to visit the UK. Hui got a Ph.D. under XF's supervision in Beijing University and became a head of the Policy Study Office in Suzhou City, to which Wujiang City belongs. He was also head of a fieldwork station in Kaixiangong. He felt that he was losing his academic links at both national and international levels. He told me that he had helped many researchers, groups and individual, national and international, to do fieldwork or documentary research in this area. He hoped this would provide chances to keep academic contacts with them. However, he did not have any feedback from any of them. On the contrary, he found a paper largely dependent on his research published in Singapore without mentioning him at all, although he had been promised recognition as co-writer before he handed his paper to the research group. He was

---

[73] See 1996, 4, Journal of Beijing University.

especially impressed by the arrangement of his visit to the UK made by SF and myself, because he had not helped us at all when we were in Wujiang. What SF did was to encourage him to carry on his topic of village studies, by directing him and giving him related books. I shared my research experiences with him and also gave him related books. After I finished my fieldwork I have been in contact with him and the village in different ways and benefited from the relationship which we established with the village and the area.

Here is another example of a mutual learning process, seen over a long period. A German anthropologist told me that although he received great help from his informants when he carried out his fieldwork in a Sichuan village, he did not see how *lishang-wanglai* works with his experience, and he did not want to be involved in *lishang-wanglai* with the villagers in the future, if he went back to the village. However, the German anthropologist's understanding of *lishang-wanglai* was mainly as regards material benefits, and the relationship which he did not want can be categorised as *guanxi* or instrumental *wanglai*. He did not recognise that his relationship with the villagers was actually an expressive *wanglai*. From my understanding of the villagers' point of view, his input was that he had accumulated profound knowledge in Chinese studies in the past, he shared his interests with the villagers and worked hard when he was there. The villagers valued this kind of spiritual wealth very much. What they could get from treating him nicely might have been the possibility that the name of the village would "go abroad (*zouxiang shijie*)" and the villagers' lives given a lasting memorial from his writing about them, or it might have just been that they enjoyed the feeling of being nice to a foreigner (generous *wanglai*).

To summarise, my fieldwork experience shows that knowing each other is a two-way process between fieldwork researcher and informants. In the mutual learning process we observed and learned from each other. The more we know each other, the better the relations with the informants, and the better the information it is possible to get from them.

XII.II. *"Lishang-wanglai"* and social creativity

This section will consider *lishang-wanglai* and social creativity in the further analysis of the above topics of gaining fieldwork access, getting to know informants, and the mutual learning process.

1. Analysis using *lishang-wanglai*

The accidental loss of my only connection with Kaixiangong Village a few days before my departure from UK to the village can be explained with *lishang-wanglai* between GS and me, as follows. Our relationship was a mixture of different kinds of *wanglai*, i.e. generous, expressive, instrumental (personalised market, personalised institutional), and negative. GS's letter to Neiguan and his other offers of help in Kaixiangong can be explained as instrumental *wanglai*, based on the criterion of rational choice, because he needed me to help him and his colleagues to visit the UK. For me, morally, I should thank (returning his past help) GS for his help by helping him and his colleagues. However, I recognise now that I was willing to create a closer relationship with him. Originally, our relationship was a kind of institutional relationship because we were both Chinese scholars. I thought I could increase the closeness of our relationship to an expressive rank because we were both involved in the same UK based project and had had many personal contacts. In other words, I was personalising an institutional relationship with him by helping him, although I did not expect a return from him. However, not all relationships can be personalised. In contrast, as a result of events the relationship between GS and me could even have deteriorated into a negative one. But after I returned to Shanghai from Kaixiangong Village GS arranged accommodation for me, and invited me for a meal at his home. This can be seen as his way of repairing the relationship and solving the misunderstanding between us. I understood that his reason for not wanting a closer relationship with me was because he had changed his research interests. So our relationship remained as an institutional one.

There were several different *lishang* criteria involved in the above *wanglai* between GS and myself. In the creative process of *lishang-wanglai* any action could involve more than one criterion. Our relationship did involve moral judgement, human feelings, and rational choice criteria, but the weight of it was not greater than we had had with other team mates in the ESRC project.

(i) Morally it would be not fair simply to say my considerable help for GS and his colleagues was only a kind of complicated long-term social investment. It is only now that I recognise that this could have been the case. It also cannot be simply explained by saying that I was generous to them. SF, my supervisor, told me that he had helped lots of Chinese scholars and students over the last twenty plus years and did not expect any material benefit in return. He thought his action mixed up different criteria: generosity, sincerity[74], commitment to the field of study, and self-adjustment to make relationships with Chinese scholars. However, he did receive different kinds of return from different people in different ways, although he did not make a social investment on purpose.

(ii) I felt very sad and shamed after I lost the link to the village (via GS) a few days before my departure from the UK. I then very much enjoyed making last-minute arrangements to enter Kaixiangong Village. It provided me with a chance to recall my old friends and maintain relationships with them. We all enjoyed our telephone conversations and meetings very much. All these feelings of sadness, shame, and enjoyment can be categorised in the human feelings criterion of *lishang*.

(iii) My involvement of *wanglai* is based on my understanding of the rational choice criterion of *lishang*. In this case I understood that to create a relationship is always a difficult business. Although I failed to make a closer relationship with GS, it would not stop me going on to help others in a similar way. In other words, even though I lost on one occasion it does not mean the whole idea of investment was wrong. I always believed I would get a return indirectly in different ways, like a kind of social investment (Fei, 1947:75), although it would be difficult to be sure of this. It would be nice if the people who benefit from my help would remember it, or help me when I asked, which would give me a direct return. And it would be hurtful if the people I helped did not want to help me in return. It might end a particular relationship, but investment cannot always be successful. It would be useful to learn something through these experiences, including the loss. For example, I should have asked for a letter from GS just in case something went wrong, or I should have directly contacted the village in advance, by myself or through other links.

(iv) I would also like to explain the failure of the instrumental *wanglai* (personalised institutional) between GS and myself with a Chinese term *wuyuan* (have not luck to do so) which is related to the religious sense of *lishang*. This *yuan* between us can be traced back to XF. There were vertical and horizontal circles among XF, SF, GS and me. GS was the first PhD student under XF's supervision and I was SF's assistant and student. GS's involvement in the ESRC project largely depended on the relationship between him and XF and he was a visiting fellow in LSE (The London School of Economical and Political Sciences) before the project

---

[74] Sincerity is the way of Heaven (*cheng, cheng zhe tian zhi dao ye* 誠，誠者天之道也).

started. The relationships between XF / GS and SF / me are vertical. The relationship between GS and me is horizontal. Whether or not the two sets of relationship would form a completely linked network (in which any two people have direct bi-directional links) and move continuously is dependent on many elements. One of the explanations might be that after the project ended GS and I have not had the luck to work in the same field because he changed his research interests, and so the horizontal *wanglai* stopped. But I have remained connected to SF to continue my research interests, so the vertical *wanglai* remains, but I am not sure how much this is determined by fate. When I discuss the religious sense of *yuan* I should point out there are two roles for me. On the one hand I treat myself as informant and use my subjectivity to understand things. I was like my informants in that I conducted myself according to a belief that my way of entering the fieldwork site was fated. On the other hand, as a social scientist, I treat this as a part of the way in which Chinese people, including I myself, use the idea of fate in understanding their lives.

Now I am going to discuss *lishang-wanglai* in the case of my gaining access to the site. The *wanglai* between me and the field sites were through different intermediaries, and did not follow the usual pattern. The normal way of entering a field site in China would be to bring a letter of introduction from one's work unit. The relationship between the field researcher and the site would be an institutional relationship. However, my gaining access to the sites was through mixed generous, expressive, and instrumental (personalised institutional) *wanglai*. Han's letter to Dingxi and Wang's family's accommodation were cases of generous *wanglai*. All the help from my friends was expressive *wanglai*. The letters of introduction from my former University were instrumental (personalised institutional) *wanglai* because I had no formal personal file (*renshi guanxi*) there but had an informal personal relationship (*geren guanxi*) with it.

A number of types of *lishang* would be always involved in gaining access in different situations. To continue with my own case: (i) both Han and Wang wanted to help me because they felt that they respected me morally. This is a moral judgement criterion of *lishang*. They told me that I must be someone who had devoted her life to social science undertakings because I chose either the poorest place or the most difficult time for my fieldwork. (ii) There were many occasions involving human feelings, sympathy, and emotional aspects, which is another criterion of *lishang*. Wang's family showed great sympathy with me when I first arrived in Kaixiangong. Actually, after the accident there had already been a number of strangers who helped me out of sympathy. One person stopped his car and brought me to his friend's flat to ring a policeman (at that time mobile phones were not in popular use). One of the policemen woke up one of his friends (not a colleague) and asked him to help me to pass the border checkpoint between Shanghai and Jiangsu Province, because we could not then find a car with permission to drive in Jiangsu. I also had a sisterly relationship, in which we called each other "sisters" and felt warm towards each other, with a number of women. These were Xie, the editor of the rural women's magazine, Han, the vice Chief editor of *Chinese Women's Newspaper*, and Zhou, the director of women's federation of Kaixiangong. I would like to lay stress on the sheer enjoyment in the human feelings criterion of *lishang*. Both Wang's family and I felt strongly that it was a great enjoyment to spend the Chinese New Year together. Wang had come from a poor village in North Jiangsu (*subei*) a few years before. After he got his current job he married his girlfriend and brought her there. This was the first Chinese New Year for the young couple with a little baby in a newly settled place. It was snowing. They felt they were so lucky that they could spend such an unusual time with their "*dajie*" (old sister, which was how they addressed me). We made dumplings, played fireworks, and made a small snowman together. I also took some photographs of them and the baby. They told me that their parents, brothers and sisters would be very pleased if they saw those photographs. (iii) However important the emotional aspect, rational choice was another criterion of *lishang* involved. For example, the policeman's choice of asking his friend to help me to pass the checkpoint rather then finding another policeman to do so was based on a rational calculation. For him it was not worth risking his own career to help someone he could never meet again, for two reasons: it was wrong to allow a non-registered car to pass the checkpoint, and it was beyond his duty to ask another policeman to do so. In this case the relationship between the policeman and me does not look like *lishang-wanglai* because there was no personalising involved. However, from my point of view there was a generous *wanglai* between us. The policeman expected nothing in return from me, but enjoyed the way he helped me. He could also share this enjoyment with his friend who actually helped me. For me the generous *wanglai* is still there. Perhaps one day we might meet each other again accidentally. (iv) Ideas of fortune which are related to the religious sense of *lishang* played a part. After the accident happened the policemen told me that it was a serious one and I was lucky not to be badly hurt. They also used a Chinese saying to comfort me. That is: after surviving a great disaster, one is bound to have good fortune in later years (*danan bu si bi you houfu*). However, a friend of mine said to me "you are so unlucky to have been involved in one accident (the lost link to Kaixiangong Village) and the other (a car accident on the way to the village)". Other people said I was so lucky because I had had several intermediaries to the sites. In short, people always like to link unexpected events with ideas of good luck or bad luck.

Next I will illustrate circles of relationships with *lishang-wanglai*. The three protagonists are: the local officials / village cadres, the villagers and me. According to a Taiwanese saying *"lishang wang* and *lishang lai"*, which means that in a reciprocal *wanglai* process each side's action should be judged by its own criteria *(lishang)*. Although there were big differences in my fieldwork arrangements between the two sites, the common element was that officials, cadres and villagers all had to work out different treatments for different people depending on *lishang* criteria, and the same was true for me. As I have already stated, the process of gaining access to a field site and getting to know informants involves three types of reciprocity, market exchange, expressive *wanglai*, and instrumental *wanglai*. In my case the market exchange was straightforward and the expressive *wanglai* with villagers easy to understand. I will touch upon it, but will concentrate on instrumental *wanglai*.

It is easy to understand the *lishang* criteria of moral judgement and human feelings. Once the local officials classified me as a researcher I passed their moral judgement. And they told me that they were moved by my choosing a poor area (Neiguan) or a bad time (the Chinese New Year) to do research, and starting work immediately in Kaixiangong regardless of my injury, etc.

However, some criteria were mixed together. For example, after I finished my fieldwork in Neiguan Village, I asked a head of the township how much I should pay for the place where I had lived. He told me that I could pay any amount which I felt it to be worth. For me the place had been convenient for my fieldwork because the township office is located in Neiguan Village. However, poverty and the lack of water resources meant that there were no bath, shower or flush toilet facilities, and the only public toilet, in the end corner of the township courtyard, was about 100 meters away from where I lived. It was dirty and cold because it was a big manure pit with simple half enclosed walls and roof, like a pavilion. The big manure pit was of course for the vegetable plots behind it. Like everybody else who lived there I was allowed to collect a single thermos bottle of boiled water per day from the boiler room for drinking and cleaning. It was not possible to get my hair washed and have a shower or bath during my whole stay. For the first two weeks I felt very itchy all over and then I got used to it, as I was told I would when I arrived. I thought I should pay 10 yuan per night for such a place because a single room in a normal hotel of Dingxi County was only about 20 *yuan* per night.

However I would feel shamed if I offered such a price. The head of the township told me that the place was a part of the permission for me to carry out my fieldwork and the cost depended on the value of my work. So it was difficult to value it, and I paid nothing. I told him that I would remember that I owe them a great deal because I learnt much from such valuable experiences in my fieldwork. He told me that it was good to be generous to me about the accommodation because he found that I was the first researcher to live there so long without a break. Furthermore he told me that he did not take care of me while I was there, as he was told to do by the higher officials, because he had wanted to see how I coped without special care. At this stage our relationship was instrumental *wanglai*. After he had observed all my work during the fieldwork period, he decided that I had passed his test, and he decided to make a closer relationship, i.e. expressive *wanglai* with me. If I had failed the test he would have stopped the process of making a closer relationship with me, he might even have had a hostile feeling towards me.

The head of the township then took me to a meeting room and showed me proudly some calligraphy by Fei Xiaotong written specially for the township, which hangs in the middle of the front wall. The content was about shaking off poverty and building up a fortune (*tuopin zhifu*). He said that Fei *lao* (a respectful way to address him) was a pioneer in developing the north west of China (*kaifa daxibei de kaituo zhe*) and I should be one of the people who carry it on (*houji zhe*) because I was educated in England too. He hoped the wind (*feng*) from England would blow real water (*shui, yingguo de fengshui*) to the dried land, literally to help them shake off poverty and build up a fortune.

This conversation shows that while I was trying to calculate the best thing to do about payment, he was thinking completely differently. On the one hand, they were generous to me and did not expect any payment from me. On the other hand, the sincere words and earnest wishes from the head of the township also moved me deeply. Although they have limited resources, they treated me as well as they could. I understood that he wanted to keep relations with me by letting me not cancel the balance (*jiezhang*) of the place where I slept, but stay in debt for it. The way in which he used the analogy of English *fengshui* in religious sense means he knows their hope may or may not become true.

My expenditure in gaining access and knowing informants also involved both vertical and horizontal *wanglai* – it was great fun (a kind of human feelings of *lishang*). The relationships between the institutions and me, and the institutions and the villagers are vertical, whereas that between the villagers and me is horizontal. I was able to gain resources from the institutions without bribing anybody. I personalised the institutional relationship and gained resources from it relying on my previous achievements when I was in China. The institutional resources on which I relied were stored up by the villagers over a long period. I then completed the triangle by paying resources directly back to the villagers. The correctness of this logic is confirmed by the Xiajia villagers (Yan, 1996b:130-31). There had been other possibilities. If I paid back to the controllers of the resources themselves, it would be counted as bribery. If I had paid back to the collective the money would have been used one way or another and might have found its way back to the local cadres. One Kaixiangong villager even said that it would be nice if we could eat as much as possible of the collective's resources until they dried out, because an ending of the collective would be a start of the eagerly anticipated private enterprise. As Li Youmei said in 2002 in a telephone conversation, the collective gave birth to the private. She had found that everybody in the village was taking things from the collective, the only difference being that the village cadres took much more than ordinary villagers. A certain degree of flexibility is always involved in the creative process of *lishang-wanglai*. I could be forgiven if I did not pay the collective because I had done my share to speed up the collapse of the collective. But if I had lived in the luxury hotel, that would have been a different case. A villager told me that I was wise not to live in the luxury hotel because that would have meant I grabbed too much from them. The villagers would have hated me in the way they hated corrupt officials.

The rational calculation of *lishang* was also involved. Although my calculation of payment in the township was useless, I was still thinking about the payment after I went to the County. However, I found that their arrangement for my accommodation involved another kind of rational calculation. When I asked Yan why he could not arrange for me to live with a villager's family by simply paying for it, he also explained to me that it was not easy to work out a suitable amount of money for me to pay a family with whom I could stay. It was also not easy to select a suitable family for me to stay with. The simplest thing for them was to find a way from official resources, without involving too much complication.

I also asked Yan why they did not want to charge me if I came back for refreshment from time to time in the grand hotel. His explanation was that he categorised me with other researchers who came from other parts of China. Although I came from the UK, he applied similar entertainment criteria to me. He asked me not to worry about it because the local government would pay a full entertainment allowance (*zhaodaifei*), as they did for many other projects which had been carried out there from all over the world for many years. He told me that project personnel either travelled around with the local officials, or lived in the county hotel and made day trips to the site, or came in small groups and lived in a village for a few days. He also said that if I had not been using them most of the hotel rooms would be empty anyway, because they are normally used for meetings, by higher authorities and guests from everywhere.

Now consider my side. During my fieldwork time the villagers were always asking me questions such as "Where do you sleep?" and "Where do you eat?" They even asked the question "Why didn't they let you live in a luxury suite in the hotel rather than leaving it empty?" I was not then sure why they asked such questions. I realise now that this was a straightforward, rational way in which they learnt about me and even from me. Here is my budget for the trips, established before I went to China. It was about total £3,000 in total, which is equivalent to RMB 37,500 *yuan,* according to the exchange rate then[75]. The internal and international travel and expenditure took about 50 per cent, 11 per cent for living expenditure in Neiguan, 27 percent in Kaixiangong, and 12 per cent for everything else. In other words, I allowed myself to spend about 4,000 *yuan* in Neiguan and 10,000 *yuan* in Kaixiangong. This budget was based on my understanding of the villages' living standards[76] and I assumed it would cover all my accommodation there. In reality, I spent more or less the amount that I budgeted, but on the villagers themselves, rather than the local officials and the village cadres.

In terms of the religious sense of *lishang,* informants told me that I had *yuan* (lot or luck by which people are brought together) with the village. It can be summarized as *tianshi, dili* and *renhe* (timeliness, favourable terrain and friendly people). As regards timeliness, the villagers told me that I should write a book about the changes of their life over the 60 years since Fei conducted his first fieldwork. For them the significance of 60 years (rather than fifty years) is that the Chinese calendar rates it as a whole cycle. Moreover, they remembered XF's lifelong regret about not writing a book about the changes in the village over half a century. As regards favourable terrain, the villagers said that although so many people had visited the village from foreign countries, only XF and I were doing Ph.D. degrees in British universities. Therefore I should publish a book about the village in England, as XF had done. As regards friendship with people, the villagers told me that I have good *renyuan* (popularity) with the village, and they would welcome me to do fieldwork there any time.

Here is one last little story related to *yuan.* SF brought back a bag of dried green beans (*xun qingdou*) for me from the village on his return from the ceremony of XF's 60 years in academia. He told me the villagers had heard that I had got married and asked him to bring the *xun qingdou* for my present. The *xun qingdou* was a special product from Kaixiangong Village, to be added to tea to enhance its flavour. I was very moved when I saw the bag of *xun qingdou*. The process of producing it would take several people several days' part-time work, picking, peeling, drying

---

[75] This came from the GBCC, UCC, City University and the WIDE for the Women's NGO Forum.

[76] The average per capita income was 977 *yuan* in Neiguan in 1994 and 4,078 *yuan* in Kaixiangong in 1995.

under sunshine, boiling with flavours, and drying over the fire. It was also one of the types of labour support listed in my research. I feel sorry that SF cannot remember from whom this came because it was given on a flying visit. I cannot thank him or her. This is an unfulfilled cherished desire of my own. It will take me back to Kaixiangong again one day[77].

2. A creative process

I have shown earlier that the mutual learning process can extend over a long period. But my fieldwork experience also shows that the field situation is subject to change, sometimes within a short period. So gaining access and getting to know informants requires creativity, insofar as it demands adaptation to change.

After I came back to Dingxi County from Neiguan Village I asked Yan why I couldn't simply live with a family, paying my own living expenses, while I was doing my fieldwork in the village. This was what I imagined would happen before I went to China. He told me that it was no longer the fashion (*bu zuoxing*) for the local officials to arrange (*anpai*) for a visitor or a visiting member of a work team to live with a peasant's family for a few months. In the People's Commune period, officials or researchers instituted the "three together" (*santong*, namely eating together, sleeping together, and working together) working pattern when they stayed in a village, for firsthand experience. It was then normal for local officials to arrange for them to stay with a family, because it was part of a bigger family – the production brigade or team.

During the post Mao era the situation began to change. Supported by Fei Xiaotong, from 1983 onwards researchers and students from Shanghai University had started to carry out fieldwork in Kaixiangong Village and a fieldwork station had been set up in the mid 1980s. As a group they lived in guestrooms in the Village Committee Courtyard for free. The project paid the cost price to Aming, a five-guaranteed old man, to cook food and look after the guestrooms. The researchers in the original study of social support, also from Shanghai University, followed the same pattern in 1991. Since then the village administration had divided into two parts: the main body moved into a new building inside the big courtyard of the enterprises, the rest remained in the old building. In the village enterprises' courtyard there was another building for entertainment. It included one kitchen, a few dining rooms, one guest suite, and warehouses. The village collective employed a chef for cooking. Three technicians shared a guest suite and ate in

---

[77] I found out the identity of the gift giver recently through telephone conversations with villagers. I agreed with him that in return I should give him a copy of my book about Kaixiangong Village in Chinese one day.

the kitchen. In the old Village Committee courtyard, the guestrooms had become a sort of inn for carters (*dache dian*). These guestrooms were for outsiders doing business in the free market in the village. Each of the guestrooms was now shared between many people, so they were no longer offered to researchers.[78]

So, my own visits to both sites had to be arranged differently to those of previous researchers. For the local authority or village collective, Chinese researchers either came with a group of people based on an institution, i.e. the original study, or through an institutional introduction, plus some personal support. Overseas visitors only stayed for a few days, which occasioned a different style of entertainment. I was an individual, coming from a British university with some informal letters of introduction, and was to stay for about three months. I did not know how they would treat me.

My behaviour was rather like that advocated by Deng Xiaoping's famous slogan: test carefully the stones under your feet step by step when you cross a river which you do not know (*mo zhe shitou guo he*). My first full night[79] in Kaixiangong was spent under the roof of BY Zhou, the Director of Women's Federation of the village, because I had returned with her son very late from the event on Chinese New Year's Eve at a temple in the township. I slept in her daughter's room. On the following day I asked Zhou whether I could share the room with her daughter if I paid for it. Her answer was that I could stay there sometimes because her daughter worked in another township and only came back once a week. However, it would mess up her relationship with her daughter who was actually an adopted daughter, and Zhou wanted to keep her life as normal as possible. She also told me that the reason she did not spend the New Year's Eve with her was because the adopted daughter stayed with her natal family. In the end, Zhou even told me that it was not easy for her to arrange any household in the village for me to stay in. I did not understand why then but I eventually found out the real reason. I will tell this later in the section.

I also asked Wang, the guard of the township enterprise, whether I could share a room with

---

[78] Another hidden reason for the village's new arrangement was caused by a conflict between the village and the Jinfeng silk factory. The factory was established in the village in 1929. It was jointly re-established in 1967 by seven neighbouring production brigades and was taken over by the township in 1972. After that it grew rapidly and built many guest suites and a luxury hotel. But in spite of being a cause of pollution it never paid anything towards village sewage purification. Since then there was an unwritten rule that researchers and visitors visiting or studying the village should be entertained at the expense of the town enterprise.

[79] I spent my first half night (17th February) when I arrived in the village and first week with Mr Wang's family, except the first night (18th February) when I started my fieldwork for the Chinese New Year's event.

a worker in the building, as I did for my first week there. He told me that it would not be proper for me to live at such a low standard (*di biaozhun*). I told him that the standards were much higher than in Neiguan Village, where I had lived for my other fieldwork. He explained to me that the arrangement of accommodation was not just a matter of a place to sleep or eat. It was a matter of treatment (*daiyu*) and to get good treatment is half the success of fieldwork. Like Yan in Dingxi, Wang also categorised me as a researcher. This matter of the importance of *daiyu* is confirmed by another incident. When I gave a talk to postgraduates in Fudan University one of the professors told me that they should have arranged accommodation for me in the luxury hotel, as they had done for him and other researchers. I thought the ensuite guestroom was quite good enough for me, although not comparable with the luxury hotel nearby.[80] But for him, where I stayed should equate with my academic status.

Although I had tried to arrange accommodation for myself, I had to accept all the arrangements made by local officials in both sites. Afterwards I felt both happy and embarrassed about it. There was a conflict inside me all the time. On the one hand, I was glad the local officials treated me so well because I wanted them to fit me in the researcher category and they did. What they had done for me was much more than I expected. I was also moved deeply by their kindness to me. I really needed their permission with whatever strings attached, including all their arrangements for my accommodation. I was unusual compared to previous researchers because I was an individual carrying out fieldwork. I could not have got anything done if everybody treated me as a stranger or even a spy. The local officials and village cadres were gatekeepers. The type of treatment I got from them was a sign of how much they accepted me. They had a very strong influence on the villagers because both places were models of the development of the collective economy.

On the other hand, I felt embarrassed because I felt that I was taking advantage by accepting both the permission and their entertainment at the same time. This was against my principles, as I understood that there would be a danger of leaving a bad name behind me. For a Chinese scholar nothing is worse than losing face in such a way. Furthermore, I might also be losing trust from the villagers. Thus I had to explore my own way to access the site and know the

---

[80] The luxury suites cost about 80-200 *yuan* each per night at the business rate. Although there were many rooms empty in the hotel, I would never have desired to live in such a place for fieldwork because it would be beyond my budget if they charged me, and I would feel morally all wrong if I did live in such a luxurious place without paying for it.

informants (see previous section).

It was up to the local officials and the heads of the village collective to organise the proper way to entertain different people. The first thing was to put me into the right category as soon as I appeared. Although I was unusual, it was not too difficult for them to decide which category I should be in. The letters I carried persuaded them that I was a researcher. And as well as respecting my spirit of hard work, they were convinced by my writing a book. Surprisingly, both the Dingxi County official and the senior official in Wujiang City talked proudly about my book to almost everybody whenever they mentioned me. Thus, my identity was sorted out.

Then they had to work out how to treat me. The entertainment in Dingxi County included allowing me to live for free in the township, a free hotel suite plus meals in the county, and a free local tour by jeep for a few days before I left there. This was simple. The arrangements in Kaixiangong were more complicated. As I mentioned before, the female manager decided to let me stay in a modest suite. I felt that she had worked out a sensible way to treat me, and was rather creative.   For her, the question of where I should sleep was not a matter of cost but of working out proper treatment of me. Afterwards I had a talk with her about it. She told me that normally researchers and other types of visitor to the village would be placed in the luxury hotel for a short period, free of charge. It would not have been proper to arrange this for me because she did not know whether or not I was qualified (*gou zige*). It was also not right for me to live there for such a long time for free. I asked her about letting me share a room with female workers, with a half joking tone. She laughed, put her arm round my shoulder and said, "come on, you are *dushu ren* (a scholar or student with a high degree) after all". Being a *dushu ren* is very distinctive in Chinese society because Chinese people respect their knowledge in general. From her point of view the correct treatment was for me to live in a modest suite for free.

I was still rather puzzled. However everything became clear when a previous head of Kaixiangong, YG Zhou, recently told me that I could now easily find reasonable food in the village because the catering service (*chuishi fuwu*) had become very popular after privatisation (*gaizhi*) from 1997 onwards. I could also rent a reasonable private place to live because the villagers were no longer afraid to earn money in such a way[81]. I now understand why BY Zhou had felt it was too difficult to arrange for me to live with any villager's family, because private

---

[81] Mr Zhou's words were soon proved true by research students from Fudan University in spring 2001. They were six males and eight females. They paid 20 yuan per day for a town room with three meals full board in seven households for four days.

business was restrained. I was glad about the freeing up of private enterprise because it was what Kaixiangong villagers had wanted for years. However, YG Zhou told me that the villagers said that everything can be changed except that the Communist Party is always correct, and Fei Xiaotong is always correct. This gives one much food for thought.

The operation of *lishang-wanglai* as a whole seems very complicated. However, as a principle in personalised relationships it can be simply defined as a creative process based on specific ascertainable criteria (*lishang*). *Lishang-wanglai* is a creative process, especially since working out actions (*wanglai*) that simultaneously satisfy different criteria of *lishang* is a difficult, often serendipitous, and satisfying operation. For example, when Wang helped me by letting me stay with his family during the Chinese New Year, he never thought that his second brother would suddenly die from liver cancer just a few days later. He had to go back home for the funeral and he also did not expect that I would make him a gift of 200 *yuan*, a sum almost equivalent to his monthly wage. For me it was natural to show my sympathy in this way because I understood that his family needed money for such an event. Surprised, they strongly refused to take it. I was confused to begin with. I felt my self-esteem was injured and I was embarrassed. I was even a little bit annoyed with this and almost allowed them to give the money back, because they seemed hypocritical. But I also felt uncomfortable with the situation and wanted to work out the best way to solve it all. So I asked them nicely to give an old sister a little bit of face (*gei dajie yidian mianzi*), and this they eventually accepted. If I had given up it might have been very different. They told me the reason they refused me was because they did not want the money to sully their generous motives when they helped me. They also told me that they were deeply moved from the bottom of their hearts by the gift. Wang's wife even told me that they did indeed need money because they had borrowed only a small amount from the enterprise which was in a depressed state (*changli bu jingqi*). They had thought they might possibly ask to borrow money from me but they would never under any circumstances ask for it as a gift because they thought it would have been immoral to "claim" something from me immediately after helping me. I was deeply moved by them and felt guilty that I had almost misunderstood them. In the end we were all pleased that we understood each other so well.

As a creative process *lishang-wanglai* may involve a bi-directional reciprocal relationship. Although the creative process of *lishang-wanglai* can be such a reciprocal relationship seen over a long-term period and through different people, the circle is not a solid line. By this I mean that in a bi-directional reciprocal relationship, the return sometimes cannot be seen at all. For example, when Han, the vice-editor of the Chinese Women's Newspaper provided a letter for me,

I thought that I was lucky it looked like a fortuitous phenomenon. This case involved a relationship between Han and me. However, it also could be understood as an inevitable outcome of the social investment input of the editor of the rural women's magazine. When she introduced me to Han, her colleague, she did not expect that she would ever get any help from me in return. However, a few years later I had a chance to help her when she was in London. She had even forgotten that she had helped me until I mentioned the story about the letter from Han. She laughed and said that good people would always have good results in return eventually (*haoren zongshi you haobao de*). She believed in the idea that helping any one person would lead to good results which could come from anybody.

My experience of gaining access to field sites shows that it is possible for anyone to create a link to any place for fieldwork in China (provided it is open to foreigners), if he or she is introduced to any one or more of those links by central or local government bodies, universities, research institutions, relatives, or friends. A thorough understanding of *lishang-wanglai* could help fieldwork researchers learn how to gain access and establish relationships for fieldwork in Chinese society. Although I introduce *lishang-wanglai* in a context of China, the same considerations may well apply for fieldworkers anywhere. Naturally there would be different ways and conventions to establish relationships in different places. But anybody who gains field access is learning about how personal relationships are established in that society, for whatever purposes, and it is always necessary to learn this in order to do fieldwork. *Lishang-wanglai* thus has methodological implications because everybody enters into interpersonal relationships in the course of doing fieldwork. In particular, anybody at any time going into the field to investigate any subject has to enter into the personal relationships which they are investigating. This obviously is not a simple purchase or market exchange, although there may be payment involved. Therefore fieldworkers must necessarily learn how to relate to the people in their places of investigation. They need to learn the principles of personalised relationship and the local system for establishing trust. Therefore, gaining access and maintaining relationships are things we should learn all the time, which will usually be different in every new piece of fieldwork. *Lishang-wanglai* is a topic for all fieldworkers, because they have to establish personal relationships in doing the fieldwork.

XII.III. A case study of "*lishang-wanglai*" beyond the village

This example comes from my observation when I was doing fieldwork in Kaixiangong

Village. My supervisor Stephan Feuchtwang (hereafter "SF") was invited to visit the village and the area for a few days. Before the visit I was told that SF would be entertained nicely because he was Fei Xiaotong's (hereafter "XF" whenever it involves him as examples rather than quoting his ideas)[82] guest, although I myself was not so sure how he would be treated. During the welcome feast the local officials kept on asking questions about the relationship between SF and XF. In the end they worked out that SF was XF's *shidi* (younger brother under the same master or junior fellow apprentice) because both of them used to be supervised by Sir Raymond Firth at LSE (the London School of Economics and Political Sciences)[83]. Although SF told them modestly that he was one generation younger than XF, I heard an official tell a waitress, after the feast, to keep the same standard (*tongyang de daiyu*) for the rest of his stay because this was appropriate treatment (*daiyu*) for XF's younger brother under the same master. The standard of the meal was 18 dishes. 8 small cold dishes (like different types of salad and similar to a starter in the West) were displayed on the inner ring of a big circular table, then 10 different types of hot dishes were served one by one as soon as each was cooked. Apart from this, all the entertainment for SF, which included meeting the vice Mayor of Wujiang City and some senior officials, visiting different places accompanied by some officials and researchers, and food and accommodation in the best hotel, Wujiang Hotel, was arranged and paid for by the Wujiang Foreign Affairs Office.

SF offered to pay for a meal for the local officials and researchers to thank them for everything on the day he was leaving. His proposed standard for this was equivalent to the welcome feast. I thought this was reasonable, asked about the cost, and was told it 500 *yuan*. When I told local officials what SF was planning, the vice Chairperson of Wujiang Political Consultative Conference thought she should find a restaurant which had a special relationship with the Government for SF, to make the 500 *yuan* more useful. The other official suggested that they did not need a special place (*suibian zhao yige difang*) for the meal, anywhere would do. In

---

[82] Fei Xiaotong (Hsiai-Tung Fei, 1910-), Professor of Peking University. He was the author of *"Peasant life in China—a field study of country life in the Yangtze Valley"*, 1939 Routledge & Kegan Paul Ltd; winner of Huxley Memorial Medal, by The Royal Anthropological Institute, 1981; and a vice-Chairman of Standing Committee of National People's Congress. Due to Fei's special academic and political position, it is impossible for me to avoid involving Fei's relationships with his academic circle, his hometown and Kaixiangong Village where he carried out his fieldwork in 1930s, as part of the subject of my restudy.

[83] B. Malinowski (1884-1942) joined the supervising with Firth after he came back from a USA trip. According to Fei (2002), Firth was the tutor (*daoshi*) who decided on the title of Fei's PhD thesis, whereas Malinowski was his director (*yeshi*) who was in charge of the supervising of Fei's thesis (19, 25 & 29).

the end, the thank you meal took place in a small restaurant in a town on the way to Shanghai, and, surprisingly, the meal turned out to be ten times worse than the welcome feast it had been supposed to resemble. I asked the officials how this could have happened. They said that the gold content of government currency (*hanjinliang*) was much higher than normal currency. This explanation did not satisfy me and I was still wondering about the meaning of the meal afterwards. I found out the real reason later, from some informal conversations on preparations for XF's ceremony to celebrate 60 years in academia. The intention of the meal was to ensure that SF remembers he owes Wujiang a *renqing,* an obligation of human feeling, by giving him a shock (*rang ta mingbai mingbai*). The officials knew SF could attend XF's ceremony and wanted to make sure that he would express his thanks by coming back to honour it. It sounds unpleasant (as well as complicated) to a non-Chinese, that the local officials treated SF in this way, but to them it was perfectly normal. My understanding then was that they had "fair play" with SF. "Fair play" is an English term, which appeared in China in the 1930s. In Chinese it is pronounced as *feiepolai*. I checked with the local official about the meaning of the meal with an explanation of *feiepolai* and he agreed, but still stressed the word *renqing*.

A *wanglai* between any scholar and the local officials should normally be an institutional reciprocity. In this case the scholar was a professor from a foreign university who came from England and the relationship between him and the local officials was still an institutional reciprocity. However, the local officials had combined generous and expressive *wanglai* with the institutional reciprocity[84] normal for guests from foreign countries (*waibin*). The local officials were proud that Kaixiangong Village and Wujiang City were able to attract a foreign professor's visit. They deserved to be the "land of ceremony and propriety (*liyi zhi bang*)" as China has long been called in the world. There is a popular Chinese saying, which originally came from the Confucian Analects, "Is it not a joy to have friends come from afar (*you peng zi yuanfang lai, bu yi le hu*)?" At this stage the *lishang* of morality and human feelings was shown in the entertainment, which mixed generous and expressive *wanglai* into the institutional reciprocity.

Having discovered a special relationship between SF and XF they began to personalise their institutional relationship with SF by increasing the standard of his entertainment.. Thus, the relationship between SF and the local officials became personalised institutional *wanglai* rather than normal institutional *wanglai*. Soon after that they discovered another link between SF and

---

[84] See Chapter XI.V for definitions of generous *wanglai*, expressive *wanglai*, instrumental *wanglai* and negative *wanglai*.

XF, which was that SF would be returning in a few months time to attend the ceremony for XF's 60 years' academic career. Thus the personalised institutional *wanglai* became mixed with generous, expressive and instrumental *wanglai.* The standard of catering showed that the rational calculation criterion of *lishang* must have been involved. In this case a religious sense of *lishang* also carried a large weight. The fact that SF was XF's younger brother under the same master (*shidi*) showed he had *yuanfen* (predestined relationship, lot, or luck) in this area. This put SF into a more likely position for his relationship to be personalised by the local officials than other professors from foreign countries. The fact that SF would soon return put another coating of *yuanfen* colour on the special relationship between XF and SF. The discovery of "younger brother under the same master" between SF and XF and the endless subsequent comments about it added more flavour into the enjoyment of creativity for the officials, and was another criterion of *lishang*.

Let us step back some distance to see what happened. According to the principle of *lishang-wanglai* or "raising pigs" there were two processes involved in this case. One was the whole process of making and maintaining *wanglai* between SF and China. Wujiang's entertainment to SF was only one point in this whole process or circle. I will illustrate this by quantifying the different reasons for the *wanglai*. I estimate that 30 per cent of its importance came because SF is a distinguished foreign academic with more than twenty years of Chinese studies. His special relationship with XF gave another 30 per cent. The respect conferred by two factors accounted for 60 per cent of his enhanced entertainment by the local officials. 10 per cent more was from their duty as the hosts; 10 per cent was from their desire to be in the "land of ceremony and propriety (*liyi zhi bang*)", 10 per cent was the enjoyment of discovering the special relationship between SF and XF; and the final 10 per cent was an instrumental input for investment (L. Yang, 1957) to strengthen the relationship between SF and XF. Thus the motives for the *wanglai* were multiple, and not all of equal importance.

However, when SF offered a meal to thank them, they played a "fair play" (*feiepolai*) with him, which caused a considerable misunderstanding and could have led to a negative *wanglai*. SF and the local officials had a different understanding of their relationship. If it were not for the fact that SF might be able to return in the near future everything would have been much simpler, because Wujiang did very well at maintaining the relationship between SF and China. The fact that SF would come back soon involved him in a more complicated situation. Although it was normal, from SF's point of view, for him to express his thanks to the local officials, for them it was not normal to accept his thank you meal. This involved another kind of calculation of *lishang*. For the local officials whether or not SF would come back was a judgement of their entertainment for SF. If they accepted SF's thank you meal it meant that they let SF "clear the balance" with them. If SF did not turn up they would be blamed for not keeping a good enough relationship with him, even though they worked very hard to strengthen his relationship with China. They actually did not expect to accept anything at all from SF, including a thank you meal, because for them the thank you meal was a repayment that would mean a full stop of their *wanglai* with him, and they did not want to be blamed for ending the relationship. This was their misunderstanding of SF's intention. Based on this, the *feiepolai* was designed to show SF that the thank you meal was not enough to "clear the balance". This, actually, was another way of saying that they wanted to keep a closer relationship with him. In fact, my understanding of *feiepolai* then was more rational than their explanation of *renqing,* which is another criterion of *lishang*. They would never have said "no" to SF's thank you meal because they thought that this kind of refusal would be too embarrassing to SF. Nor would they ever tell SF directly that he owes Wujiang a *renqing*, hence the "fair play", which was clear to the officials, but sounds silly and hurtful when retold outside China.

In the end SF did go back to Wujiang and everybody was happy about it. Afterwards a village cadre told me that the local officials thought that SF was loyal to them (*jiang yiqi*), understood their human feelings (*dong renqing*), and the predestined relationship was fulfilled (*yuanfen lingyan*), etc., which relates to the moral, human feelings, and religious senses of *lishang*. From the local officials' point of view the relationship between themselves and SF was much more expressive after his return to Wujiang. It would, however, have dropped down to a normal institutional or slightly negative *wanglai* if SF had not returned there. The local officials would have thought that SF, a Chinese specialist, did not even understand Chinese *renqing,* and therefore they did not have *yuanfen* with him. It might also have injected a little negative feeling into the local people's reaction to him, especially since they were already generally hostile to researchers who were constantly studying them.

In order to fully explain why, if SF had not returned, his relationship with local officials would have deteriorated, another process of *lishang-wanglai* or, to use villagers own metaphor, "raising pigs" has to be involved. The fact that SF would come back soon also involved him in the more general relationship between researchers and local people. The local officials had entertained many researchers over past years, both individuals and groups, from inside and outside China. SF's visit was thus one point in the whole process or circle. The local officials' hint using SF's thank you meal would work only under a certain cultural context in which both sides understood each other very well. The local officials did not know this and assumed that SF would understand it. For them it would be nice if SF could realise why it should be so (*wu chu daoli*) without explicit explanation. If SF did not come back it would reduce his relationship with the local people a little, but not do great harm to the relationship between researchers and the local area in general, because only 10 per cent of the input involved in the entertainment was instrumental. This kind of Chinese rational calculation is different from SF's. He very much wanted to go back to Wujiang for XF's ceremony. His decision to do so depended only on whether he could organise a grant for the trip.

This case shows that for the local officials it was a novel and thus creative matter to decide how to entertain SF, because SF's visit was an informal visit. This was different from formal arrangements, to which they would simply apply standard diplomatic etiquette. In the creative process there were many things that could go wrong. For example, to provide a fixed set meal in such large quantities for a few people every day was not a sensible arrangement. It would seem to be both unnecessary and repetitive for a few people to eat such a big meal everyday. However, according to a waitress, it was necessary to do so and would not be boring if one enjoyed some of the dishes each time. She told me that the set meal was very well designed for higher level leaders and honoured foreign guests (*guibin*). It could show local cooking skills, like colours, smells and taste, balance of ingredients, shapes of chopping, ways of cooking, etc. The variety of food was carefully chosen because it is very difficult to cater for all tastes (*zhong kou nan tiao*). So both cold and hot dishes included fish, pork, beef, lamb, chicken, egg, bean curd, vegetables, and so on in order to cover different requests and tastes. Here for the local officials the question of whether or not the food would be wasted can be ignored (rational calculation), but it would be considered ungrateful (*bu lingqing - renqing*) if SF told them it was wasteful or boring.

The *feiepolai* (fair play) was also unnecessarily clever. It might seem odd to a Westerner that the local officials sometimes asked questions which pry into other people's private matters, but sometimes could not even ask a question straightforwardly, but used a hint. However, after I reviewed some related cases in Kaixiangong Village, I recognized that the question under discussion, what is the relationship between XF and SF, was the kind of question they always ask about themselves. The *feiepolai* game was also one they always played with each other. It would never have entered their heads that presence or absence of a public fund or grant could affect SF's future visit. Such misunderstandings could easily happen between local officials and a Western professor. But it could also happen among Chinese people: between rural and urban dwellers, inside and outside a village, even different generations, gender, and social or economic positions within the same village. Like it or not, it was the way they lived. The endless behaviour of "raising pigs" or the fascination of *lishang-wanglai* in making and maintaining personalised relationships gets its vitality from the enjoyment of creativity. This enjoyment, in Chinese society as a whole, is not without its cost in misunderstandings and lost opportunities.

Conclusion

As I made explicit at the beginning of the book, this study examines personal relationships by looking at social support arrangements in rural Chinese people's everyday life from 1978 to 2004. In this Conclusion, I will start with matters of state and gender raised in studying *lishang-wanglai*, and then focus more specifically on the contributions made by this book, namely, the methodological implications of *lishang-wanglai*, *lishang-wanglai* as a unified principle and typology of reciprocity, *lishang-wanglai* combining a static model and dynamic networks, social creativity as the motivation of *lishang-wanglai*; and finally, as an open question, I will ask whether *lishang-wanglai* can be extended into a general analytic concept.

I. "*Lishang-wanglai*" and issues of state and gender

Echoing the question "What holds Chinese society together?", mentioned at the beginning of the book, I move onto issues raised in studying *lishang-wanglai*. This question was asked by Watson in the days before the June 4th Event in 1989, in "studies of Chinese funerals" (James L. Watson 1988:3). After the event, socialist regimes in the USSR and Eastern Europe fell from power like dominoes while the Chinese government steadfastly stood its ground under economic sanctions by many major Western countries. The question of "What holds Chinese society together?" was raised again in the context of the economy, international relations and people interested in China and Chinese studies. The study of rural Chinese people's social support arrangements and *lishang-wanglai* reflected the above question from a different angle.

As is well known, the Chinese state system has been an autocracy ever since the first Chinese Emperor united China in the Qin Dynasty (221-207 B.C.). Over the last two thousand plus years, although the dynasties changed every couple of dozen years or more, their autocratic nature has never changed. Even the Republic of China, which appeared early last century, and the People's Republic of China from the middle of the last century, are no exception. The changes of dynasties or names for the state are like a vicious circle in which every dynasty is governed by an enlightened emperor (*mingjun*) to begin with and ends with a fatuous and self-indulgent ruler (*hunjun*) or tyrant or despot (*baojun*). These changes can be one individual changing from enlightened emperor to tyrant, or later generations ruling tyrannically after an enlightened ancestor. In Chapter IX.II I introduced the Taiji Diagram and pointed out that the relationships between a ruler and people are like those between a boat and water. This cycle has repeated itself all the way through Chinese history from the Qin Dynasty to the last imperial dynasty, and reasserts itself from the Republic of China to the People's Republic of China unendingly.

My point is that the relationship between the state and people can be seen as a vertical circle: either vicious or virtuous. Although the people in the Republic of China on the mainland are still dominated by a new form of autocracy, towards the end of the last Century in the Republic of China in Taiwan there has been a gradual change to democracy. The relationship between the state and people in Taiwanese society offers an example of a virtuous circle. The Taiji Diagram oriented *lishang-wanglai* framework can demonstrate how the relationship between state and people can enter either a vicious or virtuous circle, and how changes occur within the relationship. I have demonstrated how particularism and universalism co-existed in Chinese society and how relationships change with changing situations in Chapter IX.II. In this section I will demonstrate two major issues which are raised in studying *lishang-wanglai* in Kaixiangong and, to a lesser degree, Neiguan villages. They are the relationship between the state and the people, and the relationship between males and females, in resource exchange.

1. Relationship between villagers and state

The state played an important role in villagers' lives, although in early 1990s the majority of villagers in China only received social welfare from the state system in exceptional circumstances (see section "the ESRC project on social support" in Introduction). The ESRC project looked at three main sources for villagers seeking social support, household, private and public. Public support refers to resources from the village collective, township, credit cooperative and bank. (see Table IX-1). The Statistical Report on the project shows that in Kaixiangong the numbers of contacts (*wanglai*) for financial support from public sources amounts to 9.3 percent of the total of contacts made for such purposes (Chang and Feuchtwang 1996: 8 of Kaixiangong section), mainly for emergency events. This data agrees with the state figures showing very little input into rural areas. However, there is a large difference between this quantitative data and the qualitative data that I researched.

Firstly, I need to make clear that the relationship between rural people and the state is an administrative relationship, and as such one on which *lishang-wanglai* has no bearing. However, the state's policies are delivered through its various institutions, and local officials and village cadres who actually affect rural people's lives. The category of public support in the ESRC project does not distinguish between purely administrative relationships and those involving *lishang-wanglai*. Therefore it cannot account for how individuals sought support from public sources. It is a key point to understand the relationship and interactions between the state and the rural people, because the most important "resources" from the public source are policy and power, which cannot be quantified. Both Polanyi's (1957) redistributive political exchange, another principal form of anthropological obligatory exchange, and Parsons's (1937/51) work on personal relationships (see the 5th point in subsection Clarifications of *wanglai*" in Chapter XI.IV) are relevant. For me, once an institutional relationship has been personalised it can then be expressed as a kind of *lishang-wanglai* relationship and therefore the *lishang-wanglai* model and networks (see Chapter IX.II) can be applied for further analysis. This extends the flow of social support and *lishang-wanglai* from relationships between individuals to relationships between individuals and institutions.

Secondly, since the contacts (*wanglai*) between the villagers and the various institutions, local officials, village cadres can be personalised, *lishang-wanglai* can be engaged. We call this kind of *lishang-wanglai* personalised institutional *wanglai*, which, as in all reciprocal personalized relationships, can be divided into generous, expressive, instrumental and negative *wanglai*. These *wanglai* operate vertically in either bottom up or top down directions and can be explained with *lishang* criteria. Chapters III.IV, VII.III, and VIII.I show that the state and its various institutions have a huge impact on the villagers' everyday life, not just for medical care and during times of disaster. One obvious example is the impact of the one child policy on the marriage system through the increasing frequency of taking a man into a family marriage (*zhaonuxu*). Another is the impact of policy, e.g. preferential treatment for enterprises employing the disabled and handicapped, which promoted vigorous development of the related industries and therefore became one of the main financial sources for the local official welfare system.

Thirdly, the Statistical Report on the ESRC social support project also shows that the numbers of contacts (*wanglai*) for financial support for investment from all sources makes up 77.1 percent of total resource-seeking activity in Kaixiangong village (Chang and Feuchtwang 1996: 8 of Kaixiangong section). This is mainly for house construction. However, Chapters II.III and V.III show that before 1996 house construction in Kaixiangong Village was a major family event rather than an investment. Once house construction is moved from the category of investment to that of family event, investment becomes almost non-existent. The question is, why are Kaixiangong villagers so interested in building houses and why do they ignore financial investment almost completely? The answer is that this phenomenon was driven by the invisible hand of the state rather than by the market economy. On the one hand, after the social reforms of the later 1970s the villagers were at last able to store money and materials for rebuilding and renovating homes which had been left untouched since the Liberation in 1949. On the other hand, as I have shown in the section "Kaixiangong Village" in the Introduction, up until 1996 private economy was not allowed because the village was a model of the socialist collective economy. The villagers sensibly adapt themselves to changes of policy. At the same time they create ways to protect and comfort themselves. In their words, the state controls the whole country and the villagers manage their own life (*zhengfu guanli guojia zhege dajia, women guanhao ziji de xiaojia*), implying that they manage their life within the boundaries of given conditions. In the case of burning incense on a burned honeycomb briquette outside houses, JY Yao and her neighbours found enjoyment in creating ways to keep their religious contacts with local gods when the local temples were destroyed by the local government in 1996 (see Chapter IV).

Fourthly, the villagers were not passive. Here I would like to illustrate the relationship between the state and rural people with the Taiji Diagram, the Taoism Symbol, which I borrowed for construction of the *lishang-wanglai* networks (see Chapter IX.II). The visible very limited social relief fund provided by the state can be seen as a black dot in the white section of the *yin-yang* diagram where rural people are based, whereas the invisible concern of the state on rural people can be seen as a white dot in the black section of the diagram where the state is based. It more or less represents the real situation of the state's input (the "black dot") to rural areas and the state's concern ("white dot") for rural people in 1996 when I was in Kaixiangong village. However, the proportions between the state and the villagers changed with the application of the new policy of privatization since 1997. In April 2004, after eight years (1997 to 2004) of my fieldwork, in my very brief restudy of the previous project in Kaixiangong I found the most obvious financial support was for investment. House construction was considered as a method of investment in the ESRC social support project, but my study shows it to be in fact a kind of family event (see Chapter V.III). However, after privatization Kaixiangong villagers found different ways to invest, which can also be described and analysed with the *lishang-wanglai* concept. I have shown how, over many years, the villagers' practices of *lishang-wanglai* with village cadres and local officials have influenced economic development. Another result of this *wanglai* can be seen from Table I-2, that in 2004 191,537 *yuan* of the state tax due from Kaixingong villagers was waived by the Suzhou government, eliminating no less than 40 per cent of the villagers' burden of tax and fees.

Finally, I will use the concept of *lishang-wanglai* to show how these changes between the state and the villagers occurred. The state's power can be regarded as one of its resources in its attempts to control villagers' life, the reason why Kaixiangong villagers usually adapted themselves to changes of policy. But villagers created their own way to *wanglai* with the state through their representatives – village cadres or local officials as necessary. For example, Kaixiangong villagers' state tax increased from 32,671 *yuan* in 1985 to 163,300 *yuan* in 2000. The villagers decided to have a negative *wanglai* with the state by delaying or refusing payment. Initially, the local government decided to take people to court and asked for a list of names from the village. Whereupon the head of the village did indeed provide a list, a full list showing that nearly 20 per cent of household heads refused to pay the state tax, amounting to half of the total. The village cadre suggested to the local officials that this number was likely to increase if anyone was sent to prison, since villagers would act according their firm belief that law can't be used to punish the masses (*fa bu ze zhong*). The local government then reported the real situation to central government, and a few years later the policy was changed in favour of rural people. Thus, the size of the black dot (state's input to rural area) in the white section enlarged along with the enlargement of white dot (state's concern of rural people) in the black section.

2. Gender issue in *"lishang-wanglai"* practice

The practices of gift-giving, social support and *lishang-wanglai* are heavily imbued with gender-specificity in the ethnographic chapters, although I didn't make this an issue in the chapters on theory and methodology (see chapters in Part Three). This section will discuss the gender-significance of virtually all practices of *lishang-wanglai*.

I would like to begin by returning to a piece of I did earlier work in 1995, when I presented a paper titled "Gender difference in rural social support in China in the post-Mao era (1979-1991) -- An analysis of differences between agnatic and non-agnatic kin" in a conference on Socioeconomic Transformation and Women in China. It was based on the ESRC social support project's data on ten villages. The data shows there are three tendencies on gender differences in social support arrangements: a) the number of contacts of labour support from agnates is more than from non-agnates; b) in investment (house construction) the number of contacts from non-agnates in financial support are more than from agnates; c) the number of contacts of support from agnates is higher than from non-agnates in the same village.

I tested these gender tendencies in Kaixiangong Village and found an explanation for them. a) Chapter I.III shows how fuller information reveals a customary division of different kinds of mutual support between agnatic kin and non-agnatic kin in Kaixiangong. The rest of the ethnographic chapters repeatedly show how agnatic kin provided labour for feasts, whereas non-agnatic kin attended events with gifts (*lipin*) or gift money (*lijin*). b) Chapter V.III also proved the point that non-agnatic kin provided a large amount of gifts for house construction, showing details. c) Obviously agnatic kin who live in the same village are obliged to attend every event or give labour support to every feast or house construction (see Chapters I.III, V and VI).

The test result shows that the numerous divisions between agnatic kin and non-agnatic kin in social support arrangement are based on local custom. The problem is that agnatic kin and non-agnatic kin are made up of both male and female individuals. What is the real difference between male and female? After I came back from Kaixiangong I replaced the above paper with a new paper titled "Fattening pigs and women's gifts" in the published conference collection (West at el 1999). This more precisely addressed women's role in practices of social support and linked the role to women's status. As I said then: "A woman's status in a household is based on her understanding of customs, the principle of 'fattening pigs' and the meaning of gifts, and hence her ability to provide resources through mutual support with other households", but "how much it affects the status of women and whether any causal link exists between household wealth and numbers of social support contacts are still unclear" (Chang 1999:173). In other words, a woman's family status is largely based on her understanding of *lishang* and ability to *wanglai* with others for the purpose of providing resources to the household. Although a woman's role in using *lishang-wanglai* to provide family social support is clearly important, it seems that this does not override the tendency of men to view their own activities as of primary importance! A previous head of the village told me that the above statement is also true for a man except for replacing "family status" with "social status". This, to some extent, is confirmed by the popular saying in urban China from the 1980s to 1990s that I have already quoted: "a person's success depends on three parts of ability and seven parts of special relationships" (*sanfen nengli, qifen guanxi*).

Now I am engaging the concept of *lishang-wanglai* to develop this issue further. Firstly, I will bring forward the case of Neiguan village for horizontal comparison. I tested the gender issues in Neiguan a few months before I did my fieldwork in Kaixiangong. The results of the divisions between agnatic kin and non-agnatic kin are very similar. There is however a sizeable difference in that major events, i.e. weddings, funerals, festivals, or religious activities, in Neiguan were arranged or participated in by men. I remember that when I was stopped from entering a village temple because I was a woman. I asked what difference this made, and was told that women would pollute the temple because menstrual blood made them dirty − this being clearly an issue of religious sense rather than pragmatism. The major events listed above counted as part of the Neiguan villagers' social life, at which male heads of household acted as representatives of their households, reflecting their local social status. Males are also able to provide labour support for funerals, which relates to the *lishang* criterion of rational calculation. I connected the difference between Neiguan and Kaixiangong in this respect with another tendency I found from data in the ESRC social support project: that richer areas have a larger number of social support contacts and poorer areas have fewer. I mentioned in Chapter XII.I that among the ten villages of the ESRC project Kaixiangong is one of the richest, whereas Neiguan is the poorest. Consequently feasts for major events in Neiguan were very simple and required no labour support. The phenomenon of males' participation in major events in Neiguan is similar to that of males working as secretaries or typists in Victorian times. Nowadays it is usual that this is mainly female's work. Equally, for Kaixiangong villagers it is usual that the arrangements of social support are mainly female's work.

Secondly, I will now move to a vertical time dimension of *lishang-wanglai*. Were there any differences in attitudes to gender in Kaixiangong village between times when it was poor and when it was rich? I should point out that even when in absolute terms Kaixiangong was much poorer than it is now, in Fei's time in the 1930s, it was still relatively much better off than Neiguan. In the context of China as a whole Kaixiangong has always been a rich village except for a few years during the Japanese War of the 1940s and the Great Famine period of the 1960s. However, women's status has indeed risen over the last 60 years. I noticed that there has been a movement towards greater valuation of daughters compared with sons. This can be seen in the movement from a traditional idea of rearing sons against old age (*yang er fang lao*) to one of relying on children including daughters. Traditionally in Kaixiangong Village a marriage consisting of taking a son-in-law (*zhaonuxu*) into a family was seen as a misfortune in that it showed that the family had no son, and the son-in-law was poor and had low social status. Nowadays more and more families accept this kind of marriage model. Some people even admire it, e.g. HL Wang's younger son, who said that if he was taken into a richer family he wouldn't feel poor. Although uxorilocal marriage was always for the sons of the poor, admiration of such marriages and their being widely accepted by the villagers is an obvious change. Favouring daughters rather than sons, or at least feeling easy without sons, must be partly attributed to the one child family policy applied from the early 1980s. The fact that about one half of all families had just one daughter changed the villagers' view and attitude towards uxorilocal marriage and also affected the arrangement of elderly care. A further enhancement of women's status is shown by the expectation that daughters married into other families are expected to be able to take responsibility for the arrangements of family events and updating the families' *lishang-wanglai* networks based on local customs. This custom was quite new compared to what was expected of new wives in the 1930s (Fei, 1939:45-50). The significant change of a daughter-in-law's status is a challenge for her because if she is not careful a mistake will cost her new family loss of face or a source of resources. But many women very much enjoyed themselves making such arrangements. And married out daughters could create opportunities for closeness with their natal families. Traditionally the villagers only celebrate the one month, one year and sixteen year old birthdays for children, and the 66th birthday for the elderly as family events. Nowadays, some families celebrate children's birthdays every year and elders' birthdays every five years from 60 years old onwards, influenced by new urban practices. Although the birthday ceremonies are relatively small, low-key and had not yet been widely spread in the village, married out daughters involved their natal families in them one way or the other. Like girls in Beijing or Shanghai who normally wouldn't want to move away from their natal town to other parts of China, Kaixiangong Village's girls also preferred to get married and settled locally. This gave them opportunities to *wanglai* with their natal families conveniently for both annual events and life cycle events. For the natal families the daughters are no longer "spilled water that cannot be gathered up" as in Fei's time (1939:46). Instead they are now mothers' padded body vests (literally, a daughter is truly close to a mother compared with a son, *nuer shi mama de tiexinao*). The movement towards greater valuation of daughters indicates that their status has changed significantly between now and 60 years ago. Women's participation in knitting family *lishang-wanglai* networks has helped to raise their family status and also even social status at the local level. From my fieldwork it must be noted that women are not the only practitioners of *lishang-wanglai*, but the fact that in many cases it is the women who control *lishang-wanglai* means that they have a status and importance that would not exist in a society in which *lishang-wanglai* were less important. Further investigation of the relationship between *lishang-wanglai* and gender is clearly a topic for further research.

Finally, I would like to involve the Taiji Diagram, the Taoism Symbol, again (see section IX.II.2). The basic idea of *yin* and *yang* is that the former is associated with the Chinese characters of quiet, female, intuitive and receiving force, whereas the latter is associated with the Chinese characters of strong, male, creative and giving force. According to this the male is always a black dot in the white section of the *yin-yang* diagram where the female is based, whereas the female is always a white dot in the black section of the diagram where the male is based. The dots inside the white and black halves indicate that within each is the seed of the other. It means males have female strengths and females have male strengths inside themselves. They can both carry out similar jobs e.g. typewriting or arranging resources for families. I interviewed three families without housewives: in one family the related family arrangements were all done by the husband who was a restauranteur, in another family they were done by the grandmother, and in the last family they were done by a grandfather who used to be a treasurer of one of the village groups and had retired from a township enterprise. His wife said the reason he did this for the family is because he was good at dealing with different relationships. In Kaixiangong there were families which had less strong *lishang-wanglai* networks, e.g. the village vet's family or FS Zhou's family. There were also many families which had strong *lishang-wanglai* networks, e.g. FK Yao's family or BY Zhou's family.

Kaixiangong shows that it is not necessarily village cadres' families that absorbed larger networks than others, unlike in Xiajia Village (Yan 1996b). It is also not only women that are good at making *lishang-wanglai* networks. In Chapter XII.I I have shown that my informants were old, young, male or female, and provided information from different angles. Some women acted in the traditional husband's role and vice versa. Their families were involved in the *lishang-wanglai* networks in different degrees. So although I started my research with a concern for issues of gender, I was led to enquiries in much broader non-gender-specific areas.

To summarise: gender is significant in that male and female usually act differently in arrangements of social support and practices of *lishang-wanglai*, but their roles can if necessary be changed in line with changes of situation.

II. *"Lishang-wanglai"* unified principle and typology of reciprocity

My study on social support and *lishang-wanglai* is very largely concerned with reciprocity as a principle form of anthropological obligatory exchange. I show how the concept of reciprocity is used both as a principle and a typology, which can be unified by the single notion of *lishang-wanglai*. As I mentioned in Chapter IX.I, the concept of reciprocity always mixes the principles and typology of exchange, e.g. Mauss's "the spirit of the gift" (1950), Malinowski's "pure gift" and "real barter" (1922) and "the principle of give-and-take" (1926). Levi-Strauss believes the principle of reciprocity can be a foundation for all social relations (1949). Sahlins (1965/72) made a typology of three kinds of reciprocity, whereas M. Yang (1994) distinguished principle (*guanxixue*) and types (*guanxi*) separately. Y. Yan (1996b) even further divided reciprocity into two types of expressive gift giving and instrumental expressive gift giving categories, two types of unbalanced reciprocity in imbalanced gift exchange, *guanxi* networks and three ethics of *renqing* principle. For me all of these can be unified with the *lishang-wanglai* model, which includes *lishang* criteria and *wanglai* typology. In this section I will highlight the points leading most directly to *lishang-wanglai*.

(1) *Lishang* criteria are built on previous researchers empirical studies (Chen 1996/98, Yan 1996b, Yang 1995 and Zhai 1993, etc.). In "*Guanxi*" of Chapter X.VI I have shown that Zhai Xuewei (1993) suggested that three Chinese characters *yuan* (predestined relationship), *qing* (human feelings), and *lun* (Confucian's relationships) form a Chinese style of interpersonal relationships (*renji guanxi*). Yang Yinyi (1995) used *renqing* (human feelings), *lunli* (Confucius basic relationships) and *yuan* (predestined relationship) to be the principle of *guanxi* concept. Chen Junjie (1996/98) used *lunli* (Confucius basic relationships), *ganqing* (human feelings), and *liyi* (gain, benefit, interests) as the three dimensions for *guanxi* structure. In contrast to the Chinese works listed above, Yan Yunxiang's defines *renqing* ethics (1996b) as "rational calculation, moral obligation, and emotional attachment (146)". All of the above researchers mention morality and human feelings and half mention either rational calculation or religious sense. I too agree that morality and human feelings are two important criteria or principles in human actions. Yan's "emotional attachment" is a kind of positive feeling and covers a narrow meaning, whereas the others' category of "human feelings" can be positive or negative and cover a whole gamut of human feelings, a wider definition of the same principle. For me there is no doubt about rational calculation being one of the important principles or criteria for a human being's action. This kind of rational-choice exchange theory, deriving from the universal truth that individuals always seek to maximise rewards from their interactions with others (i.e. Blau, Homans, etc.) has already been relatively fully developed. I simply use rational calculation as one of the *lishang* criteria without further explanation.

The complicated principle is "religious sense". When I looked at the questionnaire of the ESRC social support project I was puzzled as to why there were questions related to religion. Some Chinese colleagues told me this was Feuchtwang's personal interest. However, I was surprised at how helpful and useful those questions were for my fieldwork in the two villages. To my knowledge China has never had any kind of "state religion" which had any real power in government. Although China has many religious beliefs, senses and many religious organisations and textual religious traditions, there was no separation of religion from politics (*zhengjia fenli*). This is an unusual cultural phenomena compared with the West. Religion in Chinese characters is *zongjiao*. Historically there are two basic religions in China: Buddhism (*fojiao*) and Taoism (*daojiao*). Buddhism originally came from India, whereas Taoism (*daojiao*), although indigenous to China, never became an orthodox religion. However there have been times when there was a kind of "state religion" of sorts, Confucianism (*kongjiao*), which was the official religion but was never accepted by ordinary Chinese people. This "state religion" was more like a moral code or code of ethics created by rulers to rule the people, rather than a religious spirit which came from inside of them. The religious spirit has often been treated as "negative ideology" in Chinese society, especially in Socialist China where the religious spirit became a synonym for "feudal superstition" sometimes. Almost all the Chinese scholars I know have a more or less general religious sense, but it is taboo to become a religious believer[85] because even the sage Confucius and the "state religion" of Confucianism are subject to arbitrary treatment by people in power. For ordinary Chinese people there are all sorts of popular religions (*minjian zongjiao*). What I learnt from my fieldwork is that ordinary people believe in their own gods, e.g. land god, kitchen god, medicine god and silk god. I do not mean that everybody does so, or that every believer's belief is at the same level. But although statues of these gods can be smashed and temples can be destroyed, the religious sense is deeply rooted in people's hearts and can never be removed, and I accordingly include "religious sense" as the fourth criterion of *lishang*. It sheds a very useful light on the behaviour and motivation of ordinary Chinese people.

(2) Table 3 compares 16 different kinds of typology on social exchange relationships or reciprocity, including my own. For my study the influential researchers are, in historical order, Weber (1904), Parsons (1937/51), Polanyi (1957), L. Yang (1957), Sahlins (1965/72), Befu (1966/67), Mitchell (1969), Wen (1982), Lin (1986), Walder (1986), King (Jin, 1985/94), Hwang (Huang, 1987), Z. Yang (1991), M. Yang (1988/94) and Yan (1996b). The 16 typologies are fitted into five columns. As well as generous *wanglai*, expressive *wanglai*, instrumental *wanglai* and negative *wanglai*, there is a column for market exchange (Polanyi, Z. Yang, etc.) or economic exchange (i.e. King). Market or economic exchange is completely different from social or personal exchange relationships, and not part of my study. However, for me, once any

---

[85] Not the same as a religious believer being as a kind of "flower vase" of rulers, or studying religions as a job. The analogy of "flower vase" is always used as a decorative object without real usage, e.g. mistress is a flower vase of a man.

market or economical exchange relationship has been personalised then the relationship becomes a personalised market relationship. The personalised market relationship falls either into the category of "expressive *wanglai*" – as in the case of a shop owner in Kaixiangong – or "instrumental *wanglai*", as exhibited in my case of the villagers who purchased building materials through special *guanxi* (see point 5 of "Clarifications of *wanglai*" in Chapter XI.IV).

Some researchers did not take generous *wanglai* and negative *wanglai* into consideration. For example, Weber's typology of traditional, affective, value-rational or impersonal and end-rational identified with principles of customary, emotional, ultimate values, takes account of typology and principles at the same time, and has similarities to my work. However, Weber's typology took no account of the two extremes of personal relationships. Moreover, for me each type of *wanglai* can be judged by all four principles or criteria of *lishang*. I reviewed how each of the four types of *wanglai* derives from the work of previous researchers in the "*wanglai* typology" of Chapter XI.V.

I shall highlight Sahlins's (1965/72) typology of reciprocity which directly influenced mine in many ways (see Chapter IX.I). I split Sahlins's generalised reciprocity into generous and expressive *wanglai*; I also redefined balanced reciprocity as identical with instrumental *wanglai*; and clarified the negative *wanglai* by distinguishing between a relationship with negative affection and the stopping of a relationship. More importantly, I added how materials and others things flow through those relationships and how changes are made to those relationships. I also show how and why those relationships changed, not chaotically, but by calculation of a set of reasons (*lishang*) behind the changes. I used the dynamic creativity of personalised relationships, going beyond Sahlins' rather too rigid typology of reciprocity. For me, how relationships are made depends on a calculation of the kind of relationship rather than its assumed closeness or distance. Finally, I suggest the use of reciprocity as both a principle and typology unified by the single notion of *lishang-wanglai*.

Here I would like to re-emphasize that in the theory of reciprocity studied by Sahlins and following Sahlins there has been a lack of the dynamic approach that I have introduced. My approach is dynamic and longitudinal, within which there is much more mobility and creativity than can be predicted by just saying "you are close, he is distant". In my study I use networks to analyze one or more processes of starting, maintaining, co-existing, and stopping different types of relationships in the formation of personalised relationships. This example from China has therefore broadened the scope of what ought to be considered under the topic of reciprocity studied in any other places, whether outside the village or outside China. Notions of gift exchange and ego-centered networks can be described as personalised relationships, which include institutions and non-institutions. My study in Kaixiangong suggests the full range of all that can be put together by anyone doing similar work elsewhere.

III. *"Lishang-wanglai"* combines a static model and dynamic networks

This thesis develops the Chinese term *lishang-wanglai* as a general concept for analysing personalised relationships through rural Chinese people's reciprocal social support arrangements. *Lishang-wanglai* is a creative process of personalised relationships in which different types of reciprocities (*wanglai*) are judged by different criteria (*lishang*), and the flow of materials and other things through different reciprocities (*wanglai*) can be measured with time and space in vertical and horizontal ways. Figure 2 illustrates the concept of *lishang-wanglai*, a toolbox, which consists of a static *lishang-wanglai* model and dynamic *lishang-wanglai* networks. Once the two parts work together they show the changeability of reciprocity in many different ways.

(1) A static *lishang-wanglai* model. This includes the *lishang* criteria, which are moral judgment, human feeling, rational choice and religious sense, and the *wanglai* typology, which is generous *wanglai*, expressive *wanglai*, instrumental *wanglai* and negative *wanglai* (see Chapter IX.I). Different criteria of *lishang* bring about the typology of *wanglai* in which village customs are used and creatively modified to keep track of *lishang-wanglai* networks. Amongst the literally infinite number of different possible relations the *lishang-wanglai* model shows what types of basic relations we look at, identifies the basic principles that underlie such relationships and why the different cases appear in this or that way. For instance, in Chapter IV generous *wanglai* is mainly characteristic of the relationship between the Tan and the Gu families as it is based on the sense of generosity associated with the adoption of JR by the Gu family. In contrast, the *wanglai* between the Tan family and their given-up son JR was a negative one that was sometimes perceived as JR's revenge on his natal parents. Chapter VIII.I, on another hand, suggests expressive *wanglai* between BZ and RF's families after their marriage and later instrumental *wanglai* after BZ's death. Chapters V to VII demonstrate expressive *wanglai* and show that social order is normally well kept when an area, e.g. Kaixiangong, is mainly dominated by expressive *wanglai*. When negative *wanglai* is involved either between members of a family or between villagers and local institutions a conflict or source of disorder may have arisen, e.g. a policy of privatisation or registration of house construction (see Chapter VIII.II).

(2) The contents of *lishang-wanglai* networks. They are an enlargement of each element of the social support networks (Figures IX-1 and 2). This framework is largely based on Philip Seed's (1990) social support network. I identified six kinds of basic resources for exchange via different sources of social support based on previous researchers' work (see Table IX-1). I use rational choice as one criterion together with other criteria (*lishang*) to examine a set of "personalised relationships (*wanglai*)". The contents of the *lishang-wanglai* networks are analysed into sources, resources, events, range, *lishang* criteria and *wanglai* types (Table 4 and Figure 2). As sources, all my informants agreed with me that a family's *lishang-wanglai* networks should include members of a family, relatives, neighbours, friends, fellow villagers, the collective, institutions, even the ancestors, and the local gods and goddesses. The source "the collective and institutions" extended relationships between individuals to organizations (see section "Personalised institutional relationships" later in the Conclusion). The source "the ancestors and the local gods and goddesses" extended relationships from social relationships to the nether world. This is why the "religious sense" of *lishang* is very important and the numbers of vertical and horizontal *wanglai* expand from four dimensions to eight dimensions (see point 3 below). *Lishang-wanglai* networks' resources include not only finance, labour, and information, but also materials, human feelings, and religious aims and categories, having a very broad range of resources. The events in a *lishang-wanglai* network include almost everything that happens regularly in villagers' everyday life. It tells us with which sources people tend to exchange the resources, what resources people are looking for, what the resources are used for and where the people get the resources. I add ego-centered networks into the analysis of reciprocity, and use time or space dimensions to allow *lishang-wanglai* networks to work with vertical and horizontal flow together in up to eight directions. The ego-centred criss-cross globe, in the middle of Figure 2, indicates the dynamic nature of *lishang-wanglai* networks.

(3) The dynamic or mobile nature of the concept of *lishang-wanglai* brings the changeability of reciprocity into sharp relief. I introduced ego-entered networks into social support network or *lishang-wanglai* networks. As I have shown in Chapter IX.II.2, the *lishang-wanglai* network presents criss-cross patterns of horizontal and vertical circles in five basic dimensions. They are time vertical, time horizontal, space vertical, space horizontal and a pair of basic dialectic changes based on the Taiji Diagram. These dimensions can be doubled when they are applied to an imaginary world. They can also be looked at from the different directions of bottom up, top down, inside and outside for the purpose of analysis.

I should point out that for either vertical or horizontal *wanglai* the ego can be involved in different types of *wanglai* within one or more relationships at different times or even at the same time. There are four possibilities: the ego can have a relationship with a particular person or institution or spiritual being with one or more than one type of *wanglai* at the same time or at different times; the ego can have a relationship with a different person or institution or spiritual being with one or more than one type of *wanglai* at the same time or at different times. In short, each relationship of reciprocity or *wanglai* can change from one kind of *wanglai* to another (see Chapter IX.II).

Within this framework *lishang-wanglai* relates to a creative process of reciprocal personal or personalised relationships in which different types of reciprocities (*wanglai*) are judged by different criteria (*lishang*), as in the relationship between a western professor (SF) and local officials during our fieldwork (see Chapter XII.III). Each relationship of reciprocity or *wanglai* is judged with reference to four different *lishang* criteria, which are weighted differently from case to case. These criteria were refined for my analysis of reciprocity according to the testimony of the actors themselves, Kaixiangong villagers.

IV. The motivation of "*Lishang-wanglai*" is social creativity

My fieldwork shows that the motive force for driving the ego-centred *lishang-wanglai* networks is social creativity. I had a strong sense that there is a deeper level motivation, other than multi-reasons of *lishang*, driving Kaixiangong villagers' actions in making *lishang-wanglai* networks. I also feel that one difference between Chinese and Western cultures is that the reasons for actions that make or change social relationships are well understood and elaborated by Chinese people – in the West such a deliberate approach to social relationships may be thought artificial. In Northern American or Northern European countries the idea that sincerity and spontaneity are virtues is so strong that to talk about how you calculate relationships is embarrassing. Rural Chinese people are more straightforward about it. They enjoy talking about such niceties and the question of insincerity does not arise, whereas when people in Northern American or Northern European countries talk about relationships in this way they are regarded as calculating and insincere. The enjoyment of the creativity inherent in calculating relationships is a part of culture that I see in China. For the Chinese, social creativity is the innovatory sense of sheer enjoyment coming from the human heart (*renxin*, Liang's term 1949/75).

After contrasting Kipnis's (1997), Liang Shumin's (1949/95) and Davis's (1994) works I realised that they are all related to the topic of social creativity. I joined Kipnis's notion of "nonrepresentational ethics" and Liang Shumin's idea of "human heart" to Davis's social creativity and used it as motivation for *lishang-wanglai* based on both literature and my empirical studies. Kipnis distinguished another kind of *ganqing* which is more to do with human feelings, rather than *renqing* ethics, with the notion of "nonrepresentational ethics" (see "*Renqing* and *ganqing*" in Chapter IX.III). The three kinds of *ganqing*: *ganqing* (human feelings) as one of the *lishang* criteria (human feelings), *ganqing* with the meaning of "nonrepresentational ethics", and *ganqing* as an underlying motivation of *lishang-wanglai*, are all close in meaning, but must be distinguished. This is why I borrow Liang Shumin's term human heart (*renxin*) for describing this underlying motivation, to distinguish it from the *lishang* criterion of "human feelings" (see Chapter X.VII). Liang's human heart is related to three *xing*s (go-aheadism, flexibility and planning), partially confirmed by one of my important findings that *lishang-wanglai* is the way in which participants enjoy balancing the multiple criteria involved in personalising different relationships (see Chapter IX.III). *Lishang-wanglai* describes the way in which Chinese people deal with the complex process of making and using social relationships. In my work I use these concepts as an analytical tool to understand my fieldwork observations. In so doing I have formalised some ideas that explain my observations, but are not explicitly present within the Chinese socio-cultural context. The use of *lishang-wanglai* by Chinese people is an example of social creativity. The successful practice of *lishang-wanglai* is enjoyed by the practitioner, and admired by Chinese observers, quite apart from its utility in furthering the social goals of the practitioner. For example, in social events both the host and guests make judgments on relationships with each other based on *lishang*, and all my informants enjoyed this process of reviewing relationships because they regarded it as creative work, as discussed in the section "The villagers' usage of *li shang wanglai*" in the Introduction. They enlarged the content of *lishang-wanglai* not only by redefining but also by constantly reviewing their relationships within the *lishang-wanglai* networks. For them *lishang-wanglai* is a creative process. The continuous knitting of *lishang-wanglai* networks from birth to death is shown in Chapters IV to VIII.

Davis's idea of social creativity reaches the same goal as Liang's three *xing*s by different routes. According to Davis, social creativity is purposeful action because the social order people seek is a series of ramshackle contraptions and inherently unstable, but these contraptions are ingenious, clever, pleasing to contemplate and need continual affirmative re-creation and maintenance. Therefore, social creativity is the motivation for making and maintaining personalised relationships, as I found in Kaixiangong. I then demonstrated social creativity as a motivation for changing relationships in seven ways (see Chapter IX.III).

In point (4) of the above Chapter IX.III, I pointed out that Chinese people prefer to do things in a way that is indirect: hazy, dim, or allusive. This can be found from Kaixiangong villagers' everyday life in which the updating of their *lishang-wanglai* networks often involves no words, as a preferred and admired option (Chapters IV to VIII). This can also be found from Chinese scholars' academic habits tending to the allusive (*hanxu*).   Of course this might occur because of a lack of independence from political power. In the West, as is common knowledge, there was a separation of religion from politics after the Renaissance, separation of the legislative, executive and judicial powers after the Enlightenment and independence of liberal intellectuals from the 18th Century. As Yu Yingshi (1987b) pointed out, there is a cultural phenomenon in China that is perhaps unique in the world. For more than two and a half thousand years without a break (Preface: 2) Chinese scholars (*shi* – equivalent to modern intellectuals in the West) have continued, as shidafu (scholar-bureaucrats or scholar-officials) to rank at the top stratum of the Chinese hierarchical system, except for brief periods such as during the Cultural Revolution when their social status temporarily fell to the bottom of society. However this fall did not alter Chinese scholars' relative status, because they lost their high position together with equally high officials including Liu Shaoqi, the former President of the P. R. China, and were "raised to the Heaven"86 again at the same time as them soon after the Cultural Revolution finished. The relationships between Chinese scholars and officials are very close, as in Mao Zedong's analogy that they are hairs on skin (literally, a part of body). To carry out human and social science studies in China has never been a purely institutional relationship with the institution where one works and colleagues with whom one works. Personalised institutional relations between a scholar and his or her academic institutions and colleagues are always prevalent. For Chinese scholars it is only safe to say something new if it is done without great precision, to avoid political danger. Nobody wants to have a negative *wanglai* with one's work place (*danwei*) or colleagues (*tongshi*). Feelings of fear, and enjoyment of classics or other knowledge, both belong to the category of "human feeling", a *lishang* criterion, not without conflict.

Kaixiangong villagers and Chinese scholars have both continually had to create different ways of dealing with different relationships, living as they do in an inherently unstable

---

[86] A popular saying was then "the smelly scholars risen to the Heaven again (*chou laojiu you shen shang tian le*)".

environment (See Chapters III.IV, VII.II and III, and Conclusion.I).

V. Can *"lishang-wanglai"* be a general analytic concept?

The theoretical framework of *lishang-wanglai* developed here is very general and likely to be applicable throughout Chinese society. My information about personalised relationships comes from those Chinese people who were maybe more willing to talk about what they did and how they felt about it than others, and helped me forge a general concept *"lishang-wanglai"* which is deals not only with relationships between individuals, but also individuals with institutions. As I have shown that in a fairly complex and advanced society like China personalised relationships are of very great importance, and an understanding of them is the key to understanding the combination of changeability and stability in Chinese society. This new way of looking at change and exchange as well as stability can be applied to any part of China, both rural and urban.

Furthermore, it seems likely that personalised relationships have importance in all societies. Things that happen in China are likely to happen elsewhere in the world. People in other societies might be less willing to talk about their own equivalent of *lishang-wanglai*, but that does not make examination impossible. In each culture or society personalised relationships will be differently constructed, construed and created. Society is formed by different kinds of reciprocal relationships, which can be personalised in different ways by different people. Society is also formed by human beings who have human feelings, the most important criterion to distinguish personalised from other types of relationships. I have made a few references to other cultures in this text, but whether and how *lishang-wanglai*, a concept so deeply embedded in Chinese culture, is applicable outside China and its diasporas needs to be tested and retested empirically.

The fieldwork on which this study is based derives primarily from one Chinese rural village (Kaixiangong). The status of this village, as one much studied by social scientists in the past, is a mixed blessing. On the one hand, it enables longitudinal comparisons to be made which would not otherwise be possible. On the other, the influence of researchers on the object of research could in theory lead to some contamination of the fieldwork results. Further work to see how well *lishang-wanglai* captures the dynamics of social relationships in other parts of China, and indeed in other countries, is therefore motivated.

Investigation of this question in a cross-cultural context may lead to interesting new comparative perspectives between Chinese and non-Chinese societies. Traditionally, anthropology has studied relationships in terms of descent, kinship, family, and so on. These aspects are structural and abstract. The relationships concerned, essentially inherited, contain little room for choice. In contrast I am looking at aspects of choice within members of family and kinship relationships: how one person or kin can be made closer and another more distant. I can think of other, equally useful ways of studying some of the relationships that I have examined in the light of *lishang-wanglai*. Custom can be viewed as embodying what a particular culture expects in terms of rights and duties acting as laws, another traditional and useful direction that sociology and anthropology has taken, in which the expectation that somebody will play a particular kind of role within a particular set of roles– pressure to perform – is seen as definitive. Looking at custom in this way leads to a very different emphasis from my own, which often positively celebrates the autonomy within an elastic framework of custom that I found in Kaixiangong. My aim has been to formulate a new way to look at these relationships, not to subsume other ways of viewing them. But I do believe that *lishang-wanglai*, with all its possibilities of development, has some claim to be a universally applicable theory of human reciprocity.

Appendix

I. List of conversion of currencies and measures

1 *yuan* 元＝10 *jiao* 角 or *mao* 毛＝100 *fen* 分

＝0.12 US Dollar 美元

＝0.066 UK Sterling 英鎊(March 2004)

1 *jin* 市斤＝10 *liang* 兩

＝500 gm 克

1 *dan* 擔＝100 *jin* 市斤

＝½ quintal 公擔

＝50kg 公斤

1 *mu* 畝＝10 *fen* 分

＝6.667 are 公畝

＝0.165 acre 英畝

II. List of place names

Anhui Province 安徽省
Beijing City 北京市
Dingxi Prefecture 定西地區
Dingxi County 定西縣
Fanggan Village 房幹村
Fenjia Village 馮家村
Fujian Province 福建省
Fuyang Prefecture 阜陽地區
Gansu Province 甘肅省
Guangdong Province 廣東省
Guangzhou City 廣州市
Guangxi Province 廣西壯族自治區
Hangzhou City 杭州市
Hebei Province 河北省
Hehuawan Village 荷花灣村
Heilongjiang Province 黑龍江省
Heming Village 合明村
Henan Province 河南省
Hengshan Township 橫扇鎮
Huanxiqiao Village 歡喜橋村
Jiangsu Province 江蘇省
Jiangxi Province 江西省
Jinxing Village 金星村
Kaixiangong Village 開弦弓村
Miaogong Township 廟港鎮

Nanjing City 南京市
Nanning City 南寧市
Neiguan Township 內官鎮
Neiguan Village 內官村
Qidu Township 七都鎮
Shandong Province 山東省
Shanghai City 上海市
Shanxi Province 陝西省
Shaoxin City 紹興市
Shengze Township 盛澤鎮
Shenyang City 瀋陽市
Sheyang County 射陽縣
Sichuan Province 四川省
Sifangxu Village 四方圩村
Suzhou Prefecture / City 蘇州地區/市
Tianzixu Village 天字圩村
Wanping Township 莞坪鎮
Wujiang City / County 吳江市/縣
Xiajia Village 下岬村
Xiangfeng Village 先鋒村
Xicaotian Village 西草田村
Xishuangbanna Prefecture 西雙版納自治州
Yunnan Province 雲南省
Zhejiang Province 浙江省
Zhenze Township 震澤鎮

III. List of characters[1]

ai modayu xinsi chou moguoyu wuzhi
哀莫大於心死愁莫過於無志
Aiguo liang 愛國糧
aitai yuanzi 阿太圓子
anchuang 安床
anpai 安排

anxi 安息
atai mo 阿太嬤
atai tuanzi 阿太團子
atai yi 阿太衣
bai dipan 擺地盤
bai fo 拜佛

bai laoye 拜老爺

bai niangjia, liang fujia 敗娘家，亮夫家

bai shangzu 拜上祖

bai shen 拜神

bai tai 拜太

bai tiandi 拜天地

bai tudi gonggong 拜土地公公

bai xingan mo 拜心肝媖

bai xinzao 拜新灶

baibai 拜拜

baifaren song heifa ren 白髮人送黑髮人

baijin 白金

baishan 擺刪

baixi 白喜

baiyu 白玉

baizao 拜灶

ban houshi 辦後事

bang qiong bu bang fu 幫窮不幫富

bangyang de liliang shi wuqiong de
榜樣的力量是無窮的

bao sang 報喪

bao xinniang 抱新娘

bao 保

bao 報

bao'en 報恩

baochang 報償

baochou 報仇

baoda fumu de yangyu zhi en
報答父母的養育之恩

baoda renmin de yangyu zhi en
報答人民的養育之恩

baodao 報到

baofa hu 暴發戶

baofu 報復

baojia zhi 保甲制

baojia 保甲

baojun 暴君

baoliang bu 包梁布

baomen 報門

baoying 報應

baozhang 保長

baozi 包子

baxian zhuo 八仙桌

bayue ba nage ling lai bo yi bo
八月八拿個菱來剝一剝

beicun 北村

bentu hua 本土化

biantian zhang 變天帳

biaoda ganqing 表達感情

biaoxian hao 表現好

bieshu 別墅

bihu 閉戶

bing 病

binguan 賓館

bixie 避邪

bo qingdou 剝青豆

bo 薄

bogong 伯公

boli 薄禮

bu dazhen le 不打針了

bu dazhen 不打針

bu de hao si 不得好死

bu guangcai 不光彩

bu jili 不吉利

bu lingqing 不領情

bu name mixin 不那麼迷信

---

[1]   Some words are created and used by Kaixiangong villagers, e.g. *canba*, *fanyi*, *guosijie*, *wangxin*, *yueban*, etc. The corresponding Chinese characters are all confirmed with the villagers except "*daidi*" and "*lianfang*" , for which they don't know the Chinese characters. Here the given characterisation is therefore determined by me, and indicated by the use of double quotation marks around the characters.

bu qianqing 不欠情

bu qingzhang 不清帳

bu shixing 不時興

bu tong renqing de zhengce zaowan yao wandan 不通人情的政策早晚要完蛋

bu xiaoshun 不孝順

bu yao mafan le 不要麻煩了

bu zhengchang guanxi 不正常關係

bu zuo taozhai gui 不做欠債鬼

bu zuoxing 不作興

bubao 不報

budengjia jiaohuan 不等價交換

bugou yisi 不夠意思

buhao yisi xian kaikou 不好意思先開口

buhao yisi 不好意思

bujie zhi yuan 不解之緣

bukai xianli 不開先例

bula bula 不辣不辣

bushen 補身

buxiao you san, wuhou wei da 不孝有三，無後為大

buxiao 不孝

buyao buhao yisi 不要不好意思

buyao tongpo chuanghuzhi 不要捅破窗戶紙

buyao tongpo 不要捅破

buyu duizhang 不予對帳

cai 財

canba 蠶罷

canda 蠶笡

canhua niangniang 蠶花娘娘

Cao daren 曹大人

chaguan 茶館

chaigurou jiu 拆骨肉酒

chaiyi 拆衣

chang yi chang 嘗一嘗

changhe budui 場合不對

changli bu jingqi 廠裡不景氣

changli 廠裡

changming deng 長明燈

changming fugue 長命富貴

chanzui de poniang qin baizao 饞嘴的婆娘勤拜灶

chaxugeju 差序格局

cheng, cheng zhe tian zhi dao ye 誠，誠者天之道也

chengbao de kouliang tian 承包的口糧田

chenxin ruyi 稱心如意

chi nianye fan 吃年夜飯

chongshang 崇尚

chongyang jie 重陽節

chouhuo shuo zai xian 醜話說在先

chouqian 抽籤

chu fenzi 出份子

chu rizi 出日子

chu tiezi 出帖子

chu xing 出姓

chuan fuyin 傳福音

chuangzao xing 創造性

chuangzao 創造

chuanmen 串門

chuilian gainian gongju 錘煉概念工具

chuishi fuwu 炊事服務

chujia 出嫁

chuncan dao si si fang jin 春蠶到死絲方盡

chuntaixi 春台戲

chuyi yueban xiaobai 初一月半小拜

chuyi yueban 初一月半

couhe hunyin 湊合婚姻

couhe 湊合

cuigurou jiu 催骨肉酒

cuiming 催命

cunjiti 村集體

cunli 村裡

cunweihui zhuren 村委會主任

cunzhang 村長

cuo 錯

da duanming 打短命

da huigui 打回歸

da jiuxing 大救星

da laoye 大老爺

da yuan 大院

dabai 大拜

dachang chang 大腸長

dache dian 大車店

dading 大訂

dadui zhang 大隊長

dadui 大隊

dagao 大糕

dagong mei 打工妹

dagong 大工

daidao 代禱

daidi "代底"*

daike 待客

daixiao 戴孝

daiyu 待遇

daizou de qinqi 帶走的親戚

dajie 大姐

dalou 大樓

dan dapan 擔大盤

dan dongzhi fan 擔冬至飯

dan ninye fan 擔年夜飯

dan shengtang 擔生湯

dan shutang 擔熟湯

dan tiezi 擔帖子

dan xiaopan 擔小盤

dan yiluo pan 擔一摞盤

danan bu si bi you houfu
大難不死必有後福

dang he guojia lingdao ren 黨和國家領導人

dangao 蛋糕

dangdai renleixue 當代人類學

danjuan 蛋捲

dantang 擔湯

danwei 單位

dao 道

daode 道德

daogao 禱告

daojiao 道教

daomei 倒楣

daoshi 道士

daoshi 導師

daotou longshao 到頭龍梢

daoyi 道義

dasaochu 大掃除

dashi xiaoqing 大事小情

datizi 大蹄子

dazhonglian chong pangzi 打腫臉充胖子

dazu 大組

dazuzhang 大組長

de cai jianbei 德才兼備

de 德

di biaozhun 低標準

di shui zhi en dang yong quan xiang bao
滴水之恩當湧泉相報

dian dao weizhi 點到為止

dianrebei 電熱杯

didiao 抵掉

difang jiaohui 地方教會

ding 訂

dinghun 訂婚

dingqin 訂親

dingrizi 訂日子

disan tidui 第三梯隊

diu mianzi 丟面子

diuren 丟人

dixia jiaohui 地下教會

diyuan 地緣

dizangwang 地藏王

dong renqing 懂人情

dongfang hong 東方紅

dongmiao 東廟

dongtu 動土

dongyong 動用

dongyuan 動員

dongzhi 冬至

doufan 豆飯
doufu 豆腐
duan xianghuo 斷香火
duan zi jue sun 斷子絕孫
duanwu jie 端午節
dui 對
duixiang 對象
duo 多
duozhong jingying 多種經營
duozi duofu 多子多福
duozi duohuo 多子多禍
dushuren 讀書人
egui 餓鬼
en jiang chou bao 恩將仇報
en 恩
en'ai fuqi 恩愛夫妻
enhui 恩惠
enqing 恩情
erdeng gongmin 二等公民
erguotou 二鍋頭
eryue er cheng yaogao 二月二撐腰高（糕）
erzi kao buzhu 兒子靠不住
esha zai mengya zhi zhong 扼殺在萌芽之中
fa bu ze zhong 法不責眾
fa da haishi quan da 法大還是權大
fan lai zhangkou yi lai shenshou
飯來張口衣來伸手
fanggao 方糕
fanyi 翻衣
feiepolai 費厄潑賴
feigaishui 費改稅
feijunheng huhui 非均衡互惠
feishui buliu wairen tian
肥水不流外人田
feng dan huan yi, feng shuang bu huan
逢單還一，逢雙不還
feng 風
fengjian mixin 封建迷信
fengshui 風水

fengyang 奉養
feng-yu wu zu 風雨無阻
fenjia qiyue 分家契約
fenjia zhenhao zhongyu ba wo he laotouzi
fenkai le
分家真好終於把我和老頭子分開了
fenjia 分家
fenren 分人
fenzi 份子
fo guang pu hzao 佛光普照
fo 佛
fojiao 佛教
fouding xing huhui 否定性互惠
fu shezhang 副社長
fu shuji 副書記
fu xiangzhang 副鄉長
fu 福
fubai duolou 腐敗墮落
fubai wuneng 腐敗無能
fufen 福分
fulan 腐爛
fuli 附禮
fuli 福利
fulifei 福利費
fu-lu-shou-xi-cai
福祿壽喜財
fumu xin 父母心
fumu zhi ming, meishuo zhi yan
父母之命，媒妁之言
fumu 父母
funu zhuren 婦女主任
fuping 扶貧
fuqi 福氣
fuxiang 福相
fuxing 福星
fuye 副業
fuze quanmian gongzuo 負責全面工作
fuzhi 福祉
gaihua jiaohuan 概化交換

gaizhi 改制

gandong shangdi 感動上帝

ganli 趕禮

ganqing buhao 感情不好

ganqing hao 感情好

ganqing yongshi 感情用事

ganqing 感情

ganyu 贛語

gao guanxi 搞關係

gao jia gao 糕（高）加糕（高）

gao zong tuan yuan 糕粽團圓

gao 糕

gaobing 糕餅

gaoe yiliao tongchou jijinhui
高額醫療統籌基金會

gaogao xingxing 高高興興

gaolai gaoqu 糕來糕去

gaoshang 高尚

gaotang 糕糖

gaoxin yanglian 高薪養廉

gaoxing laiwang 高興來往

gei dajie yidian mianzi 給大姐一點面子

gei mianzi 給面子

geren chuxu 個人儲蓄

geren guanxi 個人關係

geti jingji 個體經濟

gong cheng ming jiu 功成名就

gongde bang 公德榜

gongde bu 公德簿

gongjia baoxiao 公家報銷

gou yisi 夠意思

gou zige 夠資格

goutong 溝通

gua 掛

guafan 掛幡

gualiangtou 掛兩頭

guandi / guandi laoye 關帝/關帝老爺

guangrong bang 光榮榜

guangrong che 光榮車

guanshiyin niangniang 觀世音娘娘

guanxi bu zhengchang 關係不正常

guanxi buhao 關係不好

guanxi gao de hao shi ni chenggong de kuai
關係搞得好使你成功得快

guanxi jinzhang 關係緊張

guanxi polie 關係破裂

guanxi 關係

guanxixue 關係學

guanyin hui 觀音會

guanyin niangniang 觀音娘娘

guanyin 觀音

gufu 姑夫

gugu / guma 姑姑/姑媽

guibai 跪拜

guibin 貴賓

guo danian 過大年

guofang 過房

guofangqin 過房親

guoji hanxue / shijie hanxue
國際漢學/世界漢學

guojia jiaohui 國家教會

guojia 國家

guomen 過門

guonian 過年

guoniang 過娘（過房母親）

guosijie 過四節

guoxiaonian 過小年

gurou qinqing 骨肉親情

gurou zhi qing 骨肉之情

gurou 骨肉

guyong 雇傭

Han 漢

hanjin liang 含金量

hanxu 含蓄

hanyu 漢語

hao baixiang 好白相

hao chu 好處

hao ganbu 好幹部

hao ren hao shi 好人好事
haoren zongshi you haobao de
好人總是有好報的
he 合
hebulai 合不來
hedelai 合得來
hefa 合法
hehu renxin 合乎人心
hehu renxing 合乎人性
hei doufu gan 黑豆腐乾
hei mingdan 黑名單
heli 合理
hen youyisi 很有意思
heqing 合情
heshang 和尚
heshui moguo qiao 河水莫過橋
hong bai xishi 紅白喜事
hongbao 紅包
hongfeng tong 紅封筒
Hongmen yan 鴻門宴
hongwei bing 紅衛兵
hongwei 紅衛
hou 厚
houjizhe 後繼者
houzang 厚葬
huahong 花紅
huajia 花甲
huancun gonglu 環村公路
huandiao 還掉
huang nangua gao 黃南瓜糕
huang quan zhi yu xian 皇權止於縣
huangdou ya 黃豆芽
huangjin 黃金
huangong 換工
huangtong zhi 黃銅紙
huansong hui 歡送會
huanzhu 花燭
huaquan 花圈
huhuan 互換

huhui jiaohuan 互惠交換
huhui 互惠
hui niangjia 回娘家
hui 回
huibao 回報
huijia 回家
huili 回禮
huimen 回門
huizeng 回贈
huli huhui 互利互惠
hun 魂
hunjun 昏君
huohua 火化
huoren jie 活人節
huqin 胡琴
hushen 護身
huxiang bangzhu 互相幫助
ji quan zhi sheng xiang wen, lao si bu xiang wanglai
雞犬之聲相聞，老死不相往來
ji wang kai lai 繼往開來
ji yingong 積陰功
ji zhong you yang 繼中有養
ji 繼
jia chuqu de nü'er ru po chuqu de shui
嫁出去的女兒如潑出去的水
jia gong ji si 假公濟私
jia louban 架樓板
jia yishuang kuaizi 加一雙筷子
jia 家
jiafeng 家風
jian li si yi 見利思義
jian li wang yi 見利忘義
jian ren jian zhi 見仁見智
jian yi yanglain 儉宜養廉
jian 間
jiang daoli 講道理
jiang yiqi 講義氣

Jiangcun jingji-Zhanguo nongmin de shenghua 江村經濟——中國農民的生活

jiangcun 江村

jiangshi 僵屍

jianqian 監簽

jianxiu 鑒休

jianzhu baogong dui 建築包工隊

jiao gongliang 交公糧

jiao shou gongliang 交售公糧

Jiao 交

jiaoche 轎車

jiaodao 交道

jiaoji 交際

jiaolu 腳爐

jiaoqing 交情

jiaotong 交通

jiaowang 交往

jiaozi 餃子

jiaozi 轎子

jiating jingji 家庭經濟

jiazu 家族

jidade 積大德

jide 積德

jidujiao 基督教

jie lutou 接路頭

jie shen zi hao 潔身自好

jie 接

jiecai hua 芥菜花

jieshouren 介紹人

jiezao 接灶

jiezhang 結帳

jigong yuan 記工員

jihua xing 計劃性

jikou 忌口

jili 吉利

jili 祭禮

jin de jin, chu de chu 進得進，出得出

jin xiaodao 盡孝道

jing 靜

jingchang baibai 經常拜拜

jingji shang buqu, ren jiuyao xialai 經濟上不去，人就要下來

jinglao yuan / yanglao yuan 敬老院/養老院

jinlin shi zuhe jiating 近鄰式組合家庭

jinqin 近親

jinxiao 盡孝

jiri 忌日

jiti jingji 集體經濟

jiu bing cheng yi 久病成醫

jiu bing chuangqian wu xiaozi 久病床前無孝子

jiu ji bu jiu pin 救急不救貧

jiu taigong 舅太公

jiu 酒

jiugong 舅公

jiujiu mai qizi 六月買七子

jiujiu wei da 舅舅為大

jiujiu 舅舅

jiuli 舅禮

jiuma 舅媽

jiuniang bing 酒釀餅

jiuyue jiu chongyang gao 九月九重陽糕

jixiang ruyi 吉祥如意

jixiang 吉祥

jiyang 寄養

jizi kuan 集資款

junheng huhui 均衡互惠

junzi 君子

kai chaguan 開茶館

kaifa daxibei de kaituozhe 開發大西北的開拓者

Kaixiangong dadui dang zhibu guanyu sheyuan jianfang de youguan guiding 開弦弓大隊黨支部關於社員建房的有關規定

kan touke 看頭客

kang 炕

kangzhuo 炕桌

kao benshi er bushi kao guanxi chifan 靠本事而不是靠關係吃飯

kao ta zhidian 靠他指點

kao zinu 靠子女

kaolao 栲栳

keji xiushen 克己修身

kelian tianxia fumu xin 可憐天下父母心

kongjiao 孔教

kuangre 狂熱

kuichou eryue chuqi wushi
癸丑二月初七五時

kuming 苦命

kunnan cun 困難村

kunnan 困難

la guanxi 拉關係

laba zhou 臘八粥

lai er bu wang fei li ye, ci chou bu bao fei
junzi 來而不往非禮也，此仇不報非君子

lai kankan 來看看

lai wanwan 來玩玩

lai 來

laidiao 賴掉

laile jiu yisi daole 來了就意思到了

laile jiu you fu 來了就有福

laiwang 來往

lakuai 辣塊

lao jiemei 老姐妹

lao pengyou 老朋友

lao taiye 老太爺

lao you suo yang 老有所養

lao zhangbei 老長輩

lao 老

laobei 老輩

laofa xinban 老法新辦

laofa 老法

laoqin 老親

laotai miao 老太廟

laotai 老太

laotian baoyou 老天保佑

laotian de yisi 老天的意思

laotian xiaogui dou yao bai
老天小鬼都要拜

laotian you yan 老天有眼

Laotian 老天

larou 臘肉

le 樂

leizu 嫘祖

li buxia shumin, xing bushing dafu
禮不下庶民，刑不上大夫

li gang tui yang 離崗退養

li shang wang lai 禮尚往來

li shang wanglai 禮尚往來

li zhi qi zhuang 理直氣壯

li 利

li 理

li 禮

lian 臉

lianfang "連方"*

liangtou gua 兩頭掛

liangtou 兩頭

liangxiao yike zhi qianjin
良宵一刻值千金

liangxin 良心

lianluo ganqing 聯絡感情

lianmian 臉面

liansan dadui 聯三大隊

liansan she 聯三社

lianxi 聯繫

lidan 禮單

lifa 禮法

lifu 禮服

lijie 禮節

lijin 禮金

limao 禮貌

ling buqing 拎不清

ling 靈

linghuo xing 靈活性

lingpai 靈牌

lingqing 領情

lingtang 靈堂

lingwei 靈位

lingwu miao 靈屋廟

lingyan 靈驗

liniang rou 離娘肉

lipao 禮炮

lipin 禮品

lishang lai 禮尚往

lishang wang 禮尚來

lishang 禮上

lishang 禮尚

lishang-wanglai 禮尚一往來

lishu 禮數

lisu 禮俗

Liu Huang pusa 劉皇菩薩

liu 留

Liuhuang (liuwan) 劉皇

liushiliu bushi yeyao diao shen rou
六十六不死也要掉身肉

liuyue liu mai lai huntun liu yi liu
六月六買來餛飩遛一遛

liwu 禮物

lixia changxin 立夏嘗新

lixia 立夏

lixing 理性

liyi zhi bang 禮儀之邦

liyi 利益

liyi 禮儀

liyu 禮遇

liyue 禮樂

lizhi 禮治

lizi mo 利子嫫

lizi 利子

longmen 龍門

longshao 龍梢

longti 籠屜

loufang 樓房

lu 祿

ludouya 綠豆芽

lue 樂

lun 倫

lunli 倫理

mai yuliang 賣餘糧

Maiogang mei miao le 廟港沒廟了

mang 盲

mangnian 盲年

mannian 滿年

manyue baitai 滿月拜太

manyue hui niangjia 滿月回娘家

manyue 滿月

matong 馬桶

mei de yisi / mei shade yisi
沒的意思/沒啥的意思

mei fuqi 沒福氣

mei ganqing 沒感情

mei liangxin 沒良心

mei shenme liaobuqi 沒什麼了不起

mei yuanfen 沒緣分

meiren zuo da 媒人坐大

meiyou tipang bucheng yan
沒有蹄膀不成宴

meiyou weidao 沒有味道

meiyou yisi 沒有意思

men 門

mengjiang hui 猛將會

mengjiang 猛將

miandiao 免掉

mianqiang 勉強

mianzi 面子

mihuntang 迷魂湯

mihunyao 迷魂藥

min ying qiye 民營企業

minbing yingzhang 民兵營長

ming buhao 命不好

ming zhong zhu ding 命中註定

ming 命

mingchong 螟蟲

mingjun 明君

mingmei zhengqi 明媒正娶

mingyun 命運

minjian zongjiao 民間宗教

minjian 民間

minyu 閩語

mixin huodong 迷信活動

mizao 蜜棗

mo zhe shitou guo he 摸著石頭過河

moushi 謀士

mujuan mingdan 募捐名單

muyu 木魚

nan hong nu lu 男紅女綠

nancun 南村

nannü xingan 男女心肝（媒）

nengren 能人

nian sanshi qiang touxiang 年三十搶頭香

niangjia de qinqi 娘家的親戚

niangjia 娘家

nianjing 念經

niannian youyu 年年有餘

ninye fan 年夜飯

ninye 年夜

nong zhuan fei zhibiao 農轉非指標

nongcun jingji hezuoshe 農村經濟合作社

nongcun jingji shouru fenpei biao
農村經濟收入分配表

nonghu wanglaie 農戶往來額

nongjiyuan 農技員

nongmang jijie 農忙季節

nongmangjia 農忙假

nü 女

nüer shi mama de tiexinao
女兒是媽媽的貼心襖

nüer wei da 女兒為大

nüxu tuanzi 女婿糰子

pan / panzi 盤/盤子

pao xinniang 拋新娘

paoliang mantou pao de gao, daidai zisun jie
de lao 拋梁饅頭拋得高，代代子孫接得牢

paoliang 拋梁

peijia 陪嫁

peiyang geming jieban ren 培養革命接班人

peizang 陪葬

ping'an dida 平安抵達

ping'an 平安

pingdeng huhui 平等互惠

pingfang 平房

pingshi bu shaoxiang, linshi bao fojiao
平時不燒香，臨時抱佛腳

pinkun cun 貧困村

pinkun 貧困

pinyong 聘用

piqi 脾氣

po jiu li xin 破舊立新

potu 破土

putong ren 普通人

puxiang 鋪廂

qi qing liu yu 七情六欲

qi 氣

qian renqing zhai 欠人情債

qiang touxiang 搶頭香

qianghua xueke yishi 強化學科意識

qianli song emao li qing qingyi zhong
千里送鵝毛禮輕情義重

qianzai fugui fuguang man fuzhai, baifeng
hehe fuwang ju shoutang 千載富貴福光滿福
宅，百風和合福望居壽堂

qianzhai yao huan 欠債要還

qiaomen tuanzi 敲門糰子

qieqie kai 切切開

qifu 祈福

qimiao 起廟

qin shang jia qin 親上加親

qin 親

qing shangzu 請上祖

qing xianren 請先人

qing 情

qing 輕

qing 請

qinggeng 請庚

qingguan 清官

qingli buliang zichan 清理不良資產

qingli 情理

qingmei 請媒

qingmei 請媒

Qingming jie 清明節

qingming 清明

qingyi 情義

qinqi yue zou yue qin, linju yue zou yue jin
親戚越走越親，鄰居越走越近

qinqi yue zou yue qin, pengyou yue zou yue
jin 親戚越走越親，朋友越走越近

qinqi 親戚

qinqing 親情

qinyuan 親緣

qiqing 七情

qishisan bashisi 七十三八十四

Qiu laotai / Qiu lali 丘老太/丘癩痢

Qiuju da guansi 秋菊打官司

qiye zhuanzi 企業轉資

qiyue ban 七月半

qiyue qi nage xigua qie yi qie
七月七拿個西瓜切一切

qizhong 七種

qizi 七子：guazi 瓜子/ lizi 梨子 lizi 李子/
juzi 桔子/ meizi 梅子/ taozi 桃子/ zaozi 棗子

qu le laopo wang le ma 娶了老婆忘了媽

qu 娶

quanli yiwu duideng guanxi
權利義務對等關係

quanli 權力

quanli 權利

quanqiu hua 全球化

que xinyaner 缺心眼兒

qundai guan 裙帶官

qunzhong jichu 群眾基礎

quqin 娶親

quyuan 趣緣

rang ta mingbai mingbai 讓他明白明白

rang yibufenren xian fu qilai
讓一部分人先富起來

re 熱

ren guofang qin 認過房親

ren linju 認鄰居

ren qiong zhi bu duan 人窮志不短

ren wei cai si, niao wei shi wang
人為財死，鳥為食亡

ren yao lian shu yao pi 人要臉樹要皮

ren yi li zhi xin 仁義理智信

ren zijia 認自家

ren zijia(ren) 認自家(人)

ren 人

ren 仁

renji guanxi 人際關係

renlei zhi qing 人類之情

renli 人力

renmin, zhiyou renmin caishi chuangzao
shijie lishi de zhenzheng dongli
人民，只有人民才是創造歷史的真正動力

renqing bu 人情簿

renqing de cilichang 人情的磁力場

renqing guanxi 人情關係

renqing haishi yao jiang de
人情還是要講的

renqing wei 人情味

renqing ya si ren 人情壓死人

renqing 人情

renren xin zhong you yi gan cheng
人人心中有一桿秤

renshi guanxi 人事關係

renxin 人心

renyuan 人緣

reqing 熱情

ru xiang sui su 入鄉隨俗

ruyi 如意

sanfen bing qifen yang 三分病七分養

sanfen nengli qifen guanxi
三分能力七分關係

sangang wuchang 三綱五常

sanqi 三七

sanqi/wuqu 三七/五七

sanshi nian hedong sanshi nian hexi
三十年河東三十年河西

santian qingming sitian jie 三天清明四天節

santong 三同

sanyue san cha jiecaihua 三月三插芥菜花

sha ji jing hou 殺雞儆猴

shan you shan bao, e you e bao
善有善報，惡有惡報

shang diwangye xiang 上地王爺香

shang you tiantang xia you Su-Hang
上有天堂下有蘇杭

shang 尚

shangfen 上墳

shangji lingdao da zhaohu 上級領導的招呼

shangji 上級

shangli 尚禮

shangliang 上樑

Shangren zhu 上人竹

shangwen 尚文

shangwu 尚武

shangzu 上祖

shanyang laoren 贍養老人

shanyang 贍養

shao 少

shazhao 紗罩

shehui diaocha 社會調查

shehui guanxi 社會關係

shehui huzhu 社會互助

Shehui ji xingwei kexue yanjiu de zhongguohua
社會及行為科學研究的中國化

shehuizhuyi jingshen wenming zhen
社會主義精神文明鎮

shehuizhuyi 社會主義

shen 神

sheng yi nu'er pei sandai
生一個女兒陪三代

shengchan shang de xiangbang
生產上的相幫

shenghuo shang de xiangbang
生活上的相幫

shengjiang 生薑

shengqi 生氣

shengqian 勝遷

shenhua ganqing 深化感情

shenme yisi 什麼意思

shepidai 蛇皮袋

shezhang 社長

shi dafu 士大夫

shi shiwu zhe wei junjie 識時務者為俊傑

shi zhe sheng cun 適者生存

shi 士

shidi 師弟

shifu 師傅

shier zhao 十二朝

shigu 世故

shiliusui baitai 十六歲拜太

shitang 食堂

shiyue yi song hanyi 十月一送寒衣

shiyue zhong niangjiu 十月中釀酒

shou dapan 受大盤

shou panzi 受盤子

shou xiaopan 受小盤

shou 壽

shougongye 手工業

shoumian 壽麵

shousui 守歲

shoutao 壽桃

shouxing 壽星

shouye 守夜

shu da zhaofeng 樹大招風

shuangxi 雙喜

shugong 叔公

shui neng zai zhou, yi neng fu zhou
水能載舟，亦能覆舟

shui ye bu qian shui 誰也不欠誰

shui 水

shuigao 水糕

shuiyao 水舀

shuji 書記

shumin 庶民

shun tianming 順天命

shuo de zheme mingxian ni zenme hai kan bu chulai 說得這麼明顯你什麼還看不出來

Shuo ni xing ni jiu xing buxing yexing, shuo ni buxing ni jiu buxing xing ye buxing 說你行你就行不行也行，說你不行你就不行行也不行

shuofa 說法

shuoqing 說情

shushi jiu 素事酒

shushi 素事

shushu 叔叔

si po lian 撕破臉

si ying jingji 私營經濟

si ying qiye 私營企業

sifangqian 私房錢

sihai zhi nei jie xiongdi y e 四海之內皆兄弟也

sihui fu ran 死灰復燃

siren guanxi 私人關係

siren lianxi 私人聯繫

sirenjie 死人節

sishi tongtang 四世同堂

sixiang gongzuo 思想工作

song / qing / jie / liu / ying 送/請/接/留/迎

song le yicheng you yicheng 送了一程又一程

song wang ying lai 送往迎來

song 送

songgao 松糕

songzao 送灶

subei 蘇北

suibian zhao yige defang 隨便找一個地方

suili 隨禮

suishen bao 隨身包

suishi / jieqi 歲時/節氣

sunan moshi 蘇南模式

sunan 蘇南

sushijiu 素事酒

sutang 酥糖

suyuan 宿怨

ta dui fumu bu xiaoshun 他對父母不孝順

ta hen gaoshang 他很高尚

ta shi yige gaoshang de ren 他是一個高尚的人

tabing 塌餅

taji 台基

tanbing 探病

tang niangao 糖年糕

tang 湯

tangtong 湯桶

tangtuan 湯糰

tao nuxutuan 討女婿團

tao tiezi 討帖子

tao tuanzi 討團子

tao waisheng tuan 討外甥團

taomaozi 討帽子

taorizi 討日子

taos hubao 討書包

tekun buzhu 特困補助

tekun hu 特困戶

tian di jun qin shi 天地君親師

tian wu jue ren zhi lu 天無絕人之路

tian 田

tiandi 田地

tianjing 天井

tianlun zhi le 天倫之樂

tianming guan 天命觀

tianshi dili renhe 天時地利人和

tianye zuoye 田野作業

tianyi 天意

tianzhu jiao 天主教

tiao dachang 挑大腸

tiaoli 挑禮

tiaoshou 挑壽

tiexin'ao 貼心襖

tiezi 帖子

tipang ti shang 蹄膀提上

tipang 蹄膀

tizi 蹄子（蹄膀）

tong gan gong ku 同甘共苦

tong qing da li 通情達理

tong xiaodui renjia 同小隊人家

tong xiaoze de renjia 同小組的人家

tong xiaozu renjia 同小組人家

tongbao piping 通報批評

tongnan tongnu 童男童女

tongqing ruozhe 同情弱者

tongqing xin 同情心

tongqing 同情

tongshi 同事

tongxing de renjia 同姓的人家

tongxing 同姓

tongyang de daiyu 同樣的待遇

tongyang xi 童養媳

tongyang xu 童養婿

touqi 頭七

tu jili 圖吉利

tu zhengce 土政策

tuan 團/糰

tuantuan yuanyuan 團團圓圓

tuanyuan jie 團圓節

tuanyuan 團圓

tuanzi 團子

tudi gonggong 土地公公

tuiqin 退親

tuo Feilao de fu 托費老的福

tuo laotian de fu 托老天的福

tuo niang de fu 托娘的福

tuo renqing 託人情

tuomeng 托夢

tuopin zhifu 脫貧致富

tupo kou 突破口

tuyuan 土圓

waibin 外賓

waisheng tuanzi 外甥糰子

waisheng 外甥

waitai 外太

wang en fu yi 忘恩負義

wang xinke 望新客

wang 往

wanglai 往來

wangluo 網路

wangxin 望信

wanwan ma 玩玩嘛

wanwei 玩味

Wei baozhang 偽保長

wei nuzi he xiaoren nan yang ye
惟女子和小人難養也

wei xiangzhang 偽鄉長

weifu sifang 微服私訪

weili 微禮

weisheng shi 衛生室

weizi 位子

wen han wen nuan 問寒問暖

wenhua zou chuqu 文化走出去

wo bu gen ni hao le 我不跟你好了

wo yang erzi wei guojia, guojia wei wo
yanglao 我養兒子為國家，國家為我養老

wo yinggai baoda dang he renmin de yangyu
zhi en 我應該報答黨和人民的養育之恩

women de guanxi shi jianli zai li shang
wanglai de yuanze jichu shang de 我們的關
係是建立在禮尚往來的原則基礎上的

women hui ba tamen quandou bianhei
我們會把他們全都變黑

women jiechu de yuanze shi li shang wangle
我們接觸的原則是禮尚往來

women shuangfang zhengzai li shang
wanglai 我們雙方正在禮尚往來

wu chu daoli 悟出道理

wu shi bu deng sanbaodian
無事不登三寶殿

wu zhi zhi fu　無知致福

wu　吳

wu　物

wu　悟

wubao hu　五保戶

wudi　吳地

wufu　五服

wufu　五福

wuhou wei da　無後為大

wuke jiuyao　無可救藥

wuneng de ren　無能的人

wuqi　五七

wushihe　無事盒

wuwei er zhi　無為而治

wuyu yuxi　吳語語系

wuyu　吳語

wuyu　無欲

wuyue wu mai tiao huangyu guo duanwu　五月五買條黃魚過端午

wuzhai yishen qing　無債一身輕

wuzhi　物質

xi cong tian jiang　喜從天降

xi　喜

xia　俠

xiagang gongren　下崗工人

xiagang nongmin　下崗農民

xian jiehun hou lianai　先結婚後戀愛

Xiandai Hanyu Cidian　現代漢語詞典

xiang qingfu　享清福

xiang yiti gaobie　向遺體告別

xiangbang　相幫

xiangfu　享福

xianghuo hen wang　香火很旺

xianghuo　香火

xiangtu shehui　鄉土社會

xiangxiang　想像

xiangzhen qiye pochan fa　鄉鎮企業破產法

xianling　顯靈

xianren　先人

xiantaiye　縣太爺

xian-tuan ji　縣團級

xianzhi　縣誌

xiao bieshu　別墅

xiao nianye　小年夜

xiao pengyou　小朋友

xiao xifu　小媳婦

xiao yisi　小意思

xiao yuanzi　小圓子

xiao zu shi lu　削足適履

xiao　孝

xiaobai　小拜

xiaobei　小輩

xiaodao　孝道

xiaoding　小訂

xiaogong　小工

xiaojiemei　小姐妹

xiaojing　孝敬

xiaojiuzi　小舅子

xiaoren　小人

Xiaosheng shi ge hao qingnian　曉聲是個好青年

xiaoshun zinu　孝順子女

xiaoshun　孝順

xiaoxin　孝心

xiaoyao　逍遙

xiaozi　孝子

xiazang　下葬

xiban　戲班

xiemei　謝媒

xiexia　歇夏

ximiao　西廟

xin nongcui guihua tu　新農村規劃圖

xin ze ling　信則靈

xinfang　新房

xinfo　信佛

xing　性

xingan mo　心肝媖

xingan　心肝

xingfu 幸福

xingge buhe 性格不合

xingmei 行媒

xingzheng cun 行政村

xingzheng quyu tiaozheng 行政區域調整

xinji 心悸

xinke 新客

xinkucha 辛苦茶

xinnian fan 新年飯

xinqi 心氣

xinqin 新親

xinqing shuchang 心情舒暢

xinshen 信神

xinxi yuan 信息員

xinyesu 信耶穌

xinyong she 信用社

xitang 喜糖

xitian 西天

xiu shen yang xing 修身養性

xiukou 休口

xu 序

xue nong yu shui 血濃於水

xueqi fang gang 血氣方剛

xueshu guifan 學術規範

xueyuan shehui 血緣社會

xueyuan 血緣

xun dougan 燻豆幹

xun qingdou 燻青豆

yang bing qianri yongbing yishi
養兵千日用兵一時

yang bing 養病

yang can 養蠶

yang di 養地

yang er fang lao 養兒防老

yang erzi 養兒子

yang fu / mu / zi / nu 養父/母/子/女

yang ge da pang erzi 養個大胖兒子

yang haizi 養孩子

yang han 養漢

yang hu yi huan 養虎遺患

yang hua / niao / yu / chong 養花/鳥/魚/蟲

yang jia hu kou 養家糊口

yang jing xu rui 養精蓄銳

yang lao song zhong 養老送終

yang lao 養老

yang lu 養路

yang shen 養神

yang sheng 養生

yang siren 養死人

yang xing 養性

yang yong chenghuan 養癰成患

yang yu yiwu 養育義務

yang yu zhi en 養育之恩

yang zhi da pang zhu 養只大胖豬

yang zhu / yang / niu / ma / mau / gou
養豬/羊/牛/馬/貓/狗

yang zhu 養豬

yang zun chu you 養尊處優

yang zuxian 養祖先

yang 養

yangchun baixue, xiali baren
陽春白雪，下里巴人

yanghuo 養活

yaogao 腰糕

yaohao de 要好的

yaxie 壓邪

yegui 野鬼

yehuo fan 野火飯

yeniang guandao hunhou sannian, zinu guan
tamen hou bansheng
爺娘管到婚後三年，子女管他們後半生

yeniang shengsi buguan 爺娘生死不管

yeshi 業師

yesu jiao 耶穌教

yeyuan 業緣

yi bubian ying wan bian 以不變應萬變

yi de bao de 以德報德

yi de bao yuan 以德報怨

yi dian jiu tou 一點就透
yi fen wei san 一分為三
yi he wei gui 以和為貴
yi ku si tian 憶苦思甜
yi qing dong ren 以情動人
yi quan mou si 以權謀私
yi yuan bao de 以怨報德
yi 益
yi 義(yang 羊 ＋ wo 我)
yiban huhui 一般互惠
yibashou 一把手
yibei hucheng 以輩互稱
yidian xiao yisi 一點小意思
yidian xiao yisi, buyao buhao yisi, doushi zijia ren ma 一點小意思，不要不好意思，都是自家人嘛
yifen 一份
yige duo yue 一個多月
yige nü tongzhi 一個女同志
yige yige di zhengqu 一個一個地爭取
yiguan hui 醫管會
yihui sheng erhui shu 一回生二回熟
yijia yihu 一家一戶
yiju 義舉
yiliao baoxian 醫療保險
yima / yiniang 姨媽/姨娘
yin / yang 陰/陽
yin huo de fu 因禍得福
yin 銀
ying renwu 硬任務
ying 迎
yingfu kuan 應付款
yingguo de fengshui 英國的風水
yingqin dui 迎親隊
yingqin 迎親
yinguo baoying 因果報應
yingyou zhi qing 應有之情
yinqing bu 銀情簿
yinyang 陰陽

yinyangshi 陰陽師
yinyuan 姻緣
yiqi yongshi 意氣用事
yiqi 義氣
yisheng ping'an 一生平安
yisi yisi 意思意思
yisi 意思
yiwu 義務
yiyao guanli jijin hui 醫療管理基金會
yiyuan 遺願
yizhang waiguo miankong 一張外國面孔
yizi 椅子
yong bieren de zangli xuanxie ziji de beishang 用別人的葬禮宣洩自己的悲傷
yonggong 用功
yongnao 用腦
yongxin 用心
you jie you huan, zai jie bunan 有借有還，再借不難
you liangxin 有良心
you peng zi yuanfang lai, bu yi le hu 有朋自遠方來，不亦樂乎
you qian peng qian chang, mei qian peng ren chang 有錢捧錢場，沒錢捧人場
you qiu bi ying 有求必應
you wei li, wu wei yong 有為利，無為用
you yisi 有意思
youdeng shibing 優等士兵
youfu anzhi 優撫安置
youfu 有福
youfuqi 有福氣
youli 有理
youqing 友情
youxia 遊俠
youyi wuli 有益無利
youyong 有用
youyuan 友緣
yu tian fendou qi le wuqiong, yu di fendou qi le wuqiong, yu ren fendou qi le wuqiong

與天奮鬥其樂無窮，與地奮鬥其樂無窮，
與人奮鬥其樂無窮
yu zhege jia wuyuan 與這個家無緣
yu zhengfu chang fandiao 與政府唱反調
yu 魚
yuan zhi yuan wei 原汁原味
yuan 圓
yuan 緣
yuanbao 元寶
yuanfen lingyan 緣分靈驗
yuanfen 緣分
yuanhua 圓滑
yuanhuo 圓活
yuanman 圓滿
yuanmeng 圓夢
yuanqin buru jinlin 遠親不如近鄰
yuanqin 遠親
yuanshi 院士
yuanshishi wuwu jiaohuan 原始式物物交換
yuanshu 圓熟
yuantong 圓通
yuanxiao jie 元宵節
yuanxiao yuanzi 元宵圓子
yuanxiao 元宵
yuanzi 圓子
yueban 月半
yueju tuan 越劇團
yuelao 月老
yuexia laoren 月下老人
yueyu 粵語
yunpian gao 雲片糕
zaijia gao fumu, zaiwai gao pengyou
在家靠父母，在外靠朋友
zangli 葬禮
zao baoying 遭報應
zao laotian baoying 遭老天報應
zao sheng guizi 早生貴子
zaojun gonggong 灶君公公
zaoshi 造勢

zaozi 棗子
zengtai 曾太
zhangbei 長輩
zhanguang 沾光
zhantian doudi chuangzao xinshijie
戰天鬥地創造新世界
zhao nüxu 招女婿
zhaodai fei 招待費
Zheng can 正餐
zheng jiu 正酒
zhengce duo bian xiang xiaohai de lian he
liuyue de tian
政策多變像小孩的臉和六月的天
zhengfu guanli guojia zhege dajia, women
guanhao ziji de xiajia 政府管理國家這個大
家，我們管好自己的小家
zhengji 政績
zhengjia fenli 政教分離
zhengqi 爭氣
zhengui 鎮鬼
zhenqing 真情
zheshi JR yingde de baochang
這是JR應得的報償
zhi daguo ruo peng xiao xian
治大國若烹小鮮
zhi en tu bao 知恩圖報
zhibao zhuren 治保主任
zhifu 致福
zhiqi 志氣
zhiyao you le ren shenme renjian qiji dou
keyi chuangzao chulai
只要有了人什麼人間奇跡都可以創造出來
zhizhu dan 蜘蛛蛋
zhizu 知足
zhong kou nan tiao 眾口難調
zhong 重
zhongfeng 中風
zhongguo shenshi 中國紳士
zhongjian quan 中間圈
zhongqiu jie / tuanyuan jie 中秋節/團圓節

zhongren shi chai huoyan gao
眾人拾柴火焰高

zhongtang 中堂

zhongxin cun 中心村

zhongyong 中庸

zhousui baitai 周歲拜太

zhuan xin zhi zhi 專心致志

zhuangmen 裝門

zhuangyuan bei 狀元被

zhuangyuan pan 狀元盤

zhuangyuan 狀元

zhuanxin 專心

zhudong xing 主動性

zhufu 祝福

zhuidao hui 追悼會

zibu pin 滋補品

zidao 自禱

zijia guonian wu wangle baibaishen
自家過年勿忘了拜拜神

zijia menzu 自家門族

zijia ren 自家人

zijia xianren zonggui shi zijiaren
自家先人總歸是自家人

zijia 自家

ziliu di 自留地

ziniantou 紫撚頭

ziran cun 自然村

ziran 自然

zisun hui 子孫會

zongci 宗祠

zongjiao 宗教

zongzi 粽子

zongzu 宗族

zou ge renqing 走個人情

zou houmen 走後門

zou renqing 走人情

zou 走

zoudai 走代

zoudong 走動

zoufang 走訪

zouwang 走往

zouxiang shijie 走向世界

zui haowan de shi 最好玩的事

zun lao ai you shi Zhonghua minzu de chuantong meide
尊老愛幼是中華民族的傳統美德

zun lao ai you 尊老愛幼

zuo jianzheng 做見證

zuo keren 做客人

zuo manyue 做滿月

zuo sushi 做素事

zuojie 做節

zuoke 做客

zuomei 坐媒

zuonie 作孽

zuoqi 做七

zuoxi chaodong 坐西朝東

zuoxinke 做新客

zuxian 祖先

zuzong 祖宗

Bibliography[1]

D'Abbs, P. 1982. Social support networks: a critical review of models and findings. Melbourne: Institute of Family Studies.

Abrams, P. et. al. 1988. *Neighbourhood care and social policy*. London: HMSO Books.

Acock, A. C. & Hurlbert, J. S. 1993. "Social networks, marital status, and well-being." *Social Networks* 15: pp. 309-334.

Afshar, H. ed. 1985. *Women, work, and ideology in the third world*. London: Tavistock Publications.

———. 1991. Women, development and survival in the third world. Longman: Harlow.

Ahern, Emily, Martin. 1973. *The cult of the dead in a Chinese village*. University of Stanford Press.

———. 1976. "Segmentation in Chinese lineage: A view from written genealogies." *American Ethnologist* 3: pp. 1-16.

———. 1981. *Chinese ritual and politics*. New York: Cambridge University Press.

Alcoff, L. 1992. "The problem of speaking for others." *Cultural Critique* (1991-92) Winter: pp. 5-32.

Alexander, J. C. 1988. *Action and its environments*, pp. 13; pp. 223. New York: Columbia University Press.

Allan, G. A. 1979. *Sociology of friendship & kinship*. London: Allen & Unwin.

———. 1986. "Friendship & care for elderly people." *Ageing & Society* 6(1): pp. 1-12.

All-China Women's Federation. 1993. The impact of economic development on rural women in China: a report of the United Nations University household, gender, and age project. Japan: United Nations University.

Alwin, D. F., Converse, P. E. & Martin, S. S. 1985. "Living arrangement & social integration." *Journal of Marriage & the Family* 47(2): pp. 319-334.

Andors, P. 1983. *The unfinished liberation of Chinese women 1949-1980*. Bloomington: Indiana University Press and Sussex: Wheatsheaf Books.

Antonucci, T., Fuhrer, R., & Jackson, J. S. 1990. "Social support and reciprocity: A cross-ethnic and cross-national perspective." *Journal of social and personal relationships* 7: pp. 519-30.

Arkush, R. D. 1981. *Fei Xiaotong and sociology in revolutionary China*. Cambridge USA/London: Harvard University Press.

Baker, Hugh D. R. 1968. *A Chinese lineage village: Sheung Shui*. Stanford: Stanford University Press.

———. 1979. *Chinese family and kinship*. London/Basingstoke: The Macmillan Press Ltd.

———. 1991. "Marriage and mediation: relations between lineage." In H. Baker & S. Feuchtwang, eds., *An old state in new settings: studies in the social anthropology of China in memory of Maurice Freedman*, pp. 11-24. Oxford: JASO.

Bailey, Carol, A. 1996. *A guide to field research*, California/London, el.: Pine Forge Press.

Balbo, L. 1987. "Family, women, and state: notes toward a typology of family roles and publics intervention." In Maier, C. S. ed., *Changing boundaries of the political*. Cambridge:

Cambridge University Press.

Barnes, J. A. 1954. "Class and committee in a Norwegian island parish." *Human relations* 7.

——. 1969. "Networks, and Political Process." In J.C. Mitchell ed., *Social networks in urban situations* pp. 51-76. Manchester: Manchester University Press.

——. 1971. *Three styles in the study of kinship*. London: Tavistock Publications.

——. 1974. "Social Networks." *Module in Anthropology* No.26. Reading, Mass.: Addition-Wesley.

Barth, F. 1967. "On the study of social change." *American Anthropologist* 69(6): pp. 661-669.

Beall, J. 1995. "Social security and social networks among the Urban poor in Pakistan." *Habitat International* 19: 4: pp. 427-445.

Befu, Harumi. 1966-67. "Gift giving and social reciprocity in Japan." *France-Asia* 21: pp. 161-77.

——. 1968. "Gift-giving in a modernizing Japan." *Monumenta Nipponica* 23(3-4): pp. 445-56.

——. 1974. "Power in exchange: strategy of control and pattern of compliance in Japan." *Asian Profile* 2 (5-6): pp. 601-22.

——. 1977. "Social exchange." *Annual Review of Anthropology* 6: pp. 255-81.

Bell, Lynda. 1985. Merchants, peasants, and the state: the organisation and politics of Chinese silk production, Wuxi County, 1870-1937. PhD. Dissertation. Los Angeles: University of California.

Belshaw, C. 1965. *Traditional exchange and modern markets*. Englewood & N.J.: Prentice-Hall.

Belsky, J. R. & Rovine, M. 1984. "Social-network contact, family support, and the transition to parenthood." *Journal of Marriage & the Family* 46(2): pp. 455-462.

Beneria, L. ed, 1982/5. Women and development: the sexual division of labour in rural societies. New York: Praeger Publications.

Bernard, H. R.; Johnson, E.C. & Killworth, P.D. 1990. "Comparing four different methods for measuring personal social networks." *Social Networks* 12 (3): pp. 179-215.

Bian, Yanjie . 1997. "Bringing strong ties back in: indirect connection, bridge, and job search in China." *American Sociological Review* 62.

——. 1999. "Getting a job through a web of *Guanxi* in urban China," pp. 255-277. In Barry Wellman ed., *Networks in the Global Village*, Boulder, CO: Westview Press.

Bian Y., & Ang, S. 1997. "*Guanxi* networks and job mobility in China and Singapore." *Social Forces* 75(3).

Bianweihui 編委會. 1995. *An overall view of the Chinese social security system (Zhongguo shehui baozhang zhidu zonglan)*, Beijing: Chinese legal publication House (Zhongguo fazhi chubanshe), p3. 《中國社會保障制度縱覽》，北京：中國法制出版社。

Biegel, D.E.; Farkas K.J.; Abell N.; Goodin J. & Friedman, B. 1989. *Social support networks: a bibliography 1983-87*. New York/Westport/Connecticut/London: Greenwood Press.

Blau, P. M. 1964. *Exchange and power in social life*, pp.88—114. New York: John Wiley & Sons Inc.

Blum, L. A. 1980. *Friendship, altruism & morality*. London et. al. : Routledge & Kegan Paul.

Blumer, H. 1962. "Society as symbolic interaction," p. 180. In A.M. Rose, ed., *Human behavior and social processes: an interactionist approach*. Boston: Houghton Mifflin.

Bodde, D. 1975. *Festivals in classical China.* Princeton: Princeton University Press.

Bohannan, P. & Middleton, J. eds., 1968. *Kinship & social organization.* Garden City/New York: The Natural History Press.

Boissevain, J. F. 1973. "Preface." In J.C. Mitchell and Boissevain, eds., *Network analysis: studies in human interaction.* The Hague: Mouton.

——. 1974. Friends of friends: networks, manipulators and coalitions. Oxford: Blackwell.

Bond, Michael H; Lee, Peter, W.H. 1981. "Face saving in Chinese culture: A discussion and experimental study of Hong Kong students," pp. 289-304. In A. Y. C. King and R. P. L. Lee, eds., *Social life and development in Hong Kong.* Hong Kong: the Chinese University Press.

Bonacich, P. 1996. "Analysis of discrete structure: an overview." *Social Networks* 18: pp. 315-318.

Boserup, E. 1970/89. *Women's role in economic development.* London: Earthscan Publications Ltd.

Bott, Elizabeth. 1955-56. "Urban families." *Human Relations* 8 and 9.

——. 1957/71. *Family and social network.* London: Tavistock Institute of Human Relations.

Bowlby, J.1969. *Attachment and loss: Vol. 1 Attachment.* New York: Basic Books.

——. 1980. Attachment and loss: Vol. 3. Loss: sadness and depression. New York: Basic Books.

Boyce, W.T. 1985. "Social support, family relations, & children," pp. 151-173. In S. Cohen & S.L. Syme, eds., *Social support & health.* Orlando, FL: Academic Press.

Brannen, J. & Wilson, G. ed. 1985. *Support networks in a caring community*, pp. 125-38. Lancaster: Kluwer Academic Publishers.

Bridge, G. 1995. "Gentrification, class and community: a social network approach," pp. 259-286. In A Rogers & S. Vertovec, eds., *The urban context: ethnicity, social networks and situational analysis*, Oxford/Washington D. C.: Berg Publishers.

Brody, E.M. et al. 1983. "Women's changing roles & help to elderly parents: attitudes of three generations of women." *Journal of Gerontology.* 38(5): pp. 597-607.

Brownell, A. & Shumaker, S. A.. 1984. "Social support: an introduction to a complex phenomenon." *Journal of Social Issues.* 40: 4: pp. 1-9.

——. 1985. "Where do we go from here? The policy implications of social support." *Journal Social Issues* 41: 1: 111-121.

Broyelle, C. 1977. Trans. France, 1973, *Women's liberation in China.* Hassocks: The Harvester Press.

Bruhn, J. G. & Philips, B. U. 1984. "Measuring social support: a synthesis of current approaches." *Journal of Behavioral Medicine* 7(2): pp. 151-169.

Brydon, L. & Chant, S. 1989. *Women in the third world: Gender issues in rural and urban areas.* Hants: Edward Elgar Publishing Ltd.

Burgess, R. G. 1984/97. *In the field: Introduction for fieldwork research*, London/New York: Routledge.

——. 1991. "Sponsors, gatekeepers, members, and friends: Access in educational settings." In B. William Shaffir and A. Robert Stebbins, eds., *Experiencing fieldwork: An inside view of qualitative research*, pp. 43-52. New York: St. Martin's Press.

Burgess, R. L. & Huston, T. L., eds., 1979. *Social exchange in developing relationships.* New

York/San Francisca/London: Academic Press.

Burns, J. P. 1988. *Political participation in rural China.* California: University of California Press.

Burt, R. S. 1984. "Network items and general social survey." *Social Networks* 6(4): pp. 293-339.

——. 1986. "A note on sociometric order in the survey network data." *Social network* 8.

——. 1990. "Kinds of relations in American discussion networks." In C. J. Calhoun, M. W. Mayer & W. R. Scott, eds., *Structure of power and constraint.* New York: Cambridge University Press.

——. 1992. *Structural holes: the social structure of competion.* Cambridge/MA: Harvard University Press.

Cai, Shangsi 蔡尚思. 1982. *A system of Counfucius thoughts* (*Kongzi sixiang tixi*). Shanghai: Shanghai People's Publishing House. 《孔子思想體系》。上海：上海人民出版社。

Cao, Guigen 曹貴根. 1991. "Development report on social security" (*Shehui baozhang shiye fazhan baogao*). In Xueyi Lu and Peilin Li, eds., *Reports of social development in China* (*Zhongguo shehui fazhan baogao*), pp. 343, 348. Shenying: Liaoning People's Publishing House. 〈社會保障事業發展報告〉，見陸學藝、李培林主編《中國社會發展報告》。瀋陽：遼寧人民出版社。頁 343、348。

Cao, Jingqing 曹錦清. 2000. *China by the Yellow Revier* (*Huanghe bian de zhongguo*). Shanghai: Shanghai Cultural Publishing House. 《黃河邊的中國》。上海：上海文化出版社。

Caplan, Gerald. 1974. Support system and community mental health: lectures on concept development, New York: Behavioural Publications.

Caplow, T. 1982. "Christmas gifts and kin networks." *American Sociological Review* 47: pp. 383-392.

Carrier, James G. 1998. "Property and social relations in Melanesian anthropology," pp. 85-103. In C. M. Hann, ed., *Property relations: Renewing the anthropological tradition.* Cambridge: Cambridge University Press.

Carter, A. T. 1984. "Household histories." In Netting, Will & Arnould, eds. *Households*, pp.44-83. Berkeley, etc: University of California Press.

Cassel, John. 1974a. "An epidemiological perspective of psychosocial factors in disease aetiology." *American Journal of Public Health* 64: pp. 1040-43.

——. 1974b. "Psychosocial Processes and 'Stress': Theoretical formulations." *International Journal of Health Services* 4: pp. 471-82.

——. 1976. The contribution of the social environment to host resistance, *American Journal of Epidemiology* 104: pp. 107-123.

Chan, A., Madsen, R. & Unger, J. 1984. *Chen village: the recent history of a peasant community in Mao's China.* California: University of California Press.

——. 1992. *Chen village under Mao and Deng.* Berkeley/Oxford: University of California Press.

Chang, Chung-li (Zhang, Zhongli) 張仲禮. 1955. *The Chinese gentry, studies on their role in Nineteenth Century Chinese society.* Seattle/Washington: University of Washington Press.

——. 1991. The Chinese gentry, studies on their role in Nineteenth—Century Chinese society (Zhongguo shenshi-guanyu qi zai 19 shiji zhongguo shehui zhong zuoyong de yanjiu). Trans. Rongchang Li. Shanghai: Shanghai Academy of Social Sciences Publishing House. 《中國紳士——關於其在 19 世紀中國社會中作用的研究》，李榮昌譯。上海：上海社科院出版社。

Chang, Xiangqun 常向群. 1992. *Makesi zhuyi shehuixue lungao* (On Marxist sociology). Zhengzhou: Henan

People's Publishing House. 《馬克思主義社會學論稿》。鄭州：河南人民出版社。

——. 1995. "Gender difference in rural social support in China in the post-Mao era (1979-1991) – An analysis of differences between agnatic and non-agnatic kin." A paper for a conference of Socioeconomic Transformation and Women in China. SOAS, London, 8 June.

——. 1999. "Fat pigs' and women's gifts: agnatic and non-agnatic social support in Kaixiangong village." In West, Zhao, Chang and Cheng, eds., *Women of China: Economic and social transformation*. Houndmills / London: Macmillan Press Ltd.

——. 2000. "Importance of intermediaries in gaining access to a Chinese village with *lishang-wanglai*." A paper for the EACS postgraduate workshop on fieldwork research methods in contemporary Chinese Studies. Oxford, September.

——. 2001. "Academic normality, dialogue, equality and tolerance" (*Xueshu guafan, xueshu duihua yu pingdeng kuanrong*). In Jieshun Xu, eds., *Nativization: the great trend of anthropology* (*Bentuhua: renleixue de da qushi*). Nanning: Guanxi Nationality Publishing House. 〈學術規範、學術對話與平等寬容〉，徐傑舜主編，《本土化：人類學的大趨勢》。南寧：廣西民族出版社。

Chang, Xiangqun & Feuchtwang, Stephan. 1996. Social support in rural China (1979-1991): A statistical report on ten villages. London: City University.

Chao, P. 1983. *Chinese Kinship*. London/Boston/Melbourne: Kegan Paul International.

Chard, R. 1979. "Folktales on the god of the stove." *Chinese Studies* 8(1).

Cheal, David. 1978. "Showing them you love them: gift giving and the dialectic of intimacy." *Sociological Review* 35: pp. 150-69.

——. 1988. *The Gift Economy*. London and New York: Routledge.

Cheater, A. P. 1989. *Social anthropology: an alternative introduction*, London & Now York: Routledge.

Chen, C. 1985. "Dowry and inheritance." In J. Hsieh and Y. Chuang, eds., *The Chinese family and its ritual behaviour*, Taipei: Institute of Ethnology, Academia Sinica.

Chen, Guidi; Chuntao 陳桂棣；春桃，2003. *The investigation of Chinese peasants* (*Zhongguo nongmin diaocha*). Beijing: People's Literature Publishing House. 《中國農民調查》。北京：人民文學出版社。

Chen, Jieming 陳皆明. 1988. "Investment and support for the elderly - an analysis of cause and effect on generational exchange among urban residents" (*Touzi yu shanyang-guanyu chengshi jumin daiji jiaohuan de yinguo fenxi*). *Chinese Social Sciences* No. 6. 《投資與贍養——關於城市居民代際交換的因果分析》。《中國社會科學》第 6 期。

Chen, Junjie 陳俊傑. 1996. Guanxi resources and non-ruralisation: a fieldwork in Yue village of Zhejiang Province (Guanxi ziyuan yu feinonghua – zhejiang yuecun de shidi yanjiu). PhD. Dissertation. Beijing: Peking University. 《關係資源與非農化——浙江越村的研究》。博士論文。北京：北京大學。

Chen, Junjie & Chen, Zhen. 陳俊傑、陳震 . 1988. "Rethinking of 'Chaxugeju' ('Chaxugeju' zai sikao)". In Rong Ma and Xing Zhou, eds., *Fieldwork and culture conscious* (*Tianye gongzuo yu wenhua zijue*). Beijing: Qunyan Publishing House. 〈差序格局再思考〉，見馬戎、周星主編《田野工作與文化自覺》。北京：群言出版社。

Chen, Shi and Mi, Youlu, eds., 沉石、米有錄主編. 1989. *Changing of peasants' families in China* (*Zhongguo nongcun jiating de bianqian*). Beijing: Rural reading materials Publishing House (*Nongcun Duwu chubanshe*). 《中國農村家庭變遷》。北京：農村讀物出版社。

Chen, Wuqing. 1997. 陳午晴. "The game implication of *guanxi* amongst Chinese" (*Zhongguoren guanxi de youxi yihan*). Sociological Researches 2: pp. 103-122. 〈中國人關係的遊戲意涵〉，《社會學研究》第 2 期。

Chen, Zhiping. 陳支平. 1991. Lineage society and culture in Fujian province over the last 500 years (*Jin 500 nian lai fujian de jiazu shehui yu wenhua*). Shanghai: Sanlian Shudian Branch. 《近五百年來福建的家族社會與文化》。上海：上海三聯書店。

Cheng, Chung-Ying. 1986. "The Chinese face and its Confucian roots." *Journal of Chinese Philosophy* 13(3): pp. 329-348.

Chow, N. W. 1983. "The Chinese family & support of the elderly in Hong Kong." *Gerontologist* 23(6), pp.584-588.

Chu, Godwin and Hsu, Francis, eds., 1983. *China's new social fabric*. London / New York, etc.: Kegan Paul international.

Chu, Godwin & Ju, Yanan. 1990. *The great wall in ruins: cultural change in China*. Honolulu: East-West Center.

Cicirelli, V.G.1983. "Adult children's attachment & helping behavior to elderly parents: a path model." *Journal of Marriage & the Family* 45(4): pp. 815-825.

——. 1983. "Adult children & their elderly parents", pp. 31-46. In T. H. Brubaker, ed., *Family relationships in later life*. Beverly Hill, CA: Sage Publications.

Cidianzu 詞典組. 1995. *A Chinese-English Dictionary (Revised Edition)* (*Han-Ying Cidian* (*Xiudingban*)), Beijing: Foreign language and research press. 《漢英詞典（修訂版）》，北外英語系詞典組編。北京：外語教學與研究出版社。

Cobb, S. 1976. "Social support as a moderator of life stress." *Psychosomatic Medicine* 3: pp.300-314.

——. 1979. "Social support and health through the life course," pp. 93-106. In M. W. Riley, ed., *Aging from birth to death: interdisciplinary perspectives*. Washington D.C.: American Association for the advancement of Science.

Cohen, I.J. 1989. Structuration theory: Anthony Giddens and the constitution of social life, Houndmills, London: MaCmillan Education Ltd.

Cohen, Myron L. 1969. "Agnatic kinship in south Taiwan." *Ethnology* 15: pp. 237-92.

——. 1970. "Developmental process in the Chinese domestic group." In M. Freedman, ed., *Family and Kinship in Chinese Society*, pp. 21-36. Stanford: Stanford University Press.

——. 1976. House united, house divided: the Chinese family in Taiwan. New York: Columbia University Press.

——. 1984. "Lineage development and the family in China." In J. Hsieh, et al. eds. *The Chinese family and its ritual behavior*, pp. 232-262. Taipei: Academia Sinica.

——. 1988. "Souls and salvation: conflicting themes in Chinese popular religion." In J. Watson and E. Rawski, eds., *Death ritual in late imperial and modern China*. Berkeley/Los Angeles/London: University of California Press.

——. 1989. "Lineage organization in north China." *Journal of Asian Studies* 4: pp. 509-534.

——. 1992. "Family management & family division in contemporary rural China." *The China Quarterly*, 130: pp. 355-377.

——. 1993. "Cultural and political inventions in modern China: the case of the Chinese 'peasant' ".

Daedalus 122: 2, pp. 151-170.

Cohen, S., Wills, T. A. 1985. "Stress, social support, and the buffing hypothesis." *Psychological Bulletin* 98: pp. 310-357.

Cohen, S. & Syme, S.L. eds. 1985. *Social support & health*. Orlando, FL: Academic Press , Inc.

Coleman, J. S. 1988. "Social capital in the creation of human capital." *American Journal of Sociology* 94 (supplement).

Collins, A.H. 1983. "Review of social networks and social support." *Social work*, 28(4): pp. 328-29.

Cook, F. L. 1979. *Who should be helped? – Public support for social services*. Berverly Hills/London: Sage Publications.

Cook, K. S. 1982. "Network structures from an exchange perspective." In Marsden and Lin, eds., *Social structure and network analysis*. Beverly Hill, Calif.: Sage Publications.

Couen, S. & Syme, S.L. 1985. *Social support and health*. New York: Academic press, Inc.

Croll, Elisabeth. 1974. The women's movement in China: a selection of readings 1949-1973. Nottingham: The Russell Press Ltd.

——. 1978. *Feminism and socialism in China*. London / Boston / Henley: Routledge & Kegan Paul.

——. 1979 Women in rural development: the People's Republic of China. Geneva: International Labour Office.

——. 1981. *The politics of marriage in contemporary China*. London: Cambridge University Press.

——. 1983. The family rice bowl: food and domestic economy in China. London: Zed Press.

——. 1985a Women and rural development in China: production and reproduction. Geneva: International Labour Office.

——. 1985b. "Introduction: fertility norms and family size in China." In E. Croll; D. Daven and P. Kane, eds. *China's One Child Policy*. London: MaCmillan.

——. 1985c. "The sexual division of labour in rural China." In L. Beneria, ed., *Women and development: the sexual division of labour in rural societies*. New York: Praeger Publications.

——. 1986. *Chinese women since Mao*. London: Zed Books Ltd.

——. 1987a. "Some implications of the rural economic reforms for the Chinese peasant household." In A. Saith, ed. *The re-emergency of the Chinese peasantry*. London: Croom Helm.

——. 1987b. "New peasant family forms in rural China." *Journal of Peasant Studies* July, no. 4: pp. 469-499.

——. 1988. "The new peasant economy in China," pp. 77-100. In S. Feuchtwang; A. Hussain & T. Pairault, eds., *Transforming China's economy in the eighties, Vol. 1: the rural sector, welfare and Employment*. London: Zed Books Ltd.

——. 1988. "The household, family and reform." In R. Benewick & P. Wingrove, eds., *Reforming the revolution: China in transition*. Hampshire / London: MaCmillan Education Ltd.

——. 1991. "Decades of redefinition: reflections on gender roles in China." In G. Lycklama Nijeholt, ed. *Towards women's strategies for the 1990s Challenging Government and the State*. Intl Specialized Book Service Inc.

——. 1994. From heaven to earth - images and experiences of development in China. London / New York: Routledge.

Crook, I.; Crook, D. 1979a. *The first years of Yangyi commune.* London: Routledge and Kegan Paul.

——. 1979b. *Mass movement in a Chinese village: Ten Mile Inn*, London and Henley: Routledge and Kegan Paul.

Cusack, D. 1958. *Chinese women speak.* London: Century Hutchinson Ltd.

Dalton, George. 1965. "Primitive, archaic, and modern economies: Karl Polanyi's contribution to economic anthropology and comparative economy." In Helm, June, el. eds., *Essays in economic anthropology: dedicated to the memory of Karl Polanyi.* Seattle: The University of Washington Press.

Damas, D. 1972. "Central Eskimo systems of food sharing." *Ethnology*, 11(3): pp. 220-240.

Davin, D. 1975. "Women in the countryside of China", in Wolf, M. & White, R. eds. *Women in Chinese society*, Stanford: Stanford University Press.

——. 1976/79 Women-work: women and the Party in revolutionary China. Oxford University Press.

——. 1988 "The implications of contract agriculture for the employment and status of Chinese peasant women," pp. 137-146. In S. Feuchtwang; A. Hussain & T. Pairault, eds. *Transforming China's economy in the eighties, Vol. 1: the rural sector, welfare and employment.* London: Zed Books Ltd.

——. 1991a. "Women, work and property in the Chinese peasant household of the 1980s." In R. Elson, ed., *Male bias in the development process.* Manchester: Manchester University Press.

——. 1991b. "Chinese models of development and their implications for women." In H. Afshar, ed., *Women, development and survival in the third world.* New York: Longman.

——. 1992. "Population policy and reform: the Soviet Union, Eastern Europe and China." in S.Rai; H. Pilkington & A. Phizacklea, eds., *Women in the face of change: the Soviet Union, Eastern Europe and China.* London/New York: Routledge.

Davis, Deborah, Harrell, S., eds. 1993. *Chinese families in the post-Mao era.* California: University of California Press.

Davis, John. 1994. "Social creativity." In C. M. Hann, ed. *When History Accelerates: Essays on Social Change, Complexity and Creativity.* London & Atlantic Highlands, NJ: Athlone Press.

Davis, M. 1977. *Support systems in social work.* London/Henley/Boston: Routledge & Kegan Paul.

Davis, W.G. 1973. *Social relations in a Philippine market: self-interest and subjectivity.* Berkeley, Los Angeles: University of California Press.

Davis-Friedmann, D. 1983. *Long lives: Chinese elderly and Communist revolution.* Cambridge: Harvard University Press.

Day, C.B. 1969. Chinese peasant cults: being a study of Chinese paper gods. Taipei: Ch'eng Wen Publishing Co.

De Glopper & R Donald. 1978. "Doing business in Lukang," pp. 291-320. In Arthur Wolf, ed., *Studies in Chinese society*, Stanford: Stanford University Press.

Dean, Kenneth. 1993. *Taoist ritual and popular cults of Southeast China.* Princeton University Press.

Dean, K. 1988. *Taoism and popular religion in Southeast China: history and revival.* Ph.D. Dissertation. Stanford: Stanford University.

Deaux, K. Wrightsman, L. S. 1988. *Social psychology* (5th Edition), Pacific Grove/California: Brooks/Cole Publishing Company.

Decicco, Gabrial. 2001. "Nativization: Chinese approach to anthropology" (*Beituhua: Zhongguo renleixue de tansuo*). In Jieshun Xu, ed., *Nativization: the great trend of anthropology* (*Bentuhua: renleixue de da qushi*). Nanning: Guanxi Nationality Publishing House. 〈本土化：中國人類學的探索〉，徐傑舜主編，《本土化：人類學的大趨勢》。南寧：廣西民族出版社。

Del Valle, T. ed. 1993. *Gendered anthropology*, London: Routledge.

Delman, J. ; Christiansen, F. & Ostergaard, C. S. 1991. *Remaking peasant China: rural China in the 1990s*. Denmark: Aarhus University Press.

Depner, C. E., Wethington, E. & Ingersoll-Dayton, B. 1984. "Social support: Methodological issues in design & measurement." *Journal of Social Issues* 40(4): pp. 37-54.

Dex, Shirley. 1985. The sexual division of work conceptual revolutions in the social sciences. Kent: Chanctonbury Press Ltd.

Diamond, N. 1975. "Collectivization, Kinship, and the status of women in rural China." In R. Reiter, ed., *Toward an anthropology of women*, pp. 372-395. New York: Monthly Review Press.

Djilas, Milovan. 1957. The New Class: An Analysis of Communist System of Power. New York: Praeger.

Domes, Jürgen. 1980. Socialism in the Chinese countryside: rural social policies in the People's Republic of China, 1949-1979. London/Montreal: C. Hurst; McGill-Queen's University Press.

Dominelli, Lena. 2000. *Feminist social work theory and practice*. London: Palgrave.

Dorn, J. A. ed. 1989. *Economic reform in China*. Chicago: University of Chicago Press.

Dreze, Jean & Sen, Amartya. 1989. *Hunger and public action*. Oxford: Clarendon Press.

Du, Jian & Zheng, Weizhen, eds. 杜儉、鄭維楨主編. 1995. *Social security system reform* (*Shehui baozhang zhidu gaige*). Shanghai: Lixin Kuaiji Publishing House. 《社會保障制度改革》，上海：立信會計出版社。

Du, Runsheng. 1989. *Many people, little land: China's rural economic reform*, Beijing: Foreign Languages Press.

Duara, Prasenjit. 杜贊奇. 1988. *Culture, power, and the state: rural north China, 1900-1942*. Stanford /Calif.: University Press.

——. 1995. *Culture, power, and the state: rural north China, 1900-1942* (*Wenhua, quanli yu guojia-1900-1942 nian de huabei nongcun*). Trans. Fuming Wang. Nanjing: Jiangsu People's Publishing House. 《文化、權利與國家——1900-1942 年的華北農村》。王福明譯。南京：江蘇人民出版社。

Duck, S. W. 1973. Personal relationships and personal constructs - a study of friendship formation, London: Wiley.

Duck, S. W. & Gilmour, R. eds. 1981. *Personal relationships, 1&2*. London/New York et.: Academic Press.

Duck, S. W. & Silver, R. C. eds. 1990. *Personal relationships and social support*. London: Sage Publications.

Dunkel-Schetter, C. 1984. "Social support and cancer: findings based on patient interviews and their implications." Journal of Social Issues 40(4): pp. 77-79.

Duojicairang 多吉才讓. 1998. "Prospects of Chinese social security for the 21st century" (Ershiyishiji zhongguo shehui baozhang zhanwang), In Zhengxin Shi & Yong Zhu, eds., *a foreword of Report on Chinese social welfare and social progress in 1998 (Zhongguo shehui fuli yu shehui jinbu baogao 1998)*. Beijing: Social

Sciences document publishing house (Shehui kexue wenxian chubanshe).〈二十一世紀中國社會保障展望〉，時正新，朱勇主編《中國社會福利與社會進步報告1998序言》。北京：社會科學文獻出版社。

Durkheim, E. 1895/1935. The rules of sociological method. New York: Free Press.

Dutton, M. 1988. "Policing the Chinese household: a comparison of modern and ancient forms." *Economy and society* 17(2): pp. 195-224.

Ebrey, P.B. 1990. "Women, marriage and the family in Chinese history", pp. 197-223. In P. Ropp, ed., *Heritage of China*. Berkeley and LA: University of California Press.

Ebrey, P. B. & Watson, J. L. eds. 1986. *Kinship organization in late imperial China: 1000-1940.* Berkeley: University of California Press.

Ekech, P. P. 1972. *Social exchange theory: the two traditions.* Cambridge/Mass: Harvard University Press. Ellwood, D. T. 1988. *Poor support: poverty in the American family.* New York: Basic Books, Inc.

Endicott, S. 1988. *Red earth: revolution in a Sichuan village.* London: I.B. & Co. Ltd.

Entwisle, B. et. al. 1995. "Gender and family businesses in rural China." *American Sociological Review* 60: pp. 36-57.

Eriksen, T. H. 1995. Small places, large issues: an introduction to social and cultural anthropology, London/East Haven: Pluto Press.

Esherick, W.; Rankin, Mary B. eds. 1990. *Chinese local elites and patterns of dominance.* California: University of California Press.

Etienne, G. 1985. Trans. France, 1982, *Rural development in Asia: meetings with peasants.* New Delhi /London: Sage Publications.

Evans, Harriet. 1992. "Monogamy and female sexuality in the People's Republic of China." In S. Rai; H. Pilkington & A. Phizacklea, eds., *Women in the face of Change: the Soviet Union, Eastern Europe and China.* London/New York: Routledge.

——. 1997. Women and sexuality in China: dominant discourses of female sexuality and gender since 1949. New York: Continuum International Publishing Group.

Faure, David. 1985. "The plight of the farmers: a study of the rural economy of Jiangnan and the Pearl River Delta, 1870-1937." *Modern China* 11, 1: pp. 3-37.

——. 1986. The structure of Chinese rural society: lineage and village in the eastern New Territories, HongKong. Oxford: Oxford University Press.

——. 1989. "The lineage as a cultural invention: the case of the Pearl River Delta." *Modern China* 15: 1: pp. 4-36.

Faure, D. and H. Siu, eds., 1995. *Down to earth: the territorial bond in South China.* Stanford, CA: Stanford University Press.

Feger, H. 1981. "Analysis of social networks." In S. Duck & R. Gilmour, eds., *Personal relationships (1).* London/New York: Academic Press.

Fehr, B. & Perlman, D. 1985. "The family as a social network and support system." In L. L'Abate, ed., *Handbook of family psychology & therapy*, pp. 323-356. Homewood, IL: Dow Jones-Irwin.

Fei, Xiaotong (Hsiao-Tung) 費孝通. 1939. *Peasant Life in China: a field study of country life in the Yangtze village*. London London/Henley: Routledge & Kegan Paul.

——. 1946. "Peasantry and gentry: an interpretation of Chinese class structure and its changes." *American Journal of Sociology* 52: 1: pp. 1-17.

——. 1947. *Folk China (Xiangtu zhongguo)*, Shanghai: Guanchashe. Fernandez, James. 《鄉土中國》。上海：觀察社。

——. 1983. *Chinese village close-up*. Beijing: New World Press.

——. 1986. *Peasant Life in China*, Trans. Dai, Kejing. Nanjing: Jiangsu People's Publishing. 《江村經濟——中國農民的生活》，戴可景譯。南京：江蘇人民出版社。

——. 1989. Rural development in China: prospect and retrospect. Chicago: University of Chicago Press.

——. 1992. "Home trip – the ninth visit to the Jiang Village in 1985" (*Guli xing-jiu fang Jiangcun* 1985). In Fei, ed. *Touwnship developmemt collection (Xingxing zhong xingxing-xiangzhen fazhan lunshu)*.〈故里行（九訪江村，1985）〉。《行行重行行——鄉鎮發展論述》。銀川：寧夏人民出版社。

——. 1996. *I love my hometown (Wo ai jiaxiang)*. Beijing: Qunyan Publishing House. 《我愛家鄉》。北京：群言出版社。

——. 2002. Succeed from masters, make up missed lessons and pursue our studies (Shicheng/buke/zhixue), Beijing: Sanlian Shudian. 《師承、補課、治學》。北京：三聯書店。

Fei, Xiaotong (Hsiao-Tung) et al. 1986. *Small town in China: functions, problems and prospects*. Beijing: New World Press.

Feng, Youlan 馮友蘭. 1984. *A history of Chinese philosophy (Zhongguo zhexueshi)*. Beijing: Shangwu yishu guan. 《中國哲學史》。北京：商務印書館。

——. 1998. *The spirit of Chinese philosophy – Essays of Feng Youlan (Zhongguo zhexue de jingshe － Feng Youlan ji)*. Ed. Lai Chen. Shanghai: Shanghai Cultural and Arts Publishing House. 《中國哲學的精神——馮友蘭集》，陳來選編。上海：上海文藝出版社。

Feng, H.Y. 1948. *The Chinese kinship system*. Cambridge: Harvard University Press.

Feuchtwang, Stephan. 王斯福. 1966. Chinese lineage and society: Fukien and Kwangtung. Athlone Press.

——. 1974. "Mortuary rituals." Chapter ten of Doctorate dissertation. SOAS, London.

——. 1987. "Changes in the system of basic social security in the countryside since 1979", in A. Saith, ed., *The re-emergence of the Chinese peasantry*, pp. 173-210. London: Croom Helm.

——. 1989. "The problem of 'superstition' in the PRC", pp. 43-68. In Benavides and Daly, eds., *Religion and Political Power*. New York: The State University of New York Press.

——. 1994. "Social support arrangements among households in rich and poor village: some preliminary results of an enquiry", p. 141-158. In R. Krieg and M. Schadler, Eds., *Social Security in the People's Republic of China*. Hamburg: Institute fur Asienkunde.

——. 1996. "Local temples and village identity", pp. 161-75. In T.T. Liu & D. Faure, eds., *Unity and diversity: local cultures and identities in China*. Hong Kong University Press.

——. 1997. "What is a village?" In E. Vermeer, F. Pieke and W. L. Chong, eds., Cooperative and Collective in China's Rural Development: Between State and Private Interests. M. E. Sharpe.

——. 1998. "A practical-minded person: Prof. Fei's anthropological calling and Edmund Leach's game", In Rong Ma, Xing Zhou, eds. *Fieldwork and culture consciousness (Tianye gongzuo yu wenhua zijue)*. Beijing: Qunyan Publishing House. 〈實踐者：費孝通教授的人類學使命與利奇的遊戲〉，見馬戎、

周星主編《田野工作與文化自覺》。北京：群言出版社。

——. 2001. "Rising to the challenge: for a critical anthropology of China." In Jieshun Xu, ed., *Nativization: the great trend of anthropology (Bentuhua: renleixue de da qushi)*. Nanning: Guangxi Nationality Publishing house. 〈中國人類學：自我批評與迎接挑戰〉，見徐傑舜主編，《本土化：人類學的大趨勢》。南寧：廣西民族出版社。

——. 2003. Popular religion in China: the imperial metaphor. London & NY: Routledge Curzon.

——. Forthcoming. *Popular religion in China: the imperial metaphor* (Diguo de yinyu-Hanren "minjian xinyang" de renleixue yanjiu). Trans. Xudong Zhao. Shanghai: Shanghai People's Publishing House. 《帝國的隱喻——漢人民間信仰的人類學研究》，趙旭東譯。上海：上海人民出版社。

Finch, Janet. 1989. *Family obligations and social change*. Cambridge: Polity Press.

Finch, Janet and Mason, Jennifer. 1993. *Negotiating Family Responsibilities*. Routledge/Tavistock. Firth, Raymond W. 1961/71. *Elements of social organization*. London: Tavistock Publications 3rd ed. reprint 1971 (1961).

——. 1969. *Families and their relatives*. London: Routledge and Kegan Paul.

——. 1970/81. Essays on social organization and Values, Beacon /New York: The Athlone Press.

——. 1973. *Symbols: public and private*. London: George Allen & Unwin.

Fischer, C.S. & Oliker, S.J. 1983. "A research note on friendship, gender, and the life cycle." *Social Forces* 62:1 : 126-133.

Flaherty, J.A., Gaviria, F. M. & Pathak, D.S. 1983. "The measurement of social support: the social support network inventory." *Comprehensive Psychiatry* 24(6): 521-529.

Foa, E. B., Foa, U. G. 1980. "Resource Theory: interpersonal behavior as exchange," pp. 78-79. In K.J., Gergen; M. S. Greenberg & R.H. Willis, eds., *Social Exchange: advances in theory and research*. New York: Plenum Press, Foa, U. G. 1971. "Interpersonal and economic resources." *Science* 171, January 29, pp. 345-51.

Fortes, M. 1949. *The web of kinship among the Tallensi*. Oxford: Oxford University Press.

Foster, R.J. 1990. "Value without equivalence: exchange and replacement in a Melanesian Society." *Man* 25: pp. 54-69.

——. 1995. Social reproduction and history in Melanesia: mortuary ritual, gift exchange and custom in the Tanga island. Cambridge: Cambridge University Press.

Frazer, James George. 1890-22. *The Golden Bough* (12 vols.). London: Macmillan.

Freeman, L. C., 1979. "Centrality in social networks: conceptual clarificion." *Social Networks* No.1.

Freeman, L. C., Roeder, D., & Mulholland, R. R. 1980. "Centrality in social networks II: experimental results." *Social networks* No. 2.

Freedman, Maurice 莫里斯·弗裡德曼.1958. *Lineage Organizations in Southeastern China*. London: Athlone.

——. 1963. "A Chinese phase in social anthropology." *British Journal of Sociology* 14:1, pp. 1-19, reprinted as essay 22 in G. William Skinner, ed., 1979. *The study of Chinese society - Essays by Maurice Freedman*. Stanford: Stanford University Press.

——. 1966. Chinese lineage organizations: Fujian and Guangdong, London: Athlone.

——. 1970. *Family and kinship in Chinese society*. Stanford/California: Stanford University Press.

——. 1979. "Kinship and religion in China", and "On the study of Chinese society", as Part four and five in G. W. Skinner, ed. *The study of Chinese society - Essays by M. Freedman*. Stanford: Stanford University Press.

——. 2000. *Lineage Organizations in Southeastern China (Zhongguo dongnan de zongzu zuzhi)*. Trans. Xiaochun Liu. Shanghai: Shanghai People's Publishing House. 《中國東南的宗族組織》，劉曉春譯。上海：上海人民出版社。

Fried, Morton, H. 1953. *The fabric of Chinese society*. New York: Praeger Inc.

Friedman, E.; Pichowicz, P.G.; Selden, M. 弗裡曼、畢克偉、賽爾登. 1991. *Chinese village, socialist state*. New Haven and London: Yale University Press.

——. *Chinese village, socialist state (Zhongguo xiangcun, shehuizhuyi guojia)*. Trans. Heshan Tao. Beijing: Social Sciences Documents Publishing House. 《中國鄉村，社會主義國家》，陶鶴山譯。北京：社科文獻出版社。

Gallin, Bernard. 1960. "Matrilateral and affinal relationships of a Taiwanese Village." *American Anthropologist* 66(4): pp. 632-642.

——. 1966. *Hsin Hsing, Taiwan: a Chinese village in change*. Berkeley: University of California Press.

Gallin, B. and Rita. 1985. "Matrilateral and affinal relationships in Changing Chinese society." In Jih-chang Hsieh and Ying-chang Chuang, eds., *The Chinese family and its ritual behavior*. Taipei: Institute of Ethnology, Academia Sinica, Monograph series B, No.15. Gao, Chenyang 高晨陽. 1994. *A study of Chinese traditional thinking methods (Zhongguo chuantong siwei fangshi yanjiu)*. Jinan: Shandong University Publishing House. 《中國傳統思維方式研究》。濟南：山東大學出版社。

Gao, Cong & Zou, Qiong 高崇 鄒瓊. 2001. "China's anthropology from the native to the world." In Jieshun Xu, ed., *Nativization: the great trend of anthropology (Bentuhua: renleixue de da qushi)*, Nanning: Guanxi Nationality Publishing House. 〈從本土走向全球的中國人類學〉，見徐傑舜主編，《本土化：人類學的大趨勢》。南寧：廣西民族出版社。

Gao, Mobo. 1999. *Gao village: rural life in modern China*. London: Hurst & Co. Ltd.

Gao, Xudong & Wu, zhongmin 高旭東、吳忠民等. 1989. *Comparison of the spirit between Confucius and Christianity (Kongzi jingshen yu jidujiao jingshen)*, Shijiazhuang: Hebei People's Publishing House. 《孔子精神與基督教精神》。石家莊：河北人民出版社。

Garbarino, J. 1983. "Social support networks: Rx for the helping professions," pp. 3-28. In J. K. Whittaker; J. Garbarino and Associates, eds., *Social support networks: Informal helping in the human services*. New York: Aldine De Gruyter.

Ge, Chengyong; Sun, Fuxi and Liang, Tao 葛承雍、孫福喜、梁濤. 1994. Cultivating people from the golden empire: traditional peasants and Chinese society (Jinse diguo de gengyuren: chuantong nongmin yu zhongguo shehui). Tianjin: Tianjin People's Publishing House. 《金色帝國的耕耘人：傳統農民與中國社會》。天津：天津人民出版社。

Geddes, W.R. 1963. *Peasant life in Communist China,* the society for applied anthropology, Monograph No.6.

——. 1986. "Peasant life in Communist China." An appendix of *Peasant Life in China*. Trans. Kejing Dai. Nanjing: Jiangsu People's Publishing. 〈共產黨領導下的農民生活〉，費孝通《江村經濟——中國農民的生活》中附錄，戴可景譯。南京：江蘇人民出版社。

Gergen, M.J.; Greenberg, and R.H. Willis, eds., 1980. *Social exchange: Advances in theories and research*. New York: Plenum Press.

Giddens, Anthony. 安東尼‧吉登斯. 1976/97. *New rules of sociological method*. Cambridge: Polity Press.

——. 1984. *The constitution of society*. Cambridge: Polity Press.

——. 1985. *The Nation-state and violence*. Cambridge: Polity Press.

——. 1991. Modernity and Self-Identity: Self and Society in the Late Modern Age. Polity Press.

——. 1993. *Sociology (second edition)*. Cambridge: Polity Press.

——. 1997. The transformation of intimacy: sexuality, love and eroticism in modern society. Cambridge: Polity Press.

——. 1998a. *The constitution of society* (*Shehui de goucheng*). Trans. Kang Li & Meng Li. Beijing: Sanlian Shudian. 《社會的構成》，李康、李猛譯。北京：三聯書店。

——. 1998b. *The Nation-state and violence* (*Minzu-guojia yu paoli*). Trans. Zongze Hu & Litao Zhao. Beijing: Sanlian Shudian. 《民族——國家與暴力》，胡宗澤、趙力濤譯。北京：三聯書店。

——. 1998c. *Modernity and Self-Identity: Self and Society in the Late Modern Age* (*Xiandaixing yu ziwo rentong*). Trans. Xudong Zhao & Wen Fang. Beijing: Sanlian Shudian. 《現代性與自我認同》，趙旭東、方文譯。北京：三聯書店。

——. 2001. The transformation of intimacy: sexuality, love and eroticism in modern society (Qinmi guanxi de biange - Xiandai shehui zhong de xing, ai he aiyu). Trans. Yongguo Chen & Min'an Wang. Beijing: Social Science Documentation Publishing House. 《親密關係的變革——現代社會中的性、愛和愛欲》，陳永國、汪民安譯。北京：社會科學文獻出版社。

Giddens, A. & Turner, J. 1987. *Social theory today*. Cambridge: Polity Press.

Gilmartin, C.K.; Hershatter, G.; Rofel, L. & White, T. eds. 1994. *Engendering China: women, culture and the state*. Cambridge: Harvard University Press.

Goddard, Michael. 2000. "Of Cabbages and Kin-the value of an analytic distinction between gifts and commodities." *Critique of Anthropology*, 20 (2).

Goffman, Erving. 1955. "On face-work: an analysis of ritual elements in social interaction." *Psychiatry*18 (August): pp. 213-31.

——. 1959. *The presentation of self in every day life*. Edinburgh: University of Edinburgh Press.

——. 1972. Interaction ritual: essays on face-to-face behaviour. London: Penguin.

Gold, Thomas B. 1985. "After comradeship: personal relations in China since the cultural revolution." *China Quarterly* 104: pp. 657-75.

——. 1993. "The study of Chinese society." In L Shambaugh David, ed., *American studies of contemporary China*. Washington D.C.: Woodrow Wilson Centre Press.

Gold, T.; Guthrie, D & Wank D, eds., 2002. *Social connections in China – institutions, culture, and changing nature of guanxi*. Cambridge: Cambridge University Press.

Goodman, D. S.G. ed. 1989. *China's regional development*. London: Routledge.

Goody, J. 1969. *Comparative studies in kinship*. London: Routledge & Kegan Paul.

——. ed. 1971. Kinship - selected readied readings. London: Penguin.

——. 1973. *The character of kinship*. Cambridge: Cambridge University Press.

Goodnow, Frank J. 古德諾.1926. *China: an analysis*. Baltimore: The Johns Hopkins Press.

——. 1998. *China: an analysis* (*Jiexi zhongguo*). Trans. Xiangyang Cai & Maozeng Li. Beijing: Internation Cultural Publishing Corporation. 《解析中國》，蔡向陽、李茂增譯。北京：國際文化出版公司。

Gottlieb, B.H. 1978. "The development and application of a classification scheme of informal helping behaviours." *Canadian Journal of Behaviour Science* 10: pp. 105-15.

——. 1985. "Social networks and social support: an overview of research, practice and policy implications." *Health Education Quarterly* 12(1): pp. 5-22.

Gottlieb, B.H. ed., 1981. *Social network and social support*. Beverly Hills/London: Sage Publications.

——. 1988. Marshaling social support: formats, processes and effects. London: Sage Publications.

Gou, Chengyi. 1994. 勾承益. *Blessing happiness, good luck, good fortune, and glad tidings (Fu, fuqi, fuyin)*. Chengdu: Sichuan People's Publishing House. 《福、福氣、福音》。成都：四川人民出版社。

Gouldner, A. W. 1960. "The norm of reciprocity: a preliminary statement." *American Sociological Review* 25 (2): pp. 161-78.

——. 1975. "The importance of something for nothing", pp. 260-290. In *For Sociology: Renewal and Critique in Sociology Today*. London: Penguin.

Gransow, Bettina [德] 柯蘭君. 1993. "Gift giving and corruption" (*Songli yu fubai*). *Sociological Researches* No. 6. 〈送禮與腐敗〉，《社會學研究》第 5 期。

Granovetter, M. 1973. "The strength of weak ties." *American Journal of Sociology* 78.

——. 1982. "The strength of weak ties: A network theory revised." In P. V. Marsden & Nan Lin, eds., *Social structure and network analysis*. Sage Publications.

——. 1974/95 *Getting a job (Second edition)*. Chicago: University of Chicago Press.

Greene, F. 1982.   The dilemmas of friendship: some personal thoughts about China. New York: Maud Russell Publishers.

Greenberg, M. S. 1980. "An theory of indebtedness," pp. 3-26. In K. J. Gergen; M. S. Greenberg and R. H. Willis, eds., *Social exchange: advances in theory and research*. New York: V. H. Winston and Sons.

Gregory, C. A. 1982. *Gift and Commodity*. London: Academic Press.

Greider, T. & Krannich, R. S. 1985. "Neighbouring patterns, social support, and rapid growth: a comparison analysis from three western communities." *Sociological Perspectives* 28(1): pp. 51-70.

Gu, Hongming (Ku, Hung-Ming) 辜鴻銘. 1915. The spirit of the Chinese people (Chunqiu dayi). Peking: Peking Daily News.

——. 1996. *The spirit of the Chinese people (Zhongguoren de jingshen)*. Trans. H. Huang & X. Song. Haikou: Hainan Publishing House. 《中國人的精神》，黃興濤、宋小慶譯。海口：海南出版社。

Gu, Jun 顧駿.1991. Human being, benevolence, and the masses: Wisdom between people's relationships (Ren, ren, zhong: ren yu ren de zhihui). Hangzhou: Zhejiang People's Publishing House. 《人、仁、眾：人與人的智慧》。杭州：浙江人民出版社。

Guisso, R.W. & Johannesen, S. eds. 1981. *Women in China: current directions in historical scholarship*. Youngstown: Philo Press.

Guldin, G.E. 1997. Farewell to peasant China: rural urbanization and social change in the late twentieth Century. M.E. Sharpe.

Gulliver, P.H. 1971. *Neighbours and networks*. University of California Press.

Guo, Chunmei; Zhang, Qingjie 郭春梅、張慶捷. 2001. *Popular religion and Chinese society* (*Shisu mixin yu zhongguo shehui*). Beijing: Religious Culture Publishing House. 《世俗迷信與中國社會》。北京：宗教文化出版社。

Guo, Ying. 郭英.1998. "Basic rules of conducting oneself in society in Chinese tradition" (*zhongguo chuantong chushi zhi dao de jiben guifan*). *Social Sciences Front* No.2. 〈中國傳統處事之道的基本規範〉，《社會科學戰線》第 2 期。

Guo, Yuhua. 郭於華. 2001. "The logic of fairness and its change in crossgenerational relations: an analysis of cases of elderly support in rural Hebei". Chinese Scholarship, no. 4: pp 221-54. 〈代際關係中的公平邏輯及其變遷：對河北農村養老時間的分析〉，《中國學術》第 4 期：頁 221-54。

Guo, Zhigang 郭志剛. 1995. Population development and the changing family and household in contemporary China (Dangdai zhongguo renkou fazhan yu jiating hu de bianqian). Beijing: Chinese People's University Publishing House.《當代中國人口發展與家庭戶的變遷》。北京：中國人民大學出版社。

Hain, P. 1980. *Neighbourhood participation*. London: Temple Smith.

Hans, O.F.; Veiel & Urs Baumann, eds. 1992. *The meaning & measurement of social support*. NY: Hemisphere Publishing Corporation.

Hass, D.F. 1979. Interaction in the Thai Bureaucracy: structure, culture, & social exchange. Boulder: Westview Press.

Hallgren, C. 1979. "The code of Chinese kinship: A critique of the work of Maurice Freedman." *Ethnos* 44(1): pp. 7-33.

Hammer, M. 1982. "Explorations into the meaning of social network interview data." *Social Networks* 6(4): pp. 341-371.

Hannerz, Ulf. 1980. *Exploring the City*. Columbia University Press.

Haralambos, Michael, ed. 1994. *Sociology: a new approach (second edition)*. Ormskirk: Causeway Press Ltd.

Harrell, S. 1981. "Social Organization in Han-Shan." In E.M. Ahern and H. Gates eds., *The Anthropology of Taiwan Society*. Stanford: Stanford University Press.

——. 1992. "Aspects of marriage in three south-western villages." *The China Quarterly* 130: pp. 323-337. Harrison, D. 1988. *The sociology of modernization and development*. London: Uniwin Hyman.

Hashimoto, A. 1996. The gift of generations: Japanese and American Perspectives on aging and the social contract. Cambridge USA: Cambridge University Press.

Hatch, S. 1986. Self-help in practice: a study of contact a family, community work & family support. Teresa Hinton.

He, Mengbi 何夢筆. 1996. Networks, culture, and economic behaviour model of Chinese society (Wangluo, wenhua yu huaren shehui jingji xingwei moshi). Shangxi Economical Publishing House. 《網路網絡、文化與社會經濟行為模式》。太原：山西經濟出版社。

He, Qinglian 何清漣. 1997. The primary capital accumulation in contemporary China (Zhongguo de xianjing). Hong Kong: Mirroe Books. 《中國的陷阱》。香港：明鏡出版社。

——. 2001. "An analysis on social environment for changes in current Chinese women's social states" (*Dangqian zhongguo funu diwei bianhua de shehui huanjing fenxi*). *Modern China Studies* No. 2. 〈當前中國婦女地位變化的社會環境分析〉，《當代中國研究》第 2 期（總第 73 期）。

He, Ruifu. 1992. *Family networks and life in Southeastern China*. Ph. D dissertation. London: City University.

Heald, T. 1983. *Networks: Who we know and how we use them*. London: Hodder and Stroughton.

Heath, A. 1976. *Rational Choice and Social Exchange*. London: Cambridge University Press.

Hemmel, V. & Sindbjerg, P. eds. 1984. Women in rural China: policy towards women before and after the Cultural Revolution. London: Curzon Press.

Highbaogh, I. 1948. *Family life in West China*. New York: Agricultural Missions, Inc.

Hill, B.; Young, N. Brookes, G. 1989. *Alternative support systems for rural areas*. London: CEAS consultant (wye) Ltd.

Ho, David Yau-fai. 1976. "On the concept of face." *American Journal of Sociology* 81: pp. 867-84.

Ho, Ping-ti. 1962. *The ladder of success in late Imperial China*, pp 49. Columbia University Press.

Ho, S.P.S. 1994. Rural China in transition: non-agricultural development in rural Jiangsu, 1978-1990. Clarendon Press.

Honig, E. & Hershatter, G. 1988. *Personal voices: Chinese women in the 1980's*. Stanford: Stanford University Press.

Hooks, B. 1984. *Feminist theory from margin to centre*. Boston: South End Press.

Hooyman, N. 1983. "Social support networks in services to the elderly." In J. K. Whittaker & J. E. Garbarino, eds., *Social support networks: informal helping in the human services*. New York: Aldine de Gruyter.

House, J. S. 1981. *Work stress and social support*. Reading, MA: Addison-Wesley.

——. 1987. "Social support & social structure." *Sociological Forum* 2(1): pp. 135-146.

House, J.S. & Kahn, R. L. 1984. "Measures & concepts of social support," pp. 83-108. In S. Cohen & L. Syme, eds., *Social support & health*. New York: Academic Press.

House, J. S., Landis, K. R., & Umberson, D. 1988. "Social relationships and health." *Science* pp. 241, 540-545.

House, J.S., Umberson, D. & Landis, K.R. 1988. "Structures and processes of social support." *Annual Review of Sociology* 14: pp. 293-318.

Hostetler, J., Huntington, G.E. 1967. *The huterites in North America*. New York: Holt, Rinehart & Winston.

Hoyt, D. R. & Babchuk, N. 1983. "Adult kinship networks: the selective formation of intimate ties with kin." *Social Forces* 62: 1: pp. 84-101.

Hsieh, J. C. & Chuang Y. C. eds. 1985. *The Chinese family and its ritual behaviour*. Taipei: Institute of Ethnology, Academia Sinica, Taiwan, Monograph Series B No. 15.

Hsu, F. L. K. 1949. Under The Ancestors' Shadow: Chinese culture and personality. London: Routledge and Kegan Paul.

——. 1970. "Eros, affect, and Pao." In F. L. K. Hsu, ed. *Kingship and culture*. Chicago: Aldine Co.

——. 1970. American and Chinese: relationships on two cultures and their people. New York: Garden City Press.

——. 1971. Under The Ancestors' Shadow-kinship, personality, and social mobility in China. California: Stanford University Press.

Hsu, F. L. K. ed. 1971. *Kinship and culture*. Chicago: Aldine Publishing Company.

Hu, Daiguang 胡代光（音）1994. "Market shouldn't rely on balance of interpersonal relationships" (*Shichang buneng kao renjiguanxi pingheng*). A Newspaper of Public Relationships (*Gonggong guanxi daobao*), 29th Oct. p 1. 〈市場不能靠人際關係平衡〉,《公共關係導報》, 10 月 29 日第 1 頁。

Hu, Hsien Chin. 1944. "The Chinese concept of 'face'." *American Anthropologist* 46: pp. 45-64.

——. 1948. The common descent group in China and its function. New York: Viking Fund Publications.

Hu, Ji 胡戟. 1994. *The ancient etiquettes and rites of China* (*Zhongguo gudai liyi*). Xi'an: Shanxi People's Publishing House. 《中國古代禮儀》。西安：陝西人民出版社。

Hu, Taili 胡台麗. 1991. "Between union and separation: rural family and industrialization in Taiwan" (*He yu fen zhijian: Taiwan nongcun jiating yu gongyehua*), pp 213-220. In Jian Qiao, ed., *Chinese family and changes*. Social Sciences School, Hong Kong Chinese University. 〈合與分之間：臺灣農村家庭與工業化〉, 第 213-220 頁。喬健主編《中國家庭及其變遷》, 香港中文大學社會科學院暨香港亞太研究所。

Hu, Yucheng 胡玉成. 1996. "The present and the past of Jiang Village as far apart as heaven and earth" (*Jiangcunjinxi panruo tianrang*). *Wujiang Cultural and Historical Documents* No5. Wujiang Political Consultative Conference. 〈江村今昔判若天壤〉,《吳江文史資料》第 5 輯, 吳江政協。

Huang, Philip, C.C. 黃宗智.1980.   *The development of underdevelopment in China*. New York: M. E. Sharpe.

——. 1985. *The peasant economy and social change in North China*. Stanford/California: Stanford University Press.

——. 1990. The peasant family & rural development in the Yangzi Delta, 1350-1988. Stanford/California: Stanford University Press.

——. 1992. The peasant family & rural development in the Yangzi Delta, 1350-1988 (Changjiang sanjiaozhou xiaonong jiating yu xiangcun fazhan). Trans. Cheng, Li & Lu. Proof-reading C.C. Huang. Beijing: Zhonghua Shuju. 《長江三角洲小農家庭與鄉村發展》, 程、李、盧譯, 黃校。北京中華書局。

——. ed. 黃宗智主編. 2003. *Rural China studies* (Vol 2) (*Zhongguo xiangcun yanjiu*). Beijing: Shangwu Yinshuguan.《中國鄉村研究（第二輯）》。北京：商務印書館。

Huckfeldt, R. R. 1983. "Social contexts, social networks & urban neighbours: Environmental constraints on friendship choice." *American Journal Sociology* 89(3): pp. 561-669.

Huggins, G. B. 1989. *Informal support networks in Soshanguve*. Pretoria: The HSRC Publishers.

Hui, Haiming 惠海鳴 1996a "Jiangcun: from the land reform to the co-operative transformation" (*Cong tugai dao hezuohua de jiangcun*). In Naigu Pan & Rong Ma, eds., *Community studies and social development* (*Shequ yanjiu yu shehui fazhan*). Tianjin: Tianjin People's Publishing House. 〈從到合作化的江村〉, 潘乃毅、馬戎主編《社區研究與社會發展（上）》。天津：天津人民出版社。

——. 1996b. "An impression of Jiang village in 1992" (*Jiangcun 1992 nian yinxiang ji*). In Wujiang zhengxie (Wujiang County branch of Chinese Political Consultative Conference), eds., *From Jiang village to Jiang Township: Developmental pace of Miaogang Township* (*Jiangcun–Jiangzhen: Maiogang fazhan de jiaobu*). Beijing: Chinese Literature and History Publishing House. 〈江村 1992 年印象記〉,《江村——江鎮：廟港發展的腳步》, 吳江市政協編。北京：中國文史出版社。

——. 1999. "A dialogue and reflection in Jiang village" (*Duihua he fanxing: Jiangcun duihua*), a paper for visiting Department Anthropology, LSE. Suzhou Policy Study Institution of Suzhou City Government, Suzhou. 〈對話與反省：江村對話〉, 訪問倫敦經濟學院人類學系論文。蘇州市政府政研室。

Humphrey, C. & Hugh-Jones, S. eds. 1992. *Barter, exchange and value: an anthropological approach.* Cambridge/New York: Cambridge University Press.

Humphrey, J. 1987. *Gender and work in the third world.* London: Tavistock.

Hwang, Jianhou 黃堅厚. 1989. "The practices of filial duty in modern life (*Xiandai shenghuo zhong xiao de shijian*)," pp 25-38. In K. S. Yang, ed., *Chinese psychology (Zhongguoren de xinli)*. Taipei: Guiguan Press.〈現代生活中孝的實踐〉，見楊國樞主編《中國人的心理》。臺北：桂冠圖書公司。

Hwang, Kwang-kuo (Huang Guang-guo) 黃光國. 1982/89. "*Renqing* and *mianzi*: Chinese power games (*Renqing yu mianzi: zhongguoren de quanli youxi*). In K. S. Yang, ed., The psychology of the Chinese (*Zhongguoren de xinli*). Taipei: Taiwan Guiguan Press.

——. 1987. "Face and favour: the Chinese power game." *American Journal of Sociology* Vol. 92 (4).

Hyde, L. 1979/83. The gift: imagination and the erotic life of property. New York: Vintage Books.

Jacka, T. 1997. Women's work in rural China: change and continuity in an era of reform. Cambridge: Cambridge University Press.

Jacobs, J. Bruce. 1979. "A preliminary model of particularistic ties in Chinese political alliances: *ganqing* and *guanxi* (Kan-ch'ing and Kuan-his) in a rural Taiwanese township." *The China Quarterly* 78: pp. 237-273.

——. 1980. Local Politics in a Rural Chinese Cultural Setting: A Field Study of Matzu Township. Canberra: Contemporary China Centre, Australia National University.

——. 1982. "The concept of *guanxi* and local politics in a rural Chinese cultural setting", pp. 209-236. In S. L. Greenblatt; R.W. Wilson & A. A. Wilson, eds., *Social Interaction in Chinese Society*. N.Y.: Praeger.

Jacobson, D. E. 1987. "The cultural context of social support and support networks." *Medical Anthropology Quarterly* (New Series), 1(1): pp. 42-67.

Jarrett, W.H. 1985. "Care giving within kinship systems: is affection really necessary? *Gerontologist* 25(1): pp. 5-10.

Jary, David & Julia. 1991. *Collins Dictionary of Sociology*. Glasgow: Harper Collins Publishers.

Jaschok, M. & Miers, S. eds.1994. Women and Chinese patriarchy: submission, servitude and escape. London: Zed Books.

Jerrome, D. 1990. "Frailty and Friendship." *Journal of cross-cultural Gerontology* 5(1): 64. Ji, Xiangxiang 計翔翔. 2002. "Clarifications on 'Sinology' " ('*Hanxue' zhengming*). *Zhejiang Social Sciences* No. 5. 〈「漢學」正名〉，《浙江社會科學》第五期。

Jiang, Bin 蔣斌. 1996. "Kinship and social organisation" (*Qinshu yu shehui zuzhi*). In Xing Zhou & Mingming Wang, eds., *Collection of social cultural anthropology (Shehui wenhua releixue jiangyan ji)*. Tianjin: Tianjin People's Publishing House. 〈親屬與社會組織〉，見周星、王銘銘主編《社會文化人類學講演集》。天津：天津人民出版社。

Jin, Guangyi 金光億. 1996. "Religion and ritual under modern background" (*Xiandai beijing xia de zongjiao he liyi*). In Xing Zhou & Mingming Wang, eds., *Collection of social cultural anthropology (Shehui wenhua releixue jiangyan ji)*. Tianjin: Tianjin People's Publishing House. 〈現代背景下的宗教和禮儀〉，見周星、王銘銘主編《社會文化人類學講演集》。天津：天津人民出版社。

——. 1998. "Family and lineage in contemporary China" (*Dangdai zhongguo de jiating yu zongzu*). In Rong Ma, Xing Zhou, eds. *Fieldwork and culture consciousness (Tianye gongzuo yu wenhua zijue)*. Beijing: Qunyan Publishing House. 〈當代中國的家庭與宗族〉，見馬戎、周星主編《田野工作與文化自覺》。

北京：群言出版社。

Jin, Shenghua 金盛華. 1997. "Personal space and interpersonal connection" (*Renjin kongjian yu renjin jiaowang – weiguan shehui shengtaixue daoyin*). *Sociological Researches* No. 1. 〈人際空間與人際交往 ——微觀社會生態學〉，《社會學研究》第 1 期。

Jin, Zheng 金錚. 1990. *Imperial examination system and Chinese culture* (*Keju zhidu yu zhongguo wenhua*). Shanghai: Shanghai People's Publishing House. 《科舉制度與中國文化》。上海：上海人民出版社。

Jing, Jun 景軍. 1996. The temple of memories: history, power, and morality in a Chinese village, Stanford/California: Stanford University Press.

——. 1998. "Knowledge, Organization, and Symbolic Capital: A Field Study of Two Confucius Temples in Northwest China" (*Zhishi, zuzhi yu xiangzheng ziben-zhongguo beifang liangzuo kongmiao zhi shidi kaocha*). Sociological Research (1): 5-22. 〈知識、組織與象徵資本——中國北方兩座孔廟之實地考察〉，《社會學研究》第一期，第 5-22 頁。

——. *The temple of memories* (*Shentang jiyi*). Trans. Jun Jing. In webpage of Department Sociology, Tsinghua University: http://www.tsinghua.edu.cn/docsn/shxx/site/teacher/jingjun/shentang/temple.htm 《神堂記憶》，景軍譯。載清華大學社會學系網頁。

Johnson, C. L. 1974. "Gift-giving and reciprocity among the Japanese Americans in Honolulu." *American Ethnol* 1(2): pp. 295-308.

Johnson D. ed. 1995. *Ritual and scripture in Chinese popular religion: five studies*. Berkeley, CA: Chinese Popular Culture Project. University of California Press.

Johnson, Elizabeth L.1988. "Grieving for dead, grieving for the living: Funeral Laments of Hakka Women." In J. L. Watson & E. S. Rawski, eds. *Death ritual in late imperial and modern China*. Berkeley: University f California Press.

Johnson, Kay A. 1983. *Women, the family & peasant revolution in China*. Chicago/London: University of Chicago Press.

Johnson, Nathan, and Rawski, eds. 1986. *Popular culture in late imperial China*. Berkeley: University of California Press.

Judd, E. R. 1989. "*Nianjia*: Chinese women and their natal families." *Journal of Asian Studies* 48:3: pp. 525-44.

——. 1990. "Alternative development strategies for women in rural China." *Development and Change* 90:21: pp. 23-42.

——. 1994. *Gender & power in rural North China*. Stanford/California: Stanford University Press.

Kahn, R. L., & Antonucci, T. C. 1980. "Convoys over the life course: Attachment, roles, and social support," pp. 253-86. In Baltes & Brim, eds., *Life-span development and behaviour*. New York: Academic Press.

Kallgren, J. K. 1992. *Strategies for support of the rural elderly in China: a research and policy agenda*. Hong Kong Institute of Asia-Pacific Studies. Hong Gong: The Chinese University of Hong Kong. Kaniasty, K., & Norris, F.H. 1993. "A test of the social support deterioration model in the context of natural disaster." *Journal of Personality and Social Psychology* 64: pp. 395-408.

Kelliher, D. 1993. *Peasant power in China: the era of rural reform, 1979-1989*, New Haven/London: Yale University Press.

Kendig, H. L., Hashimoto, A., & Coppard, L., eds. 1992. *Family support for the elderly: the international experience.* Oxford: Oxford University Press.

Kendig, H.L. & Rowland, D.T. 1983. "Family support of the Australian aged: a comparison with the United States." *Gerontologist* 23 (6): pp. 643-649.

King, Ambrose (Jin Yaoji or Yao-chi) 金耀基. 1989a "An analysis *renqing* in the interpersonal relationships" (*Renji guanxi zhong renqing zhi fenxi*), pp. 75-104. In Guoshu Yang, ed., *Chinese psychology* (*Zhongguoren de xinli*). Taipei: Guiguan Press. 〈人際關係中人情之分析〉，見楊國樞主編《中國人的心理》。臺北：桂冠圖書公司。

——. 1989b. "*Mian, chi* and the Chinese social behaviour" (*Mian, chi yu zhongguoren xingwei zhi fenxi*), pp. 319-345. In Guoshu Yang, ed., *Chinese psychology* (*Zhongguoren de xinli*). Taipei: Guiguan Press. 〈面、恥與中國人行為之分析〉，見楊國樞主編《中國人的心理》。臺北：桂冠圖書公司。

——. 1994. "Kuan-hsi (*Guanxi*) and networks building: a sociological interpretation." In Wei-ming Tu, ed., *The living tree: the changing meaning of being Chinese today.* Stanford: Stanford University Press.

King, A. Yeo-chi and Myers, John. T. 1977. *Shame as an incomplete conception of Chinese culture: a study of face.* Social research centre, Hong Kong: Chinese University of Hong Kong.

Kipnis, Andrew. 1995. " 'Face': An adaptable discourse of social surfaces." *Positions: East Asia Cultures Critique*, 3(1): pp. 119-148.

——. 1997. Producing Guanxi: Sentiment, self, and subculture in a North China village. Durham/London: Duke University.

Knipscheer, C. P. M. & Antonucci, T. C. eds. 1990. *Social network research: substantive issues & methodological questions.* Amsterdam/Lisse: Swets & Zeitlinger B.V.

Komter, A. ed., 1996. "Women, gifts and power." In Komter, A. ed., *The gift: an interdisciplinary perspective*, Amsterdam: Amsterdam University Press.

Korn, F. 1973. Elementary structures reconsidered—Levi-Strauss on kinship. London: Tavistock Publications.

Krackhart, D. 1992. "The Strength of strong ties: the importance of Philos in organizations." In Nitin Nohria & Robert G. Eccles, eds., *Networks and organisation.* Harvard Business School Press.

Kraus, N., Liang, J. 1993. "Stress, social support, and psychological distress among the Chinese elderly." *Journals of Gerontology* 48 (6): pp. 282-91.

Krieg, R. and Schadler, M. Eds. 1994. *Social Security in the People's Republic of China.* Hamburg: Institute fur Asienkunde.

Kristeva, J. 1977/86. (trans. from France, 1974) *About Chinese women.* New York: Marion Boyars.

Kulp, D. H. 1925. *Country Life in South China.* New York: Columbia University Press.

Kuper, A. 1978. "Lineage Theory: A Critical Review." *Annual Review of Anthropology* 11: pp. 71-95.

Labra, Takie Sugiyama. 1969. "Reciprocity and the asymmetric principle: an analytical reappraisal of the Japanese concept of *on.*" *Psychologia* 12: pp. 129-38.

——. 1975. "An alternative approach to reciprocity." *American Anthropologists* 77: pp. 550-65.

Land, H. 1986. "Social support networks." *Social work* 31(1).

Lando, R. P. 1979. The gift of land: irrigation and social structure in a Toba Batak village. Ph.D Dissertation. University of California.

Lang, O. 1946. *Chinese family and society*. New Haven: Yale University Press.

Lavely, W. & Ren, X. 1992. "Patrilocality & early marital co-residence in rural China." *The China Quarterly*130: pp. 378-391.

Leach, Edmund. 1961. Rethinking anthropology. London: The Athlone Press.

——. 1983. *Social anthropology*. London: Fontana Press.

Leach, J.W. & Leach, E. eds. 1983. *The Kula: new perspectives on Massim exchange*. Cambridge: Cambridge University Press.

Lee, M., Lin, H., & Chang, M. 1995. "Living arrangements of the elderly in Taiwan: qualitative evidence."*Journal of Cross-Cultural Gerontology* 10 (1 &2), April.

Legge, James, trans. 1885. *The Li Ki* (Book of Rites), pp65. In The Sacred Books of the East, Max Muller, ed. Vols. 27-28, Oxford: Clarendon Press.

Lein, L. & Sussman, M. B. eds. 1983. *The ties that bind: men's & women's social network*. Hawarth Press.

Leong, Y. K. & Tao, L. K. 1923. *Village & town life in China*. London: George Allen & Unwin.

Levy, Marion J. 1949. The family revolution in modern China, Cambridge: Harvard University Press.

Levi-Strauss, Claude 克勞德‧李維史托. 1949. *The Elemental Structures of Kinship*. Eng. Trans. 1969. Boston, MA: Beacon.

——. 1963. *Structural anthropology*. Trans. Jacobson, C. & Schoepf, B.G., New York: Doubleday Anchor.

——. 1989. *Structural anthropology*. Trans. Xiaohe Lu & Xiguang Huang, at el. Beijing: Culture and Arts Publishing House. 《結構人類學》。陸曉禾、黃錫光等譯。北京：文化藝術出版社。

Lewis, M. 1975. *Friendship & peer relations*. New York: Wiley-Interscience.

Li, Anzhai 李安宅. 1931. The sociological study of the Yili and the Li ji ("Yili" yu "liji" zhi shehuixue de yanjiu). Shanghai: Shanlian Yinshuguan. 《「儀禮」與「禮記」之社會學的研究》上海三聯印書館.

Li, Changping 李昌平. 2002. I speak truthfully to the Primier (Wo xiang zongli shuo shihua). Beijing: Guangming Daily Publishing House. 《我向總理說實話》，北京：光明日報出版社。

Li, Peiliang 李佩良. 1998. "Nuclear model and *chaxu* relationships of Hong Kong families" (*Xianggang jiating de hexin moshi yu chaxu lianxi*). In Rong Ma, Xing Zhou, eds. *Fieldwork and culture consciousness* (*Tianye gongzuo yu wenhua zijue*). Beijing: Qunyan Publishing House. 〈香港家庭的核心模式與差序聯繫〉，見馬戎、周星主編《田野工作與文化自覺》。北京群言出版社。

Li, Peilin 李培林. 1996. "Social network and social status of migration labour" (*Liudong mingong de shehui wangluo he shehui diwei*). *Sociological Researches* 4: pp. 42-52. 〈流動民工的社會網路網絡和社會地位〉，《社會學研究》pp. 42-52。

——. 2004．*Ending of the village (Cunluo de zhongjie)*. Beijing: Shangwu Yinshuguan. 《村落的終結》。北京：商務印書館。

Li, Peilin ed., 李培林主編. 1995. *Social stratification in the market transition in China (Zhongguo xinshiqi jieji jieceng baogao)*. Shenyang: Liaoning People's Publishing house. 《中國新時期階級階層報告》。瀋陽：遼寧人民出版社。

Li, Qingshan 李慶善. 1994. " 'Precautions onself': a maze of Chinese interpersonal actions" ('*Fangren*': *guoren renji jiaowang de wuqu*)". *Sociological Researches* No.3. 〈「防人」：國人人際交往中的誤區〉，《社會學研究》第 3 期。

Li, Renyu & Liu, Kaixiang 李仁愈 劉凱祥. 1995. *Sense of contract and creation of social order* (*Qiyue guannian yu zhixu chuangxi*). Beijing: Peking University Publishing House. 《契約觀念與秩序創新》。北京：北京大學出版社。

Li, Yinhe 李銀河. 1994. *Bearing children and village culture* (*Shenyu yu cunluo wenhua*). Beijing: Chinese Social Sciences Publishing House. 《生育與村落文化》。北京：社會科學出版社。

Li, Yiyuan 李亦園. 1989. "Traditional popular beliefs and modern life" (*Chuantong minjian xinyang yu Xiandai shenghuo*). In Guoshu Yang, ed., *Chinese psychology* (*Zhongguoren de xinli*). Taipei: Taiwan Guiguan Press. 〈傳統民間信仰與現代生活〉，見楊國樞主編《中國人的心理》。臺北：桂冠圖書公司。

——. 1998. "Religions, ritual, and symbolic" (*Zongjiao, yishi yu xiangzheng*). In Rong Ma, Xing Zhou, eds. *Fieldwork and culture consciousness* (*Tianye gongzuo yu wenhua zijue*). Beijing: Qunyan Publishing House. 〈宗教、儀式與象徵〉，見馬戎、周星主編《田野工作與文化自覺》。北京：群言出版社。

——. 1999. Fieldwork portrait – a self-collected work on a life long career of anthropology (Tianye tuxiang-wo de renleixue yanjiu shengya). Jinan: Shangdong Pictorial Publishing House. 《田野圖像—我的人類學研究生涯》。濟南：山東畫報出版社。

Li, Youmei 李友梅. 1996. "The organisation and social environment of family economy in Jiang village" (*Jiangcun jiating jingji de zuzhi yu shehui huanjing*). In Naigu Pan & Rong Ma, eds., *Community studies and social development* (*Shequ yanjiu yu shehui fazhan*). Tianjin: Tianjin People's Publishing House. 〈江村家庭經濟的組織與社會環境〉，潘乃穀、馬戎主編《社區研究與社會發展（上）》，天津：天津人民出版社。

Li, Yu-ning, ed. 1992. *Chinese women through Chinese eyes.* Armonk, NY: M.E. Sharpe.

Li, Zehou 李澤厚.1980. "A re-evaluation of Confucius" (*Kongzi zai pinglun*). *Chinese Social Science* No. 2: pp. 77-96. 〈孔子再評論〉，《中國社會科學》第 2 期。

——. 1985. On the history of ancient Chinese thoughts (Zhongguo gudai sixiangshi lun). Beijing: People's Publishing House.《中國古代思想史論》。北京：人民出版社。

——. 1979. On the history of contemporary Chinese thoughts (Zhongguo gudai sixiangshi lun). Beijing: People's Publishing House.《中國近代思想史論》。北京：人民出版社。

Liang, Zhiping 梁治平.1997. "Law and order in popular society"(Xiangtu shehui zhong de falu yu zhixu). In Mingming Wang & S. Feuchtwang, eds., Order, justice, and authority of popular society (Xiangtu shehui de zhixu, gongzheng yu quanwei). Beijing: Chinese Political and legal University Publishing House. 〈鄉土社會中的法律與秩序〉，見王銘銘、王斯福主編《鄉土社會中的秩序、公正與權威》。北京：中國政法大學出版社。

Liang, Shuming 梁漱溟. 1922/94. "Culture and philosophy between the East and the West" (Dongxi wenhua jiqi zhexue). In Jingqing Cao, ed., The road of Confucius' rejuvenation – Sellected work of Liang Shuming (Ruxue fuxing zhilu – Liang Shuming wenxuan). Shanghai: Far East Publishing House. 〈東西文化及其哲學〉，見曹景清《儒學復興之路——梁漱溟文選》。上海：遠東出版社。

——. 1949/95. *The main ideas of Chinese culture* (*Zhongguo wenhua yaoyi*). Shanghai: Xuelin Publishing House. 《中國文化要義》。上海：學林出版社。

——. 1975/94. *Mind, Heart and life* (*Rexin yu rensheng*). Shanghai: Xuelin Publishing House. 《人心與人生》。上海：學林出版社。

Lin, Nan 林南. 1982. "Social resources and instrumental action", in Marsden, P. V. & Lin, Nan, eds, *Social structure and network analysis*. Sage Publications.

——. 1983. "Social resources & social actions: a progress report." *Connection* 6(2): pp. 10-16.

——. 1986. "Modeling the effect of social support." In N. Lin; A. Dean & W.M. Ensel, eds., *Social support, life events, and depression*. Orlando, FL: Academic Press.

——. 1990. "Social resources and social mobility: a structure theory of status attainment," pp. 247-71. In R. Breiger, ed., *Social mobility and social structure*. Cambridge University Press.

Lin, N. & Dean, A. & Ensel, W.M. eds. 1986. *Social support, life events, and depression*. Orlando, FL: Academic Press.

Lin, N. Ensel, W. M., & Vaughn, J. C. 1981. "Social resources and strength of ties: structural factors in occupational status attainment." *American Sociological Review* 46.

Lin, J.Y. 1990.Collectivization and China's agricultural crisis in 1959–1961. *Journal of Political Economy* 98 6 (1990), pp. 1228–1252.

Lin, J.Y. and Yang, D.T. 1988. On the causes of China's agricultural crisis and the great leap famine. *China Economic Review*. Volume 9, Issue 2, Autumn, Pages 125-140.

——. 2000. Food availability, entitlements, and the Chinese famine of 1959–1961. *Economic Journal*. Volume 110, Issue 460, pp:136-158.

Lin, Yueh-Hwa (Lin Yaohua) 林耀華. 1948. *The Golden Wing: A sociological study of Chinese familism*. London: Kegan Paul, Trench, Trubner & Co.

——. 2000. *The Golden Wing: A sociological study of Chinese familism*. Trans. Kongshao Zhuang & Zongcheng Lin. Beijing: Sanlian Shudian. 《金翼——中國家族制度的社會學研究》，莊孔韶、林宗成譯。北京：三聯書店。

Lin, Yutang 林語堂. 1935. *My country and my people*. New York: John Day Company.

——. 1994. *My country and my people* (*Zhongguoren*). Trans. Zhidong Hao & Yihong Shen. Shanghai: Xuelin Publishing House. 《中國人》。郝志東、沈益洪譯。上海：學林出版社。

Lin, Xudian 林徐典. 1995. Looking backward and forward of sinology studies (Hanxue yanjiu zhi huigu yu qianzhan). Beijing: Zhonghua Shuju. 《漢學研究之回顧與前瞻》。北京：中華書局。

Li Puma, E. 1988. *The gift of kinship: structure and practice in Maring social organization*. Cambridge/New York el.: Cambridge University Press.

Little, V.C. et. al. 1983. "International symposium: the family as a support for elderly." *Gerontologist* 23(6): pp. 573-596.

Liu, Guangming 劉廣明. 1993. *Patriarchal lineage Chinese Society* (*Zongfa zhongguo*). Shanghai: Sanlian shudian. 《宗法中國》。上海：三聯書店。

Liu, Guangming & Wang, Zhiyue 劉廣明、王志躍. 1995. *A criticism of Chinese traditional personalities* (*Zhongguo chuantong renge pipan*). Nanjing: Jiangsu People's Publishing House. 《中國傳統人格批判》。南京：江蘇人民出版社。

Liu, Haoxing 劉豪興. 1996. "Between agriculture and industry – a survey of 60 years in Jiang village" (*Nonggong zhijian – jiangcun fuye 60nian de diaocha*). In Naigu Pan & Rong Ma, eds., *Community studies and social development* (*Shequ yanjiu yu shehui fazhan*). Tianjin: Tianjin People's Publishing House. 〈農工之間——江村副業 60 年的調查〉，潘乃穀、馬戎主編，《社區研究與社會發展(上)》。天津：天津人民出版社。

Liu, Shipei 劉師培. "On changes in contemporary sinology" (*Jindai hanxue bianqian lun*). "*Journal of the quintessence of a country*" (Guocui xuebao) No 31. 〈近代漢學變遷論〉，《國粹學報》第 31 期。

Liu, W.T. 1986. "Culture & social support." *Research on Aging* 8(1): pp. 57-83.

Liu, Xin 劉新. 1995. Zhao villagers — everyday practices in a post-reform Chinese village. Ph.D. Dissertation. SOAS, London University.

——. 2000. In one's own shadow: An ethnographic account of the condition of post-reform rural China. Berkeley & Los Angeles: University of California Press.

Liu, Ying 劉英. 1986. "Initial analysis of Tianjin Huningrong neighbourhood in the five-cities family survey" (*Tianjin Huningrong wu chengshi jiating diaocha chuxi*). *Sociological Researches* 4. 〈天津 Huningrong 五城市家庭鄰裏調查初析〉，《社會學研究》第 4 期。

Liu, Ying, Xue Shuzhen, eds., 劉英、薛素珍等主編.1987. *Studies of Chinese marriage and family* (*Zhongguo hunyin jiating yanjiu*). Beijing: Social Science Documents Publishing House. 《中國婚姻家庭研究》。北京：社科文獻出版社。

Lomnitz, L.A. 1988. "Informal Exchange Networks in Formal Systems: A Theoretical Model." *American Anthropologist* 90: pp. 42-55.

Long, N. & Long, A. eds. 1992. Battlefields of knowledge: the interlocking of theory and practice in social research and development. London: Routledge.

Loscocco, K. A., & Spitze, G. 1990. Working conditions, social support, and the well–being of female and male factory workers. *Journal of Health and Social behaviour* 31, pp. 313-27.

Lu, Dequan 陸德全. 1991. "Guanxi–An exchange form in contemporary Chinese society" (*Guanxi – dangdai zhongguo shehui de jiaohuan xingtai*). *Sociology and Social survey* No 5. 〈關係——當代中國社會的交換形態〉，《社會學與社會調查》No 5。

Lu, Feiyun 陸緋芸. 1993. "An investigation into social support and security in Jinxing village and Kaixiangong village in Wujiang County, Jiangsu Province", A paper for the conference of the City University project funded by ESRC on "Rural Social Support Arrangements & the Transformation of Local Traditions in China." July.

Lu, Wei 魯威. 1990. *Absurd writing of the Imperial official examination system* (*Keju qiwen*). Shenyang: Liaoning Educational Publishing House. 《科舉奇聞》。瀋陽：遼寧教育出版社。

Lu, Xueyi. ed. 陸學藝主編. 1992. *Rural areas and peasants in social reform* (*Gaige zhong de nongcun yu nongmin*). Beijing: CCP School Publishing House. 《改革中的農村與農民》。北京：中央黨校出版社。

——. ed.1993. *Traditional agricultural country's social transition* (*Chuantong nongyexian de shehui zhuanxing*). Beijing: Beijing Agricultural University Publishng House. 《傳統農業縣的社會轉型》。北京：北京農業大學出版社。

Lu, Xun 魯迅. 1973. "On mianzi" (S*huo mianzi*), pp. 127-130. In *The complete works of Lu Xun* Vol. 6. Beijing: People's Literature Publishing House. 〈說面子〉，見《魯迅全集》第 6 卷。北京：人民文學出版社。

Luo, Guojie, ed., 羅國傑.1995. Chinese traditional morality: 5 volumes (*Zhongguo chuantong daode*). Beijing: Chinese People's University Publishing House. 《中國傳統道德（五卷本）》。北京：中國人民大學出版社。

Luo, Hanxian.1985. *Economic changes in rural China*. Beijing: New world press.

Luo, Hongguang 羅紅光. 1995. "Forming of social classes: a case study of Yangjiagou village, Shanxi province" (*Shanbei mizhi xian Yangjiagou cun jieceng xingcheng de baogao*). In Peilin Li, ed., *Social stratification in the market transition in China*. Shenyang: Liaoning People's Publishing House. 〈陝北米脂縣楊家溝村階層形成的報告〉，見李培林主編《中國新時期階級階層報告》。瀋陽：遼寧人民出版社。

——. 1997. "The exchange of moral—soul: an analysis on ritualization of wealth in rural northern China"

(*Daode linghun de jiaohuan*). In Xing Zhou & Mingming Wang, eds., *Collection of social cultural anthropology* (*Shehui wenhua releixue jiangyan ji*). Tianjin: Tianjin People's Publishing House. 〈道德靈魂的交換〉，見周星、王銘銘主編《社會文化人類學講演集》。天津：天津人民出版社。

——. 2000. Exchange of unequal values: wealth around the work and consumption (*Bu dengjia jiaojuan: weirao caifu de laodong yu xiaofei*). Hangzhou: Zhejiang people's publishing house. 《不等價交換——圍繞財富的勞動與消費》。杭州：浙江人民出版社。

Lynam, M. J. 1985. "Support networks developed by immigrant women." *Social Science & Medicine* 21(3): pp. 327-333.

Ma, Guoqing 麻國慶. 1998. "Family and society in a Huabei village – A discussion from a case study in Beiwang village, Hebei" (*Huabei cunluo de jia yu shehui – cong hebei beiwangcun gean tan'qi*). In Rong Ma & Xing Zhou, eds. *Fieldwork and culture consciousness* (*Tianye gongzuo yu wenhua zijue*). Beijing: Qunyan Publishing House. 〈華北村落的家與社會——從河北北王村個案談起〉，見馬戎、周星主編《田野工作與文化自覺》。北京：群言出版社。

——. 1999. "Family division: there are some things inherited and somethings shared after the division" (*Fenjia: fen zhong you ji ye you he*). *Sociological Researches* No.1. 〈分家：分中有繼也有合〉，《社會學研究》第一期。

MacCormack, G. 1976. "Reciprocity." *Man* 11: pp. 89-103.

Macaulay, S. 1963. "Non-contractual relations in business." *American sociological Review* 28: pp. 55-67.

Madsen, Richard. 1984. *Morality and power in a Chinese Village*. Berkeley/Los Angeles/London: University of California Press.

Maguire, L. 1983. *Understanding social networks*. Bevely Hills/ CA: Sage Publications.

Mai, Gaiwem J. [英] 麥高溫. 1998. *Men and manners in modern China* (*Zhongguoren shenghuo de ming yu an*). Originally published in English in Shanghai in 1909 and in England afterwards. Trans. Tao Zhu & Jing Ni. Beijing: Current Affairs Publishing House (*Shishi Chubanshe*). 《中國人生活的明與暗》，朱濤、倪靜譯。北京：時事出版社。

Mai Tianshu 麥天樞. 1998. *Guesses in Heaven— A new route to learn China* (*Renshi zhongguo de yitiao xin lu*). Beijing: Sanlian Shudian. 《天國猜想——認識中國的一條新路》。北京：三聯書店。

Majumder, A. 1987. Poverty, development and exchange relations. Radiant Publishers.

Malinowski, B. 1922. *Argonauts of the western Pacific*. London: Routledge.

——. 1944. *A scientific theory of culture*. New York: Galaxy Books.

Marsden, P. V. 1982. "Brokerage behaviour in restricted exchange networks." In P. V. Marsden & Nan Lin, eds., *Social structure and network analysis*. Sage Publications.

——. 1987. "Core discussion networks of America." *American Sociological review* 52.

——. 1990. "Network data and measurement." *Annual Review of Sociology* 16.

Marsden, P. V. and Lin, N. eds. 1982. *Social structure and network analysis*. Beverly Hill, Calif.: Sage.

Marsden, P. V., & Campbell, K. E. 1984. "Measuring tie strength." *Social Forces* 63.

Marsden, P. V., & Hurlbert, J. S. 1988. "Social resources and mobility outcomes: a replication and extension." *Social forces* 66.

Marsh, C.; Arber, S. 1992. *Families and households: divisions and change*. New York: Saint

Martin's Press.

Marshall, Gordon, ed. 1994. *The Concise Oxford Dictionary of Sociology*. Oxford/New York: Oxford University Press.

Martin, Emily. 1981. *Chinese ritual & politics*. Cambridge: Cambridge University Press.

——. 1988. "Gender and ideological difference in representations of life and death." In J. L. Watson & E. S. Rawski, eds., *Death ritual in late imperial and modern China*. Berkeley: University of California Press.

Mauss, Mircel. 1950/90. *The Gift*, Trans. Halls, W.D., (original in France, 1950), London: Routledge.

——. 1972. *A General theory of Magic*. Trans. Brain R., (original in France, 1950), London/Boston: Routledge & Kegan Paul.

Mayo, Mlton. 1933. *The Human Problems of an Industrial Civilization*. Cambridge, Mass: Harvard University Press.

——. 1945. *The social problems of an industrial civilization*. London: Routledge and Kegan Paul.

McCallister, L. & Fischer, C. 1978. "A procedure for surveying personal networks." *Sociological methods and research* 7.

McDougal, C. 1979. The kulunge Rai: a study in kinship and marriage exchange. Kathmandu: Ratna Pustak Bhandar.

McDowell, L. & Pringle, R. eds. 1992. *Defining women: social institutions and gender divisions*. Cambridge: Polity Press.

McGee, R. J. & Warms, R. L. eds. 1996. *Anthropological theory: an introductory history*, London: Mayfield Publishing Company.

Mckenzie R. 1926. "The ecological approach to the study of human community." In Park & Burgess, eds., *The city*. Chicago: University of Chicago Press.

McKinley, T. 1995. The distribution of wealth in rural China, M. E. Sharpe.

McNeill, Daniel, 1998. *The face*. New York: Little, Brown & Co.

——. 1998. *The face* (*Miankong*). Trans. Jichao Wang; Heng Liu & Yi Shi. Beijing: China Freidship Publishing Corporation. 《面孔》，王積超、劉珩、石毅譯。北京：中國友誼出版公司。

Meredith, W. H. & Abbot, D. A. 1995. "Chinese family in later life," pp. 213-230. In S. Smith, ed., *Families in multicultural perspective*. New York: Guilford Press.

Michekke, Z. R. el. at. eds., 1974. *Women, culture and societies*. Stanford: Stanford University Press.

Miller, Daniel; Jackson, Peter; Thrift, Nigel; Holbrook, Beverly and Rowlands, Michael. 1998. *Shopping, Place and Identity*. Routledge.

Mitchell, J.C. 1969. "The Concept and Use of Social Networks." In J.C. Mitchell, ed., *Social Networks in Urban Situations*. Manchester: Manchester University Press.

——. 1969. *Social networks in urban situations*. Manchester: Manchester University Press.

——. 1973. "Networks, Norms and Institutions." In J. C. Mitchell and Boissevain, eds., *Network Analysis: Studies in Human Interaction*. The Hague: Mouton.

Mead, G. H. 1934. Mind, self, society from the standpoint of social behaviourists. Chicago: UP Chicago.

Mitter, S. 1986. Common fate, common bond —women in the global economy. London: Pluto.

Mogey, J. M. 1956. *Family & neighbourhood—two studies in Oxford*. Oxford: Oxford University Press.

Momsen, J. H. 1991/93. *Women and development in the third world*. London/New York: Routledge.

Montgomery, J. D. 1994. "Weak ties, employment, and inequality: an equilibrium analysis." *American Journal Sociology* Vol. 99, No. 5.

Moore, H. L. 1988/94. *Feminism and anthropology*. Cambridge: Polity Press.

Moreno, J. L.1934. *Who Shall Survive?* New York: Beacon Press.

Morton, K.L. 1973. *Kinship, economics and exchange in Tongan village*. Ann Arbor: University Microfilms.

Mugford, S.; Kendig, H. 1984. "Social relations: networks and ties," pp. 38-59. In H. Kendig, eds. *Ageing and Families: a social networks perspective*. Sydney: Allen and Uniwin.

Naquin, Susan. 1988. "Funerals in North China: uniformity and variation." In J. Watson and E. Rawski, eds., *Death ritual in late imperial and modern China*. Berkeley and Los Angeles: University of California Press.

Naran, R. V. 1991. The Social support system and social network characteristics of a group of low-income single mothers identified as users and non-users of social services. Pretoria: The HSRC Publishers.

NBS (National Bureau of Statistics, also see SSB) 國家統計局. 2002. *China statistical yearbook* (*Zhongguo tongji nianjian*). Beijing: China statistical Publishing House. 《中國統計年鑑》。北京：中國統計出版社。

Nee, V. 1991. Social exchange and political process in Maoist China. New York/London: Garland Publishing.

Needham, R. ed. 1971. *Rethinking kinship and marriage*. London: Tavistock.

Netzer, D. 1978. *The subsidised muse: public support for the arts in the United States*. Cambridge/London/New York: Cambridge University Press.

Nicholson, L. 1986/94. "Feminism and Marx: integrating kingship with the economic," pp. 16-30. In S. Benhabib & D. Cornell, eds., *Feminism as critique*. Cambridge: Polity Press.

Nie, Lili 聶莉莉. 1996. "Exam Confucius culture through a small tradition" (*Cong xiao chuantong kan rujia wenhua de yingxiang*). In Naigu Pan & Rong Ma, eds., *Community studies and social development* (*Shequ yanjiu yu shehui fazhan*). Tianjin: Tianjin People's Publishing House. 〈從小傳統看儒家文化的影響〉，潘乃穀、馬戎主編，《社區研究與社會發展》。天津：天津人民出版社。

Ning, Yegao; Ning, Yequan & Ning, Telong 甯業高、甯業泉、甯業龍.1995. *Discussions on Chinese filial culture* (*Zhongguo xiao wenhua mantan*). Beijing: Chinese Nationalities University Publishing House. 《中國孝文化漫談》。北京：中央民族大學出版社。

Oi, Jean. 1989. State and peasant in contemporary China: the political economy of village government. Berkely: University of California Press.

——. 1999. Rural China Takes Off: The Institutional Foundations of Economic Reform. Berkeley: University of California Press.

Olson, Philip. 1986. "A model of eldercare in the People's Republic of China." *International Journal of Aging & Human Development* 1986-87, 24(4): pp. 279-300.

Omari, C.K. 1988. Rural women, informal sector, and household economy in Tanzania. Helsinki:

WIDER.

Orcutt, G., Merz, J. & Quinke, H., eds. 1986. *Microanalytic simulation models to support social and financial policy*. Amsterdam/New York/Oxford: North-Holland.

Oxley, D., Haggard, L. M., Werner, C. M., & Altman, I. 1986. "Transactional qualities of neighbourhood social networks: a case study of 'Christmas street'." *Environment & behavior* 18(5): pp. 640-677.

Paci, M. 1987. "Long waves in the development of welfare systems." In C.S. Maier, ed. *Changing boundaries of the political*. Cambridge: Cambridge University Press.

Pahl, J. 1991/94. "Money and power in marriage," pp. 41-57. In P. Abbott & C. Wallace, eds., *Gender, Power & Sexuality*. Houndmills/London: The MaCmillan Press Ltd.

Pan, Guangdan 潘光旦. 1947. "On *lun*" (*Shuo lun zi*). *Social Studies* No. 19. 〈說侖字〉，《社會研究》第 19 期。

——. 1995. *A selected work of Pan Guangdan, Vol. I* (*Pan Guangdan wenji*). Beijing: Peking University Publishing House. 《潘光旦文集》第一卷。北京：北京大學出版社。

Pan, Yunkang, ed., 潘允康.1987. *Chinese urban marriages and families* (*Zhongguo chengshi hunyin yu jating*). Jinan: Shandong People's Publishing House. 《中國城市婚姻與家庭》。濟南：山東人民出版社。

Pan, Yunkang & Lin, Nan. 1987. "A model of contemporary Chinese urban families (*Zhongguo chengshi xiandai jiating moshi*)." *Sociological Researches* 3.

Parish, W. L. & Whyte, M. K. 1978. *Village and family in contemporary China*. Chicago/London: University of Chicago Press.

Parish, W. L. 1985. *Chinese rural development*. M. E. Sharpe, Inc.

Parsons, Talcott. 1937/49. *The structure of social action*, pp. 550-51.Glencoe, IL: The Free Press.

——. 1963. *Essays in sociological theory*, p. 230. New York: Free Press.

——. 1966. *Societies: evolutionary and comparative perspectives*, pp.5.Englewood Cliffs, New Jersey: Prentice-Hall.

Parsons, T. and Shils, E. 1951. *Toward a general theory of action*. Cambridge: Harvard University Press.

Pasternak, Burton. 1969. "The Role of Frontier in Chinese Lineage Development." *Journal of Asian Studies* 28: pp. 551-61.

——. 1972. *Kinship and Community in Two Chinese Villages*. Stanford/California: Stanford University Press.

——. 2000. "The disquieting Chinese lineage and its anthropological relevance." In J. Hsieh, et. al. eds. *The Chinese family and its ritual behaviour*. Taipei: Institute of Ethnology, Academia Sinica.

Payne, M. 1991. *Modern social work theory*. London: Macmillan.

Payne, R. L. & Jones, J. G. 1987. "Measurement and methodological issues in social support," pp. 167-205. In S.V. Kasl & C.L. Cooper, eds., *Stress and health: issues in research methodology*. New York: John Wiley.

Pearson, R. E. 1990. Counselling & social support: perspectives & practice. Newbury Park: Sage.

Peng, X.Z. 1987. Demographic consequences of the Great Leap Forward in China's provinces.

Population and Development Review 13 4 (1987), pp. 639–670.

Pieke, Frank 彭軻. 1996. *The ordinary and the extraordinary*. London/New York: Kegan Paul International.

——. 2001. "Nativization: new relevance and equality strategy of China's anthropology." In Jieshun Xu, ed., *Nativization: the great trend of anthropology (Bentuhua:renleixue de da qushi)*. Nanning: Guangxi Nationality Publishing house. 〈本土化：中國人類學追求新的關聯與平等的策略〉，見徐傑舜主編，《本土化：人類學的大趨勢》。南寧：廣西民族出版社。

Pilisuk, M., Boylan, R., & Acredolo, C. 1987. "Social support, life stress, and subsequent medical care utilization." *Health Psychology* 6: pp. 273-288.

Poel, M. G. M. 1993. "Delineating personal support networks." *Social Networks* 15: pp. 49-70.

Polanyi, Karl. 1957. *The great transformation*. Beacon Hill/Boston: Beacon Press.

——. 1968. *Primitive, archaic and modern economies*. Garden city/New York: Doubleday & Company, Inc.

Popkin, S. L. 1979. *The Rational Peasant*. Berkeley: University of California Press.

Potter, J. M. 1968. Capitalism and the Chinese Peasant: social and economic change in a Hong Kong village. Berkeley: University of California Press.

——. 1970 "Land and Lineage in Traditional China," pp. 121-138. In M. Freedman, ed., *Family and Kinship in China Society*. Stanford: Stanford University Press.

Potter, Salamith, H. 1983. "The position of peasants in modern China's social order." *Modern China* 9, 4: pp. 465-499.

Potter, Salamith and Jack. 1990/93. *China's peasants: the anthropology of a revolution*. Cambridge University Press.

Procidano, M.E. & Heller, K. 1983. "Measures of perceived social support from friends & from family: three validation studies." *American Journal of Community Psychology* 11(1): pp. 1-24.

Pynoos, J., Hade-Kaplan, B., & Fleisher, D. 1984. "Intergenerational neighbourhood networks: a basis for aiding the frail elderly." *Gerontologist* 24(3): pp. 233-237.

Qian, Wenbao. 1996. Rural-Urban migration and its impact on economic development in China. Aldershot: Avebury Ashgate Publishing Ltd.

Qiang, Shigong; Zhao, Xiaoli & Zheng, Ge 強世功、趙曉力、鄭戈. 1997. "Comments on a legal practice event" (*Yixiang falu shijian shijian de pinglun*). In Mingming Wang & S. Feuchtwang, eds., *Order, justice, and authority of popular society (Xiangtu shehui de zhixu, gongzheng yu quanwei)*. Beijing: Chinese Political and legal University Publishing House. 〈一項法律實踐事件的評論〉，見王銘銘、王斯福主編《鄉土社會中的秩序、公正與權威》。北京：中國政法大學出版社。

Qiao, Jian (Chiao, Chien) 喬健. 1989. "A preliminary discussion of *guanxi*" (*Guanxi chuyi*). In Guoshu Yang, ed., *Chinese psychology (Zhongguoren de xinli)*. Taipei: Taiwan Guiguan Press. 〈關係芻議〉，見楊國樞主編，《中國人的心理》。臺北：桂冠圖書公司。

——. 1999. The immutability of vagabondize – anthropological fieldwork notes (Piaobo zhong de yongheng-renleixue tianyue diaocha biji). Jinan: Shangdong Pictorial Publishang House. 《飄泊中的永恆——人類學田野調查筆記》。濟南：山東畫報出版社。

Qiao, Yan 喬岩. 1999. "What is 'Permanent resident overseas' and 'Citizenship of foreign countries'?—related PRC policies to Overseas Chinese (I) " (*Hewei 'huaqiao', 'waiji huaren'? Zhongguo dui huaren huaqiao youguan zhengce wenda (I)*). *People's Daily* (Overseas) 17th Dec. 〈何謂「華僑」、「外籍華人」？

中國對華人華僑有關政策問答（一）〉，《人民日報海外版》12 月 17 日。

Qin, Hui 秦暉. 1999. What a cultivator said: a self-collected work on peasant studies (Gengyunzhe yan- yige nongminxue yanjiuzhe de xinlu). Jinnan: Shangdong Educational Publishing House. 《耕耘者言：一個農民學研究者的心路》。濟南：山東教育出版社。

Qin, Hui; Su Wen 秦暉、蘇文.1996. Pastorals and rhapsodies: research for peasant societies and peasant culture (Tianyuanshi yu kuangxiangqu: guanzhong moshi yu qianjindai shehui de zai renshi). Beijing: Central Compilation and Translation Press.《田園詩與狂想曲——關中模式與前近代社會的再認識》。北京：中央編譯出版社。

Quittner, A. L., Glueckauf, R. L., & Jackson, D. N. 1990. "Chronic parenting stress: Moderating versus mediating effects of social support." *Journal of Personality and Social Psychology* 59: pp. 1266-78.

Radcliffe-Brow, A. R. 1930-31. "The social organisation of Australian tribes." *Oceania* 1: pp. 34-63, pp. 206-246, pp. 322-341, pp. 426-456.

——. 1940. "On social structure." Journal of the Royal Anthropology Society of Great Britain and Ireland 70: pp. 1-12.

——. 1940/52. *Structure and function in primitive society*, pp.190, 200. London: Cohen & West.

Raheja, Gloria G. 1988. The poison in the gift: ritual, prestation, and the dominant caste in a North India village. Chicago: University of Chicago Press.

Rai, S.; Pilkington, H. & Phizacklea, A. eds. 1992. *Women in the face of change: the Soviet Union, Eastern Europe and China*. London/New York: Routledge.

Reiter, R. ed. 1975. *Toward an anthropology of women*. New York: Monthly Review Press.

Ren, Jiyu 任繼愈. 1963. *A history of Chinese philosophy, 4 volumes (Zhongguo zhexue shi)*. Beijing: People's Publishing House. 《中國哲學史：4 卷本》。北京：人民出版社。

——. 1995. "Sinological studies in China" (*Hanxue yanjiu zai zhongguo*). In Xudian Lin, ed., *Looking backward and forward of sinology studies (Hanxue yanjiu zhi huigu yu qianzhan)*. Beijing: Zhonghua Shuju. 〈漢學研究在中國〉，見林徐典主編，《漢學研究之回顧與前瞻》。北京：中華書局。

Ritzer, George. 1996. *Sociological theory* (fourth edition). New York, etc.: The Mcgraw-hill Companies, Inc.

Roberts, P. C. and Stephenson, M. A.. 1983. *Marx's theory of exchange, alienation, and crisis*. New York: Praeger Publishers.

Rogers, Vertovec, Gledhill, Kapferer and Bender, eds. 1995. *The urban context: ethnicity, social networks and situational analysis*. Oxford/Washington D.C.: Berg Publishers.

Roloff, M. E. 1982. *Interpersonal communication: the social exchange approach*. Beverly Hills CA: Sage Publications.

Rook, K.S. & Dooley, D. 1985. "Applying social support research: theoretical problems & future directions." *Journal of Social Issues* 41(1): pp. 5-28.

Rosaldo, M. Z. & Lamphere L. 1973/93. *Women, culture & society*. Stanford / California: Stanford University Press.

Rosel, N. 1983. "The hub of a wheel: a neighbourhood support network." *International Journal of Aging Human Development* 16(3): pp. 193-200.

Ross, Edward Alsworth. 1911. The changing Chinese: the conflict of oriental and western cultures in

China. The Century Co.

———. 1998. *The changing Chinese: the conflict of oriental and western cultures in China* (*Bianhua zhong de Zhongguoren*). Trans. Maohong Gong and Hao Zhang. Beijing: Current Affairs Publishing House.《變化中的中國人》，公茂虹、張皓譯。北京：時事出版社。

Ruan, Danqing 阮丹青. 1993. "Interpersonal networks and workplace controls in urban China." *The Australian Journal of Chinese Affairs* 29: pp. 89-105.

———. 1998. "The content of the GSS discussion network: an exploration of GSS discussion name generator in a Chinese context." *Social Network* 20.

Ruan, D.; Freeman, L.C.; Dai, X.; Pan, Y. & Zhang, W. 1997. "On the changing structure of social networks in urban China." *Social Networks* 19: pp. 75-89.

Ruan D, Zhou Lu, P. M. Blau, A. G. Walder. 1990. "Initial analysis of resident social networks in Tianjin" (*Tianjin chengshi jumin shehuiwang chuxi*). *Chinese Social Science* 2: 157-76. 〈天津城市社會網初析〉，《中國社會科學》，第二期。

Russell, Bertrand 伯特蘭‧羅素. 1922. *The problem of China*. London: Allen and Unwin.

———. 1996. *The problem of China* (*Zhongguo wenti*). Trans. Yue Qin. Shanghai: Xuelin Publishing House.《中國問題》。秦悅譯。上海：學林出版社。

Saari, J.L. 1982.   "Breaking the hold of tradition: the self-group interface in transitional China." In S. L. Greenblatt; R. W. Wilson & A. A. Wilson, eds., *Social Interaction in Chinese society*. Praeger.

Sahlins, Marshall 馬歇爾‧薩林斯. 1965a. "On the sociology of primitive exchange." In Michael Banton ed., *The relevance of models for social anthropology*. London: Tavistock Publications.

———. 1965b "Exchange-value and the diplomacy of primitive trade," pp. 95-129. In June Helm, ed, *Essays in economic anthropology: dedicated to the memory of Karl Polanyi*. Seattle: The University of Washington Press.

———. 1972/74. *Stone age economics*. London: Tavistock Publications.

———. 1996. "The sadness of sweetness: the native anthropology of Western Cosmology with CA* comments", pp. 395-428. *Current Anthropology* Vol 37 (3). The University of Chicago Press.

———. 2000. "The sadness of sweetness: the native anthropology of Western Cosmology with CA* comments" (*Tianmin de bei'ai*). Trans. Mingming Wang & Zongze Hu. Beijing: Sanlian Shudian.《甜蜜的悲哀》。王銘銘、胡宗澤譯。北京：三聯書店。

Said, Edward W. 愛德華 W.‧薩義德. 1978. *Orientalism*. London: Routledge & Kegan Paul Ltd.

———. 1999. *Orientalism* (*Dongfangxue*). Trans. Yugen Wang. Beijing: Sanlian Shudian.《東方學》，王宇根譯。北京：三聯書店。

Saifuddin, A. F. 1992. Stability and change: a study of support networks and household flexibility among the poor of Jakarta, Indonesia. Ph.D. Dessertation. University of Pittsburgh.

Saith, A. ed. 1987. *The re-emergence of the Chinese peasantry*. London: Croom Helm.

Sainiya 賽妮亞. ed. 2002. *The myth of rural philosophy* (*Xiangcun zhexue de shenhua*). Wulumuqi: Xinjiang People's Publishing House.《鄉村哲學的神話》。烏魯木齊：新疆人民出版社。

Sandison, H. R. & Williams, eds. 1981. *Tax policy and private support for the arts in USA, Canada and UK*. A publication of British American Arts Association (USA & UK), Washington, D. C./London.

Sangren, P. S. 1987. "Orthodoxy, heterodoxy, and the structure of value in Chinese rituals." *Modern China* 13: 1: pp. 63-89.

——. 1987. History and magical power in a Chinese village. Stanford: Stanford University.

Sarason, I. G., Sarason, B. R. eds. 1985. *Social support: theory, research and applications.* Dordrecht Boston/Lancaster: Martinus Nijhoff Publishers.

Sarason, I. G., Sarason, B. R. & Pierce, G. R. eds. 1990. *Social support: an interactional view.* New York/Chichester/Brisance el. at: John Wiley & Sons.

Sauer, W. J. & Coward, R. T. eds., 1985. *Social support networks & the care of the elderly: theory, research, & practice.* New York: Springer Publishing Company.

Scheirer, M. A. 1983. "Household structure among welfare families: correlates & consequences." *Journal of Marriage & the Family* 45(4): pp. 761-771.

Schilling, R. F. 1987. "Limitations of social support." *Social Service Review* 61(1): pp. 19-31.

Schipper, K. 1977. "Neighbourhood cult associations in traditional Tainan," pp. 651-676. In Skinner, ed., *The city in late imperial China.* Stanford University Press.

Schoppa, K. 1990. "Power, legitimacy, and symbol," pp. 140-161. In Esherick and Rankin, eds., *Chinese local elites and patterns of dominance.* University of California Press.

Schrift, A.D. 1996. Logic of the gift: towards an ethics of generosity. London: Routledge.

Schusky, E. L. 1965. *Manual for kinship analysis*, New York/London et.: Holt, Rinehart and Winston, Inc.

Schuster, T. L. 1988. "Social networks or social support: clarification & consequences." Dissertation Abstracts International, A: *The Humanities & Social Sciences* 49(4): p. 958.

Schweizer, Thomas. 1991. "The power struggle in a Chinese community, 1950-80: A social network analysis of the duality of actors and events." *Journal of Quantitative Anthropology* 3: pp. 19-44.

——. 1996. "Actor and event orderings across time: lattice representation and Boolean analysis of political disputes in Chen Village, China." *Social Networks* 18: pp. 247-266.

Schweizer, T. el., 1993. "Ritual as action in a Javanese community: a network perspective on ritual and social structure." *Social Networks* 15: pp. 19-48.

Scott, John. 1991/94. *Social network analysis: a handbook.* London/Thousand Oaks/ New Delhi: Sage Publication.

Seabrook, J. 1984. The idea of neighbourhood—what local politics should be about. London: Pluto Press.

Seed, Philip. 1987. Applied social network analysis: a set of tools for social services research and practical. Kent: D. J. Costello Publishers Ltd.

——. 1990. *Introducing network analysis in social work.* London: Jessica Kingsley Publishers.

Selden, M. 1993. "Family strategies and structures in rural north China." In D. David and S. Harrell, eds., *Chinese families in the post-Mao era.* Berkeley: University of California Press.

Shanin, T. ed. 1987. *Peasants and peasant societies.* London: Penguin Books.

——. 1990. *Defining peasants.* Basil Blackwell.

Shen, Guanbao 沈關寶. 1993. A quiet revolution: village industry and society in South Jiangsu province

(Yichang jingqiaoqiao de geming: sunan xiangcun de gongye yu shehui). Kunming: Yunnan People's Publishing House. 《一場靜悄悄的革命：蘇南鄉村的工業與社會》。昆明：雲南人民出版社.

——. 1995. "Jiang village economy before liberation and land reform" (*Jiefangqiang de jiangcun jingjin yu tudi gaige*). In Naigu Pan & Rong Ma, eds., *Community studies and social development* (*Shequ yanjiu yu shehui fazhan*). Tianjin: Tianjin People's Publishing House. 〈解放前的江村經濟與土地改革〉，潘乃毅、馬戎主編《社區研究與社會發展（上）》。天津：天津人民出版社。

Sheridan, M & Alaff, J.W. eds. 1984。 *Lives: Chinese working women*。 Bloomington: Indiana University Press.

Shi, L. Y. 1993. "Family financial and household support exchange between generations: A survey of Chinese rural elderly." *Gerontologist* 33(4): pp. 468-480.

Shinn, M.; Lehmann, S. & Wong, N.W. 1984. "Social interaction and social support." *Journal of Social Issues* 40: 4: pp. 55-76.

Shore, B. 1985. "Extended kin as helping networks," pp. 108-120.In W.J. Sauer & R.T. Coward, eds., *Social support networks & the care of the elderly: theory, research, & practice*. New York: Springer Publishing Company.

Shu, Jingnan 束景南. 1994. *Chinese Taiji Diagram and Taiji culture* (*Zhonghua Taiji tu he Taiji wenhua*). Suzhou: Suzhou University Publishing House. 《中華太極圖與太極文化》。蘇州：蘇州大學出版社。

Shue, Vivienne. 1988. *The reach of the state: sketches of the Chinese body politic*. Stanford/Calif.: Stanford University Press.

Shumaker, S. A. & Brownell, A. 1984. "Toward a theory of social support: closing conceptual gaps." *Journal of Social Issue*s 40: 4: pp. 11-36.

——. 1985. "Introduction: social support interventions." *Journal of Social Issues*, 41: 1: pp. 1-4.

Singh, A. M. 1976. Neighbour and social networks in urban India. New Delhi: Marwah.

Siu, B. 1982. *Women of China*. London: Zed Press.

Siu, Helen, F. 1984. Agents and victims in South China: accomplices in rural revolution. Yale University Press.

Skinner, G. William. 1964-65. *Marketing and social structure in rural China*. Reprinted from the *Journal of Asian Studies*, No. 1. Ann Arbor: Association for Asian Studies.

——. 1971. "Chinese peasants and the closed community: An open and shut case." *Comparative Studies in Society & History* (13): p. 277.

——. 1977. "Regional urbanization in nineteenth-century China." In G. W. Skinner, ed., *The City in Late Imperial China* Stanford: Stanford University Press.

——. 1994. "Differential development in Lingnan." In T. Lyons and V. Nee, eds., *The economic transformation of South China: reform and development in the Post-Mao-Era*. Ithaca: Cornell East Asia Series No. 70.

Skvoretz, J. 1991. "Theoretical and methodological models of networks and relations." *Social Networks* 13: pp. 275-300.

Smart, Ninian. 1989/95. The world's religions—Old traditions and modern transformations. Cambridge University Press.

Smith, Arthur, H. 明恩溥. 1894. *Chinese characteristics*. New York: Fleming H. Revell Company.

——. 1899. *Village life in China*. NY/Chicago/London/Edinburgh: Fleming H. Revell Company.

——. 1998a. *Village life in China* (Zhongguo xiangcun shenghua). Trans. Wuqing & Jun Tamg. Beijing: Current Affairs Publishing House (Shishi Chubanshe). 午晴、唐軍譯，中國鄉村生活》。北京：時事出版社。

——. 1998b. *Chinese characteristics* (*Zhongguoren de suzhi*). Trans. Yue Qin. Shanghai: Xuelin Publishing House. 《中國人的素質》，秦悦譯。上海：學林出版社。

Smith, C.J. 1978. "Self-help and social networks in the urban community." *Ekistics* 45:268: pp. 104-114.

Song, Lina. 1993. "A study of China's welfare system." A paper from the RES of Oxford University.

Song, Qiang; Zhang, Zangzang and Qiao, Bian, 宋強，張藏藏，喬邊. 1995. China can say No – the choices between political and human feeling after the cold war (Zhongguo keyi shuo bu: lengzhan hou shidai de zhengzhi yu qinggan jueze). Beijing: Chinese united industry and business publishing house. 《中國可以說不》。北京：中華工商聯合出版社。

Specht, H. 1986. "Social support, Social network, Social exchange in social work practice." *Social Services Review* 60: 2: pp. 218-240.

Spencer, Herbert. 1897. *The Principles of Sociology,* 2 volumes. New York: D. Appleton.

SSB (State Statistics Bureau, also see NBS) 中國國家統計局. 1991. *China statistical yearbook* (*Zhongguo tongji nianjian*). Beijing: China statistical Publishing House.《中國統計年鑒》。北京：中國統計出版社。

——. 1996. idem. Stacey, J. 1983. *Patriarchy and socialist revolution in China*. Chicago: University of Chicago Press.

Stafford, Charles 石瑞. 1995. *The road of Chinese childhood*. Cambridge: Cambridge University Press.

——. 1998. "A swan's trace in snow: unexpected visits, fieldwork, and anthropology of FeiXiaotong". In Rong Ma, Xing Zhou, eds. *Fieldwork and culture consciousness* (*Tianye gongzuo yu wenhua zijue*). Beijing: Qunyan Publishing House. 〈雪泥鴻爪：意外訪問、田野工作與費孝通的人類學〉，見馬戎、周星主編《田野工作與文化自覺》。北京：群言出版社。

——. 2000a. "Chinese patriliny and the cycles of *yang* and *laiwang*." In Janet Carsten, ed., *Cultures of relatedness: New approach to the study of kinship*. Cambridge: Cambridge University Press.

——. 2000b. "Deception, corruption and Chinese ritual economy." *Working Paper* Asia Research Centre, LSE WP3.

——. 2000c. *Separation and reunion in Modern China*. Cambridge: Cambridge University Press.

Stanley, W. ed. 1994. Advances in social network analysis: research in the social and behavioral sciences. Sage Publications.

Starker, J. 1986. "Methodological & conceptual issues in research on social support." *Hospital & Community Psychiatry*. 37: 5: pp. 485-490.

Stockman, N.; Bonney, N. & Sheng, X. 1995. *Women's work in east and west*. London: UCL Press Ltd.

Stover, L.E. & Stover, T.K. 1976. *China: an anthropological perspective*. Pacific Palisades/California: Goodyear Publication Company, Inc.

Strathern, M. 1988/90. *The gender of the gift*. Berkeley/ Los Angeles/London: University of California Press.

——. 1992. "Qualified value: the perspective of gift exchange." In C. Humphrey & S. Hugh-Jones, eds., *Barter, exchange and value: An anthropological approach.* Cambridge/New York/.: Cambridge University Press.

Su, Ping 蘇萍. 1996. "Following and changing the Chinese peasants' interaction model" (*Zhongguo nongmin jiaowang moshi de yanxi yu bianqian*). *Social Sciences Front* 4. 〈中國農民交往模式的沿襲與變遷〉，《社會科學戰線》第 4 期。

Sun, Liping 孫立平. 1996. " 'Guanxi', social relationships and social structure" (*'Guanxi', shehui guanxi yu shehui jiegou*). *Sociological Researches* No.5. 〈「關係」、社會關係與社會結構〉，《社會學研究》第 5 期。

Sun, Lung-kee (Sun Longji) 孫隆基. 1987. The deep structure of Chinese culture (Zhongguo wenhuade shenceng jiegou). Hong Kong: Ji Xian She. 《中國文化的深層結構》。香港：集賢社。

——. 1991. "Contemporary Chinese culture: Structure and emotionality." *Australian Journal of Chinese Affairs* 26: pp. 1-41.

Sun, Shangyang 孫尚楊.1994. *Christian and Confucian at the end of the Ming dynasty* (*Jidujiao yu mingmo ruxue*). Beijing: The Eastern Publishing House. 《基督教與明末儒學》。北京：東方出版社。

Sussman, M. B. 1965. "Relationships of adult children with their parents in the United States." In E. Shanas and R. Streib, eds., *Social Structure and the Family: Intergenerational Relationships*. Englewood Cliffs, NJ: Pretice-Hall.

Sussman, M. B.; Burchinall, L.G. 1962. "Kin and Family Network: Unheralded structure in current conceptualization of family functioning." *Journal of Marriage and Family Living* 24: pp. 231-240.

Szelenyi, Ivan. 1978. "Social Inequalities Under State Socialist Redistribution Economics." *International Journal of Comparative Sociology* I: pp. 61-78.

Tang, Jun; Zhu, Yaoyin & Ren, Zhenxing 唐鈞、朱耀垠、任振興. 1999. "Social security and social support networks in urban families who live in poverty" (*Chengshi pinkun jiating de shehui baozhang he shehui zhichi wang*). *Sociological Researches* No.5. 〈城市貧困家庭的社會保障和社會支持網〉，《社會學研究》第 5 期。

Tang, Ning. 2002. "Interviewer and interviewee relationships between women." *Sociology* Vol. 36 No. 3.

Taylor, R. J. 1985. "The extended family as a source of support to elderly blacks." *Gerontologis* 25: 5: pp. 488-495.

Teng, J. E. 1996. "The construction of the 'traditional Chinese women'in the Western Academy: a critical review." SIGNS, 22:1: pp. 115-151.

Taylor, S. E., Peplau, L. A., Sears, D.O. 1994. *Social Psychology* (8th edition). Englewood Cliffs/New Jersey: Prentice Hall.

The Food and Agriculture Organization of the UN. 1987. Women in agriculture and rural development: FAO's program directions. Rome.

The Friedrich Naumann Foundation. 1994. The impact of the economic reforms on the situation of women in China. Beijing.

The World Bank. 1988. *The World Bank's support for the alleviation of poverty*. Washington: A world bank publication.

Thireau, I. 1988. "Recent change in a Guangdong village." *Australian J. of Chinese Affairs* No.19-20.

Thompson, K. 1996. *Key quotations in sociology*. London & New York: Routledge.

Thompson, S. E. 1988. "Death, food, and fertility." In J. Watson and E. Rawski, eds., *Death ritual in late imperial and modern China*. Berkeley/Los Angeles/London: University of California Press.

Toryer, C.; Rojek, eds. 1989. *Social control in the People's Republic of China*. NY/ Westport: Praeger.

Traube, E. G. 1986. Cosmology and social life—ritual exchange among the Mambai of East Timor. Chicago/London: The University of Chicago Press.

Tu, E. J., Liang, J. & Li, S. 1989. "Mortality Decline and Chinese family structure: implications for old aged support." *Journal of Gerontology* 44(4): pp. 157-68.

Tu, Wei-ming (Du weiming) 杜維明. 1995. "Culture Chinese—the third kinds of Chinese" (*Wenhua Zhongguoren – di sanzhong leixing de zhongguoren*). a paper for the 8th ACSE International Academic Conference, by Association of Chinese Scholars in Europe (ACSE), 30th July-5th August, Paris.

——. ed. 1994. *The living tree—the changing meaning of being Chinese today*. Stanford/California: Stanford University Press.

——. 1996. Confucius tradition in East Asian modernity. Harvard University Press.

Uehara, E. & Chicago, I. 1990. "Dual exchange theory, social networks & informal social support." *American Journal of Sociology* 96:3: pp. 521-557.

Ueno, H. 1995. "Daughters and the natal family in Taiwan: affinal relationships in Chinese society," pp. 48-66. In J.S. Eades Suenari and Daniels, ed., *Perspectives on Chinese society—anthropological views from Japan*. Kent: CSAC, University of Kent.

Unger, J. 1985-86. "The decollectivisation of Chinese countryside: A survey of twenty-eight villages." *Pacific Affairs* 58: p. 4.

——. 1993. "Urban families in the eighties: An analysis of Chinese surveys." In D. Davis & S. Harrell, eds., *Chinese families in the post-Mao era*. California: University of California.

Van de Poel, M. G. M. 1993. "Delineating personal support networks." *Social Networks* 15.

Vaux, Alan. 1985. "Variations in social support associated with gender, ethnicity, and age." *Journal of Social Issues* 41(1): pp. 89-110.

——. 1988. *Social support: theory, research, and intervention*. New York/London, etc.: Praeger Publishers.

Village Masses (Nongcun Dazhong) 《農村大眾》. 1988. "The gifts couldn't knock open the door to the Agricultural bank" (*Liwu qiao bu kai nonghang de men*). December 10.

——. 1989. "Gifts become life insurance fee" (*Lipin biancheng renshen baoxian jin*). April 22.

Walby, S. 1990/94. *Theorizing patriarchy*. Oxford UK /Cambridge USA: Blackwell.

Walder, Andrew. 1983. "Organized dependency and cultures of authority in Chinese industry." *Journal of Asian Studies* 43(4): pp. 51-76.

——. 1986. Communist neo-traditionalism: work and authority in Chinese industry. Berkeley: University of California Press.

——. 1989. "Social change in post-revolution China." *Annual Review of Sociology* 15: pp. 405-24.

Wallace, T. & March C. ed. 1991. Changing perceptions-writings on gender and development. Oxford: Oxfam.

Wallman, Sandra. 1984. *Eight London households*. London/New York: Tavistock Publications.

Wales, Gibbard/Gibberd; Norman, Henri/Henrie/Henry 吉伯特・威爾士；亨利・諾曼. 2000. The subjects under a dragon flag—Contemporary Chinese society and custom (*Longqi xia de chenmin-jindai zhongguo shehui yu lisu*). Trans. Haiping Deng; Yijun Liu. Beijing: Guangming Daily Publishing House. 《龍旗下的臣民——近代中國社會與禮俗》，鄧海平、劉一君譯。北京：光明日報出版社。

Wan, Jieqiu 萬解秋. 1993. *Governmental pushing and economic development (Zhengfu tuidong yu jingji fazhan)*. Shanghai: Fudan University Publishing House. 《政府推動與經濟發展》。上海：復旦大學出版社。

Wang, Hansheng; Liu, Shiding; Sun, Liping & Xiang, Biao 王漢生、劉世定、孫立平、項彪. 1997. "'Zhejiang village': A special way of rural Chinese peasants entering into urban areas" ('*Zhejiangcun': zhongguo nonmin jinru chengshi de yizhong dute fangshi*). *Sociological Researches* 1: pp. 56-67. 〈「浙江村」：中國農民進入城市的一種獨特方式〉。《社會學研究》第 1 期。

Wang, Huibing 王淮冰. 2002. "An investigation of Jing village" (*Jiangcun Diaocha*). In a self-collected work (*Dianshuiji*). Nanjing: Jiangsu Association of Philosophy and Social Sciences. 〈江村調查〉，《點水集》。南京：江蘇省哲學社會科學聯合會。

Wang, Huning 王滬寧. 1991. *Village lineage culture in contemporary China (Dangdai zhongguo cunluo jiazu wenhua)*. Shanghai: Shanghai People's Publishing House. 《當代中國村落家族文化》。上海：上海人民出版社。

Wang, Kang 王康. 1994. *Wealth, the God of wealth, and luck of making wealth (Cai, caishen, caiyun)*. Chengdu: Sichuan People's Publishing House. 《財、財神、財緣》。成都：四川人民出版社。

Wang, Mingming 王銘銘. 1993. *Flowers of the state; grasses of the people*. Ph.D. Dissertation. SOAS, University of London.

——. 1996. A process of community: a case study of han lineage in Xin village (Shequ de licheng: xicun hanren jiazu de ge'an yanjiu). Tianjin: Tianjin People's Publishing House. 《社區的歷程：溪村漢人家庭的個案研究》。天津：天津人民出版社。

——. 1997a. Social anthropology and its studies of China (Shehui renleixue yu zhongguo yanjiu). Beijing: Sanlian Shudian. 《社會人類學與中國研究》。北京：三聯書店。

——. 1997b. "Gods, symbolic, and ritual: a cultural understanding of popular religions" (*Shenling, xiangzheng, yu yishi: minjian zongjiao de wenhua lijie*). In Mingming Wang & Zhongdang Pan, eds., An exploration of Chinese popular culture (*Xiangzheng yu shehui: zhongguo minjian wenhua de tantao*). Tianjin: Tianjin People's Publishing House. 〈神靈、象徵與儀式：民間宗教的文化理解〉，見王銘銘、潘忠黨主編，《象徵與社會：中國民間文化的探討》。天津：天津人民出版社。

——. 1997c. "Lineage, state, and society of village view" (Cunluo shiye zhong de jiazu, guojia yu shehui). In Mingming Wang & S. Feuchtwang, eds., Order, justice, and authority of popular society (Xiangtu shehui de zhixu, gongzheng yu quanwei). Beijing: Chinese Political and legal University Publishing House. 〈村落視野中的家族、國家與社會〉，見王銘銘、王斯福主編，《鄉土社會中的秩序、公正與權威》。北京：中國政法大學出版社。

——. 1997d. *Cunluo shiye zhong de wenhua yu quanli* (Culture and power of villages view), Beijing: Sanlian Shudian.

——. 1998. "Happiness, self power and social ontology: the concept of '*fu*' in a Chinese village" (*Xinfu, ziwo quanli he shehui bentilun: yige zhongguo cunluo zhong 'fu' de gainian*). *Sociological Researches* No. 1.

〈幸福、自我權力和社會本體論：一個中國村落中的「福」的概念〉，《社會學研究》第 1 期。

Wang, Qizhen 王琦珍.1995. *Propriety and Chinese traditional culture (Li yu chuantong wenhua)*. Nanchang: Jiangxi High Educational Publishing House. 《禮與傳統文化》。南昌：江西高教出版社。

Wang, Sibin 王思斌. 1995. "Functions of lineage ideas in rural industrialisation (*jiazu yishi zai nongcun gongyehua zhong de zuoyong*)." In Jian Qiao& Naigu Pan, eds., *Chinese ideas and behaviour (Zhongguoren de guannian yu xingwei)*.Tianjin: Tianjin People's Publishing House. 〈家族意識在農村工業化中的作用〉，見喬健、潘乃穀主編《中國人的觀念與行為》。天津：天津人民出版社。

Wang, Xiaoyi 王曉毅. 1993. *Ties of blood and locality (Xueyuan yu diyuan)*. Hangzhou: Zhejiang People's Publishing House. 《血緣與業緣》。杭州：浙江人民出版社。

Wang, Yihao; He, Yinfeng, Tian, Cuiqin. 王、何&田. 1989. "The recent situation of rural marriage and family relationships and its trend" (*Jinnian lai nongcun jiating guanxi zhuangkuang he fazhan qushi*). People's University Books and Periodicals Resource Centre (*Renmin daxue shubao ziliao zhongxin*) C-4 *Sociology* 5: pp. 145-152. 〈近年來農村家庭關係狀況和發展趨勢〉，人大複印報刊中心《社會學》第 5 期。

Wang, Zhixin 王治心. 1988. A brief history of Chinese religious thoughts (Zhongguo zongjiao sixiangshi dagang). Beijing: Zhonghua shuju. 《中國宗教思想史大綱》。北京：中華書局。

Ward, R.A., Lagory, M., & Sherman, S.R. 1985。"Neighbourhood & network age concentration: does age homogeneity matter for older people?" *Social Psychology Quarterly* 48:2: pp. 138-149.

Warner, W. Lloyd. 1937. A black civilization: a social study of Australian tribe. London: Harper.

Warner, W. Lloyd and Lunt, P. S. 1941. *The social life of a modern community*. New Haven, Conn.: Yale University Press.

Wasserman, S. & Faust, K. 1994. *Social network analysis: method and applications*. Cambridge: Cambridge University Press.

Watanabe, Shin. 1987. "Job-searching: a comparative study of male employment relations in the United States and Japan." Ph.D Dissertation. University of California.

Watson, A. ed. 1992. Economic reform and social change in China. London: Routledge.

Watson, James L. 1975. *Emigration and the Chinese Lineage*. Berkeley: University of California Press.

——. 1976. "Anthropological analysis of Chinese religion." *The China Quarterly* 66: pp. 355-364.

——. 1982. "Chinese kinship reconsidered: Anthropological perspectives on historical research." *The China Quarterly*. 92: pp. 589-627.

——. 1986. "Anthropological overview: The development of Chinese descent groups", pp. 274-292. In P. B. Embrey and J. L. Watson, eds., *Kinship Organization in Late Imperial China: 1000-1940*. Berkeley: University of California Press.

——. 1988. "The structure of Chinese funerary rites: Elementary Forms, Ritual Sequence, and the Primacy of Performance." In J. L. Watson & E. S. Rawski, eds. *Death ritual in late imperial and modern China*. Berkeley: University of California Press.

Watson, J. L. & Rawski, E. S. eds. 1988. *Death ritual in late imperial and modern China*. Berkeley: University of California Press.

Watson, R. S. 1981. "Class differences and affinal relations in south China." *Man* 16: pp. 593-615.

——. 1985. Inequality Among Brothers: Class and Kinship in South China. Cambridge: Cambridge

University Press.

——. 1986. "The named and the nameless: gender and person in Chinese society." *American Ethnologist* 13: pp. 619-32.

——. 1988. "Graves and politics in Southeastern China." In J. Watson and E. Rawski, eds., *Death ritual in late imperial and modern China*. Berkeley/Los Angeles/London: University of California Press.

Weber, M. 1947. *The theory of social and economic organization.* (original Ger. 1922), pp. 88. Trans. Henderson, A. M.; Parsons. 1964. New York: Free Press.

——. 1951. *Religion of China*. Glencoe: Free Press (original Ger. 1920-1).

Wei, Xinghua; Wei, Jie, eds., 衛興華、魏傑主編. 1994. *Studies of Chinese social security system* (*Zhongguo shehui baozhang zhidu yanjiu*). Beijing: Chinese People's University Publishing House. 《中國社會保障制度研究》。北京：中國人民大學出版社。

Wellman, B. 1981. "Applying Network Analysis to the Study of Support." In B.H. Gottlieb, eds., *Social Networks and Social Support*. Beverly Hill, CA,: Sage Publications.

——. 1983a. "Network analysis: some basic principles," pp. 155-200. In R. Collins, ed., *Sociological theory*. San Francisco: Jossey-Bass,

——. 1983b. "The basic principle of network analysis." In R. Collin, ed., *Sociological theory*. San Francisco.

——. 1992. "Men in networks: private communities, domestic friendships." In P. N. N. Park, ed., *Men's friendships*. CA: Sage Publication.

Wellman, B. ; Berkowitz, S.D. eds. 1988. *Social Structures: Network Approach*. Cambridge: Cambridge University Press.

Wellman, B., & Leighton, B. 1979. "Networks, neighbourhoods and community: approaches to the study of the community question." *Urban Affairs Quarterly* 15.

Wellman, B. & Wortley, S. 1990. "Different strokes from different forks: community ties and social support." *American Sociology Review* 96.

Wen Chongyi (Chung-I) 文崇一. 1982. "Repay an obligation and revenge: an analysis of social exchange behaviour" (*Bao'en yu fuchou*). In K. S. Yang ed., *Chinese psychology* (*Zhongguoren de xinli*). Taipei: Taiwan Guiguan Press. 〈報恩與復仇〉，見楊國樞主編《中國人的心理》。臺北：桂冠圖書公司。

——. 1995. "Richness and morality: re-stress the value conflict and conformity" (*Fugui yu daode: zailun jiazhi de chongtu yu zhenghe*). In Jian Qiao & Naigu Pan, eds., *Chinese ideas and behaviour* (*Zhongguoren de guannian yu xingwei*). Tianjin: Tianjin People's Publishing House. 〈富貴與道德：再論價值的衝突與整合〉。見喬健、潘乃穀主編《中國人的觀念與行為》。天津：天津人民出版社。

Wenger, G.C. 1987. *Relationships in Old Age: Inside Support Networks*. CSPRD Report, Bangor: University of Wales.

——. 1990. "The Special Role of Friends and Neighbours." *Journal of Ageing Studies* 4(2): pp.149 et seq.

——. 1991. "A network typology: from theory to practice." *Journal of Ageing Studies* 5(1): pp. 147-62.

——. 1991. "Survivors: Support Network Variation and Sources of Help in Rural Communities." *Journal of cross-cultural Gerontology* 6(1): pp. 41-82.

——. 1992. Help in old age-facing up to change: a longitudinal network study. Liverpool University Press.

——. 1993. "The formation of social networks: self-help, mutual aid and old people in contemporary Britain". *Journal of Aging Studies* 7(1): pp. 25-40.

——. 1994. *Support networks of older people: A guide for practitioners.* Centre for social policy research and development, Bangor: University of Wales.

——. 1994. Understanding support network and community care: Network Assessment for Elderly People. Ashgate Publishing.

——. 1995. "A Comparison of urban with rural support networks: Liverpool and North Wales." *Aging and Society* 15: pp. 59-81.

Wenger, G. C. & St. Leger, F. 1992. "Community structure and support network variation." *Ageing and Society* 12(2): pp. 213-36.

Wenger, G. C. & Scott, A. 1994. "Change and stability in support network type: finding from the Bangor longitudinal study." A paper for XIII World Congress of Sociology, Bielefeld, Germany.

Wentowski, G. J. 1981. "Reciprocity and the coping strategies of older people: cultural dimensions of network building." *Gerontologist* 21: pp. 600-609.

West, J., Zhao, Chang and Cheng, eds., 1999. *Women of China: Economic and social transformation.* Macmillan Press Ltd.

White, D.R. & Jorion, P. 1996. "Kinship networks and discrete structure theory: applications and implications." *Social Networks* 18: pp. 267-314.

White, H. C. 1963. *An anatomy of kinship.* Englewood Cliffs, NJ: Prentice-Hall.

——. 1981. "Where do markets come from?" *American Journal of Sociology* 87.

Whittaker, J. K. 1983. "Mutual helping in human service practice." In J. K. Whittaker; J. Garbarino and associates, eds., *Social support networks: Informal helping in the human services.* New York: Aldine De Gruyter.

Whittaker, J. K., Garbarino, J., and associates, eds. 1983. *Social support networks: Informal helping in the human services.* New York: Aldine De Gruyter.

Whitten, N.; Wolfe, A.W. 1973. "Network Analysis," pp. 717-746. In Honigmann ed., *Handbook of Social and Cultural Anthropology.* Chicago: Rand McNally.

Whyte, M.K. 1984. *Small groups & political rituals in China.* University of California Press.

——. 1988. "Death in the People's Republic of China." In J. Watson and E. Rawski, eds., *Death ritual in late imperial and modern China.* Berkeley/Los Angeles/London: University of California Press.

——. 1992. "Introduction: rural economic reforms and Chinese family patterns." *The China Quarterly*, 130: pp. 317-322.

Whyte, M. K., Parish, W. 1983. *Urban life in Contemporary China.* Chicago: University of Chicago Press.

Wilhelm, Richard 衛禮賢. 1998. Original published in Germany in 1926. It can be translated into English as *Chinese Heart (Zhongguo xinling).* Trans. Yujie Wang, Min Luo & Jinping Zhu. Beijing: International Cultural Publishing Corporation.《中國心靈》，王宇潔、羅敏、朱晉平譯。北京國際文化出版公司。

Wilkinson, H. 1976. *The family in classical China*. Arlington, Va.: University Publications of America.

Willmott, P. 1987. *Friendship networks and social support*. London: Policy Studies Institute.

Wills, T. A. 1991. "Social support and interpersonal relationships," pp. 265-289. In M.S. Clark, ed., *Personal behaviour: review of personality and social psychology, Vol. 12*. Newbury Park, CA: Sage.

Wilson, Edward O. 1975. *Sociobiology: The New Synthesis*. Cambridge, MA: Belknap Press of Harvard University Press.

Wilson, Richard W. 1970. Learning to be Chinese: The political socialisation of children in Taiwan. Cambridge, Mass: The M. I. T. Press.

Wolf, A. P. ed. 1975. *Religion and ritual in Chinese society*. Stanford: Stanford University Press.

Wolf, D. L. 1992. Factory daughters: gender, household dynamics, and rural industrialization in Java. Berkeley/LA/Oxford: University of California Press.

Wolf, M. 1972. *Women and the family in rural Taiwan*. Stanford: Stanford University Press.

——. 1973/93. "Chinese women: old skills and a new context," pp. 157-172. In M. Z. Rosaldo & L. Lamphere, eds. *Women, Culture & Society*. Stanford/California: Stanford University Press,

——. 1975. "Women and suicide in China." In M. Wolf & R. White, eds., *Women in Chinese society*. Stanford: Stanford University Press.

Wolf, M. & White, R. eds. 1975. *Women in Chinese society*. Stanford: Stanford University Press.

——. 1985. Revolution postponed: women in contemporary China, Stanford: Stanford University Press.

——. 1994. "Uterine families and the woman's community." In J.P. Spradley & D.W. McCurdy, eds., *Conformity & conflict: readings in culture anthropology*. Harper Collins: College Publishers.

Wolfman, E. 1968. The local cultures of south and east China. B.J.Brill.

Wright, P. H. 1969. "A model and a technique for studies of friendship." *Journal of experimental Social Psychology* 5: pp. 295-309. Wu chengshi jianting yanjiu xiangmu zu (Research project group on the family of five cities) 五城市家庭研究專案組. 1985. *Chinese urban family (Zhongguo chengshi jiating)*. Jinan: Shandong People's Publishing House. 《中國城市家庭》。濟南：山東人民出版社。

Wujiang shi difangzhi bianzhuan weiyuanhui (Editing Committee for *Wujiang general records*) 吳江市地方誌編纂委員會. 1994. *Wujiang general records (Wujiang xianzhi)*. Nanjing: Jiangsu Science and Technology Publishing House. 《吳江縣誌》。南京：江蘇科學技術出版社。

Wujiang zhengxie (Wujiang County branch of Chinese Political Consultative Conference), eds., 吳江政協. 1996. *Jiangcun—Jiangzhen: Maiogang fazhan de jiaobu* (From Jiang village to Jiang township: Developmental pace of Miaogang township), Beijing: Chinese Literature and History Publishing House.

Wu, Xiang 吳象. 2001. *Chinese rural reform records (Zhongguo nongcun gaige shilu)*. Hangzhou: Zhejiang People's Publishing House. 《中國農村改革實錄》。杭州：浙江人民出版社。

Xiang, Biao. 1999. "The networking logic of power-big men in a migrant community in contemporary China." A paper presented in British Association of Chinese Studies (BACA) conference, 6th Sep, SOAS, London.

Xiao, Zhenyu 蕭振禹. 1988. *Elderly care, whom do you rely on?* (*Yanglao, ni zhiwang shui?*). Beijing: Social Reform Publishing House. 《養老，你指望誰？》。北京：改革出版社。

Xin, Guanjie 辛冠潔. 1996. "Confucius and human being (*Kongzi yu ren*)." In Chinese Confucius Foundation (*Zhongguo kongzi jijinhui*), ed. *Confucius and the twenty-first century* (*Ruxue yu ershiyi shiji*). Beijing: Huaxiao Publishing House. 〈孔子與人〉，見中國孔子基金會編：《儒學與二十一世紀》。北京：華夏出版社。

Xu, Wenchu 徐文初. 1996. "Culture" (*Wenhua*). Wujiang Branch of Political consultative conference of China, Eds., Jiang village-Jiang Township: The developing footsteps of Miaogang (*Jiangcun-Jiangzhen:Miaogang fazhai de jiaobu*). Beijing: The Culture and History Publishing House of China. 〈文化〉，見吳江市政協編：《江村——江鎮:：廟港發展的腳步》。北京：中國文史出版社。

Xu, Ping 許平. 1990. *The ritual and customs of gift-giving* (*Kuizeng lisu*). Beijing: Chinese Huaxia Publishing House. 《饋贈禮俗》。北京：中國華夏出版公司。

Xu, Jieshun 徐傑舜 ed., 2001. Nativization: the great trend of anthropology (*Bentuhua: renleixue de da qushi*). Nanning: Guanxi Nationality Publishing House.《本土化：人類學的大趨勢》。南寧：廣西民族出版社。

Xu, Yong ed.徐勇主編. 2002. *China rural studies (Vol. 2001)* (*Zhongguo nongcun yanjiu*). Beijing: Chinese Social Sciences Publishing House. 《中國農村研究（2001 卷）》。北京：中國社科出版社。

Xuan, Jun 玄峻. 1994. Connection and corroboration: A reinterpretation of Chinese thoughts (Lianxiang yu yinzheng: dui zhongguo sixiang de chongxin lijie). Beijing: Eastern Publishing House. 《聯想與印證：對中國思想的重新理解》。北京：東方出版社。

Xue, He 薛和. 2004. Jiangcun zizhi-shehui bianqian zhong de nongcun jiceng minzhu (Villagers autonomy in Jiang Village – rural democracy in social change). Nanjing: Jiangsu People's Publishing House. 《江村自治——社會變遷中的農村基層民主》。南京：江蘇人民出版社。

Xue, Suzhen; Zhao, Xishun; Fei, Junhong; Zhou, Kaili 薛素珍、趙喜順、費涓洪、周開麗. 1993. *Rural families in China* (*Zhongguo nongcun jiating*). Printed by Institutes of sociology of Shanghai and Sichuan Academy of Social Sciences. 《中國農村家庭》。上海社會科學院。

Yan, Yunxiang 閻雲翔. 1996a. "The culture of *guanxi* in a north China village." *The China Journal* 35:1: pp. 1-26.

——. 1996b. The flow of gifts-reciprocity and social networks in a Chinese village. Stanford/California: Stanford University Press.

——. 1997. "The triumph of conjugality: structural transformation of family relations in a Chinese village." *Ethnology* 36(3): pp. 191-212

——. 1998. "Money and morality in family politics: the case of family division in rural north China." *Sociological Researches* No. 6: pp. 74-84. 〈家庭政治中的金錢與道義：北方農村分家模式的人類學分析〉，《社會學研究》第 6 期。

——. 2000. *The flow of gifts*. Trans. Fangchun Li & Yu Liu. Shanghai: Shanghai People's Publishing House. 《禮物的流動——一個中國村莊中的互惠原則與社會網路網絡》，李放春、劉瑜譯。上海：上海人民出版社。

——. 2003. Private life under socialism—love, intimacy, and family change in a Chinese village. Stanford: Stanford University.

Yang, C. K. 1959. Chinese communist society: the family and the village. Cambridge, MA: M. I. T. Press.

——. 1961. *Religion in Chinese society*. California: University of California Press.

Yang, Cuntian 楊存田. 1994. *General survey of Chinese customs* (*Zhongguo fengsu gaiguan*). Beijing: Peking

University Publishing House. 《中國風俗概觀》。北京大學出版社。

Yang, Guoshu (Kuo-shu) 楊國樞. 1989a. "An analysis of the concept of Chinese filial duty" (*Zhongguoren xiaodao de gainian fenxi*)." In K. S. Yang ed., *Chinese psychology* (*Zhongguoren de xinli*). Taipei: Taiwan Guiguan Press. 〈中國人孝道的概念分析〉，見楊國樞主編《中國人的心理》。臺北：桂冠圖書公司。

——. 1989b. "The ideas and functions of Chinese *yuan*" (*Zhongguoren zhi yuan de guannian yu gongneng*), pp. 123-155. In K. S. Yang ed., *Chinese psychology*(*Zhongguoren de xinli*). Taipei: Taiwan Guiguan Press. 〈中國人之緣的觀念與功能〉，見楊國樞主編《中國人的心理》。臺北：桂冠。

Yang, Haiou. 1990. "The family support system for the elderly in rural China." In *The Humanities and Social Sciences*. Honolulu: University of Hawaii, 50, 7. Jan., Dissertation Abstracts International, A: The Humanities and Social Sciences 50:7: pp.2259 A - 2260 A..

Yang, Lien-sheng. 1957. "The Concept of *Bao* as a Basis for Social Relations in China", pp. 291-309. In J.K. Fairbank, ed., *Chinese Thought and Institutions*. Chicago: University of Chicago Press.

Yang, Martin M. C. 1945. *A Chinese Village: Taitung, Shantung Province*. N.Y.: Columbia University Press.

Yang, Mayfair Meihui 楊美惠. 1989. "The gift economy and state power in China." *Comparative Studies in Society and History* 31(1): pp. 25-54.

——. 1994. Gifts, favors and banquets — the art of social relationship in China. Ithaca and London: Cornell University Press.

——. Forthcoming. *Gifts, favors and banquets — the art of social relationship in China* (*Liwu, renqing yu yanxi—Zhongguoren shehui guanxi de yishu*). Trans. Xudong Zhao. Shanghai: Shanghai People's Publishing House. 《禮物、人情與宴席——中國人社會關係的藝術》，趙旭東譯。上海：上海人民出版社。

Yang, Yiyin 楊宜音. 1995. "Initial analysis of interpersonal relationships and typology" (*Shixi renjiguanxi jiqi fenlei*). *Sociological Researches* No. 5. 〈試析人際關係及其分類〉，《社會學研究》第 5 期。

——. 1999. " 'Selves': a case study of constructing trust" (*'Ziyiren': xinren jiangou guocheng de ge'an yanjiu*). *Sociological Researches* No. 2. 〈「自己人」：信任建構過程中的個案研究〉，《社會學研究》第 2 期。

Yang, Zhongfang and Peng, Siqing 楊中芳，彭泗清. 1999. "Conceptualization of Chinese interpersonal trust: a viewpoint of interpersonal relationship" (*Zhongguoren renji xinren de gainianhua: yige rejiguanxi de guandian*). *Sociological Researches* No. 2. 〈中國人人際信任的概念化：一個人際關係的觀點〉，《社會學研究》第 2 期。

You, Laiyin. 1995. Unequal rights: social welfare in contemporary China 1949-1993. Ann Arbor: UMI Dissertation Sevices.

Young, M. B. ed. 1973. Women in China: studies in social change and feminism. Michigan: Ann Arbor.

Yu, Jianrong 於建嶸. 2001. *Politics in Yue Village* (*Yuecun zhengzhi*). Beijing: Shangwu Yinshuguan. 《嶽村政治》。北京：商務印書館。

Yu, Shou 於碩. 2004. Preface of Chinese translation of *De la Nature, pour penser l'écologie*, Serge Moscovici Métailié, 2002. 《還自然之魅——對生態運動的思考》塞爾日·莫斯科維奇著，於碩中文版序，莊晨燕、邱寅晨譯。北京：三聯出版社。

Yu, Yingjie 1987. "An exploration of the *guanxi* network" (*Shilun guanxiwang*). People's University Books and Periodicals Resource Cnetre (*Renmin daxue shubao ziliao zhongxin*), C-4 *Sociology* 1: 103-7. 〈試論關係網〉，人大報刊複印資料中心，《社會學》第 1 期。

Yu Yingshi 余英時. 1987a. "Viewing modern meanings of Chinese culture from volume system" (*Cong jiazhi xitong kan zhongguo wenhua de xiandai yiyi*). Beijing: Sanlian Shudian. 〈從價值系統看中國文化的現代意義〉，《文化：中國與世界》。北京：三聯書店。

——. 1987b. 《士與中國文化》。上海：上海人民出版社。

Yue, qingping 岳慶平. 1995. "Filial and modernisation" (*Xiao yu xiandaihua*). In Jian Qiao & Naigu

Yuen-Tsang, Angelina W. K. 1997. Towards a Chinese conception of social support a study on the social support networks of Chinese working mothers in Beijing. Aldershot, Hants, England; Ashgate.

Pan, eds., *Chinese ideas and behaviour* (*Zhongguoren de guannian yu xingwei*). Tianjin People's Publishing House. 〈孝與現代化〉，見喬健、潘乃毅主編：《中國人的觀念與行為》。天津：天津人民出版社。

Yuan, Fang 袁方.1987. "The status and function of the Chinese elderly in the family and society" (*Zhongguo laonianren zai jiating, shehui zhongde diwei he zuoyong*). *Beijing University Studies (Philosophy and social Science edition)* 3 no. 1. 〈中國老年人在家庭社會中的地位和作用〉，《北京大學學報（哲社版）》第 3 期。

Zeggelink, E. 1995 "Evolving friendship networks: an individual-oriented approach implementing similarity." *Social Networks* 17: pp. 83-110.

Zeng Yi, Li Wei, Liang Zhiwu 曾毅、李偉、梁志武. 1993. "The regional difference and changing trends in current Chinese family structure" (*Zhongguo jiating jiegou de xianzhuang quyu chayi jiqi biandong qushi*). *China Population Sciences* No.2. 〈中國家庭結構的現狀區域差異及變動趨勢〉，《中國人口科學》第 2 期。

Zhai Xuewei 翟學偉. 1993. "The characteristics of Chinese interpersonal relationships: native concepts and model" (*Zhongguo renjiguanxi de tezhi: bentu de gainian jiqi moshi*). *Sociological Researches* 4: pp. 74-83. 〈中國人際關係的特質：本土的概念及其模式〉，《社會學研究》第 4 期。

——. 1994. *Mianzi, renqing, and guanxi networks* (*Mianzi · renqing · guanxiwang*). Zhengzhou: Henan People's Publishing House. 《面子，人情，關係網》。鄭州：河南人民出版社。

——. 1995. The face idea of Chinese (*Zhongguoren de lianmian guan*). Taibei: Guaiguan tushu gongsi. 《中國人的臉面觀》。臺北：桂冠圖書公司。

——. 1996. "Problems of balance in Chinese interpersonal relationships networks: a case study" (*Zhongguo renjiguanxi wangluo zhongde pinghengxing wenti: yixiang ge'an yanjiu*)." *Sociological Researches* No.3. 〈中國人際關係網路網絡中的平衡性問題：一項個案研究〉，《社會學研究》第 3 期。

——. 1997. "A functional analysis of 'Local Policy': from particularism to universalism" ("*Tuzhengce" de gongneng fenxi-cong pubianzhuyi dao teshuzhuyi*). *Sociological Researches* No. 3. 〈「土政策」的功能分析——從普遍主義到特殊主義〉，《社會學研究》第 3 期。

——. 1999. "Personal status: a concept and its analytical framework" (*Geren diwei: yige gainian jiqi fenxi kuangjia*). *Chinese Social Sciences* No.4. 〈個人地位：一個概念及其分析框架〉，《中國社會科學》第 4 期。

Zhang, B. 1990. *Decision support system in China: a clash of cultures*. The London School of Political Sciences and Economy (LSE), London.

Zhang, Deqing. 1993. *Shanbian zhong de hunyin jiating* (Marriage and families in change) Lanzhou: Lanzhou University Publishing House.

Zhang, Guansheng 張冠生. 1996. Step voice in villages – Fei Xiaotong's footprints, records and "heart prints" (Xiangcun zuyin – Fei Xiaotong zuji, biji, xinji). Beijing: Qunyan Publishing House. 《鄉村足音——費孝通足跡，筆跡，心跡》。北京：群言出版社。

Zhang, Junzuo 張君佐. 1993. "Development in a Chinese reality: rural women's organization in China", a conference paper.

Zhang, Letian 張樂天.1998. Leave-taking Utopia: a study of People's Commune System (Gaobie lixiang: renmin gongshe zhidu yanjiu). Shanghai: Orient Publishing Centre. 《告別理想：人民公社制度研究》。上海：東方出版中心。

Zhang, Wenhong; Ruan, Danqing & Pan, Yunkang 張文宏、阮丹青、潘允康. 1999. "Tianjin rural residents' social networks" (Tianjin nongcun jumin de shehuiwang). Sociological Researches No.2. 〈天津農村居民的社會網〉，《社會學研究》第 2 期。

Zhang, Yinghua 章英華. 1995. "The combination of *jia* and *hu* and the changes in family values" (*Jiahu zucheng yu jiating jiazhi de bianqian.*" In Jian Qiao & Naigu Pan, eds., *Chinese ideas and behaviour* (*Zhongguoren de guannian yu xingwei*). Tianjin People's Publishing House. 〈家戶組成與家庭價值的變遷〉，見喬健、潘乃穀主編《中國人的觀念與行為》。天津：天津人民出版社。

Zhang, Zhirong; Yang, Haijiao 張志榮、楊海蛟. 2001. *Local democracy and social development* (*Jicheng minzhu yu shehui fazhan*). Beijing: World Affairs Press. 《基層民主與社會發展》。北京：世界知識出版社。

Zhao, Lin 趙林. 1992. *Xietiao yu chaoyue* (Harmonise and surmount). Xi'an: Shanxi People's Publishing House. 《協調與超越》。西安：陝西人民出版社。

Zhao, Ruizheng; Wang,Aili & Ren, Ling 趙瑞政、王愛麗&任伶. 2002. *A secured route for the elderlycare of Chinese peasants* (*Zhongguo nongmin yanglao baozhang zhi lu*). Ha'erbin: Heilongjiang People's Publishing House. 《中國農民養老保障之路》。哈爾濱：黑龍江人民出版社。

Zhao, Xudong 趙旭東. 1997. "'Idea of justice' in popular society" (*Xiangtu shehui de "zhengyiguan"*). In Mingming Wang & Sifu Wang (S. Fuechtwang), eds., *Xiangtu shehui de zhixu, gongzheng yu quanwei* (Order, justice and power of rural society). Beijing: Chinese Political and legal University Publishing House. 〈鄉土社會的「正義觀」〉，見王銘銘、王斯福主編《鄉土社會的秩序、公正與權威》。北京：中國政法大學出版社。

——. 2003. *Power and justice* (*Quanli yu gongzheng*). Tianjin: Tianjin Ancient Books Publishing House. 《權力與公正》。天津：天津古籍出版社。

Zhe, Xiaoye 折曉葉. 1997. *The Rebuilding of a village* (*Cunzhang zaizao*). Beijing: Chinese Social Sciences Publishing House. 《村莊的再造》。北京：中國社科出版社。

Zheng, Yefu 鄭也夫. 1984. An exploration of *guanxixue* (*Shilun guanxixue*). *Sociology and Social Survey* No. 2-3. 〈試論關係學〉，《社會學與社會調查》第 2-3 期。

——. 1993. "Particularism and universalism" (*Teshuzhuyi yu pubianzhuyi*). *Sociological Researches* No. 4. 〈特殊主義與普遍主義〉，《社會學研究》第 4 期。

——. 1995a. On cost: A new view of sociology (Daijia lun – yige shehuixue de xin shijiao). Beijing: Sanlian shudian. 《代價論——一個社會學的新視角》。北京：三聯書店。

——. 1995b. *Presoner's dilemma and other essays* (*Zouchu qiutu de kunjing*). Beijing: Guangming Daily Publishing House. 《囚徒的困境》。北京：光明日報出版社。

Zhongguo *kongzi jijinhui* (Chinese Confucius Foundation) 中國孔子基金會. 1996. *Confucius and the twenty first century* (*Ruxue yu ershiyi shiji*). Beijing: Huaxiao Publishing House. 《儒學與二十一世紀》。北京：華夏出版社。

Zhou, Yun 周雲. 1998."The changing population quantity and lineage kinship relationships" (*Renkou shuliang de biandong yu jiazu qinshu guanxi*). In Rong Ma; Xing Zhou, eds., Fieldwork and culture conscious (*Tianye gongzuo yu wenhua zijue*). Beijing: Qunyan Publishing House. 〈人口數量的變動與家族親屬關係〉，見馬戎、周星主編《田野工作與文化自覺》。北京：群言出版社。

Zhu Dongliang 朱冬亮. 2003. Land system changes at village level along with social change (Shehui bianqian zhong de cunji tudi zhidu). Xiamen: Xiamen University Publishing House. 《社會變遷中的村級土地制度》。廈門：廈門大學出版社。

Zhu, Lijia 竹立家. 1989. *Culture and surmount (Wenhua yu chaoye*). Beijing: Chinese News Publishing House. 《文化與超越》。北京：中國新聞出版社。

Zhu, Ruiling 朱瑞玲. 1989. "Chinese interactiong: *mianzi*" (*Zhongguoren de shehui hudong: lun mianzi de wenti*). In K. S. Yang, ed., *Chinese psychology* (*Zhongguoren de xinli*). Taipei: Guiguan Press. 〈中國人的社會互動：論面子問題〉，見楊國樞主編：《中國人的心理》。臺北：桂冠圖書公司。

Zhu, Tonghua, Wu Kequan 朱通華、吳克銓 1994. *A study on the development of Southern Jiangsu model (Suna moshi fazhan yanjiu*). Nanjing: Nanjing University Publishing House. 《蘇南模式發展研究》。南京：南京大學出版社。

Zhu, Weimin 朱為民. 1993. "Enterprise, leadership and poverty in Anhui." A paper for the conference of The City University project funded by ESRC on "Rural Social Support Arrangements & the Transformation of Local Traditions in China", July.

Zhuang, Kongshao 莊孔韶. 2000. The silver wing – Social and cultural changes in local Chinese society (Yinchi – Zhongguo de difang shehui yu wenhua bianqian). Beijing: Sanlian Shudian. 《銀翅——中國的地方社會與文化變遷》。北京：三聯書店。

Zhuang, yingzhang 莊英章. 1995. "Ancestors worship in modernisation" (*xiandaihua guocheng zhong de zuxian chongbai*). In Jian Qiao & Naigu Pan, eds., *Chinese ideas and behaviour (Zhongguoren de guannian yu xingwei*). Tianjin People's Publishing House. 〈現代化過程中的祖先崇拜〉，見喬健、潘乃毅主編《中國人的觀念與行為》。天津：天津人民出版社。

---

[1] This large bibliography was collected over more than ten years. It is interdisciplinary containing material in general references; methodology; sinology; social psychology; sociology - social support, social networks, social welfare and security, social exchange, social change, etc., and also social anthropology – reciprocity, Chinese studies on rural China, state, family and kinships, women and gender, social interaction, ritual and religion, etc. It is much larger than strictly necessary for this book. I kept this bibliography because it represents a useful reference for further study.

Currently there are two common ways of organising references which involve Chinese language using English as the primary language. One way is to have two separate sets of Bibliography in Chinese and English, i.e. 何瑞福 (R. He) 1993; M Yang 1994, etc. The problem with this is that some researchers publish their work in both Chinese and English under different names and this may not be recognised. For example, Ambrose King appears to have four names, apart from the English name mentioned earlier his Chinese name in modern *pinyin* is Jin Yaoji, in an old fashioned spelling this is King Yao-chi, or in Chinese characters 金耀基. Moreover, it is always necessary to involve a translator's understanding and re-creation when a book, which originally was written in English, has been translated into Chinese. It is very useful to be able to read the same book in both languages, i.e. X. Fei 1939 in English and 1986 in Chinese, Y. Yan 1996b in English and 2000 in Chinese. Even one author who writes the same work in both Chinese and English can be understood with different meanings, i.e. G. Hwang 1982 in Chinese and 1987 in English, A. King 1989a and b in Chinese and 1994 in English. Therefore, it is important to make sure the same author's work, whether written in or translated to Chinese or English, always stays together. This is why I have mixed references in Chinese and English together in this book.

However, my method is different from another commonly used way of organising a Bibliography which also mixes Chinese references with English, i.e. Y. Yan 1996, A. Kipnis 1997, etc. These authors used a small number of Chinese references and simply translated them into English. The problem is that it is almost impossible to re-translate Chinese authors' names from English (*pinyin*) back to Chinese characters accurately. For example, Jun Jing's (景軍, the author of *The temple of Memories* 1996) name has been translated as 軍靜 in Chinese (J. Xu 2001, p51). This does not just put his surname or first name in the wrong order. The name is completely different. The more Chinese references used the more serious this problem. Moreover, all the translated work from foreign languages into Chinese will either give the authors' names in Chinese characters, i.e. 莫里斯·弗里德曼 for Maurice Freedman, 安東尼·吉登斯 for Anthony Giddens, etc., or use the authors' own Chinese names if they have them, i.e. Prasenjit Duara (杜贊奇), Stephan Feuchtwang (王斯福), Charles Stafford (石瑞), etc. However, sometimes the authors' English names disappear completely, i.e. *Men and manners of modern China* (《中國人生活的明與暗》) was originally published in English in Shanghai in 1909 and then in England afterwards. The book's other name can be translated into English as *Modern Chinese people and their life style* (《現代中國的人及其生活方式》). The author's name on the Chinese translation appeared as [英]J.麥高溫 in 1998, Beijing: Current Affairs Publishing House (Shishi Chubanshe 時事出版社). In this case, there is almost no way to find the author's English name and the English book. So it is important for readers who read both English and Chinese to recognise related authors' names in English or *pinyin* and Chinese characters. Therefore, in my book all the Chinese references will give an English translation first, followed by *pinyin* in brackets, and finally the Chinese characters.

Postscript

Based on empirical studies on rural Chinese society this book introduces and discusses the conceptualisation and content of *lishang-wanglai*. I hope this attempt to combine three themes in one work will be able to play the role of "eliciting the jade by throwing out the brick" (*pao zhuan yin yu*, literally, to offer out one's piece of work in order to learn better and valuable things from others). This Postscript is based on the acknowledgement and abstract in my doctoral dissertation. Herein it is necessary to draw a summary of "*lishang-wanglai*", to explain the merit of producing Chinese and English versions, and to acknowledge family, relatives, friends, colleagues, and all the people who helped me in the process of doing this research over the years.

1. Summary of "*lishang-wanglai*"

This book develops the Chinese term *lishang-wanglai* as a general concept in the analysis of personalised relationships in China, through the detailed study of rural Chinese people's social support arrangements since the early 1980s. Based on an ESRC social support project in ten Chinese villages (1991 – 1994) and my restudy on two of these villages between 1995 and 1996, the book concentrates on one of them: Kaixiangong village which was introduced to the anthropological field by Fei Xiaotong in the 1930s. The combination of previous researchers' studies and original fieldwork and post-fieldwork over the past few years makes it possible to present a longitudinal study of the village which covers nearly 70 years (1936 to 2004). This allows an up-to-date and broad-ranging ethnography with a highly detailed empirical study on villagers' personalised relationships and reciprocity (see Chapters IV to VIII).

Previous researches, e.g. Fei Xiaotong's *chaxugeju* (social egoism), Marshall Sahlins's typology of reciprocity, 1972; Mayfair Yang's *guanxi* and *guanxixue*, 1994; Yunxiang Yan's *guanxi* network and *renqing* ethics, 1996b; Andrew Kipnis's *guanxi* and *ganqing*, 1997 and Charles Stafford's cycles of *yang* and *laiwang*, 1995, 2000a and c, etc have already made progress in analysing personalised relationships in China. This book extends and broadens this previous work, using *lishang-wanglai* as a general analytical tool.

The notion *li shang wanglai,* used during the fieldwork by a Chinese villager, is deeply rooted in Chinese culture. In May 2009, Yunyun Zhu, a co-author of the book *Social Changes of the Kaixiangong Village* (forthcoming, 2010, see Appendix 2) expressed his opinion on "*li shang wanglai* from grassroots" (*minajian*). According to Zhu:

Ancient thinkers, such as Confucius and Laozi, philosophised social relationships based on family units as early as 2000 years ago. Running through generations after generations these philosophies have become the essence of Chinese thoughts. On the one hand, *li shang wanglai* gave form to the philosophical idea of 'harmony is a supreme good (*yi he wei gui*)' in a popular society (*minjian*); on the other hand, the idea 'harmony is a supreme good' is a social basis for *li shang wanglai*. Philosophical ideas did not come from Heaven, nor did the philosophers make them out of thin air, but they are rather a summation of the practical life experiences of the society. *Li shang wanglai* incarnates a specific character of the Chinese people and it is deeply rooted in the society.

Zhu's explanation of the meaning of *li shang wanglai* has been further informed by study of Kaixiangong villagers' own understanding and practice. From this starting point, this book develops the novel concept of *lishang-wanglai* by interpreting certain implicit cultural models and patterns of social relationships in Kaixiangong. *Lishang-wanglai* models the creative process of personalised relationships in which different types of reciprocities (*wanglai*) are judged by different criteria (*lishang*).

This book has contributed to general knowledge in the following ways: it is a very thorough and detailed ethnography of a Chinese village with longitudinal comparisons; it has methodological implications for fieldwork, although *lishang-wanglai* is not itself a research method; it has highlighted the importance and significance of state and gender in personalised relationships between individuals, and personalised institutional relationships between individuals and institutions; it has brought together previous researchers' studies on personalised relationships, i.e. *mianzi*, *bao*, *chaxugeju*, *ganqing*, *guanxi*, *renqing*, *yuan*, *fu*, *yang* and *laiwang*, etc. within a single unified model; it has developed a new analysis of reciprocity in which principles and typology are combined; it has demonstrated a dynamic network model of reciprocity (*lishang-wanglai* networks); and finally it has also demonstrated through detailed ethnography that the motivation of *lishang-wanglai* is social creativity.

As a concept *lishang-wanglai* was developed from studies made in China of social cultural aspects of everyday life. How can it possibly be accepted by anthropology and sociology worldwide? Feuchtwang suggested two English translations for the concept, "contacts-ethics", or "the calculus of changing reciprocal relationships". For me, these translations fail to convey the universality of *lishang-wanglai*, which is linked to so many English words connection, communication, interaction, reciprocity, relatedness, relationship, social exchange, social creativity, social capital, social support, and social network. This comprehensiveness adds to its great usefulness, but increases barriers to universal recognition.

I prefer to keep the usage of *lishang-wanglai* as a foreign term, like Kula ring in anthropology, or *guanxi,* which is known worldwide in different disciplines. But coinage of a compound term such as *lishang-wanglai* to cover a set of complicated ideas has its own disadvantages. During the publication process this book changed its main title from '*Li shang wanglai'* to '*guanxi* or *li shang wanglai*?' in an attempt to establish a connection between the familiar term *guanxi* and the unfamiliar Chinese phrase *li shang wanglai,* to make the new concept (*lishang-wanglai*) easier to introduce.

2. The merit of producing Chinese and English versions simultaneously

Like many physical products "made in China", this "made in China" intellectual product is also designed abroad, with materials and manufacturing nonetheless based in China. Therefore, both the Chinese and English versions still lack refinement. I have accepted the advice of many friends not to pursue perfection. In spite of the desirability of refinement, publication is of greater importance. Existence precedes quality, as a Chinese saying puts it. In English there are similar sayings, "the perfect is the enemy of the good", or "it's better than nothing".

This book was written in English, but translated into Chinese by someone else. My proofreading of the Chinese version was carried out in a rather hurried manner during my field trips in China. Plus, I had no Chinese or English original works and field notes to verify the content, and am myself responsible for any errors and mistakes. However, compared with "products" on studies of China made by foreigners abroad, Chinese readers may find it easier to understand, and non Chinese readers may find something different from the work of Western writers, or work written in a Western style.

Unlike physical products made in China, this book will be published in Chinese and English simultaneously. I hope that they will be complementary. English readers will immediately detect the Chinese-ness of this book, while Chinese readers may sense this "import" feeling of the Chinese version. While proofreading, my corrections and rewording of the translation from English to Chinese covered about 20 per cent of the content.

After you read this book patiently if you find the "brick" is worthwhile for getting "jade" or building into the architecture of human knowledge, I would like to use this opportunity to reveal a "secret" that you might not find in English or Chinese textbooks. Reading both Chinese and English versions of a book is a short cut to deepening understanding of studies of China, for both advanced researchers and general readers. Based on my own experiences of reading Chinese and English versions of the same book, and proofreading this book, I found that translation delivers at most 80 per cent of the original contents. Difficult ideas which are often core messages may get lost, twisted, and misinterpreted during translation. These difficult passages – let us say 20 per cent of the text – have a wholly disproportionate importance. The possession of both English and Chinese versions of a work can be of great use to advanced researchers trying to understand difficult parts of the contents.

For Chinese readers capable of reading English, or foreigners capable of reading Chinese, these books might be supplementary works, or materials on social sciences read as an aid to learning English or Chinese. I apologise for some places that are not identical in both versions, because the English version has been slightly edited after the Chinese version went to print.

The special characteristic of this book is that the author has both published sociological works in Chinese amounting in total to more than a million words, and carried out research continuously for 18 years at two British universities. Nevertheless, I should emphasise that compared with such classic works as *The Flow of Gifts*, by Yunyxiang Yan, this book is far from exemplary: 95 per cent of its contents directly came from my PhD dissertation which was written five years ago; it covers too many issues; there are areas of not-so-strict analysis, and insufficient explication of certain issues; especially in both Chinese and English versions there might be still many grammatical and rhetorical problems caused by time pressure before the publication. However, these are the very reasons that make the book, with its two versions, a good target for training and practice in communication between Chinese and non-Chinese scholars – communication essential if Chinese sociology and anthropology are to become part of general knowledge worldwide.

3. Acknowledgement

My deep gratitude to Professor Fei Xiaotong for his great influence on this work will be expressed in another book.[1] Here, I must acknowledge numerous people who kindly provided me with invaluable direct and concrete assistance throughout my research over the years.

I am tremendously grateful to my supervisor and lifelong academic adviser Stephan Feuchtwang, for without his constant encouragement, and invaluable advice and criticism

---

[1] *Lishang-wanglai* and Relationship Research –*Study of Fei Xiaotong's theories and restudies on Kaixiangong Village*, will be published by the Foreign Language and Teaching Research Press in October 2010.

throughout the period of all my research work from 1991 to 2009[2], this book would never have been written. I would like to thank the City University, the ESRC (The Economics and Social Research Council), the UCC (the Universities' China Committee), the GBCC (the Great Britain China Centre), and the BFWG (the British Federation of Women's Grant) for their financial support; the Centre of Chinese Studies, School of Oriental and African Studies (SOAS), University of London, for giving me borrowing rights from SOAS Library, one of the biggest collections of Chinese resources in the UK; the Asia Research Centre, Department of Anthropology, and many related departments at London School of Economics and Political Science, which provided me wonderful opportunities and excellent services, and stimulated me to make greater efforts to contribute to the world class academic community.

I owe a special *renqing* debt to the villagers in Kaixiangong village, as well as Neiguan village, whose understanding and help are crucial to my fieldwork, to the local cadres of the villages, officers of township, and Wujiang City and Dingxi County, especially, Yu Menda, Shen Zhirong, Zhou Yuguan, Wang Jianmin, Yao Fukun, Xu Guoqi, Zhou Yonglin and Zhou Baoying, etc. who supported me during the periods of my fieldwork and post-fieldwork. Fukun Yao and Yunyun Zhu also checked all the details of the first eight chapters of the book and corrected some errors at the stage of proofreading its Chinese version. I am grateful to local officials in Dingxi Prefecture and County, Neiguan Township, and Neiguan Village Cadres and villagers for their support of my fieldwork, although I only used vary small portion of materials in this book.

My thanks also to my colleagues in the ESRC project for letting me share their fieldwork notes and reports, and their comments on my work: Kent Deng, Zhenglai Deng, Xiaolin Guo, Feiyun Lu, Yinghao Lu, Zongying Lu, Minghua Mao, Jianxiong Pan, Wenbao Qian, Guanbao Shen, Mingming Wang, and Weimin Zhu. My thanks also goes to my former work unit, Chinese People's Public Security University, for it gave me letters of introduction to enter fieldwork sites; I am also grateful to the following people who have helped me in different ways, Dolly Bailey, Feng Chen, Lixing Chen, Yuan Cheng, Gina Cuciniello, Jianzhong Dai, Kent Deng, Zhenglai Deng, Harriet Evens, Linda Free, Gordon Grant, Ping Huang, Henry Weidong Han, Xiangjing Han,

---

[2] From October 1998 when Stephan moved to Department of Anthropology at the London School of Economics and Political Sciences (LSE) I extended my research interests towards anthropology. I continued my research work at Department of Sociology while I was completing my PhD dissertation in 2004. Since then I have continuously received his academic advice from time to time.

Haiming Hui, William Jankowiak, Bingqin Li, Peilin Li, Qiang Li, Xiaojiang Li, Xin Liu, Chun Lin, Xi Lin, Haoxing Liu, Chengwu Lou, Hanlong Lu, Fiona McConnon, Anne McGrath, Zeqi Qiu, Lina Song, Peter Savundra, Charles Stafford, Norman Stockman, Ning Tang, Huaibing Wang, Qi Wang, Lihua Xie, Chenggang Xu, He Xue, Yunxiang Yan, Mayfair Yang, Nanke Ye, Shuo Yu, Haiou Zhang, Letian Zhang, Xuewei Zhai, Wei Zeng, Jinghao Zhou and Xiaohong Zhou.

Finally, I must thank my family and close relatives. In particular, Eleanor Mayger, my sister-in-law, and my mother-in-law, Shirley Clarke, for their "labour of love", respectively, in reviewing and correcting the hugely long original draft of my PhD dissertation and manuscript of the book, and helping with some of the more difficult parts of the text in this book under great time pressure before the publication of the book. They both are Cambridge graduates, but not professional proofreaders, so I take responsibility for any of the errors; Thomas, my dearest husband, not only for displaying considerable self sacrifice and patience in our family life and tolerating my consistent underestimates of the time and effort required to complete this piece of research work - more importantly his intelligent questions stimulated my thoughts, and his critical mind sharpened my arguments and promoted better understanding of cultural, gender and personal differences; Neil / Changcheng, my lovely son, for loving me in spite of the long hours I have had to spend in front of my desk or from time to time away from home for fieldwork or conferences as he grows up, for which I feel guilty. My great gratitude also goes to my close relatives from my natal family including my father's spirit in the Heaven, especially, Xiangdong Chang, my elder brother, who shared the family responsibilities with my mother at only 11 years of age, when my father was in jail during the Cultural Revolution, and has given me many kinds of support during the arrangement of publication. Last but not least, I am deeply grateful to my beloved mother, Jizhai Yang, for her love and strength throughout my unusual upbringing and her invaluable support and wisdom while living with us as I completed and published this work.

On all accounts, I wish to emphasise that this book is a result of my research on reciprocity, social support networks, and social creativity. It is also a product of reciprocity, social support networks, and social creativity between myself (ego) and all the family, relatives, classmates, friends, colleagues, and people who were involved in helping me with the research.

Thank you for reading and comments are welcome!

CHANG Xiangqun

China in Comparative Perspective Network, London School of Economics and Political Science, April 2010

Guanxi or *Li shang wanglai?*

--- Reciprocity, Social Support Networks, & Social Creativity in a Chinese Village

ISBN: 978-986-6286-18-6

Publishing Date: June 2010

Price: NT$ 1000 / USD$ 35

Author: Xiangqun Chang 常向群

Publisher: Airiti Press Inc.

Editor-in-Chief: Eliza Chang

Editor: Judie Ku

Cover Illustration & Design: Yayu Wu

Airiti Press Inc.

18 F, No. 80, Sec. 1, Chenggong Rd. Yonghe City, Taipei 234, Taiwan

Tel: +886-2-2926-6006 / Fax: +886-2-2231-7711

E-mail: press@airiti.com